*The Soviet Union and
National Liberation
Movements in the
Third World*

The Soviet Union and National Liberation Movements in the Third World

Galia Golan

Boston
UNWIN HYMAN
London   Sydney   Wellington

Allen & Unwin, Inc.
8 Winchester Place, Winchester, Mass. 01890, USA

Published by the Academic Division of
Unwin Hyman Ltd
15/17 Broadwick Street, London W1V FP, UK

Allen & Unwin (Australia) Ltd,
8 Napier Street, North Sydney, NSW 2060, Australia

Allen & Unwin (New Zealand) Ltd in association with
the Port Nicholson Press Ltd,
60 Cambridge Terrace, Wellington, New Zealand

First published in 1988

Library of Congress Cataloging-in-Publication Data

Golan, Galia.
  The Soviet Union and National Liberation Movements in the Third World/Galia Golan.
    p. cm.
Includes index.
ISBN 0–04–445111–3 : $45.00
1 Developing countries—Foreign relations—Soviet Union.
2 Soviet Union—Foreign relations—Developing countries.
3 National liberation movements. 4 Soviet Union—Foreign
relations—1945— I. Title.
D888.S65G64 1988

British Library Cataloguing in Publication Data

Golan, Golia
  The Soviet Union and National Liberation Movements in the Third World.
1 Nationalism—Developing countries
2 Soviet Union—Foreign relations—Developing countries
3 Developing countries—Foreign relations—Soviet Union
I Title
322.4'2'091724   JE60
ISBN 0–04–445111–3

Typeset in 10 on 12 print Bembo
and printed in Great Britain by Biddles of Guildford

19 055

Contents

Acknowledgments

A number of people were particularly generous and helpful with their time and comments, particularly with regard to the various national liberation movements. For such assistance, I should like to thank Jerry Bender, Phillip Nel, Weinrich Kuhne, Paul Henze, Hagai Ehrlich, Arthur Klinghoffer, and Wayne Limberg. I am especially grateful to George Breslauer for his extremely useful criticism of the whole manuscript, to Naomi Chazan for insightful work on the theoretical framework, and to Condolezza Rice, Mike MccGwire, and Frank Fukuyama for their thoughtful comments. A group of wonderful assistants helped me ferret out the material at different times: Jonathan Kamen, Feliks Fuks, Alek Millman, Debby Rothfield, Brenda Sheffer, and Zak Levy. I should also like to thank the librarians Jeannette Avraham and Cecile Panzer, as well as my typists Judith Friedgut, Michele Cheslow, and Jean Deacon.

Research for this work was made possible by the funds and facilities of the Hebrew University's Mayrock Center for Research on the Soviet Union and Eastern Europe, the Truman Institute for the Study of Peace, and the Schonbrun Fund. Completion of the work and the writing were made possible by the generosity of the Ford Foundation and the Berkeley–Stanford Project on Soviet International Behavior. Thanks are also due to the University of California, Berkeley, and the Van Leer Jerusalem Institute for the stimulating and pleasant surroundings in which to write.

I should like to dedicate this book to the memory of my good friend Dr Naomi Kies.

Jerusalem, 1987

Introduction

Marxism, as an analysis of capitalist society and a theory for proletarian revolution, is by definition concerned with modern industrialized society. While Marx himself did write sporadically about what is today called the Third World, and about national struggles by subjugated peoples,[1] it was to Lenin that the first socialist state, the Soviet Union, had to turn to find guidelines for relating to this phenomenon.

Soviet theory regarding the Third World evolved over the years, sometimes in zigzags; Khrushchev, for example, reverted to some of the pre-Stalin Leninist notions. Indeed, Khrushchev initiated a fresh Soviet interest in the Third World which generated new policies and involvement in this area as well as doctrines and theoretical investigation. The Brezhnev period brought a reassessment of the theoretical underpinning of these policies, resulting eventually in a still more vigorous involvement in the Third World based on some new, pragmatically oriented principles.[2] The Brezhnev period itself, stretching over eighteen years, exhibited further evolution in Soviet thinking, or what might be interpreted as a retreat to a more ideologically based approach to this area (in the late 1970s). This in turn was abandoned, according to some, in the post-Brezhnev period, with a return to the more pragmatic, possibly even less involved, policy toward the Third World.[3]

The first problem with the above account of Soviet policy is the fact that it is basically linear. A most significant feature, in fact, of Soviet policy and thinking regarding this area is its complexity and multi-dimensionality. This has been perceived by some, most recently Jerry Hough, who have noted the debates among Soviet theoreticians. What the debates reveal is a lack of consensus, not only among the theoreticians but also among Soviet decision-makers themselves, which defies the pure linear periodization or evolution approach to this subject. A policy or theoretical position is not abandoned in one day; contradictory approaches continue to exist side by side, reversals or shifts in dominance blurring clear delineations and characterizations. Dealing with the post-Khrushchev period, we shall see a striking lack of consistency or uniformity in Soviet theoretical works and even in leadership attitudes toward the Third World, culminating in what appears to be a general shift not in the post-Brezhnev period but, rather, in the last years of Brezhnev's rule. Reinforced or continued by the post-Brezhnev leaderships, this shift may not in fact be fully formed, definitive, or fully accepted.

The second problem with the standard (and not-so-standard) histories of Soviet policy toward the Third World is their failure to distinguish among the various objects of this policy, specifically to deal with national liberation movements. Part of the reason for this is the dearth of information available on Soviet relations with such movements. Another part of the reason is that Soviet literature itself makes little or no distinction. The Soviet use of the term "national liberation movement" refers to a broad historical process, from colonial subjugation through independence up to socialism, that is, a broad interpretation of the term "liberation" which includes not just formal independence but genuine independence in every sense, of the type which, according to Marxism–Leninism, can only come with scientific socialism. Thus, even the term "national liberation revolution" means not just the act of achieving statehood or national sovereignty but also the entire process, even subsequently, of achieving the kind of freedom deemed possible only under socialism, or the absence of any kind of capitalist exploitation, be it internal or external (neo-colonialism). Inadvertently, Western experts have tended to perpetuate this approach insofar as they usually study, indiscriminately, the Third World or specific Third World countries as a phenomenon or objects in Soviet foreign policy without distinguishing between movements and states, pre-independence national liberation and the post-independence period. Western studies on Soviet foreign policy in fact tend to concentrate on the post-independence period, usually mentioning only in passing the Soviet attitude toward the pre-independence movements;[4] or, in the case of the separatist movements, the Soviet role usually is treated only briefly.

What is missing, then, from both Soviet works and Western analyses, is a coherent Soviet theory of national liberation movements in the strict sense of the term, that is, the struggle for liberation from foreign rule. Such a theory can be deduced only from an analysis of and often an extrapolation from a wealth of Soviet theoretical works on the Third World in general, in addition to empirical research on Soviet relations with specific movements. A working model for a comprehensive Soviet theory of national liberation movements may be obtained from Soviet statements themselves, even in the absence of Soviet acceptance of the strict definition of the term. A Soviet foreign broadcast series on "The Theory and Practice of the National Liberation Movements" posited the following "premises" for national revolution:[5]

1 growth of the popular masses' resistance to colonialist rule;
2 diffusion among the masses of the liberation ideal;
3 awakening of national awareness;
4 maturing of political forces which stand for the people's interests and are capable of leading their struggle for independence;

5 all-round support rendered by the Soviet Union and other socialist
   countries.

Rearranged, these internal and external factors provide a model to
be used in the development of the theory.[6] Thus, the "awakening of
national awareness" may be termed the study of the *conditions*, internal
and external, that produce national liberation movements, specifically
the "subject" of national liberation and its evolution. The "maturing
of political forces" to represent and lead the people may be termed the
social composition, leadership, and organizational structure of the movement
and its relationship with other organizations or parties. The diffusion
of the liberation ideal encompasses the question of the *ideology* of the
movement, including its basic ideological principles, the vision of the
future society which it postulates, and the objectives it posits. The
growth of mass resistance may entail the forms of the struggle itself
or the *means* employed, be they armed (conventional warfare, guerrilla,
terror, sabotage), unarmed, political, and so forth.

   Finally, Soviet and socialist support addresses the question of outside
assistance and the *role of the Soviet Union*, including the relationship
between national liberation movements and the world proletarian revolution. A further distinction which becomes analytically useful, particularly
in the empirical research but also in the theoretical, is a breakdown
of the movements into two categories: anti-colonial movements, such
as the Zimbabwean movements ZAPU/ZANU or the Mozambique
FRELIMO, and separatist movements, such as the Eritreans or the
Kurds. A third, more problematic, category is distinguishable: this might
roughly be called "internal" movements such as the ANC or the PLO,
which are not strictly anti-colonial but also are not separatist. While the
Soviets do not officially make such distinctions, their behavior and to
some degree their theoretical works do exhibit different approaches to
the different categories, depending upon circumstances.

   Of the various issues or components of the Soviet theory of national
liberation, there are those that are less and those that are more controversial in Soviet literature. On subjects such as the conditions for
the emergence of these movements there appears to be relatively little
controversy, although there does appear to be a more conservative
Marxist economically oriented approach as distinct from a more modern,
sophisticated ethnic approach. This is connected with disagreements
over the meaning of the term "nation", and it also involves somewhat
different emphasis on internal and external influences. The last is by
no means a new issue: it is as old as the communist movement
itself. Moreover, it becomes entangled with the politics of détente and
superpower competition—and accusations. On the whole, however, it
is not a subject that seems to have aroused serious controversy.

Only slightly more dispute revolves around the issue of composition and particularly leadership, the old Roy–Lenin and Comintern debates over the role of the national bourgeoisie joined by newer controversies over the role of the military and the intelligentsia. Nor is the role of the peasants a simple matter in view of modern Third World, especially Chinese, theories of revolution, where the issue of town versus countryside is still an active one. And then, the phenomenon of the so-called middle strata, including the intelligentsia and the petty bourgeoisie but defying strict class delineation, is also to be accommodated.

The subject of organization is less complicated up to the point of creating a vanguard Marxist–Leninist party. This idea is surprisingly complex and controversial, spilling over into the area of ideology as well, where this encroaches upon the constituent parts of future society envisaged by the ideologies of the movements. This subject of ideologies is a far more controversial one, with different approaches in Soviet literature to the ideology of nationalism, as well as to religion and other Third World ideologies or belief systems. The controversy sharpens over the possibility of socialism evolving from the national movements, the character of the societies envisaged, and even, to a lesser degree, the objectives of these movements' ideologies. This includes the definition of self-determination, the forms it can take, and the conditions necessary for it.

Equally controversial and complex is the issue of methods or means of struggle, not only because of traditional arguments over violent versus peaceful means, terror versus political action, but also because of modern Third World emphasis on methods associated with the peasantry rather than the workers, based on the Chinese or Fanon doctrines of revolution. The issue of means is connected with the equally controversial subject of local wars and the risks involved in such conflicts, such as the possibility of escalation and superpower involvement. These in turn touch on the whole issue of the role of the Soviet Union, specifically on just how much and in what way the Soviets should be involved. On this last issue there appears to be a good deal of controversy, with views varying over the years, although basically revolving around the questions of détente and revolution. Thus, while it is not the intention of this study to describe the debates within the Soviet literature,[7] these controversies generate a variety of views which defy a unitary or monolithic presentation of "the Soviet view."

The controversies are generally concentrated in Soviet theoretical literature. Nonetheless, upon occasion they are reflected in the views of foreign communists. More important, albeit infrequently, they are also reflected in leadership pronouncements. These at least provide some clues as to which view is favored by the members of the Soviet leadership at a given time, although there do appear to have been varied opinions within the Soviet leadership itself on some of these issues. Moreover, in some cases the theoreticians preceded what was to become a leadership position, presaging if not necessarily precipitating evolution of Soviet official thinking. It is indeed difficult clearly to determine the exact relationship between the theoretical discussions and the views of the policy-makers, or, for that matter, the relative weights among the theoreticians themselves.

The Soviet system of research institutes, outside and inside the CPSU, which has flourished particularly since the 1960s, is quite well known by now.[8] Just how these institutes are related to the actual decision-making process is somewhat less clear. Formally, there is a series of non-party research institutes in the Academy of Sciences, such as the Africa Institute, the Oriental Institute, the Far East Institute, the Latin America Institute, the Institute for World Economic and International Relations, the Institute of the International Workers Movement, and so forth. The CPSU Central Committee, for its parts, has a series of institutes such as the Institute for Social Sciences and the Marxism–Leninism Institute, both within the Ideology Department; while the International Department is broken down into regional units, many of which clearly deal with research as well as policy.[9]

Yet there does not appear to be a solid wall between the party and non-party bodies. In terms of personnel, we know that at least three leading officials (deputy chiefs) of the International Department—Rostislav Ul'ianovskii, Karen Brutents, and Ivan Kovalenko—were appointed from non-party research institutes to the Central Committee's International Department. Similarly, the two types of units frequently hold joint meetings or conferences, with the party commissioning or ordering research from the Academy of Sciences, as well as employing a group of consultants from the Academy institutes, although there are also occasions upon which lack of cooperation has also been singled out for criticism.[10] In some circumstances there are simultaneous joint appointments, as in the case of Petr Fedoseev, deputy president of the Academy of Sciences and head of the Marxist–Leninist Institute of the Central Committee's Ideology Department, although few of the non-party institutes' heads have actually been Central Committee members until recently. Georgii Arbatov, head of the Academy of Sciences' USA and Canada Institute, was named to the Central Committee in 1981; the late head of the Institute for World Economy and Internal Relations, Nikolai Inozemtsev, was named candidate member in 1971; his successor for a brief period, Aleksandr Iakovlev, was also a member; and Evgeny Primakov, who took over the same institute in 1985, was also named candidate member at the twenty-seventh CPSU Congress. Yet many of these institute heads, such as Primakov, Inozemtsev in his time, or Anatolii Gromyko of the Africa Institute, are considered to have excellent connections with the party leadership (Gromyko if for no other reason than that he is Andrei Gromyko's son). Similarly, there is also cooperation between Soviet government ministries and these research institutes, occasionally in the form of joint research projects or conferences.[11]

On the other hand, the Central Committee is the recipient of, and to some degree the channel for, information from non-party units (the institutes, the ministries, even the KGB) to the party Secretariat and Politburo. More specifically, it has some supervisory role with regard to the research institutes, at least insofar as it has high-level representatives on the editorial boards of the institutes' journals and, presumably, control over personnel appointments.[12]

In short, whatever the influence of the institutes on the Communist party—and there is some difference of opinion on this in the West—the party units are the Soviet Union's most authoritative bodies in the formulation of foreign policy attitudes. The International Department may compete with the Ideological or other departments on some issues, and it may rely on materials and personnel from the institutes, but it would appear to be the most important unit for informing foreign policy leadership decisions. This would be particularly so for the realm of national liberation movements, if not for the Third World itself, for this department was originally designed to deal with non-ruling communist parties, and was expanded to include movements and, eventually, the non-communist regimes that grew out of these movements.

If the party units, and specifically the International Department, are the most authoritative within the theoretical discussions, one might be tempted simply to view their works as "the" line. It would probably be inaccurate to draw such a conclusion, however, inasmuch as the above-mentioned controversies and varied positions often cut across organization lines, both within the party and between the party and various institutes. Although it is tempting to make a party=conservative/institutes=flexible distinction, one finds some conservative attitudes among the institute scholars and, even more so, what might be called flexibility or originality among the Central Committee analysts. The most notable of these has been deputy chief of the International Department, Karen Brutents, elevated to candidate membership in the Central Committee at the 1986 CPSU congress, and believed to be close to certain members of the Soviet leadership (particularly Andropov until his death).

Some institutional consistency in attitudes does exist, but even when this appears it is not always entirely clear just what *policy* option the relatively consistent attitude would indicate. For example, a negative attitude toward the possibility of the national liberation movements evolving into socialist governments might indicate a hands-off, non-supportive Soviet role' but it could also serve as a basis for advocating Soviet involvement so as to ensure the ultimate direction of the movement.

A similar dichotomy may exist in the arguments for and against the creation of a Marxist–Leninist party, in that some would argue that these movements, even after achieving power, are far from proletarian or socialist and therefore are not yet suited for the creation of such a party, while others would find in these same circumstances the very reason for setting up such a party forthwith. Others, who have argued that the movements would not inevitably bring in socialism, have done so to advocate neither intervention nor the abandonment but rather, simply, a more realistic attitude with lower expectations. By the same token, there have been those who have invoked détente as a facilitating factor, moderating the West and thereby relieving the socialist bloc from an obligation to intervene and from any need for *armed* struggle. Other commentators invoking détente, however, have seen it as providing a calmer international atmosphere in which the Soviet Union need not be fearful of becoming involved in or encouraging armed struggle. Conversely, an image of an aggressive West could be evidence of the need for a cautious, non-interventionist policy for fear of escalation and confrontation; yet an aggressive interfering Western policy could be said to demand a strong Soviet rebuff and defense of friends abroad.

These are just a few of the apparent contradictions that appear in the not unusual situation of individuals, possibly institutions, drawing different (in this case, policy) conclusions from basically the same set of facts. The problem is that the theoretical works, be they of party or academic origin, tend to concentrate on what they see as facts, with their policy recommendations remaining either secret or merely implied. Certain code words or phrases do appear, in leadership speeches as well, which ostensibly indicate policy preferences. The proper interpretation on the outside analyst's part presumably could be derived only from an empirical study of Soviet behavior itself. Yet, while the study of Soviet behavior is certainly instructive as to which policy option or interpretation has actually been chosen, a continued or apparent dissonance with the theoretical discussions is not without significance, especially when those discussions are conducted by the very body formulating foreign policy recommendations for the party – the International Department. That controversy or variety of views persist—and are permitted to be expressed—suggests that the policy itself has not been wholeheartedly embraced and may well be subject to change. Indeed, as stated above, theoretical debates have preceded changes in leadership pronouncements, and possibly even policies.

Thus, the study of the theoretical works may well shed some light on future as well as present Soviet policies. What has been delineated by some as the middle and late Brezhnev period, as well as the post-Brezhnev period, have been chosen for concentration, for they contain the major themes and lines of debates (and controversy) after the initial post-Khrushchev reassessment of the late 1960s.[13] Indeed, these would appear to be particularly rich periods for a flourishing of Soviet thinking on the subject of the Third World as a whole, in which Soviet theoreticians, inside and outside the party apparat, appeared to be seeking the most "realistic" policy, in part in response to failures as well as to new challenges in the Third World.

A study of actual Soviet policies toward the various national libera-tion movements provides the opportunity to examine the relationship between theory and practice or, at least, evidence of the actual theoretical position chosen for implementation. A comparative analysis of actual Soviet behavior in relation to national liberation movements in different regions, as well as within a specific region, may provide theoretical conclusions which are no less instructive regarding Soviet foreign policy considerations than the Soviet theoretical discussions themselves. The degree of actual Soviet involvement, and the types of Soviet responses and positions toward the movements, may vary along a scale, all the way from actual opposition to propaganda support only, to proxy intervention, to advisers in place or Soviet intervention. The position taken or type of response and behavior chosen by the Soviets may be determined by a number of factors, both internal and external. Thus, a comparative study can examine the relative importance of these factors outlined, explicitly or implicitly, in the theoretical discussions. The importance of the internal factors, such as ideology, organization, composition, leadership, and the means chosen by the movement for its struggle, can be tested against outside factors, such as the Sino-Soviet competition, local, regional, or global factors, including not only the Soviets' relationship with and interests in the ruling government but also East–West considerations and risk-taking.

From this type of analysis certain patterns or trends emerge, distin-guishable to a large degree by the categorization of anti-colonial and separatist movements, as well as the more problematic but definable third "internal" category. The first category includes the following move-ments: the NLF of Vietnam, the anti-Portuguese movements, FRELIMO of Mozambique, PAIGC of Guinea-Bissau-Cape Verde, the MPLA of Angola, and the southern African movements ZAPU of Zimbabwe and SWAPO of Namibia. The rival or additional movements in each country, such as ZANU of Zimbabwe, COREMO of Mozambique, SWANU of Namibia, and UNITA and FNLA of Angola, are dealt with in relation to the Soviet-supported movement.

The secessionist or separatist category is much larger, encompassing in many cases several movements or peoples within one state, such as the Karen in Burma, the Baluchis, Kurds, and Arabs of Khuzistan in Iran, the Baluchis and Pathans in Pakistan and Afghanistan, and the Eritreans and Tigreans of Ethiopia. In addition, there are the East Bengalis of Pakistan, the Kurds of Turkey and Iraq, the Ibos in Nigeria, the Tamil in Sri Lanka, the Sikhs in India, the Moros in the Philippines, the southern Sudanese (Anyanya) in the Sudan, the Katangans in Zaire, the FROLINAT in Chad, and the Dhofaris in Oman (although the last two groups may well be revolutionary rather than, strictly speaking, national liberation movements). Three movements seem to fall into a category all of their own: the PLO, the ANC, and the Polisario—in some instances bearing the signs of anti-colonialist movements, in other instances bearing those of secessionists insofar as Soviet behavior and the factors governing this behavior are concerned.

As in the study of Soviet theory, so too a study of actual Soviet behavior does not necessarily produce a clear, totally consistent, airtight—or dogmatic—model. What does emerge from both types of analysis is a picture of complexity, relative pragmatism, or flexibility, characterized nonetheless by certain tendencies and preferences connected with various factors within each category. These in turn have dictated both Soviet behavior and positions vis-à-vis the movements themselves, in some cases precipitating disagreement and/or abrupt changes in policy. They also determined the degree or lack of Soviet control in Moscow's relationships with the various movements, as well as the degree or lack of Soviet commitment.

While covering a large number of movements, this study is not exhaustive. There are some movements, such as those of the Canary Islands or Micronesia or New Caledonia, which are rarely, if ever mentioned by Soviet or other sources, defying any kind of systematic study. The focus is mainly on the 1970s and early 1980s, in part because this is the period represented by Soviet theoretical debate which *followed* the post-Khrushchev discussions. The major reason for the choice of this period, however, is the fact that it appears to encompass changes in overall Soviet Third World policies including a more activist approach, ending in the last years of Brezhnev's rule and the transition to a new Soviet leadership.[14] Moreover, it is a period in which decisive steps were incumbent upon the Soviets subsequent to Khrushchev's opening of contacts with various movements and in response to actual events in the Third World, be they connected with Cuba or China, with regional or global actors, from the civil war in Nigeria and the Indian–Pakistan war to the revolutions in Portugal, Ethiopia, and Iran, or to other events in southern Africa or the Middle East.

Notes*

1. See Shlomo Avineri (ed.), *Karl Marx on Colonialization and Modernization*, Doubleday, New York, 1968.
2. See Elizabeth Kridl Valkenier, "Soviet Economic Relations with the Third World", in Roger Kanet (ed.), *The Soviet Union and the Developing Nations*, Johns Hopkins University Press, Baltimore, 1974, pp. 215–36; or Jerry Hough, *The Struggle for the Third World: Soviet Debates and American Options*, Brookings Institution, Washington, D.C., 1986.
3. Francis Fukuyama, "Moscow's Post-Brezhnev Reassessment of the Third World", Rand, February 1986; Elizabeth Kridl Valkenier, "Revolutionary Change in the Third World: Recent Soviet Reassessments", *World Politics* 38, no. 3 (April 1986): 419–24.
4. S. N. MacFarlane, *Superpower Rivalry and Third World Radicalism*, Johns Hopkins University, Baltimore, 1985, is in part an exception to this. The only full-length studies of Soviet relations with a national liberation movement are Galia Golan, *The Soviet Union and the Palestine Liberation Movement*, Praeger, New York, 1980 and an unpublished M.A. thesis by Arthur Jay Klinghoffer, "The Indian Communist Party and the Indian National Congress."
5. Moscow radio in Portuguese to Africa, 22 April 1974.
6. The following model was worked out with Dr. Naomi Chazan in a course which we taught jointly on National Liberation Movements at the Hebrew University of Jerusalem, 1983–84, 1984–85.
7. This has been done amply in the broader study of the Soviet Union and the Third World by Jerry Hough, *Struggle for the Third World*.
8. Oded Eran, *The Mezhdunarodniki*, Turtledove Publishers, Tel-Aviv, 1979; Seweryn Bialer, "The Political System," in Robert Byrnes (ed.), *After Brezhnev: Sources of Soviet Conduct in the 1980s*, Indiana University Press, Bloomington, 1983, pp. 61–2; Milton Morris, "The Soviet Africa Institute and the Development of African Studies," *Journal of Modern African Studies* 2, no. 2 (1973): 247–65; Hough, *Struggle for the Third World*; and Jerry Hough, "Soviet Policymaking Toward Foreign Communists," *Studies in Comparative Communism* 15, no. 3 (Autumn 1982): 176–80.
9. On the International Department see Robert Kitrinos, "International Department of the CPSU," *Problems of Communism* 33 (1984): 47–67; Wallace Spaulding, "Addenda on the International Department," *Problems of Communism* 33 (1984): 68–75; Leonard Schapiro, "The International Department of the CPSU: Key to Soviet Policy," *International Journal* (Winter 1976–77): 41–55; Hough, "Policy-making," 167–83; Vladimir Petrov, "Formation of Soviet Foreign Policy," *Orbis* 17 (1973): 819–50; Philip Nel, "Soviet African Policy: The Role of the International Department," *Africa Insight* 12, no. 3 (1982): 132–6, 141.
10. A. I. Borisov and N. B. Aleksandrov, "Obsuzhdenie knigi N.A. Simoniia 'Strany Vostoka: puti razvitiia," *Narody Azii i Afriki*, no. 3 (1977): 54–5.
11. E.g., V. L. Tiagunenko et al., *Vooruzhennaia bor'ba narodor Afriki za svobodu i nezavisimost'*, Ministerstvo obrony-SSSR, Nauka, Moscow, 1974.
12. Kitronos, "International Department of the CPSU," p. 63, says that Brutents is on the editorial board of *Aziia i Afrika segodnia* and, with Zagladin, on the board of *SShA: ekonomika, politka, ideologiia*.
13. For a discussion of this debate see, for example, Roger Kanet (ed.), *The Soviet Union and Developing Nations*, Johns Hopkins University Press, Baltimore, 1974; Roger Kanet and Donna Bahry (eds.), *Soviet Economic and Political Relations with the Developing Countries*, Praeger, New York, 1974; Raymond Duncan (ed.), *The Soviet Union in the Third World: Successes and Failures*, Westview, Boulder, Colo., 1981; John Keep, "The Soviet Union and the Third World," *Survey* (Summer 1969): 21–8.

---

* Transliterations according to the Library of Congress. Differences appear when the original source employed a different transliteration system. All references to radio and television are from FBIS (Washington D.C.) and BBC (London).

14 David Albright (ed.), *Africa and International Communism*, Macmillan, London, 1980; John Copper and Daniel Papp (eds.), *Communist Nations' Military Assistance*, Westview, Boulder, Colo., 1983; Stephen Hosmer and Thomas Wolfe, *Soviet Policy and Practice toward Third World Conflicts*, Lexington Books, Lexington, Mass., 1983; Walter Laqueur (ed.), *The Pattern of Soviet Conduct in the Third World*, Praeger, New York, 1983; John Mauer and Richard Porth, *Military Intervention in the Third World*, Praeger, New York, 1984; Bruce Porter, *The USSR in Third World Conflicts*, Cambridge University Press, Cambridge, 1984.

PART I

Toward a Soviet Theory of National Liberation

1
Origins of National Liberation Movements

Introduction

Basic to the Soviet approach to national liberation movements, even to specific movements, were the conceptions as to just what, legitimately, constitutes such a movement. A "national liberation movement" would appear to be, by definition, a framework for the conduct of the liberation struggle of a nation. At the outset, however, the term "nation" itself requires definition; for, presumably, the characterization of a particular group as a "nation" would qualify it for a positive Soviet approach. The issue of just what qualifies as a nation has, however, been a controversial one in Soviet thinking, primarily because of Soviet internal concerns as a federal state composed of numerous "nations". The dispute and the final definitions accepted at any one time have had relevance for—and indeed, have been applied to—Soviet attitudes regarding movements in the Third World. Usually this has been in the form of rejecting the legitimacy of a given movement on the grounds that the "subject" did not in fact constitute a nation.

The dispute itself, in recent years, revolved around two approaches. First, there was the more conservative approach which defined nationhood in strict Marxist categories, that is, socioeconomic terms. In time, however, a new approach emerged which allowed for, and in some cases even focused on, more subjective factors, such as psychological or traditional influences expressed in such categories as ethnicity and ethnos. The newer approach opened the way for a more sophisticated analysis of phenomena in the Third World, including separatism, in an effort to cope with peoples or groups in other than a colonial framework.

The varied approaches to just what constituted a nation had their counterparts in the theories regarding the emergence of movements for national liberation. Just as there was the more conservative school, applying an economic, class-based definition of nationhood, so too, the conditions that produced the awakening and organization of a nation for struggle were seen by some as purely objective socioeconomic factors and processes. Variations appeared among Soviet theoreticians, however, drawing attention to additional—more subjective—factors, which were in fact emphasized by still others as the central factors. To some degree this debate, which saw leading officials of the party's International Department on opposite sides, was generated by a dissatisfaction with classical Marxist–Leninist categories with regard to developing societies as such. Armed with new categories, the emergence of movements could be explained in socio-political and psychological as well as economic terms, in accord with the new ideas of ethnicity. Thus, here too separatist movements could be accommodated, though not fully accepted.

An additional approach to the way in which national liberation movements were formed focused on a totally external factor: the October Revolution. The role of this event, its essentiality, its relevance, and its universality, were in fact viewed in varied ways, to the point of causing some controversy among Soviet theoreticians. The issue had much relevance for policy, not only because the view of the importance of outside factors would determine the role of the Soviet Union, but also because each view implied a particular set of expectations regarding both the struggle itself and the type of society that might emerge from the movement—including its potential for socialist development. Foreign policy statements by Soviet leaders, however, dwelt little on these issues, avoiding, as might be expected, most of the theoretical analyses and implications. Exhibiting far less variety, they tended to pattern their approach to suit their audience, on the whole adhering to the more conservative socioeconomic approach. Nonetheless, leadership pronouncements to some extent did reflect the ongoing debate.

The "Subject" of Liberation: The Conservative or Socioeconomic Approach

The conservative Soviet approach was invariably based on Stalin's 1913 definition of the nation, which remained virtually unchanged until the late 1960s. As promulgated as late as 1950, this definition asserted that a nation was "an historically evolved, stable community of people, formed on the basis of a common language, territory, economic life, and psychic make-up manifested in a common culture."[1] Ultimately, a nation was either "bourgeois" or "socialist" depending upon its social structure, with the socialist nation obviously constituting the higher form. On the basis of Stalin's definition of nation, Soviet international law specialist and deputy director of the Africa Institute Gleb Starushenko elaborated a relatively complex explanation of national liberation or the subject of self-determination in the Third World. Writing before the debates of the late 1960s, Starushenko distinguished between tribes, races, and nations, the last appearing only with the emergence of capitalism.[2] He described race as "a large group of people with common biological characteris- tics...consequently a *biological category*."[3] A tribe was a "consanguineous group of people of one and the same race [with] its language, customs, morals, traditions, etc....consequently an *ethnographical category*."[4]

In this scheme of things, there was no national community of people in either primitive, communal society or early feudal society, that is, not until private property and early commodity production broke down tribal bonds—or led to tribal unions—and brought class divisions. People then mixed and united into national groups, rather than tribes, on the same territory. This was a qualitatively new community of people because it was formed on a territorial basis rather than on that of consanguinity. These national groups in time merged or redivided to include people not only of different tribes but also of different races. This then was a national community, which was not just a racial or tribal community but rather an historical community. The nation into which a national group evolved was, therefore, an "*historical category*," characterized by the fact that it existed "a relatively long time"; in other words, it was a stable community of people. It was distinguished from other communities by virtue of its common language and, in time, by a common psychological makeup manifested in a common culture.[5]

The key element of this evolution was economic, for only close eco- nomic ties could convert isolated, autonomous, self-sufficient national groups into a nation. And the initiative for this came from the capitalist mode of production (appearing within the feudal society); for "in its thirst for profits, the bourgeoisie centralizes the means of production and concentrates property...gets the customs barriers abolished, and supports absolutist power in its drive to put an end to feudal disunity and unite the country."[6] The economic factor not only accounted for the territorial mutality but also influenced the developing language (one common language being needed for commercial intercourse and eco- nomic concentration), while even the emerging psychological mutality was the product of the material conditions inasmuch as, according to Starushenko, "psychological makeup is a coagulation of impressions derived by people from environment."[7]

From all this, one may conclude that the development of the nation was "an objective law of social development."[8] This process, although inevitable, could be accelerated if the emerging nation, even at an earlier stage such as that of a "national grouping," were freed from outside (fo- reign) constraints. In this sense, all peoples, not just fully formed nations, had the right to self-determination or freedom from aggression. "People" was a broader concept than "nation," defined as a "large body of persons...inhabiting a common territory."[9] According to Starushenko, "the population of a colony representing a conglomeration of tribes and national groups, is not a 'nation', but it is a 'people' and as such is a subject of the right to self-determination. Such a people has a common territory, a common historic destiny, and a common aim, which it wants to achieve by availing itself of the right to self-determination."[10] Starushenko was willing to exchange community of aims for some other mutality, such as a common economic or social life or common statehood—peoplehood being defined basically by territoriality and at least one common feature.[11] The national liberation struggle, therefore, was not limited to nations but encompassed a broader category in which at least some of the attributes of nationhood were as yet unformed.

The debates of the late 1960s were intended less to challenge this view of national liberation than to cope with the concept of nation as such (in connection with Soviet nationality problems).[12] In this debate, the editors of *Voprosy istorii* posited economic community (including the existence of a proletariat) as the decisive element which converted a people into a nation, downgrading the importance of language and adding "a self-consciousness of ethnic identity," a national character (defined much like Stalin's psychic makeup), and a national tradition.[13] Ethnicity and tradition were significant innovations, the former being associated with the common economy, territory, and language. Ethnicity provided, according to most of the debate's participants, the source of strength of a given nation, while tradition was considered a somewhat vague but historically and culturally binding feature.[14] One contributor—the ethnographer Iu. Semenov—dissented from the above, defining nation primarily as a "political structure," existing only when there was a unified "social organism."[15] The final form of this "organism" was to be determined by the state, when it came. Presumably this was an attempt to accommodate the more amorphous Third World nations as distinct from Stalin's division of nations into "bourgeois" and "socialist." Thus, in time, a transitional category—neither bourgeois nor socialist—was added to the qualification of types of nations, referring to the developing countries.[16]

A central point in the debate, and one that may have separated the conservative, more ideologically bound, from the more innovative theoreticians, was the relative importance of economic (social) characteristics versus psychological (consciousness-centred) criteria. Petr Fedoseev, head of the Marxist–Leninist Institute of the Central Committee's Ideology Department, cited Lenin's criticism of the Narodniki and of Otto Bauer on this issue.[17] First, he explained the dialectical evolution of the term "nation," based on the "identity of social and ethnic" factors. The social elements were defined as, primarily, the economic ties and the class (and political) relations created by these ties; the ethnic elements were "chiefly" the language, territory, and "features (but not the entire content) of the culture, way of life, beliefs, traditions, mentality and psychology shaped by the geographic environment, common origin and centuries of historical development, frequently still in the clan or tribe."[18] Although the social–ethnic essence of the nation was a dialectical whole, the *social* factor played the dominant role, with the economic factor being the one responsible for the emergence of a nation as such.[19] The Narodniki had been guilty of ignoring the social (economic) element, reducing the essence of nations to ethnic phenomena; while Bauer, guilty of the same thing, had seen the nation not as an historic community but as a cultural one, emphasizing the ethnic in a "psychological" theory of nation.[20]

Fedoseev justified his elevation of the idea of economic community to first place in the hierarchy of determinants of the nation on the grounds that times had changed, necessitating new formulations.[21] This new formulation reduced or more restrictively defined the role of "psychological makeup," and called for less dogmatism as to the necessity of *all* the attributes of the nation to be equally present. Thus, Fedoseev's proposed definition of nation was: "a lasting historical community of people constituting a form of social development based on the continuity of economic life in combination with the community of language, territory, culture, consciousness, and psychology."[22] According to this definition, not only were language and territory secondary to and determined by economic life, but national culture, consciousness, and psychology were basically class-defined concepts. Bearing in mind that nations themselves emerged only with the capitalist mode of production, national culture, consciousness, and psychology were fated to be dualistic (bourgeois and proletarian), torn by contradictions so long as there was class society. The important point was that even national consciousness and psychology were determined by class factors, with no independent existence. At least, Fedoseev was to concede a difference between national consciousness (or self-awareness)—with an essentially socio-class content—and ethnic consciousness, which was "based first and foremost on ethnic properties."[23]

An ethnic group was defined as a community, small in number, often dispersed, and only loosely connected in terms of ethnic properties such as language, territory, sense of common origin, community of culture, life-style, and traditions.[24] Even these properties were said to be most stable only in the family, in rites and traditions. Distinct from this were ethnographic groups, classified as "constituents of nations and nation- alities" which have merged with them but retained certain "distinctive traits."[25] Ethnic groups, existing generally in an environment different from their own, were said to be more stable than ethnographic groups, whose more familiar surroundings led to relatively rapid assimilation. National groups were defined by Fedoseev, as by Starushenko, as transient phenomena; but, unlike Starushenko, the Fedoseev study saw national groups as "splinters" of foreign nations or nationalities, destined to merge with the new, dominant nation rather than retain ties with their original nation. (Examples given were the Koreans, Slovaks, Turks, etc., living in the Soviet Union.[26]) Ethnic, ethnographic, and national groups, then, were all transient, and ultimately little different from the nations and nationalities among which they lived. Said to provide "variety into the overly monotonous homogeneity of the national character," they do not appear to have been perceived as "subjects" of history or liberation.

The term "nationality" here was said to have had two meanings. One was the same as the term "national group" employed by Starushenko, namely, an historical stage on the way from tribe to nation.[27] The second meaning was the broader term "people"—including ethnic or national groups and/or nations. In the more limited meaning, a nationality begins "when it has enough strength, enough unity, and the capacity and opportunity to assure national development."[28] National existence then depended, according to Fedoseev's quote of Lenin, on "considerable numbers, one territory, and a developed national feeling, which on the socio-economic plane means a striving for unity and independence."[29] The properties of a nationality were basically the same as those of a nation, but because they were at an earlier stage of development (and of the division of labor), they were qualitatively different—socially. Moreover, if the properties were not sufficiently strong, or conditions not suitable, a nationality would *not* develop into a nation. A nationality could develop into a nation before or after independence or without independence altogether.

A few pages later, the Fedoseev study offered another definition of nationality: "the national bonds of individual people to the aggregate of traits and properties that identify them with a nation, nationality, national or ethnic group."[30] This definition, which appeared in a sub-section which may have been written by a different author, thus defined nationality in terms of identification and self-awareness, albeit "shaped by social factors" as well as ethnic ones.[31] By this definition, however, origins did not necessarily coincide with nationality, for national identity could be formed by ethnic or social factors. Yet ethnic ties could or could not outweigh national ties, or the reverse.

While the Fedoseev study provided, on the whole, a conservative appraisal of the nation—elevating social (economic) factors above all others—it did at least address the more subtle issues of ethnicity and national identification or self-awareness. The same could be said for a slightly earlier study, edited by Central Committee International Department's first deputy chief Vadim Zagladin and Fedor Ryzhenko, head of the Ideology Department's Social Sciences Institute, which grew out of a symposium held by Ryzhenko's Institute.[32] This study explicitly took issue with the conclusions of the 1960s debate, arguing that "national" attributes appeared long before the nation. Thus, it was posited that the "national" (defined as "socio-ethnic") element was present from the very beginning of society, even in the primeval communal system. Indeed, it remained the most important aspect of society until a fully class-differentiated society evolved—even up to the present day in many Third World societies.[33] Although the study went on to emphasize the predominance of the class factor over the national, categorically dismissing nationalism (which was a class phenomenon),[34] the effort to distinguish between "national" and "nationalist" did produce greater attention to—and legitimacy for—concepts such as national identity, national self-awareness, and the like. "National feelings," for example, were described as "the aggregate of sentiments and feelings of affection for a social–ethnic community, for the peculiar natural environment in which it develops, of respect for its positive traditions and culture, of affinity with its historic destiny, and solidarity with other members of the same social-ethnic community."[35] "National self-awareness" was a consciousness which was emotional rather than conceptual, dominating all other relationships.[36] In time, this could produce a national ideology, that is a more conceptually structured national consciousness. Once classes developed, however, all of these were influenced by and perceived through "the prism of class interest."[37] Thus, for Zagladin as well as Fedoseev, national consciousness was, on the whole, a class or socially influenced phenomenon, even if self-awareness and ethnic identification were noted.

The New Ethnic–Psychological Approach

Quite a number of definitions of national self-consciousness, if not of nation, were to appear in the 1970s, but the most subjective (and therefore innovative) would appear to have been that of Iu. V. Bromlei.[38] Bromlei was head of the Academy of Science's Scientific Council on National Problems and of its Institute for Ethnography. Given these positions, his view might be considered the major challenge to the Central Committee studies.

For Bromlei, national consciousness was first of all ethnic consciousness, that is, a person's perception of himself as a member of an ethnic community regardless of his affiliation with a tribe, a nationality, or a nation. The measuring of this was contained in Bromlei's appeal for "'ethnic'" terminology, whereby the term "narod" (nation and people) would be replaced by the term "'ethnos'" (people), ethnic community being a still broader concept.[39] In this manner, the term "ethnic community" could be removed from the specific pre-nation description to a more permanent category characterized by different levels and typologies. "Ethnos," defined as people, would then replace the common usage of the word "narod" and include all types of communities from tribes to nations. "Ethnos" was defined as an "historically established community of people, characterized by common, relatively stable cultural features, certain distinctive psychological traits and also by an awareness of their identity and distinctiveness from other similar communities."[40] Bromlei urged a distinction between these components of ethnos on the one hand, and the conditions contributing to the origin of an ethnos on the other hand, namely, geographic, economic, and state–political factors.[41] These, he argued, might play a part in the rise of an ethnos, but after this they remained significant "only as auxiliary forms." So much for the Stalinist attributes of a nation, although Bromlei did allow for interaction between an ethnos and its environment or, in other words, social influences.[42]

Bromlei also noted "synthetic formations," that is, the interpenetration of the ethnos and a social organism (independent societies or independent macro units of social development such as tribal units in primitive society or socio-political units in clan society).[43] These synthetic formations were called ethno-social organisms, and they were characterized by the traditional attributes of a nation: common economic, social, territorial, and political features. Generally, the ethnic outlived the socio-political characteristics of a community. The difference with an ethno-social organism, however, was in its connection with a particular social organism or socio-political form (such as slave-owning or feudal society). The advent of classes did not necessarily change the ethnic character of a community, although it could lead to class or group features within the ethnic community. Nor did an ethno-social organism have to be ethnically homogeneous. Bromlei spoke of three types of ethno-social organisms:

type one: with own territory and social organism but the same ethnos existing also outside this territory or socio–economic unit (e.g., Turks, Slovaks);

type two: the socio-political formation forms several ethno-social organisms out of one ethnos (e.g., several Arab states moulding the Egyptian, Iraqi, Syrian, etc. ethno-social organisms);

type three: one socio-political community (state) with several homogeneous ethnoi with relative independence (e.g., the USSR).[44]

This was not meant to exhaust all the types of ethno-social organisms, ethnos appearing in various forms and varieties of ethnic communities. It was intended, however, to provide a more inclusive conceptual

framework than the traditional tribe–nationality–nation formula criticized explicitly by Bromlei.[45]

The debate continued throughout the 1970s and into the 1980s, with
numerous contributors advocating more or less subjective, more or less
"socially" oriented, more or less conservative definitions.[46] With regard
to the Third World, the important point was that the subject of national
liberation could be not only the national group but also the ethnos, while
the historical approach left room for the national group or nationality
or people to seek liberation and self-determination. Within the bounds
of the more standard historical, economically dominated approach, it
was granted that, despite the fact that a national economy had not yet
developed and therefore that nationhood had not yet been reached by
many peoples of the Third World, this process—as Starushenko had
said—could actually be accelerated if something less than a nation became
the subject of a liberation struggle.

Nonetheless, this idea of an entity, be it an ethnos or a national
grouping—that is, anything less than a nation acting as the subject
of liberation—did pose some problems. In a *Narody Azii i Afriki*
discussion in 1973, A. D. Litman said, somewhat disdainfully, that
often "what pretends to be a formed national community is just a racial
or ethnic community," lacking a basis for independent existence.[47] V.
S. Shevtsov, in a book on national sovereignty, also warned against
independence for a nation that was still being formed and lacking
in self-awareness, although he did not totally reject the idea.[48] The
more authoritative Rostislav Ul'ianovskii, deputy chief of the Central
Committee International Department, was less hesitant but cautionary.
He conceded and approved of the fact that many countries seeking
liberation were at a pre-capitalist, even pre-feudal, stage, lacking the
economic community essential for nationhood. Thus, he said, "not
only the formed nations or those that were in the process of formation
proclaimed independence *but also* conglomerates of nationalities, tribes,
and ethnic groups."[49] More significantly, Ul'ianovskii, the senior party
theoretician on Third World affairs, went on to argue that not all of
these fighting units actually deserved independence. He attributed this not
only to the underdeveloped level of their nationhood, but also to the
unevenness of their economic and cultural development, the diversity
of their religions and languages, and the arbitrariness of the borders
inherited from the colonial era (specifically in Africa).[50]

Nations, Peoples, and Separatism

What Ul'ianovskii was warning against was separatism, movements
which he claimed sought secession not from a colonialist metropole

but from a new state itself or an anti-imperialist state. For this reason, a caveat should be placed on the right to liberation or self-determination, subordinate, as Lenin had decreed, to the broader interests of the whole or "the interests of socialism."[51]

Ul'ianovskii's opposition to separatist as distinct from purely anti-colonialist movements was by no means an isolated phenomenon; criticism of separatism was an integral part of Soviet thinking on the Third World. Starushenko, for example, in an article written with Anatoli Gromyko, head of the Academy of science's Africa Institute since 1977, condemned what he called the "bourgeois concept" of nation-state on the grounds that such a principle was "inapplicable in many areas of Asia and Africa because often not yet formed nations and ethnic groups are such mottley mosaics that they cannot promise, even in the future, solutions along strictly ethnic lines."[52] This was not, however, so much a challenge to the rights of ethnic communities or pre-nation groupings to be the "subject" of liberation or self-determination. Indeed, all of the above theoreticians defended the right of every "people," however defined, to self-determination.[53] The challenge was, rather, to the form that this self-determination should take, that is, the objective to be pursued: independence, autonomy, or some other form of relationship with other nations or peoples. I shall, therefore, discuss the issue of separatism below, in connection with the objectives posed by the ideologies of national liberation movements.[54] It was, nonetheless, indicative of the problem the Soviets had with their own multinational state, as well as with the phenomenon of separatism in the Third World, that they found it necessary to distinguish between liberation and self-determination on the one hand, and statehood or independence on the other, the former (but not the latter) being the right of every people.[55]

A pedagogical journal summed things up in the most general terms in an article in 1977 which nonetheless condemned separatism. The author, V. F. Gryzlov, explained that the subject of liberation could be a state, an ethnic group, or a nation, or none of these: it could be communities of heterogeneous ethnic formations, or simply "large groups of people united by a community of goals in the liberation struggle."[56] The word "people" then was to be used to include "all communities," and all people had "the right to self-determination."[57]

Conditions for Emergence of a Movement: Objective Factors

While the circumstances in which nations were created received a certain attention among Soviet theoreticians, relatively little attention was given to the circumstances that caused the formation of national liberation movements themselves. The emergence of such movements was basically seen as an integral function of the historical process of imperialism. According to Lenin, imperialism virtually saved capitalism from the revolutionary dialectic prophesied by Marx and Engels, but nonetheless spawned its own destruction. According to a strict interpretation, imperialism introduced capitalism into the colonies, beginning there the inevitable revolutionary process by creating the cycle of capitalist exploitation, impoverishment, and a large dissatisfied body of working people (mainly peasants) within the colonies themselves. This interpretation, presented, for example, by Iu. Gavrilov (of the Social Sciences Institute), writing in *Aziia i Afrika segodnia* in 1980, gave little attention to the national element, emphasizing rather the dialectically opposed interests of the working people of the colonial and dependent countries, on the one hand, and capitalism on the other.[58]

For the most part, however, Soviet theoreticians, no less anxious to emphasize the social side of anti-colonialism, nonetheless explained imperialism's role in national as well as social terms. The Fedoseev study, with its generally conservative line, sought to accommodate this by stating that national and racial oppression, part of colonial exploitation, were built-in features of capitalism, gaining in intensity when capitalism reached its final, monopoly stage.[59] According to this study, the bourgeoisie, fearing the progress made in its own country because such progress tended to strengthen the proletariat, nonetheless sought to use this progress "for the purpose of plundering and enslaving other people. And for this it had to corrupt its own nation with nationalism and chauvinism, and *the peoples it oppressed with national nihilism.*"[60] The pedagogical journal explained this national nihilism as the obstruction of people's rights to express their own will.[61] Then head of the Africa Institute, Vasilii Solodovnikov, writing with Viktor Bogoslovskii in 1975, was a bit more explicit, making the link with the formation of national movements: "Colonial domination with its plunder and violence, racial discrimination and scorn for the culture of the peoples of the East inevitably gave rise to the growth of nationalism."[62] Ul'ianovskii added to these factors the strengthening of local reaction, explaining that virtually all social strata of the colonial population found itself oppressed or exploited.[63]

Expanding Lenin's theory of the uneven development of capitalism around the world, Ul'ianovskii explained how a revolutionary situation was created.[64] Under imperialism, a world economy developed; capitalism became international and centralized in a few monopolies of a handful of capitalist states. This shift from free competition to monopolistic domination no longer suited the capitalist system of private property and private production relations. Thus, two contradictions (the catalyst of revolution) emerged: (1) the contradiction between the social nature of labor and the private capitalist method of appropriation of the results of labor; (2) the contradiction between the tendency of production forces toward expansion and the totality of property relations fettering such growth. The national solution was the overthrow of the owners, be they foreign bourgeoisie or landowners.

This revolutionary situation—the contradiction between the creation of the material prerequisites for socialism and the persistence of the capitalist mode of production—was compounded by the contradiction between the international, centralized nature of monopoly capital on the one hand, and nationalist aspirations and competition or particularism on the other, leading to wars for the redivision of colonial empires. This too contributed to the revolutionary situation by weakening the imperialist powers and rendering at least the weakest among them vulnerable to revolution at home.[65] Thus Ul'ianovskii reiterated Lenin's theories of imperialism and the "weakest link" to explain the interaction between a revolutionary situation in the colonies and the metropole at the same time.

Evgenii Primakov, then influential head of the Academy's Oriental Institute, went beyond the classical Marxist–Leninist delineation of a revolutionary situation.[66] Writing in the 1980s, he spoke of three conditions for a revolution (although he failed to elaborate on them): the material/economic preconditions; the objective socio-political preconditions; and the subjective factors. He pointed to the uneven development of these three conditions in order to explain the different paths or orientations adopted by national liberation movements once they came to power. Nonetheless, by the adding socio-political and subjective factors, Primakov was going beyond the somewhat straitjacketed classical Marxist–Leninist approach. This is not to say that Ul'ianovskii rejected these factors: he wrote at length on the leaders of the national liberation movements,[67] and he did investigate to some degree socio-political conditions. Nonetheless, even in these studies Ul'ianovskii was critical, for example of Franz Fanon, with regard to what he called an "anti-historical" approach which favored a socio-ethnic interpretation.[68] Reviewing a 1975 full-length Soviet study on Fanon, written by A. V. Gordon (and which made exactly the same point), Ul'ianovskii criticized Fanon's definition of colonialism as "the focus of ethnic rather than class contradictions."[69] According to this view, Ul'ianovskii and Gordon argued, a "we/they" relationship was perceived between colonialized and colonializer which translated also into black/white, Third World/Europe, countryside/town[70] dichotomies, placing both the proletariat (town) and, implicitly, the Soviet bloc (Europe) in the "they" oppressor category. Further, according to Gordon, the concentration on the socio-ethnic rather than the socioeconomic essence of society identified the economic base with the superstructure: white became synonymous with wealthy, black with poor. The causal relationship was altogether ignored; social relations, in Fanon's work, were determined not by the base but by the superstructure.[71]

Conditions: Subjective Factors

Karen Brutents, as a deputy head of the International Department and apparent successor (if not challenger) to Ul'ianovskii's position as the Communist party's leading Third World expert, explicitly went beyond the more conservative socioeconomic approach. In keeping with accepted procedures, Brutents elucidated the economic conditions for a national liberation revolution or the emergence of such movements, specifically in the Third World.[72] He spoke of the contradiction between the requirements of the production forces, which, he claimed, required "an independent national framework for their development, and foreign domination, which ", he said, went "hand in hand with the plunder of the oppressed country, subjugation of its economic life to the purposes of this domination, and preservation of backward socio-economic forms."[73] The corresponding social basis, therefore, was the conflict between the interests of the ruling class or social forces of the oppressed country and its people as a whole on the one side, and the interests of the ruling class of the oppressor state—recipient of the benefits from exploiting the oppressed country—on the other.

In the purely economic sphere, there was little difference between the rise of national movements under capitalism or under imperialism: the basic motivating force was the bourgeoisie's need to capture the home market and to have a politically united territory with a common language. "Therein is the economic foundation of national movements," Brutents quoted Lenin,[74] be it in the era of capitalism or imperialism. Yet there were differences between such movements in the two eras, and in the realm of these differences Brutents added the specifically national factor, generated by socio-political and subjective conditions or, as he put it, "ideological, cultural and psychological factors [which] are of especial importance in the origin and development of national liberation revolutions."[75]

These factors were explained by Brutents in the following way. With regard to the socio-political sphere, the colony was deprived of its ability to act as a "subject" in the international arena or historical processes, as well as to govern its own affairs domestically, inasmuch as it was under imperialist subjugation and domination. In the realm of social relations, the colonies were "doomed to growing backwardness and social stagnation" because the colonial rulers sought to preserve

backward and feudal social relationships the in hope of stifling the emergence of any social forces capable of challenging the foreign domination
or competing with the imperialist monopolies.[76] In the ideological and
spiritual realm, the colonialists implanted racism and encouraged the
artificial preservation of racism and obsolete ideologies (presumably
religious and cult faiths or rituals), as well as active resistance to
the development of education. At the same time, they engendered the
humiliation of the national dignity of the subjugated peoples and the
destruction of their cultural values, "resulting in stagnation and even
regress in the spiritual development of many peoples."[77] Thus, a people's
very national existence became a question of opposing colonialism or
imperialism. All of this was actually no more than a somewhat more
explicit rendition of the term "oppression," but in it Brutents went
further than the purely socioeconomic interpretation given to the term
in the past. In this sense, such an explanation was comparable with
the somewhat more sophisticated approach to the idea of nations,
national identity, and the like.

It is also possible, however, that the addition of non-economic
factors was necessitated by the appearance of some confusion among
Soviet theoreticians over just how to characterize colonial society in
socioeconomic terms. There emerged in discussions in the 1960s and
1970s a certain discomfort with classical Marxist categorizations of
socioeconomic evolution, from primitive–communal, through slave-
owning, to feudal, capitalist, and finally socialist modes of production,
with corresponding superstructures.[78] In this scheme colonial Third
World societies tended to be lumped into the feudal pre-capitalist stage,
with the possibility of skipping capitalism in a non-capitalist progression
to socialism, given certain circumstances.

This oversimplification of Third World society became increasingly
unacceptable to sophisticated Soviet theoreticians.[79] Some preferred to
return to the idea of a special Asiatic mode of production, relevant
to Africa as well as Asia; others debated the nature of feudalism.[80]
On the whole, however, the conclusion was that these societies were
in fact mixed, or "multi-structural," necessitating somewhat different
terminology.[81] For example, one Africanist, L. M. Entin, spoke of pre-
capitalist and pre-feudal societies, which he called "traditional-colonial
society," defying the standard classification of primitive–communal,
slave-owning, or feudal.[82] Another scholar spoke of a type of society
formed around a "chiefdom-proto-state."[83] Still other forms and many
sub-structures were proposed, but basically the idea of a multi-structured
pre-capitalist society was generally accepted. This could be accommodated by Lenin's theory of the uneven development of capitalism, with
various differing forms of ownership and production modes existing
simultaneously in different countries—now even in the same country.

It also fitted into the idea of societies or peoples seeking independence at a stage prior even to the formation of a nation, without the appearance of a fully developed economic life and, therefore, not necessarily typified by any one exclusive mode of production—or mature class differentiation. The implications of this for the social or class composition of a national liberation movement will be discussed below, but acceptance of the multi-structural formation did obviate the need for an exclusively socioeconomic analysis of the conditions generating national liberation movements in favor of other more subjective factors.

Ethnicity and Separatism

In all of the above, the key to the era of national liberation struggle and the emergence of national liberation movements was imperialism or colonialism. Most Soviet literature satisfied itself with this explanation, thereby accounting implicitly only for anti-colonialist movements. Yet, even if separatism was not regarded favorably, more narrowly ethnic-based movements occasionally were also considered legitimate, demanding something different from the purely colonialist-related explanations. Few such explanations were in fact attempted, the standard argument being a negative one which blamed imperialism and outside reaction for, as the Zagladin–Ryzhenko study put it, "kindling conflicts between national, ethnic, religious, tribal and linguistic groups."[84] While this conservative approach persisted, nonetheless, as ethnicity gained attention and legitimacy, a framework evolved for more objective differentiation and analyses. Few in number, even these were by no means entirely positive, reluctant as they were to justify secessionism or separatist tendencies. One such analysis was offered by Africanist R. N. Ismagilova in a 1974 book by I. R. Grigulevich and S. Iu. Kozlov on "ethnic and racial" problems.[85] Ismagilova reduced ethnic conflicts to intertribal friction at the pre-nation stage, leading to "nationalism" on the part of the tribe or ethnic group.[86] In keeping with the traditional Soviet approach, she explained these ethnic conflicts as the result of socioeconomic causes, but she nonetheless admitted that subjective factors were also at play, including what were called ethnic prejudice. Ethnic friction both was the result of and led to an "exaggerated emotional attachment" to one's own language and culture.[87] Ismagilova gave the following basic reasons for ethnic conflicts:

1 colonialist policies, either of the type which foster the tribal system and tribal separatism leading to "nationalism" or the type which forces assimilation producing tension over and exaggerated attachment to a local language and culture;

2 uneven social and economic development (sometimes fostered by the imperialists on a tribal basis);

3 tribal customs, traditional institutions, rites, myths and legends; tribal morality and loyalty;

4 the role of traditional authorities, i.e., tribal chiefs.[88]

She also pointed out that colonial borders did not always correspond to ethnic lines, often cutting across single ethnic organisms, harming national consolidation.[89] She added, however, that political motives of a self-interested rising bourgeoisie or feudal circles might also lie behind ethnic demands. On the whole critical of this type of ethnically based "national" struggle, Ismagilova's was at least an attempt to understand a phenomenon that did not fit the pure anti-colonialist mould.

A somewhat more positive analysis was an article published in *Aziia i Afrika segodnia* in 1980 by M. Lazarev, also exploring the rise of non-anti-colonialist national liberation movements.[90] Lazarev dealt primarily with what he called "multinational" societies, and the phenomenon of "multinationalism" as a basis for conflict and, therefore, "national" awareness. Employing a typology close to that of Bromlei, he subdivided multinationalism into three types of states: those with a poly-ethnic population (India); countries that had one ethnic group composing several states (Arab states), and a transitional type of multinational state with an indigenous, more or less ethnically homogeneous, population (the Phillipines, Indonesia). Like Ismagilova, he too explained ethnic awareness and "nationalism" as the result of uneven economic develop-ment which produced inequalities and grievances. Moreover, economic upheavals and fluctuations aggravated such internal grievances, often leading to exploitation, inequality, and oppression of an ethno-national type. These in turn could generate political crises.

Ideological factors were joined to the economic ones. In the absence of a common anti-colonialist binding ideology and with the collapse of the political and moral principles inherited from the pre-colonial and colonial period, "national" feelings achieved predominance. Nationalism then "contributes to the awakening or abruptly activating national awareness among the Eastern ethnoses. The interests of a given ethnic group, identified with 'ones' own' nationalism, have always been given priority at all levels of the economic, political, and cultural life of society."[91] This in turn encouraged national (ethnic) conflict and tension, enhancing "the role of the moral–psychological factor in ethnic inter-relations." Moreover, tensions within Asia and Africa as a whole, which included rapid shifts, upheavals and collisions, led to or accelerated a "politization" which split the formerly "single-stream" national liberation movements. Ethno-political conflicts, often of worldwide significance, were the result, inasmuch as they could not be solved within the confines of existing borders or administrative units. Among these were the ethno-political problems of the Palestinians, the Kurds, the Tamil, the Baluchi, the Pathans, and the Bengali, as well as the overseas Indians and scores of smaller ethnic conflicts.[92]

This article did not, however, neglect the formerly standard, more negative, explanation of the phenomenon. Lazarev spoke also of the outside contribution, namely efforts by the West (and reactionaries in the East) to stir up ethnic trouble, "either to whip up ethnic separatism...or to suppress the legitimate struggle of the minorities for their rights."[93] To these conflicts were added the Chinese, who sought to exacerbate existing ethnic conflicts and stir them to aggressive actions, in order to achieve their own "hegemonistic ends." This was an accusation cast against the Chinese on too many occasions to warrant specific citations; almost no article on China failed to mention it in one context or another. It was, however, part of the criticism of China, and not necessarily or even frequently an integral part of the explanation of the emergence of separatist or ethnic movements.

External Factors: The role of October

There were those who accorded greater influence to external than internal factors, not just with regard to separatist movements but also with regard to anti-colonial movements. Even while explaining the internal factors and conditions that spawned such movements, Fedoseev, for example, explained the essentiality of the external factors. In Europe, the Fedoseev study explained, nation-states had been born through the maturing of intrinsic national processes nurtured by the development of capitalism, which produced an economic base, a developed national consciousness and political unity around parties or governmental bodies.[94] In the colonies, however, because the growth of capitalism was different and the nation remained unformed, external rather than internal factors became essential to the national awakening, organization, and struggle. These were primarily of an ideological nature, entering these societies through the intelligentsia from the developed (socialist) world.[95] In the same vein, Sh. Sanakoev, writing in 1984, said that the decisive factor in the political awakening of the colonial peoples was the spread of the ideas of freedom and independence and "the exposure of the rapacious policies of all colonialists," through the "liberating ideas" of the October Revolution.[96] Anatolii Gromyko too spoke of the influence of the ideas of October as an essential factor in the awakening of the peoples of Africa.[97] Nikolai Kosukhin (department head at the Africa Institute) wrote in *Aziia i Afrika segodnia* about this infiltration of ideas, facilitated by local communist parties or Marxist study groups either locally or in the metropole, or even in the Soviet bloc.[98] A *Pravda* May Day editorial explained how the October Revolution had awakened the national liberation movement in that it was Communists who "initiated the national liberation struggle."[99]

Generally, however, the invocation of the October Revolution as the external key to the emergence of national liberation movements was not quite so explicit, taking less an ideological direction than three other views of the role of the revolution: (1) as a catalyst for national awakening; (2) as a facilitator by virtue of its challenge to imperialism; (3) as an example. Anatolii Gromyko, for instance, spoke of October also as a catalyst, as did Oleg Dreier, who claimed that Africa was "stirred into activity" by the October Revolution.[100] More common was the view, also espoused by Gromyko, of October as facilitator.[101] Shevtsov and Primakov, for example, emphasized the weakening of imperialism as a result of the October Revolution and the growth of the socialist camp, leading to the possibility of the struggle for national liberation.[102] Primakov saw an "organic connection" between the two events because of the change in the balance of forces in the world as a result of the Bolshevik Revolution.[103] He depicted stages in the connection. The first, in the two decades after the revolution, was more demonstrative (i.e., demonstrating that imperialism could be defeated) than facilitative. The second stage followed World War II and the creation of the socialist bloc, which significantly changed the world balance of forces. Contributing to this also was the destruction of "the foremost detachment of imperialism represented by fascist Germany and Italy, militarist Japan, thereby weakening the positions of the major colonial powers. The decline of the economic and military strength, as well as the socio-political strength, present before the war led to the disintegration of the colonial system of imperialism."[104] This situation, according to Primakov, combined with the ripening of internal conditions to make for the emergence of national liberation movements.

Georgii Kim, deputy to Primakov at the Oriental Institute, added a further stage to Primakov's two: that of the 1950s, when, he claimed, the socialist system became the decisive influence in the world and the swift collapse of colonialism began.[105] (Primakov put the stage of socialist preponderance only in the 1970s.) According to Kim, the October Revolution created "exceptionally propitious conditions" for a general offensive against colonialism because it provided an internationalization of the liberation struggle. The blow to one empire had an effect on the strength of other empires, revolutions in one aiding as well as encouraging revolutions in another, transforming the national liberation movements from a local phenomenon to a universal one.[106] Kim pointed out the value of the Soviet example in that the October Revolution demonstrated "for the first time" that it was "possible not only to get rid of colonial oppression but that people could win state power and be in a position to solve economic, political and social questions of development."[107] What Kim did not say explicitly, but may have intended by this explanation, was that the October Revolution demonstrated the power of subjective factors over objective ones, the elimination of the need to await suitable objective (socioeconomic) conditions, such as the full development of capitalism, in order to revolt. The more conservative Evgenii Tarabrin coupled the crisis of the capitalist economic system with the weakening of imperialism caused by the strength of socialism which was the key to the factors precipitating national liberation movements.[108] He too added the power of the Soviet example (as did Gavrilov[109]) and, for the later period, the restraining influence of détente on imperialism.

While Tarabrin, and to some degree Kim and Gromyko, emphasized these external factors to the exclusion of internal factors, the International Department Africanist Petr Manchkha took a somewhat different position. In a book published in 1979, he appeared to give priority to what he called the "regular" (law-governed) process of the rise of anti-colonialism in Africa, which occurred at the same time as, but by implication not necessarily as a result of, the strengthened position of socialism in the world and a general crisis of imperialism—which improved conditions for the outcome of the liberation struggle.[110]

On this issue of regularity and the value of the Soviet example, something of a debate emerged around a book, published in 1975, by Nodari Simoniia of the Oriental Institute.[111] This debate focused mainly on what might be expected from national liberation movements *after* independence, with Simoniia arguing that the absence even of pure feudalism, much less capitalism, in the Third World meant that the necessary economic base for a transformation to socialism was still lacking.[112] We shall consider this debate below, in relation to the prospective transformation to socialism.[113] With regard to the issue of regularity and the October Revolution, however, Simoniia argued that, while the "weak-link" theory was accurate, the October Revolution was nonetheless something of a special case—not necessarily transferable elsewhere. For him, the more typical revolution was that of 1905, the 1917 revolution being special because the proletariat was at the helm. This meant that socialism could be introduced, albeit after a transition period (because of the underdeveloped economic base). Because of the proletarian leadership, no new socialist revolution was necessary. In the Third World, with the national liberation revolution resembling more a 1905 revolution, a second revolution would be necessary, both because of the prevailing backward economic conditions and because of the social composition of the movements.[114]

Ul'ianovskii took issue with Simoniia, as did a number of theoreticians of the Marxist–Leninist Institute who objected to any implication that the October Revolution might have been an historical exception.[115] Begging the question somewhat, Ul'ianovskii merely asserted that the October Revolution could serve as an example because it demonstrated the possibility of revolution in a less than fully developed society and the transformation to socialism after only a brief transition period, without recourse to a fully developed capitalist system. The difference between the October Revolution and national liberation revolutions, in relation to Simoniia's argument, would appear to have been that, while Russia, albeit a "weak link," was nonetheless more advanced economically, the new countries could make up this difference by receiving assistance from the existing socialist states and by the weakening of imperialism. In this sense Ul'ianovskii saw the value of October as an example, but perhaps primarily as that event, coupled with World War II, which "triggered off the crisis and disintegration of the colonial system as a whole"[116] (although in an earlier book Ul'ianovskii credited the 1905 Revolution with awakening the Eastern masses).[117] Simoniia, in his articles after the 1975 book, seemed to accept this more standard approach of the October Revolution as a catalyst for change elsewhere—even serving as an example and, subsequently, weakening imperialism—although he appeared to credit World War II more for the disintegration of the colonial system.[118]

Brutents did not enter into the debate over the universality of the October Revolution; indeed, he appeared to give much higher priority to internal rather than external conditions for the formation of national liberation movements. Nonetheless, he did ascribe an essential role to external conditions as created by the October Revolution. First of all, he saw October as a catalyst or "awakening" of the colonial peoples. In this sense it was also an example, for it demonstrated that the defeat of imperialists could be achieved, or in other words that subjective factors could outweigh objective ones. Moreover, it weakened imperialism by providing the possibility for an alliance of forces—the new socialist state, the world proletariat, and the oppressed peoples—which would be hard to defeat. "Evidence" of this vital link was said to be the fact that the first victorious national movements were located in geographic proximity to the new Soviet state.

All of this, according to Brutents, marked the beginning of the "crisis of the colonial system of imperialism," which proceeded in the following order: first, the anti-colonialist, national liberation struggle of the nations of czarist Russia and the establishment of their own states, the Soviet republics; second, the rise of liberation movements over the whole colonial periphery of imperialism; and third, the successful outcome, "for the first time in the Twentieth Century," of national battles such as those in Turkey and Afghanistan (which, as stated earlier, were triggered by October and achieved, possibly, because of Soviet proximity).[119] The fourth step was the cessation of further enslavement in many colonial countries and the emergence of tendencies toward liberation. Specifically, October assisted this in that it "gave the decisive impetus to the formation of forces capable of bringing organization and purpose to the massive struggle—national revolutionary organizations and, in particular, the Communist parties."[120] The rise in strength of the socialist world and the second crisis of imperialism, presumably World War II, created "*particularly* favorable" conditions for successful national liberation struggle.[121]

Because of October, then, it became possible for national liberation movements to emerge and even win *before* a proletarian revolution destroyed the capitalist system in the imperialist metropole.[122] And, as we shall see below, this also made the non-capitalist path of development possible for the newly independent countries. The relationship between the national liberation struggle and the proletarian revolution was historically a highly debated one, and one that I shall discuss below at greater length. So far as it was applicable to the issue of conditions for the *emergence* of national movements, however, Brutents clearly took the position that the first proletarian revolution (October) was prior to and essential (even if, as he sought to prove, the national movements also played a positive role for the advance of subsequent proletarian revolutions). This having been said, rather succinctly, Brutents then went on to give much greater attention to the internal conditions necessary for, or at least coincident with, the emergence of national liberation movements, as we have already seen.

On the whole, there were few—most notably Anatolii Gromyko, Kim, and Tarabrin—who gave exclusive significance or even priority to the external factors. There was the obvious need to credit the contribution of the role of the October Revolution, the Soviet Union, and the international proletariat. There was also, however, the need to counter accusations both of voluntarism (the forcing of a situation or leftism) and of exporting revolution (a Western accusation). To answer both such charges, the internal or historically intrinsic conditions had to be elucidated and emphasized. Beyond this, there was also an apparently serious attempt on the part of Soviet Third World theoreticians in the 1970s to analyze and come to grips with the evolving realities—which were not always pro-Soviet or socialist—in the Third World. Simoniia's book was one such attempt, as were the discussions on ethnicity, dependency, and economic structures. Foreign communists and Soviet leaders themselves were significantly less involved in these debates. The former, at least when writing in official Communist organs, demonstrated their loyalty to the Soviet Union by emphasizing the external, Soviet, factor, some crediting World War II with the death blow to imperialism.[123] The only noteworthy exception to this was the position of the South African communists. Although no less willing to acknowledge the importance of October and the socialist world,[124] party chairman Yusuf Dadoo also emphasized internal social and racial conditions.[125] Given the nature of the situation in South Africa, such a reference could hardly have been omitted, although the emphasis of the South African communists was generally on indigenous conditions.

Leadership Views

Leadership pronouncements were triggered mainly by Western accusations of Soviet responsibility for revolutions in the Third World, and therefore were not necessarily indicative of a position regarding objective or subjective factors or even internal versus external conditions. Moreover, some of their pronouncements had more to do with outside assistance than with factors contributing to the origins of national liberation movements, indicating perhaps a particular leader's attitude as to what role the Soviet Union should or should not take in the national liberation struggle once it developed.[126] As far as can be determined from the relevant leadership pronouncements, there was, for example, a decided difference between the then head of the International Department, Boris Ponomarev (at the time candidate Politburo member and a party secretary) and his two deputies, Ul'ianovskii and Brutents. More in line with his chief deputy Zagladin and with the Ideology Department's Fedoseev, Ponomarev took the conservative approach to the rise of national liberation movements. While Brutents and Ul'ianovskii explained the lack of fully formed nations or class differentiation in most Third World countries, Ponomarev asserted categorically that "the liberation movements...are the inevitable and completely natural results of the build-up of internal contradictions in an antagonistic society that has been divided into hostile classes." Arguing that all revolutions had an economic basis, he offered the orthodox Marxist explanation regarding contradictions between production forces and production relations leading to an acute conflict, primarily because of the effort by the ruling class to maintain its position and "exploit the workers."[127] Ponomarev's only acknowledgment that there might be an impetus connected with national rather than purely socioeconomic factors was the somewhat declaratory statement that one could see in the revolutionary process "the mighty expression of the internal force of the masses of the people, the brightly expressed striving for national independence, their inflexible will to achieve their independent historic creativity, to confirm the sovereignty of their country."[128]

Ponomarev at least credited internal factors rather than external ones. In answer to accusations of Soviet incitement, he did say that a revolution required a revolutionary situation which could not be created artificially or from outside. The October Revolution could serve as inspiration and an example, but this would be "refracted through the prism of internal conditions, which vary [he did not say why] from various countries." Any attempt to "export revolution," impose, or incite had been dubbed by Lenin, he pointed out, as leftist adventurism.[129] In fact, he described a combination of internal and external factors as the conditions attendant upon the rise of democratic, anti-imperialist, and anti-capitalist movements. These were all "objective historic factors" which included the "development of the productive forces, the scientific–technical revolution, the consolidation of the positions of world socialism...the aggravation of the overall crisis of capitalism...the overall change in the ratio of forces in the world...[and] *the growth of the political awareness and consciousness of the masses,*" this last presumably the result of the socioeconomic contradictions within society.[130] Ponomarev was fairly consistent in this position, as evidenced by speeches and articles in the 1970s.[131] On one occasion, however, he reversed himself, perhaps because he was addressing foreign communists. Speaking to a conference sponsored by the *World Marxist Review,* he emphasized an external factor—the existence of the socialist world—as the essential element without which "the colonial system would not have been destroyed."[132] This may have referred to chances for success, however, rather than conditions for formation of a national liberation movement, which Ponomarev apparently saw as primarily internal and objective.

Surprisingly few Soviet leaders were even to refer to the October Revolution as an example or catalyst for the national liberation movements. Only when the sixtieth anniversary of the revolution required some reference did Brezhnev, for example, speak of October as the catalyst for the awakening of the peoples of the East, augmented by the victory over fascism in World War II. Even on this occasion, however, Brezhnev emphasized internal factors. As he put it: "Revolutions start and triumph by virtue of each country's *intrinsic development* and the will of its people."[133] Brezhnev had said exactly the same thing to the twenty-fifth CPSU Congress a year earlier, in response to accusations that détente might lead to a "freezing" of the revolutionary process. He said then: "every revolution is primarily the natural result of the internal development of the society in question," and therefore could be neither exported nor stopped. In a similar context, he had said the same thing four years earlier when Castro visited the Soviet Union.[134]

Brezhnev was less explicit by the time of the twenty-sixth CPSU Congress in 1981, perhaps because there was no longer a need to defend détente; but he did abjure the export of revolution (and of counter-revolution).[135] With regard to what were seen by theoreticians as ethnic movements, Brezhnev took the more conservative position.

He described them as the result of the stirring up, by outside (Western) factors, of disputes left over from the colonial period.[136] He explicitly, therefore, ruled out any encouragement of separatism in the 1981 speech in which he spelled out "rules of conduct" appropriate for the superpowers.[137] The positions both on the predominance of internal factors (or at least "objective historical processes") and on the outside causes of ethnic conflict were embodied in the June 1978 Soviet statement on Africa.[138]

During his trip to Africa in 1977, Soviet President Podgornyi did invoke October—primarily as an example, however, for the new African states. In Africa itself, he was sensitive enough to circumstances to avoid in any way minimizing domestic factors in favor of crediting outside factors. Rather, he invoked the mutuality of the uprising against colonialism which was characteristic, he claimed, of both October and the national liberation movements.[139] Similarly, when addressing the predominantly Third World United Nations, Gromyko too emphasized internal over external factors, giving a bit more credit to the "correlation of forces" and socialist aid when addressing domestic Soviet audiences.[140]

Generally, looking at the speeches of most Soviet leaders—Brezhnev, Podgornyi, Suslov,[141] Gromyko, and Ponomarev (i.e., those who addressed the issue at all)—one finds very little analysis and basically nothing more than general references to "objective laws" or "intrinsic developments" designed to exonerate the Soviet Union either from organizing (in violation of détente) the emergence of national liberation movements or from refusing to organize them (because of the constraints of détente). The two exceptions to this were, at one end, Ponomarev, who, as we have seen, did attempt an analysis, albeit the conservative socioeconomic one; at the other end, Andropov. Andropov, too, was basically responding to Western accusations of Soviet incitement, positing instead the "intrinsic process" or "internal development of society" arguments and opposition to the export of revolution.[142] Yet he did provide a somewhat more colorful—and possibly national as well as socially oriented—explanation when he said: "No, it is not the 'hand of Moscow' but the long hand of hunger, not the 'intrigues of communists' but deprivation, oppression, and suffering that force people to take up arms and take to the streets, that make radical change inevitable."[143] In a later speech, on the sixtieth anniversary of the USSR, Andropov did acknowledge the existence of subjective factors, namely, the persistence of psychological, ethnic, and traditional influences.[144] This was, however, in a purely domestic Soviet context and cannot be said with any certainty whatsoever to represent Andropov's view of national liberation movements abroad.

It cannot be ruled out that the leadership's general emphasis on internal factors served not only as a response to Western accusations or an answer to opponents of détente, but also possibly as an expression of some reservations as to how involved the Soviet Union should become. This issue will be discussed in another chapter, although, given the near universality of leadership pronouncements against the export of revolution, it would appear that the leadership was more concerned with promoting a certain image of Soviet foreign policy than with tackling the issues raised by the theoreticians. In keeping with this, the issues of ethnicity and nationhood, that is, the subject of national liberation, were—if touched on at all by the leadership—reserved solely for the domestic Soviet situation, foreign experience remaining entirely separate from leadership pronouncements on the nationality issue.

Conclusions

The Soviet view of the origins of national liberation, the conditions that give rise to them, and the very subject of national struggles (the definition of a "nation") was not an entirely uniform one. The standard line was the more conservative, orthodox Marxist view, which gave priority, in some cases exclusivity, to socioeconomic factors which operated within a colonial society as part of the objective historical process connected with imperialism as the highest stage of capitalism. To this might be added such external factors as the example of the October Revolution or its role in weakening imperialism; but the overall thrust of the conservative approach, including that expressed most frequently by Soviet leaders, ignored any subjective internal features and minimized external factors. If hardship, poverty, discrimination, and the like give rise to national liberation movements, these problems themselves were seen as the result of a particular economic and class situation, just as the molding of a group into a nation or nationality was a basically socioeconomic function.

In time, however, a more sophisticated, less orthodox, approach emerged. This approach came to grips both with the lack of class development or differentiation within most colonial societies and with a more complex set of subjective factors at play in these societies. Altering the definition of "nation" to include such concepts as ethnicity, psychological and national awareness or identification, and tradition, the more innovative theoreticians gave prominence, even priority, to the subjective national element generating national liberation movements. Without neglecting economic factors, spiritual oppression and the preservation of emotional attachments were accorded a role in the awakening of peoples and the formation of national movements. This multi-dimensional approach produced a more sophisticated view of the phenomenon of separatism. Without altering the basic rejection of separatism, the new approach allowed more room for some such movements, based as they were, at the least, on ethnic or varieties of ethnic associations.

The new approach was by no means accepted by all; it was reflected, possibly, in only one leadership speech (that of Andropov in December 1982). Yet it did cut across institutional lines, reaching into senior cadres of the Central Committee. Brutents, for example, was an exponent of this approach, even as his superior in the International Department, Zagladin, adhered to the conservative approach and his senior colleague, Ul'ianovskii, took a somewhat middle position. No such division was apparent in the generally more orthodox Ideological Department of the Central Committee. In the research institutes, deputy director of the Africa Institute, Starushenko, was a major promulgator of the conservative approach, while the more influential Primakov, as head of the Oriental Institute, expressed elements of the newer approach. Yet on the issue of the value of external factors, specifically the October Revolution, members of the one institute were on different sides (Kim and Simoniia of the Oriental Institute), although those of the Africa Institute (Gromyko and Tarabrin) were apparently of one mind. Here a dispute occurred between an institute researcher, Simoniia, and a Central Committee official, Ul'ianovskii, but Ul'ianovskii's colleagues, Brutents and Manchkha, did not apparently share his evaluation of external versus internal factors.

Thus, on the whole, the differing views among Soviet theoreticians dealing with the Third World tended to defy institutional classification. There would appear also to have been some cross-germination of ideas between those dealing with Soviet nationality policy and those dealing with Third World matters, for the debate among the former on the essence of a nation, ethnicity, and the like was directly reflected among the latter—and possibly vice versa.

Differences of basic approach in the above distinctions notwith-standing, the conditions that produce national liberation movements were not the subject of *major* controversy. The fact that the two approaches could coexist, even complement, one another may have mitigated against too great a controversy. Yet the debate itself indicated a certain dissatisfaction with the classical Soviet approach and an effort to adapt Soviet theory to a more realistic picture of the phenomenon of national liberation movements. The result was the beginnings, at least, of a more sophisticated theory of the factors influencing the emergence of such movements, and of nationhood itself.

Notes

1 Boris Meissner, "The Soviet Concept of Nation and the Right of National Self-Determination," *International Journal* 34, no. 1 (Winter 1976–77): 58n. See also Charles Herod, *The Nation in the History of Marxian Thought*, Martinus Njhoff, The Hague, 1976; Michael Lowy, "Marxism and the National Question," in Robin Blackburn (ed.), *Revolution and Class Struggle*, Fontana, London, 1977.

2 G. Starushenko, *The Principle of National Self-determination in Soviet Foreign Policy*, Foreign Languages Publishing House, Moscow, n.d.

3 Ibid., p. 14.

4 Ibid.

5 Ibid., pp. 15–16.

6 Ibid., p. 18.

7 Ibid., p. 21.

8 Ibid., p. 30.

9 Ibid., p. 196.

10 Ibid.

11 Ibid., p. 197.

12 For discussion of this debate see Meissner, "Soviet Concept," pp. 66–71; Roger Kanet (ed.), *The Soviet Union and Developing Nations*, Johns Hopkins University Press, Baltimore, 1974; Roger Kanet and Donna Bahry (eds.), *Soviet Economic and Political Relations with the Developing World*, Praeger, New York, 1974; Raymond Duncan (ed.), *Soviet Policy in Developing Countries*, Ginn-Blaisdell, Waltham, 1970; Robert Donaldson (ed.), *The Soviet Union in the Third World: Successes and Failures*, Westview Press, Boulder, Colo., 1981.

13 D. M. Rogachev and M. A. Sverdlin, "O poniatii 'natsiia'" *Voprosy istorii*, no. 1 (1966): 35–7.

14 Ibid., p. 45; M. S. Dzhunusov, "Natsiia kak sotsial'no-etnicheskaia obshchnost' liudei," *Voprosy istorii*, no. 4 (1966): 24–5.

15 Iu. I. Semenov, "K opredeleniiu poniatiia 'natsiia'," *Narody Azii i Afriki*, no. 4 (1967): 88; cited in Meissner, "Soviet Concept," p. 70.

16 Meissner, "Soviet Concept," p. 71.

17 P. N. Fedoseev et al., *Leninizm i natsional'nyi vopros v sovremennykh usloviiakh*, Politizdat, Moscow, 1974 (citations from English translation: P. N. Fedoseyev, *Leninism and the National Question*, Progress Press, Moscow, 1977), pp. 20–2.

18 Ibid., p. 18 n.

19 Ibid., p. 19.

20 Ibid., p. 20.

21 Ibid., p. 25.

22 Ibid., p. 27.

23 Ibid., p. 37.

24 Ibid., p. 48.

25 Ibid., p. 49.

26 Ibid.

27 Ibid., p. 44.

28 Ibid., pp. 45–6.

29 Ibid., p. 45.

30 Ibid., p. 50.

31 Ibid., pp. 50–1.

32 V. V. Zagladin and F. D. Ryzhenko, *Sovremennoe revoliutsionnoe dvizhenie i natsionalizm*, Politizdat, Moscow, 1973.

33 Ibid., p. 45.

34 See chapter 4 below.

35 Zagladin and Ryzhenko, *Sovremennoe revoliutsionnoe dvizhenie*, p. 34.

36 Ibid., pp. 34–5.

37 Ibid., pp. 36–7.

38 Iu. V. Bromlei, *Sovremennye problemy etnografii*, Nauka, Moscow, 1981; *Etnos i etnografiia*, Moscow, 1973; cited in Martha Brill Olcott, "Yuri Andropov and

42   *A Soviet Theory of National Liberation*

the 'National Question'," *Soviet Studies 37, no. 1 (January 1985): 107–8.*
39   Iu. V. Bromlei in I. R. Grigulevich and S. Iu. Kozlov, *Rasy i narody: Sovremennye etnicheskie i rasovye problemy,* Nauka, Moscow, 1974 (citations from English translation: I. R. Grigulevich and S. Y. Kozlov, *Races and Peoples: Contemporary Ethnic and Racial Problems,* Progress Press, Moscow, 1977), p. 19.
40   Ibid., pp. 33–4.
41   Ibid., p. 34.
42   Ibid., p. 35.
43   Ibid., p. 35.
44   Ibid., p. 38.
45   Ibid., p. 40.
46   See for example V. I. Kozlov, "Etnos i kultura," *Sovetskaia etnografiia,* no. 3 (1979): 71–86; V. I. Kozlov, "Problema etnicheskogo samosoznaniia i ee mesto v teorii etnosa", *Sovetskaia etnografiia,* no. 2 (1974): 79–92; M. I. Kulichenko, *Rastsvet i sblizhenie natsii v SSSR,* Mysl', Moscow, 1981; M. I. Kulichenko, *Sotsializm i natsii,* Mysl', Moscow, 1975; M. I. Kulichenko, "Razvitie natsii i natsional'nykh otnoshenii v SSSR na sovremennom etape," *Voprosy istorii,* no. 9 (1971): 3–10.
47   A. D. Litman, "Ob opredelenii poniatiia i klassifikatsii tipov natsionalizma v osvobodivshikhsia stranakh (k postanovke voprosa)," *Narody Azii i Afriki,* no. 1 (1973): 46.
48   V. S. Shevtsov, *Natsional'nyi suverenitet i Sovetskoe gosudarstvo,* Nauka, Moscow, 1974 (citations from English translation: V. S. Shevtsov, *National Sovereignty and the Soviet State,* Progress Press, Moscow, 1974), p. 20.
49   Rostislav Ul'ianovskii, *Ocherki natsional'no-osvoboditel' noi bor'by: voprosy teorii i praktiki,* Nauka, Moscow, 1976 (citations from English translation: Rostislav Ulyanovsky, *National Liberation:*Essays on Theory and Practice, Progress Press, Moscow, 1978), pp. 136, 322.
50   Ibid., p. 137.
51   Ibid.
52   A. A. Gromyko and G. B. Starushenko, "Sotsial'nye i natsional'nye faktory rasvitiia osvobodivshikhsia stran," *Sotsiologicheskie issledovaniia,* no. 1 (1983): 5. See also D. Baratashvilli, "Lenin's Doctrine of Self-determination of Nations and the National Liberation Struggle," *International Affairs,* no. 12 (1970): 11.
53   Ulyanovsky, *National Liberation,* p. 332; Starushenko, *National Self-determination,* pp. 31, 64–7; Gromyko and Starushenko, "Faktory rasvitiia", p. 4.
54   See chapter 3 below.
55   See chapter 3.
56   V. F. Gryzlov, "Protiv fal'sifikatsii antikommunistami FRG leninskoi teoriiopreve narodov na samoopredelenie," *Nauchnyi kommunizm,* no. 3 (1977): 113.
57   Ibid.
58   Iu. Gavrilov, "V. I. Lenin i istoricheskie sud'by antikolonial'noi bor'by," *Aziia i Afrika segodnia,* no. 3 (1980): 2.
59   Fedoseyev, *Leninism,* p. 469.
60   Ibid., p. 59.
61   Gryzlov, "Protiv fal'sifikatsii," p. 115.
62   V. G. Solodovnikov and V. V. Bogoslovsky, *Non-capitalist Development,* Progress Press, Moscow, 1975, p. 144. The ideology of nationalism is discussed in Chapter 4 below.
63   Ulyanovsky, *National Liberation,* pp. 8, 27. (On the class aspect see chapter 2 below.)
64   Ibid., p. 27.
65   Ibid., p. 31.
66   *Pravda,* 11 August 1982. See also E. Primakov, "Strany sotsialisticheskoi orientatsii: trudnyi, no real'nyi perekhod k sotsializmu," *Mirovaia ekonomika i mezhdunarodnye otnosheniia,* no. 7 (1981): 3–16; E. Primakov, *Vostok posle krakha kolonial'noi sistemy,* Nauka, Moscow, 1982, pp. 88–90. Citing Primakov on this matter, see N. A. Simoniia, "Sovremennyi etap osvoboditel'noi bor'by," *Aziia i Afrika segodnia,* no. 5 (1981): 14.
67   R. A. Ul'ianovskii, *Bortsy za natsional'nuiu svobodu,* Politizdat, Moscow, 1983. Interestingly, this book of biographic profiles included chapters published first in

English as an appendix to a Ul'ianovskii book, in the English edition only, and not in the original Russian (Rostislav Ulyanovsky, *Present-day Problems in Asia and Africa*, Progress Press, Moscow, 1980; first published as R. A. Ul'ianovskii, *Sovremennye problemy Azii i Afriki*, Nauka, Moscow, 1978). Some did appear earlier in Russian as articles: R. Ul'ianovskii, "Nauchnyi sotsializm i Frants Fanon," *Aziia i Afrika segodnia*, no. 5 (1978): pp. 20–2; R. Ul'ianovskii, "Nauchnyi sotsializm i Amilkar Kebral," *Aziia i Afrika segodnia*, no. 12 (1978): 29–32.

68 Ul'ianovskii, "Fanon," p. 21.

69 Ibid., p. 20.

70 Ul'ianovskii, "Kabral," pp. 31–2; and A. V. Gordon, *Problemy natsional'no-osvoboditel'noi bor'by v tvorchestve Frantsa Fanona*, Nauka, Moscow, 1977, pp. 26, 39.

71 Ibid., p. 40.

72 K. N. Brutents, *Sovremennye natsional'no osvoboditel'nye revoliutsii*, vol. I, Nauka, Moscow, 1974 (citations from the English version: K. N. Brutents, *National Liberation Revolution Today*, Progress Press, Moscow, 1977), p. 29.

73 Ibid. (emphasis in original).

74 Ibid.

75 Ibid., pp. 34–5.

76 Ibid., pp. 40–1.

77 Ibid., p. 41.

78 For a discussion of this issue see Jerry Hough, *The Struggle for the Third World*, Brookings Institution, Washington, D.C., 1986.

79 Ibid. for discussions of the 1960s and later discussions of the Asiatic mode of production, summed up in V. N. Nikiforov, *Vostok i vsemirnaia istoriia*, Nauka, Moscow, 1977, pp. 320–5.

80 Hough, *Struggle*. N. A. Simoniia, *Strany Vostoka: puti razvitiia*, Nauka, Moscow, 1975, pp. 13–35; R. A. Ul'ianovskii, "O nekotorykh voprosakh marksistsko–leninskoi teorii revoliutsionnogo protsessa," *Novaia i noveishaia istoriia*, no. 4 (1976): 61–83; and to a lesser degree I. M. Mikhailov and E. V. Tadevosian, "O ser'eznykh metodologicheskikh oshibkakh v osveshchenii marksistsko–leninskoi teorii istoricheskogo protsessa," *Voprosy istorii KPSS*, no. 5 (1977): 105–14; A. I. Borisov and N. B. Aleksandrov, "Obsuzhdenie knigi N. A. Simoniia 'Strany Vostoka: puti razvitiia'," *Narody Azii i Afriki*, no. 3 (1977): 54–65.

81 N. A. Simoniia, "Natsional'no–gosudarstvennaia konsolidatsiia i politicheskaia differentsiatsiia razvivaiushchikhsia stran Vostoka," *Mirovaia ekonomika i mezhdunarodnye otnosheniia*, no. 1 (1983): 84–5. See also chapter 3 below.

82 L. M. Entin, *Politicheskie sistemy razvivaiushchikhsia stran*, Mezhdunarodnye otnosheniia, Moscow, 1978, p. 85.

83 Hough, *Struggle*, citing L. S. Vasil'ev, "Stanovlenie politicheskoi administratsii ot lokal'noi gruppy okhotnikov i sobiratelei k protogosudarstvu-chifdom," *Narody Azii i Afriki*, no. 1 (1980): 172–86; L. S. Vasil'ev, "Proto gosudartsvo-chifdom kak politicheskaia struktura," *Narody Azii i Afrika*, no. 6 (1981): 159–75.

84 Zagladin and Ryzhenko, *Sovremennoe revoliutsionnoe dvizhenie*, p. 94. See also Ulyanovsky, *National Liberation*, p. 309.

85 Grigulevich and Kozlov, *Races and Peoples*, pp. 190–228.

86 Ibid., pp. 191–2.

87 Ibid., p. 200.

88 Ibid., pp. 200–2.

89 Ibid., p. 225.

90 M. Lazarev, "Sovremennyi etap natsional'nogo razvitiia stran zarubezhnogo Vostoka," *Aziia i Afrika segodnia*, no. 12 (1979): 22–5.

91 Ibid., pp. 23–4.

92 Ibid., p. 24.

93 Ibid., p. 25.

94 Fedoseyev, *Leninism*, p. 474.

95 Ibid., p. 477.

96 Sh. Sanakoyev, "The Great Transforming Force in World Relations," *International Affairs*, no. 6 (1984): 10.

97   An. Gromyko, "Sovetskoi assotsiatsii druzhby s narodami Afriki — 20 let," *Aziia i Afrika segodnia*, no. 5 (1979): 2; Anatoly Gromyko, *Africa: Progress, Problems, Prospects*, Progress Press, Moscow, 1983, p. 13.

98   N. Kosukhin, "Rasprostranenie idei nauchnogo sotsializma v Afrike,": *Aziia i Afrika segodnia*, no. 7 (1981): 3.

99   *Pravda*, 1 May 1979.

100 Gromyko, "Sovetskoi assotsiatsii," p. 2; Oleg Dreier, "Lenin and Africa," *Asia and Africa Today*, no. 5 (1978): p. 2.

101 Gromyko, *Africa*, pp. 13–14; Gromyko, "Sovetskoi assotsiatsii," p. 2; Anat. Gromyko, "Lenin i Afrika," *Aziia i Afrika segodnia*, no. 5 (1980): 2.

102 Shevtsov, *National Sovereignty*, pp. 24–5; Primakov, *Pravda*, 11 August 1982; see also Primakov, *Vostok*, pp. 89–90.

103 Primakov, *Vostok*, pp. 89–90.

104 *Pravda*, 11 August 1982.

105 G. Kim, "Sovetskii Soiuz i natsional'no–osvoboditel'noe dvizhenie," *Mirovaia ekonomika i mezhdunarodnye otnosheniia*, no. 9 (1982): 23.

106 G. Kim, "World Socialism and the National Liberation Movement," *Far Eastern Affairs*, no. 2 (1976): 43. See also G. Kim, "Razriadka i sotsial'nyi progress v stranakh Azii i Afriki," *Aziia i Afrika segodnia*, no. 11 (1978): 2–6.

107 Kim, "Razriadka," pp. 2–6.

108 E. Tarabrin, "Neokolonializm na sovremennom etape," *Aziia i Afrika segodnia*, no. 1 (1978): 12.

109 Gavrilov, "Lenin," p. 2.

110 P. I. Manchkha, *Aktual'nye problemy sovremennoi Afriki*, Politizdat, Moscow, 1979, p. 333.

111 Simoniia, *Strany Vostoka*; Ul'ianovskii, "O nekotorykh voprosakh"; Mikhailov and Tadevosian, "O ser'eznykh metodologicheskikh"; Borisov and Aleksandrov, "Obsuzhdenie knigi."

112 Simoniia, *Strany Vostoka*, pp. 22–61; Simoniia, "Konsolidatsiia," pp. 84–5.

113 See chapter 4.

114 Simoniia, *Strany Vostoka*, pp. 91–139, 312–31.

115 Ul'ianovskii, "O nekotorykh voprosakh." See the Borisov and Aleksandrov, "Obsuzhdenie knigi," account of discussion on the book, November 1976, by party and Academy of Science researchers, See especially Aleksandrov of the Marxist–Leninist Institute (pp. 58–9) and V. I. Kuz'min and V. N. Egorov of the same institute (pp. 60–2). More sympathetic to Simoniia were S. L. Agaev of the Institute of the International Workers Movement (p. 61), A. V. Meliksetov of the Foreign Ministry's Institute of International Affairs (p. 59) (i.e., persons dealing more with day-to-day affairs regarding the Third World), and G. I. Mirskii of IMEMO (pp. 57–8). Much of the criticism in *Voprosy istorii KPSS* (Mikhailov and Tadevosian, "O ser'eznykh metodologicheskikh") also focused on Simoniia's analysis of October.

116 Introduction by Ul'ianovskii to I. Andreyev, *The Non-capitalist Way*, Progress Press, Moscow, 1977, p. 13. See also Ul'ianovskii, *Sovremennye problemy*, pp. 33–4.

117 Ulyanovsky, *National Liberation*, p. 30.

118 Nodari Simoniya, "The October Revolution and the National Liberation Movements," *International Affairs*, no. 12 (1979): 60–1; Simoniia, "Sovremennyi etap," p. 14; S. N. Simoniya, "Mighty Tide of National Liberation," *New Times*, no. 50 (1980): 21–3.

119 Brutents, *National Liberation Revolution*, vol. I, pp. 62–3.

120 Ibid., p. 62.

121 Ibid., p. 63.

122 Ibid., p. 64.

123 E.g. Seydou Cissoko, "Lenin—Theorist of the National Liberation Movement," *World Marxist Review* 23, no. 4 (1980): 36–7; "A Communist Call to Africa," *African Communist*, no. 75 (1978): 6–7; Michael Harmel, "Lenin and African Liberation," *New Times*, no. 21 (1970): 22; Ezekias Papaicannon, "Lenin and Some Problems of the National Liberation Movement," *World Marxist Review* 13, no. 4 (1970): 14; Zaki

Karkabi "Against Imperialism, For Social Progress," *World Marxist Review* 24, no. 2 (1981): 49.

124 See "A Communist Call to Africa," or Harmel, "Lenin and African Liberation," or A. Azad, "What Proletarian Internationalism Means to Africa," *African Communist*, no. 70 (1977): 51–2.

125 In Berlin Conference discussion, "Right to Decide One's Own Future," *World Marxist Review* 24, no. 4 (1981): 70–1.

126 See chapter 5 below.

127 B. Ponomarev, "Neodolimost' osvoboditel'nogo dvizheniia," *Kommunist*, no. 1 (1980): 15.

128 Ibid., p. 12.

129 Ibid., p. 16.

130 Ibid., p. 12; emphasis mine.

131 *Pravda*, 18 October 1979; Boris Ponomarev, "The World Situation and the Revolutionary Process," *World Marxist Review* 17, no. 6 (1974): 3–10; Boris Ponomarev, "Under the Banner of Marxism–Leninism and Proletarian Internationalism," *World Marxist Review* 14, no. 6 (1971): 1–6.

132 *Pravda*, 13 December 1978.

133 *New Times*, no. 45 (1977): pp. 8–9, on the sixtieth anniversary, to the Central Committee, Supreme Soviet, and Russian Soviet.

134 Moscow domestic radio, 24 February 1976; *Pravda*, 18 June 1972.

135 *Pravda*, 24 February 1981.

136 Interview with *Le Monde*, in *Pravda*, 16 June 1977.

137 TASS, 27 April 1981.

138 *Pravda*, 23 June 1978.

139 TASS, 29 March 1977; 31 March 1977.

140 E.g., A. Gromyko, "Programma mira v deistvii," *Kommunist*, no. 14 (1975): 3–20; A. Gromyko, "Leninskaia vneshniaia politika v sovremennom mire," *Kommunist*, no. 1 (1981): 13–27; to UNGA, *Izvestiia*, 27 September 1978.

141 Soviet domestic radio, 23 November 1983.

142 *Pravda*, 16 June 1983; 1 September 1978; 23 April 1976.

143 *Leninskoe znamia*, 23 February 1979 in FBIS-III, 5 April 1979, R-8.

144 See Olcott, "Yuri Andropov," pp. 111–15.

2

Composition, Leadership, and Organization of National Liberation Movements

Introduction

Any theory of national liberation would require reference to the structure of the movement—specifically, the types or classifications of persons involved, the nature of the leadership, and the overall organizational framework. Even more so, a Soviet theory of national liberation must relate to these issues inasmuch as basic Marxist and Leninist strictures go beyond the conditions that produce a revolutionary movement to the questions of just how a revolution is to be organized and led, by whom, and with whom. The overall class and social composition of the society itself will to a large degree determine or influence the actual composition of the cadres or groups adhering to a national liberation movement.

Even on this basic point, however, there were, on the one hand, those accepting the standard Marxist, class description of society in the Third World and, on the other hand, those advocating a more differentiated or sophisticated approach to the subject. The latter pointed to the existence of numerous social strata, and to production- or even non-production-related groups and categories of jobs which defied classical Marxist typology.

This variation notwithstanding, Soviet analyses of the composition of national liberation movements focused on an only somewhat broadened list of classes: the national bourgeoisie, the petty bourgeoisie (broadened to include what were called intermediate strata, such as the intelligentsia and the military), the peasantry, and the proletariat. Each class was analyzed or rated in terms of its interest and role in a liberation movement, including its essentiality or marginality as well as its influence and political potential. The spectrum of views regarding each class was not particularly broad, but in each case it reflected nuances ranging from a conservative, proletarian-based, anti-bourgeoisie approach, through a more enlightened but cautious approach skeptical, for example, of too great an emphasis on the peasantry (expressed in criticism of Franz Fanon), all the way to acknowledgment of the centrality of the non-proletarian classes, including the bourgeoisie.

Attitudes toward the leadership qualifications of each class generally fell along the same spectrum, but the various approaches were determined somewhat differently. Leadership by the peasantry was rejected by all for many reasons, not least of which was the Soviet–Marxist priority for the town over the countryside. There were those who rejected the leadership of any one group, regarding them all negatively with regard to numbers, experience, influence, political–organizational potential, or any other leadership qualities. Others, the usual conservative commentators, rejected all but the proletariat. Still others, however, acknowledged the negative aspects of all the non-proletarian classes but adopted a more pessimistic approach to the proletariat, rejecting it for the role of leader. Rather, they argued that, despite the negative attributes of the national and petty bourgeoisie (including the intermediate strata), the leadership of a national liberation movement would come from one or another of these classes.

Given this dichotomy between the two basic approaches, there were also differing attitudes as to the ultimate importance or influence of the class composition of a movement's leadership. Beyond this, there was the question of personalities rather than a class characterization of leadership, "leaderism" being a phenomenon often associated with such movements, for better or for worse.

The organization of a movement could follow one of two models: an elitist, vanguard party, or a mass movement or party. The mass model could be based on class, ethnic, religious, or other organizing principle, but this model called for a national-front-type framework. There was also the question of internal organization, that is, the division into and relationship between political, military, administrative, and ideological organs. The relationship between leadership and cadres could be a problematic facet of the mass movement or party. The second model, that of a vanguard party, was less applicable to the pre-independence struggle, viewed basically as an exception for national liberation movements. Organizations of the working class such as trade unions had a role to play, as did communist parties. The inapplicability of a communist party, and the subordinate role of such a party where it already existed, were matters of surprisingly little controversy, as the united front tactic implicit in the mass movement model was proposed. Only one slight deviation appeared in this regard, and that, a cautionary voice rather than an advocate of a different approach.

Composition: The Society

National liberation movements presumably in some way reflected the societies in which they developed and whose struggle they sought to represent or conduct. In turn, these societies were, in Marxist terms, determined by the historical stage reached in their production base. Herein lay the major difference between classical (nineteenth-century) national movements and those of the Third World; for, given the relatively early developmental stage of the Third World societies (which, as we have seen, in some cases lacked the prerequisites even for "nationhood"), their economies had not developed sufficiently to have led to the formation of classes or class relations. If not actually pre-class societies, they were at best societies with only "embryonic divisions into social groups and classes."[1] As Ul'ianovskii put it, their liberation struggle was waged "in a pre-capitalist and largely pre-feudal social structure thinly veiled in bourgeois relations developed mostly in the fields of commodity production and money circulation."[2] As a result, these societies were still under the tribal system; or, as Brutents explained, they were frequently still governed by "family and tribal ties, caste preconceptions, [and] religious attachments" which obscured class relations.[3]

The importance of the traditional social structure of Third World societies was therefore recognized and on occasions even analyzed.[4] The continued dominance of the clan or tribal relationship even among the large numbers of persons who sought work in towns, the persistence of and even reaffirmation of traditional ties and identity, were also acknowledged.[5] Brutents, for example, admitted that "very frequently it is not the actual social condition but these ties and attachments that determine the behaviour of men."[6] In some cases these ties, such as religious ones, might even generate an interest in national liberation as a struggle against the imposition of outside (Western) faith and customs.[7] Nonetheless, generally speaking, these traditional ties were perceived as negative, retrograde factors, standing in the way of class formation. Indeed, colonialism was accused of purposely fostering the persistence of the traditional social structure so as to prevent progressive development.[8] And it was pointed out that traditional elites, such as tribal chiefs, not only remained aloof from the national liberation process but even permitted themselves to be co-opted into the service of the colonialists so as to protect their own flagging status.[9]

In addition to the traditional division of society, the existence of semi-traditional or marginal strata was also acknowledged. These strata, according to Orientalist Georgii Kim, included "paupers, lumpen groups, the pre-proletariat," in other words, groups or strata that had broken off from the traditional structure but had not yet been absorbed into any other structure.[10] Moreover, an intermingling of different social groupings or types was also noted, wherein an individual might be a member of more than one social grouping at the same time. For example, remaining within the framework of a "patriarchal commune," a peasant might be a "feudally enthralled debtor, a farmhand temporarily working for an agro-entrepreneur, and a small producer of goods for the market," while an urban worker might maintain primary loyalty to his tribe, clan, religious community, or sect, returning to his traditional village at frequent intervals.[11] In pointing out these complexities, Kim (as well as others) appeared to be arguing for a more sophisticated approach to the structure of Third World societies even while proclaiming the continued validity of classical Marxist categories.[12]

Semi-proletarians were occasionally called non-proletarian working masses, a term used by Central Committee experts Ul'ianovskii and Manchkha.[13] It was clearly stated that this grouping needed analyzing,[14] for, as Orientalist Vladimir Li claimed in 1978, there were "unique social groups emerging at the junction or in the process of interaction between various economic patterns which do not always correspond to 'classic' models of the early capitalist society."[15] According to Li, Soviet Orientalists had not yet settled the problem of the class application of this large, socially important mass of non-proletarian working people. Presumably for the purposes of legitimacy, he generally defined or likened this group to Lenin's category of "oppressed masses of exploited working people in non-capitalist Eastern countries," who were "not workers who have passed through the school of capitalist factories."[16] It was just this group, however, which, according to Li, Lenin had emphasized among the motive forces for national liberation.

Unlike other observers, who spoke of the "toiling masses" as a catchall phrase for a worker–peasant alliance,[17] Li included in this grouping seasonal workers, migrant laborers, "half-peasants and half-workers" (connected with both industrial production and agriculture), the lumpenproletariat, and the "pauperized peasants." These were gainfully employed but non-hired workers; they were non-agricultural workers who nonetheless did not fit precisely into the petty bourgeoisie, though they did include small entrepreneurs, owners of tiny peasant households and artisan shops.[18] Household servants formed a separate category of non-proletarian workers. While they were not identical with the petty bourgeoisie, Li claimed that the non-proletarian workers were influenced by petty bourgeois views, and that they were drawn into the revolutionary struggle at least to some degree as part of the political awakening of the petty bourgeoisie, engendered by a nationalistic consciousness against foreign (imperialist) domination. Thus, there was a similarity, even a connection, between the petty bourgeoisie (and the broader category, called the intermediate or medium social strata) on the one hand, and the non-proletarian masses on the other. Rather than explain this relationship, or even provide a full and wholly coherent discussion of this "unique" social grouping, Li directly called for further examination on the grounds that this group, the non-proletarian working masses, in fact constituted a social base for future revolutionary development.

For the most part, however, differentiated analyses of the social structures of these societies, and their national liberation movements, were based on the more limited, classical Marxist approach, with only minor modifications. This approach divided society into what were described as "tendencies" or social groupings, if not actual classes.[19] They consisted of the national bourgeoisie, the petty bourgeoisie, broadened into the intermediate or medium strata, the peasantry, and the proletariat, as well as those not involved in the national liberation struggle, such as feudal and landowning groupings, clan or tribal chiefs, the comprador bourgeoisie (that bourgeoisie which cooperated with the colonialists), and, according to some, the bureaucracy.[20]

Composition of Movements

THE NATIONAL BOURGEOISIE

The national bourgeoisie was different in a number of aspects from a classical bourgeoisie known to European society. The primary difference was that the local or national bourgeoisie of the Third World did not consist of capitalist owners or bourgeois businessmen, as such, exploiting workers. This local bourgeoisie was not perceived as exploitative, for the employer-owners were in fact foreign investors and entrepreneurs.[21] Rather, the national bourgeoisie was composed of persons confined to trade, services, and credit (money-exchanging and lending), that is, persons who might be called little more than petty-bourgeois trades-men.[22] This was due in part to the low level of production forces in what was a predominantly pre-capitalist system, the strength of which mitigated against the emergence of a bourgeoisie.[23] It was also due to the fact that capital was in the hands of foreigners. Indeed, this class was in most societies quite small, if it existed at all. Foreign capital with foreign entrepreneurs gave the local bourgeoisie little chance to develop; local markets were small, and the local bourgeoisie had little capital, their countries having been plundered by foreigners.[24] Moreover, they were discriminated against and subjected to restriction by the colonial authorities.

Unable to develop or prosper in these conditions, perceiving them-selves oppressed by foreign interests, the national bourgeoisie joined the national liberation struggle. Their motivation was, however, purely economic, their nationalism purely selfish.[25] As the more conservative study edited by Zagladin and Ryzhenko put it, the national bourgeoisie joined the national liberation struggle because it did not want to share profits with the foreign imperialists.[26]

Zagladin's assessment was among the more extreme,[27] but it did express the general ambivalence toward this class as a component of the national liberation movement. The dual nature of the national bourgeoisie was pointed out, for example, by Ul'ianovskii, who explained that, on the one hand, this class had "an objective stake" in the abolition of foreign political and economic domination, while, on the other hand, it tended to equate the national liberation movement with its own narrow class interests, cooperating with and entering into compromises with foreign capital.[28] A highly cautious attitude, because of this dual nature, was advocated by B. Gafurov, when head of the Oriental Institute, and by the 1970 Zhukov study;[29] the study by the Marxist–Leninist Institute of the CPSU, under the supervision of Petr Fedoseev, supported the more conservative view in its pronouncement that the revolutionary potential of the national bourgeoisie was in fact an illusion, since this class would always act according to its class interests.[30]

The unreliability of the national bourgeoisie and the purely temporary, particularistic nature of its interest in the liberation struggle meant that this was a most unstable component. Its relative importance to the struggle was, however, still the subject of debate, as it had been in the early years of the international communist movement. It was pointed out that the national bourgeoisie's influence on other classes or groups in society varied, depending on concrete circumstances. There were those who allotted them little if any importance, because they were basically underdeveloped as a class.[31] Some said their influence was limited because of the strength of the traditional elements of society and the persistence of the tribal, patriarchal, or feudal structure of society, although it was also said that they could have influence over the ranks of petty bourgeoisie and peasants (with whom they were in commercial contact).[32] It was also argued, however, that the peasants, at least, viewed them as exploiters, given their role as money-lenders and barterers for credit.[33]

Similarly, there were varied evaluations of the national bourgeoisies' political potential. Some argued that they were politically as well as economically weak in most parts of the Third World, possessing political parties only in a very small number of countries.[34] They were said to have been cowered by the colonialists, and to be lacking in courage. It was also said, however, sometimes even by the same observer, that they were characterized by a high degree of political activity, their political influence enhanced by the lack of a differentiated class structure and, therefore, the absence of class antagonism.[35]

The ambiguities and ambivalence notwithstanding, the CPSU stance of the 1960s on the importance of the national bourgeoisie was basically reconfirmed by the Central Committee's two senior Third World experts, Ul'ianovskii and Brutents. Brutents actually rehashed the old Lenin–Roy dispute, criticizing Roy's rejection of this class on the grounds that, whatever its dual nature, this class, objectively, played a significant anti-imperialist role. Thus, Brutents argued:

> The profound contradiction between the urge of the national bour-geoisie to enhance its material and political condition, to rise to dominance in the country, to set up a national state, develop the national economy, organize a national market and secure control of it, on the one hand, and the interests of the colonialists, on the other, determine the national bourgeoisie's participation in the liberation struggle.[36]

Ul'ianovskii too affirmed this assessment, even as he spoke of the dual nature of this class. He emphasized the heterogeneity of the national bourgeoisie, that is, the existence of a positive, revolutionary aspect, and its anti-imperialist nature, despite the presence also of elements willing to compromise with the imperialists.[37] In his 1976 book, Ul'ianovskii argued that one simply had to adjust to the vacillations of the national bourgeoisie, and that their participation in the liberation struggle could not be rejected or ignored just because they had caused problems in such places as China or India.[38] Two years later Ul'ianovskii took the same position, maintaining that this class still possessed a progressive potential—and that it would be "unrealistic" to write it off "even after independence."[39] Also, noting the negative experience of China, an *Asia and Africa Today* Lenin Anniversary editorial in 1982 (only in English) nonetheless emphasized Lenin's belief that the national bourgeoisie, because of its oppression by the imperialists, could take an active role in the liberation struggle. The verdict here was that "on the whole...the national bourgeoisie is able to stage courageous anti-imperialist acts."[40]

THE PETTY BOURGEOISIE

While there was disagreement over the size and importance of the national bourgeoisie as part of the national liberation struggle, there was much more agreement on the idea that the *petty bourgeoisie*, expanded to include the "intermediate strata" or "urban middle section" of society, was an important element of Third World society and of the liberation struggle. There were a few who linked the semi-proletarian or pre-proletarian masses to this category, while most included the intellectuals, army officers, and in some cases clerks (bureaucrats) in the broadened category of intermediate strata.[41] In one work, for example, Kim spoke of the petty bourgeoisie as a broad spectrum of social forces including traditional and modern, rural and urban elements as well as "adjoining strata" such as semi-traditional marginal elements from below, the intelligentsia, and the modern middle strata from above.[42] In another piece, Kim spoke of the "middle urban strata," which included the intelligentsia, army officers, petty proprietors, and white-collar workers;[43] and a less authoritative later study, for example, included the petty bourgeoisie as such in the urban middle strata.[44] Gafurov, like others, added students to the intelligentsia and military but employed the less differentiating term of the "patriotic strata" in describing them (a term employed less frequently in later years, when greater differentiation became standard).[45] The Oriental Institute's Andreasian spelled out the "intermediate strata" to include many not connected with production, such as teachers, clerks, and officers, that is, the "non-proletarian, non-Marxist strata" which were influenced by the petty bourgeoisie.[46] And the petty bourgeoisie "proper" was defined as former peasants turned small producers or traders, handicrafts people turned owners.[47] The exact composition or clarification was indeed confused, with some including the petty bourgeoisie within the intermediate strata, some reversing this with the intermediate strata (intellectuals, military, etc.) subsumed under the urban petty bourgeoisie, some placing the rural petty bourgeoisie there as well, some separating all of them as allied but separate categories.

Part of this classification problem was explained by Ul'ianovskii as resulting from the earlier tendency among scholars simply to view the intelligentsia and military as part, albeit the left-wing part, of the national bourgeoisie.[48] Or, as Brutents explained, some Soviet scholars (he named Mirskii and Pokataeva) had earlier classified small traders and small independent farmers not as part of the petty bourgeoisie but as pre-capitalist phenomena.[49] And he pointed out that, on the other hand, small traders, artisans and the like were often indistinguishable from the national bourgeoisie.[50] Both Kiva (of the Oriental Institute) and Primakov explained the difficulty by the different relationships the various components had to production, with some, such as clerks, intellectuals, and the military, having no links with private enterprise, while traders, artisans, and small producers clearly did have.[51] Inasmuch as class was determined by one's relationship to the means of production, Primakov pointed out that, the petty bourgeoisie or intermediate strata could not be considered one class simply because they were all urban non-proletarians in similar situations.[52] Be that as it may, the petty bourgeoisie and middle strata comprised some 65 percent of the urban population and, therefore, had to be reckoned with as an important, if differentiated, group, according to Brutents.[53] As a conglomerate, however, it was a temporary, ad hoc group rather than a class.

The petty bourgeoisie proper was said generally to consist of tradespeople, small shopowners, artisans, and other small producers, and as such was, in fact, a strong force in the national liberation struggle. As members of the lower-income sector of society (indeed, sometimes poorer than the proletariat), they were opposed to imperialism on economic grounds. According to Brutents, "they were induced to join the struggle by the colonial oppression, the exploitation and the ruinous competition from foreign countries, and also from well-to-do compradors and the pressure from the moneylenders."[54]

Yet, even more than the national bourgeoisie, the petty bourgeoisie was characterized by a dual nature. Petty bourgeois tradesmen, artisans, and the like tended to be both owners and laborers, proprietors and workers at the same time; even when employing others, they themselves worked alongside their employees or apprentices and, therefore, were not exploiters.[55] Their link with private property objectively nurtured, or connected them with, a bourgeois mentality or the bourgeoisie; but, inasmuch as they were directly involved in the labor process, they also developed or possessed a sympathy for and link with the working people, and joined them in the anti-capitalist struggle.[56] Because of this dual nature, members of the petty bourgeoisie were anti-capitalist, but not wholly so, for they were also sympathetic toward small capitalists; they were against the bourgeois philosophy of exploitation but were not Marxist–Leninist.[57] Having only recently been peasants, they had ties with the peasantry as well as the proletariat, who themselves were only recently peasants. But for this same reason they still had strong tribal, religious, caste, and other ties.[58] Thus, the petty bourgeoisie brought to the liberation struggle not only their class ambiguity but also, as Lenin said, "their prejudices, reactionary fantasies, weaknesses and errors."[59]

Citing Lenin, Ul'ianovskii asserted that the petty bourgeoisie—even the apparently revolutionary part of the petty bourgeoisie—could not help but vacillate between the bourgeoisie and the proletariat in its outlook and values.[60] Brutents and others added that as a result it was also politically divided and unorganized, and that its political attitudes reflected this duality, leading to collaborationist as well as leftist tendencies.[61] Its leaders were often a mixed bag of radicals, nationalists, or revolutionary democrats, but certainly not Marxist–Leninists.[62] Citing its inherent dualism and social instability, Andreev spoke of the petty bourgeoisie's vacillations between passive or reformist conciliation and wild outbursts of petty bourgeois revolutionism, anarchism, and extremism.[63] Indeed, Ul'ianovskii said, in his introduction to Andreev's book in English, that it would "take a whole historical epoch to overcome the dualism of the small producer."[64] And, as Kim and others put it, the inherent instability in a group that played such an important role in the national liberation struggle gave such movements themselves an unstable character, with the potential for going in either a bourgeois capitalist (counter-revolutionary) or proletarian socialist (revolutionary) direction after independence was won.[65]

These negative features of dualism and instability notwithstanding, the petty bourgeoisie and the proletariat were said to have mutual interests.[66] The petty bourgeoisie's actual social and economic situation brought it closer to the non-proletarian sectors of the working people, making its interests "objectively" different from those of foreign capitalists (or the local bourgeoisie).[67] As many cited from Lenin, for all its vacillation, prejudices and so forth, the petty bourgeoisie "objectively will attack capital."[68] Going even further, Tumanova, in a 1982 article in *Aziia i Afrika segodnia*, claimed that, because of the influence of socialist ideas in the world (and the lack of exposure of the Third World petty bourgeoisie to capitalism's "progressive image"), this grouping was capable of cooperating with the proletariat in the direction of social progress.[69] Brutents explained that it had political as well as social ties with the proletariat, possessing a great deal of political mobility even if highly vulnerable to nationalist attitudes.[70] Therefore, as Tumanova concluded, the petty bourgeoisie was a social grouping that could not be disregarded and was indeed a driving force of the national liberation movement.[71] Ul'ianovskii gave this a more official stamp when he asserted that it was essential for the proletariat (and Marxists) to cooperate with the petty bourgeoisie in the struggle for liberation.[72]

THE INTELLIGENTSIA

According to Brutents, the petty bourgeoisie generally followed the national intelligentsia, which gave political expression to these aspirations.[73] The national intelligentsia, part of the intermediate strata (along with, or according to some, as part of, the petty bourgeoisie), was said to be a relatively independent grouping with no class status or base as such. Described by Kim as occupying a position in the lower and middle strata of society, it was said to consist of "proletarians in white collars", including students (though elsewhere Kim spoke of intellectuals and white-collar workers as two separate categories within the intermediate strata).[74] Brutents, however, spoke of the intelligentsia as having come from well-to-do elites, and included members of the free professions, technicians, and bureaucrats (clerks or civil servants in the employ of the colonial administration).[75] The social origins or placement were not of great significance, however, with regard to the characterization of the national intelligentsia, for it was usually not subject to any concrete social forces.[76] Often standing apart from the social classes, it was usually not in need of association with one class or another.

Despite its small size, the intelligentsia's importance was a function of its wide influence. This influence was due primarily to the fact that, in what were basically illiterate societies, the intelligentsia possessed a monopoly on education and culture among its own people.[77] Moreover, it had good connections with other sectors of society. Often coming from the tribal or aristocratic elites, according to Brutents, it had influence among the tribal castes and at least a link with the peasant masses.[78] Its links with the colonial administration and army broadened its influence, while its combination of connections with both the tribal structure and the modern institutions clearly enhanced its position.[79] At the same time, it was often close to the national bourgeoisie from which it emerged; and, in general, it could be said to be in social proximity to the petty bourgeoisie whom it resembled by virtue of the transitional quality of its social status.[80]

The views of the intelligentsia were not necessarily determined by its social connections, however. According to Brutents, its social orientation emerged and formulated by itself, and, as pointed out by others, it could voice the interests of virtually any social group. Kim referred to the intelligentsia as the bearer of a hybrid combination of contrasting principles and beliefs.[81] Among these, according to Andreev, because of their proximity to the petty bourgeoisie, were often petty bourgeois "voluntarism" and extremism, or their opposite, politically shortsighted solutions.[82] Yet on the more positive side, according to Andreev himself and almost all other theoreticians, the intelligentsia was not in fact infected by bourgeois or petty bourgeois ideas and profit-seeking motivation.[83] It was agreed that clear distinctions must in fact be made between the attitudes of the petty bourgeoisie proper (shopkeepers, small producers, etc.) and those such as the intelligentsia who were not connected with private enterprise.[84] In fact, they were often sympathetic to the working masses and responsive to their deprivation, even to the point of assuming their point of view.[85]

Brutents and Andreev (who quoted Brutents) explained the intelligentsia's adherence to the national liberation struggle as the result of its service to the colonials.[86] Colonial administrations, in need of clerks, civil servants, and so on, trained and employed the national intelligentsia—to serve them. This effort, however, backfired, so to speak, for a number of reasons. In the colonial service, the intellectuals were exposed to ideas; often, sent abroad for training, they returned with new viewpoints and ideologies. Moreover, in the service of the colonial regime, they became aware of the horrors of the system, so that their national consciousness was raised. To this was added the humiliation they suffered in the form of discrimination or, at the very least, limitations on their advancement in colonial service. Thus, their national pride was hurt by the phenomenon of colonialism, leading them to join—indeed, in many cases to form—the national liberation struggle.

Inasmuch as they were consolidated early, because of the needs of the colonialists, the intellectuals were among the first to raise the nationalist banner. As a result, they were the group with the greatest political experience in terms of both time and function.[87] They exhibited a high degree of political activity, filling the political vacuum of a society of undifferentiated classes and the absence of an organized (or any) proletariat.[88] Specifically, according to Brutents, they acted as initiators, as organized and active participants, in setting up parties, organizations, and even trade unions. By means of their parties, they united the urban population with the peasant masses.[89]

Most of all, as Kim explained, the national intelligentsia fulfilled the role of the bearer and spokesperson of the general national ideals of independence, social justice, and anti-capitalism.[90] This was not always entirely positive, because of the variety of ideas and generally non-class outlook the intellectuals promulgated.[91] They were also vulnerable to the pressure of the tribal elites and the bourgeois atmosphere from which they emerged. As with the petty bourgeoisie (of which some considered them a part), they possessed an ambiguity which could influence them in either direction after independence. The more conservative Fedoseev study seemed to contradict Brutents' analysis when it argued that the reason post-independence bureaucrats, who were often cited as a group that became counter-revolutionary after independence, were pro-colonialist was because of their services to the colonialist authorities prior to independence.[92] Nonetheless, almost all agreed that the role of the intelligentsia in the liberation struggle was not only a key role and "objectively" positive, but also a progressive one, particularly when a differentiation was made for the "vanguard sections" of this group.[93]

THE MILITARY

Military officers, often referred to as the military intelligentsia, were also seen as a part of the intermediate strata, sometimes subsumed under the petty bourgeoisie, more often given separate status of their own. For the most part, the characteristics of this grouping were included among those of the intelligentsia (often distinguished only by the terms civil and military intelligentsia) and, therefore, could generally be said to have been similar or even identical. This absence of a differentiated approach or separate analysis regarding the military meant that, for most analysts, virtually everything said about the civilian intelligentsia was true for the military as well, be it with regard to its social origins, status, relations and influence, its views and attitudes, its role and importance. Ul'ianovskii, for example, tended to discuss military officers and the national intelligentsia together, even stating that they had identical social background, education, psychology, and practical experience which welded them together independently of concrete social forces or status or classes.[94] There were many exceptions to this, however, probably because of the debate over the role of armies in Third World states after independence—a debate prompted by the numerous military coups in the newly independent states.[95] For example, Solodovnikov and Bogoslovskii, probably under the influence of the major study on armies in Third World states by Georgii Mirskii, singled out the military for more cautious treatment.[96] Solodovnikov and Bogoslovskii, as well as Mirskii, allowed that military officers might play an important, even progressive, role in the liberation struggle, but warned (quoting Mirskii) that they could go in either direction—progressive or reactionary—the implication being that they were even less trustworthy than the other intermediate strata.[97] This was in line with Mirskii's conclusion that bourgeois and petty bourgeois influence came to dominate the post-independence army, a conclusion accepted by Kim as well.[98] Gavrilov, too, may have implied this when he limited his references only to "the progressive military" when discussing the composition of national liberation movements.[99] Thus, a reviewer of Mirskii's 1970 book rejected what could be interpreted as Ul'ianovskii's relatively homogeneous image of the military (and intelligentsia), emphasizing Mirskii's admonitions regarding the heterogeneity of the military from every point of view.[100] An equally critical article in *Narody Azii i Afriki* did, nonetheless, list some of the positive aspects of the role of the military, such as the prevention of bourgeois influence on the politically naive masses, or, even more positively, the organization of a backward society around a revolutionary order.[101] It was not explained, however, how or why the military could play such a role.

While Mirskii's analysis apparently did have a serious impact, and may well have reflected official uneasiness over military regimes as such, these analyses did not produce a general change in the way in which most commentators, including the most authoritative Central Committee theoreticians such as Ul'ianovskii and Brutents, related to the military at the stage of the liberation struggle.[102] The Soviet military itself is said to have taken up the issue in argument with Mirskii, implicitly defending the role of the military at the early liberation stage in what was an explicit defense of it at the post-independence stage.[103] One military study was more mixed inasmuch as it was more detailed, distinguishing between the military drawn from the colonial period and those from an army formed by the national liberation movement itself during the course of its struggle. The former was said to contain many "representatives of the exploiter classes, their lackey and imperialist agents" providing the raw material for future counter-revolutionary tendencies. Those of the national liberation struggle itself were of a mixed nature but generally positive in their anti-imperialist quality.[104]

The Zhukov study, which appeared the same year as Mirskii's work, provided what was in fact a rare analysis of how and why the military became involved in the liberation struggle and its positive contribution to this struggle. According to this analysis, the military was drawn to the national liberation cause in much the same way as the civilian intelligentsia.[105] Sent abroad for training, usually to the colonialists' home country, military people became exposed to ideas and other realities. Often they were sent abroad to fight the imperialists' war, which produced the same effect. Moreover, they were used at home by the colonialists to put down local disorders against their own people, thereby raising their national consciousness and sense of injustice. To this was added a blow to their national and individual pride in the form of discrimination and limitations on their advancement in the army and the indignity of having to take orders, always, ultimately, from foreign officers. Indeed, Mirskii himself explained the adherence of the military, stating that "no one feels the backwardness of the state as does an officer....Recognition of the backwardness of his country to the rise of nationalistic patriotic feelings leads him to struggle for the liquidation of foreign control."[106] The military, therefore, was among the first to be drawn to the national liberation struggle along with the civil intelligentsia, as we have seen from all the studies which simply dealt with both groups together. Military officers brought to this struggle their close-knit sense of loyalty, organization, and experience.[107] Indeed, in societies with little class differentiation, they were possibly the only well organized and disciplined group, a group which, according to Zhukov, was also highly political.

THE PEASANTRY

The peasantry comprised the vast majority of the population, or masses, in Third World societies. In terms of its size, it formed the base of the whole social pyramid.[108] Therefore, by virtue of their sheer numbers, the peasants could not be ignored. In fact, they were said to form the social basis for the national liberation movement itself, rendering it nationwide. Without this participation, no movement could be a mass movement or gain sufficient numbers of supporters to wage the liberation struggle or carry off a national liberation revolution.[109] As Brutents put it in a *Pravda* article in 1970, the position of the peasantry was "decisive for a mass revolutionary upsurge."[110] And, indeed, both Lenin and Brezhnev were quoted as to the centrality of the peasantry in national liberation movements because they constituted the "bulk" of the population.[111] Lenin was also invoked to attest to the revolutionary potential of this class, that is, to not only the quantitative but also the qualitative reasons for their inclusion in the liberation struggle. For example, Ul'ianovskii referred to the "vast revolutionary potential" of the peasantry as one of Lenin's "fundamental conclusions" with regard to the national liberation movements.[112] This potential was due to the fact that antiquated and semi-feudal relations existed in the countryside, rendering the peasants the most deprived, oppressed, and exploited sector of colonial society.[113] The countryside was so undeveloped that commodity production had not yet emerged, and most peasants lived at mere subsistence level and were, for the most part, landless.[114]

The peasants generally bore the brunt of foreign rule, exploited by foreign capital and the colonial authorities, by the feudal and tribal elite and landowners, by usurers and merchants, and even, occasionally, by rich peasants (kulaks).[115] As Brutents put it: "The peasantry, living and working in arduous conditions, being driven off the land by foreign companies and settlers, subjected to oppression, arbitrary acts and levies by the colonial administration, exploited by the landowners, the tribal elite and the money-lenders, were driven to take part in the national movement, which held out the prospect of obtaining land and a radical improvement of their condition."[116]

According to Ul'ianovskii, their depression drove the peasants to political awareness, starting with "patriotic feelings of anti-imperialist nationalism."[117] Indeed, he claimed elsewhere, since the October Revolution peasants had been fighting against feudal landowners for land and for new agrarian relations.[118] This intimate connection between colonial rule and peasant rights accounted for the fact, according to Solodovnikov and Bogoslovskii, that many national liberation struggles were preceded or accompanied by peasant revolts and uprisings.[119]

Nonetheless, for all that the peasantry had a revolutionary potential and was essential to the struggle in the Third World, there were certain problems with this class. It was by no means a uniform class. An article in *Aziia i Afrika segodnia* pointed out that it was a class composed of smallholders, landless peasants, and agricultural workers. But Primakov was more doubtful about the possibility of defining it as a class at all.[120] He argued that, in fact, in many places it was impossible to distinguish peasants from tribal groups. Where the tribal system was breaking down, a differentiation formed whereby there were poor peasants, middle peasants, and kulaks, or what Primakov called peasants of the tribal system, the feudal system, and the capitalist villages. Each type of peasant was characterized by different social content and interests. Thus, according to Primakov, the term "peasantry" referred not to a class as such, but merely to all those operating within the agricultural economy. Ul'ianovskii implicitly accepted the differentiated view when he said that the most important group to win over was the poorest peasantry, who, he said, formed the majority of the peasantry.[121]

Rather than actual differentiation, the coexistence of contradictory attributes in the peasant, as in the petty bourgeoisie, was also acknowledged. Referring to Lenin, Solodovnikov and Bogoslovskii, for example, spoke of the duality of the peasant as worker as well as proprietor; Andreev likened the small peasant producer to the urban petty bourgeois producer who joined in the work himself rather than practicing bourgeois exploitation.[122] Ul'ianovskii described this duality somewhat differently when he said that, like the urban petty bourgeoisie, the peasant had proprietory attributes, but also collective attributes.[123] While Ul'ianovskii interpreted this positively, to say that there was at least a potential for collective forms of agriculture in the dual nature, the more conservative Fedoseev study pointed to this duality as evidence of the peasantry's unreliability.[124] Ul'ianovskii did not disagree with this entirely, however, for he wrote of the lack of certainty as to just how revolutionary the peasantry would remain in the future, employing the following quote from Lenin:

> "The more backward the country, the stronger is the hold of small scale agricultural production, patriarchalism and isolation, which inevitably lend particular strength and tenacity to the deepest of petty-bourgeois prejudices, that is, to national egoism and national narrowmindedness."[125]

Ul'ianovskii even went further and said that the peasantry was often tied to tribal backwardness.[126]

Others were also to refer to the patriarchal qualities of the peasantry, and the Central Committee's Africanist Manchkha, for example, also believed the peasants to be "weighed down by backward nations."[127] In this same vein, Ul'ianovskii, in a glowing article on Amilcar Cabral, praised the African leader for recognizing that this handicap of backwardness often prevented the peasants from developing a socio-political or national awareness, making it very difficult to mobilize the peasantry for the national liberation struggle. Brutents explained the peasants' weaknesses as members of the liberation struggle according to the following reasons:[128] their isolation, or the fact that they were scattered throughout the countryside; the fact that they were swayed by petty proprietory and patriarchal tendencies; their frequently low level of political awareness; their inclination to precipitous action; their lack of familiarity with organization and discipline. Moreover, they were totally illiterate and were steeped in superstition and prejudices. As a result of all this, large sections, even the bulk of peasants, never joined the liberation movement, and those who did often did so not for its national political platform but for local reasons. Those who joined played no role in the movement as an independent class force; nor did they organize any political parties to further their demands.

There was a certain defensiveness in the Soviet theoreticians' appraisal of the peasantry as a factor in the national liberation struggle. This was due to what they described as the exaggeration or "absolutization" of the role of the peasantry among some Third World thinkers (the urban leftists and "Maoists") at the expense of the proletariat or in juxtaposition to Marxism–Leninism.[129] Detailed discussion of the issue was triggered by the publication in 1977 of a major Soviet work on Franz Fanon by A. V. Gordon. While taking care to be generally positive in their appraisal, because of Fanon's prestige and importance, particularly in Africa, Gordon and the book's reviewers were critical of Fanon's attitude toward the peasantry. Gordon particularly criticized Fanon for "absolutizing" the peasantry as the only revolutionary force in Third World society. One of the reasons for this, according to Gordon and reviewers Ul'ianovskii and Landa, was that Fanon employed violence as the measure of revolutionariness, and inasmuch as the kind of violence most common to the liberation struggle was guerrilla warfare and guerrilla warfare was centered in the countryside, the peasants were the group most involved.[130] A second reason was Fanon's "glorification" of the traditionalism and patriarchalism of the countryside, according to Landa. As Gordon explained Fanon, the proletariat and the middle strata in the city were ultimately influenced by the bourgeoisie in the cities, seeking only to improve their own lot. Peasant society, on the other hand, represented colonialized society: underdeveloped, conservative, feudal, medieval but pre-colonial, the only purely "national" reality. Given its isolation and traditional life, as well as its traditional communal structures, which Fanon claimed provided discipline and a collective mentality, the peasant was not interested in or influenced by the colonials. Because of his poverty, however, he had nothing to lose, and therefore became the only bearer of the revolution.[131]

As Gordon and Ul'ianovskii pointed out, Fanon reversed the peasant and proletarian roles; the proletariat took on petty bourgeois traits of the city, the peasant took on the revolutionary traits.[132] The peasant rather than the proletariat was seen as exploited because, according to Gordon, Fanon defined "exploited" as poor, and the peasant was the poorest element in society. Poverty, in turn, was associated with spontaneous revolutionarism, and, on the basis of this spontaneity, the main revolutionary role went to the peasantry.[133] The peasantry encompassed the vast majority of society, the main and largest force against colonialism, capitalism, and modernization, which had "de-nationalizing" effects on the people.[134]

The problems with this theory were numerous, according to Gordon and his reviewers. First of all, aside from a logical inconsistency—defining "exploited" by its consequence, poverty—extreme poverty and oppression did not automatically create a revolutionary consciousness or lead to political activity (for Fanon also said that the consciousness could be gained through activity), according to Gordon.[135] Like Marx in the Communist Manifesto, Fanon described the revolutionary class as the largest one, but the numbers did not themselves make for this revolutionariness; the character of the class was the determining point and, on this point, the peasantry was in fact found lacking.[136] Indeed, according to Ul'ianovskii, it was not even a unified social group as Fanon envisaged it.[137] Moreover, in his article on Cabral, Ul'ianovskii commented that Fanon (unlike Cabral) failed to understand that, while the peasantry provided the manpower for the armed struggle, there was an essential difference between physical force and revolutionary force: the peasantry provided the former, not the latter.[138] Despite Landa's criticism that Gordon did not attack Fanon's glorification of village traditionalism sufficiently, Gordon did in fact take issue with Fanon's condemnation of modernization as distinct from traditional life.[139] He summed up Fanon's mistakes on this issue with the explanation that Fanon tried to see something special in the Third World and therefore rejected everything European. This understandable opposition to Eurocentrism had led him to reject modernization and emphasize the peasantry; in other words, Fanon absolutized the points of distinction between Europe and the Third World, specifically the peasantry.[140]

The above criticism, and defensiveness, notwithstanding, almost all the Soviet commentaries, with the notable exception of the Fedoseev study, found some redeeming feature in the peasantry. Brutents, for example, argued that this, albeit backward, group was undergoing a change and need not be merely an appendage to other classes.[141] There was, he said, a political awakening of the "advanced section" of the peasantry and an "overall enhancement" of its social and revolutionary potential as well as the growth of "social forces concerned with raising the peasants' political activity and initiative."[142] According to Brutents, the economic basis for this changing situation was "provided by the growing colonial and imperialist oppression and exploitation, the development of social antagonisms in the countryside...and the deepening crisis of agrarian structures. In these conditions, the progressive forces intensify their efforts aimed politically to activate the peasantry, international factors exert an influence, and there is an influx of democratic and socialist ideas."[143] In other words, the peasants could be awakened; oppression could lead to consciousness as well as a realization of their importance to the liberation struggle; outside political forces could activate them; and outside ideas could reach them. Thus, for all their inconsistencies and hesitations, *Narody Azii i Afriki* and *Aziia i Afrika segodnia* pointed out editorially at different intervals that Lenin (and Brezhnev) nonetheless saw the peasant as playing a very important revolutionary role.[144] Solodovnikov and Bogoslovskii explained that, even when the peasantry was not involved in active socio-political life, its importance to the national liberation movement "should not be underestimated." Its size alone, according to Brutents, rendered it the one factor that could determine, by its support, by whom and in what direction the movement would be led.[145] Moreover, the peasants' allegiance and involvement also held the key to ultimate victory.[146]

THE PROLETARIAT

As in the traditional dispute since the earliest days of the Comintern, the role of the proletariat in the Third World and in the national liberation movement was the subject of some controversy. It was generally agreed that the proletariat was minuscule at the stage of the liberation struggle. Because of the pre-capitalist, semi-feudal state of the economy, the concentration of people in service industries and small production, as well as the general lack of industry, a proletariat simply would not have emerged in any size.[147] Revealing the existence of the controversy, Brutents said that there were those who tried to exaggerate the number of workers by including virtually all wage-earners in the category of workers. ("One must object, therefore, to the now and again pronounced tendency—apparently for the purpose of emphasizing the role of the working class—to argue its large size on the strength of the data concerning the number of wage-workers with an approach similar to that used for the developed capitalist countries."[148]) Brutents argued that civil servants, administrative personnel, engineers, technicians, and the like were simply different—in political attitudes as well as economic conditions—from the workers and, therefore, could not be included in the latter category.[149] As we have seen, the groups listed by Brutents were, rather, to be categorized among the "intermediate strata."

A similar tendency for accuracy, over what might be called the more conservative ideological approach, was evident in the distinctions already pointed out regarding the "non-proletarian masses," which, according to many, simply defied classical Marxist categorization or, at the very least, could not be called proletarians. As Vladimir Li pointed out, Lenin's broad category of "toiling masses" or "exploited masses" or "working population" included huge groups of small producers, half-proletarians, pre-proletarians, and non-proletarians, in other words, much more than the proletariat as such.[150] What Andreev termed the "minuscule" or "embryonic" proletariat, at the stage of the national liberation struggle, constituted only a small fraction of the population.[151] According to Solodovnikov, the "working class" comprised only 1–1.5 percent of the African population, for example; but according to Brutents, this 1–2 percent itself was for the most part agricultural laborers, only 9 percent of the labor force (wage laborers) actually being what could be called proletarians.[152]

Moreover, even this minuscule proletariat was something of a mixed, amorphous group. At one end of the spectrum, according to Andreev, what skilled workers there were tended to be foreigners and, therefore, not part of what could be called the local proletariat. At the other end of the spectrum, there were particularly high numbers of migrant laborers, a group which Andreev saw more as a lumpenproletariat, a semi- or pre-proletarian group—somewhere between peasant and worker.[153] The genuine proletarian sprang from the traditional handicraftsmen of the village, the farmhands and the day-laborers, and those who had broken loose from the traditional village community.[154] Brutents contended, however, that even this group remained bound to the countryside and to the petty bourgeois ideology of small plants, handicrafts (etc.), and tribal relations. For example, the worker might relate to his boss as a member of a tribe or a patriarchal family rather than as a member of a social group or class.[155]

On the positive side, with regard to the national liberation struggle, the proletariat was said to develop more quickly than the national bourgeoisie, for example, as an anti-imperialist factor.[156] The major reason for this, according to Brutents, was the fact that the proletariat was concentrated in the factories—which belonged to foreign capitalists. The workers, therefore, came into daily, direct contact with foreign oppression. Because of this, the worker's response to exploitation, his immediate work-related demands, rapidly assumed political, anti-imperialist over-tones.[157] The fact that they were concentrated in factories also meant that there was contact and solidarity among the workers themselves, and that they had an organizational advantage in the form of the creation of trade unions and communist parties. Add to this their continued contact with their village origins, if seen as a positive factor,[158] and their role could be quite significant in the national liberation struggle. Indeed, Ul'ianovskii argued that the proletariat was the only true social class and, as such, the only group capable of waging a consistent struggle for complete liberation.[159]

This quality of consistency, which was singularly lacking in the descriptions of the other social strata involved in the national liberation struggle, was pointed out by others.[160] And the more conservative Fedoseev study echoed Brutents's analysis when it claimed that the ranks of the working class were cemented by the objective conditions of their work, which encouraged concentration of their (albeit small) numbers and engendered class solidarity, rendering them the advantages of good organization, firm discipline, and strong conviction.[161] Thus Solodovnikov, too, argued that the proletariat played a determining role in the national liberation movement, despite its small numbers.[162]

There was a certain amount of defensiveness in these arguments, particularly in response to the Third World and Chinese preference for the peasantry over the proletariat and, specifically, Fanon's criticism of the Third World proletariat. For example, Rumiantsev addressed the issue of the possibility of a revolutionary consciousness and role for the proletariat in basically pre-capitalist countries.[163] He explained that the formation of the proletariat as a separate class had two distinct aspects: a socioeconomic aspect, determined by the capitalist mode of production, and a socio-political aspect, that is, the consciousness of being a revolutionary force. The latter could be determined by many things, he argued, besides socioeconomic conditions, although he explained these only as "the specific historical conditions" of the struggle against the exploiter system.

Gordon, in his criticism of Fanon, argued that only "vulgar sociologism" could claim that the level of semi-economic development was the only determinant of one's attitude toward revolution.[164] And, as we have seen, he rejected the argument that sheer numbers imbued a group with revolutionary fervor. Ul'ianovskii, too, argued that a proletarian minority could, nonetheless, be aware of its historical mission even if this group were small in numbers.[165] Both Gordon and Ul'ianovskii rejected Fanon's claims that the proletariat was not a revolutionary force because of its small size or because it had become influenced by the bourgeois city, therefore becoming less eager to join the liberation struggle. According to Gordon, Fanon ignored the fact that the proletariat was in fact exploited in the Third World city no less than he was in Europe.[166] Moreover, as Ul'ianovskii explained citing Cabral, there was such a thing as a prototype or "ideal proletariat," that is, a carrier of proletarian ideology and consciousness even without a purely proletarian socioeconomic background.[167]

Similarly, Gordon took issue with Fanon's argument that the Third World proletariat was not truly revolutionary because he obtained his revolutionary ideas from books and theory (since he was literate), while the illiterate peasant was truly revolutionary because his consciousness came spontaneously. Gordon pointed to the lack of any necessary connection between literacy and opposition to or support for the liberation struggle or the juxtaposition of consciousness to emotional revolutionariness.[168] Both Ul'ianovskii and Gordon did admit, however, that there might be something to Fanon's reference to a privileged city proletariat or workers' aristocracy. Ul'ianovskii explained that this might be due to "trade unionism," that is, the seeking of immediate worker benefits on the part of such an elite; and Gordon admitted that this did create something of a problem with regard to the proletariat's political potential.[169]

There were others, such as Gavrilov and Kortunov, who acknowledged the political and organizational weakness of even those small numbers of proletarians that did exist, thereby contradicting the Fedoseev study, for example.[170] Andreev spoke of the low class awareness of the workers,[171] and Gavrilov said that, whereas other groups were objectively the carriers of socialist ideals in the national liberation movement, the nearly non-existent proletariat was "in the best case" merely an object of exploitation and oppression.[172] Solodovnikov even contradicted the Brutents thesis when he said that the absence of large enterprises in most Third World countries militated against large concentrations of workers, and, together with the low level of both the education and qualifications of the workers, seriously hindered the organization and class consciousness of the proletariat.[173] Brutents did not necessarily deny all of this; like Rumiantsev, he seemed to argue that awareness, organization, and revolutionariness could be induced, or assisted, by a vanguard group, specifically a communist party.[174] Even the Fedoseev study admitted that the proletariat did not exist as an independent political force,[175] and Ul'ianovskii, for all his belief in its revolutionary potential, concluded that the proletariat had inadequate experience and revolutionary activity, requiring more ideological, political, and organizational work. All appeared to agree that alliance with other classes or groups was necessary, although the frequent assertions that a purely proletarian movement was out of the question in the Third World and the frequent rationalizations of the need for such alliances suggested that there were still some doubters somewhere.[176] About them, Ul'ianovskii said: "In our day only hopeless dogmatists and sectarians can insist on the so-called 'revolutionary intransigence' to the non-proletarian national democratic forces."[177]

Leadership

TOWN VERSUS COUNTRY

More or less axiomatic to the Soviet theoretical position on the leadership of the national liberation movement was the priority of the town over the countryside. Virtually no one challenged the Leninist tenet that the town led the countryside. In a brief historical review, Kim did allow that feudal tribal elites had led the national struggles of the 1918–22 period; but, he added, later, particularly after World War II, the national movements had no such leadership.[178] Merdel claimed that the peasantry, along with the proletariat, had been "pushed away" from leadership positions, although he did not actually state where or in what circumstances they would otherwise have held such positions.[179]

On the whole, this dominance of the town over the countryside was attributed, in a negative argument, to the character of the rural population itself, the peasantry. Those qualities—or a lack of them—that prevented the peasantry from leading have been pointed out above in our discussion of the peasantry's potential role in national liberation movements. Thus, this was a group described as scattered, influenced by the antiquated, semi-feudal character of the countryside; often illiterate, prejudiced, superstition-ridden; swayed by petty bourgeois and patriarchal tendencies; inclined to spontaneous action; and lacking in organization, discipline, and political awareness or experience.[180] Fedoseev argued that the peasantry could not create anything new.[181] Ul'ianovskii explained that the very status of the peasantry inhibited its understanding of the "revolutionary vistas."[182]

However severe the judgment, the peasantry, for the above reasons, did not act as an independent force, but rather followed other social groups.[183] Their allegiance or support, because of their sheer numbers, might determine just which group would in fact be leader of the struggle, but their numbers, as we have already seen in the criticism of Fanon, did not in themselves qualify the peasantry for leadership.[184] Challenging Fanon's claim for peasant leadership, Ul'ianovskii asked rhetorically what (or who) set the peasant masses in motion and what gave their struggle consistency.[185] He and others (criticizing the Chinese as well) concluded that, despite its revolutionary potential, the peasantry, as Lenin had already ordained, would inevitably follow the town.[186]

The leadership for the national liberation struggle was to be found in the town for a number of reasons, detailed by the Zhukov study.[187] The town was the center of all cultural, economic, and political life. Although a relatively small unit, it nonetheless served as a unifying factor for the whole country, inasmuch as it was the commercial (marketing) and administrative seat. This centrality not only served as a unifying factor but also accounted for the fact that the major, determining battle had to be for the town—the center of power. Moreover, given the compact structure and close living quarters in the towns, organization and solidarity were more easily achieved there. Indeed, the oppression implicit in these conditions constituted direct and immediate evidence of foreign rule, leading to the development of national consciousness. Townspeople became the vehicles for nationalist and progressive ideologies.[188] Thus, "by virtue of the material and spiritual way of life of the urban population," this public was more united, more organized, and more aware than the peasantry, and the "towns assumed the guiding role in the shaping of people's national consciousness."[189] This was what "made it incumbent" upon the town to take upon itself the leadership of the peasant masses.[190]

THE NEGATIVE APPRAISALS

The question was, Which urban social group was to have this role? There were those who claimed that no one group could in fact lead. The peasantry having been ruled out, no other group existed in sufficient number or with sufficient organized strength to take a dominant role as sole leaders.[191] Leadership, therefore, like the composition of the movements themselves, could only arise out of coalitions or a socially mixed group. Generally, however, each group (the national bourgeoisie, petty bourgeoisie including the intermediate strata, the proletariat) was examined for its leadership potential.

From a theoretical point of view, the national bourgeoisie was rejected as leader. First, there was the argument that this class was, in most cases, extremely small, unformed, and weak; therefore, it was unable to lead.[192] It was also unqualified for leadership because of its political weakness organizationally, and its lack of influence in the face of tribal or patriarchal bonds.[193] Brutents claimed that the national bourgeoisie also lacked political courage and initiative, having been cowered by the colonialist rulers.[194] Moreover, as already pointed out, the national bourgeoisie was an unstable group, vacillating between social directions, with too great a potential for or tendency for compromise. Therefore, although the national bourgeoisie might (and did) claim to speak in the name of the whole people, its ultimately narrow interest, which would lead it to compromise, disqualified it from any legitimate claim to leadership.[195]

The petty bourgeoisie, including the intermediate groups, was rejected on similar grounds. Basically, its dual nature, and therefore inherent instability, were the greatest obstacles to leadership by the petty bourgeoisie proper.[196] According to Ul'ianovskii, the petty bourgeoisie could not long maintain a leadership position because of its tendencies toward the opposing poles of the bourgeoisie or the proletariat, collaborationism or leftism.[197] It was also, according to Ul'ianovskii, not only an uncertain, unreliable class but also a politically immature one, internally divided and unorganized.[198] All of this made it unqualified to lead. At best, it could be said to follow the intelligentsia.[199]

The intelligentsia, however, was also seen by some in too negative a light to warrant a leadership position. Andreev, as we have seen pointed to the intellectuals' penchant for abstractions, as well as their political shortsightedness, voluntarism, or extremism.[200] There was also a social ambiguity (as well as social independence) about the intelligentsia which could result in its tending in a non-progressive direction, even, according to Fedoseev, in the direction of collaboration, at least on the part of those serving in the colonial administration.[201] These qualities, by implication, placed the desirability of their leadership in some doubt.

The military showed some of these negative features, particularly the class ambiguity and instability, the potential for going in either a reactionary (bourgeois) or progressive direction.[202] Politically, they were considered vulnerable to "petty bourgeois" ideological influences, that is, to precipitous, extremist action.[203] Moreover, their ability to lead was hampered by their small size and, more important, by their exclusiveness or isolation from the masses they were presumably to lead and whose support they did not have.[204] Mirskii pointed out that "the psychological mould of military men is not favorable to their development of the qualities essential for political work, both amongst the intelligentsia and amongst the masses; to count on the leadership of the military would be a serious mistake."[205]

THE PROLETARIAT

Against the background of these negative attributes of all the above-mentioned urban candidates for leadership, the proletariat emerged—in theory—as a possible alternative. Brutents cited specific attributes which provided at least a potential for leadership among the proletariat. As we have seen, this was the only group that could be counted on *consistently* to place the general interest above its own. It suffered, and therefore saw the social and national question as one; inasmuch as it possessed no private property, it was unhampered by proprietory attitudes which might interfere with a principled, uncompromising stand. As we have seen, the proletariat had the advantage of awareness, solidarity, and organization, its consolidation often having preceded that of other social groups, such as the national bourgeoisie at least. Moreover, because of its peasant origins, it had good contacts with the peasant masses and the countryside. It had the further advantage of the organization provided by trade unions and communist parties, the latter lending it also the weight and assistance of international forces.[206]

For these objective reasons, the proletariat was the vanguard of the revolutionary masses, whether this was recognized by other groups or not.[207] And, as Kortunov asserted, citing Lenin, the proletariat did have the capacity to unite and direct the mass, multi-class movement.[28] There were those who stopped here, almost anachronistically (even for the Soviet Union) insisting on the leading role of the proletariat in the national liberation movements. The Fedoseev study took this point of view, virtually ignoring all classes but the peasantry and then insisting that the latter needed proletarian leadership.[209]

As might be expected, another source for this view was *Voprosy istorii KPSS*, where Troitskii defended the leading role of the proletariat against Western detractors who, he claimed, spoke only of the small numbers, illiteracy, and religious and traditional influences hampering the proletariat.[210] Troitskii did not, however, go so far as to claim that the proletariat had actually led all the successful national liberation movements. Another example of this attitude was expressed in *Krasnaia zvezda*, where "bourgeois ideologists, opportunists and revisionists" were criticized for scorning the role of the working class (and the communist parties) in the revolutionary struggle.[211] On the whole, however, such assertions of proletarian supremacy were reserved for the post-independence stage of the struggle, that is, the struggle for full freedom, which entailed social change and even socialism. For this later stage, proletarian leadership was generally deemed necessary, at the very least at some distant point in the future.[212]

Even among those who claimed proletarian capacity and possibility for leading the national liberation struggle, it was generally agreed that such a role had materialized in only a minority of movements. According to Brutents, the proletariat rose to leadership in some movements, but in many others it was a vanguard force without holding the leadership; in still others, it did not reach even vanguard status, and in some it did not play a role at all.[213] This was, in fact, admitted in almost all the literature on the subject, including, indirectly, even the Troitskii article in *Voprosy istorii*. Ul'ianovskii pointed out that the proletariat in the Third World was small and "at times historically unprepared" to perform its mission of a political vanguard.[214] Speaking even of the post-independence period, he said that it was still "too early" for the working class to lead, inasmuch as it was not yet fully formed, necessitating leadership from others.[215] In his argument for united-front tactics, the goal of which was to achieve eventual proletarian leadership, Ul'ianovskii made it clear that "the toiling people" were still under the influence of non-proletarian sections of society.[216] In fact, speaking of the tasks of communist parties, he criticized "sectarianism, which manifests itself in an *a priori* demand to extend recognition of the leading role to one or another party without due consideration for the concrete situation."[217]

Tarabrin, writing in *MEMO*, also argued that even after independence the proletariat was unable to take the lead because of its small size, insufficient organization, and (according to Kortunov) lack of political experience.[218] Journalist Kudriavtsev, deputy chairman of the Soviet Afro-Asian Solidarity Committee, echoed this view, while Central Committee Africanist Manchkha explicitly proclaimed in *Voprosy istorii KPSS* that, because of ill-defined class differentiation in Third World societies, the weakness of proletariat tradition, inadequate organization, substantial influences of tribal traditions low level of literacy, the working class could not become the decisive force.[219] Kim even went so far as to say that this weakness of the proletariat created certain "contradictions" when a proletarian, Marxist–Leninist ideology was adopted, presumably by what passed for proletarian leadership over the non-proletarian masses after independence, because the proletariat simply was not sufficiently large or organized to lead.[220]

NATIONAL BOURGEOISIE

Reviewing history, Brutents was critical of over-optimistic young communists in the colonies who thought that only the working class could bring liberation, and that only working-class leadership, rather than that of the national bourgeoisie, was called for even in the Third World:

> Some Marxists also drew the conclusion that the colonial regimes could be eliminated only if the national bourgeoisie was ousted from the leadership of the struggle...ignoring the theses adopted by the Sixth Congress [of the Comintern], warning that an underestimation of the special significance which the bourgeois national–reformist, as distinct from the feudalist–imperialist camp, possesses, owing to its mass influence on the ranks of the petty bourgeoisie, peasantry, and even a portion of the working class, at least in the first stages of the movement, may lead to a sectarian policy and to the isolation of the Communists from the toiling masses.[221]

Adding the concession that the proletariat was capable of a leading role, as for example in certain cases in post-World War II Asia, nonetheless, "the idea that the proletariat is prepared *everywhere* to play such a role in these [national liberation] revolutions, and that the national bourgeoisie cannot provide leadership in the anti-colonial movement leading to independence, *has not been confirmed.*"[222]

Thus, Brutents maintained that, despite his own acknowledgment of the failings of the national bourgeoisie, the national bourgeoisie had sufficient qualifications, in the present circumstances, to take the leading role. The absence of clear class differentiation favored it, while its own self-interest was sufficient to propel it. Combined with the national bourgeoisie's influence, particularly over the petty bourgeoisie but perhaps also over other groups, and its relative (to the peasants') political experience and organization, these factors could militate toward national bourgeois leadership. Kim echoed just this analysis on at least one occasion, focusing, however, on the negative features of the other groups in society, which left the national bourgeoisie to lead more or less by default.[223]

Defense of the national bourgeoisie's leadership was not too frequent, however, perhaps because most of the Soviet literature that touched on the subject at all was more concerned with the post-independence period—for which the national bourgeoisie was regarded somewhat differently. Thus, many of the studies already cited added no caveats to their negative analysis of the national bourgeoisie's ability or right to lead. Indeed, even Brutents's authoritative work, and Kim's remarks somewhat later, noted the negative—primarily unreliable—aspect of such leadership, a weakness which Brutents claimed created a situation in which other groups might take the leadership.

THE PETTY BOURGEOISIE

Both Brutents and Merdel pointed out that, of the nations that had achieved independence, the vast majority had done so under the leadership of the petty bourgeoisie or intermediate strata. Brutents claimed that, of seventy such nations, only thirty had been led by either the proletariat or the national bourgeoisie, while a full forty had been led by the intermediate strata.[224] Merdel quoted American Africanist Richard Sklar's analysis of two African countries in which 75 percent of the leadership was composed of persons from the free professions (27 percent), the educational system (20 percent), and business (28 percent), with no breakdown between small and large business (petty and national bourgeoisie).[225]

Ul'ianovskii was critical of the phenomenon of petty bourgeois leadership, but he acknowledged that this group both could and usually did lead the liberation struggle.[226] In one article, he made a case for the petty bourgeoisie's offsetting the proletariat's lack of experience by assuming the mission of an "ideal proletariat."[227] Seeing little alternative to petty bourgeois leadership, he nonetheless cited this as a weakness of the national liberation movements themselves, because of the petty bourgeoisie's unreliability and failings. Others tended to note the phenomenon of petty bourgeois leadership as more or less inevitable, without analyzing it—or recommending it,[228] although Solodovnikov and Bogoslovskii, for example, saw it as merely one of the possibilities along with those of peasant or intermediate-strata leadership.[229] Thus, the negative appraisal of the petty bourgeoisie as leadership material was not qualified, but rather was accepted as part of a certain reality.

The appraisal of the intermediate strata, on the other hand, was somewhat more positive, despite thee acknowledgement of their negative aspects. There were those, apparently among the Soviet military, who at least would not rule out the possibility that military leadership could lead to progressive development.[230] The Zhukov study pointed out that the system of military organization suited such people to tight organization and conspiratorial activity, thereby qualifying them at least in some ways for leadership.[231] Without recommending it, the military as well as the civil intelligentsia were said to be the most politically active groups and, therefore, to contain a strong potential for leadership where a large or organized proletariat was lacking.[232]

As in the case of the composition of the national liberation movements, so too with regard to the leadership question, the military was in some instances subsumed under the category of intelligentsia, lending it a somewhat more positive evaluation than might otherwise have been the case. For the intelligentsia, perhaps more than any other group, was treated positively as the beneficiary of the power vacuum created by the lack of a strong proletariat and a differentiated class system. The intelligentsia's leadership qualifications derived from the fact that it had developed more rapidly as a nationally conscious social entity and, therefore, had greater experience than the other social groups in the national struggle.[233] It could and did act as initiator and organizer of trade unions and parties as well as other organizations, raising the national consciousness. It was suited to this task by virtue of its education and talents, its ability to understand modern society and theory, and its ability to interpret these to the masses, and to create or express a national culture and national aspirations, in the role of something of a supra-class or independent social force.[234] With its contacts in several social strata, and through the parties it created, the intelligentsia united the peasant masses with the urban population, while acting as chief political and social spokesman.[235] This, according to Brutents, was in fact the most common form of hegemony in the national liberation movements, and it possessed at least an equal potential for going in either social direction, vulnerable to, but not as intrinsically or inherently influenced by, bourgeois tendencies as the other non-proletarian strata.[236]

IMPORTANCE OF CLASS

While it was generally agreed that the intermediate strata, rather than the proletariat, or even the national bourgeoisie or the peasantry, carried the leadership of the struggle for national liberation, there were those who believed that, in terms of the tasks to be achieved, it did not make any difference which group held the leadership. This was probably the most likely conclusion for those who were most realistic in their appraisal of Third World societies. Understanding or arguing that the proletariat could not assume a leadership role, they sought to downplay the importance of the class composition of the leadership. This might explain why two researchers from the Institute for the International Workers Movement, Semen Agaev and Inna Tatarovskaia, expressed this view. They contended that, since the goal at this stage was independent statehood, it made no difference if national bourgeois or pro-bourgeois forces stood at the helm. The social composition of the leadership became important only in subsequent, post-independence, stages.[237]

Yet there were some who deemed it significant, possibly even critical, just which group did lead even at the early stage, because of the later direction in which their leadership would take the post-independence entity. Solodovnikov and Bogoslovskii, for example, believed that the future power tended to be formed by those forces that had already led the national liberation movement in the independence struggle.[238] In his 1973 book, Solodovnikov said that:

> [the] depth and dimensions of the national liberation movement depends on which class stands at its head. If the head of this movement is the national bourgeoisie, then it will strive to lead it only to a victory of political independence and the establishment of a bourgeois social order in the country. If, on the other hand, the national liberation movement is led by the working class and peasants, guided by a Marxist–Leninist party, then the national liberation movement can grow into a socialist revolution.[239]

Nonetheless, Solodovnikov himself allowed that this was, and could be, the case in only a few places, and that therefore such leadership would have to come at the later stage. According to Ul'ianovskii, "the political prerequisites of non-capitalist development, the forms it takes and the time needed for transition to it [i.e., the future direction] are largely determined by the balance of class forces already in the period of the liberation struggle."[240] Yet Ul'ianovskii himself went on to argue for class alliance, as we have seen, because of the absence of a strong proletariat.

Zagladin, representing the more consistently conservative view, said that:

> [the] presence of democratic [i.e. positive] elements in the concrete historical content of a variety of nationalisms depends not only on the national but on the class factor, on what class is at the head of the national movement, on its aims and on the methods suggested to resolve the social and national problems. The more progressive the social group or class at the head of the social and national liberation movement, the more extensive are the democratic elements in its ideological and political concepts.[241]

While few may have been willing to argue with this thesis in theory, the extensive references to the absence of clear class differentiation in the Third World, including the absence of a large or strong proletariat, all suggested what Brutents stated explicitly: that the future direction could not necessarily be discerned in (and therefore was not necessarily determined by) the social makeup of the movement or its leadership prior to independence. As we shall see below, Brutents even claimed that it was just this absence or weakness of local social factors to influence the overall orientation that created the need or opportunity for outside class influences.[242] The dualistic or unformed nature of the various social groups that might make up the leadership meant, by definition, that the future orientation was not yet certain.[243]

PERSONAL LEADERSHIP

Leadership, from the personal rather than the class or strata point of view, was not extensively discussed, even though specific leaders were quite often singled out for comment. The phenomenon of "leaderism" had, in fact, been negatively treated since the 1960s (because of setbacks to Soviet policies arising from the overthrow of Third World leaders with whom Soviet relations had been established).[244] Typical of the critical attitude was the comment in the *World Marxist Review* that the low level of development generally led to a situation wherein the masses followed a leader rather than a platform or an ideology.[245] Ul'ianovskii explained in one article: "leaders always play no mean role in the political struggle [of the East]. They are of special importance, for the leader is a symbol of mass consciousness, stable popular instinct, personal trust, and even of reverence. Here, in the eyes of the rank and file voters, even the most progressive political course cannot exist independently unless it is associated with a certain personality."[246] Presumably because of this view of the situation, Ul'ianovskii added, in the English version of his 1978 book, several chapters on individual nation liberation figures.[247] These biographies eventually appeared as a separate volume, with both explicit as well as implicit criticism of the centrality of the leaders' personalities and personal leadership vis-à-vis their own movement.[248]

Brutents was somewhat inconsistent on this issue. In a 1972 article he expressed "regret" that the "social back-wardness" of the developing countries facilitated the emergence of "so-called strong personalities" who "exert a definite influence" on progressive regimes.[249] Yet in his 1974 study he appeared to consider the issue of the leader more positively as well as more realistically, presenting a list of seven factors which influenced the future evolution of the leading party group (of a socialistically oriented country after independence). Sixth in this list was "the personality of the leader of the revolution, of the revolution's most influential figures."[250] Citing the enormous influence of leaders such as Castro and Nasser, Brutents explained that the outlook and "even the personal features of the leader or leaders of the revolutionary movement, his or her political ties, can be of great significance for both ideological and practical developments."[251] Unlike Ul'ianovskii, who had indeed acknowledged this significance, Brutents did not add any words of criticism—at least not until 1979, when he criticized Nasser's failure to go (institutionally) beyond the personal quality of his leadership.[252]

Organization

There can be little doubt that the Soviets considered organization of key importance in any estimation of national liberation movements. The foregoing analysis of the advantages and disadvantages of the various social components of the movements and their leadership qualifications often revolved around the organizational strength or potential of each class or social group. Ul'ianovskii, writing on Cabral, spoke of the necessity of a party organization, that is, a political vanguard "trained for the task of mobilizing the people and promoting their knowledge of the aims and methods of the struggle."[253] This group had to be capable in organization and in propaganda. Indeed, both Ul'ianovskii and Brutents criticized Nasser for failing to understand the importance of a strong organization.[254] Gordon's book on Fanon criticized the concept of "spontaneity," that is, revolutionary action without the benefit of political parties and organization; he called for the organization and education of the masses rather than Fanon's more amorphous idea of consciousness through self-administration.[255] Yet, for all the importance of organization, which we shall also see later in Soviet appraisals of specific movements, the theoretical literature devoted very little attention to types of organization or structures existing or advocated for the national liberation movement. Such discussion was generally reserved for the post-independence stage, focusing on the issue of a vanguard party, as we shall see below.

In theory, at least, there were basically two models for organizational structure available for the national liberation movements: that of the mass party or movement, and that of the elitist "vanguard" party. As the *World Marxist Review* put it in an unsigned comment:

> For most leaders of the national liberation movement in Africa, there is no question of weighing a party representing a broad national democratic front uniting all sections of the nation aspiring to anti-imperialist, democratic reconstruction against a vanguard party orienting the masses on long-term social reconstruction. Both concepts, as they see it, are relevant in Africa, and which of the two predominates depends on the stage of the national liberation revolution and the concrete conditions in the countries.[256]

This did indeed sum up the Soviet position, which was more or less unanimous in accepting the mass party as the model for the stage of the struggle for independence, the vanguard model being applicable at some later (post-independence) stage depending upon local conditions. The necessity or desirability of a communist party, and its relationship to other parties, was a special question in itself (as we shall see below).

THE MASS PARTY

Acceptance of the mass party model for the liberation struggle was dictated primarily by the conditions of Third World societies, that is, by the lack of class differentiation and the multi-class nature of the national liberation struggle itself. In describing the emergence of this model, it was recognized that parties in Third World societies were not class-based: they did not in fact represent the interests of any one class or social group. Although an article in the *World Marxist Review* on the subject of these parties claimed that the class criterion was "the crucible of any scientific classification," it went on to explain that, nonetheless, it was too early for parties in the Third World to display class allegiance, and they were, in fact, based more on ethnic lines.[257] Entin also claimed that the national liberation organizations were often based on ethnic or religious, rather than class or wholly national, lines.[258] Manchkha, however, explained that there were many such parties, but that the national liberation struggle had in fact generally achieved a coalition or union of them, creating a national front type of "revolutionary democratic" party.[259] As he put it, "it was necessary to put an end to intra-party strife and direct the efforts of the widest masses to the achievement of national independence."[260] Kiva explained that it was necessary to provide unity of all the population against the imperialists.[261] Moreover, no one class was in fact strong enough to undertake the struggle alone.[262]

Thus, rather than representing any one class or social stratum, these parties, or "fighting political organizations," as Manchkha called them, expressed the interests of the vast majority of the population, or virtually the whole adult population, including non-party organizations and individuals of a heterogeneous social and political background.[263] Ul'ianovskii, writing about the Indian Congress Party, said that a national coalition mass party of this type was able to exert a powerful influence over hundreds of millions of people.[264] And, basing himself on Lenin, he cited the second Comintern dictate that "the formation of mass organizations of the toiling people in the countries of the East" be the Communists' most important task.[265]

A rare study of organizations, devoted to the specific topic of the organization of armed struggle, pointed to various types of organization for the mass party or national group itself. These varied from those with only amorphous military organs and virtually no political leadership, to those with stable military and administrative organs but no centralized political organization, to those with all three. It allowed that the military organs could be fused with the political; the critical point was that there be a political structure that could provide leadership, control, and ideological guidance.[266] According to this study, published jointly by the Defense Ministry's History Department and the Academy of Sciences' Africa Institute (under the chief editorship of IMEMO's leading Third World specialist, V. L. Tiagunenko):

> Experience of armed struggle in Africa confirms that the level of military organization of revolutionary activity is closely dependent upon the level of political maturity and organization of the movement as a whole...[there was] a need for multi-faceted party leadership of this struggle. Only such a correspondence of political and military factors gives the party the possibility to secure a close relationship between the armed forces of the revolution and the popular masses, i.e., to secure the development of the liberation struggle in accordance with one of the most important laws of revolutionary wars.[267]

The Algerian example of creating two bases for military action, one inside, one outside the country, was noted, while other models of organization only within the country were also noted, with no preference expressed.[268] Ul'ianovskii detailed the type of organization employed by Cabral for PAIGC in the Guinea Bissau–Cape Verde struggle, with party organizations throughout the zones and districts of the liberated areas exercising direct responsibility for the military units in each area as well as for political, ideological, economic, and social activities in the area.[269] None of these descriptions offered more than the general idea of political control over the military[270] and the need for strong organization for political, ideological and military activities.

A mass organization or national front type coalition had its disadvantages, mainly in the post-independence period, but also in the liberation struggle itself. The major weakness lay in the heterogeneous social and, therefore, ambiguous ideological nature of such an organization.[271] This would lead to only loose organization and the inability to train cadres.[272] Moreover, as Kiva pointed out, because of the illiteracy and low cultural level of the masses, only a small part of the population was politically mature enough to take an active part in the movement. Therefore, the functioning of the organization was dependent upon a small group of activists and their ties with the masses as well as the party structure. These same circumstances, according to another analysis, also led to a situation wherein the masses tended to follow a leader rather than his platform or ideas.[273] Thus, according to Kiva's analysis, the problem was not only the national (rather than class) character of the organization, but also objective circumstances.

VANGUARD PARTY—WORKING CLASS ORGANISATIONS

By contrast, a vanguard party, taking the Leninist model of an elite of ideologically motivated professional revolutionaries operating on the basis of democratic centralism, was inherently better organized, better disciplined, and better able ultimately to maintain contact with the masses.[274]

One description of how a vanguard party should look was provided by *Narody Aziia i Afriki* in 1976: it should have "a clear goal...socialism" and know the laws of social development; it should be based on scientific socialism ideologically, with only minor deviations on "non-essential theoretical points"; it must predominate over the mass organizations and unions and represent the "progressive classes and social groups" of the country; "its membership must be limited to those" capable of assuming all the obligations of the vanguard detachment of society"; and, finally, it must be organized on the basis of democratic centralism, with personal initiative combined with discipline, "subordination of the minority to majority and of the lower organizations to the higher ones."[275]

Soviet literature was indeed rich on the attributes and advantages of a vanguard party, but, as already pointed out, this type of organization was not in fact suggested for the pre-independence stage. The examples of China, Vietnam, Korea, and the Philippines were given as cases in which a vanguard Marxist–Leninist party had led the liberation movement, its organizational qualities having aided the proletariat to take shape as a national class force and, therefore, to take the leadership of the liberation struggle.[276] Yet Soviet theorists tended to view these as exceptions, advocating a different role for communist parties in the Third World.

Working-class organizations such as trade unions were definitely seen as playing a positive role in the liberation struggle. Brutents, for example, said that they served not only as instruments of the nascent working class, but also provided support "for the anti-imperialist, patriotic parties," acting as political organizers and providing a cover the the banned patriotic parties to work among the masses.[277] Gordon, in response to Fanon's neglect of these organizations, cited trade unions as the "school for democracy and the administration of industry."[278]

As for communist parties themselves, however, there were possibly various views. There were those who did not appear to believe that a communist party could or necessarily should exist at this stage, at least if one can extrapolate—backwards—from the discussion of the issue of a vanguard Marxist–Leninist party in the post-independence period. Drawing on that discussion, it can be seen that Simoniia and Shastitko invoked Lenin's admonition to the Mongolians in 1921 to the effect that the absence of a proletariat precluded the idea of a communist party.[279] In answer to their question as to whether or not to transform their party into a communist one, Lenin answered: "I should not recommend it, because one party cannot be transformed into another...the revolutionaries will have to put in a good deal of work in developing state-economic and cultural activities before the herdsman elements become a proletarian mass, which may eventually help to 'transform' the People's Revolutionary Party into a Communist Party. A mere change of signboards is harmful and dangerous."[280]

Kim, too, on occasion, linked such a party to the emergence of a large proletariat.[281] More important, perhaps, were the views of Solodovnikov and his successor as head of the Africa Institute, Anatolii Gromyko, son of the then Foreign Minister Gromyko. They, too, quoted Lenin's comments to the Mongolians, warning against precipitously trying to convert the existing mass organization into such a party.[282] Manchkha gave this view Central Committee backing when he stated in his 1979 book that, although a Marxist–Leninist party was absolutely necessary for the passage to scientific socialism, the time was not yet ripe to raise the question of the creation of such a party.[283] Ul'ianovskii, too, employed Lenin's admonition to the Mongolians, going so far as to say that, where the proletariat was weak, it could be "harmful, even to try to put a new Communist coloring on to the national liberation revolution." This, he said, might even be dangerous, although where the proletariat was developed a communist party should be established.[284] In another book, however, he said that the time for this had not yet come.[285]

Not to belittle the role of communist parties, at least where they already existed, Domenger and Letnev extolled the role played by these parties in the colonial countries themselves as purveyors of "advanced views." Cited as an example was the creation of Marxist study groups by the French Communist party after World War II, groups that were said to have later merged with other organizations to form the "forward-looking parties."[286] An *Aziia i Afrika segodnia* article also noted the study groups as well as the local sections created by the French Communist party in the colonies, sections that formed the core of the future communist parties.[287] Pointing to the twenty-three communist parties that existed in the colonies before liberation, Brutents gave some of them even more credit, as we have seen, for organizing the proletariat into leadership positions of the liberation struggle.[288] Manchkha argued that the communist parties—where they were able to exist—wielded power beyond their small numbers, acting as a vanguard force of the national liberation struggle, expressing the general, national aspirations of all the working people.[289] This same description was given in the Ministry of Education's exegesis on the subject, claiming that the communists merged "all the revolutionary currents" in their activities.[290]

Yet all of these commentators, however praiseworthy of the role the communist party might play, went on to explain that it was incumbent upon these parties, because of conditions in the Third World, to create and/or join a united front coalition with the other parties and organiza-tions.[291] As Manchkha put it, the small size of the proletariat made it "utopian" to think of anything but a united front of all the anti-imperialist forces;[292] Solodovnikov, as well as Ivanov, Ul'ianovskii, and Brutents, all said that it was the task of the communists to help create such a united front.[293] Brutents and Ul'ianovskii both went to some lengths to explain that what was meant was not some sort of short-term alliance which the communists should seek to dominate and take over. On the other hand, the communists were to maintain their political, ideological, and, for the most part, organizational independence, taking care not to become infected by the views of their non-proletarian partners.

As Brutents put it, the "key line" for the communists was the setting up of a united national front of "all patriotic and progressive forces" which would be on a voluntary, coalition basis.[294] This united front would be based on a compromise, which was more realistic and advantageous for the struggle, and meant that there would be coopera-tion on the common goal with a shelving of the differences between them.[295] The way in which to do this was to clearly define the tasks of each component and describe how each job was to be accomplished. It was recommended that a joint concrete action be organized to achieve jointly defined goals. This joint effort on a concrete task could be the vehicle through which the united front could be set up.

The dominant component of the united front would most likely come from the social class or group that was dominant in the national movement as a whole. Thus, the communists would not necessarily be the dominant party but merely a partner in the coalition.[296] This implied a long-term alliance for a broad range of tasks, and short-term cooperation for less important and specific aims. It also meant a "differentiated" approach to each of the allies, without adopting their views. The communists would, however, have to adopt a "strategic line" which would "take into account" the real potential of each ally and motivate them to participate. For this reason, as Manchkha also stated, the organization and structure would have to be on a democratic basis.[297] Ignoring or stepping on the interests of the allied parties would only hurt the joint struggle: "Sectarian self-complacency and haughtiness, and an under-estimation of the potential of one's allies amount to perhaps the worst that can be done to frustrate the efforts to set up an anti-imperialist front."[298]

This united front approach was to apply at the mass, lower levels as well as at the leadership level, though there should be respect for the organizational, political, and ideological independence of all the parties in the front. Regarding the organizational independence of the communist party itself, Brutents did comment indirectly in one place that the communist party might merge with the other parties, although this possibility was mainly in the context of a post-independence one-party system which otherwise might exclude the communists.[299]

While Ul'ianovskii was unequivocal about the communists' maintaining their ideological and political independence, he was equally clear about their refraining from trying to take over. Speaking even about the post-independence period, he warned that an effort to win power immediately, at whatever cost, would not be "consonant with the actual state of affairs, could split the national front, isolate the communists from the masses." He admonished communists not to try to take over the united front., but rather to try to win the masses over to the movement as a whole—and not as a means of helping the communist party take the leadership. "It is not a tactic of leadership, that is, a tactic designed to form a bloc of leaders, but a mass tactic designed to bring together the entire proletariat and non-proletariat toiling masses." The ultimate goal of the communist party was, after independence, to gain the leadership, but it would be harmful to its own interests to try to go over the heads of the recognized non-proletarian leaders.[300] Criticizing Trotskii's opposition to united front tactics, Ul'ianovskii argued that a revolution "logically and historically" needed a united front of all classes and social strata in order to achieve a mass base.[301] He explained Lenin's concept of a united front as envisaging "nascent Marxist groups which historically would become the nuclei of Marxist–Leninist parties working for the unification of the patriotic forces in their respective countries."[302] According to Ul'ianovskii, Lenin did not envisage that the united front would lead to the beginning of the still undeveloped working class and communist parties, just as it was not envisaged that an immediate establishment of communist parties would be the main task in all countries. The Second Comintern congress, according to Ul'ianovskii, determined that the communists' most important task in the Third World was the formation of mass organizations which would not be communist at first but could in time acquire a popular, anti-imperialist, and anti-capitalist nature. "From the very beginning the national anti-imperialist front was viewed as a coalition of hetero-geneous socio-political forces, *otherwise it would not have been a question of setting up a united front but simply of ensuring the growth of the numerical composition* and influence of the communist parties in the colonies and semi-colonies."[303]

The more conservative journal, *Rabochii klass i sovremennyi mir*, did warn that such cooperation in the Third World meant increasing the opportunities for "alien influences" on members of the communist parties. Indeed, the documents of such coalitions often were devoid of the Marxist–Leninist ideas of the communists.[304] Entin, too, pointed out that the united front might lead to the communists' being influenced by the "petty bourgeois and peasant patriarchal" milieu and, therefore, taking "sectarian positions."[305] The remedy he suggested, however, was not the abandonment of this coalition approach, but, rather, more ideological–political work within the communist parties.[306]

Zagladin was more doctrinaire, perhaps, in his warnings regarding the potential evil influences of such cooperation, arguing that communists' support of unity should not be "at the cost of renunciation of their own principled positions, which would lead to the weakening of the international workers' movement as a whole."[307] United action could not be at the expense of the communists' own unity and revolutionary nature.[308] Yet this warning, like the myriad of literature on the issue of the creation of a vanguard party, clearly deemed necessary for the achievement of socialism, was directed to the post-independence period. Whether or not conditions were ripe for a communist party, and however problematic its cooperation with others was perceived, there appeared to be little question that the suitable organizational form for the liberation struggle was, by virtue of the circumstances in the Third World societies, a mass party, perceived as a loose coalition, including the communist party in a united front, where a communist party could or in fact did exist.

Conclusions

Debates over the relevant importance of the bourgeoisie or even the petty bourgeoisie and the centrality of the proletariat were not a new phenomenon for Soviet theoreticians. In the discussions regarding both composition and leadership, the classical proletariat-based approach, going so far even as to demand not only proletarian dominance but communist party leadership, could still be found. The most important advocates of this conservative approach were the International Department's first deputy chairman Zagladin and the Ideological Department's Fedoseev—as was the case with regard to the origins of movements. This did not mean, however, that the Central Committee held the conservative view, as distinct from non-party institutions. In fact, the conservative view was not held by many even within the Central Committee hierarchy. What clearly was emerging was an attempt to forge a more realistic, up-to-date, sophisticated view not only of the social structure of Third World societies, but also of those forces that were necessary to a movement, and of those that in fact were dominant and likely to lead.

The most realistic and innovative of those to undertake a new approach, at the opposite end of the spectrum from Zagladin, for example, was indeed one of the next highest officials of Zagladin's own department, Karen Brutents. And others at the top (such as

Ul'ianovskii) or near the top (such as Manchkha) of this department took a middle position, on the whole much closer to that of Brutents than that of Zagladin.

To summarize, the national bourgeoisie was given a much greater role by the more realistic analysts, with Ul'ianovskii showing more reservations than Brutents, for example, but nowhere approaching the conservative view, which was shared in part, in the early 1970s at least, by Academy of Science institutes' theoreticians Zhukov and Gafurov. There was much less disagreement over the dual (negative) nature of the petty bourgeoisie, and recognition of the fact that this group, nonetheless, dominated national liberation movements. The early controversy was over the degree to which the proletariat should cooperate with this class; the conservative view (Zagladin and Fedoseev) demanded proletarian leadership, while the "realistic" school, by far the majority (including Ul'ianovskii), accepted proletarian subordination. There was some variation with regard to the intelligentsia, the generally positive appraisal of this group being questioned by one or two analysts (including Fedoseev). There were greater differences regarding the military, a number of institute theoreticians such as Kim and Solodovnikov picking up Mirskii's warning about the negative potential of this group, echoed by Gavrilov of the Ideology Department's Social Science Institute. Yet the International Department's Brutents and Ul'ianovskii saw this group more positively.

While no one claimed a leadership role for the peasantry, there was a whole spectrum of positions regarding their importance to a movement. With Fedoseev and Brutents at opposite poles, and the then Africa Institute chief Solodovnikov being close to Brutents' position, Ul'ianovskii and Manchkha took a more middle position, presumably being more concerned over a Fanon-type absolutization of the peasantry, though rejecting the conservatives' more damning criticism of this class.

There was almost total agreement that the organizational model for a national liberation movement was that of the mass party as distinct from a vanguard party. It was generally agreed that this was to be nationally rather than class-based, although some pointed out that these parties were in fact more narrowly based, along ethnic or religious lines. The vanguard party model was rejected for the pre-independence stage, as was the creation of a communist party. Where such parties already existed, there was general agreement that they should pursue a united front tactic with the other groups and parties involved in the national liberation struggle. Brutents appeared even to condone merger, and Ul'ianovskii argued against any attempt by a communist party to take over a united front alliance. A few conservative voices warned against such cooperation, but even Zagladin appeared to accept the united front approach. Ul'ianovskii's lengthy admonition against a cynical view of such a tactic and a communist attempt to take over suggests, however, that the conservatives' continued belief in the centrality and leadership of the proletariat continued to be a challenge to the mass party–united front approach of the realists.

Notes

1   K.N. Brutents, *Sovremennye natsional'no—osvoboditel'nye revoliutsii*, Politizdat, Moscow, 1974 (citations from the English translation: K. N. Brutents, *National Liberation Revolutions Today*, Progress, Moscow, 1977), vol. 1, p. 72.
2   Rostislav Ul'ianovskii, *Ocherki natsional no-osvoboditel'noi bor'by: voprosy teorii i praktiki*, Nauka, Moscow, 1976 (citations from the English translation: Rostislav Ulyanovsky, *National Liberation: Essays on Theory and Practice*, Progress Press, Moscow, 1978), p. 113.
3   Brutents, *National Liberation Revolutions*, vol. I, p. 72. See also Georgii Kim, *The Socialist World and the National Liberation Movement*, Novosti, Moscow, 1978, pp. 28–31.
4   E.g., Aida Moseiko, "Traditsii i ikh rol' v sovremennoi Afrike," *Aziia i Afrika segodnia*, no. 5 (1978): 36–9. See also A. Malashenko, "Religioznaia traditsiia i politika revoliutsionnoi demokratii," *Aziia i Afrika segodnia*, no. 9 (1979): 20.
5   Malashenko, "Religioznaia traditsiia,": 20; I. L. Andreev, *Nekapitalisticheskoe razvitie*, Politizdat, Moscow, 1974 (citations from the English translation: I. Andreyev, *The Noncapitalist Way*, Progress, Moscow, 1977), pp. 52–63.
6   Brutents, *National Liberation Revolutions*, vol. I, p. 72.
7   See chapter 3 for the attitude toward religious nationalism, specifically Islam.
8   Brutents, *National Liberation Revolutions*, vol. I, pp. 41, 71–2.
9   Andreyev, *The Noncapitalist Way*, p. 58; V. V. Zagladin and F. D. Ryzhenko, *Sovremennoe revoliutsionnoe dvizhenie i natsionalizm*, Politizdat, Moscow, 1973 (citations from the English translation: V. V. Zagladin (ed.), *The Revolutionary Movement of Our Time and Nationalism*, Progress, Moscow, 1975), p. 61.
10   Kim, *The Socialist World*, p. 31; G. F. Kim and A. S. Kaufman, "XXV s"ezd KPSS i problemy natsional'no-osvoboditel'nykh revoliutsii," *Narody Azii i Afriki*, no. 3 (1976): 6–7; K. Merdel, "Politicheskie organizatsii v antikolonial'noi bor'be," in G. A. Nersesov and V. A. Subotin, *Afrika v novoe i noveishee vremia*, Nauka, Moscow, 1976, p. 48; Iu. Gavrilov, "V. I. Lenin i istoricheskie sud'by antikolonial'noi bor'by," *Aziia i Afrika segodnia*, no. 3 (1980): 4.
11   Kim, *The Socialist World*, p. 30; also Moseiko, "Traditsii," p. 38.
12   See, for example, the Conference of the Scientific Council of the Academy of Sciences on "Classes and Class Struggle in Eastern Countries," published in *Asia and Africa Today*, no. 5 (1979): 58–9; Vl. Li, "Neproletarskie sloi v sotsial'noi strukture osvobodivshikhsia stran," *Aziia i Afrika segodnia*, no. 1 (1978): 29–32; Kim, *The Socialist World*, pp. 29–32; even Brutents, *National Liberation Revolutions*, vol. I, pp. 71–2.
13   P. I. Manchkha, *Aktual'nye problemy sovremennoi Afriki*, Politizdat, Moscow, 1979, p. 190; Ulyanovsky, *National Liberation*, pp. 55, 67.
14   Kim and Kaufman, "XXV s'ezd," p. 6.
15   Li, "Neproletarskie sloi," p. 29.
16   Ibid.
17   E.g., Zagladin, *Revolutionary Movement*, p. 62.
18   Li, "Neproletarskie sloi," p. 30.
19   Brutents, *National Liberation Revolutions*, vol. I, p. 72. See also L. M. Entin, *Politicheskie sistemy razvivaiushchikhsia stran*, Mezhdunarodnye otnosheniia, Moscow, 1978, p. 21.
20   There were those who placed other social groups such as the bureaucracy (Zagladin), comprador bourgeoisie (Ul'ianovskii), and occasionally the army (Ul'ianovskii)

among the opponents to the national liberation movement; see below (Zagladin, *Revolutionary Movement*, p. 61; Rostislav Ul'yanovsky, "An Epochal Predication that Has Come True," *New Times*, no. 22 (1977): 21). See also V. G. Solodovnikov, *Afrika vybiraet put'*, Nauka, Moscow, 1979, p. 59. The bureaucracy tended to be excluded from the ranks of the movement only after independence.

21 Andreyev, *The Noncapitalist Way*, p. 58; Brutents, *National Liberation Revolutions*, vol. I, p. 94.

22 Andreyev, *The Noncapitalist Way*, pp. 57–8; Brutents, *National Liberation Revolutions*, vol. I, p. 97.

23 Andreyev, *The Noncapitalist Way, p. 61; Brutents, National Liberation Revolutions, vol. I, p. 94.*

24 Brutents, *National Liberation Revolutions*, vol. I, pp. 31, 94; Solodovnikov, *Afrika*, p. 86; Entin, *Politicheskie sistemy*, p. 22.

25 P. N. Fedoseev, *Leninizm i natsional'nyi vopros v sovremennykh usloviiakh*, Politizdat, Moscow, 1974 (citations from English translation, P. N. Fedoseyev, *Leninism and the National Question*, Progress, Moscow, 1977, p. 490).

26 Zagladin, *Revolutionary Movement*, p. 62.

27 See also Fedoseyev, *Leninism*, pp. 489–92.

28 Rostislav Ulyanovsky, "The Developing Countries; Aspects of the Political Scene," *New Times*, no. 38 (1976): 19; see also Vadim Kortunov, "The Working Class—The Leading Revolutionary Force of Our Time," *New Times*, no. 11 (1972): 20.

29 B. Gafurov, "Lenin and the Liberation of the Peoples of the East," *International Affairs*, no. 6 (1970): 37; Y. Zhukov, L. Delyusin, A. Iskenderov, and L. Stepanov, *The Third World*, Progress, Moscow, 1970, pp. 44–5.

30 Fedoseyev, *Leninism*, p. 490.

31 Iu. Gavrilov, "The New Africa Emerging," *International Affairs*, no. 7 (1980): 33; R. N. Andreasian, "Protivorechiia i kriterii nekapitalisticheskogo razvitiia," *Narody Azii i Afriki*, no. 2 (1974): p. 38; Solodovnikov, *Afrika*, p. 86 (although in another book Solodovnikov said that the national bourgeoisie had an "objective interest" in the liberation struggle: V. G. Solodovnikov, *Politicheskie partii Afriki*, Nauka, Moscow, 1970, p. 160).

32 Brutents, *National Liberation Revolutions*, vol. I, p. 103.

33 Andreyev, *The Noncapitalist Way*, p. 61.

34 Entin, *Politicheskie sistemy*, p. 22; Brutents, *National Liberation Revolutions*, vol. I, p. 98.

35 Zhukov et al., *The Third World*, p. 44–5; Brutents, *National Liberation Revolutions*, vol. I, p. 100.

36 Brutents, *National Liberation Revolutions*, vol. I, p. 105.

37 Ulyanovsky, "The Developing Countries," pp. 18–22.

38 Ulyanovsky, *National Liberation*, pp. 76–8. (See below for more on China and India.)

39 R. A. Ul'ianovskii, *Sovremennye problemy Azii i Afriki*, Nauka, Moscow, 1978, p. 72. See also V. Khoros, "V. I. Lenin i revoliutsionnoe dvizhenie narodov Vostoka," *Aziia i Afrika segodnia*, no. 7 (1984): 3.

40 Editorial, "Lenin and the National Liberation Movement," *Asia and Africa Today*, no. 2 (1982): 4.

41 Including semi-proletarians: Brutents, *National Liberation Revolutions*, vol. I, p. 107; E. M. Primakov, *Vostok posle krakha kolonial'noi sistemy*, Nauka, Moscow, 1982, p. 105.

42 Kim, *The Socialist World*, pp. 32-3.

43 G. Kim, "World Socialism and the National Liberation Movement," *Far Eastern Affairs*, no. 2 (1976): 50.

44 L. Tumanova, "Melkaia burzhuaziia afrikanskogo goroda," *Aziia i Afrika segodnia*, no. 11 (1982): 36.

45 Gafurov, "Lenin," p. 38; see also Brutents, *Pravda*, 23 January 1970.

46 Andreasian, "Protivorechiia," pp. 39–40.

47 Ibid.; Brutents, *National Liberation Revolutions*, vol. I, p. 107.

48 Ulyanovsky, *National Liberation*, p. 77.

49 Brutents, *National Liberation Revolutions*, p. 119.
50 Ibid., p. 117. Andreev argued against labelling all tradesmen, artisans, and small-property-owners as petty bourgeois when these existed in basically precapitalist societies (Andreyev, *The Noncapitalist Way*, p. 58).
51 Primakov, *Vostok*, p. 105; A. Kiva, "Nekotorye tendentsii evoliutsii revoliutsionnoi demokratii," *Aziia i Afrika segodnia*, no. 3 (1975): 24.
52 Primakov, *Vostok*, p. 105.
53 Brutents, *National Liberation Revolutions*, vol. I, p. 107.
54 Ibid.; see also G. Kim, "Vo imia sotsial'nogo progressa," *Aziia i Afrika segodnia*, no. 11 (1972): 26.
55 For a detailed study of this status, see Tumanova, "Melkaia," p. 36; unsigned, "Antiimperialisticheskii front v razvivaiushchikhsia stranakh," *Aziia i Afrika segodnia*, no. 7 (1970): 2–4.
56 Brutents, *National Liberation Revolutions*, vol. I, p. 119; Kim, "Vo imia," p. 27; Tumanova, "Melkaia," p. 36; "Antiimperialisticheskii front," p. 3; Rostislav Ulyanovsky, "Paths and Prospects of National Democracy," *New Times*, no. 14 (1978): 19; Andreasian, "Protivorechiia," p. 40.
57 Andreasian, "Protivorechiia," p. 39; Kim, *The Socialist World*, p. 46.
58 Brutents, *National Liberation Revolutions*, vol. I, p. 120.
59 Kortunov, "The Working Class," p. 20; Rostislav Ulyanovsky, "Leninism, Soviet Experience and the Newly-Free Countries," *New Times*, no. 1 (1971): 20.
60 Ulyanovsky, *National Liberation*, p. 384.
61 Brutents, *National Liberation Revolutions*, vol. I, p. 120; Tumanova, "Melkaia," p. 37.
62 Ul'ianovskii, introduction to Andreyev, *The Noncapitalist Way*, p. 37.
63 Ibid., p. 58.
64 Ibid., p. 22.
65 Kim, "Vo imia," p. 27; Brutents, *National Liberation Revolutions*, vol. I, p. 124; Tumanova, "Melkaia," p. 37; Iu. Sumbatian, "Gosudarstvo sotsialisticheskoi orientatsii: sushchnost', zadachi i funktsii," *Aziia i Afrika segodnia*, no. 8 (1973): 24. See chapter 3.
66 Ulyanovsky, "Leninism, Soviet Experience," p. 20.
67 Tumanova, "Melkaia," p. 37.
68 E.g., Ulyanovsky, *National Liberation*, p. 384; Kortunov, "The Working Class," p. 20.
69 Tumanova, "Melkaia," p. 37.
70 Brutents, *National Liberation Revolutions*, vol. I, p. 120.
71 Tumanova, "Melkaia," p. 37.
72 Ulyanovsky, *National Liberation*, pp. 54, 384.
73 Brutents, *National Liberation Revolutions*, vol. I, p. 120.
74 Kim, "Vo imia," p. 27; Kim, "World Socialism," p. 51.
75 Brutents, *National Liberation Revolutions*, vol. I, pp. 108, 111; Andreyev, *The Noncapitalist Way*, p. 62, quoting Brutents.
76 Ulyanovsky, *National Liberation*, p. 169; Brutents, *National Liberation Revolutions*, vol. I, p. 108.
77 Brutents, *National Liberation Revolutions*, vol. I, p. 108; Andreyev, *The Noncapitalist Way*, p. 61.
78 Brutents, *National Liberation Revolutions*, vol. I, p. 108.
79 Andreyev, *The Noncapitalist Way*, p. 63.
80 Ibid., p. 62; Brutents, *National Liberation Revolutions*, vol. I, p. 107.
81 Kim, *The Socialist World*, p. 46.
82 Andreyev, *The Noncapitalist Way*, p. 62.
83 Iu. Gavrilov, "Ideino-politicheskoe razvitie sovremennoi natsional'noi i revoliutsionnoi demokratii," *Aziia i Afrika segodnia*, no. 1 (1979): 26; Brutents, *National Liberation Revolutions*, vol. I, pp. 111–13; Andreyev, *The Noncapitalist Way*, pp. 57, 94.
84 A. Kiva, "Revoliutsionno-demokraticheskie partii: nekotorye tendentsii razvitiia," *Aziia i Afrika segodnia*, no. 3 (1978): 24.
85 Ibid.

86 Andreyev, *The Noncapitalist Way*, p. 62 quoting Brutents; Brutents, *National Liberation Revolutions*, vol. I, p. 110.
87 Andreyev, *The Noncapitalist Way*, p. 57; Brutents, *National Liberation Revolutions*, vol. I, p. 110.
88 Sumbatian, "Gosudarstvo," p. 25; Zhukov et al., *The Third World*, p. 49
89 Brutents, *National Liberation Revolutions*, vol. I, p. 114.
90 Kim, *The Socialist World*, p. 33.
91 See chapter 3.
92 Fedoseyev, *Leninism*, p. 472.
93 Andreyev, *The Noncapitalist Way*, p. 94; Brutents, *National Liberation Revolutions*, vol. I, pp. 114–15 and *Pravda*, 23 January 1970.
94 Ulyanovsky, *National Liberation*, p. 169.
95 For discussion of this debate, see Charles C. Petersen, "Third World Military Elites in Soviet Perspective," Center for Naval Analysis, Professional Paper no. 262, November 1979; Mark Katz, *The Third World in Soviet Military Thought*, Johns Hopkins, Baltimore, 1982, pp. 81–2, 104–5, 134; David Albright, "Vanguard Parties and Revolutionary Change in the Third World: The Soviet Perspective," unpublished paper, 1985, pp. 18-20.
96 V. G. Solodovnikov and V. V. Bogoslovsky, *Non-Capitalist Development*, Progress Press, Moscow, 1975, p. 138; Georgii Mirskii, *Armiia i politika v stranakh Azii i Afriki*, Nauka, Moscow, 1970, and later, with no significant changes, *Tretii mir: obshchestvo, vlast', armiia*, Nauka, Moscow, 1976.
97 Solodovnikov and Bogoslovsky, *Non-Capitalist Development*, p. 138; Mirskii, *Armiia*, p. 336.
98 Kim, "Vo imia," p. 27. See also R. E. Sevortian, "Armiia i obshchestvo v molodom gosudarstve," *Mirovaia ekonomika i mezhdunarodnye otnosheniia*, no. 6 (1970): 105; R. E. Sevortian, *Armiia v politicheskom rezhime stran sovremennogo Vostoka*, Nauka, Moscow, 1973, pp. 115–22; R. E. Sevortian in Vl. Li, *Srednie sloi gorodskogo obshchestva v stranakh Vostoka*, Nauka, Moscow, 1975, pp. 60–2.
99 Gavrilov, "New Africa," p. 33.
100 G. Usov, "Armiia v Razvivaiushchikhsia stranakh," *Aziia i Afrika segodnia*, no. 12 (1970): 54.
101 Andreasian, "Protivorechiia," p. 42.
102 See Petersen, "Military Elites," pp. 25–30.
103 See Katz, *Third World*, pp. 81, 104, citing articles by Col. E. Dolgopolov in *Krasnaia zvezda*, 21 April 1978 and *Kommunist Vooruzhennykh Sil*, no. 21 (1976): 90–2, or Petersen, "Military Elites," citing Dolgopolov in *Kommunist Vooruzhennykh Sil*, no. 6 (1975): 76, and *Natsional'no-osvoboditel'nye voiny na sovremennom etape*, Voenizdat, Moscow, 1977, p. 91; Maj.-Gen. B. G. Sapozhnikov, "Klassy i armiia v razvivaiushchikhsia stranakh," in B. G. Gafurov, *Leninizm, klassy i klassovaia bor'ba v stranakh sovremennogo Vostoka*, Nauka, Moscow, 1973, p. 252; Col. Iu. G. Sumbatian, "Armii v politicheskoi strukture stran sotsialisticheskoi orientatsii," *Aziia i Afrika segodnia*, no. 4 (1974): 18. A later article by Dolgopolov was more critical, speaking of the military's origins in well-to-do families (Col. Ye. Dolgopolov, "National Democratic Revolution and the Army," *Soviet Military Review*, no. 4 (1984): 49–50).
104 Maj.-Gen. V. Mozolev, "Rol' armii v razvivaiushchikhsia stranakh," *Voenno-istoricheskii zhurnal*, no. 4 (1980): 63. See also Capt. 1st rank N. Chikhachev, "Na strazhe progressivnykh zavoevanii," *Kommunist Vooruzhennykh Sil*, no. 13 (1981): 83–4.
105 Zhukov et al., *The Third World*, pp. 50–1.
106 Mirskii, *Armiia*, pp. 9–10.
107 See also P. Shastitko, "Revoliutsiia dolzhna umet' zashchishchat'sia," *Aziia i Afrika segodnia*, no. 1 (1982): 4.
108 Brutents, *National Liberation Revolutions*, vol. I, p. 88.
109 Gafurov, "Lenin," p. 38; R. Ul'ianovskii, "Nauchnyi sotsializm i Amilkar Kabral," *Aziia i Afrika segodnia*, no. 12 (1978): 31.
110 *Pravda*, 23 January 1970.

111 R. Ul'ianovskii, "O natsional'nom osvobozhdenii i natsionalizme," *Aziia i Afrika segodnia*, no. 10 (1980): 4; Ulyanovsky, "Leninism, Soviet Experience and the Newly-Free Countries," pt. II, *New Times*, no. 2 (1971): 20; Ulyanovsky, "Epochal Predictions," p. 20; A. V. Gordon, *Problemy natsional'no–osvoboditel'noi bor'by v tvorchestve Frantsa Fanona*, Nauka, Moscow, 1977, p. 141; unsigned, "Leninskii, sotsialisticheskii, internatsionalistskii kurs," *Narody Azii i Afriki*, no. 2 (1974): 10.

112. Ulyanovsky, "Perspective Opened by Socialism," *New Times*, no. 27 (1977): 22; Ulyanovsky, "Leninism," pt. II, p. 20; editorial, "Lenin," *Asia and Africa Today*, p. 3.

113 Gavrilov, "New Africa," p. 33; Iu. Gavrilov, "Ob"ektivnye osnovy soiuza rabochego klassa i krest'ianstva v natsional'no–osvoboditel'noi bor'be," *Narody Azii i Afriki*, no. 1 (1979): 6.

114 Brutents, *National Liberation Revolutions*, vol. I, pp. 89–90.

115 Ibid., pp. 90–1; Solodovnikov and Bogoslovsky, *Non-Capitalist Development*, p. 251.

116 Brutents, *National Liberation Revolutions*, vol. I, p. 91.

117 Ul'ianovskii, introduction to Andreyev, *The Noncapitalist Way*, p. 1.

118 Ulyanovsky, "Perspective," pp. 21–2.

119 Solodovnikov and Bogoslovsky, *Non-Capitalist Development*, p. 251.

120 Sumbatian, "Socialist Oriented State," p. 24; Primakov, *Vostok*, p. 104.

121 Ulyanovsky, "Perspective," p. 22.

122 Solodovnikov and Bogoslovsky, *Non-Capitalist Development*, p. 130; Andreyev, *The Noncapitalist Way*, p. 50.

123 Ul'ianovskii, introduction to Andreyev, *The Noncapitalist Way*, p. 16.

124 Ibid.; Fedoseyev, *Leninism*, p. 471, quoting Brezhnev to the 1969 meeting of Communist and workers' parties.

125 Ulyanovsky, *National Liberation*, p. 215; Ul'ianovskii, "O Natsional'nom," p. 4.

126 Ulyanovsky, *National Liberation*, p. 320.

127 Manchkha, *Aktual'nye problemy*, p. 40.

128 Brutents, *National Liberation Revolutions*, vol. I, p. 92.

129 Gavrilov, "Ob"ektivnye osnovy," p. 6; V. Sofinsky and A. Khazanov, "PRC Policy in Tropical Africa," *Far Eastern Affairs*, no. 3 (1978): 73–4; Solodovnikov and Bogoslovskii, *Non-Capitalist Development*, p. 132; V. Bushuev, "The National Liberation Movement and Neocolonialism," *International Affairs*, no. 3 (1975): 114; A. Rumiantsev, "Sovremennaia epokha—epokha perekhoda ot kapitalizma k kommunizmu," *Aziia i Afrika segodnia*, no. 10 (1982): 3; V. G. Solodovnikov, *Problemy sovremennoi Afriki*, Nauka, Moscow, 1973, p. 196.

130 Gordon, *Problemy*, p. 109; R. G. Landa, "A. V. Gordon, Problemy natsional'no-osvoboditel'noi bor'by v tvorchestve Frantsa Fanona," *Narody Azii i Afriki*, no. 6 (1977): 215; R. Ul'ianovskii, "Nauchnyi sotsializm i Frants Fanon," *Aziia i Afrika segodnia*, no. 5 (1978): 21.

131 Gordon, *Problemy*, pp. 110–18.

132 Ibid., p. 86; Ul'ianovskii, "Fanon," p. 21.

133 Gordon, *Problemy*, pp. 120–1, 125.

134 Ibid., p. 130.

135 Ibid., pp. 125–6.

136 Ibid., p. 128.

137 Ul'ianovskii, "Fanon," p. 21.

138 Ul'ianovskii, "Kabral," p. 31. Solodovnikov had said of these views, without specifying Fanon, that the peasants "are far from being bearers of progressive tendencies" (Solodovnikov, *Problemy*, p. 196).

139 Gordon, *Problemy*, p. 132.

140 Ibid., pp. 133–4.

141 Brutents, *National Liberation Revolutions*, vol. I, p. 93.

142 Ibid., p. 93. Therefore, there was an even greater need for their participation, he said.

143 Ibid.

144 "Lenin," *Asia and Africa Today*, p. 3; "Leninizm" *Narody Azii i Afriki*, p. 10; "Antiimperialisticheskii front," *Aziia i Afrika Segodnia*, p. 3.

145 Brutents, *National Liberation Revolutions*, vol. I, p. 92.

146 Ibid.
147 E.g., Solodovnikov, *Afrika*, p. 85; Andreyev, *The Noncapitalist Way*, p. 55; Ulyanovsky, "Perspective," p. 22; Rumiantsev, "Sovremennaia epokha," p. 3; "Lenin" *Asia and Africa Today*, p. 3.
148 Brutents, *National Liberation Revolutions*, vol. I, p. 75.
149 Ibid
150 Li, "Neproletarskie sloi," p. 30.
151 Andreyev, *The Noncapitalist Way*, pp. 53, 55.
152 Solodovnikov, *Afrika*, p. 85; Brutents, *National Liberation Revolutions*, vol. I, p. 75.
153 Andreyev, *The Noncapitalist Way*, p. 56; see also Solodovnikov, *Afrika*, p. 85.
154 Andreyev, *The Noncapitalist Way*, p. 57.
155 Brutents, *National Liberation Revolutions*, vol. I, p. 75.
156 Ibid., p. 83–4.
157 Ibid.; Zhukov et al., *The Third World*, p. 47.
158 Ibid., p. 45.
159 Ulyanovsky, "Perspective," p. 22; introduction to Andreyev, *The Noncapitalist Way*, p. 21.
160 E.g., "Lenin" (*Asia and Africa Today*), p. 3.
161 Fedoseyev, *Leninism*, p. 471.
162 Solodovnikov, *Afrika*, p. 59; Solodovnikov, *Partii*, p. 160.
163 Rumiantsev, "Sovremennaia epokha," p. 3.
164 Gordon, *Problemy*, pp. 127–8.
165 Ul'ianovskii, "Fanon," p. 22.
166 Gordon, *Problemy*, p. 119.
167 Ul'ianovskii, "Fanon," p. 22.
168 Gordon, *Problemy*, pp. 84, 126.
169 Ibid., p. 137; Ul'ianovskii, "Fanon," p. 21.
170 Gavrilov, "Ideino-politicheskoe," p. 26; Gavrilov, "New Africa," p. 33.
171 Andreyev, *The Noncapitalist Way*, p. 56.
172 Gavrilov, "Ideino-politicheskoe," p. 26; Gavrilov, "New Africa," p. 33.
173 Solodovnikov, *Afrika*, p. 85. He said that where there were large enterprises, as in Zambia for example, the workers did play an important role.
174 Brutents, *National Liberation Revolutions*, vol. I, pp. 85–6; Rumiantsev, "Sovremennaia epokha," p. 3; Kortunov too said that one must work on raising awareness ("The Working Class," p. 20).
175 Fedoseyev, *Leninism*, p. 472.
176 Ulyanovsky, *National Liberation*, p. 56; Anatolii Gromyko, "Lenin i Afrika," *Aziia i Afrika segodnia*, no. 5 (1980): 4.
177 Ulyanovsky, *National Liberation*, p. 326.
178 G. Kim, "Social Development and Ideological Struggle in the Developing Countries," *International Affairs*, no. 4 (1980): 68.
179 Merdel, "Organizatsii," p. 48. Brutents and the Solodovnikov–Bogoslovsky study both mentioned peasant participation in the leadership, with other non-proletarian groups, but both explicitly minimized and virtually ruled out peasant leadership (Brutents, *National Liberation Revolutions*, vol. I, p. 123; Solodovnikov and Bogoslovsky, *Non-Capitalist Development*, p. 135).
180 Gavrilov, "New Africa," p. 33; Brutents, *National Liberation Revolutions*, vol. I, p. 86.
181 Fedoseyev, *Leninism*, pp. 471–2.
182 Ul'ianovskii, "Kabral," p. 32.
183 Kortunov, "The Working Class," p. 20; Zhukov et al., *The Third World*, p. 40; Brutents, *National Liberation Revolutions*, vol. I, p. 92.
184 Ibid., pp. 39–40; Ul'ianovskii, "Kabral," p. 32; Ul'ianovskii, "Fanon," p. 21; Gavrilov, "Ob'ektivnye osnovy," p. 6.
185 Ul'ianovskii, "Fanon," p. 22.
186 Solodovnikov and Bogoslovsky, p. 133; Kim, "Vo imia," p. 26; Zhukov et al., *The Third World*, p. 40; Ul'ianovskii, "Kabral," p. 31.
187 Zhukov et al., *The Third World*, pp. 39–40.
188 Ul'ianovskii, "Kabral," p. 32.

92 A Soviet Theory of National Liberation

189 Zhukov et al., *The Third World*, p. 40.
190 Ibid.
191 Gavrilov, "V. I. Lenin," p. 4; Gavrilov, "New Africa," p. 33; Kortunov (in part), "The Working Class," p. 20; Entin, *Politicheskie sistemy*, p. 22; P. I. Manchkha, "Kommunisty, revoliutsionnye demokraty i nekapitalisticheskii put' razvitiia v stranakh Afriki," *Voprosy istorii KPSS*, no. 10 (1975): 57–69; G. Kim, "Razvivaiushchiesia strany: usilenie sotsial'no-klassovoi differentsiatsii," *Aziia i Afrika segodnia*, no. 11 (1981): p. 8.
192 Entin, *Politicheskie sistemy*, p. 22; V. Li, "The Newly-free Countries' Problems of Social and Political Development," *International Affairs*, no. 11 (1980): 45; K. Maidanik and G. Mirskii, "Natsional'no-osvoboditel'naia bor'ba: sovremennyi etap," *Mirovaia ekonomika i mezhdunarodnye otnosheniia*, no. 6 (1981): 24; Andreasian, "Protivorechiia," p. 38; Brutents, *National Liberation Revolutions*, vol. I, p. 100.
193 Brutents, *National Liberation Revolutions*, vol. I, pp. 98–9; Ulyanovsky, "Developing Countries," p. 19.
194 Brutents, *National Liberation Revolutions*, vol. I, p. 99. He said there were, of course, exceptions, such as China and India.
195 See, for example, Ulyanovsky, "Developing Countries," p. 19; Kortunov, "The Working Class," p. 20.
196 Sumbatian, "Socialist Oriented State," p. 25; Ul'ianovskii, "Fanon," p. 22.
197 Ul'ianovskii, "Fanon," p. 22; Tumanova, "Melkaia," p. 37; Andreyev, *The Noncapitalist Way*, p. 58.
198 Ulyanovsky, *National Liberation*, pp. 319–20; Ul'ianovskii in Andreyev, *The Noncapitalist Way*, p. 22; Brutents, *National Liberation Revolutions*, vol. I, p. 120; Tumanova, "Melkaia," p. 37.
199 Brutents, *National Liberation Revolutions*, vol. I, p. 120.
200 Andreyev, *The Noncapitalist Way*, p. 62.
201 Fedoseyev, *Leninism*, p. 472.
202 Solodovnikov and Bogoslovsky, *Non-Capitalist Development*, p. 138.
203 Kim, "Vo imia," p. 27; Usov, "Armiia," p. 54 (review of Mirskii's first book).
204 Zhukov et al., *The Third World*, p. 51.
205 Mirskii, *Armiia*, pp. 307, 336. Also Mirskii, *Tretii mir: obshchestvo, vlast', armiia*, Nauka, Moscow, 1976, pp. 385, 389–91; Dolgopolov, "National Democratic Revolution," pp. 49–50.
206 Brutents, *National Liberation Revolutions*, vol. I, pp. 83–6. This last point, the international character of the proletariat, was stressed by Gordon (*Problemy*, p. 139) in his criticism of Fanon's underestimation of the proletariat.
207 Ulyanovsky, *National Liberation*, p. 384; Sumbatian, "Socialist Oriented State," p. 25.
208 Kortunov, "The Working Class," p. 20; Brutents, *National Liberation Revolutions*, vol. I, p. 122; see also Sumbatian, "Socialist Oriented State," p. 25, and Rumiantsev, "Sovremennaia epokha," p. 5 (if under a Marxist–Leninist party).
209 Fedoseyev, *Leninism*, pp. 471–2. Gavrilov said the same, but he also argued that no class was sufficiently strong to lead. (Gavrilov, "Ob"ektivnye osnovy," p. 6; "New Africa," p. 33).
210 E. S. Troitskii, "Kritika neokolonialistskikh fal'sifikatsii idei V.I. Lenina po problemam natsional'no-osvoboditel'nogo dvizheniia," *Voprosy istorii KPSS*, no. 7 (1980): 77.
211 *Krasnaia zvezda*, 21 April 1974.
212 See chapter 3.
213 Brutents, *National Liberation Revolutions*, vol. I, pp. 86–7.
214 Ulyanovsky, *National Liberation*, p. 229.
215 Ibid., p. 182.
216 Ibid., p. 68.
217 Ibid., pp. 75–6.
218 E. Tarabrin, "Afrika na novom vitke osvoboditel'noi bor'by," *Mirovaia ekonomika i mezhdunarodnye otnosheniia (MEMO)*, no. 2 (1979): 38–9.
219 Manchkha, "Kommunisty," p. 62. See also Zhukov et al., *The Third World*, pp. 46–7.
220 G. Kim, "The National Liberation Movement Today," *International Affairs*, no. 4 (1981): 35.

221 Brutents, *National Liberation Revolutions*, vol. I, p. 104.
222 Ibid., p. 122 (emphasis mine).
223 Kim, "Social Development," p. 68.
224 Brutents, *National Liberation Revolutions*, vol. I, p. 123.
225 Merdel, "Organizatsii," p. 48.
226 Ulyanovsky, *National Liberation*, pp. 319–20.
227 Ul'ianovskii, "Kabral," p. 32.
228 Viktor Kudriavtsev, "Africa Fights for its Future," *International Affairs*, no. 5 (1978): 33; Andreasian, "Protivorechiia," p. 38; Solodovnikov and Bogoslovsky, *Non-Capitalist Development*, p. 137; Tumanova, "Melkaia," p. 37.
229 Solodovnikov and Bogoslovsky, *Non-Capitalist Development*, p. 137.
230 See Col. E. Dolgopolov, "Molodie armii i sotsial'nyi progress", *Kommunist Voosuzhennykh Sil*, no. 21 pp. 90-2 (1976), Sapozhnikov, "Klassy"; Sumbatian, "Armii," or comments in a conference published by *Latinskaia Amerika*, no. 3 (1977): 69–75.
231 Zhukov et al., *The Third World*, p. 51; see also Andreasian, "Protivorechiia," p. 42.
232 Andreasian, "Protivorechiia," p. 38; Sumbatian, "Socialist Oriented State," p. 25. See also Rostislav Ul'ianovskii, "Idei Velikogo Oktiabria i sovremennye problemy natsional'no-osvoboditel'nogo dvizheniia," *Novaia i noveishaia istoriia*, no. 3 (1977): 6.
233 Andreyev, *The Noncapitalist Way*, p. 57; Brutents, *National Liberation Revolutions*, vol. I, p. 110.
234 Andreyev, *The Noncapitalist Way*, p. 61; Kim, *Socialist World*, p. 33.
235 Brutents, *National Liberation Revolutions*, vol. I, pp. 107, 114, 121, 123; Andreyev, *The Noncapitalist Way*, p. 62.
236 Brutents, *National Liberation Revolutions*, vol. I, p. 123; Kim, *Socialist World*, p. 46; Andreyev, *The Noncapitalist Way*, p. 62; Kiva, "Nekotorye tendentsii," p. 24.
237 S. Agaev and I. Tatarovskaia, "Puti i etapy revoliutsionnogo protsessa v stranakh Azii i Afriki," *Aziia i Afrika segodnia*, no. 7 (1978): 28. See chapter 3.
238 Solodovnikov and Bogoslovsky, *Non-Capitalist Development*, p. 249.
239 Solodovnikov, *Problemy*, p. 167.
240 Ul'ianovskii, *Sovremennye problemy*, p. 42.
241 Zagladin, *Revolutionary Movement*, p. 79.
242 Brutents, *National Liberation Revolutions*, vol. I, p. 124.
243 Ibid., pp. 124-5. The issue of an individual leader is discussed below, as part of the problem of organization.
244 E.g., A. A. Kutsenkov, *Rabochii klass i anti imperialisticheskaia revoliutsiia v Azii, Afrike i Latinskoi Amerike*, Nauka, Moscow, 1969, p. 20, or the discussion in Thomas Zamastny, "Moscow and the Third World: Recent Trends in Soviet Thinking, *Soviet Studies* 36, no. 2 (1984): 223–35.
245 R. Domenger and A. Letnev, "Tropical Africa: Its Parties and Problems of Democracy," *World Marxist Review* 13, no. 10 (1970): 31.
246 R. Ul'ianovskii, "Vliiatel'naia politicheskaia sila Indii," *Aziia i Afrika segodnia* no. 9 (1982): 22.
247 Rostislav Ulyanovsky, *Present-day Problems in Asia and Africa*, Progress, Moscow, 1980, pp. 163–240. See also R. Ul'ianovskii, "O natsional'noi i revoliutsionnoi demokratii: puti evoliutsii," *Narody Azii i Afriki*, no. 2 (1984): 14–16.
248 R. Ul'ianovskii, *Bortsy za natsional'nuiu svobodu*, Politizdat, Moscow, 1983.
249 K. N. Brutents, "Praviashchaia revoliutsionnaia demokratiia: nekotorye cherty prakticheskoi deiatel'nosti," *Mirovaia ekonomika i mezhdunarodnye otnosheniia*, no. 12 (1972): 124.
250 Brutents, *National Liberation Revolutions*, vol. II, p. 222.
251 Ibid.
252 K. N. Brutents, *Osvobodivshiesia strany v 70-e gody*, Politizdat, Moscow, 1979, p. 68.
253 Ul'ianovskii, "Kabral," p. 30. See also V. Solodovnikov and O. Martyshin, "Nasledie Amilkara Kabrala," *Aziia i Afrika segodnia*, no. 7 (1983): 42–5.
254 Ibid., p. 29; see also Solodovnikov and Martyshin, "Nasledie Amilkara Kabrala," *Aziia i Afrika segodnia*, no. 7, 1983, p. 43; Ul'ianovskii, "O natsional'noi i revoliutsionnoi demokratii," pp. 14–16; Brutents, *Osvobodivshiesia strany*, p. 68 (said Nasser "understood" but failed to act on it).

255 Gordon, *Problemy*, pp. 144–5, 152.
256 "The Ways of the Anti-Imperialist Struggle in Tropical Africa" (unsigned), *World Marxist Review*, 14, no. 8, 1971, p. 30.
257 Domenger and Letnev, "Tropical Africa," p. 29.
258 Entin, *Politicheskie sistemy*, p. 27.
259 Manchkha, *Aktual'nye problemy*, p. 195. "Revolutionary democrats" usually referred to a class bloc excluding the national bourgeoisie, but in reference to pre-independence period the national bourgeoisie was generally included, as we have seen, and the term "national democratic" was employed somewhat more frequently. See chapter 4.
260 Ibid.
261 Kiva, "Revoliutsionno-demokraticheskie partii," p. 31.
262 Report on Prague conference, "New Stage in the National Liberation Movement; Problems of Anti-Imperialist Unity." *World Marxist Review*, 15, no. 11 (1972): 26–7; Brutents, *National Liberation Revolutions*, vol. I, p. 210.
263 Manchkha, *Aktual'nye problemy*, p. 196; A. A. Ivanov, "Avangard revoliutsionnogo dvizheniia v Afrike," *Nauchnyi kommunizm*, no. 4 (1976): 90; Solodovnikov, *Problemy*, p. 182.
264 Ul'ianovskii, "Indii," p. 20.
265 Ulyanovsky, *National Liberation*, p. 75.
266 V. L. Tiagunenko, *Vooruzhennaia bor'ba narodov Afriki za svobodu i nezavisimost'*, Ministerstvo Oborony SSSR, Nauka, Moscow, 1974, pp. 337–8.
267 Ibid., p. 338.
268 Ibid., p. 350.
269 Ulyanovsky, *Present-day Problems*, pp. 223–4.
270 See Katz, *Third World*, p. 106.
271 Ul'ianovskii, "Indii," p. 19; L. Entin, "Orientiruias' na sotsializm," *Aziia i Afrika segodnia*, no. 1 (1972): 6.
272 Entin, "Orientiruias'," p. 6; Kiva, "Revoliutsionno-demokraticheskie partii," p. 33. Praising Cabral, Solodovnikov and Martyshin also spoke of the need for "ideological clarity" provided by a party: Solodovnikov and Martyshin, "Nasledie Amilkara Kabrala," p. 43.
273 Domenger and Letnev, "Tropical Africa," p. 31.
274 Kiva "Revoliutsionno-demokraticheskie partii," p. 33. See also Fedoseyev, *Leninism*, p. 471.
275 G. I. Shitarev, "Nekotorye problemy evoliutsii revoliutsionno-demokraticheskikh organizatsii v napravlenii partii avangarda," *Narody Azii i Afriki*, no. 2 (1976): 39.
276 E.g., Solodovnikov, *Problemy*, p. 168; Brutents, *National Liberation Revolutions*, vol. I, p. 86.
277 Brutents, *National Liberation Revolutions*, vol. I, p. 85.
278 Gordon, *Problemy*, p. 162.
279 P. Shastitko, "Vstrecha s Leninym," *Aziia i Afrika segodnia*, no. 4 (1980): 7; N. Simoniia, "Sovremennyi etap osvoboditel'noi bor'by," *Aziia i Afrika segodnia*, no. 5 (1981): 16. See chapter 3 for the discussion on post-independence revolutionary parties.
280 Simoniia, "Sovremennyi etap," p. 16.
281 G. F. Kim, "The National Liberation Movement Today," *International Affairs*, no. 4 (1981): 35.
282 Solodovnikov and Bogoslovsky, *Non-Capitalist Development*, p. 141; A. Gromyko, "Socialist Orientation in Africa." *International Affairs*, no. 9 (1979): 10.
283 Manchkha, *Aktual'nye problemy*, p. 332.
284 Ulyanovsky, *National Liberation*, p. 215.
285 Ul'ianovskii introduction to Andreyev, *The Noncapitalist Way*, p. 21. Even the above-mentioned *Narody Azii i Afriki* outline of a vanguard party contained the caveat that this was mainly a theoretical description, such parties existing more in potential than in reality (Shitarev, "Nekotorye problemy," p. 39).
286 Domenger and Letnev, "Tropical Africa," p. 29.
287 N. Kosukhin, "Rasprostranenie idei nauchnogo sotsializma v Afrike," *Aziia i Afrika segodnia*, no. 7 (1981): 2.

288 Brutents, *National Liberation Revolutions*, vol. I, p. 86.
289 Manchkha, *Aktual'nye problemy*, pp. 188–9.
290 Ivanov, "Avangard revoliutsionnogo," p. 88. Foreign communists too praised the role played by Marxist–Leninist parties; e.g, Algerian communist Larbi Bouhali, "The Lenin-type Party and the Struggle for National and Social Liberation," *World Marxist Review* 13, no. 5 (1970): 1–2; Jordanian Communist Naim Ashhab, "Exchange of Views" (Berlin Conference on The International and National in the Working Class Movement), *World Marxist Review* 24, no. 8 (1981):59; South African Communist Yusuf Dadoo, "Against Imperialism, For Social Progress" (Berlin Conference), *World Marxist Review* 24, no. 4 (1981): 70–1. However, many of them appear to have been referring to post-independence states.
291 This was true of foreign communists as well. See Khaled Bagdesh, "Lenin and the Struggle Against Opportunism and Revisionism in the National Liberation Movement," *World Marxist Review* 13, no. 4 (1970): 48–9; Seydon Cissoka, "Lenin—Theorist of the National Liberation Movement," *World Marxist Review* 23, no. 4 (1980): 42; Georges Haoui, "Flexibility of Form, Firmness of Principle," *World Marxist Review* 22, no. 9 (1979): 15–17; "A Communist Call to Africa," *African Communist*, no. 75 (1978): 22–3 (document of African communist parties, 1978).
292 Manchkha, *Aktual'nye problemy*, p. 190; Ivanov, "Avangard revoliutsionnogo," p. 89.
293 Solodovnikov, *"Problemy,"* p. 160; Ivanov, "Avangard revoliutsionnogo," p. 89.
294 Brutents, *National Liberation Revolutions*, vol. I, pp. 210–11.
295 Ibid., p. 212.
296 Ibid., p. 213.
297 Manchkha, *Aktual'nye problemy*, p. 196.
298 Brutents, *National Liberation Revolutions*, vol. I, p. 214.
299 Ibid., vol. II, p. 209.
300 Ulyanovsky, *National Liberation*, pp. 52–70.
301 Ibid., pp. 70, 216–18.
302 Ibid., p. 73.
303 Ibid., p. 75.
304 Iu. A. Krasin, "Uzlovaia problema strategii communistov," *Rabochii klass i sovremennyi mir*, no. 1 (1977): 36.
305 Entin, *Problemy*, p. 108.
306 Krasin, "Uzlovaia problema," pp. 36, 45.
307 V. V. Zagladin, "XXVI s"ezd KPSS i mirovoi revoliutsionnyi protsess," *Mirovaia ekonomika i mezhdunarodnye otnosheniia*, no. 4 (1981): 14.
308 Ibid.

3

Ideology of National Liberation Movements

Introduction

For the purposes of analysis, an ideology may be broken down into three component parts: (1) the basic conceptualization, that is, the conceptual prism through which one views and analyzes the world; (2) the image of the future society to which one aspires; and (3) the objectives set for achieving this society.

Within the category of basic conceptualization, the major if not sole relevant theory to be considered was that of nationalism. This was a theory common to virtually all national liberation movements, which saw the nation as the central conceptual element for understanding society. Nationalism could be viewed conservatively, i.e., rejecting, from a Marxist point of view, anything but a strict class analysis of society; a second, more subtle approach applied a differentiated analysis, discerning certain positive tendencies in the non-class analysis applied by nationalism. Thus, where one school saw national superiority and exclusiveness, the other saw anti-imperialism and even progressiveness, while a middle ground saw the negative features of nationalism as circumstantial and, therefore, temporary. Nationalism was also perceived as spawning a number of offshoots associated with a particular group beyond or within the nation, for example, pan-Africanism, pan-Arabism, Negritude, religious nationalism (including Islam), populism, and "social nationalism." Here too the conservative, blanket rejection of these views was challenged by those who saw pragmatic, even theoretical, value of such conceptualizations, or at the very least viewed them with somewhat greater tolerance. These offshoots included not only Third World philosophies but also the unique approach of the Chinese, against which criticism was more uniform.

Various models of a future society were considered, a central one being that of some type of "national" socialism, which could be, more specifically, African socialism or, more generally, a "third way"—

non-capitalist but not scientific socialism. Here, too, the more conservative approach simply rejected anything short of scientific socialism, denying any truly socialist quality or potential for national socialism. Others, however, even though theoretically rejecting any "third way", saw a positive side to what was claimed as at least some form of socialism. These theoreticians, therefore, applied a differentiated approach here as well, categorizing national socialisms according to their progressiveness or conservativeness.

Within this categorization, the most positive or progressive form of Third World socialism was national revolutionary democracy. Actually defining this model was not an easy matter, even for those who viewed it positively. The distinctions between national democracy and revolutionary democracy were not clear, and the actual form of revolutionary democracy was described in various ways—as a wing of national democracy, a stage of national democracy, or something beyond national democracy. Its content was also described or prescribed in a variety of ways, dealing with attributes such as public ownership, small-scale capitalism, or merely a minimum requirement of anti-imperialism. The importance of these issues devolved from the question of just how much potential there was in revolutionary democracy for the development of scientific socialism. Just as, in the case of the negative features of nationalism and national socialism, the response of the more innovative or optimistic theorists was differentiation, so too with revolutionary democracy. Criticism of this model and its potential for scientific socialism was answered by differentiation even of revolutionary democracy, along the lines of "left" and "right". The ensuing debate, which was generated by the search for a realistic appraisal of the revolutionary democratic model, led to a challenge to both the optimists and the conservatives, as well as producing a new schematic definition of national and revolutionary democracy.

The solution that emerged from this debate was the addition of another attribute to the model, and that attribute was a vanguard party. Variously defined but generally accepted as an essential element for the emergence of scientific socialism, the vanguard party idea nonetheless prompted no little controversy with regard to its applicability, suitability, and timeliness. The Soviet leadership itself took certain positions on the issue, inasmuch as it represented or symbolized the controversy between what could be termed the ideological purists' (conservative) point of view versus the pragmatic approach to Third World societies and movements.

The more immediate objectives of, or framework for, realizing a movement's aspirations regarding a future society were entirely less controversial than the model proposed for this society. These objectives could be summed up by the term "self-determination," the definition of which involved the determination of the idea of national sovereignty and state sovereignty. The latter raised the issue of independent statehood as an essential or non-essential component of self-determination, a crucial point with regard to separatism. Separatism as an ideological objective was a complex issue, with some (albeit few) exhibiting somewhat greater tolerance than others. Alternative objectives, such as autonomy, federation, and confederation, were also posed, completing the picture of the possible ingredients of a movement's ideology.

Basic Conceptualization

As we have already seen, nationalism was perceived as the motive force of the national liberation movements, and, as such, it provided the basic conceptualization for most if not all of these movements. While this fact was undisputed even by those who noted that communist parties and Marxist–Leninist ideas had some influence,[1] the problem of cooperation with bourgeois or petty bourgeois national movements was reflected in the attitude toward nationalism itself. The ideology of the national liberation movements was no less difficult to condone than the composition and leadership; indeed, they were all connected. There appears to have been two schools of thought on the subject: those who acknowledged the negative aspects of nationalism but called for a differentiated approach to this ideology (criticizing those "Soviet scholars" who condemned all nationalisms out of hand), and those who acknowledged the differentiations but nonetheless condemned nationalism virtually in all its forms.[2]

Nationalism: Two Approaches

THE NEGATIVE (CONSERVATIVE) APPROACH

An example of the second, negative, school of thought could be found in the book edited by Zagladin. The theoreticians here began and ended by condemning the nationalist error of placing nation above class as the determining factor with regard to social relations and the individual consciousness:

> Nationalist idelogy, exclusively rendered on the national element, or evaluating all other social processes and defining political and other objectives from the national angle, is invariably a distorted form of

reflecting the social being. It is therefore incorrect, unscientific, conservative, or reactionary, and represents a passage to nationalism.

Consequently, the essence of any historical variety and form of
nationalism amounts to distortion and over-emphasis on the national
element for egoistic class purposes. In this sense nationalism is always
an inadequate and distorted reflection of reality, and therefore an
egoistic social activity by a definite class.[3]

While rejecting the opposite extreme of denying any role to the
nation, this study viewed nationalism as primarily a class phenomenon,
determined at any given historical stage by the class relations and
socioeconomic circumstances of the nation.

The question was: Were there any exceptions to this blanket condemnation of nationalism? In answer to this, the authors addressed themselves
to Lenin's distinction between "reactionary" and "progressive" nationalism, claiming that in many works Lenin nonetheless condemned any
and all forms of nationalism.[4] Lenin, they argued, advocated supporting
the generally democratic *content*, directed against oppression, of any
oppressed nation—thereby distinguishing between the concrete historical
content of nationalism and the *essence* of nationalism. The essence of
nationalism remained negative. ("The essence of every historical variant
of nationalism is distortion and over-emphasis of the national element
by one or more of the exploiting classes or social groups, which, in the
final analysis, conflicts with the truly revolutionary tendency."[5]) The
specific historic content, however, was broader and with some parts of it
possibly containing "relatively progressive, democratic elements."[6] But
the presence of such elements "depends not on the national, but on the
class factor...the more progressive the social group or class at the head
of the social and national liberation movement, the more extensive are the
democratic elements in its ideological and political concepts."[7] Only the
democratic elements were to be supported, however, while nationalism
itself was to be combated.

As for the non-democratic elements in the nationalism of the oppressed, one could find the "conservative and protective" nationalism of the
local oligarchy, for example the local tribal chiefs, whose nationalism
was "no more than tribalism." There was also rightist nationalism,
which included "religious nationalism (Buddhist, Islamic, etc.), black or
coloured racism, and different forms of so-called continental nationalism
(Asian, African, and Latin American)."[8] Albeit understandable anti-
imperialist responses to colonialist (white, European) oppression, they
nonetheless represented retrograde, often racist, forms of nationalism.
Moreover, some of these non-democratic forms of nationalism or
elements might be found interwoven with relatively democratic anti-
imperialist elements. Indeed, even the nationalism of the revolutionary

democrats, whose ideology comprised many democratic elements, was void of class content.[9] Thus, despite one or two sentences acknowledging the progressive role of nationalism in the liberation struggle, the over-riding conclusion of the Zagladin study was that nationalism remained nationalism, by definition incorrectly conceptualizing the nation as the focal point of society.

The study conducted by the Ideological Department's Institute of Marxism–Leninism, edited by the Institute's head, Central Commit-tee member Petr Fedoseev, also emphasized the negative aspects of nationalism.[10] This study, too saw the national element as formed by socioeconomic factors and resulting from class relations.[11] "The national aspects in people's lives, in the life of society, are only a form of social development whose content depends on the mode of production prevailing in the respective formation."[12] It condemned nationalism as an ideology associated with the bourgeoisie, which—even in the liberation struggle—used it to promote its own class interests. Thus, nationalism was defined as "national superiority, exclusiveness".[13] It was recognized that nationalism was composed of "an intricate blend" of the democratic and the reactionary, and that the democratic elements of nationalism might be predominant in the liberation struggle, but they were to be supported only "temporarily and within strictly designated limits."[14]

Like the Zagladin work, this study took the narrow interpretation of Lenin's distinction between progressive and reactionary nationalism. Citing Lenin to the effect that the awakening of the masses from feudal lethargy was progressive in itself and therefore to be supported, it went on to cite Lenin in that the effort to democratize the nationalist issue was a "largely negative" task. It was limited insofar as the proletariat should go in supporting nationalism; "for beyond that, begins the positive activity of the bourgeoisie striving to *fortify* nationalism."[15]

Joining those like Zagladin and Fedoseev, who might be termed hard-line preservers of ideological purity, was the then editor of the *World Marxist Review*, K. I. Zarodov. He summed up a Prague conference on national liberation movements in 1972 with a blanket condemna-tion of nationalism on the grounds that it tended toward isolation and exclusiveness. He did make a distinction between the ideology of nationalism and patriotism, allowing the latter as a legitimate concern for one's country.[16]

Academicians and theoreticians dealing with Asian–African studies had various views on the subject of the nationalist ideology. Some theoreticians generally more positive in their attitude toward Third World movements were more objective but nonetheless critical. Aleksei Kiva, Georgii Kim, and A. S. Kaufman all specified the negative side of nationalism, even in the struggle for national liberation, insofar as it, together with religion (according to Kiva), blocked the way for class development, or (according to Kim and Kaufman) reflected the influence of traditional institutions "connected with the patriarchal way of life."[17] A debate on the pages of *Narody Azii i Afriki* in 1975 reflected some of Zagladin's arguments as to the idea that the historical and other differentiations which might be drawn regarding nationalism did not change the *essence* of the ideology. This essence remained negative, exclusive, and purely transient, depending upon class and socioeconomic factors.[18]

THE POSITIVE APPROACH

Another school of thought, however, rejected the blanket condemnation of nationalism, seeking by differentiated typologies to find a basis for more than begrudging support (if not outright acceptance). Explicit criticism of what could be called the ideological purists' (such as Zagladin's) approach was expressed on the pages of *Narody Azii i Afriki*, prompting the discussion, mentioned above, on differentiation versus essence.[19] Most significant of the adherents to the more flexible approach were the two deputy chiefs of the Central Committee's International Department, Brutents and Ul'ianovskii. Brutents claimed that it was a mistake to overlook the national aspect or to see it as no more than a form for the expression of the social content of the national liberation movement.[20] Citing Lenin, he argued that "the oppressed nation's struggle against the oppressing nation for its liberty was the *'real* social content' of uprisings in annexed countries."[21] While the social aspect was crucial to characterizing revolutions, this thesis "has been wrongly used as a basis for mechanically regarding the national factor in any revolution as being a subordinate one and no more."[22] Indeed, there were even cases where the factors were reversed, with the socioeconomic factor being secondary to the national. Recognizing that the ideology of nationalism envisaged a harmonious national unity of all components of society, Brutents presented that as a positive rather than negative characteristic of nationalism. The reason was that nationalism traditionally had been seen as divisive, fanning distrust and hostility—a view that applied only to "reactionary nationalism."[23] Lenin, Brutents claimed, changed this view.

Brutents acknowledged that nationalism was nonetheless associated with the interests of a particular class or social group and contained latent ideas of national superiority and national exclusiveness. He argued, however, that, while nationalism had been used by classes, it "does not always express only narrow class interests. The character of nationalism and its socio-historical role as ideology and policy tend to change with the social position, social nature, and role of these class forces, their ties with the people, the historical state of development in progress and the balance of class forces" outside as well as within a given country.[24] Thus he did not simply allow for some of the content of nationalism to be temporarily acceptable even while the essence of nationalism was to be rejected. Rather, he argued that some forms of nationalism itself were to be accepted.

This was Brutents's interpretation of the same Lenin quotes employed by Zagladin and Fedoseev. Indeed, he used the same sentence as Fedoseev on nationalism's progressive role of awakening the masses from feudal lethargy, though omitting the subsequent lines quoted by Fedoseev as to the negative and limited nature of this role.[25] Brutents even went so far as to say that bourgeois nationalism could regain its lost progressive character in certain circumstances.[26] This is not to say that he accepted the basic flaw in all nationalist conceptualization: the placement of the national above the class factor as the ultimate determinant of society. He did, however, see two key elements which could provide a positive evaluation. The first was the basically petty bourgeois, rather than bourgeois, nature of the nationalism of the liberation movements. Although this did not make for a fundamental difference, it did "ensure...more substantial premises for the development of progressive tendencies within it." Because of the dual nature of the petty bourgeoisie, "petty bourgeois nationalism is more 'open' for progressive ideological and political influences."[27] Moreover, the social unity espoused by the nation, even if it contradicted a class analysis of society, placed all citizens as equal. Thus, even bourgeois nationalism was positive as a move against the feudal system and aristocracy.

Similarly, petty bourgeois nationalism united the people for a struggle against the outside exploiter, the imperialist, and even universalized this to be a struggle against imperialism as such. The second factor that provided for a positive evaluation, therefore, was "the direction of the edge" of nationalism—against whom or which type of oppression it was directed.[28] Ideas of national superiority and exclusiveness remained present in *all* types of nationalism, but they were slowed down by the anti-imperialist tenor and conditions of the liberation struggle (including the need for outside allies). Moreover, racism and chauvinism were kept in check, because they had been discredited as a result of their association with the colonial oppressors. This was not to say that such phenomena could not or had not appeared among the national liberation movements. Left radicalism and chauvinism could appear, as could religious fanaticism, but they were to be seen as aberrations, a response to past suppression and the subsequent need for national self-assertion. The general direction of the nationalism of the liberation movements reflected a surge for independence and even social progress as well as anti-imperialism.[29]

The publication of Brutents's book (which was positively reviewed in *Pravda*[30]) a year after the Zagladin book and at roughly the same

time as the Fedoseev book may have been an indication of the direction
the Communist party wished to have taken on this issue. Ul'ianovskii's
volume, which appeared the following year (1975), tended to substan-
tiate this view. Condemning those who rejected nationalism out of
hand, Ul'ianovskii too resorted to typology to justify certain forms of
nationalism.[31] As stated in a later (1980) article, the major criterion for
accepting or rejecting any of these forms was the presence or absence
of an anti-imperialist potential.[32]

Ul'ianovskii's arguments, however, appeared to be directed not toward internal critics, but rather toward anti-communist accusations
that the Soviet Union opposed nationalism and therefore could not be
a reliable ally. Allowing that "Marxist–Leninists fully understand and
take into account the prejudices, reactionary fantasies, and errors that
are unavoidable when the national is absolutized," Marxist–Leninists
nonetheless stand for alliance between socialism and anti-imperialism—refraining from "contraposing" socialism to the national feelings
of oppressed peoples.[33] The reasons for this tolerance of nationalism,
insofar as they could be found in Ul'ianovskii's analysis, were that (1)
Leninists "have confidence in the revolutionary and creative potential
of mass movements"; and (2) "anti-colonialist nationalism has not yet
become outdated, nor has it ceased to be a progressive factor in definite
spheres of struggle."[34]

Where Ul'ianovskii's arguments appear to have been directed toward
the discussions among Soviet Third World specialists was in his adamant-
ly expressed opposition to any effort to substitute a proletarian, socialist
ideology for that of nationalism at too early a stage.[35] Indeed, this idea
did not even appear to be pertinent for the stage of national liberation
but rather was a point of debate, with regard to the post-independence
stage, as we shall see below. Just as non-proletarian elements had to be
accepted for the leadership of the movement, so too the non-proletarian
ideology of nationalism could not be replaced.

Solodovnikov occupied something of a middle ground, leaning nonetheless toward the more tolerant, flexible approach. Arguing in his
books of the early 1970s that the ideology of the national movements
could grow into a socialist one depending upon the class nature of the
leadership, he did not see much hope for bourgeois or even petty bourgeois nationalism.[36] But his was the argument favoring a differentiated
approach, which clearly saw anti-imperialist nationalism as the essential
unifying factor in the national liberation struggle.[37] Moreover, in a book
written with Viktor Bogoslovskii in 1975, Solodovnikov used the usual
quotes from Lenin and the idea of differentiation to justify some forms
of nationalism. Indeed, his positive attitude went so far as to advocate a
differentiated approach even to the nationalism of the oppressor nation,
on the grounds that it nonetheless included progressive forces such as

communists.[38] Using the historical argument, he unequivocably stated that nationalism, at the anti-imperialist stage of the struggle, "expressed the interests of the peoples."[39] Nationalist prejudices and egoism, acknowledged to exist, were explained as the result of the prolonged colonial oppression. They were not, however, to be perceived as a serious problem, for, according to Solodovnikov and Bogoslovskii, they grow weaker—not stronger—in the course of time.[40]

Offshoots of Nationalism

These "national prejudices or national egoism" were mentioned in almost all the theoretical works as components or offshoots of the nationalism to be found among the national liberation movements. Thus, the category of nationalist ideology included such offshoots as pan-Africanism, pan-Arabism, Negritude, religious nationalism (including Islam), populist nationalism, and something called "social nationalism." As we have seen, the first three—pan-Africanism, pan-Arabism, and Negritude—were often lumped together and universally condemned for their exclusiveness and even racist qualities. One variation in the approach to them, however, was the already-noted tolerance on the part of the less doctrinaire, explaining if not excusing them as "over-reactions" produced by prolonged oppression. The more tolerant thus explained that, inasmuch as nationalism was built on the aspirations of the nation, not the class, it was natural that liberation for an Arab meant "Arab liberation," for an African, "African liberation," and so on.[41] The emphasis on their "special" quality or particularness served the function of defining the nation's independence or integrity; it served not only to justify but also to rally the masses against the oppressors of their nation.[42] At the same time, these ideologies were nonetheless condemned on a pragmatic as well as theoretical level for their exclusiveness, which barred cooperation with or help from outside sources.

The same negative but mixed attitude was apparent with regard to religious nationalism. Brutents, for example, argued that national liberation movements were simply wisely putting existing religious beliefs to good use—the service of a progressive goal—rather than permitting these beliefs of the masses to be used by and for reactionaries.[43] Thus, religion was often instrumentally used by nationalist leaders to secure the broadest popular support. In an article that carried the unusual caveat by the editor that the author was expressing "his own views," Kim analyzed the resurgence of traditional religious feelings (as a result of enforced capitalist modernization from above.) While he noted the limitations of such ideologies (failure to offer a "comprehensive program of positive transformation"), he did acknowledge that religious tradition had become "a conduit and a means for the expression of mass social protest, giving coherence to its anti-exploitative main thrust."[44] Others, such as Zagladin, made a blanket condemnation of all religious ideologies as "rightist nationalism."[45] Somewhere in between was Ul'ianovskii, who tended to condemn the generally reactionary and obstructionist (regarding progress) role of the religions of the East, although remaining adamant about the need to avoid underestimating their role and importance.[46]

Islam, because of its broad importance in the Third World, was accorded particular attention—at least by those who urged a differentiated approach to nationalism. Primakov offered an authoritative interpretation in a 1980 *Voprosy filosofii* article (occasioned by the revolution in Iran).[47] He attributed the importance of Islam to the national liberation struggle generally to the fact that Islam was not simply a religious system, but a way of life; its tenets provided not only a guide to moral and ethical behavior, but also norms relating to the areas of personal, economic, and social life. Thus, its influence went well beyond the religious sphere. Moreover, it encompassed hundreds of millions of people, with a long history as a guiding factor.

The influence of Islam, however, was due primarily to the historical, economic, and political conditions of the Islamic countries. Inasmuch as imperialism was identified with the Western, non-Islamic world, Islam served as a rallying point in the struggle for independence, religious slogans becoming an integral part of this struggle. In that sense Islam was positive, but this anti-imperialist aspect had a negative side because of its juxtaposition of the religious–exclusive principle over the international class principle. As with nationalism, the opposition to the outsider engendered anti-capitalist tones as the foreigner was identified with exploitation and the poor conditions within the country. In the case of Islam, however, this exploitation was compounded by what was seen as "Westernization," which was also weakening the religious principles of Moslem society. Thus, Islam provided a further impetus in a positive direction. But in this same context, Primakov said, it was the defenders of tradition, including the clergy, who led the anti-imperialist struggle, using religion as a means of reaching and rallying the masses.

Beyond this, however, Islam itself changed in the course of socioeconomic changes; social elements began to take precedence over religious ones. Thus, the idea of an "Islamic state" or an "Islamic economy" were positive concepts in that they offered an alternative—"albeit utopian"—to the exploitative system of the economy and the state. There were problems with the content of each of these ideals, especially as the economic ideas represented the mistaken notion of a "third way," while the political ideas could be used by the bourgeoisie in a conservative direction. As Brezhnev decreed at the twenty-sixth CPSU

Congress (quoted by Primakov), Islam had to be seen as both potentially progressive and conservative at one and the same time, depending on the specific content.[48]

Primakov explained this in terms of Lenin's distinctions regarding the bourgeois nationalism of an oppressed nation, with its democratic but also its conservative current. More specifically, he explained that Islam had historically comprised diverse class and political interests; there was the petty bourgeois current with certain revolutionary potential, and the capitalist landowner current with a reactionary, counter-revolutionary role. In this sense, the same principles of the Koran concerning "peoples power," "Islamic justice," and the "Islamic path of development" could be interpreted differently by each current, either against capitalism or against communism. And even each current, specifically the petty bourgeois one, had the dual potential of going in a conservative or a revolutionary direction. If the revolutionary element dominated, conditions could be created for non–capitalist development.[49] This element, therefore, was to be supported, without, however, supporting the religious ideology itself. This was to say, as with nationalism, the revolutionary trend should be strengthened in hopes that the religious movement would progress from religion to socialism.

While Kim did not express such direct aspirations for Islam in its radical stream, he did agree that the religious and tradition-bound ideology of Islam could be filled with a progressive content in an attempt to solve acute social and national problems.[50] Another observer, Aleksandr Malashenko, in reference to Algeria, argued that, "since Islam is closely associated with the egalitarian concepts of social justice" merging with nationalism in the national liberation struggle, "awakening the patriotic feeling among people, religious traditions can nowadays be used to mobilize believers for fully secular undertakings."[51] Referring specifically to Islam in Lenin's attitude toward the religious convictions of the peoples of the East, a *Voprosy istorii KPSS* article spoke of the "positive role" played by those in the national liberation movement "who came forward under the religious, nationalist flag."[52] And Brutents, citing the Syrian Communist distinction between the conservative "Moslem Brothers" and the "true faithful," urged communists to "show respect for Islam and its customs, and prove that they [the Communists] truly stand for translating into reality the ideals of social justice which express the social and material interests and aspirations of the people and are reflected in various religious canons."[53]

By 1981, however, as developments in Iran became increasingly disappointing, the commentaries on Islam became somewhat more pessimistic. The basic dualist line regarding Islam did not change, but Ul'ianovskii referred to the "highly contradictory...politisation of Islam" with the increasing strength of the conservative wing in Iran, and the totally counter-revolutionary character of Islam in a country like Afghanistan.[54] He nonetheless saw two opposite directions for Islam in the two countries and continued to urge analysis of the anti-imperialist and anti-feudal potential of religious nationalism "for the benefit of the revolutionary process."[55]

The journalist Bovin, often a maverick but nonetheless considered to be close to Brutents, and in the past to Andropov, said in an interview (on the occasion of receiving the Order of Lenin) that the Islamic revival was "an attempt to return to those times when Islamic dogmatists determined the character and system of political life." This was in essence a "theocractic renaissance." He made no distinction between the conservative form of religious power as pursued by the Moslem Brotherhood or the Shi'ite clergy and that pursued by Khomeini in Iran.[56] Earlier, comments in a *Narody Azii i Afriki* discussion on religion had delivered a somewhat similar verdict. S. Erasov described Islamic revivalism (like that of Buddhism and Hinduism) as a call for the return to the original precepts of Islam which were considered the just foundation of society. Reflecting the mood of the masses, it called for a "just reconstruction of society" on the basis of the "omnipotence of God, democracy, and justice."[57] Uniting with the nationalist and popular radical movements, however, revivalism was the "heir to popular heresies and sectarian rebellion...messianic and eschatological, millenistic movements," demanding a return to religious purity and the elimination of the defects of the world.

Primakov and Kim also began slightly to shift their emphasis to the negative aspects of Islam in articles they wrote in 1982.[58] Calling the Islamic revival a "renovation of the traditionalist forces," Kim said that the "retraditionalization of the policy in the East...has a mass democratic, 'plebian' [sic] basis, is a form of social protest, and can set in motion considerable reserves of political extremism."[59]

Populism and Social Nationalism

Another offshoot of nationalism, criticized mainly in the later literature on developing countries, was populism. By extrapolation, this criticism was applied to the national liberation movements as well. The most serious approach to this ideology would appear to have been a 1978 article on populism by V. G. Khoros, of the Oriental Institute,[60] although in this type of literature populism was usually subsumed under the more general category of petty bourgeois nationalism. Seen by Khoros as an ideology which combined bourgeois democratic anti-feudal features with anti-capitalist tendencies, it was said to adapt and modernize "traditional collectivist methods and values."[61] According to Khoros, this modernizing feature was the distinguishing mark between "pro-peasant ideas of prebourgeois times" and the new petty bourgeois populism.[62]

To its credit, Third World populism was juxtaposed to Western populism on the grounds that the latter was designed to protect and glorify the private farmer. This did not necessarily, or in all cases, mean a glorification of the peasant. Khoros argued that often populism was the ideological expression of groups that emphasized "statist, elitist tendencies," because of the "passivity of the peasants" and the leaders' desire for modernization and industrialization.

On the whole, Khoros appeared to be relatively positive with regard to the populist trend, citing experiments in socialist-type collectives and cooperatives, and arguing that the form taken depended upon the social–political coloring of the leadership. Another somewhat less positive analysis likened populism in the Third World to Russian Narodism in its "criticism of bourgeois civilization, the idea of non-capitalist development through the adaptation and modernization of the traditional communal institutions, orientation on the peasantry, emphasis on the special role of the intelligentsia, etc."[63] This type of populist thinking was explained by the low level of capitalist development, which led to the predominance of traditional or semi-traditional strata. Ul'ianovskii expressed similar criticism of populism, viewing it as a type of national egoism of those in the Third World who saw their own peoples as somehow unique (spiritually superior) and therefore able to avoid capitalism.[64] Later analyses published by *Aziia i Afrika segodnia* in 1982 and 1983 were even more critical, tending to see the contradictory, open-ended character of the ideology and declaring this typical of the petty bourgeois approach itself.[65] But again, in 1984, Khoros published a positive view of populism, quoting Lenin on the "positive characteristics of Populist teachings and [Populist-] type movements."[66] This was in the context of Lenin's support for Gandhi against criticism by Roy—criticism that had been echoed in Ul'ianovskii's portrait of Gandhi in the 1980 English version of his 1978 book.[67]

Ostensibly due to populism, at least in its attitude toward the peasantry, was the ideology of Franz Fanon. Termed by Soviet analysts "social nationalism," Fanon's views were comprehensively and critically treated in the volume by Gordon which appeared in 1977.[68] According to this work, the major ideological problem with Fanon's "social nationalism" was his perception of the world in class rather than national terms, to the point where only two categories emerged: colonialized and colonialist, a "we" and "they" view whereby the Third World was glorified and pitted against "Europe"—the developed world.[69] Moreover, the colonialized–colonialist dichotomy, black-white, natives–Europeans, took on a "social class category" as universal antagonism. The reason, according to Gordon, was that for Fanon the economic base was in fact the superstructure as well: cause equalled reason; white equalled wealthy. Social relations, therefore, were determined not by "economic reality," but by "human reality."[70] Within this framework, the town was identified with the colonizer, the superstructure over the rural world, which was the village. The rural world "kept intact the traditional, pre-colonial system of relations...[71] Thus, the village was the anti-colonial, "national" element, and as such was superior to the corrupted city.[72]

Discussing Gordon's book, Ul'ianovskii sought to find positive elements in Fanon's ideology, pointing out (as had Gordon to some extent) that Fanon's "national consciousness" was not meant to be nationalism, but rather had a social content of justice, equality, and democracy.[73] Criticism was nonetheless expressed regarding Fanon's village–town dichotomy and his non-class approach.[74] The latter was said to reflect the influence of two "nationalistic errors" on Fanon's part: the perception of the ethnic rather than class contradictions in colonialism, and the rejection of any but the "wretched"—the colonized—of the world. Writing in a journal designed for overseas consumption, Ul'ianovskii repeatedly asserted that the positive side of Fanon outweighed the negative, but the unacceptability of such an exclusive ideology was made clear. Another review of Gordon's book, by R. G. Landa in *Narody Azii i Afriki*, was also praiseworthy but actually criticized the Gordon book for not sufficiently emphasizing the negative aspects of Fanon's glorification of the village vis-à-vis the town (including the proletariat).[75]

Until the Gordon book, it had been more or less customary to lump Fanon's views together with other "extreme left" ideologies, especially those of the Chinese.[76] What was similar, and was consistently condemned in the Soviet literature, was the idea, sometimes directly associated with Maoism, of the juxtaposition of the "world village" against the "world city" or the rich versus the poor.[77] In 1972 this was described by the Soviets as Mao's theory of "intermediate zones," that is, two intermediate zones between the United States and the socialist countries. The first included the underdeveloped countries of Asia, Africa, and Latin America, the second, the developed states of Western Europe, Japan, Canada, and Australia. The first of these intermediate zones, led by China, was to be the decisive one.[78] Later the Soviets claimed Maoism changed, with the espousal of a "three-world" concept: the superpowers, the developed world, and the underdeveloped world.[79] While there could be an alliance between the "Third World" and the countries of the developed "Second World," the chief contradiction of our times was defined as that between imperialism and hegemonism, or between the rich on the one hand and the peoples of the Third World on the other—with the latter to be ultimately victorious.[80]

Like the ideas of Fanon, the Chinese ideology was condemned not only for ignoring the class determinant but also for failing to take into account social or ideological differences in all societies, be they of the First, Second, or Third World. Thus, not only did the Chinese lump the socialist countries into the same, hostile, developed world basket, but they were also guilty of encouraging nationalism. Chinese ideology, with its glorification of the Third World, was said to pit the colored races against the white, encouraging such "racist ideologies" as pan-Africanism.[81] Quoting Mao to the effect that "the clashes between the peoples of Asia and Africa on the one hand, and the peoples of Europe and America, on the other, will be the main clashes in the world," China specialist Krivtsov explained that this meant that "the main contradiction of the contemporary epoch was viewed in China not from class but from nationalistic and even racialist positions."[82]

On the other hand, faced with the change in Chinese policies in the 1970s, Soviet analysts such as Krivtsov claimed that Peking "dampened down the propaganda idea of the surrounding of the 'world town' by the 'world village,' and of other ultra-revolutionary theses," so as to cooperate with the imperialists.[83] This did not make Chinese ideology more acceptable, but the Soviet condemnations shifted from attacks on ultra-left adventurism to those on opportunism and exploitation. Inasmuch as Chinese policy was still anti-Soviet, it continued to be condemned for promulgating a nationalistic, racist ideology. Still another change regarding the Chinese conception occurred during the 1980s' period of progress in Sino-Soviet relations. This was evident in the 1983 translation of Brutents's 1979 book: the earlier, Russian, version spoke of the "Maoists'" superpowers (First World) idea; the later, English, version spoke of the theory without identifying its origin.[84]

Future Society

The nationalist conceptualization of the world, with the nation as the determining factor in society, clearly affected the image of the future society to be achieved after independence in the ideologies of the national liberation movements. For purists like Zagladin and Fedoseev, there were few subtleties. For them, nationalism was the ideology of a class, employed by it for its class interests, with the nationalism of the petty bourgeoisie of the Third World bearing no essential difference from that of the bourgeoisie. Therefore, the future society envisaged by nationalism would be a class-divided society, characterized by class strife and exploitation. The ideas of national harmony, national solidarity, and national unity inherent in nationalism would, as in classical bourgeois states, simply be slogans for the use of the ruling class to keep the masses "in ideological subjection."[85]

The other school of analysts would not contest that ultimately class differentiation and class strife would occur in the newly independent states. In judging nationalism as an ideology, however, they considered it a more positive—even if fallacious—vision. Brutents, for example, noted positively the nationalists' idealized concept of class harmony, of a society based on class peace and cooperation born of national solidarity.[86] This aspect of the ideology was to be combated for its effort to contain the class struggle, but it did provide a somewhat more subtle approach than that of Zagladin and Fedoseev, who saw only the purposely divisive objective. Solodovnikov stood somewhere between these two positions, identifying the vision of a classless, harmonious society with the idea of national exclusiveness and uniqueness.[87] Those who subscribed to this vision, according to Solodovnikov writing on Africa, "build their schema of a new African society on the basis of theories of classlessness, social harmony, and assert the possibility of the integration of social forces on the basis of exclusive qualities of the Negro personality, the value of which they see as its spiritual–emotional properties."[88]

National Socialisms

With the above characterization, Solodovnikov introduced the subject of "African socialism," which was part of the theory of "national socialism" or the "third path" generally criticized in Soviet literature. This type of socialism, he explained, was an ideology primarily of the non-proletarian strata which had not yet worked out an independent political theory but nonetheless rejected capitalism. Attitudes toward "national socialism" in Soviet literature to some degree resembled that on nationalism, reflecting differences between those who expressed blanket disapproval and those who argued for a more sophisticated or flexible, differentiated approach. Indeed, the ideological purists often refrained from using the term "national socialism," as if refusing to admit the existence of any kind of socialism within the nationalist movements; rather, they (but not only they) condemned the idea of a "third way." In either case, their criticism related to the "exclusive" idea that special conditions pertained in the Third World, ruling out the relevancy of class-based theories such as scientific socialism.[89]

Aleksei Kiva, for example, discussed "national socialism," or the various "unique types of socialism" (e.g., "African socialism"), as incorrect theories born in the liberation struggle, which would prevent cooperation with, and therefore help from, the rest of the anti-imperialist world.[90] Kim (and Gromyko), too, tended to dismiss the phenomena of "national socialisms" as nothing more than bourgeois ideology clothed in socialist terminology so as to "convince the masses that the steps they are taking to modernize society on bourgeois lines are aimed at realizing the working people's age-old aspirations...for real social justice."[91] In a later article, Kim called this, rather, "pre-proletarian petty bourgeois socialism, with their emphasis on supraclass populism, nationalist romanticism, and traditionalist outlooks."[92] Khoros, in his article on populism, linked that ideology with the appearance of "numerous varieties of 'national socialism" in Africa, an area where "capitalism had made few inroads and communal structures remained firmly entrenched."[93] And Manchkha, with his authority as Central Committee International Department African specialist, stated that the struggle against such deviations as "bourgeois-national concepts of African socialism" was "the most important task of Communists and revolutionary democrats" in Africa.[94]

Solodovnikov, not as critical as some, argued for a differentiated approach. Discussing African socialism, he saw two trends: the conservative trend, described above with regard to classlessness and national exclusiveness, and the radical trend, which aspired to scientific socialism though not necessarily being Marxist–Leninist.[95]

Brutents, too, took a differentiated approach toward "national socialism," reflecting his generally more tolerant approach. First, he acknowledged that "national socialism" was a vague, somewhat all-inclusive, term for what were in fact a number of ideologies claiming the mantle of socialism.[96] Indeed, several theorists, including Brutents, pointed to the arbitrary use of socialist terminology by Third World movements without any real understanding, but Brutents found positive significance even in this.[97] He explained that one of the common points to all the theories of "national socialism" was the advocating of socialism—of some form or another—for fulfilling the tasks of national liberation, rapid independent development, and national revival. Capitalism, for its part, had become identified with imperialism and colonialism, rather than primarily with the idea of social injustice.[98] Despite the fact, however, that many of these ideologies were influenced by Marxism, particularly as an explanatory model of colonialism and as a technical model for economic growth, "the conceptions of 'national socialism' are characteristically bound up with nationalistic ideas."[99] By this was meant anti-Marxist as well as anti-foreign ideas, advocating some indigenous form of socialism based on claims to "innate" or pre-colonial socialist tendencies.[100]

According to Brutents, moral and ethical as well as religious elements played a large role in the "national socialist" conception of socialist society. Kenya's Mboya was cited as defining socialism as a "frame of mind" designed "to establish rational relations and harmony in society," while others, like Senghor or Cambodia's Sihanouk, emphasized the religious basis. These views of class relations and even their definition of class were far from correct, with many "national socialisms" emphasizing the "special" and "leading role of the small producer," opposing the elimination of private property and small landholdings.[101]

Nonetheless, despite these theoretical similarities, there were great differences—and therefore a need to differentiate—when it came to the policies associated with the various terms of "national socialism." Like Solodovnikov, Brutents divided "national socialism" into two trends: the reformist, or conservative reformist, and the revolutionary democratic.[102] The former was based on and oriented toward the bourgeoisie or petty bourgeoisie; the latter toward the peasantry, petty bourgeoisie, and semi-proletariat.[103]

The reformist or conservative reformist theories did not go beyond bourgeois–democratic reformism. With the idea of overcoming socioeconomic backwardness and reducing dependence on imperialism, they established (sometimes unwittingly or temporarily) capitalist relations, at times within the framework of state capitalism.[104] Rejecting (be it for tactical or ideological reasons) classical capitalism, this trend adopted some measures and characteristics of socialism, though in so so doing "they tend to kill their true, socialist content."[105] Thus, while this model included the establishment of a state sector, the use of planning principles, and the creation of cooperatives in the countryside, its implementation was geared in a way to favor the bourgeoisie while debilitating the revolutionary or radical elements of society.[106] Moreover, it allowed for a mixed economy, and private capital was protected.

On a theoretical level, the conservative–reformist trend of "national socialism" rejected historical and dialectical materialism, denying class struggle and proclaiming class collaboration. Indicative of its nationalist basic conceptualization, this trend advocated a "non-class" socialism applicable to "the whole of humanity," of "equal concern to all social sections of the nation."[107] Moreover, this trend was characteristically anti-Marxist, anti-Communist, and opposed to "scientific socialism" as a conception, though the methods of scientific socialism were not totally rejected. Communism was regarded as "obsolete" or "not genuine," while the emphasis on national uniqueness pitted them against Marxism as a class ideology not applicable to African or other Third World nations.[108] To its credit, this trend of "national socialism" was also anti–imperialist, and could even evolve in a progressive direction in certain conditions (such as the radicalization of the petty bourgeois component); but this possibility was seen as no more likely than its exact opposite.[109]

There were some theoreticians who added to this "conservative-reformist" trend of "national socialism" other intermediary categories or types of ideology, such as bourgeois-liberal (Kim) or petty bourgeois

Utopian socialism (Ul'ianovskii), so separating them from the purely bourgeois reformism. Like the conservative–reformist trend, bourgeois liberalism, according to Kim, more accurately belonged in the capitalist type of development category. Yet it had progressive aspects—as well as socialist goals. [110]

Ul'ianovskii argued that petty bourgeois Utopian socialism should be a separate category halfway between the two trends outlined by Solodovnikov and Brutents. [111] He explained that this trend was characterized by "the illusions of the main mass of the petty bourgeois population in the spirit of the patriarchal 'Golden Age' and 'family' relations between classes." [112] These were concepts of both anti-imperialism and anti-capitalism, combined nonetheless with a mistrust of scientific socialism. At first glance purely retrograde and tradition-bound, this petty bourgeois Utopian socialism could nonetheless be progressive, depending upon which of the two major trends it veered toward, bourgeois reformism or national (revolutionary) democracy. [113] By advocating a separate category, Ul'ianovskii was basically trying to prevent a blanket dismissal of this ideology, which would occur if it were unceremoniously dumped together with bourgeois reformism.

Ul'ianovskii's effort went beyond the discussion of "national socialism" into the broader realm of the theory of non-capitalist development, which was basically none other than the "third way" between capitalism and scientific socialism (although the Soviets denied this was a "third way"—defining it rather as a transition stage). [114] The purpose of the differentiation provided by Solodovnikov (conservative/radical); Brutents (conservative–reformist/national–revolutionary democratic); and Kim and Kaufman (national bourgeois ideology/liberal petty bourgeois ideology/revolutionary democratic ideology) apparently was to demonstrate that, just because an ideology was not Marxist–Leninist scientific socialism, it did not mean that it was simply conservative or bourgeois-reformist. While the model of scientific socialism was of course the preferred one, and the one against which every other model of the future society was to be measured, there were gradations in the non-capitalist model.

Revolutionary Democracy

FORM

The preferred of these gradations in the non-capitalist model was that of national-revolutionary democracy. The discussion of national–revolutionary democracy was one of complex semantics and entailed no little confusion as well as controversy. It dominated Soviet literature on the Third World particularly in the late 1970s, primarily as an effort to come to grips with the ideologies and policies of the new states. From this discussion, one can at least extrapolate that image of the future society which the Soviets advocated or at least tolerated for the national liberation movements.

The issue at stake in the late 1970s appeared to be just how revolutionary national or revolutionary democracy could be; that is, would it or would it not develop into scientific socialism? On one side stood those who tended to lump national–revolutionary democracy together with all the non-capitalist social visions other than scientific socialism, seeing, as Ul'ianovskii accused them, no difference between revolutionary democracy and simple bourgeois reformism (or conservative reformism). The other school argued for the differentiation, explaining that it was a mistake to claim that revolutionary democracy was the equivalent of scientific socialism, but that it could develop in that direction. Thus, the argument appeared to be over the value or degree of socialist content of revolutionary democracy, and how it could develop into scientific socialism.

Before addressing the controversy, let us examine just what was meant by revolutionary democracy. The term itself evolved in the 1960s to characterize the revolutionary or socialist nature (or orientation) of some Third World states which nonetheless were not ruled by Marxist–Leninists.[115] The term was used by some, such as Ul'ianovskii, interchangeably with "national" democracy, but even the same author just as often referred to revolutionary democracy as a branch of national democracy.[116] Often it was delineated as the type of regime or rule in a national democratic state. In any case, national–revolutionary democracy was perceived as a temporary type of society in which the state expressed the will of a "single national democratic front and all the patriotic forces of the nation."

Georgii Kim, editor of *Aziia i Afrika segodnia* and one of the authoritative theoreticians on the Third World (specifically Asia), early described revolutionary democracy as developing within national democracy,[117] but he generally referred to it as the type of rule or ideology of national democracies which paved the way for scientific socialism.[118] Manchkha and Entin also saw revolutionary democracy as the type of rule (leaders and their ideology) in the national democratic state, with the latter described as a broad democracy.[119] Gavrilov, however, saw revolutionary democracy perhaps as a form of rule, but one connected more with the stages of national democracy. He described national democracy as that form of rule of the state which ensured the advance to socialism in societies where conditions were not yet ripe for the creation of a socialist state.[120]

In its first stage, however, the national democratic state was basically negative, not only because of its bourgeois and petty bourgeois nature, but primarily because of its essentially nationalist ideology, which dictated anti-capitalism owing to its subjective nationalist interests.[121] Revolutionary democracy constituted the second, more positive, stage of national democracy, because in it "national socialism" gave way to socialism of a "national type." Presumably, this was a more genuine form of socialism, inasmuch as it was described as being influenced more by the working class.[122] Revolutionary democracy continued into the third stage of national democracy as well, but in this stage revolutionary democracy itself was defined as Marxist–Leninist-inspired, that is, as following the model of scientific socialism.[123]

Aleksei Kiva also ascribed to the idea of distinctions between national democracy and revolutionary democracy being a matter of stages, connected with the class composition and interest represented at each stage. On one occasion, he added to these distinctions the level of development of any given society, defining national democracy as the form of the state in the stage of pre-capitalist conditions, not yet ripe for socialism, while revolutionary democracy was suitable for countries of a medium level of development, headed by a coalition of anti-imperialist and anti-feudalists led by the working class.[124] On another occasion, he cited the authority of Ul'ianovskii to the effect that national democracy was composed of all the progressive, anti-imperialist elements, some of whom might well fall victim to the idea of a "third way," while revolutionary democracy was composed of the direct predecessors of Marxism–Leninism and scientific socialism. These last might be considered the left wing of national democracy.[125]

Ul'ianovskii himself, upon occasion, lumped the two terms together, speaking of national–revolutionary democracy as a society or stage between national reformism and scientific socialism.[126] On the other hand, in the same and other works he spoke of the revolutionary democratic (left) wing of national democracy, the dominance of which accounted for the revolutionary character of national democracy and the possibility of its developing into scientific socialism. If this wing were absent or weak, national democracy could deteriorate into "reactionary democracy."[127] Thus, national democracy itself could be identified, wholly, neither with scientific socialism nor with national (bourgeois) reformism. Rather, it was by nature contradictory and subject to lapses, depending upon the strength of its revolutionary democratic, that is, anti-imperialist or socialist-oriented, wing.[128]

Brutents, too, argued that national democracy could go either socialist or capitalist, but held that its very potential for socialist development differentiated it from past bourgeois revolutions.[129] And, with Ul'ianovskii, Brutents understood revolutionary democracy as that wing of national democracy, or that group, which could lead it to socialist construction (as distinct from proletarian leadership, which would assuredly and directly lead it to socialism, or the bourgeois leadership, which clearly would not).[130]

CONTENT

On the whole, revolutionary democracy was understood as a particular form of national democracy associated with a particular ideology and group which subscribed to it. For Kim, the ideology of revolutionary democracy consisted of a rejection of capitalism; an espousal of socialism and other principles such as elimination of exploitation, public ownership, distribution according to work, cooperatives, and so on; revolutionary rather than reformist methods, including radical recon-struction of the economy against imperialism, feudalism, and national capitalism while building a public sector; socioeconomic and political measures in accord with the interests of the working people, including changes in the social structure and system; anti-imperialist foreign policy; and general agreement with the socialist bloc.[131] This ideology generally accorded with the model of national democracy presented by Kim. The model was defined by the tasks of national democracy, with the general purpose being "the outgrowing of the bounds of bourgeois democratic tasks"[132] along the following lines:

1 elimination or drastic reduction of foreign capital in all branches of the economy (which does not rule out, of course, equal economic relations with Western capitalist countries); considerable reduction of the sphere of activity of national (especially big) capital and establish-ment of government control over it; the setting up of a democratic state sector and its conversion into the leading economic formation; uniting small producers in town and county into cooperatives; social measures in favor of urban and rural working people;
2 establishment of democratic political institutions, including a van-guard national–patriotic party and a mass organization of working people; the securing of the direct participation of the masses to some or other extent in the solution of economic and political problems;
3 adoption of a foreign policy oriented towards and allied with the world socialist system.[133]

In a *Pravda* article of 20 June 1981, Kim stated the tasks of the "national–revolutionary democratic struggle" more succinctly:

1 elimination of the position of imperialist monopolies, local big bourgeoisie, and feudal lords;
2 state control of the commanding heights of the economy;
3 planned development of the productive forces;

4 encouragement of the cooperative movement in the countryside;
5 growth of the working people and peasants' role in managing society.

There were, apparently, different opinions over the first task, that is, over how thoroughly or rapidly capitalism was to be eliminated, the example of Soviet Russia's (NEP) period being recommended by some for emulation. The references to NEP were akin to various theorists' approval of at least temporary persistence of small-scale capitalism and even state capitalism. This tolerance was explained by the dangers inherent in precipitous socioeconomic reorganization and was explicitly defended by, for example, Primakov.[134] Primakov even went so far as to say that, so long as revolutionary democrats were in charge, it was not totally negative if they introduced various forms of state capitalism, for capitalism might be bad in comparison with socialism but not in relation to feudalism, from which these societies were emerging.[135] Brutents later added that the existence of capitalist forms did not contradict the anti-imperialist character of such societies.[136]

To the above list, agrarian reform was added by a number of experts such as Ul'ianovskii, Primakov, Kaufman, Brutents, and Starushenko, the last also adding the nationalization of primary resources; Kaufman, Ul'ianovskii, and Manchkha all added the creation of a national army (Manchkha added security forces).[137] While Starushenko, for example, listed all of the above as tasks of national democracy, and Brutents, Ul'ianovskii, and Solodovnikov listed them as part of the general democratic transformations undertaken by revolutionary democracy,[138] still others, such as Manchkha and Primakov, attributed them to revolutionary democracy's preparing of the ground for socialism.[139]

Did revolutionary democracy in fact prepare society for socialism? This question was increasingly raised in the 1970s. Just as the concept of revolutionary democracy had been introduced in the early 1960s to accommodate the phenomenon of countries with a socialist orientation without the benefit of communist leadership or communist parties, so in the 1970s the same concept was re-examined, presumably to account for the retreat of some of these same societies from the path of socialism and/or their anti-communist policies. It became increasingly clear that revolutionary democracy was not sufficient to ensure the progress of national democracy to scientific socialism. Criticism of revolutionary democracy came from many quarters and was interpreted by some as criticism of the whole notion of non-capitalist development.

AN APPRAISAL

It was predictable that the Fedoseev collection would contain criticism of revolutionary democracy, which it did on the grounds that it was eclectic

and inconsistent, because of the petty bourgeois nature of the revolutionary democrats themselves.[141] Surprisingly, however, Fedoseev went on to
concede the transitional value of revolutionary democracy, even allowing
that it might be a long process, subject to reversals, which nonetheless
might be increasingly influenced by scientific socialism despite the strong
influences of nationalism and Utopian socialism.[142] In terms of the debate
over the non-capitalist road of development, the significant point was
that even revolutionary democracy was no guarantee of an orientation
toward socialism, for even revolutionary democrats (and not just national
democrats) were subject to the ideas of a "third way."

Mirskii, in his inimical way, bluntly described revolutionary democrats as "leftist radical nationalists...which may or may not take the road
of socialism." He explained that, although they rejected capitalism, they
might "get stuck" rather than progress further to scientific socialism.
Manchkha admitted that many revolutionary democrats did not regard
socialism as an historically inevitable socioeconomic formation, but
merely as the most effective method for organizing society against
backwardness and dependency upon imperialism. As early as 1972,
Entin discussed the petty bourgeois nature of revolutionary democrats as manifest in their ideology, which usually rejected the idea
of the dictatorship of the proletariat, and in some cases the ideas of
scientific socialism altogether.[143] In his 1978 book, he spoke of the
"fierce struggle" among revolutionary democrats over ideology—even
as revolutionary democrats distinguished themselves from bourgeois
reformists.[144] Gavrilov claimed that some revolutionary democrats "lost
touch with the masses," falling back into reformism and nationalism
(as well as positive relations with the imperialist world), despite their
use of scientific socialist terminology (which was often accompanied
by anti-communist prejudices).[145] Kim, too, allowed that revolutionary
democracy was a varied ideology, with only some aspects of it or adherents to it approaching scientific socialism, exhibiting "serious ideological
and political weaknesses."[146] These may include even anti-communism,
denial of the revolutionary role of the proletariat in favor of the peasantry, religious and idealistic philosophies, "ethical socialism," "vulgar
sociologism," "anthropological philosophy," and other ideas connected
with the "third way."[147]

The most authoritative Ul'ianovskii, as we have seen, sometimes
employed the terms "national democracy" and "revolutionary democracy" interchangeably, so it was not always easy to determine his attitude
toward revolutionary democracy as such. Nonetheless, one could find
such statements as: "Revolutionary democracy can be a staunch ally of
the proletariat if it does not slide back to the positions of the national
bourgeoisie but breaks away from them."[148] In discussing the tasks
and problems facing revolutionary democracy, Ul'ianovskii appeared

to believe that revolutionary democracy, like national democracy, could go in any direction.[149] Yet, on at least one occasion, he stated that one could not speak of "real revolutionary democracy" if it were not developing in the direction of socialism, though even here he said that national democracy and its left wing, revolutionary democracy, could go either way.[150]

Brutents, on the other hand, devoted a great deal of attention to the problems with revolutionary democracy, clearly stating that revolutionary democracy did not guarantee development into scientific socialism.[151] He pointed out the inconsistencies in this form of society, inconsistencies that contradicted "the very social orientation of revolutionary democracy."[152] And he warned against assuming "that revolutionary democrats can evolve politically only in a progressive direction."[153]

Brutents explained the inconsistencies and negative features of some revolutionary democracies as the result of a number of factors: *objective factors* such as the complexity of the social and economic tasks, the level of development of the country, and the persistence of (mainly economic) dependence on the imperialist countries; *subjective factors* such as the socio-political heterogeneity of the revolutionary democrats themselves. The heterogeneous political nature of revolutionary democracy (even in the same country) was the result primarily of their class or social composition.[154]

Kim expanded on these factors to include the social origin of the revolutionary democracy, the social, political, historical, and ideological conditions in the country, and external influences which resulted from the outside struggle between two world systems.[155] However, he joined Ul'ianovskii in concluding that the differences between revolutionary democracies from one country to the next were a question of stages or maturity; that is, they were dependent upon "how far the national democratic revolution has progressed in every given country"—thus implying a positive overall direction of revolutionary democracy.[156]

Indeed, the critical appraisal outlined above was not apparently intended as blanket condemnation. Kim, for example, may have challenged such condemnation when he said:

> Despite the historically conditioned limitations of the revolutionary democracy, it would be wrong theoretically and short-sighted politically not to see the positive role of revolutionary democracy.... There is no doubt that, basically, the social function of revolutionary democracy is profoundly progressive.[157]

Kaufman argued that the "non-socialist character of revolutionary democracy does not mean it lacks progressive elements."[158] More important, perhaps, were Ul'ianovskii's and Brutents' conclusions. Ul'ianovskii, who generally refrained from adopting a particularly critical approach to revolutionary democracy to begin with, said: "national or revolutionary democracy is a promising revolutionary trend...distinguished by intransigence towards modern capitalism and assimilating many elements of scientific socialism."[159] Again without specifying revolutionary democracy, Ul'ianovskii argued:

> To give up the non-capitalist alternative just because in its practical expression it differs from the outstanding examples of the already accomplished social revolutions means a refusal consciously to take advantage of those objective laws of the development of capitalism which tend to expedite its own doom, and above all refusal to use the law of the uneven economic and political development of countries at the present stage of the general crisis of capitalism....[160] It is impossible to say where a major breakthrough to socialism will take place.[161]

Brutents was on the same side of the debate even as he called for a realistic appraisal of the limitations of revolutionary democracy. Thus, he asserted:

> The fact that the anti-imperialist position of revolutionary democracy is not a position identical to that of the Communists, as well as the fact that socialism and the movement toward it are in much conceived differently by them, is not, at the present stage, of overriding importance.[162]

Brutents devoted many pages to his thesis that, despite its shortcomings, revolutionary democracy was capable of paving the way for scientific socialism as well as objectively serving this purpose as a stage on the road to socialism.[163] He cited Lenin to the effect that one might arrive "at profound socialist convictions 'not through Marxism, not starting with the idea of the class struggle of the proletariat.'"[164] Thus, revolutionary democrats used socialist formulations because of their revolutionary experiences, not because of their "mastering of the theory of scientific socialism." Brutents defended this, however, because of the overall direction and implications, explaining that "the capacity for progressive evolution is one of the most important features of revolutionary democracy, a feature that determines its historical prospects."[165]

There were those who accounted for the negative phenomena in revolutionary democracy—or the reversals—by differentiating between types of revolutionary democracy itself. For example, Anatolii Gromyko, head of the Africa Institute, acknowledged that revolutionary democracy was a form of government which paved the way for socialism; but he specified that it was the "advanced sections" of the revolutionary democracies that "often" (i.e., not always) "go over to scientific social-ism."[166] These "advanced sections" were more often called the left wing, revolutionary democracy being divided into left and right wings. This formulation could be found in works by Kim, Gavrilov, Kiva, and Kaufman. According to Kiva, the left wing of revolutionary democracy was closer to Marxism than to right-wing revolutionary democracy, while Gavrilov actually claimed that the left wing sought creation of a people's democracy.[167] For Kiva, right-wing revolutionary democracy was in fact no more than bourgeois democracy.[168]

Kim and Kaufman claimed that the existence of both wings accounted for the simultaneous presence of both scientific socialism *and* "petty bourgeois prejudices" such as nationalism and anti-communism in revolutionary democracy.[169] Africanist Nikolai Kosukhin also spoke of left-wing, progressive revolutionary democrats as that part of revolu-tionary democracy which adapted Marxist–Leninist scientific socialism, subdividing them into those who accepted this ideology prior to the achievement of independence, those who became Marxists as a result of the liberation struggle experience, and those who adopted the ideology after independence—the "second generation of revolutionaries," who tended openly to identify themselves as communists.[170] Kaufman, for his part, added to right– and left-wing types of revolutionary democracy a third type, which he called a "vacillating center."[171] Brutents, in his 1979 book, elaborated on this new differentiation, claiming that the centrist trend was in fact predominant in the new states, but that for all its vacillation it still retained its "progressive potential."[172]

As with nationalism and national democracy, however, these efforts at differentiation came not so much as criticism of the concept of revo-lutionary democracy, but rather as an effort to avoid oversimplification which might result in outright rejection of the concept, including its broader theoretical framework: the non-capitalist path of development. Thus, virtually every theoretician who supported this model argued that it was—and would be—a mistake simply to identify revolutionary democracy with scientific socialism. Many of them argued that it would be a mistake to try to push this form of society too far, too fast. Ul'ianovskii, for example, warned against overtaking revolutionary democracy "from the left," arguing that this form had not yet fully ripened (i.e., that it had not finished its tasks as a transitional society creating the pre-conditions for socialism).[173]

As we have already seen, the thrust of the argument was that, by expecting too much of revolutionary democracy, there was the danger that its failure to live up to these expectations (the temporary lapses, the absence of genuine socialism, the appearance of such phenomena as nationalism, religious philosophies, and the like) would lead to the opposite conclusion: that revolutionary democracy or the whole non-capitalist path was purely bourgeois in content and direction.

The Socialist Potential—The Simoniia Challenge

The above position lay at the core of a controversy over the very nature of the national liberation revolution itself: was it just another, bourgeois, democratic revolution, or was it "special," different and, therefore, possessing the potential for developing into socialism?

A catalyst for debate on this issue was N. A. Simoniia's book *Strany Vostoka: puti razvitiia* (Countries of the East: Roads of Development), which appeared in 1975.[174] Simoniia departed from the usual approach of Soviet theoreticians on the Third World in that he attempted to employ a strict but also innovative Marxist analysis of the national liberation struggle, employing comparisons with revolutions in Europe, including the Bolshevik revolution, beyond the relatively superficial references usually employed. Delving into texts by Marx, Engels, and Lenin, he compared the national liberation movements with bourgeois revolutions such as the one in Russia in 1905, denying them any special character. Moreover, in so doing he claimed that Lenin's theory of the development of bourgeois revolutions into socialist ones was intended only for the post-1917 Russian reality in which a revolutionary government was already in power.[175] Lenin, he claimed, did not see the 1905 revolution—which was comparable to the national liberation revolution—in the same way; it was a purely bourgeois revolution, which, despite large proletarian participation, was destined to remain bourgeois, incapable of being developed into a socialist revolution. Thus, the Third World national liberation revolution also was not to be expected to "grow up" into a socialist revolution.

There were many other points raised by Simoniia which provoked the ire of the ideological purists; debate ensued on the pages of *Voprosy istorii KPSS* and other journals, and a formal discussion was organized in which people from the Party's Ideological Department (mainly the Institute of Marxism–Leninism) criticized Simoniia for entering an area he failed to understand.[176] These critics may not have been concerned so much with the substance of Simoniia's theory vis-à-vis the Third World. (His conclusions were not in fact far from some of their own.) Rather, they objected to his intrusion into their own field of Marxist–Leninist revolutionary doctrine proper, as well as to his analyses of the Bolshevik Revolution, particularly his characterization of the Bolshevik Revolution as a special case.[177] Of importance for our discussion, however, was the criticism levied by Ul'ianovskii, for whom the conclusions regarding Third World states were crucial—and unacceptable.[178] Simoniia had argued that, inasmuch as Lenin did not apply the idea of the transformation of a bourgeois revolution into a socialist one to the 1905 revolution (because the economic base had not been sufficiently developed), he had urged his party not to support it. Ul'ianovskii argued that Simoniia was misquoting and misunderstanding Lenin, who, he said, *did* believe the 1905 revolution could grow into a socialist one and merely warned against expecting it to implement a maximalist (socialist) program. On this point, it was of less importance to Ul'ianovskii if the national liberation movements were considered bourgeois or not; what was at stake was the concept of the potential of such a revolution to develop into socialism.

Connected with this was Simoniia's discussion of political, as distinct from social, revolution. He made the point that what happened in the Third World was political revolution, that is, revolution in the superstructure only; for, so long as the economic base had not matured sufficiently, there could be no coincident social revolution.[179] Inasmuch as the ripened conditions were missing, the national liberation revolution was a change of a political but not social nature; in other words, it would not produce socialism. Furthermore, as already argued, it was more akin to the classical bourgeois revolutions, necessitating, later, a purely socialist revolution (and in the interim, the continued use rather than elimination of pre-socialist economic institutions such as the NEP).

On this point Simoniia employed the analogy of the 1917 Russian revolution, likening the level of development in Russia to that of the Third World (generalizing the theory of the "weak link"), claiming that, as in Russia, even for the Bolsheviks, a transition period had been necessary to complete the tasks of the bourgeois social revolution (the ripening of conditions, i.e., development of the production base including NEP) before going on to socialist construction.[180] In the case of Russia, as we noted, a new political revolution had not been necessary, as by implication it would be in the Third World, because the revolutionary forces had already come to power there and were carrying out the unfinished tasks of the bourgeois social revolution.

Ul'ianovskii argued that this view misinterpreted the theory of ripened conditions and that revolution did more than "release" the potential for socialism: it radically changed the production base itself. In other words, he argued that the political revolution could subsequently change the economic base and bring about the eventual transformation to socialism without the need for a "new" revolution or an inordinately long transition period. He accused Simoniia of rejecting Lenin's theory of the possibility of developing countries to skip the stage of capitalism, and of rejecting the whole idea of the non-capitalist path for the Third World. Thus, the image of the future society advanced by theoreticians such as Ul'ianovskii was also called into question. The national–revolutionary democracy produced by the national liberation revolution was no more than bourgeois democracy, with (according to Simoniia) more potential for developing into capitalism than anything else; the "socialist orientation" of these countries was no more than a "running ahead of itself" of the basically bourgeois revolution, thus explaining what subsequently appeared to be lapses or retreats. According to Ul'ianovskii, if this were the case, the socialist orientation could not be considered "serious."[181]

It is not certain that it was Simoniia's intention to discredit the socialist-oriented non-capitalist path altogether. As admitted by critics and supporters alike, Simoniia had intended his arguments as a weapon against "left opportunism," that is, those who sought to go too fast in the Third World, presumably those who demanded a genuine socialism even at the present stage of the societies of the Third World states, when conditions were not yet ripe. Generally less optimistic than other theoreticians, he was apparently arguing against any idea of precipitously trying to convert these regimes to scientific socialism. This might explain the fact that he was supported by his academic colleagues, who clearly did advocate the idea of the non-capitalist path (national–revolutionary democracy), and by the people associated with the concrete problems of Third World countries.[182] On the other hand, others besides Ul'ianovskii, specifically party people of the less flexible, more "purist," tendency (from the Ideological Department, for example), *criticized* Simoniia, not just for seeing the Bolshevik Revolution as a special case, but also for failing to see the "principally new character" of the national liberation revolutions in their proximity to proletarian revolutions.[183]

A New Definition of Revolutionary Democracy

Much of the debate over Simoniia was esoteric, digressing a good deal into exegesis on the nature of the Bolshevik Revolution and the exact meaning of this or that statement of Lenin with regard to Russia. The issues raised in the debate with regard to the national liberation movements were stated more directly and clearly in an article that appeared in *Aziia i Afrika segodnia* in 1978, by Semen Agaev of the Institute of the International Workers Movement and Inna Tatarovskaia.[184] Agaev had supported Simoniia in the 1978 debate, criticizing him only for underestimating the socialist potential of the non-capitalist path.

In their article, Agaev and Tatarovskaia described the two sides in the debate as (1) those who saw the national liberation revolution, that is, national democracy, as objectively bourgeois and remaining so, and (2) those who saw national democracy as that system which introduced radical transformations all the way up to the stage of socialism, thereby distinguishing it from past bourgeois democratic revolutions. Their schema for explaining and perhaps bridging the two schools of thought was based on the premise that "national liberation revolution," as a concept, should not be confused with "national democratic revolution." Those who did so tended to use the term "national liberation revolution" to cover the whole process right up to the building of socialism, dividing it into one stage of political independence (the struggle for national independence or statehood) and a second stage of economic independence (the post-statehood struggle against neo-colonialism). For those who used it in this way, the term "national democratic revolution" merely signified a particular pattern of a general democratic revolution as applied in Asia and Africa, or simply interchangeably with "national liberation movements." The authors called for a three-stage approach:

Stage 1: national liberation struggle (eliminating colonial oppression, winning independence, setting up national state);

Stage 2: national democratic revolution;
         Phase 1: general, democratic transformation;
         Phase 2: radical socialist change or the development of social-
                   ist transformation;

Stage 3: socialist revolution (building of socialism).

In this schema, the national democratic revolution was an independent stage, for states with a socialist orientation; it was an intermediate stage between the national liberation revolution proper and the socialist revolution. Where revolutionary democrats led the national liberation struggle, some would argue, stage 1 itself had a national democratic character. On the whole, however, (according to the authors) all tended to agree that stage 1 was dominated by the national factor, uniting all classes and interests. Implicitly referring to Simoniia's distinctions, stage 1 was classified a "political revolution" as distinct from stage 2 which was, presumably, the social revolution.

   This schema solved the problem of the contending schools of thought for the following reasons. Those who "extended the national liberation revolution" through stage 2, right up to the stage of socialist change, including the radical social transformation, obviously saw this whole non-capitalist path as different from bourgeois democracy, leading to socialism. This "extended" interpretation of the national liberation revolution did not mean that the national liberation revolution *proper*, the chief aspect of which was in fact the nation, was of a special non-bourgeois nature. Indeed, it was usually argued that what made this revolution "special" was the fact that (in its extended interpretation to include what should be stage 2) the tasks of the revolution were undertaken and solved by a democratic power representing the broad working masses. But, according to the authors (and siding with Simoniia), Lenin had not seen the proletarian participation in the revolution of 1905 as sufficient reason to consider its content anything but bourgeois–democratic. Even the people's democratic revolutions of post-World War II (presumably in Eastern Europe), under the leadership of the proletariat, were in essence only bourgeois–democratic regarding the content of the tasks they had to resolve.

Limiting the national liberation revolution to the tasks of achieving statehood, and seeing national democracy as a subsequent separate stage, solved the problem, according to Agaev and Tatarovskaia. Thus, stage 1 did *not* exceed the limites of a bourgeois revolution (even when non-bourgeois elements played a leading role). The question was how to proceed to stage 2. If the bourgeoisie or even the petty bourgeoisie led stage 1 there might *not* be any shift to stage 2, national democracy, but rather a lapse into reformism. As we have already seen, the petty bourgeoisie could go in either direction, so it might be necessary for a new revolutionary democratic power to take over and make the shift. Not only leadership but also the situation in the world, as we shall see below, might influence the progress (or lack of it) into stage 2.

Stage 2 itself was apparently, by definition, not only "national" democracy but also "revolutionary" democracy, for two reasons: (1) it continued the revolution beyond stage 1, and (2) its basically socioeconomic tasks were anti-capitalist because of the national, anti-imperialist struggle against the persistence of pre-independence economic structures and international ties. Thus, the tasks of stage 2, that is, of national revolutionary democracy, were (a) to set up a public sector, (b) to weaken and eliminate feudal prejudices, and (c) to undermine the positions of big capital. This was not sufficient, however, for the building of socialism (stage 3); for in stage 2 there was often a preservation of capital production relations even in the public sector, and the public sector itself could go either socialist or state capitalist.

Thus, the tasks outlined above were delineated for stage 2, phase 1, while stage 2, phase 2, was necessary for the development into socialism, that is, for radical social transformations. These were described as the elimination of capitalist property, the development of the public sector and its conversion into the basis for a socialist structure, land reform, the encouragement of collectivization, the consolidation of the positions of the working class in public life, cohesion of the vanguard forces, and ties with the socialist world.

According to Agaev and Tatarovskaia, not all revolutionary democracies entered or implemented stage 2, phase 2. Rather, the revolutionary potential of each revolutionary democratic leadership determined passage. Only "left-wing" revolutionary democrats entered phase 2, paving the way for later transition to stage 3. "Right-wing" revolutionary democrats, on the other hand, lost their "revolutionariness" in stage 2, phase 1, lapsed into reformism, and thus drew a halt to the progress toward socialism. The key factors that enabled the left-wing revolutionary democrats to implement phase 2 were the cohesion of the vanguard forces into a vanguard revolutionary democratic party, based on scientific socialism and the drawing closer to the socialist world. It was the move into phase 2 that changed national democracy from "petty bourgeois democracy" to "proletarian revolutionary democracy." The ideology of the former, in phase 1, was "national socialism," while the ideology of the latter, in phase 2, was Marxism–Leninism.

One may deduce from this article the vision of the future society as national (revolutionary) democracy which went beyond the general democratic changes of phase 1. For, regardless of its socialist orientation, national democracy which remained at phase 1 did not create the prerequisites for socialism. Only the conscious addition of new content to the general democratic changes of phase 1 would make the process irreversible and eliminate the bourgeois aspects of the national liberation revolution altogether.

Brutents, too, had argued that this addition of new content to the general democratic changes accounted at least in part for the difference between this and a purely bourgeois revolution.[185] Manchkha, in his 1979 book, also adhered to the three-stage schema offered by Agaev and Tatarovskaia, as had Entin in his book of 1978.[186] Both Kim and Primakov, however, appeared to translate this schema into a new typology, distinguishing between a "national–revolutionary" model and a "revolutionary democratic" model, roughly corresponding to stage 2, phases 1 and 2, respectively, of the Agaev–Tatarovskaia schema.[187] The major differences between the two models, according to both Kim and Primakov, lay in the class and ideological nature of the leadership. National revolutionary states were led by nationalist parties espousing socialism, including anti-imperialism, anti-feudalism, and anti-capitalism. Revolutionary democracies were led by vanguard working people's parties espousing scientific socialism. In a slightly later article, Kim retreated from this typology somewhat, returning to the old conceptualization which had the national–revolutionary and revolutionary democratic models in one all-inclusive category, with only a sub-category ("special place") for those states guided by Marxism–Leninism and vanguard parties.[188]

This new definition of revolutionary democracy (or Kim's subcategory and Agaev and Tatarovskaia's stage 2, phase 2 of national democracy led by revolutionary democrats, otherwise called by them "proletarian revolutionary democracy") could be said to be actually creating the foundations for socialism. But now still another stage or model appeared—that of people's democracy. Primakov, Kim, and, in at least one article, Simoniia all claimed that the new type of revolutionary democracy approached people's democracy, which even in classical Soviet literature was that form of government which completed the tasks of the democratic revolution while laying the foundations for socialism, under the leadership of the working class.[189] The distinction between Kim and Primakov's revolutionary democracy and their category of people's democracy was not, however, clear. This lack of clarity probably accounted for the fact that the same states were placed in various categories by different theorists: Kim, for example, placed Angola and Ethiopia in his new revolutionary democratic category, while Gavrilov and Starushenko called them people's democracies; Kim, Starushenko, and Mirskii described both Angola and Mozambique as states led by Marxist–Leninist parties, while Anatolii Gromyko explicitly denied them this status; Simoniia had Angola, South Yemen, Ethiopia, and Mozambique developing from revolutionary democracy into people's democracies.[190] Perhaps by way of explanation, Gavrilov appeared to see Third World people's democracies in a somewhat different way from the classical concept: he placed them in the overall category of national democracies, with the same tasks as those already outlined for such national democracies. The only distinctive feature, then, would be the composition of the leadership. Using the very same distinction, Starushenko reduced the categories to two models of socialist orientation: national democratic and people's democracy.[191]

The discussion of people's democracies did not significantly alter the general concepts of national and revolutionary democracy, however. It was more an effort to define the place not of countries that had lapsed (which had prompted the re-examination of revolution democracy), but of those countries that had gone a step further in declaring their loyalty to Marxism–Leninism and to the Soviet Union. Whether the model was called revolutionary democracy or proletarian revolutionary democracy, or even people's democracy, the major feature was the laying of the foundations of socialism. And the one common factor said to account for their move toward socialism was the existence of a Marxist–Leninist vanguard party.

The Vanguard Party Controversy

The issue of the creation of such a party, as we saw in the previous chapter, was also controversial inasmuch as it reflected the traditional Lenin–Roy dispute over bourgeois national versus proletarian leadership, national liberation versus the non-capitalist path. The debate of the 1960s had to a large degree been typified by the party orientation versus the

revolutionary democratic orientation. The 1970s debate revived this
issue. It was not a question of whether or not a party should be created
in the new states. Revolutionary democracy by definition had a party,
often a one-party, system, but this party was not the communist party.
Indeed, some were still mass parties, while some were vanguard parties.
The issue appeared to be over the class composition and ideology of
the party: was this a vanguard party, a Marxist–Leninist party, even a
communist party, or a proletarian party?

At a 1980 Berlin conference on the Third World, CPSU International
Department chief Ponomarev listed the creation of a "revolutionary
vanguard party founded on scientific socialism" as the first requirement
for progress in the new state.[192] As might be expected, the journal
Voprosy istorii KPSS picked up this theme in an article which stressed
the need for communist leadership of any leftist or revolutionary
democratic bloc of forces, and in another article which emphasized the
necessity of the leading role of the working class and the dictatorship
of the proletariat.[193] This was echoed later by a 1982 Lenin anniversary
editorial in the English version of *Aziia i Afrika segodnia*, which specified
among the tasks of the national liberation movement the creation of a
vanguard party based ideologically on scientific socialism.[194] Mirskii and
Latin Americanist Maidanik joined this call in a *MEMO* article which
derided revolutionary democracies that "got stuck" at something like
state capitalism because of the failure to create a vanguard party based
on scientific socialism.[195]

Foreign communists appeared to follow suit, as evidenced by an article
in the *World Marxist Review* by a leading official of the Yemen Socialist
party, expounding the necessity of the formation of a working-class
party for the advance of the national democratic revolution toward
socialism.[196] Yet this was by no means the line of that journal, even
in its accounts of the same conference addressed by Ponomarev.[197]
Indeed, most other comments by Third World communists maintained
the national front line of cooperation with non-communists, as had
been specifically stated, for example, by the Lebanese Communist party
general secretary in 1979 and by the document adopted and published
by a meeting of African communist parties in late 1978.[198]

Soviet literature on the Third World in the late 1970s and early 1980s
was in fact permeated with references to the need to create a vanguard
party. Yet, as we have seen, a closer look at the analyses presented
reveals a general hesitancy or reluctance to make this a demand for
Marxist–Leninist or communist party dominance. While the general
desirability, and indeed necessity, for a Marxist–Leninist party in order
to bring a society fully along to scientific socialism was acknowledged,
the timeliness or applicability of such a demand for the Third World
was questioned and even rejected by some.

A vanguard party, which was indeed necessary for there to be progressive development, was not always seen as synonymous with a Marxist–Leninist party. Primakov explained that revolutionary democracy did not mean that the proletariat or communists were at the helm, but they were preparing the ground for scientific socialism.[199] He saw it as a matter of stages, the first stage being a society led by "national revolutionary elements," the second by "vanguard revolutionary parties" moving in the direction of people's democracy, "many" (i.e., not all) with Marxist–Leninist ideology.[200] Warning against going too fast and against leftist "adventurism" in efforts at social as well as economic change prior to the ripening of the necessary conditions, Primakov explained that it was still necessary for local Marxists to cooperate with the revolutionary democrats. He nonetheless concluded that a vanguard party based on Marxist–Leninist ideology was the only solution for the transition to socialism, but the implication and thrust of his arguments were that this was still a premature demand.[201]

Kosukhin also urged an approach by stages, from a mass party at the stage of the liberation struggle to a revolutionary democratic party at the next stage, based not on national but on social class organizational principles, to a vanguard party at the third stage—possibly but not always based on Marxism–Leninism, inasmuch as revolutionary democrats held varying views on the nature of the vanguard party.[202] Moreover, Kosukhin, like Primakov, warned against sectarianism and going too fast, that is, beyond the potential of objective and subjective conditions among the masses.

Thus, while the necessity of creating a vanguard party, approaching if not actually espousing Marxism–Leninism, was advocated, here too there seemed to be some reservations on the issue. As Kosukhin put it:

> The process of establishing ruling parties with scientific socialist ideologies in countries of non-capitalist development, parties which mirror the new stage of ideological and political evolution of the revolutionary democrats, and their transition to the positions of the working class as well as the assimilation of Marxist–Leninist theory is *highly complicated and contradictory*...the dissemination of scientific socialism meets with strong resistance from traditional communal and nationalistic views. The overcoming of archaic prejudices is *painstaking and delicate work which can take only a long period of time, and any attempts to accelerate this process artificially are fraught with negative consequences.*[203]

Starushenko expressed the same reservations when he warned that "far from all countries are ripe for building states of the latter [people's democracy] type" and therefore recommended that one should limit efforts to strengthening the existing national democratic states.[204] The answer to these hesitations, at least regarding the subjective conditions, was, according to Primakov, Kosukhin, and Kaufman, vigorous ideological and propaganda activity among the masses, as indeed was outlined by Ponomarev in 1980 in Berlin.[205] Petr Shastitko of the Oriental Institute called this a "cultural revolution," and Anatolii Gromyko listed it as one of the matters for Soviet Africanists to add to their research.[206]

The Africanist Entin, who assiduously outlined the tasks of a vanguard revolutionary democratic party, ignored any reference to a Marxist-Leninist or proletariat character, despite the fact that the role he outlined bore a striking resemblance to the classical role allotted the communist party in the Soviet Union or Eastern Europe.[207] Kiva was much more precise when he described not only the idea of stages for the emergence of the various types of parties, but also the idea of an abundance of models or types of parties even at the same stage. Having described the different types (and the problems involved), including the "new type" of revolutionary democratic party based on scientific socialism, Kiva asserted that "the crux of the matter lies not so much in the parties as in the nature of the revolutionary process itself."[208] He went on to distinguish between "a vanguard revolutionary–democratic party" and "a party of the proletarian vanguard." The former, which was basically the "new type" described as emerging in some African countries, was still not a truly Marxist–Leninist proletarian party, despite the similarities. The differences lay both in the full understanding of Marxism–Leninism and in the class composition. The important point was that this transformation was still only a gradual process, determined primarily by local conditions and developments. Moreover, even the creation of the lower "new type," or vanguard revolutionary democratic, party could only be the result of a gradual, apparently long, process.[209]

This general skepticism over the authenticity of the new supposedly Marxist–Leninist parties in Africa was apparently the expression of opposition to the demand for the transformation of the revolutionary parties into Marxist–Leninist, communist parties. Thus, as we saw in the discussion of organization, both Simoniia and Shastitko quoted Lenin's warning to the Mongolians in 1921 against the creation of a Marxist–Leninist party.[210] In a later article, Shastitko specified that only a unified vanguard party could carry through the revolution to fulfillment; but, noting the absence of communist parties in the less developed world, he urged the long-term policy of the united front or class blocs to bring about the transformation of society.[211]

As we have seen, Kim distinguished between the advanced type of revolutionary democracy and people's democracy, on the one hand, and simply national revolutionary regimes, on the basis of the leadership by a Marxist–Leninist party guided by scientific socialism. The transformation of the revolutionary democratic vanguard party into a vanguard Marxist–Leninist party was linked to the emergence of a large, organized proletariat.[212] Yet Kim did little more than note, favorably, this development. For the most part, he advocated cooperation with the revolutionary democratic parties rather than attempts to supplant them, expressing relative optimism as to their eventual ideological evolution.[213]

Anatolii Gromyko was not even willing to go as far as Kim, for in 1979 he explicitly rejected the idea that virtually any state in Africa was ruled by a Marxist–Leninist party.[214] While espousing the ultimate desirability of such leadership, he saw it as something to be achieved— or capable of being achieved—only gradually, over the very long run. Thus, like his predecessor Solodovnikov, he too quoted Lenin's 1921 warning to the Mongolians about *gradual* transformation of the revolutionary democratic party into a Marxist party.[215] And later, in 1981, he was willing to speak only of "the aspirations" of some revolutionary democratic parties to arm themselves with Marxism–Leninism.[216]

Gromyko's position would appear to have been in line with that of Manchkha. Manchkha stated (quoting Brezhnev) that a Marxist–Leninist party was absolutely necessary for the realization of scientific socialism. But, he added, it would be incorrect in the countries of Africa, the peoples of which had chosen the socialist orientation, "already now to raise the question of the necessity of immediate creation of a party of the working class, i.e., a Marxist–Leninist party."[217] Gavrilov, too, implied this when he said that such parties "undoubtedly *make it easier* for the revolutionary democrats to pursue a progressive course and ensure closer links between the tasks of the national democratic revolution and those of social liberation," but warned that the economic, social, and cultural level of African states was "extremely low."[218]

Brutents, for all his attention to revolutionary democracy and its weaknesses, did not appear to advocate an attempt to convert these parties to pure Marxism–Leninism or subordinate them to communist domination. Rather, he urged continued communist cooperation with the revolutionary democratic parties (even to the point of subordinating themselves or merging with the revolutionary democratic party).[219] In fact, Brutents's two-volume study, admittedly published early— in 1974—but revised and issued in English in 1977, almost totally ignored the whole idea of a vanguard party and the role of a party in correcting the errors of the revolutionary democracies or leading them onward. This same non-party approach was evident in a long *Pravda* article published by Brutents in 1978, which made no reference whatsoever to a vanguard, much less a Marxist–Leninist party.[220] In his 1979 book, Brutents spoke of the importance of—indeed, the urgent need for— a vanguard party (noting its absence as a cause of Egypt's retreat) to ensure the development of socialism, and he noted the creation of Marxist–Leninist vanguard parties in such countries as Angola and South Yemen. Yet he did not list either party as a feature of a socialist-oriented state. Rather, he warned against going too fast and *against* trying to substitute Marxism–Leninism or a communist party for the basically nationalist goals of the revolutionary democratic parties.[221] On the whole, Brutents gave very little attention to the issue.

Ul'ianovskii too, in his major volume of 1976 (revised and translated in 1978) had almost nothing to say about the need for a party, merely listing the creation of a "progressive party" as one of the tasks of national democracy.[222] Instead, he emphasized united front alliances and cooperation with the revolutionary democrats,[223] explaining that: "Communist parties in Asian and African countries have not set themselves the task of winning power immediately, and at whatever cost. If adopted, this course, which is inconsonant with the actual state of affairs, could split the national front, isolate the Communists from the masses, and result in the adoption of putschist tactics amplified by opportunistic aspirations..."[224] Thus, he warned that communists should not attempt to "overtake" revolutionary democracy "from the left."[225] Ul'ianovskii had said, in the foreword to a book by I. Andreev in 1974 (translated and revised in 1977), that the socialist stage of the national liberation revolution could only occur with a proletarian Marxist–Leninist leadership; but even then, without specifically mentioning a party, he said that this stage had yet to be reached in the socialist-oriented countries.[226] Here and elsewhere, Ul'ianovskii specified the existence of such a party as the distinguishing feature of socialist revolutions,[227] but on other occasions he failed to make any reference to a party in connections with revolutionary democracy and its development.[228]

In his 1979 book Ul'ianovskii gave the subject greater attention, but, again, it was basically to warn against going too fast, against establishing such a party before there was a "social, political or ideological basis for it."[229] Here as well as later, in 1984, he was highly skeptical if not downright contemptuous as to the genuinely Marxist–Leninist nature of the parties claiming to be Marxist–Leninist vanguard parties in Africa.[230] As he said in a *Kommunist* article in 1979:

> The creation of a truly vanguard party gravitating towards Marxism–Leninism and working under the conditions of a post-colonial yet still extremely socioeconomically backward society, *is an exceptionally complex process*. It cannot be reduced to the approval and proclamation of a program for scientific socialism...it is considerably more difficult to truly master scientific socialism at all party levels, make it the base of party practical activities and acquire an awareness of the social, ideological–political, and organizational structure of the vanguard

party in accordance with the task of directing the majority of the people in a socialist direction.[231]

The official conclusions of the CPSU leadership with regard to this issue and the whole debate over the potential of the non-capitalist path or model were outlined in Brezhnev's report to the twenty-sixth CPSU Congress in February 1981, and amplified somewhat by Zagladin in *MEMO*.[232] Devoting extremely little attention to the theoretical issue, Brezhnev spoke of two categories only: the revolutionary democracies or states with a socialist orientation and states which chose the capitalist, pro-imperialist, path. The characteristics of the former were those of relatively minimalistic demands of the type the theoreticians allotted to the early stages of national democracy: gradual elimination of the positions of imperialist monopolies, the local big bourgeoisie, and the feudal elements, and restriction of foreign capital; the securing by the state of the commanding heights in the economy; progress to planned development of the production forces; encouragement of the cooperative movement in the countryside; enhancement of the role of the working masses in society and the gradual reinforcement of the state apparatus with "national personnel, faithful to the people"; adoption of anti-imperialist foreign policy; and, lastly, strengthening of the "revolutionary parties expressing the interests of the broad masses of the working people."[233]

Thus, though Brezhnev made references to a party, he did not mention the idea of a Marxist–Leninist or even a vanguard party. Nor did he make any distinction between countries at various stages of national or revolutionary democracy—Angola, Ethiopia, Mozambique, and Syria were indistinguishable from each other, and there was no reference to "people's democracies."

Zagladin corrected this slightly by mentioning the "recent appearance" of a group of countries which were "continuing the formation of vanguard revolutionary parties recognizing Marxism–Leninism and proletarian internationalism as their basis." Zagladin was careful, however, to explain that "what is meant here is not the creation in these countries, today, of the material–technical base of socialism and, even more, of its social structure. Simply, social changes have taken on a greater scale."[234]

Thus, the more modest, realistic appraisal of the ideological content of the national liberation movements, even with regard to the image of the societies they could produce, remained the official line. The tasks to be added to the efforts of Soviet Africanists in 1981 did include the whole issue of the Marxist–Leninist tendencies of some vanguard parties and the importance of the dissemination of Marxist–Leninist ideology. These tasks were immediately qualified, however, by an emphasis on national, ethnic, and other influences in the Third World; and all, in dividing the political sphere, appeared to take second place to the study of the economic and production spheres as the key component of the society of non-capitalist socialist orientation.[235]

Andropov, however, on at least one occasion prior to his succession to Brezhnev, took a very different and clear position. In his 1982 Lenin Day speech, he called for the creation of a "fundamentally new Leninist-type" party, a communist party.[236] Arguing that such a party was essential if a country were not to "remain in the system of capitalism," he said that only such a party could "win the recognition of the masses for its role in the vanguard and lead the working people to socialism." Yet once in power, Andropov made no direct reference to this issue. Rather, at the June 1983 Central Committee plenum, he virtually quoted Ul'ianovskii (who may have provided the text) when he said: "It is one thing to proclaim socialism as a goal and another to build it.[237]

Gorbachev made no references to this issue in any of his public pronouncements during the first year of his power. The draft CPSU program published in October 1985 and approved by the twenty-seventh Congress in February 1986 did, however, accord first priority to relations with revolutionary democratic parties "striving to build their activity on the basis of scientific socialism."[238] While this indicated a clear preference, the program went on to favor ties with "all national progressive parties occupying anti-imperialist and patriotic stands." Moreover, this same program sanctioned cooperation with new states following the capitalist path, suggesting that, despite Soviet preferences, the more demanding position regarding the component features of the ideologies' future society had not returned.

Objectives: Self-determination

One may deduce from the image of the future society advocated in Moscow's approach to the ideologies of the national liberation movements that the objective posited by these ideologies should be to rid oneself of imperialist as well as local feudalist rule. The political objective could be defined as independence from the colonialists, the socioeconomic objective as independence from feudal and nascent capitalist exploitation, the socioeconomic being integrally linked with the political sphere. In either, or both, cases the overall objective might be called independence. In fact, however, independence was probably a concept too strictly or clearly defined—the implication being independent statehood. The term preferred by the Soviets as an overall, all-inclusive type of objective was self-determination. Indeed, the term "self-determination" is probably more functional generally when describing the ideological objectives of national liberation movements, for it permits inclusion of movements that sought no more than autonomy, or solutions less than those of fully independent statehood.

A basic issue connected with self-determination was that of the *subject* of self-determination, as we have seen in the discussion of the origins of national liberation movements. Of greater relevance for the ideological question, that is, the question of the objectives posited by the ideology, was the actual definition of self-determination advocated by the Soviet Union, and the various forms this might take. A book published in the 1960s by the Soviet legal authority on the subject, Gleb Starushenko, offered a comprehensive definition of self-determination:

> the principle of self-determination of peoples and nations means the right of every people and every nation to decide all questions concerning its relations with other peoples and nations up to and including secession and formation of independent states, as well as all questions concerning the internal system without interference from other states.[239]

Internally this meant, specifically, the right to decide one's own political and social system, to dispose freely of one's natural resources and manage the economy, and to "decide all other domestic issues concerning culture, religion, etc."[241] Later definitions did not vary significantly from this. Starushenko himself, writing nearly twenty years later with Africa Institute chief Gromyko, merely added some details when he summed up self-determination as the right independently to solve one's own destiny, including the "internal aspects of self-determination: the right of peoples and nations to freely dispose of their natural riches, the right to an independent solution of all questions of internal organization, including also the questions of the social system, and, finally, the right to a choice of the path of development," as well as the right to determine "their internal and foreign political status...to carry out according to their wishes their political, economic, social and cultural development."[240]

The definition of self-determination was closely associated with the concept of "national sovereignty." For example, writing in the 1960s, Starushenko saw self-determination as a form of expression of national sovereignty, defining the latter as "the expression of the over-all interests of the masses of a given national group or nation."[242] Among these interests, he placed the right to self-determination as well as the right to international protection against genocide and the right to defense by international law in case of hostilities. Some years later, two other legal experts added to this a nation's right to choose its social and political system and its right to territorial integrity, economic independence, respect for culture, honor, and dignity as well as equal rights with other nations and peoples.[243] These additions were basically just a spelling out of the right of self-determination, which was itself seen as part of the concept of national sovereignty.

Another Soviet legal expert, V. S. Shevtsov, defined national sovereignty as "a nation or nationality's independence in the political, territorial, cultural and linguistic fields...determined and ensured by socio-economic measures and the political and state system of a given society."[244] What was meant here was that nations were not inherently sovereign. Sovereignty implied national freedom and equality, as well as self-determination, and these were integrally linked with political democracy, which itself was based, ultimately, on the economic system. Therefore, without political democracy, there was no national sovereignty, and by extrapolation we have the Leninist position that without a particular economic system, namely socialism, there would be no genuine democracy—and, therefore, no national sovereignty.[245] Once again, the social revolution was to be organically linked to national liberation.

Yet Soviet discussions of the concept of national sovereignty, from which the right to self-determination was derived, generally were designed to provide a distinction from another concept, which was also expressive of self-determination: state sovereignty. Rights, including the right to self-determination, existed, even if a nation did not have statehood, by virtue of the concept of national sovereignty.[246] By the same token, however, self-determination as a form of expression of national sovereignty did not necessarily mean independent statehood (which could claim the right to state sovereignty). National sovereignty might well stop short of state sovereignty while still fulfilling its rights of self-determination, national freedom, and equality. Thus, for Starushenko everything concerning the internal aspects of self-determination were expressive of national, not state, sovereignty and therefore were attainable without statehood.[247]

The above should not be construed to mean that Starushenko opposed the right to statehood as part of self-determination. Indeed, most Soviet discussions of self-determination presented appropriate quotations from Lenin on the equation of self-determination with the creation of an independent state. Shevtsov, for example, said, "Lenin held that, from an historico-economic standpoint, the self-determination of nations means only political self-determination, state independence and the formation of a national state."[248] Or, as Baratashvili paraphrased it, "Lenin repeatedly pointed out that the right of nations to self-determination 'implies exclusively the right to independence in the political sense, the right to free political separation from the oppressor nation,' that is, the establishment of an independent state."[249] Or, in the Fedoseev collection: "The self-determination of nations means the political separation of the nations from alien national bodies, and the formation of an independent national state."[250] Limiting this only somewhat, Gryzlov asserted that, for peoples living under capitalism, especially its highest stage of imperialism (as distinct from peoples living under socialism), "there is only one way to oppose colonialism—creation of an independent state." Inasmuch as the colonial oppressor would place "all sorts of obstacles" to the implementation of the people's free will, the only solution was full independence.[251]

Separatism

Gryzlov's distinction was connected with the by now familiar arguments by Soviet theoreticians regarding Lenin's call for self-determination up to and including secession on the one hand, and the justification for the multinational system of the Soviet Union on the other.[252] In dealing with Third World peoples, however, it would appear that very few accepted even Gryzlov's formula, preferring a more restrained attitude toward secession even for the objectives of Third World national liberation movements.

In his early discussion of secession as the most frequent form of self-determination for peoples under foreign domination, Starushenko directed his criticism against the demands for statehood, via secession, posed by imperialists in order to divide and weaken Third World states. Thus, the principle of self-determination was not to include secession and statehood if based merely on a minority decision or the decision of an imperialist power. In such a case, the self-determination of the whole nation would be hampered by the self-determination of one of its parts; "such separatist movements have nothing in common with self-determination, when decisions are taken by the majority."[253] Writing in 1983, Starushenko, in his article with Gromyko, went beyond the "imperialist provocation" argument, speaking rather in the name of pragmatism. He explained that it was "unrealistic" for every nation and nationality to have its own state.[254] Indeed, the idea was "totally inapplicable in many areas of Asia and Africa where often there are not yet formed nations; and ethnic groups comprise such motley mosaics that also in the future any possibility for forming states only on a strictly ethnic basis is ruled out."[255] Thus, separation did "not always correspond to the real interests of the principle of self-determination on an ethnic basis," which might in fact merely intensify socioeconomic difficulties. One must examine just which group would be the benefactor in such a case. Therefore, "to prevent the interpretation of self-determination only as a right to separation, that is, without taking into account social factors," one must respect "the principle of the integrity of state and national territory."[256] And in another journal Starushenko categorically condemned "outside support for any separatist movements seeking partition of these [newly free and other] countries."[257]

On this same point, Shastitko argued that "Attempts to create a multitude of small states on the basis of ethnic principle weaken the national liberation movement," often leading to states economically, financially and militarily dependent upon the imperialists....Only the enemies of the young states will fan nationalist and separatist trends."[258] These were almost word for word the sentiments expressed by R. N. Ismagilova in an earlier book, when she had said that:

> the inalienable right of self-determination, including the right to secede and form independent states, must not be confused with the practical and political expediency of secession or autonomy in each given case....The implementation of the self-determination principle on an ethnic basis in forms that would increase separatism would not only aggravate the difficulties of the present situation, but would lead to further fragmentation of the [African] continent.[259]

As the Starushenko–Gromyko article noted, it was not just a matter of the ethnic basis that was to rule out separatism. (They said it was "unrealistic" for every nation and nationality to have its own state.[260]) As we have seen from the discussion of the "subject" of national liberation, legitimate demands for national liberation might be expressed by groups or peoples that had not yet reached the status of nationhood, with nation-building coming after independence.[261] The above condemnation, in part justified by aversion to the ethnic (or language or religious) criterion, was, rather, a condemnation of separatism or the objective of statehood for those peoples whose national aspirations did not coincide with the territorial border delineated by their colonial past. Thus most, like Starushenko, accepted the African Organization of Unity's principle of inviolability of borders for states that have already won their independence. This was stated clearly by Brezhnev himself in 1981, when he outlined "rules of conduct" for the superpowers regarding the new states of the Third World. One of the rules was: "no external support for any separatist movements aimed at partitioning these countries."[262]

For those peoples who had not yet gained independence, or those unsatisfied with the borders of the independent states, the above condemnation of separatism would appear to have ruled out statehood. Indeed, Gryzlov explicitly stated that, despite the ethnic or inter-national problems that might result, division along the former colonial administrative borders was the only "real possibility" for "breaking away from direct colonial dependence."[263] Baratashvili was more flexible (in 1970) when he said that "when the problems of new frontiers and the formation of new states is actually demanded by nations in their struggle for the liquidation of colonialism, then this is fully justified." However, condemning separatism, which served the imperialists' interests, he concluded that "the majority of African states decisively repudiate any attempts to review the frontiers of their continent."[264]

Ul'ianovskii, however, was willing to qualify the above principle.[265] Agreeing that self-determination did not necessarily require statehood —and that statehood did not always guarantee self-determination—he nonetheless asserted that some separatist solutions, or solutions demanding border changes, might be justified and even necessary in particular cases (such as those of Bangladesh or the Palestinians). On the whole, he favored "other solutions" on the grounds that "non-homogeneity" within the existing state was not sufficient reason for demanding a separate state and might well lead to the negative phenomenon of fragmentation.[266] Tarabrin, however, spoke of the unjust character of borders drawn by the colonial powers, although he limited his approval of demands for change only to the need for peaceful negotiations.[267] Acknowledgment of the insolubility of certain national or "ethno-political" problems within existing state boundaries could also be found in articles in *Aziia i Afrika segodnia*.[268] These articles did not, however, actually express approval of secession as such, while "separatism" remained a negative term.

Alternative Objectives

Alternative objectives advocated by Soviet theoreticians for national liberation short of actual secession or statehood were self-determination via a unitary state, confederation, federation, or autonomy. While all these form were often listed,[269] the only one discussed at any length was that of federation, interpreted to include the idea of autonomy. The reason for this was most likely the preference for the Soviet federal model for application in the Third World. This model was outlined in some detail for Third World readers in the English edition of *Aziia i Afrika segodnia* in 1978, explaining the new Soviet constitution's concept of federation.[270]

Quoting Cabral, Starushenko and Gromyko claimed that the national liberation movements themselves accepted the applicability of this form of self-determination to their own experience.[271] The purpose was to provide broad powers of autonomy within a federal structure, so as to prevent national differences within a multinational state from becoming antagonistic contradictions. Autonomy in a federal structure was to guarantee that no one nationality ruled over another, with each nationality's history, culture, language, and religion being recognized within its own regional (autonomous) borders. Theoretically, at least, this was also to mean control over additional internal matters, such as the other components of Starushenko's "national sovereignty": one's own political and social system, one's own natural resources and economy. Starushenko explained that the above rights could be retained in a multinational state, although the individual nation might delegate some of them to the state.[272] Thus, as Fedoseev explained, the concept of federation that was (only gradually) accepted by Lenin was based on autonomy as "a form of regional self-government."[273]

Autonomy within a federal solution, or adherence to a unitary state, was assumed to be obligatory for nations that formed an enclave within a country.[274] Theoretically, at least, any other situation required a voluntary decision by the nation to accept this alternative. Regional autonomy was to be considered only if the nation did not *choose* to secede, or, as Ul'ianovskii put it, on the condition that there was no direct suppression of the minority nation or, even more vaguely, if the unitary state or federation were not an "artificial" union.[275] These conditions were included, however, almost as afterthoughts rather than as theoretical categories which might provide a guide as to when to advocate autonomy over independent statehood or vice versa. As we have seen, the overall thrust in Soviet literature was against secession or separatism, by implication limiting the voluntary aspect of autonomy to accepting the most "practical" or "realistic" solution, if not leaving it to the realm of pious platitudes altogether.

This general opposition to separatism has been attributed by some Western observers to Moscow's fear of a challenge from within its own federal system.[276] Nonetheless, as with the ideology of nationalism, so too with the meaning of the objective of self-determination: Soviet theory did invoke Lenin's reluctance to grant blanket approval or disapproval for any one solution without regard for concrete circumstances and tactical interests.[277] This provided the sanction for Soviet policy-makers to make "exceptions" by redefining or classifying the particular group involved.

Conclusions

Two basic schools of thought are discernible throughout the discussions of the ideologies of national liberation movements; the conservative or purist adherents to strict Marxism–Leninism, and the more flexible pragmatists who sought to come to grips with Third World realities. There were variations within the second school, even a middle approach, but a certain pattern tended to repeat itself. This pattern was one of a rejectionist position, on the one hand, which condemned nationalism or anything but the ideology of Marxism–Leninism, condemned national types of socialism or anything short of scientific socialism, and even condemned revolutionary democracy or anything but a Soviet-type model. Against each of these rejectionist positions was posed an approach which argued for differentiation. Thus, by breaking down each -ism, this school could find at least one internal category of a positive nature (e.g., national socialism among the types of nationalism; revolutionary democracy among the types of national socialism; left-wing revolutionary democracy among the types of revolutionary democracy).

In this way, the negative features of these ideologies could be accounted for without rejecting the ideology itself. In a sense, both conservatives and pragmatists appeared to come full circle and meet on the conclusion that the only guarantee that scientific socialism would emerge was through the addition of a vanguard party to the components of the type of society envisaged by a national liberation movement. Yet on this issue too there was disagreement between the proponents of a genuine Marxist–Leninist vanguard party based on scientific socialism and those who spoke in more general terms, questioning the realism, at the present time, of adding such a requirement.

To a large degree, the same breakdown of persons and positions discernible on other issues (conditions, composition, leadership) emerged with regard to ideology. The two extremes, both to be found within the Central Committee and even within the same department, were once again represented by Zagladin and Fedoseev at one end, together with others of the Central Committee's Ideological Department, and Brutents at the other end of the spectrum. Ul'ianovskii remained close to Brutents on most of the ideological issues, and even those theoreticians who took a middle ground, for example institute directors such as Solodovnikov and Primakov, expressed positions closer to those of Brutents than those of Zagladin. Slightly lower-level theorists, such as Kim, Oriental Institute deputy director, or Manchkha, Central Committee International Department Africa chief, took middle positions which tended to shift between the two poles, on some issues even approaching the extreme conservative position but on the whole defying classification.

On the issue of a vanguard party, however, there was surprising consistency, Zagladin standing virtually alone in his adherence to the more ideologically demanding position. All the Africanists, including the more conservative Starushenko, Africa Institute deputy director, and the Central Committee's Manchkha, as well as Kim and the more general Third World specialists, argued against too stringent an ideological demand. In the debate on Simoniia's book, even Agaev, the head of the International Workers Movement Institute, and a Foreign Ministry official took this position. The Soviet leadership itself, at least in Brezhnev's pronouncements, appeared to accept the dominant hesitation regarding vanguard parties, coming down on the side of the more realistic or pragmatic appraisals of national and revolutionary democracies rather than the ideological purists' overestimation of how far and how fast one could go in demanding ideological conformity. While Andropov appeared to be an exception to this on one occasion before coming to power, once in power his pronouncements followed the line of the pragmatists, as did those of Gorbachev and the new party program.

With regard to the objectives advanced by the ideologies of national liberation movements, there was far less controversy. It was agreed that self-determination did not necessarily dictate independent statehood, since national sovereignty was not identical to state sovereignty. Autonomy, and federative and confederative solutions, were acceptable and were even recommended for those peoples for whom independent statehood might violate greater interests. Thus, separatism was generally rejected at the theoretical level, even explicitly by Brezhnev. There were two somewhat dissenting voices on this issue: those of the Central Committee's Ul'ianovskii and the more conservative institute researcher Tarabrin. Without challenging the undesirability of separatism, they nonetheless allowed for circumstances that might justify such an objective. This was not, however, a central issue in the debates over ideology, a pragmatic approach suiting each of the schools—the conservative as well as the more realistic—inasmuch as it merely called for judging the specific case against some broader interest which could be defined in more or less Marxist terms as each school saw fit.

The dominant school, throughout the 1970s and early 1980s, endorsed eventually by Brezhnev and subsequently by Andropov and Gorbachev, was the pragmatic school. Offering a more realistic view of the ideological nature of Third World movements (and societies), this school eschewed the demand for ideological purity. Thus, the dominant view might be summed up by Ul'ianovskii's comment that Marxism–Leninism did not reject out of hand "any other ideological trends and social theories"; while Brutents put it even more clearly: "In a word, what we are saying is that ideological agreement is not viewed as a preliminary condition for cooperation in the liberation struggle."[279] This pragmatism did not preclude efforts to achieve ideological agreement or conformity with the concepts espoused by Moscow, but it did characterize Soviet thinking, to the dismay, perhaps, of purists who saw ideological dissonance as the source of future deviation from a genuinely socialist (pro-Soviet) orientation.

Notes

1 E.g., V. G. Solodovnikov, *Afrika vybiraet put'*, Nauka, Moscow, 1970, p. 86.
2 V. V. Zagladin and F. D. Ryzhenko, *Sovremennoe revoliutsionnoe dvizhenie i natsionalizm*, Politizdat, Moscow, 1973 (citations from the English translation: V. V. Zagladin (ed.), *The Revolutionary Movement of Our Time and Nationalism*, Progress, Moscow, 1975), p. 52; G. S. Akopian, "O dvukh tendentsiiakh natsionalizma ugnetennykh i razvivaiushchikhsia natsii," *Narody Azii i Afriki*, no. 5 (1970): 15–16; Rostislav Ul'ianovskii, *Ocherki natsional'no-osvoboditel'noi bor'by: voprosy teorii i praktiki*, Nauka, Moscow, 1976 (citations from the English translation: Rostislav Ulyanovsky, *National Liberation: Essays on Theory and Practice*, Progress, Moscow, 1978), p. 113; A. D. Litman, "Ob opredelenii poniatiia i klassifikatsii tipov natsionalizma v osvobodivshikhsia strankakh," *Narody Azii i Afriki*, no. 1 (1973): 45.
3 Zagladin, *Revolutionary Movement*, p. 77.
4 Ibid., p. 78.
5 Ibid., p. 78.
6 Ibid., p. 78.
7 Ibid., p. 79.
8 Ibid., pp. 61, 260.
9 Ibid., p. 62.
10 P. N. Fedoseev, *Leninizm i natsional'nyi vopros v sovremennykh usloviiakh*, Politizdat, Moscow, 1974 (citations from English translation,: P. N. Fedoseyev, *Leninism and the National Question*, Progress, Moscow, 1977).
11 Ibid., pp. 20, 50.
12 Ibid., p. 57.
13 Ibid., p. 492.
14 Ibid., p. 494.
15 Ibid., p. 490.
16 Z. I. Zarodov, "New Stage in the National Liberation Movement: Problems of Anti-imperialist Unity," *World Marxist Review* 15, no. 11 (1972): 30. Zarodov died in April 1982.
17 G. F. Kim and A. S. Kaufman, "Ob ideologicheskikh techeniiakh v stranakh tret'ego mira," *Narody Azii i Afriki*, no. 5 (1972): 40; A. V. Kiva, "Nekotorye tendentsii evoliutsii revoliutsionnoi demokratii," *Aziia i Afrika segodnia*, no. 3 (1975): 23.
18 M. V. Igolkin, "K metodologii izucheniia natsionalizma v razvivaiushchikhsia strankakh," *Narody Azii i Afriki*, no. 1 (1975): pp. 44–8; M. V. Iordan, "O svoeobrazii natsionalizma v strankakh 'tret' ego mira," *Narody Azii i Afriki*, no. 1 (1975): 49–53.
19 Litman, "Opredelenii," pp. 37–49; Akopian, "Tendentsiiakh," pp. 13–16.
20 K. N. Brutents, *Sovremennye natsional'no-osvoboditel'nye revoliutsii*, Politizdat, Moscow, 1974 (citations from English translation; K. N. Brutents, *National Liberation Revolutions Today*, Progress, Moscow, 1977), vol. 1, p. 27. An appraisal very similar to that of Brutents could be found in Kh. Merdel, "Politicheskie organizatsii v antikolonial'noi bor'be," in G. A. Nersesov and V. A. Subbotin, *Afrika v novoe i noveishee vremia*, Nauka, Moscow, 1976, pp. 49–52.
21 Brutents, *Revolutions*, vol. I, p. 27; emphasis in original.
22 Ibid., p. 27.
23 Ibid., p. 128.
24 Ibid., p. 129.
25 Ibid., p. 130; Fedoseyev, *Leninism*, p. 490. (They also cited different pages of Lenin's writings for the same quote.)
26 Brutents, *Revolutions*, vol. I, p. 131.
27 Ibid., p. 143.
28 Ibid.
29 Ibid., pp. 142–3.
30 *Pravda*, 25 April 1974.

146   *A Soviet Theory of National Liberation*

31   Ulyanovsky, *National Liberation*, pp. 113, 383.
32   Rostislav Ul'ianovskii, "O natsional'nom osvobozhdenii i natsionalizme," *Aziia i Afrika segodnia*, no. 10 (1980): pp. 3, 5.
33   Ulyanovsky, *National Liberation*, p. 113.
34   Ibid., p. 383. Se also R. A. Ul'ianovskii, *Sovremenne problemy Azii i Afriki*, Nauka, Moscow, 1978, pp. 35, 79–84.
35   Ulyanovsky, *National Liberation*, pp. 56–7.
36   Solodovnikov, *Afrika*, p. 86; V. G. Solodovnikov, *Problemy sovremennoi Afriki*, Nauka, Moscow, 1973, pp. 167–8; 181–5.
37   Ibid., Solodovnikov, *Problemy*, pp. 167–8, 81–5.
38   V. G. Solodovnikov and V. V. Bogoslovsky, *Non-capitalist Development: An Historical Outline*, Progress, Moscow, 1975, p. 143.
39   Ibid., p. 144.
40   Ibid., p. 154. This view was shared by Brutents, *Revolutions*, vol. 1, p. 154, although on p. 269 of the same work Brutents expressed the opposite view.
41   E.g., Brutents, *Revolutions*, vol. 2, p. 81. See also Merdel, "Organizatsii," p. 49 for a positive evaluation of pan-Africanism.
42   Merdel, "Organizatsii," pp. 57–69; Solodovnikov, *Problemy*, pp. 181–2; B. Yerasov, "Concepts of Culture in the Nationalist Ideology of the Developing Countries," in R. Ulyanovsky, *National Liberation Movement: Current Problems*, Novosti, Moscow, 1979, pp. 159–76.
43   Brutents, *Revolutions*, vol. II, p. 28.
44   G. Kim, "National Liberation Movement: Topical Problems," *International Affairs*, no. 9 (1984): pp. 46–7. See also G. Kim, "Ideological Struggle Concerning the Newly-free States' Road of Development'" *International Affairs*, no. 1 (1984): 100.
45   Zagladin, *Revolutionary Movement*, p. 61. See also P. Shastitko, "Revoliutsiia dolzhna umet' zashchishchat'sia," *Aziia i Afrika segodnia*, no. 1 (1982): 3, who rejected religion as a basis for national unity.
46   R. A. Ulyanovsky, *Present-day Problems in Asia and Africa*, Progress, Moscow, 1979, pp. 118–19. This whole section on the backward nature of tradition and religion in the East was added for the English edition; it was not in the original (R. A. Ul'ianovskii, *Sovremennye problemy Azii i Afriki*, Nauka, Moscow, 1978).
47   E. M. Primakov, "Islam i protsessy obshchestvennogo razvitiia stran zarubezhnogo Vostoka," *Voprosy filosofii*, no. 8 (1980): 60-71.
48   *Pravda*, 24 February 1981.
49   There was some attempt to identify the different elements with the schism in Islam between Shi'ites and Sunnis. E. Doroshenko, "Iran: musul'manskie (shiitskie) traditsii i sovremennost'," *Aziia i Afrika segodnia*, no. 8 (1980): 59–61; P. Demchenko, "Iran Takes a New Road," *International Affairs*, no. 10 (1979): 80–6; Ul'ianovskii, "O natsional'nom," pp. 5–6.
50   G. Kim, "Social Development and Ideological Struggle in the Developing Countries," *International Affairs*, no. 4 (1980): 73.
51   A. Malashenko, "Religioznaia traditsiia i politika revoliutsionnoi demokratii," *Aziia i Afrika segodnia*, no. 9 (1979): 21.
52   E. S. Troitskii, "Kritika neokolonialistskikh fal'sifikatsii idei V.I. Lenina po problemam natsional'no-osvoboditel'nogo dvizheniia," *Voprosy istorii KPSS*, no. 7 (1980): 77.
53   Karen Brutents, *the Newly Free Countries in the Seventies*, Progress, Moscow, 1981, p. 152. This whole chapter was not in the original Russian edition (*Osvobodivshiesia strany v 70-e gody*, Politizdat, Moscow, 1979).
54   Ul'ianovskii, "O natsional'nom," p. 6.
55   Ibid., p. 3.
56   *Literaturnaia gazeta*, 1 January 1981.
57   B. S. Erasov, in "Religiia v stranakh Azii i Afriki: Kruglyi stol," *Narody Azii i Afriki*, no. 1 (1980): 43.
58   *Pravda*, 11 August 1982 (Primakov); G. F. Kim, "Razvivaiushchiesia strany: usilenie sotsial'no-klassovoi differentsiatsii," *Aziia i Afrika segodnia*, no. 11 (1981): 5.
59   Kim, "Razvivaiushchiesia strany," p. 5.

60 V. G. Khoros, "Populistskie dvizhenia v razvivaiushchikhsia stranakh, "*Voprosy filosofii*, no. 1 (1978): 108–20. A shorter version appeared a year earlier in *Aziia i Afrika segodnia*, no. 8 (1977): 30–3, entitled "Populizm ili narodnichestvo?"

61 A. Rumiantsev, "Sovremennaia epokha—epokha perekhoda ot kapitalizma k kommunizmu," *Aziia i Afrika segodnia*, no. 10 (1982): p. 3.

62 Khoros, "Populistkie dvizhenia," pp. 108–20.

63 Georgii Kim, *The Socialist World and the National Liberation Movement*, Novosti, Moscow, 1978, pp. 34–5. See also Kim, "Ideological Struggle," p. 102.

64 Ul'ianovskii, *Sovremennye problemy*, pp. 38–9, 128, 134–6.

65 Rumiantsev, "Sovremennaia epokha," p. 3; L. Polanskaia, "Osvobodivshiesia strany: osnovnye napravleniia ideologicheskoi bor'by," *Aziia i Afrika segodnia*, no. 10 (1981): 2–5.

66 V. Khoros, "V.I. Lenin i revoliutsionnoe dvizhenie narodov Vostoka," *Aziia i Afrika segodnia*, no. 7 (1984): 4.

67 Ulyanovsky, *Present-Day Problems*, pp. 163–96.

68 A. V. Gordon. *Problemy natsional'no—osvoboditel'noi bor'by v tvorchestve Frantsa Fanona*, Nauka, Moscow, 1977.

69 Ibid., pp. 8–9.

70 Ibid., pp. 39–40.

71 Ibid., pp. 69–70.

72 Ibid., p. 72.

73 R. Ul'ianovskii, "Nauchnyi sotsializm i Frants Fanon," *Aziia i Afrika segodnia*, no. 5 (1978): 21.

74 Ibid., p. 22.

75 R. Landa, "A. V. Gordon. Problemy natsional'no–osvoboditel'noi bor'by v tvorchestve Frantsa Fanona," *Narody Azii i Afriki*, no. 6 (1977): 216.

76 E.g., Brutents, *Revolutions*, vol. I, pp. 270–1; O. Iuriev, "Sources and Substance of Non–Marxist Socialism," *New Times*, no. 32 (1973): 18.

77 E.g., V. Bushuyev, "The National Liberation Movements and neocolonialism," *International Affairs*, no. 3 (1975): 114; Y. Alimov, "The Newly Free Countries in World Politics," *International Affairs*, no. 9 (1981): 23–5.

78 Evgeni Tarabrin, "Peking's Manoeuvres in Africa," *New Times*, no. 6 (1972): 18–20.

79 V. Krivtsov, "The Maoists' Foreign Policy," *Far Eastern Affairs*, no. 3 (1978): 49–50.

80 Ibid., p. 56; or Y. Semionov, "Peking and the National Liberation Movement," *International Affairs*, no. 1 (1980): 30–1; *Izvestiia*, 8 September 1978.

81 V. Sofinsky and A. Khozanov, "PRC Policy in Tropical Africa," *Far Eastern Affairs*, no. 3 (1978): 73; Solodovnikov and Bogoslovsky, *Non-capitalist Development*, p. 162.

82 V. Krivtsov, "China's Anti-socialist Policy vis-à-vis Developing States," *Far Eastern Affairs*, no. 3 (1980): 33.

83 Ibid., pp. 34–5.

84 E.g., Brutents, *Revolutions*, vol. I, pp. 137, 143; Brutents, *Osvobodivshiesia strany*, p. 148; Brutents, *Newly Free Countries*, p. 267.

85 Fedoseyev, *Leninism*, pp. 491–2.

86 Brutents, *Revolutions*, vol. I, pp. 139, 143.

87 Solodovnikov, *Problemy*, pp. 188–9.

88 Ibid.

89 E.g., Zagladin, *Revolutionary Movement*, Fedoseyev, *Leninism*; R. N. Andreasian, "Protivorechiia i kriterii nekapi talisticheskogo razvitiia," *Narody Azii i Afriki*, no. 2 (1974): 38–49. See also Shastitko, "Revoliutsiia," p. 4; E. Tarabrin, "Neokolonializm na sovremennom etape," *Aziia i Afrika segodnia*, no. 1 (1978): 14; Iu. N. Gavrilov, "Ob"ektivnye osnovy soiuza rabochego klassa i krest'ianstva v natsional'no-osvoboditel'noi bor'be," *Narody Azii i Afriki*, no. 1 (1979): 6; An. A. Gromyko, "Afrika v mirovom razvitii i problemy sovetskoi afrikanistiki," *Narody Azii i Afriki*, no. 3 (1980): 12; A. A. Gromyko, "Lenin i Afrika," *Aziia i Afrika segodnia*, no. 5 (1980): 4; Kim, "Ideological Struggle," pp. 99–103.

90 Kiva, "Tendentsii," pp. 24–5.

91 Kim, "Social Development," p. 69; Anatoly Gromyko, *Africa: Progress, Problems, Prospects*, Progress, Moscow, 1981, p. 119.

92 Kim, "Tropical Problems," p. 48.
93 Khoros, "Populist Movements," p. 118.
94 P. I. Manchkha, *Aktual'nye problemy sovremennoi Afriki*, Politizdat, Moscow, 1979, p. 199.
95 Solodovnikov, *Problemy*, pp. 188–9.
96 Brutents, *Revolutions*, vol. I, p. 277.
97 Ibid., p. 277.
98 Ibid., p. 278.
99 Ibid., p. 281.
100 Ibid.
101 Ibid., pp. 281–2.
102 Ibid., p. 282.
103 Outside of this categorization, presumably not to be included in the categories of "national socialism," were the conceptions maintained by the "feudal and comprador" elements, which were in fact reactionary, according to Brutents: *Revolutions*, pp. 282–3.
104 Ibid., p. 284.
105 Ibid.
106 Ibid., p. 285.
107 Ibid.
108 Ibid., pp. 285–6.
109 Ibid., p. 286.
110 Kim, "Social Development," p. 71; G. F. Kim and A. S. Kaufman, "XXV s'ezd KPSS i problemy natsional'no-osvoboditel'nykh revoliutsii," *Narody Azii i Afriki*, no. 3 (1976): 7–8.
111 Ulyanovsky, "National Liberation," pp. 378–81.
112 Ibid., p. 381.
113 Ibid., pp. 379–80.
114 Cf., for example, Manchkha, *Aktual'nye problemy*, p. 335.
115 For excellent coverage of the 1960s debate, see Roger Kanet, *The Soviet Union and the Developing World*, Johns Hopkins, Baltimore, 1974, pp. 27–50; Ishwer Ojka, "The Kremlin and Third World Leadership," in W. Raymond Duncan, *Soviet Policy in Developing Countries*, Ginn Blaisdell, Waltham, 1970, pp. 9–28; and John Keep, "The Soviet Union and the Third World," *Survey* (Summer 1969): 21–8.
116 Ulyanovsky, "National Liberation," pp. 282–3; R. Ulyanovsky, "Paths and Prospects of National Democracy," *New Times*, no. 14 (1978): 19.
117 Discussion, "New Stage in the National Liberation Movement: Problems of Anti-imperialist Unity," *World Marxist Review* 15, no. 11 (1972): 23.
118 Kim, *The Socialist World*, p. 42; G. Kim, "World Socialism and the National Liberation Movement," *Far Eastern Affairs*, no. 2 (1976): 50.
119 Manchkha, *Aktual'nye problemy*, p. 337; L. M. Entin, *Politicheskie sistemy razvivaiushchikhsia stran*, Mezhdunarodnye otnoshennia, Moscow, 1978, pp. 23, 201.
120 Iu. Gavrilov, "The New Africa Emerges," *International Affairs*, no. 7 (1980): 33–4.
121 Iu. Gavrilov, "Ideino-politicheskoe razvitie sovremennoi natsional'noi i revoliutsionnoi demokratii," *Aziia i Afrika segodnia*, no. 1 (1979): 25–6.
122 Ibid., p. 26.
123 Ibid.
124 A. Kiva, "O nekotorykh osobennostiakh sotsialisticheskoi orientatsii," *Aziia i Afrika segodnia*, no. 1 (1976): 4–6. See also his review of a book by Martyshin in *Narody Azii i Afriki*, no. 4 (1972): 168–72.
125 A. Kiva, "'Tretii mir': protivorechivye tendentsii," *Narody Azii i Afriki*, no. 4 (1975): 51.
126 Ulyanovsky, *National Liberation*, p. 383.
127 Ulyanovsky, "Paths and Prospects," p. 19; Ul'ianovskii, *Sovremennye problemy*, p. 61.
128 Ul'ianovskii, *Sovremennye problemy*, p. 61; and Ulyanovsky, *National Liberation*, pp. 383–6.
129 Brutents, *Revolutions*, vol. I, pp. 145–7, 150.
130 Ibid., p. 150.

131 Kim, *The Socialist World*, p. 43.
132 Ibid., p. 58.
133 Ibid., p. 57. See also Kim, "Social Development and Ideological Struggle," pp. 73–4.
134 The debate over NEP and the persistence of capitalism is analyzed, differently, by Thomas Zamostny, "Moscow and the Third World: Recent Trends in Soviet Thinking," *Soviet Studies* 36, no. 2 (1984): 223–35, and Zenovia Sochor, "NEP Rediscovered: Current Soviet Interest in Alternative Strategies of Development," paper presented at 1980 Annual Meeting of the American Political Science Association. Zamostny places Ul'ianovskii among the conservatives opposed to the NEP example and any persistence of capitalism, basing his interpretation on Ul'ianovskii's comments in "Dvadtsatyi vek i natsional'no–osvoboditel'noe dvizhenie," *Narody Azii i Afriki*, no. 2 (1980): 8. Sochor, and I myself find Ul'ianovskii on the "liberal" side of the debate, at least as reflected in Ul'ianovskii's comments in his book, *National Liberation*, pp. 124–5 on NEP and pp. 56–7 criticizing too rapid conversion to a socialist economy. Nonetheless, in his slightly later book, *Sovremennye problemy Azii i Afriki* (Nauka, Moscow, 1975, p. 26), Ul'ianovskii took the hard line on the persistence of capitalism even while criticizing the "blind copying" of the experience of states at a higher level of development in the progress towards socialism. Others who took the more liberal or tolerant approach were E. M. Primakov, *Vostok posle krakha kolonial'noi sistemy*, Nauka, Moscow, 1982, pp. 99–101; N. Simoniia, "Sovremennyi etap osvoboditel'noi bor'by," *Aziia i Afrika segodnia*, no. 5 (1981): 15–16; A Butenko, "Nekotorye teoreticheskie problemy perekhoda k sotsializmu stran s nerazvitoi ekonomikoi," *Narody Azii i Afriki*, no. 5 (1982): 77. See also Elizabeth Valkenier, *The Soviet Union and the Third World*, Praeger, New York, 1983, pp. 73–103.
135 Primakov, *Vostok*, p. 100. By the late 1970s a debate emerged on the issue of the persistence of capitalist features, with Brutents, for example, defending such phenomena. (See Zamostny, "Moscow and The Third World," pp. 226–8.)
136 K. Brutents, "Osvobodivshiesia strany v nachale 80-kh godov," *Kommunist*, no. 3 (1984): pp. 105–6, 111. By the June 1983 plenum Andropov was speaking of Third World capitalist states as "objectively" anti-imperialist, and the new party program of 1985 paved the way for positive relations with Third World states of a capitalist orientation (*Pravda*, 26 October 1985).
137 Ulyanovsky, *National Liberation*, pp. 161, 325; Primakov, *Vostok*, pp. 91–9; A. S. Kaufman, "Sovremennaia revoliutsionnaia demokratiia i natsional'nye revoliutsii," *Rabochii klass i sovremennyi mir*, no. 6 (1979): 68–9; Brutents, *Revolutions*, vol. II, p. 109; Gleb Starushenko, "Chosen Path," *New Times*, no. 40 (1980): p. 19; G. Starushenko, "Taking Up a Point," *New Times*, no. 29 (1978): 31; Manchkha, *cit.*, pp. 31–3.
138 Ulyanovsky, National Liberation, pp. 161, 325; Brutents, *Revolutions*, vol. II, pp. 107–29; Solodovnikov and Bogoslovsky, *Non-capitalist Development*, p. 102.
139 Manchkha, *Aktual'nye problemy*, pp. 31–3; Primakov, *Vostok*, pp. 91–9.
140 Fedoseyev, *Leninism*, p. 499.
141 Ibid., p. 500.
142 K. Maidanik and G. Mirskii, "Natsional'no–osvoboditel'naia bor'ba: sovremennyi etap," *Mirovaia ekonomika i mezhdunarodnye otnosheniia*, no. 6 (1981): 25.
143 L. Entin, "Orientiruias' na sotsializm," *Aziia i Afrika segodnia*, no. 1 (1972): p. 5.
144 Entin, *Politicheskie sistemy*, pp. 160–1.
145 Gavrilov, "Ideino-politicheskoe," pp. 27–8.
146 Kim, "Social Development," p. 74; Kim, *The Socialist World*, pp. 43, 49.
147 Kim, *The Socialist World*, pp. 45–6.
148 Ulyanovsky, *National Liberation*, p. 384.
149 Ibid., pp. 52–64, 152–64, 378–86.
150 Ulyanovsky, "Paths and Prospects," p. 20.
151 Brutents, *Revolutions*, vol. I, pp. 306–7; vol. II, pp. 122, 130–53.
152 Ibid., vol. II, p. 130.
153 Ibid., p. 218.

150   *A Soviet Theory of National Liberation*

154   Ibid., pp. 130–3. Entin argued that this did not mean the strict identification
of revolutionary democracy with the petty bourgeoisie: rather, he called for an
analysis of the various social influences at play in revolutionary democracy (Entin,
Politicheskie sistemy, pp. 161–3).
155   Kim, *The Socialist World*, pp. 47–9.
156   Ibid., p. 49.
157   Ibid., p. 53.
158   A. S. Kaufman, "O roli rabochego klassa i ego partii v strankakh sotsialisticheskoi
orientatsii," *Narody Azii i Afriki*, no. 4 (1976): 8.
159   Ulyanovsky, *National Liberation*, p. 379.
160   Ibid., p. 64.
161   Ibid., p. 63. Ul'ianovskii, in fact, summed up the two schools or two extremes
in the analysis of the national democracies: those who identified "the platform of
national democracy with scientific socialism," which assessment "failed to take into
account the entire complexity of the transition period of non-capitalist development
and gave a mistaken description of the class strata directing the exceedingly important
socioeconomic and political experiment...Such an estimation is linked with the
idealisation of national democracy and oblivion of the serious differences between
the national democrats and the Marxists, which, however, are not decisive at the
present stage and do not inevitably lead to a division between them.
    "On the other hand, a nihilistic, rigidly dogmatic, sectarian negation of non-capitalist
development as a step towards socialism is also dangerous. The logical outcome of
this stand is full denial to national democracy of any socialist content whatsoever.
The revolutionary, anti-capitalist character of national-democracy is rejected; it
is alleged to be a common manifestation of national-reformism, i.e. bourgeois
nationalism, and no distinction is drawn between national-revolutionary democracy
and other, reformist, national-bourgeois trends..." (Ulyanovsky, *National Liberation*,
pp. 383–4; emphasis mine).
162   Brutents, *Revolutions*, vol. II, p. 196 (emphasis in original).
163   Ibid., pp. 85–93, 96–129.
164   Ibid., p. 217 n.
165   Ibid., p. 217.
166   Anatoly Gromyko, "Socialist Orientation in Africa," *International Affairs*, no. 9 (1979):
97–8.
167   Gavrilov, "The New Africa," p. 34.
168   Kiva, "Tendentsii," p. 27.
169   Kim and Kaufman, "Ideologicheskikh techeniiakh," pp. 9–11.
170   N. Kosukhin, "Rasprostranenie idei nauchnogo sotsializma v Afrike," *Aziia i Afrika
segodnia*, no. 7 (1981): 3.
171   Kaufman, "Sovremennaia revoliutsionnaia demokratiia," p. 71.
172   Brutents, "Osvobodivshiesia strany," pp. 63–5.
173   Ulyanovsky, *National Liberation*, pp. 56–7.
174   N. A. Simoniia, *Strany Vostoka: puti razvitiia*, Nauka, Moscow, 1975.
175   Ibid., p. 97.
176   E.g., I. M. Mikhailov and E. V. Tadevosian, "O ser'eznykh metodologicheskikh
oshibkakh v osveshchenii marksistsko–leninskoi teorii istoricheskogo protsessa,"
Voprosy istorii KPSS, no. 5 (1977): 105–14; A. I. Borisov and N. B. Aleksandrov,
"Obsuzhdenie knigi N. Simoniia," *Narody Azii i Afriki*, no. 3 (1977): 54–65.
177   For example, Mikhailov and Tadevosian, "Ser'eznykh metodologicheskikh," pp.
110–13, or L. M. Minaev (of the Central Committee Ideological Department's
Institute of Social Sciences) in *Narody Azii i Afriki* discussion, no. 3 (1977): 56–7.
178   R. A. Ul'ianovskii, "O nekotorykh voprosakh marksistsko–leninskoi teorii revoliutsionnogo protsessa," *Novaia i noveishaia istoriia*, no. 4 (1976): 61–83.
179   Simoniia based himself on Marx and Engels's idea that each historical system
produced its own contradictions; for example, the production forces and relations
necessary for socialism to develop in advanced capitalism needed only the revolutionary change in ownership to permit the establishment of socialism, just as capitalism
itself had emerged dialectically from feudalism.

180 Simoniia, *Strany Vostoka*, pp. 119–20. For a discussion of the pertinence of the NEP experience, with Ul'ianovskii siding with the conservatives who did not tolerate any persistence of capitalism in developing states, see Zamostny, "Moscow and the Third World," pp. 227–8.

181 Ul'ianovskii, "Marksistsko–leninskoi teorii," pp. 79–80. Ul'ianovskii did not claim that these countries could inevitably and necessarily become socialist, but he rejected the opposite conclusion as well. See, for example, R. Ul'ianovskii, "O stranakh sotsialisticheskoi orientatsii," *Kommunist*, no. 11 (1979): 118, where he argued for combining "historical optimism" with "healthy realism."

182 For example, M. O. Mnatsakaian of the Foreign Ministry, and B. I. Koval and S. L. Agaev of the Institute of the International Workers Movement, supported Simoniia (Borisov and Aleksandrov, "Obsuzhdenie knigi," pp. 57, 61, 63).

183 Mikhailov and Tadevosian, "Ser'eznykh metodologicheskikh," p. 113.

184 S. Agaev and I. Tatarkovskaia, "Puti i etapy revoliutsionnogo protsessa v stranakh Azii i Afriki," *Aziia i Afrika segodnia*, no. 7 (1978): 28–31.

185 Brutents, *Revolutions*, vol. I, pp. 150–3.

186 Manchkha, *Aktual'nye problemy*, p. 337; Entin, *Politicheskie sistemy*, p. 33.

187 G. Kim, "The National Liberation Movement Today," *International Affairs*, no. 4 (1981): 34–5; Primakov, *Vostok*, p. 107.

188 Kim, "Razvivaiushchiesia," p. 7.

189 Primakov, *Vostok*, p. 107; Kim, "Razvivaiushchiesia," p. 7, or Kim, "National Liberation Movement today," pp. 34–5; N. A. Simoniia, "Sovremennyi etap osvoboditel'noi bor'by," *Aziia i Afrika segodnia*, no. 5 (1981): 15. Kiva had linked people's democracy to relatively developed countries with a revolutionary bloc led by the communist party; Kim, Brutents, and Ul'ianovskii tended to list only such countries as Vietnam, Mongolia, Laos, North Korea, and possibly China in this category of people's democracies. In a 1981 *Aziia i Afrika segodnia* discussion, both Kim and Simoniia expressed skepticism over the applicability of the term "people's democracies" in the African cases ("Natsional'no-osvoboditel'noe dvizhenie: nekotorye voprosy differentsiatsii," *Aziia i Afrika segodnia*, no. 2 (1981): 32).

190 Kim, "National Liberation Movement," p. 34 and Kim, "Razvivaiushchiesia," p. 7; Gavrilov, "The New Africa," p. 34; Gromyko, "Sovremennyi etap," p. 97; Simoniia, "The Present Stage," pp. 15–16; Maidanik and Mirskii, "Bor'ba," p. 26.

191 Starushenko, "Chosen Path," p. 19.

192 B. Ponomarev, "Sovmestnaia bor'ba rabochego i natsional'no-osvoboditel'nogo dvizhenii protiv imperializma, za sotsial'nyi progress," *Kommunist*, no. 16 (1980): 42. Eric Honecker echoed this theme for a "revolutionary party guiding society and acting on the basis of scientific socialism" (*World Marxist Review* 24, no. 1 (1981): 18).

193 A. I. Sobolev, "Leninskaia kontseptsiia mnogoobraziia putei sotsial'nogo razvitiia," *Voprosy istorii KPSS*, no. 4 (1980): 52; Troitskii, "Kritika," pp. 77–8.

194 (Unsigned), "Lenin and the National Liberation Movement," *Asia and Africa Today*, no. 2 (1982): 5.

195 Maidanik and Mirskii, "Bor'ba," pp. 25–7.

196 Farook Ali Ahmed in "The International and National in the Working Class Movement," *World Marxist Review* 24, no. 8 (1981): 59.

197 See, for example, the account of the Berlin Conference on the Struggle Against Neocolonialism, "For a Democratic Restructuring of International Economic Relations," *World Marxist Review* 24, no. 2 (1981): 48–65; no. 3 (1981): 57–80.

198 George Haoui, "Flexibility of Form, Firmness of Principle," *World Marxist Review* 22, no. 9 (1979): 15–22; (unsigned), "A Communist Call to Africa," *African Communist*, no. 75 (1978): 5–33.

199 Primakov, *Vostok*, p. 99.

200 Ibid., pp. 107–8.

201 Ibid., pp. 110–13.

202 Kosukhin, "Rasprostranenie idei," pp. 4–5; N. Kosukhin, "Kharakternye cherty avangardnykh partii trudiashchikhsia," *Aziia i Afrika segodnia*, no. 2 (1983): 2–5. See also A. A. Ivanov, "Avangard revoliutsionnogo dvizheniia v Afrike," *Nauchnyi kommunism*, no. 4 (1976): 85–93.

203 Kosukhin, "Rasprostranenie," pp. 4–5 (emphasis mine).

204 Starushenko, "Chosen Path," p. 19.

205 Kosukhin, "Rasprostranenie," pp. 4–5; Primakov, *Vostok*, p. 91; Kaufman, "Revoliutsionnaia demokratiia," p. 69; Ponomarev, "Sovmestnaia bor'ba," p. 42.

206 P. Shastitko, "Revoliutsiia dolzhna umet' zashchishchat'sia," *Aziia i Afrika segodnia*, no. 1 (1982): 5; An. A. Gromyko, "XXVI s'ezd KPSS i zadachi sovetskoi afrikanistiki," *Narody Azii i Afriki*, no. 4 (1981): 7–9.

207 Entin, *Politicheskie sistemy*, pp. 186–9.

208 A. Kiva, "Revoliutsionno–demokraticheskie partii: nekotorye tendentsii razvitiia," *Aziia i Afrika segodnia*, no. 3 (1978): 31–5. Kiva, in a 1974 review of a book by O. V. Martyshin, had said that, while the transformation to a vanguard Marxist–Leninist party was desirable, the social base was still lacking (Kiva, *Narody Azii i Afriki*, no. 4 (1974): 170).

209 Kiva, "Revoliutsionno-demokraticheskie partii," pp. 33–4.

210 P. Shastitko, "Vstrecha s Leninym," *Aziia i Afrika segodnia*, no. 4 (1980): 7; N. Simoniia, "Sovremennyi etap," p. 16.

211 Shastitko, "Revoliutsiia dolzhna umet' zashchishchat'sia," p. 3.

212 Kim, "Razvivaiushchiesia," pp. 7–8; Kim, "National Liberation Movement," pp. 34–6.

213 Kim, *The Socialist World*, pp. 54–60.

214 Gromyko, "Socialist Orientation," p. 97. Singled out as not led by Marxist–Leninist parties were Angola, Mozambique, and the Congo—which states others, and even Gromyko himself a year earlier, had said were at least on their way to setting up revolutionary–democratic parties "pledged to the principles" of Marxism–Leninism (Gromyko, "Afrika: sovremennyi etap natsional'no-osvoboditel'noi revoliutsii," *Aziia i Afrika segodnia*, no. 5 (1978): 2).

215 Gromyko, "Socialist Orientation," p. 104; Solodovnikov and Bogoslovsky, *Noncapitalist Development*, p. 141. There was one mention in the latter of the need for a vanguard revolutionary party to steer a course along the principles of scientific socialism (p. 102).

216 Gromyko, "XXVI s'ezd," p. 9; Gromyko, *Africa*, pp. 81, 89; though in this last source he also said (p. 97) that Marxists headed revolutionary-democratic parties in a number of countries.

217 Manchkha, *Aktual'nye problemy*, p. 232.

218 Gavrilov, "The New Africa," p. 37 (emphasis mine).

219 Brutents, *Revolutions*, vol. II, p. 209.

220 *Pravda*, 10 February 1978.

221 Brutents, *Revolutions*, vol. II, pp. 53–5, 76; Brutents, *Osvobodivshiesia strany*, pp. 63–5. See also K. Brutents, "Osvobodivshiesia strany v nachale 80-kh godov," *Kommunist*, no. 3 (1984): 102–13, in which Brutents devotes greater attention to Third World states under non-Marxist–Leninist parties and even capitalist ones.

222 Ulyanovsky, *National Liberation*, p. 325.

223 Ibid., pp. 52, 218.

224 Ibid., p. 56.

225 Ibid., p. 57.

226 I. L. Andreev, *Nekapitalisticheskoe razvitie*, Politizdat, Moscow, 1974 (citations from the English translation: I. Andreyev, *The Noncapitalist Way*, Progress, Moscow, 1977), p. 21.

227 Ibid., p. 21, and R. Ulyanovsky, "Perspectives Opened in Socialism," *New Times*, no. 27 (1977): 20; "An Epochal Prediction That Has Come True," *New Times*, no. 22 (1977): 21.

228 For example, R. Ulyanovsky, "Paths and Prospects," pp. 18–20; R. Ulyanovsky, "The Developing Countries: Aspects of the Political Scene," *New Times*, no. 38 (1976): 18–22; Ul'ianovskii, *O natsional'nom*, pp. 2–6.

229 Ulyanovsky, *Present-day Problems*, p. 87. (This section was not in the Russian version.)

230 Ibid., pp. 85–7; Ul'ianovskii, *Sovremennye problemy*, pp. 42, 48, 93; R. Ul'ianovskii, "O revoliutsionnoi demokratii, ee gosu darstve i politicheskoi sisteme," *Voprosy filosofii*, no. 4 (1984): 27–8.

231 R. Ul'ianovskii, "O stranakh sotsialisticheskoi orientatsii," *Kommunist*, no. 11 (1979): 120.

232 *Pravda*, 24 February 1981; V. V. Zagladin, "XXVI s'ezd KPSS i mirovoi revoliutsionnyi protsess," *Mirovaia ekonomika i mezhdunarodnye otnosheniia*, no. 4 (1981): 3–9.

233 *Pravda*, 24 February 1981 (emphasis mine; official translation from Supplement to *Soviet Weekly*, 7 March 1981, pp. 9–10). There had been no mention of any kind of a party in Brezhnev's speeches to the 1971 and 1976 congresses. Interestingly, an *International Affairs* article in 1984 quoted all of these characteristics verbatim, omitting only one, the reference to parties (A. Dzasokhov, "Developing Countries: A New Stage in the Struggle for Peace and Social Progress," *International Affairs*, no. 1 (1984): 36).

234 Zagladin, "XXVI s'ezd KPSS," p. 7.

235 Gromyko, "XXVI s'ezd KPSS," p. 7.

236 Andropov, Moscow radio, 22 April 1982.

237 *Pravda*, 16 June 1983.

238 *Pravda*, 26 October 1985.

239 Gleb Starushenko, "The Principle of National Self-determination," in *Soviet Foreign Policy*, Foreign Language Publishing House, Moscow, n.d., pp. 169–70.

240 Ibid., p. 180.

241 A. A. Gromyko and G. B. Starushenko, "Sotsial'nye i natsional'nye faktory razvitiia osvobodivshikhsia stran," *Sotsiologicheskie issledovaniia*, no. 1 (1983): 5–6. See also Starushenko, "International Law and National Liberation," *International Affairs*, no. 2 (1983): 84.

242 Starushenko, "Principle of National Self-determination," p. 172.

243 V. K. Sobakin and R. A. Tuzmukhamedov, in F. I. Kozhevnikov (ed.), *Kurs mezhdunarodnogo prava*, Mezhdunarodnye otnosheniia, Moscow, 1972, p. 70; as cited in Boris Meissner, "The Soviet Concept of Nation and the Right of National Self-determination," *International Journal* 32, no. 1 (1976–7), p. 79.

244 V. S. Shevtsov, *National Sovereignty and the Soviet State*, Progress, Moscow, 1974, pp. 11–12.

245 Ibid., pp. 12–13.

246 Starushenko, "Principle of National Self-determination," pp. 170–2.

247 Ibid., p. 180.

248 Shevtsov, *National Sovereignty*, p. 16.

249 Baratashvili, "Lenin's Doctrine of the Self-determination of Nations and the National Liberation Struggle," *International Affairs*, no. 12, 1970, p. 10.

250 Fedoseyev, *Leninism*, p. 240.

251 B. F. Gryzlov, "Protiv fal'sifikatsii antikommunistami FRG leninskoi teorii o prave narodov na samoopredelenie," *Nauchnyi kommunizm*, no. 3 (1977): 115.

252 Usually based on Lenin's dicta on the need to examine each concrete case and its service to socialism or contribution to the whole. See, for example, Shevtsov, *National Sovereignty*, pp. 18–19.

253 Starushenko, *The Principle*, p. 174.

254 Gromyko and Starushenko, "Faktory razvitiia," p. 3.

255 Ibid., p. 5.

256 Ibid., p. 7.

257 Starushenko, "International Law," p. 84.

258 P. Shastitko, "Revoliutsiia dolzhna umet' zashchishchat'sia," p. 5.

259 R. N. Ismagilova, in I. R. Grigulevich and S. Iu. Kozlov, *Rasy i narody: sovremennye etnicheskie i rasovye problemy*, Nauka, Moscow, 1974 (citations from the English translation: I. R. Grigulevich and S. Y. Kozlov, *Races and Peoples: Contemporary Ethnic and Racial Problems*, Progress, Moscow, 1977), p. 225.

260 Gromyko and Starushenko, "Faktory razvitiia," p. 3.

261 See chapter 1 above.

262 TASS, 27 April 1981.

263 Gryzlov, "Fal'sifikatsii," p. 113.

264 Baratashvili, "Doctrine of the Self-determination," p. 13. Ul'ianovskii wrote in the same vein when he said that the state secessionist demand served the anti-imperialist

struggle for independence, but "now, under certain conditions, often tends to weaken the national liberation movement and plays into the hands of imperialism" (Ulyanovsky, *National Liberation*, p. 137).

265   R. Ul'ianovskii, "Sovetskaia sotsialisticheskaia federatsiia i osvobodivshiesia strany," *Narody Azii i Afriki*, no. 6 (1982): 17–18.

266   Ibid. and Ulyanovsky, *National Liberation*, p. 141. In a 1971 article, Ul'ianovskii had allowed for no exceptions, quoting Lenin against separatism and invoking the example of the Soviets' "unified, centralized socialist state" (Ulyanovsky, "Lenin, Soviet Experience and the Newly-free Countries," *New Times*, no. 2 (1971): p. 24).

267   E. A. Tarabrin (ed.), *The USSR and the Countries of Africa*, Progress, Moscow, 1980, p. 72.

268   E. G., Mikhail Lazarev, "Sovremennyi etap natsional'nogo razvitiia stran zarubezh-nogo Vostoka," *Aziia i Afrika segodnia*, no. 12 (1979): 25; Dm. Eremeev, "Anatomiia etnicheskikh konfliktov," *Aziia i Afrika segodnia*, no. 6 (1981): 16.

269   E.g., I. Ismagilova, *in Rasy i narody*, p. 226; Starushenko, *The Principle*, p. 173; Gromyko and Starushenko, Faktory razvittiia," pp. 5, 7.

270   M. Krutogolov, "The Soviet Multi-national State," *Asia and Africa Today*, no. 2 (1978): 28–31.

271   Gromyko and Starushenko, "Faktory razvittiia," p. 8.

272   Starushenko, *The Principle*, p. 180.

273   Fedoseyev, *Leninism*, p. 245.

274   Starushenko, *The Principle*, p. 177.

275   Ul'ianovskii, "I Sovetskaia sotsialisticheskaia federatsiia," pp. 17–18. Ul'ianovskii may have been expressing his dissatisfaction with this type of situation when he referred to the early Communists' advocacy of "full national independence" at a time when "bourgeois–national forces were hesitating to advance it and limiting themselves to such aims as self-government dominion status, and so on" (Ul'ianovskii, *Sovremennye problemy*, p. 46).

276   Ilya Levkov in Y. Alexander and R. Friedlander (eds.), *Self-determination Within the Community of Nationas*, Sijthoff, Leiden, 1967, pp. 53–5; U. Umozurike, *Self-determination in International Law*, Archon Hamden, 1972, pp. 161–8; and Meissner, "The Soviet Concept of Nation."

277   E.g., Ulyanovsky, *National Liberation*, pp. 136–45.

278   Ibid., p. 117; Brutents, *Revolutions*, vol. II, p. 207.

4

Strategy and Tactics: The Means

Introduction

There existed a large range of means open to national liberation movements, from passive resistance through civil disobedience, all the way up to all-out warfare. For the Soviet theoreticians, however, the question of means tended to be reduced, generally, to one of political versus military means, or, more explicitly for national liberation movements, to the use or non-use of armed struggle. Beyond this, the finer points of just what constituted political means (demonstrations, strikes, propaganda, coalitions, negotiations, etc.) or armed means (sabotage, terror, guerrilla warfare, conventional warfare) were only rarely treated—at least openly—or were elucidated only in connection with specific situations or movements. Nonetheless, certain preferences were discernible within each category, the pros and cons of both reflecting both Marxist priorities of the city (proletariat) over the countryside (peasantry) and Leninist abhorrence for spontaneity and anarchy. On the broader, more central, issue of the use of force, positions tended to be expressed in direct references to armed struggle or in less direct but clearly related discussions of (1) various revolutionary theories, such as those of Franz Fanon or the Chinese, (2) the atmosphere of détente as a factor for or against the use of force, (3) Western accusations or actions, and (4) the categorization of war, local wars, and the possibility of escalation. The views of the military were particularly relevant to this last set of issues, while the views of the Soviet leadership on the entire matter of armed struggle were only barely discernible.

Peaceful Means versus Armed Struggle

The arguments against the use of force or armed struggle were not categorical; they did not rule out armed struggle altogether. Rather, they were couched in terms of preferences and suitability. The Zhukov study, for example, allowed that all means, including national liberation wars and armed uprisings, were legitimate. It went on to say, however, that: "The concept of violent revolution, which the ultra-left opportunists seek to impose on the national-liberation movement, has nothing in common with Marxism–Leninism."[1] According to this work, the Comintern had determined that the use of such action should come only when the revolutionary situation was ripe, for only then would the movement be able to lead the masses. Without this mass support, armed revolts might simply lead to a loss of contact between the small armed detachments involved and the people.[2] Such an approach, it was claimed, "is in the spirit of putsches and petty-bourgeois gambles."[3] The conclusion was that the forms of struggle depend, therefore, upon local conditions and political expediency, which, in general, were not deemed appropriate for the use of armed struggle "at the current phase" of the national liberation movement.[4]

This would appear to have been the attitude of Primakov as well. In his book on the countries of the East, he castized "adventurism," primarily in post-independence social–economic policy, but also as "a social and historical phenomenon."[5] This phenomenon, he explained, was in part attributed by Lenin to the "petty bourgeois" character of the national liberation movements, which "resembles anarchism or borrows something from it." Primakov spoke of the "lamentable results of political adventurism," perhaps unexpected by those who encouraged them, and of the need for caution with regard to risk-taking.

In 1982 and 1983, *Aziia i Afrika segodnia* echoed the line taken in the Zhukov study. A Lenin Day editorial in its English edition explained that, regarding armed struggle, Lenin had "passionately opposed the absolutization of any particular form of struggle."[6] Though Lenin was quoted as advocating all forms (not just armed struggle), the editorial's list of Lenin's strategy and tactics omitted any reference to armed struggle, emphasizing rather the need for a progressive ideology and a vanguard party.[7] The Russian as well as foreign editions of the journal dwelt at greater length on the subject the following year, criticizing the "identification of violence with insurgent struggle" characteristic of "ultra-'left' groups."[8] Writing mainly of Asia, an article by Vladimir Fedorov maintained:

> *No doubt in some cases*, especially in countries with military-dictatorial fascist regimes, well-organized actions of armed anti-government forces, even if conducted on a limited scale, may serve as an important *supplement to the political mobilization* of the people. Experience shows that if there is a revolutionary situation, these forms of struggle may develop into a large-scale armed popular struggle against the

reactionary pro-imperialist dictatorships. It is for this reason that genuine revolutionaries justify *some forms* of violence and regard such violence as a response to the violence of the repressive anti-popular regimes, *if violence is part and parcel of the revolutionary mass movement against social and national oppression.*

Making a fetish of violence, "left-wing" extremists proclaim armed struggle to be the highest form of class struggle capable of ensuring "immediate transition to socialism." That is why many of them seized at the erroneous notion that "war is the mother of revolution," that war determines the course of history and therefore that revolution stems from war alone.[9]

Such expressions of opposition to armed struggle were not isolated phenomena. Nor were they limited to one period or another, at the beginning and end of the 1970s for example. The major works published in the mid- and late 1970s by the Central Committee's authorities, Brutents and, to a somewhat lesser degree, Ul'ianovskii, made most of the same points. Brutents condemned the influence of "petty bourgeois" tendencies toward "spontaneous rioting, 'leftist' adventurism and extremism," which he cited as occurring in many Arab and Latin American countries.[10] That he intended this as advocacy of peaceful over armed means for national liberation movements was indicated by his comment that "roughly three-quarters of the countries of the old colonial periphery of imperialism succeeded in rising to independence *without resorting to arms.*"[11] Spelling out the forms that might be used to achieve independence, he spoke of "armed or unarmed" protracted struggle for liberation, or intermittent political explosions or even reformist evolution.[12]

Brutents's basic argument appeared to be that armed force, although not to be totally condemned, was no longer necessary because of the new balance of power in the world, that is, the growth of the socialist camp and the disintegration and disunity of the colonialist world, leading to the weakening of imperialism. In these circumstances he concluded, the imperialists' "opportunities for resorting to sheer violence and armed suppression against the national liberation movement have been sharply curtailed," thereby creating the possibility for achieving independence by peaceful means.[13] Brutents did speak, specifically, of the legitimacy of acts of armed resistance in the cities and countryside in South Africa, but he placed the idea of violent overthrow of the racist regime by means of an "armed uprising" in the future—by implication, the distant future.[14]

Ul'ianovskii, in an earlier (1972) work, had actually spoken directly in favor of armed struggle, explaining that different rules applied to national liberation movements than to states, the former having every legal right to employ force against a colonialist state.[15] Such a war would be, by definition, defensive, regardless of who began it. Yet in his 1976 book, Ul'ianovskii spoke of armed struggle with greater reservation, as an "extreme measure," to be employed only when absolutely necessary and when the conditions were ripe.[16] He repeatedly warned that "a principle of Communism" held that "no form of struggle should be absolutized," that "Marxists–Leninists never absolutized the role and significance of armed strength."[17] Without fearing or ruling out the use of armed struggle (in what he called "an historically prepared uprising"[18]), Ul'ianovskii recalled the fact that Lenin had criticized not only those who idealized the peaceful, parliamentary road, but also "'left'-wing Communists who in principle repudiated peaceful methods of struggle, refusing to take part in parliamentary activity and in reformist trade unions, and turning down all compromises."[19]

Defending peaceful means, Ul'ianovskii argued that "economics, politics, ideology and culture comprise the vast field in which the struggle against capitalism takes place."[20] Commenting on the issues debated by others in indirect arguments over the use of force, he employed the argument that détente precluded the necessity for armed struggle; for, in the atmosphere of peaceful coexistence achieved because of the deterrent force of the strength of the socialist camp, the imperialist world "cannot expect to attain its aims by unleashing an armed conflict...In a situation of peace, international cooperation, mutual respect, sovereignty and territorial integrity, any manifestation of oppression and exploitation and any effort to suppress the national liberation movement are particularly intolerable."[21] He took what could be interpreted as a position against local wars when he acknowledged the risk of escalation of such conflicts, chastising those who encouraged "hawks and adventuristic circles" in an effort to return to the cold war and cause the "internationalization of local armed conflicts."[22]

Criticism of Fanon, the Ultra-left, and the Chinese

On the whole, Ul'ianovskii advocated a mixture of tactics, depending on the local conditions and timing.[23] Indeed, he was critical of Gandhi's absolutization of non-violence, but mainly because of its peasant–religious origins and defeatist overtones.[24]

Ul'ianovskii's more negative attitude toward armed conflict was readily apparent in his criticism of Franz Fanon.[25] In his review of A. V. Gordon's book on Fanon, the first tenet of Fanon to be criticized was the "absolutization" of violence. While not criticizing the advocacy of armed struggle, Ul'ianovskii did object to Fanon's belief in violence as the only—and essential—method of struggle: not an alternative to be chosen on occasion among other methods in accord with circumstances, but a goal in itself, equated with revolution itself. Fanon's social–psychological interpretation of the role of violence was, at best, a gross exaggeration: "One need hardly go to any lengths to argue that armed struggle alone, in whatever form and on whatever scale, cannot ensure all these things [emancipation of the masses politically and spiritually, safeguarding against post-independence bureaucratic perversion of party and government]," Ul'ianovskii claimed. Rather, political war, the political situation, the level of political consciousness, the political devotion, and the broad involvement of the masses—these all were to have greater importance, according to Ul'ianovskii. Allowing that Fanon did not juxtapose "armed methods to political ones, as was subsequently done in the mid-1960s by the guerrilla war ideologists in Latin America," Ul'ianovskii said, "[Fanon], too, underestimates the importance of political work."[26] Thus, Ul'ianovskii's praise for Amilcar Cabral, explicitly in contrast to his opinion of Fanon, was for the former's understanding of the importance and priority of political work even when armed struggle was also employed.[27]

The Gordon book on Fanon emphasized a point discussed by Ul'ianovskii as well, namely, the voluntaristic character of the national liberation struggle (the forcing of events, so to speak) should the idea of violence be absolutized rather than seen merely as the result of, and as subordinate to, a thorough analysis of the political situation and socioeconomic conditions.[28] And, like Ul'ianovskii, Gordon decried Fanon's underestimation of political methods, particularly those traditionally associated with and proposed by the proletariat: strikes and demonstrations, as well as propaganda and meetings.[29] Gordon argued that Fanon's disdain for such methods was the result of his preference for the countryside over the city, the peasant over the proletariat, for whom these non-violent forms of struggle were neither applicable nor comprehensible.[30] (Elsewhere, however, Gordon made the opposite claim, that Fanon's interest in violence generated his preference for the peasant and the countryside because of the need for them for armed struggle.[31])

An earlier *New Times* critique of Fanon and other "ultra-'left'" theories criticized the "exaggeration of the role of armed action" for its advocacy of revolution "at any cost, even at the cost of millions of lives."[32] Regis Debray was quoted as having said that the masses would always rise against the existing system if "aroused by armed actions of groups of professional revolutionaries."[33] This, according to the *New Times*, ran counter to the Marxist–Leninist approach, which depended upon "the maturing of a revolutionary situation" in "a lengthy and complicated process in which the decisive role is played by objective factors independent of people's will... The initiative of the vanguard can lead to the desired end—the rising of the masses in struggle against capitalism—only when it is based on objective processes forming a revolutionary situation."[34] Thus, the emphasis on armed action paved the road once again back to voluntarism, risk-taking, and little likelihood of success, as well as to the ignoring of political work and proletariat-related forms of struggle.[35]

Many of the critical references to Fanon and the ultra-left, as well as the more general condemnations of the "absolutization" of armed struggle, were aimed at the Chinese as well. Indeed, it was on the issue of the use of force, as well as the emphasis on the peasantry, that the Soviets attacked the Chinese and in fact differed from them. Whatever the intricacies and exigencies of the Sino-Soviet debate, the singling out of this issue presumably was also a sign of objections to armed struggle. The Zhukov study, for example, attacked the Chinese for advocating armed struggle as the sole means of achieving national freedom, rather than the use of "diverse means."[36] Tarabrin also condemned this reliance on armed struggle, criticizing Chinese encouragement of armed action "without regard for the specific conditions and the preparedness of the masses. On the plea that Africa was 'perfectly ripe for revolution' the Maoists have doomed to death many patriots..."[37] Articles in *Izvestiia*, *Sovetskaia Rosiia*, and *New Times* employed exactly the same arguments in referring to the "senseless sacrifices" caused by Chinese encouragement of "national liberation uprisings."[38]

Solodovnikov and Bogoslovskii also came out strongly against the armed struggle as advocated by the Chinese. Stating clearly not only that it was erroneous to say, as the Chinese did, that national liberation could come only by armed struggle and by armed struggle alone, they argued like Brutents that it was entirely possible to succeed without the use of violence at all.[39] They castigated the Chinese theory of "people's warfare," which failed to take into account "the concrete situation and real possibilities," and thus sought to jump over necessary stages of revolutionary change.[40] They condemned as "adventurism" Chinese efforts to provoke "ultra-leftists" (in the PLO, for example) to the use of non-peaceful means.[41]

Even as the critique of China was increasingly (by 1976) speaking of China's collaboration with imperialism, the issue of armed struggle continued to be raised—and opposed. In 1980 Kiva, for example, acknowledged the change in Chinese policies (to more "cautious and flexible" tactics) because of their failures, but nonetheless condemned the Maoist dictum that "'the gun barrel gives birth to power.'"[42] *Izvestiia* journalist Koriavin accused the Chinese of "encouraging and provoking local wars," of pursuing "a dangerous adventurist" path threatening a "global military clash."[43] And a 1981 article in *Far Eastern Affairs* claimed not only that China had encouraged such conflict "at all stages" of its foreign policy, regarding the national liberation movements in Africa, but that it continued its effort to "heighten tensions [in southern Africa] and aggravate the international situation in general."[44]

Virtually all of the preceding arguments against the use of armed struggle were summed up and elucidated in an article by A. I. Sobolev (then a deputy head of the Ideology Department's Institute for Marxism–Leninism and editor of *Rabochii klass i sovremennyi mir*) which appeared in 1980 in *Voprosy istorii KPSS*.[45] Without condemning or ruling out the use of force, Sobolev said:

> Experience shows that in contemporary conditions the armed path of development of the revolution is very effective for the achievement of victory, but, recognizing [this]...Communists come out against its absolutization. Marxist–Leninist teachings on revolution show that armed struggle can be justified, successful, and effectively only under certain conditions, amongst which are (1) the existence of a revolutionary situation and (2) crisis of the political domination of the reactionary classes, (3) when the possibilities for peaceful development of the revolution are already exhausted, (4) when mass, active discontent amongst the masses is present, (5) when there exists a solid link between the vanguard and the masses and (6) wide support from the masses, (7) when there are present real forces able to lead an unreserved struggle against the exploiters. Readiness of the vanguard alone to enter into battle...is not enough.[46]

Thus, the article continued, one had to oppose "scientifically baseless conceptions" such as "Maoist conceptions of the armed path...in which this path is absolutized for all countries and peoples, regardless of conditions." Also to be opposed were both "Trotskyite views which preach 'revolutionary violence' as the only way of active struggle" and "the whole conglomerate of leftist–extremist groups [particularly in Latin America, e.g., the Tupamaros] which propagated the adventuristic conception of armed struggle...'violence against violence'...and so on."[47] Criticizing specific forms of armed struggle, Sobolev went on to reiterate his "full rejection" of "the positive importance of any armed actions not conditioned by all the necessary objective and subjective conditions."[48]

The same article outlined other forms of struggle, such as combined political and armed means through an alliance between the peacefully, politically active masses and democratic contingents of the military. This form was viewed with skepticism because of the social and ideological makeup of the military, but nevertheless was listed as an increasingly employed option. The third form of struggle examined was the parliamentary path, defined primarily as an electoral struggle combined with mass non-parliamentary action. This path stood better chances for success given the general crisis of capitalism connected with, and in addition to, the shift in the correlation of forces in the world toward socialism. Nonetheless, according to Sobolev, "the most widespread opinion is that conditions for effective utilization of the possibilities of the parliamentary path have not yet ripened" (as evidenced by Chile).[49]

Sobolev's fourth, preferred, means of struggle was "the peaceful road, in the center of which is the unarmed political activity of the working masses" under the leadership of the proletariat. The description of this form (in relative detail) appeared, implicitly, to qualify it for genuinely proletarian revolution only in advanced countries or at the least for revolutionary action at a stage beyond that of national liberation.[50] From the examples provided, in the case of both the parliamentary path and the peaceful road, one might conclude—though it was not explicitly stated—that Sobolev advocated the mixed form of armed plus political struggle for the Third World, with a preference for unarmed struggle.

Détente and Local Conflict

An additional issue which prompted, or reflected, opposition to armed struggle was that of détente. This was implied in much of the criticism of China, in which Chinese encouragement of armed struggle was said to be a threat to détente.[51] Yet the relationship between détente and armed struggle was a complicated one. As the criticism of China would imply, there were presumably those who supported détente, and therefore opposed armed struggle, in the belief that local conflicts would interfere with the progress of East–West relations. There were probably others, however, who evoked détente as a supporting factor in their arguments against armed struggle. And there were probably some who fell into both categories. In any case, given the Third World sensitivities (as well as those of other opponents to détente within the communist movement, probably even inside the Soviet Union), there was an attempt by some to demonstrate that it was not a question of one interfering with the other, but that détente eliminated the need for armed struggle.

Zhukov, for example, writing in 1973, explained that the absence of détente, in other words, cold war, merely increased the determination of the imperialists to stamp out liberation movements.[52] An atmosphere of tension and hostility served to "inculcate particular stubbornness" in their employment of armed intervention in the Third World. The logical conclusion was, as the title of this article indicated, that détente was good for the national liberation struggle in its elimination of armed intervention against them. As Kim was to put it in his 1978 study, any other alternative to détente, from cold war to local military conflicts, "leads to tremendous losses"; cold war, with its hostile and militaristic atmosphere of international tension, blocked the "normal development" of the laws of social development, thus impeding rather than assisting the revolutionary process.[53] According to Zhukov, socialism did not need war to prove itself; only imperialism gained from the absence of détente.[54]

Basically, then, these were the two détente-related arguments in connection with armed struggle: (1) détente restrained the imperialists, thereby reducing the occurrence of or need for armed struggle; and (2) détente provided a peaceful atmosphere which was more conducive to revolutionary success and development, and free choice, than the cold war atmosphere which demanded military preparedness and action. The latter attitude, characteristic of the Orientalist Kim, was presented also by Africa Institute chief Anatolii Gromyko and Ivan Ivanov, then deputy director of IMEMO.[55] Ivanov took the position that détente's struggle against militarism and tension meant relief from "costly" military struggle—a factor primarily of significance for states, but for movements as well.[56] Gromyko emphasized the possibilities for free choice and development under conditions of peace, operating against imperialist interference. His arguments were perhaps less clearly directed against armed struggle than were those of the Zhukov détente-restrains-the-West type. An *Izvestiia* editorial on Africa 1975 made that type of argument, saying that "détente not only has not hindered the liberation movement, as is slanderously asserted by Peking, but it has, on the contrary, promoted the liberation movements insofar as it has restrained the aggressive circles of imperialism and limited the possibilities of their interference in the affairs of other countries and peoples."[57]

N. Inozemtsev, then head of IMEMO, advocated détente *because* it rendered the "export of counter-revolution" on the part of the imperialists "more difficult."[58] V. V. Zhurkin, deputy director of the USA and Canada Institute, apparently an advocate of détente because of the dangers of military escalation from local conflict,[59] cited the "restraining influence" exerted by détente on the United States.[60] His colleague at the USA Institute, Kremeniuk, expressed a similar view.[61] Articles in *New Times* reflected this position as well, such as comments by Aleksei Kiva in 1976 that détente "was tying [the imperialists'] hands," or by Dmitiri Vol'skii, who praised Nchon and "other national liberation leaders" for realizing the dangers of military conflict and the fact that cold war "spawned local 'hot wars' on the former colonial periphery."[62] Vol'skii went on to offer détente, indeed the "fact of negotiations as a means of settling disputes," as a "good example" for the Third World.[63] In a later article, he asserted that "the stronger peace is, the easier it is for the peoples to uphold their independence. For it is coercion and the force of arms that constitute the basis, for example, of the racists' rule in South Africa..."; and he argued that détente served to "prevent imperialism from openly using force against the emergent states."[64]

Writing in the same journal, intended for popular Third World as well as Soviet consumption, Vladimir Shelepin argued after the Helsinki accords that the recognition of such principles as non-threat of or use of force, self-determination, and equality would create guarantees in international law for the independence of the Third World nations and protect national liberation movements from imperialism.[65] He, too, cited this as a "useful" example for the Third World on solving problems by negotiation.

The *New Times* articles may not have been the most authoritative, but they received more weight when the same line was, albeit somewhat more generally, espoused by Brutents and Ul'ianovskii. Commenting on the 1980 Berlin Conference on the workers' struggle and national liberation movements, Brutents praised the representatives of the Third World parties and national liberation movements for realizing that "détente and the consolidation of the foundations of peaceful coexistence accord with the interests of the struggle for national liberation."[66] Although the West was described in its most aggressive and hostile form, the Soviet Union's pursuit of peaceful coexistence was described as providing "the conditions necessary for the historical victories scored by the national liberation movements," as distinct from the anti-détente "intrigues" of the West and the Chinese.[67]

Ul'ianovskii too saw détente as a positive factor militating against the use of violence. He agreed that "Precisely under the conditions of peaceful coexistence and not under conditions of universal war" would the national liberation movements be able to advance their cause, for "in a situation of peace, international cooperation, mutual respect, sovereignty, and territorial integrity any manifestations of aggression and exploitation and any effort to suppress the national liberation movement are particularly intolerable." Like others, therefore, he concluded that only imperialists—monopolies and arms producers—and warmongers (such as the Chinese) opposed détente and favored cold wars, because they feared the positive effect that reduced tensions would have for the national liberation movements.[68]

Presumably, those persons who were opposed to armed struggle held these positions even prior to or independently of the détente issue, in the belief that such conflicts—local even if just wars—could escalate and thereby endanger the Soviet Union with the risk of superpower confrontation. The whole issue of local wars and the danger of escalation was primarily a subject of military commentators, and their discussion will be examined below. There were, however, civilians whose opposition to the use of force or armed struggle was

perhaps identifiable by their view of local conflict leading to local wars
and the risk of escalation.

The two major civilian studies on the subject of international conflicts
fell into this category: the first published by Zhurkin and Primakov in
1972, the second by a large collective under the chief editorship of V. I.
Gantman in 1983. Both studies divided conflicts into (1) those involving
the two social systems in the world arena, (2) those in which imperialism
attempted to suppress national liberation movements, and (3) those of
a purely inter-imperialist nature.[69] The earlier study viewed the second
type of conflict—that of efforts to suppress national liberation, or what
could also be described as local or regional conflicts—as the most likely
to occur and to trigger a broader conflict of the first type.[70] Basically, the
concern was that such conflicts were not easily controlled or contained,
threatening escalation to the point of superpower involvement.[71] Indeed,
this was perceived by Zhurkin and Primakov as a growing problem,
that is, an ever increasing risk, despite the advent of détente (supported
by both these authors) and the deterrent quality of the socialist camp in
the world correlation of forces. And Gantman, in 1983, appeared to be
no less apprehensive.

Some of this concern was evident in comments by Arbatov and
Kremeniuk, as well as Gantman, in favor of some sort of crisis prevention
mechanism, the former explicitly warning against the danger of escalation and a threat to world peace from "events in the Third World."[72]
Zagladin joined Arbatov in this estimate, but appeared to be less willing,
in conclusion, to oppose wars of national liberation than to recommend
détente as a means of containing the risks.[73] Bovin, too, argued that
revolutionary processes, including, by implication, wars of national
liberation, were not to be sacrificed for the sake of détente. He seemed to
qualify this, however, in a direction that did imply opposition to armed
struggle, when he urged "reason," self-control, and caution—in view of
Western aggressiveness.[74] And, as we have seen, Kim on at least one
occasion condemned "local military conflicts" because of the losses and
costs involved, urging, on another occasion, "maximum flexibility both
in strategy and tactics"—a euphemism usually associated with the effort
to dissuade movements from concentrating on armed struggle.[75]

A *Mirovaia ekonomika i mezhdunarodnye otnosheniia* article in 1977
summed up and explicitly stated Soviet preference for political over
armed means of struggle in the following way:

> The experience of the postwar period testifies that the historic process
> of the elimination of colonialism can be accomplished both in the
> course of protracted armed struggle and as a result of the relatively
> bloodless, forced retreats by imperialism when it comes up against
> superior pressures from local and world anti-imperialist forces. *It is*

perfectly obvious that the second alternative is preferable from the viewpoint of the interests of both the oppressed peoples themselves and all mankind.[76]

It went on to imply that this preference need not hold in the case of southern Africa.

This was typical of a number of Soviet articles which made the briefest, but positive, mention of armed struggle in reference to the various African anti-colonial struggles, or retrospectively in reference to Vietnam. Such one-liners appeared to acknowledge rather than advocate, but nonetheless did not condemn, the idea of armed struggle. This viewpoint could be found in the works of those generally opposed to the use of armed struggle, such as Ul'ianovskii, Brutents, and Solodovnikov, but who, as we have already noted, were careful not to categorically dismiss the idea of armed struggle. In this category too were those who refrained from elaborating on the subject, such as Zagladin, who mentioned it as one of several options, and Manchkha, who simply indirectly mentioned it as part of the contemporary reality.[77]

Support for Armed Struggle

There were many Soviet commentators, however, for whom armed struggle was not merely a reluctant necessity, or worse. Whether they were opposing Soviet efforts to channel the national liberation struggle into non-violent means or simply more tolerant of the movements' choice of armed struggle was not entirely clear. Several articles of support for armed struggle appeared in 1974, in response to the fall of Allende. This was more of a debate over the use of violent means or "extra-legal" action to achieve a socialist revolution, and as such was relatively limited to the Latin American specialists (with some exceptions, such as Ponomarev[78]) rather than those dealing with national liberation movements proper.[79] In that context, however, there was the publication of some positive comments on armed struggle.

A similar discussion emerged at the end of the 1970s, this time in response to the successful revolution in Nicaragua, focusing on the issue of guerrilla warfare, which we shall examine below.[80] In this discussion, support for the idea of armed struggle was clearly expressed. One observer, for example, appeared to counter the argument of "absolutization of violence" generally employed against "left-wing extremists." Discussing the post-revolution situation in Iran, S. Agaev, of the Institute for the International Workers Movement, urged that a distinction be made between "left-wing extremism" and just "left-wing radicalism." Both, he said, absolutized armed struggle, but in the case of "left-wing radicalism," "the methods of struggle are consistent with the goal." And he even recommended these methods over the more traditional methods (propaganda and agitation) of the Iranian communists, who had come to resemble "educational societies."[81] Agaev had taken a similarly pro-armed-action position in the post-Allende debate as well.

Independently of what was probably a Nicaraguan-inspired discussion, and even preceding it, there were expressions of support for the use of armed struggle by national liberation movements. The clearest, most explicit, argument favoring armed struggle could be found in the works of Africa Institute deputy chief Starushenko, who, in articles in the 1970s and as late as 1983, enthusiastically provided legal grounds for the movements' right to use force. He defined efforts to hold back the national liberation process as "acts of aggression," thereby justifying as "defense against aggression" any counter-efforts by the movements.[82] This legitimate "self-defense" was further justifiable, according to Starushenko, in view of the United Nations' proscriptions "outlawing colonialism."[83] He argued that the right to insurrection and revolution is directly recognized in the UN's Universal Declaration of Human Rights. He also cited the UN Charter's article 51 and the Declaration on Principles of International Law and other UN decisions as authorizing the movements (in southern Africa) to use "all possible means for the seizure of power by the people and the realization of their inalienable right to self-determination," including armed struggle.[84]

Interestingly, Starushenko did not repeat his customary line in the article he co-authored with Anatolii Gromyko in 1983, which would suggest that Gromyko did not share Starushenko's view of armed struggle.[85] Generally, Gromyko did avoid the subject, but on at least one occasion, discussing the twenty-sixth CPSU Congress in 1981, he reiterated, albeit without discussion, his deputy's assertion that UN resolutions upheld "the right of colonial peoples to wage a struggle for self-determination...by all means available to them, including armed struggle."[86] And in his book of 1981, Gromyko, referring to Soviet aid to "all contingents of the real national liberation movements," cited Lenin on just and unjust wars, saying that "the struggle of enslaved peoples for liberation is always a just struggle, as is also armed resistance to aggression."[87]

Tarabrin, who was willing to chastise the Chinese for their belief in armed struggle, nonetheless was equally willing to invoke Lenin for what he apparently did believe, after all, to be the justified use of force by national liberation movements. There is no obvious explanation for this contradiction in the generally conservative approach to Tarabrin (both views were expressed at roughly the same time), except perhaps that he was willing to employ *any* argument against the Chinese without in fact being particularly opposed to the idea of armed struggle itself. In any case, both in an article he published in 1979 and in his 1977 book on Africa, Tarabrin spoke of the legitimacy of "just wars" in the case of national liberation movements, citing the case of Angola's "just...armed rebuff of aggression" and the struggles in southern Africa, where the movements' offers of peaceful solutions were rejected, leading them to armed struggle.[88]

Simoniia, while not of Tarabrin's conservative bent, apparently shared his support for armed struggle. In an article far less skeptical of the national liberation movements' potential than in his 1975 book, Simoniia quoted Lenin in favor of the movements as such and arguing: "'National wars *against* the imperialist power are not only possible; they are inevitable, *progressive* and revolutionary."[89] While he did not amplify on this, he also did not qualify it to mean anything less than war.

Also indirect, but perhaps of the same persuasion, were two critics of Gordon's book on Fanon who apparently did not share Gordon or Ul'ianovskii's concern over Fanon's views on violence. R. G. Landa, writing in *Narody Azii i Afriki*, argued that Gordon had been a bit too hard on Fanon on the issue of violence. Without actually supporting the idealization of violence, Landa explained that Fanon may have got carried away "when he realized the impossibility of changing human relations without violence [whereas] he had previously considered violence to be an attribute of colonialism."[90] Maksimenko, on the other hand, praised Gordon's treatment of the issue of violence in Fanon's philosophy on the grounds that Gordon understood and presented the dialectically positive aspects of Fanon's concept of violence, which functioned in a Hegelian sense as the ultimate midwife of democracy and non-violence. He also implied acceptance of this aspect of Fanon's work in his assertion that this might be the only road possible "for a large social entity such as an oppressed people" struggling against the violence of oppressors.[91]

Other signs of support for armed struggle could be found, for example, in an article by Shastitko in *Aziia i Afrika segodnia* which dealt mainly with independent states but vigorously defended as "just" "wars in defence of sovereignty and the consolidation of national liberation movements," allowing that independence might be gained by political but also by armed struggle.[92] The educational periodical *Nauchny kommunism* contained an article in 1976 which explained that communists and democrats in South Africa were forced to resort to armed struggle because of the "conditions of police terror" there. Yet this article also described the communists' main task there as "organizational and propagandistic work."[93]

The *World Marxist Review*, intended for foreign—usually communist—consumption, was not so hesitant when it published an ANC spokesman's call for intensification of the armed struggle.[94] Indeed, the journal's conservative editor at the time, Konstantin Zarodov, proposed the revolutionary violence of the Bolshevik Revolution as an example to be followed by all.[95] Two other Soviet observers appeared to differentiate as to when armed struggle could be used legitimately in the Third World. The *New Times* Africanist Viktor Sidenko strongly condemned this form of struggle when speaking of Third World states and separatist movements, as did D. Baratashvili in 1970. The latter, however, quoted Lenin on people's rights to stage uprisings and even wars of national liberation against colonialism, with no limitation on the choice of methods, including "the use of force,"[96] while Sidenko was quite positive in reference to armed struggles conducted by various *anti-colonial* movements.[97]

While Sidenko's enthusiasm had a somewhat defensive quality, expressed in response to what he called Western attempts to undermine Africans' trust in the Soviet Union and détente-related accusations, it did correspond to a number of other responses to the challenge of détente. As was to be expected, some of those favoring the use of armed struggle advocated—or explained this as—the divisibility of détente. According to this argument, détente was a policy relevant to relationships between states. It therefore did not, and need not, apply to or limit the actions of revolutionary forces, specifically national liberation movements. Conversely, the continued struggle of such forces, including armed struggle, would not interfere with or harm détente. The second part of this argument may be totally irrelevant (as well as spurious), for presumably there were those who advocated revolutionary, even armed, struggle regardless of the superpower relationship—indeed, probably in opposition to détente. Thus, whatever the sincerity of their claims as to the possibility of dividing détente, there were commentators such as Starushenko, Tarabrin, and to a lesser degree Simoniia who invoked the divisibility of détente argument in connection with their advocacy of armed struggle.[98]

For others, the connection was perhaps less direct, but the divisibility of détente theme may have represented advocacy of such forms of struggle. There was a spate of articles of this type in 1978, some in response to accusations by President Carter regarding Soviet violations of détente, some engaging in counter-accusations of Western aggressiveness in connection with the Shaba crisis, and some in defense of Soviet support for a UN non-use of force agreement. A *New Times* editorial entitled "Who is Hindering Détente" was typical of this position in this period, as were a number of *Izvestiia* articles and TASS releases.[99] TASS, for example, on 9 September 1978, explained that the proposed non-use of force treaty "does not restrict in any way the right of the peoples still under colonial–racialist rule to fight for their liberation with the use of all means at their disposal."[100] *Izvestiia*, discussing a new book of Brezhnev statements, said that "there can be no peaceful coexistence where the internal processes of the class and national liberation struggle in the capitalist countries or colonies are concerned."[101] It would appear, however, that on the whole the divisibility of détente argument was employed more commonly as general support for the national liberation struggle, or for Soviet aid to this struggle, as we shall see below, rather than more specifically as advocacy of one particular form of struggle (armed) over another.[102]

The Military and Local War

More directly to the point were the discussions among the military regarding local wars, including wars of national liberation and the risk of escalation. There has ben a certain genesis of Soviet categorization of wars, the most recent discussion of which can be found in Mark Katz's volume *The Third World in Soviet Military Thought*.[103] There has been basically no change in the Soviet characterization of wars of national liberation as "just," because of the ideological nature of the struggle and the participants involved, namely, oppressed people fighting against colonialists for independence. Thus, the traditional categories were (1) wars between opposing social systems; (2) civil wars, between the proletariat and the bourgeoisie (of capitalist states), (3) wars of national liberation. Problems arose, however, when Soviet military thinkers began to categorize wars not only according to these ideological, or socio-political, criteria, but also by such parameters as scale of war, nature of combat, and the like. Indeed, even prior to this, Khrushchev had complicated matters by using a mixed categorization, speaking of world war, wars of national liberation, and local wars, the first and last being "unjust."[104] Thus, there was at least theoretical confusion between "just wars" of national liberation and "local wars," inasmuch as the latter category, albeit defined as wars between states, could presumably also be applied to national liberation wars. Indeed, this was actually pointed out by a Soviet general in the early 1960s.[105] It was of course an important point, inasmuch as local wars were condemned because of the risk of escalation to world war, a fact that cast some doubt on the desirability of national liberation wars if they were placed in the category of local wars.

Both Khrushchev's and the traditional typologies were altered in the 1960s and 1970s, particularly with regard to various types of wars between states in the Third World—no longer wars of national liberation, but not necessarily falling into the other categories, either (wars between the proletariat and bourgeoisie or even between imperialists and socialists). A major change occurred with articles and then a volume by General I. Shavrov (head of the General Staff Academy) on local wars, which appeared in 1975 and 1981.[106] The greatest significance of Shavrov's works was their solution of the problem of the various types of inter-state and inner-state conflicts within the Third World, beyond the traditional national liberation struggle; but they were also significant for the nature of this solution, that is, the combination of ideological and non-ideological factors characterizing wars, including the scale and nature of weapons and forces.

Thus, Shavrov finally clarified the point that all Third World conflicts were indeed "local wars," including local wars and nations fighting for their national liberation."[107] While this referred to the socio-political nature of such wars (under his criterion of social composition and political aims of the participants), there was a further breakdown possible according to scale, which in the case of wars of national liberation presumably referred to the territory enveloped by military actions (one country) and the number of participating troops, as well as duration. A further criterion was that of the nature of the forces and weapons, ranging from conventional local wars with the partici-pation of regular armies, through conventional local wars with the participation of regular and irregular formations, up to conventional local wars with the threat of use of nuclear arms or escalation into nuclear war (see table 4.1). According to this scheme, the evaluation of the justice of a war depended on several criteria. Nonetheless, the implication was that, inasmuch as the socio-political criterion was still operative, even if it was only one of several to be applied, wars of national liberation against imperialists were presumably "just" wars.[108]

Before examining other, including dissenting, Soviet views of local war and the risk of escalation, another refinement of Soviet typologies must be noted in connection with a different type of national liberation struggle: that of separatists. While Soviet literature made no distinction between types of national liberation movements, we have seen from the discussion of objectives that there was a distinction between separatists seeking full independence and national groups seeking only autonomy (quasi-separatists) or some other situation within a state. While separa-tism was condemned, this distinction provided no tools for coping, at least theoretically, with the difference between a classical anti-colonial struggle for national liberation and a separatist or quasi-separatist strug-gle by a people against the central government of a Third World state (which presumably had already gained independence) or for the more problematic in-between categories such as the Palestinian, western Saharan, or South African situations. The best that traditional Soviet typologies of war could offer was not "wars of national liberation," which were by definition against imperialism, but perhaps the category

Table 4.1 Classification of local wars

Classification features	Criteria for evaluating the wars	Types of wars
Socio-political	Social composition of the participants	Local wars between individual imperialist states and individual socialist states fighting in defense of the socialist fatherland
	Political aims of each side	Local wars between imperialist states and young non-capitalist-type sovereign states fighting for their national independence
		Local wars between imperialist states and nations fighting for their national liberation
		Local wars between individual capitalist states
		Civil wars between antagonistic classes within one state with or without overt interference by a major imperialist power[a]
Scale	Number of participating states	Local wars between two states of one geographic region
	Territory enveloped by military actions	Local wars between one [sic] or several states of different regions of the world
	Number of participating troops	Wars within one country
	Duration	
Nature of participating armies and weapons used in the war	Regular or irregular armies	Conventional local wars with the participation of regular armies
	Conventional weapons or weapons of mass destruction	Conventional local wars with the participation of regular and irregular formations
		Conventional local wars with the threat employment of nuclear weapons or escalation into nuclear war

[a] This type of local war may be subdivided in turn into subtypes. (For more details on this see *Voyenno-istoricheskii zhurnal*, no. 5 (1974): 93.)

Source: Gen. I. Shavrov, *"Lokal'nye voing i ikh mesto v global'noi strategii imperializma,"* Part I, *Voenno-istoricheskii zhurnal*, no. 3 (1975): 63. (Shavrov's reference was to Col. G. Malinovskii, "Lokal'nye voiny v zone natsional'no-osvoboditel'nogo dvizheniia," *Voenno-istoricheskii zhurnal*, no. 5 (1974): 91-8.) Translation of table reproduced with permission from Mark Katz, *The Third World and Soviet Military Thought*, Johns Hopkins University Press, Baltimore, 1982, p. 75.

of civil war. Originally described in the narrow sense of class war in capitalist countries, this category was broadened in the 1960s and 1970s to include wars between the people and a reactionary regime, presumably anywhere, and regardless of imperialist support or lack of support for the reactionary regime.[109]

Military theorist Colonel E. Rybkin made a brief, but unsuccessful, attempt also to include under civil wars regional and tribal struggles that had no class basis (thereby eliminating the socio-political criterion upon which the justice of a conflict could be determined).[110] Colonel Malinovskii provided a middle position, which placed this kind of struggle back in the national liberation category, by injecting the imperialists. Thus, he subdivided national liberation wars into (1) what we saw above as the classical anti-imperialist type; (2) wars by imperialists and *puppet regimes* against the people; and (3) war by imperialists against independent Third World nations; plus a special sub-category for inner- and inter-state wars (often based on ethnic or religious differences) *caused* by the imperialists.[111] The injection of the imperialists rendered these wars "just" and gave them the quality of national liberation; it was not, however, entirely accurate. Nor did it fully cover separatist wars. The Shavrov typology did not help much in this regard, listing only civil wars between antagonistic *classes* within one state, with or without imperialist interference, making a direct reference to the Malinovskii sub-categories.[112]

The problem appeared to be solved by a fairly exhaustive typology offered by a joint volume on armed struggle published by the Military History Institute of the Ministry of Defense and the Africa Institute of the Academy of Sciences in 1974. Here conflicts in the Third World were characterized as (1) national liberation wars of oppressed peoples against colonial oppression and for political independence (Malaya, the Philippines, Algeria, Angola, Mozambique, Guinea-Bissau, and others),; (2) revolutionary and armed uprisings of broad popular masses against reactionary regimes which are politically and economically dependent on imperialism (China, South Vietnam, Iraq, Egypt, Yemen, Zanzibar, and others); (3) repulsion of the aggression of imperialist powers and their satellites, defense of independence and socialist victories (North Korea, North Vietnam, Cuba); (4) armed uprising against racist regimes of a special type, when the indigenous population lives together in the same territory as the colonizers (South Africa, Rhodesia); (5) liberation of young independent states of individual territories and bases in the hands of the imperialists (India's liberation of Goa, and others); (6) national liberation wars of young independent states against imperialist aggression; (7) suppression of reactionary elements striving to overthrow the progressive regime from within or to smash independent states in the interests of imperialists; and (8) support of peoples against colonizers (Egyptian troops in Yemen; Indian army in Bangladesh).[113]

Rybkin later amplified on categories (3) and (7), adding to category (3) wars by states with a socialist orientation in defense of socialism, and to (7) "civil wars of a special nature...waged between forces acting for the unification, consolidation or independent development of nations taking shape and opposing forces "striving to hinder this process."[114] With these additions, virtually every kind of conflict was covered, including state oppression of separatist movements not favored by the Soviets, although a certain amount of theoretical manipulation would still be necessary for those separatist or quasi-separatist movements which the Soviets *were willing* to support on occasion, such as the Kurds or the Eritreans prior to 1974. Indeed, the relatively exhaustive chart of armed struggle in Africa published in the Defense Ministry–Academy of Sciences volume omitted all but anti-colonial and internal (South Africa, Rhodesia) struggles; that is, it contained no separatist movements.[115]

With the exception of the ambiguity over internal struggles, particularly of the separatist type, the typologies revealed no dispute over the justice of wars of national liberation or the right of national liberation movements to employ armed struggle. In this regard, references to détente or peaceful coexistence were generally accompanied by the divisibility of détente argument, defending the right to revolutionary struggle, specifically wars of national liberation even in the conditions of détente. Usually such arguments were presented in conjunction with the issue of Soviet assistance to such movements, despite détente; these will be examined in the next chapter. Colonel E. Dolgopolov addressed the matter directly, however, when he explained that "the principle of peaceful coexistence...only takes place in the sphere of interstate relations and does not nor can it abrogate the laws of class struggle. In its course, each nation has the right to respond to aggressive imperialist policy by all means available to it, including the defense of its interests by starting a national liberation war with guns in hand."[116]

Deputy chief of the Main Political Administration, Major-General D. Volkogonov, also said that "peaceful coexistence does not mean prohibiting revolutionary...or national liberation wars against imperialist aggression."[117] This was stated also by the Defense Ministry–Academy of Sciences study, which, as we shall see below, was nonetheless somewhat more reserved regarding the use of armed struggle.[118] Absent from the military literature was the view, apparently held by some civilians, that détente eliminated the need for armed struggle because it restrained the imperialists. When the military spoke of restraining imperialism, it tended to mean Soviet deterrence, with the implication that this might prevent escalation and thereby render armed struggle less risky rather than unnecessary.[119]

There were, however, some differences in the approach even of military sources regarding the inevitability or necessity of armed struggle. On the one hand, in his 1974 article Malinovskii cited Lenin to the effect that national liberation wars were not only lawful and progressive but were the "inevitable" continuation of the national liberation struggle against imperialism.[120] Rybkin argued a few years later that wars of national liberation were so numerous because of "the fact that they are a necessary condition for destroying the world colonial system created by imperialism up to the twentieth century."[121] On the other hand, the joint volume published by the Defense Ministry and the Academy of Sciences about the same time as the 1974 Malinovskii article echoed most of the civilian arguments against the absolutization of armed struggle, the need for mixed forms of struggle depending upon sound analysis of the particular situation, the importance of peaceful, political means (citing national liberation leaders Cabral and Mondlane), and the irresponsibility of "leftist" views such as those of the Chinese regarding the use of force as the midwife of revolution.[122]

It may be argued that the latter were not, strictly speaking, views held by purely military theorists—the contributors, indeed, appear to have been a mixed group. There were, however, at least two military observers who did express what seemed to be reservations about the inevitability of the use of force. Colonel Dolgopolov, writing in *Voenno-istoricheskii zhurnal* in 1980, strongly supported the right of national liberation movements to use force, but he said that the decision to use this form of struggle depended upon "the specific historical conditions in each country."[123] Moreover, he criticized the Chinese for their "idealization" of violence, their exclusive emphasis on armed struggle for the Third World, and their irresponsible support of local wars and conflicts.[124] Similarly, Colonel G. Kirilenko, writing in *Kommunist Vooruzhennykh Sil* in 1983, also defended national liberation wars when supported by the masses; but, in opposition to the imperialists' belief in force, he went on to quote a Warsaw Pact Consultative Committee declaration that "there were no regional or world problems which could not be justly solved by peaceful means."[125]

This was where the question of escalation entered, for once national liberation war had been denoted as a category of local war, the desirability of such means of struggle, however just, was not assured. Standard Soviet military thinking, as already mentioned, clearly feared the escalation of local wars into global, nuclear conflicts. This view was expressed by various people in the fifth edition (1968) of *Marksizm–Leninizm o voine i armii*, the English version of which appeared in 1972, and in the authoritative Sokolovskii *Voennaia strategiia*, 1963 and 1968 editions.[126] There were those who persisted in this view in the 1970s and 1980s, as well—notably Col. N. Nikitin, who, in a 1978 article discussing Western actions against national liberation movements (and other Third World conflicts), maintained that "the lessons of local wars and military conflicts show that such aggressive actions by imperialist military circles carry a threat to peace and have an inherent danger of *escalating into global conflict*."[127] This was the typical way of handling the problem, that is, referring to local war only as the actions of imperialists and, therefore, as aggressive by definition, refraining from explicit reference to the other side in the local war, which might be the national liberation movement fighting a just, but nonetheless equally "local," war.

Colonel Dolgopolov, however, appeared to make the connection between concern over escalation and reservations about the use of armed struggle by national liberation forces in a 1980 article. Criticizing Chinese emphasis on armed struggle and imperialist-launched local wars, Dolgopolov argued that local war "threatens the cause of universal peace," and that the Chinese encouraged "local wars and conflicts...as a means of aggravating the international situation and provoking a head-on confrontation between the USSR and the United States" in world war.[128] A *Krasnaia zvezda* article by Major I. Gavrilov in 1978, speaking of Western actions in Africa, argued that "The Vietnam adventure...has provided sad testimony to the fact that the gulf is not so great between broadening imperialist military interference in the affairs of other countries and the subsequent escalation of aggression.[129]

A 1985 *Soviet Military Review* article by Colonel A. Levchenkov (described also as "assistant professor") was even more explicit in his more theoretical approach. Arguing against the applicability of the Clausewitz (and Leninist) belief that war constituted the continuation of politics in another form, Levchenkov claimed that in the nuclear era war was simply "madness." No longer conceivable as an instrument for the accomplishment of political means, all wars including local wars, he maintained, were too destructive and dangerous. He opposed "the advocates of militarism [who] have been trying to persuade the peoples to accept the false theses of local wars being safe." Such wars, he maintained, could lead to nuclear war, as evidenced by the fact that the United States had indeed considered such escalation and the use of nuclear weapons "many times."[130]

More authoritatively, if not quite as explicitly, this view was reaffirmed by the then Soviet chief of the general staff, Marshal Nikolai Ogarkov. Engaging in what could be interpreted as double-think, given the classification of national liberation wars as local wars, Ogarkov wrote in the 1979 edition of the *Soviet Military Encyclopedia*:

> Soviet military strategy takes into account also the possibility of local wars arising, the political nature of which will be determined according to the classic position and Leninist theses on just and unjust wars. While supporting national-liberation wars, the Soviet Union decisively opposes the unleashing by imperialists of local wars, taking into account not only their reactionary danger but also the *great danger connected with the possibility of their escalation into world war*.[131]

A somewhat ambivalent attitude with regard to the risks of local wars in the Third World was also evident among some Soviet military thinkers. A 1972 study edited by Major-General A. Milovidov and

Colonel V. Kozlov asserted that escalation of local wars could be prevented, but went on to say that "there exists no insurmountable barrier or solid wall between limited war and world war. Each local adventure [by the imperialists] carries within it the danger of escalation."[132] Similar ambivalence could be found in the works of General Shavrov, perhaps the leading authority on local wars (in which he included wars of national liberation, as we have seen). Shavrov maintained that each type of war in his typology was transformable into another type, most of which were in fact wars between states or involving more than one state, even socialist states. He even listed the possibility of the use of nuclear arms, at least with regard to one type of local war, explaining in one article that there was no certain means of limiting the types of arms that might be used.[133] These positions at least implied concern over the possibility of escalation, and Shavrov even said that the "lessons of local wars and military conflicts" demonstrate that such aggressive acts by imperialism carry "within themselves a threat to peace and entail the danger of their transformation into world war."[134] Yet Shavrov has also been cited as being relatively optimistic about the possibility of containing the various types of local war—as nothing more than local wars, without escalation to world war[135]—when he said: "In comparison to world war, it [local war] can be limited by the number of participant countries and the limits of a defined geographic region of military actions and, as a rule, is waged with conventional weapons."[136]

Less ambiguous than Shavrov, however, were a number of military commentators who appeared to believe that escalation could be avoided or prevented, thereby implying, if not explicitly expressing, their approval of the use of armed struggle by national liberation movements. Two pieces expressing this view and frequently cited in the West were a 1972 volume written by the retired Colonel V. M. Kulish (working at the time at IMEMO) and the 1974 article by Colonel Malinovskii. Allowing that local wars contained "the danger of developing into a wider international conflict," Kulish made the assertion that such a conflict, which might become nuclear, would be so devastating and "dangerous for humanity, the probability of its being launched is limited."[137] The threat of escalation was the very factor that would in fact *prevent* local war from spreading. Malinovskii took this a step further when he explained that, "with the change in balance of forces...in favor of socialism, another possibility is increasing more and more—that of preventing the development of local wars into a tremendous clash on a worldwide scale."[138] He reaffirmed and sharpened this later in his contribution to the *Soviet Military Encyclopedia*: "...with the growth of the economic and military might of the countries of the socialist commonwealth, grows the possibility of preventing the transformation of local wars into a conflict of worldwide scale."[139]

This was also the position at least implied by a number of articles in the *Soviet Military Review*—in 1984, for example, two by then Lieutenant-General D. Volkogonov. Volkogonov had earlier (1977) maintained that "the possibility of the use by imperialism of means of mass destruction weapons in similar situations [Vietnam] is fraught with the danger of local wars growing into world wars," but he also said that the change in the world correlation of forces made world war too great a risk for the West. [140] In 1984 he amplified this to some degree when he stated that the United States would not dare launch a nuclear war (in Europe) because of the Soviet deterrent and that, although the West launched local wars and conflicts, it had been forced each time to retreat because of the Soviet deterrent. [141] Major-General V. Matsulenko, in an article on lessons of local wars, also claimed that the United States had been deterred by the Soviet Union from using nuclear weapons in Vietnam. [142] Though less explicit than Malinovskii, the implication of such statements was that local wars could be limited, a conclusion substantiated by the fact that both Volkogonov and Matsulenko advocated an active Soviet role in assisting the national liberation movements, as we shall see below.

These views of the prevention or avoidability of escalation were certainly a departure from the standard Soviet military thinking on local wars prior to the 1970s. It is not clear that they represented an overall change in Soviet thinking, inasmuch as they appeared at various times in the 1970s and early 1980s, during which the opposite standard view was also being expressed. At the very least, then, they would suggest a debate or differences of opinion among the military, with a clear if not unanimous opening toward the idea that escalation could be avoided. Such a conclusion would therefore render local wars, including the use of force by national liberation movements, less dangerous and more acceptable, as well as just.

Leadership Views

The Soviet leadership, including those responsible for the military, such as Grechko and then Ustinov, was far less explicit in its pronouncements relating to the issue of armed struggle. Ustinov, for example, seemed to imply concern over escalation when discussing the adventuristic quality of American regional activity and the unleashing of local wars. [143] His accusations that the US actions threatened world stability—together with declarations that the Soviet Union would never initiate a nuclear war—may have reflected a concern over escalation; and indeed, they have been interpreted by some as support for a position favoring international stability as distinct from the advocacy of local wars, including national liberation wars. [144] Be that as it may, public pronouncements were far from clear, even on the part of Ustinov's predecessor Grechko and possibly Gorshkov, although the latter reportedly was less concerned about escalation than the former.[145] The same ambiguity was more or less the case for the civilian leadership, which refrained from anything but generalized statements regarding "the struggle" of national liberation movements. Only rarely did a leading party–government figure specify armed struggle as such or elucidate types of struggle.

At the 1971 twenty-fourth CPSU Congress, for example, no mention was made of armed struggle, although both Gromyko and Andropov (in a December 1971 speech) were calling to divide détente to the point of condoning ideological and political struggle even with peaceful coexistence.[146] This divisibility of détente did not, however, appear to indicate advocacy of armed struggle. Even on the occasion of Castro's visit to the Soviet Union, Brezhnev was unwilling to go beyond the division of détente to the ideological realm (citing that as the main realm of competition), refraining from any specific mention of armed struggle. In contrast, on the same occasion, Kosygin did make what was for him a rare reference not only to the divisibility of détente, but actually to the right of people, "weapons in hands, to oppose aggression or to strive for liberation from foreign oppression."[147] In subsequent speeches, however, Kosygin, even in speaking of Algeria, made no mention of "armed" struggle.[148] Nor did Suslov's more frequent—indeed, standard for him—division of détente go beyond ideological struggle. Given that ideology was his area of responsibility, this position was not surprising, and need not have indicated any position one way or another as to the form the struggle of the national liberation movements was to take.[149]

Reflecting the discussion occasioned by the defeat of Allende in 1973, Ponomarev, specifically referring to Chile—and therefore to the defense of a social rather than national liberation revolution as such—nonetheless implied general support for armed struggle when he said:

> Those events [Chile] are also a reminder of the need to approach the issue of the peaceful non-armed road to a victorious revolution from a correct Leninist position. The peaceful development of the revolution is guaranteed not only by an alignment of social forces under which the bourgeoisie would not venture to start a civil war, but by the constant preparedness of the revolutionary vanguard and the masses—in deed and not in words—to use the boldest means of struggle should the situation require it.[150]

Later comments by Ponomarev suggested, however, that he was not in fact advocating a general shift to armed action in the Third World.[151]

Just prior to the twenty-fifth CPSU Congress of 1976, Andrei Gromyko published an article in *Kommunist* which presaged the line to be taken by the Congress. Expressing at least a partial divisibility of détente argument, he also at least mentioned the "armed struggle" conducted by the national liberation movements.[152] Brezhnev, at the Congress, did not use the words themselves, but he did lay out the divisibility of détente line.[153] At this time, he clearly stated that détente was intended to prevent the use of force at the inter-state level, but that "détente does not in the slightest abolish, and it cannot abolish or alter, the laws of the class struggle." Revolution, being the result of inexorable processes, could not be halted, he argued, praising the "heroic struggle" waged by specific movements in Africa. He did not specify armed struggle, but the implication was relatively clear, at least in the explanation of the divisibility of détente.

Two months later, Andropov appeared to echo this line (almost word for word) when he too spoke of the divisibility of détente; he also expressed sympathy for peoples "forced to fight the colonialists" (in 1979 he said "forced to take up arms and take to the streets").[154] Andropov nonetheless went on to speak against the use of force in the nuclear era, the necessity of preventing ideological struggle from undermining peace, and the (implied) irresponsibility of those opponents of détente who spoke of "positions of strength."[155] These comments could raise some doubt as to Andropov's general position regarding the use of force even by national liberation movements. Inasmuch as the 1976 CPSU Congress did mark a high point in Soviet support for the national liberation struggle, as we shall see in the next chapter, it might have been expected to produce somewhat less ambiguous pronouncements on types of struggle than it did, even in the remarks of Brezhnev.

Somewhat greater clarity was to come with Podgornyi's unprecedented (for the Soviets) tour of Africa in 1977. Speaking in Zambia, Podgornyi said, in support of the national liberation struggle in southern Africa, "As for the question of forms and methods of struggle...it is the business of the peoples of South Africa, Zimbabwe, and Namibia themselves."[156] He repeated this in Mozambique, but he went on to express Moscow's preference: "Needless to say, a political settlement of all problems would be desirable" (TASS); or, as *Pravda* published the same speech to make it somewhat clearer, "Of course, the peaceful political solution of all these problems would be desirable."[157] Having said this, Podgornyi, nonetheless, continued that circumstances in southern Africa were such that "one can understand their desire to resort to armed struggle" (TASS) or, in *Pravda*, "it is perfectly natural that they want to resort to armed struggle." In a second speech in Mozambique, Podgornyi defended détente at some length and then added that the Soviet Union, "as a consistently peaceable state," supported a "peaceful settlement" of the problem in southern Africa but rejected the imperialists' accusations that the armed struggle there was to blame for the tension in the area. This launched him into a defense of armed struggle: "There is a radical difference between armed aggression and the lawful right to give a firm rebuff to this aggression, between criminal actions by the racist regimes and the just, legitimate struggle of the peoples against racism."[158]

Podgornyi's comments were unusually explicit; they were not to be found, for example, in the Soviet Government Statement on Africa of June 1978 (delivered in conjunction with the Shaba crisis). Here, as in the CPSU Congress, the defense of armed struggle was implicit rather than explicit, defending the rights of states and movements to rebuff imperialist aggression and force, particularly in the context of the divisibility of détente argument.[159] Just a few days after this statement was issued, though, Brezhnev seemed to believe it necessary to soften the tone. On the occasion of a speech honoring visiting Madagascar President Ratsiraka, Brezhnev asserted that Soviet support for the national liberation movements "of course in no way means that the USSR is opposed to the efforts, including diplomatic steps, aimed at achieving a peaceful solution of the arising problems, if such a solution meets the lawful interests of the peoples."[160] Brezhnev had said in his sixtieth anniversary speech in November 1977 that it was "no longer a simple matter for [imperialists] to decide on direct armed intervention" in the new states because of the "crushing defeat rendered them in Vietnam."[161] It is difficult to judge, however, whether this was meant in support of armed action because there was no danger of escalation, or in opposition to armed action, in the sense that force would not be necessary in view of America's new restraint.

Official Soviet tolerance of armed struggle but preference for political means, as presented by Podgornyi in Africa, was also apparent in a *Kommunist* article published by Ponomarev in 1980. In a discussion of the relationship between war and revolution, Ponomarev noted the positive effects that the Portuguese colonialist war against the peoples in Africa had had as a catalyst for the Portuguese revolution. He went on to explain, however, that:

the followers of Marxism–Leninism did not and do not believe that wars are needed for the development of revolution. Marxists by no means seek a war, do not attempt to cause a war for the sake of starting revolutions. This is all the more true today when there is added to the so-called conventional calamities linked with war the threat of the use of nuclear weapons, the catastrophic consequences of which are difficult to imagine.[162]

Ponomarev, ignoring his earlier response to the overthrow of Allende, provided examples of revolution—such as Chile, Iran, Afghanistan—

won *without* war or, in the case of Cuba, without foreign war. These examples still left some question regarding genuine wars of national liberation, as distinct from social revolutions. Indeed, the article itself contained contradictions; for, while Ponomarev argued vehemently against "adventuristic," "Trotskyite" ideas of "permanent warfare against the entire capitalist world," he also criticized those who preached a stable international atmosphere at the expense of the revolution and the national liberation struggle. Thus he presented a divisibility of détente argument with relative ambiguity on the question of means.

If Ponomarev was critical of the proponents of stability (couched in an anti-Western, anti-imperialist diatribe), Brezhnev's speech to the 1981 CPSU Congress was one of just such a proponent.[163] While failing to mention the national liberation movements, as such, he did acknowledge the "mounting intensity of the struggle" in South Africa and Namibia, and in the section on the world communist movement (but not the Third World section) he referred to the various forms used for coming to power, including armed struggle. Yet Brezhnev spent some time warning of the risks of escalation and war arising from world tension and "flashpoints of military conflict, often threatening to grow into major conflagration" around the globe. "Experience has shown," he argued, "that it is not easy to extinguish them. It would be far better to take preventive measure to forestall them." He persisted in what might be called an activist view regarding Soviet policy in assisting the Third World, as we shall see below, but there did appear to be in his speech signs of concern over escalation and something of a retreat from the twenty-fifth Congress's enthusiasm over the "heroic struggle" waged by various movements in Africa. The "rules of conduct" speech which followed a few months later made no direct reference to forms of struggle but in itself appeared to be an indication of concern over escalation and a desire for stability, as were Brezhnev's speeches in September and October 1982.[164]

The post-Brezhnev period did not differ much, insofar as the general lack of specific comment on armed struggle in leadership speeches was the rule. What did appear, in the Andropov period at least, was a decline in any reference to the national liberation movements and a rise in the concern expressed over the possibility of escalation. Andropov continued to express himself as he had in 1971, 1976, and 1979 in support of those forced to fight for their independence, and in this sense one might conclude some sort of support for armed struggle.[165] Yet Andropov's speeches were characterized by his warnings regarding war, the dangers of conflicts, and the need for peaceful competition.[166] This would suggest that he did not welcome armed conflict even on the part of national liberation movements. Indeed, the first Warsaw

Pact summit called under Andropov, in January 1983, warned of "the danger of local conflicts erupting into armed confrontation on a world-wide scale."[167] Aliev, Andropov's appointee to the Politburo, said in Vietnam in October 1983 that there were "no problems in Southeast Asia which could not be resolved through negotiations," and party secretary Zimianin asserted that "no world problems...can be solved by military means."[168] With the end of détente, it may not have been particularly significant that the divisibility of détente arguments disappeared from leadership pronouncements in the Andropov period; it did not return under Chernenko or the early pronouncements of Gorbachev, either.

The new party program issued in 1985 contained Andropov's earlier formulation warning against the spread of ideological conflict to the sphere of international relations. In this statement, and in the repeated call for negotiations as the solution to disputes and conflicts, the program appeared to continue the general preference for political over armed means of struggle, although nothing was said explicitly. Thus, the right of revolution against exploitation, while explicitly and strongly supported, was *not* presented in a divisibility of détente context (which might have implied other than peaceful means for such revolutions).[169] Gorbachev's speech to the twenty-seventh Party Congress was even less explicit than the program. The absence of the divisibility of détente argument, or even mention of the national liberation movements, combined with repeated references to the dangers of war, the risks of crises, and the call for peaceful solutions exclusively, all confirmed this post-Brezhnev attitude. This attitude was apparent in Gorbachev's CPSU Congress call for the "vitalization of collective quests for ways of defusing conflict situations in the Middle East, Central America, Southern Africa, in all of the planet's turbulent points." Inasmuch as this was the only message for the movements, including those in southern Africa, it clearly registered opposition to the use of armed struggle.

On the whole, there was a general paucity of official pronouncements or even hints regarding the form of struggle to be employed by the national liberation movements. A somewhat more tolerant attitude regarding armed struggle might be detectible during the peak year of détente, presumably because of the reduction of risks. Even at that time, however, the paucity of comments, lack of clarity, and occasional expressions of preference for political over armed means all suggested that armed struggle was more tolerated than actually advocated or actively encouraged by the civilian leadership. How this was reflected in actual Soviet policies toward specific movements and events will be examined below.

Types of Armed Struggle: Guerrilla and Regular Warfare

Leadership pronouncements were too general to even suggest what criteria might be applied for accepting or advocating armed action or a particular type of armed action. This was not entirely the case with regard to both civilian and military works, some (albeit few) of which actually did provide analyses and preferences regarding types of armed struggle. From these few published sources, one may build a Soviet typology of armed struggle, which would include: sabotage, terror, guerrilla warfare, and conventional warfare (civil war–national liberation war). Practically speaking, this appeared to be a continuum from sabotage through guerrilla warfare to conventional warfare, with terror (and even sabotage) seen only as an offshoot of guerrilla warfare.

The one major work actually devoted to the subject was the joint study published by the Defense Ministry and Academy of Sciences entitled *The Armed Struggle of the Peoples of Africa for Freedom and Independence*.[170] Published in 1974, this comprehensive study offered the following typology or stages of revolutionary armed struggle: "guerrilla war [in Russian, partisan warfare], armed uprising [of insurgent army of workers in towns], nationwide liberation war, self-defense [after political victory, after independence], and also such secondary forms of armed violence as sabotage, terror, etc."[171]

The study began with Lenin's distinction between guerrilla warfare and civil war, the latter clearly preferred by Lenin. Yet, inasmuch as civil war was defined by Lenin as the armed struggle of one class against another, specifically of the proletariat against the bourgeoisie, or "of hired workers against capitalists of a given state," it was not, strictly speaking, applicable to the national liberation struggle. It was possible, however, that wars of national liberation would eventually assume a social as well as national character, becoming a civil war against local reaction as well. This having been said, civil war was, as the standard military typologies of war indicated, a different category from the types of armed struggle employed by national liberation movements.

Given Lenin's juxtaposition of guerrilla warfare with civil war, the latter a clearly class war, it was not surprising that the former would come out the undesirable. Thus, in this context guerrilla warfare was only one form of struggle, employable once the general armed insurrection was underway (by workers in the towns) but bogged down in sporadic battles. In Lenin's view, guerrilla warfare could be useful during the long intervals *between* the battles of the civil war already sparked by the armed uprising. In this sense guerrilla warfare, broadly defined as "unabating strikes, exhaustion of the enemy by means of attacks and street battles first in one then at another end of the country," could be used by the proletariat "as one of the means, which should be proportional to the main means of struggle...At the same time, the guerrilla struggle cannot become the primary, or especially the exclusive, form of social struggle," as (according to this study) "'extreme left' theoreticians" would have it.[172]

Extrapolating from Lenin's theses on civil versus guerrilla war, it was stated that, "in a prolonged contemporary war with a strong and experienced opponent, armed with the latest word in technology, it is impossible to use guerrilla methods. A regular war is necessary, military specialists are necessary, regular armed forces are necessary."[173] Thus, Lenin's distinction was not so much one of city warfare by workers versus fighting in the countryside (by guerrillas), but of regular warfare by conventional regular units, albeit in the city, versus "irregulars" of the strictly partisan type—bearing in mind that the Russian term employed for "guerrilla warfare" is "partisan warfare" (partizanskaia voina).

Going beyond Lenin, into the contemporary era of national liberation struggle, Lenin's order was reversed somewhat, with guerrilla warfare preceding armed uprising, but nonetheless subordinate to it. The cases of Yugoslavia, China, and Vietnam were cited as mass guerrilla wars, but, it was added, they developed into "the activity of regular national liberation armies." The experience of Vietnam was invoked as one model, consisting of a preparatory phase of political propaganda work, leadership training, and the creation of both legal and underground resistance organizations; then the stage of guerrilla struggle proper with the creation of guerrilla units, supported by the local population and organized insurgency bases; then development of the large-scale guerrilla war into a regular war of mobility with the use of attacks or military formations, employing regular armed forces (division, regiment, battalion, company) and, for auxiliary tasks, para-military forces such as guerrilla units and people's militia.[174]

The Cuban model was also invoked, with the same basic preference for conventional or regular forces. That is, the Cuban's struggle was defined as "armed struggle" in the agricultural countryside *and* mass political demonstrations in the cities, Che Guevara being quoted to the effect that "'guerrilla war is only a stage of regular war and, therefore, guerrilla struggle alone cannot achieve final victory.' Only the transformation of guerrilla units into units of a regular type and dealing crushing blows to government troops are capable of securing the final victory of the insurgents."[175] The South African struggle (of the Communist Party and the ANC) was also cited as an example of guerrilla activity plus political work as the *preparatory stage* for a general uprising or nation-wide war of liberation.[176]

While this was a question of stages, it was also a matter of countryside versus city, as evidenced by the explanation given by the authors for the preponderance of guerrilla warfare as the form of armed struggle chosen by modern national liberation movements. This explanation was based on four factors which favored warfare in the countryside over armed struggle in the cities: the numerically superior rural population, the paucity of proletarians, the absence of Marxist–Leninist parties (presumably to guide the struggle along classical lines of worker agitation in the cities), and the concentration of the colonialists' best military troops in the city.[177] From these, one may deduce that the struggle was taken to the countryside, which, according to the authors, was the reason for the choice of guerrilla warfare.

This did not mean that the authors were satisfied with this deduction. They were careful to criticize the Chinese for their absolutization of the countryside, arguing that the African experience had contradicted "Maoist [more likely Fanon] claims of the 'counterrevolutionary' role of the cities, the claim that the cities can only serve as supply bases for insurgent-peasants." How did the African experience contradict this view? By the fact that it was the cities that had provided the leadership (petty bourgeoisie or workers) for the movements. This somewhat flimsy claim reflected the authors' weakness for traditional Marxist positions, which was the basis, or at least the likely explanation, for the Soviets' belief that the ultimate battle would, nonetheless, be for the cities, guerrilla warfare therefore having to give way ultimately for conventional (regular) forces.

There were a number of other factors that characterized and determined armed struggle. The strategy or objectives of the struggle, on an operative rather than ideological level, was considered a variable, depending upon the area, character of the uprising, and timing. In Algeria, for example, the objective had been to arouse the masses through country–wide guerrilla actions, though these objectives broadened to socio-political aims in the course of the war. Military strategy there had been based on the formation of two bases in neighboring countries and coordination of external and internal armies with the goal of achieving sufficient military strength from which to negotiate for independence.[178] A second model was that of the Portuguese colonies and southern Africa, where armed struggle was an internal affair. In Guinea the military strategy called for a move from the center outwards toward the borders; in Mozambique the strategy was to create provincial areas of resistance near the border and move inwards. Choice of the military strategy was said actually to be dependent upon five factors:

1 the goals and tasks set by the political and military leadership;
2 conditions of the struggle and the balance of forces at each stage of the war;
3 availability and type of weapons, technical equipment, and training;
4 degree of support of the masses;
5 direct influence of international and diplomatic factors.

On the whole, the choice of strategy would be determined largely by the "gross military–technical inequality of the forces posed against the colonizers," with the wars beginning as local guerrilla actions spreading to nationwide war. Ultimately, however, as once again stated by the authors, "victory in national liberation wars cannot be achieved as a result of direct armed clashes with imperialist forces; it is the result of a combined military, political, and diplomatic struggle."[179]

Returning to the other factors influencing armed struggle, the authors dealt with the question of spontaneity versus organization, the former perceived as early as Lenin as a negative phenomenon, synonymous with anarchism and frivolity or adventurism. The study did admit that modern national liberation wars had been or were characterized by a great deal of spontaneity, owing both to the lack of class differentiation sufficient to supply clear class leadership of the movements and to the lack of clear ideological tenets, political and military preparation, and organization. Using this criterion, another typology of armed struggle was suggested:

1 spontaneous or semi-spontaneous armed uprisings of the peasant masses with only amorphous military organization and virtually no centralized direction of the struggle or political leadership;
2 armed uprisings based on a branching and stable military and administrative organization but lacking political leadership and ideology, leading to the primacy of military questions (often incorrectly solved) at the expense of ideological and political education of the insurgents and masses;
3 armed uprisings or national liberation wars led by a national party (patriotic front), military capabilities and leadership depending upon specific conditions and the ideological–organizational level of the leadership, with in some cases a fusion of the military and political organization and in others, separate military and political structures; in all cases with cooperation between the party and the army, though in some cases only weak, virtually nonexistent centralized party control of the military;
4 national liberation wars headed by revolutionary democratic parties with relatively high level of political and military leadership and stable ties with the masses, the military capabilities of which are determined by the approach of the views of their leadership to Marxist–Leninist ideology, by cooperation with communist parties and Marxist–Leninist groups.[180]

Thus, according to the authors, "the level of military organization…is closely dependent on the level of political maturity and organization of the movement as a whole." Party leadership of the armed struggle was deemed necessary so as to secure a close relationship between the armed forces and the masses, as well as centralized organization of the struggle.[181] "To begin armed struggle without explanatory work amongst the masses is to condemn the national liberation movement to unavoidable failure," the authors argued; but such preparation was not always provided, because of "the lack of strategic leadership in armed struggle, connected with the lack of political aims, with weak political education and level of military preparedness of the leaders...and the lack of ruling political parties."[182] One of the results of this was spontaneity and insufficient coordination between city and countryside, and between different regions.

The additional factor influencing armed struggle was that of weapons and training. Both of these were to come, on the whole, from outside, specifically from the socialist countries, as distinct from "the Maoist slogan of 'dependence on one's own forces.'"[183] While types of weapons were described primarily as light weapons and anti-aircraft systems, the authors also spoke of heavy artillery, suggesting weaponry for more than guerrilla warfare. They seemed to be skeptical about the ability of local forces to handle sophisticated weapons systems when they commented that "problems of training these cadres persist."[184] And in fact, more important than weapons, according to the study, was the training of troops and command cadres. This referred not only to training in the use of weapons, but to political education as well. The latter could be provided by the movements themselves, specifically by revolutionary–democratic parties (presumably where they existed), but the communist parties and "progressive circles" of the ruling countries could also play a role. Indeed, international socialist assistance (by the socialist states) was also an important factor, in the form of supplies of weapons and training, in the form of restraining the imperialists from interfering in the national liberation struggle, and in the form of political support in international arenas.[185]

One form of armed struggle not covered by this exhaustive study was the concept of "people's war." This concept was not frequently mentioned by Soviet commentators, except in reference to the Chinese, although the *World Marxist Review* did publish an article by a FRELIMO official, in 1981, which discussed the idea of "people's revolutionary war." According to the article, the distinction between this type of war and a simple war for liberation was the revolutionary (social) characterization of its objectives, often with the realization of such objectives even before final victory, in areas already liberated.[186]

Given the resemblance of this to the Chinese concept of people's war, it was surprising that the Soviets published the article, although similar thinking by Cabral was favorably reported by the Soviets.[187] Usually, references to people's war were in fact directed at—and against—the

Chinese concept.[188] A long article on the subject was published in a military journal in 1979, by G. Mos'ko (identified only as candidate of history). Roughly equating the Chinese "people's war" with guerrilla war ("the principal, and almost the only, form of people's war"), this article contained much the same criticism of guerrilla war as the Defense Ministry–Academy of Sciences study. Indeed, the first line of criticism was the very fact that people's war meant guerrilla warfare: Mao demanded that even a war of "manoeuver" with regular formations remain "partisan" in form, that is, remain guerrilla warfare.[89] According to Mos'ko, the Chinese absolutization of guerrilla warfare as the only form of struggle for national liberation movements prevented these movements from addressing the important issue of "creating an army of a new type."[190] Invoking Lenin to the effect that guerrilla warfare was neither the only nor "even the most important means of struggle," he went on to characterize Mao's devotion to the idea as something of an antiquated remnant from the past, anti-Japanese, struggle.

Mos'ko claimed that a decisive change occurred in military thinking as a result of the Soviets' military performance in World War II. This, in turn, led to a modernization and conversion of the Chinese military itself to a regular force, until Mao reversed this and restored the guerrilla (irregular) nature of the army. This was founded on the principle of "all people—soldiers," based on the peasantry creating bases in the village, surrounding the city by the village, and finally, taking the cities. This was then advocated as the sole military doctrine to be employed by national liberation movements, combined with the principle of self-reliance—in other words the rejection of outside assistance.[191] In the post-Mao era, however, there were, according to Mos'ko, some Chinese commentators who appreciated the importance of regular formations and conventional warfare (and modern weaponry) over guerrilla warfare.[192]

Other broader studies contained references to guerrilla warfare which generally confirmed the overall attitude outlined above. For example, writing approximately the same time as the 1974 Defense Ministry–Academy study, Colonel Malinovskii expounded the continuum approach to armed struggle with its implied preference, at least ultimately, for conventional warfare. Without criticizing guerrilla warfare as a means of struggle, Malinovskii merely referred to it as part of a continuum or progression from "armed uprisings of progressive forces" (a return to Lenin's order?), development of a guerrilla movement," later growing into national liberation war.[193] Ten years later *Voenno-istoricheskii zhurnal* praised this progression in Algeria, from guerrilla to regular army tactics, as a model for such struggles.[194] Among the civilian observers, Tarabrin also stated, without discussion, this view of guerrilla warfare as a stage on the road to the formation of a regular liberation army, at least as he claimed that it had occurred in specific African cases.[195]

Some, however, avoided even the continuum approach, expressing more direct criticism of guerrilla warfare altogether. For example, Kim, in a rare (perhaps only) reference to types of armed struggle, said in a 1971 article that "today colonizers are better able to cope with guerrilla warfare, so a well-armed, disciplined army is needed in today's circumstances."[196] Sobolev, generally opposed to armed struggle and exhibiting a tendency to characterize all such forms as guerrilla warfare, argued not only against Mao's "village encircles city" principle, but also "against the conception of the 'guerrilla base' as a source for revolutionizing the masses, which 'stands above the party.'"[197] Regis Debray was criticized for expounding such a view and for advocating the "universality of the 'guerrilla base' as a means for unleashing the revolutionary energy of the masses and as the highest form of organization of revolutionary activity."[198] Fedorov, in his 1983 criticism of armed struggle, was more terse, merely quoting Lenin: "In characterizing guerrilla warfare Lenin pointed out: 'This form of struggle was adopted as the preferred and even *exclusive* form of social struggle by the vagabond elements of the population, the lumpen-proletariat and the anarchist groups."[199]

Ul'ianovskii probably put his finger on the real source of Soviet opposition to guerrilla warfare, however, in his article on Gordon's book on Fanon.

> When an anti-imperialist movement assumes the form of a guerrilla or people's war its focus is inevitably in the rural areas because the peasantry constitutes its main manpower. It could not be otherwise since the cities, according to the definition of the guerrilla war ideologists, are strongholds of colonialism...the guerrilla war has always drawn its strength from the rural areas and peasants formed the bulk of the insurgent units. It could not have been otherwise.[200]

But given Ul'ianovskii's—and Marxist–Leninist—preference for the city, for the workers, as distinct from the highly dubious revolutionary potential and level of the peasantry, the identification of guerrilla warfare with the rural areas rendered it suspect. Even if it was to be tolerated, as Ul'ianovskii said, and even if—or in fact because—the cities were the locum of "all the [colonialists'] repressive power," success could come for armed struggle only if guerrilla warfare "evolved into a national liberation war," led by and in alliance with urban forces, against the cities.[201]

Despite the overall preference for regular over guerrilla forces, there were some dissenting voices. A 1975 article in a military journal, for example, was quite positive in its appraisal of the contribution made by guerrilla warfare to the success of "progressive forces" in the anti-imperialist struggle. Mentioning, as was the norm, the cases in which there had been transformation of the guerrilla units into "a regular cadre army", this article also spoke positively about the cases in which the entire struggle had been waged, successfully, only by guerrilla forces.[202] Similar to the post-Allende discussion of armed struggle, there were also some articles in *Latinskaia Amerika*, for example, one in 1980 and one in 1982, which referred positively to the successful experience of guerrilla warfare in Nicaragua, explicitly suggesting that past opposition to this form of struggle be reconsidered.[203] These articles would appear, however, to have been relatively isolated views, not generally repeated or apparently shared either by the military or even by all the Latin American specialists.[204] At most, they may have indicated pressures by some for a reappraisal; they do not appear to have signalled an actual change in attitude on the part of the Soviets.

Terrorism

If conventional (regular) warfare was preferred over guerrilla warfare, particularly in the Defense Ministry–Academy study, sabotage was clearly preferred over terror. As in the case of guerrilla warfare, the authors of this study began with Lenin, citing Bolshevik opposition to terror, as employed both by the Narodniki and the Social Revolutionaries. "'Propagation of terror as a means of the revolutionary awakening of the masses,' V. I. Lenin pointed out, 'represents worship of spontaneity by the intelligentsia, which has no connection with the revolutionary work of the workers' movement.'" Yet, according to this study, Lenin did not categorically rule out some use of terror, even mass terror, "at particular moments of battle, under certain conditions of the troops and under certain circumstances," provided its use was under strict control of the communist party.[205]

In speaking of the modern movements, the study pointed to the choice made by the movements in southern Africa for "underground sabotage activity" rather than terror. The logic of this decision was based on the idea that, by hitting infrastructure targets such as industry and transportation, there would be an outflow of capital from the area, sorely hurting the local racist regime.[206] Sabotage of government institutions and other centers of power "could inspire the masses" as well as exert pressure on the white public. This was preferable to the use of terror, for "the lack of human victims would avoid embittering the white population" and allow for future cooperation.[207] Allowing that other movements in Africa *had* used "mass terror," as distinct from the South Africans' preference for avoiding human victims, the study criticized

> certain progressive historians [who] have somewhat exaggerated the importance of mass terror in the general arsenal of means of armed struggle, attributing to it qualities of operative-tactical means which permit the diversion of large forces of the enemy from the areas of the guerrilla movement. In reality, African experience testifies to the fact that terror is an *auxiliary* means of armed struggle, that without broad political work among the masses it is incapable of arousing the masses and securing their revolutionary rise.

The study concluded that even the use of sabotage, much less terror, in southern Africa had "turned out to be ineffective, even for attracting the attention of the world public." Such actions were "used by the colonizers for propaganda sensations"; and, in any case, international political and diplomatic pressures, in conjunction with internal pressures—"political or military"—produced greater results.[208]

This view was apparently standard Soviet thinking on the subject. As Western sources have pointed out, the Soviets perceived political change as the result of socioeconomic processes, with revolution coming as an act of the people moving at the proper historical moment. Thus, as the above arguments against the use of violence suggested, any act of violence had to be systematic, directed toward precisely defined targets, at a precisely defined time, serving possibly as a trigger for or accompanying the general armed uprising.[209] Acts of terrorism—by definition, indiscriminate blows against persons as well as property—were too diffuse to be particularly effective with regard to the goal of overall socio-political change. While theoretically they might serve to arouse the masses, attract international attention, and demoralize the regime, Soviet theoreticians rejected these hypotheses. This was the case in specialized texts in Russian as well as more general works, suggesting that the position was not merely propaganda for foreign consumption.

Colonel Dolgopolov, for example, explained that the choice of methods actually dpended upon a number of factors, the major criterion being the extent of the character of social changes accomplished, their contribution to the "economic liberation and social progress" of the nation. Much depended also on the "correlation of forces" in the particular country and the world arena, the class "and other contradictions," colonial resistance and internal reaction and the degree of violence used by them.[210] The key for Dolgopolov, which ruled out terrorism, was the massive character of the struggle; "national liberation uprisings and wars are massive, deeply popular movements having nothing in common with adventuristic, conspiratorial acts, putschism, or terrorism," he argued.[211] Rejecting the use of terror, he maintained that only mass action—by means of a liberation army and guerilla detachments operating with the absolutely essential element of broad popular support—could and did defeat the imperialists.

The Sobolev article was more negative—and specific—in its rejection of terrorism. Where the Defense Ministry–Academy study, for example, had cited Lenin against the use of terror, the Sobolev article of 1980 condemned "Trotskyite views," favoring "political terrorism" against representatives of the state apparatus. Where the earlier study had deemed terrorism counterproductive because the killing of civilians would merely arouse hostility, Sobolev claimed that it was "provocative" and "beneficial to the ruling classes which thus obtained occasions for repression."[212] He used the same argument against the "terrorist war against the staff of repressive apparatus" conducted by the Tuparmaros.

The *World Marxist Review* account of a 1979 conference on revolution and peace carried similar condemnations of terrorism. One participant condemned the use of terrorism by some in Western societies as the pursuit of "chimeras which have nothing in common with the complicated realities of the civil society and the revolutionary process."[213] An Irish participant, asked about terrorism in Northern Ireland, was quoted as attributing the use of terrorism to the "disappointment of petty bourgeois groups in the possibility of attaining legitimate goals by means of the constitutional methods of bourgeois democracy, rejection of the forms and methods of the working-class struggle and refusal to carry on painstaking work among the masses." Explaining that this phenomenon had support among part of the population of Northern Ireland, as well as the Provisional IRA, he added that the acts of terrorism "promote the growth of sectarian attitudes and prevent the establishment of an anti-imperialist alliance"; that is, they alienate people and set them against the cause. Moreover, "these acts enable the British government to intensify its repression on the plea that it is protecting the population." Concluding that terrorism was the symptom rather than the main problem, the need for fundamental change, he concluded the discussion: "Terrorism is the very opposite not only of democratic, but also of revolutionary, methods and goals of struggle."[214]

A number of these themes against terrorism were to be found in the 1983 article by Fedorov, which also called it counter-productive and identified the use of terror with "'left-wing' extremists," citing the Red Brigades and Turkish terrorists.[215] Like Sobolev, he saw acts of terrorism as providing pretexts for the "repressive authorities [to] justify consolidation of the old and creation of new repressive bodies, the tightening of control over the population, restriction of the rights of

the working people and broader, military interference of imperialists."
Indeed, terrorism was so useful to the enemy that the latter even sought
to gain control over "left-wing extremists (particularly terrorists)", so
as to guide their activities in this provocative direction.

This last point was similar to claims made by Soviet observers
regarding various acts of Palestinian terrorism as so counter-productive
as to surely have been the work not of Palestinians but of the Israeli
secret service.[216] Indeed, there were a number of Soviet condemnations
of Palestinian terrorism as assisting the enemy and harming the interests
of the national liberation movement.[217] One of the rare references by
a Soviet leader to any specific form of armed struggle was just such a
condemnation of a Palestinian terrorist act in 1972 by Andrei Gromyko
speaking at the UN.[218] Similarly, *Izvestiia* editor Tolkunov, just prior
to an Arafat visit in 1974, rejected the use of terrorism, recommending
instead "proper forms" of struggle, such as sabotage against military
targets.[219] And it was in the guise of just such "sabotage against military
targets" that the Soviet media presented those Palestinian acts of terror
which it did not condemn outright.[220]

We shall examine the Soviet position on Palestinian terrorism in
our analysis of Soviet policies toward individual national liberation
movements, but the Palestinian case did occasion more references to
the issue of terrorism than were normally to be found in Soviet sources.
These references, unlike the comments contained in the more general
discussions of armed struggle, did make some distinction between
domestically employed terrorism and international terrorism. Neither
was expressly condoned, but it was a great deal more difficult to
portray international terrorism as sabotage or legitimate acts against
military targets. Moreover, the Soviets may have felt no less vulnerable
to such things as hijackings, kidnappings, embassy occupation, and
the like than any other state—particularly after Lithuanian nationalists
hijacked a Soviet airliner in 1970. At least at this time the Soviets
became willing strongly to support a United Nations General Assembly
Resolution against hijacking (over the opposition of some Third World
states).[221] And one can find nothing but Soviet condemnation for acts
of international terrorism, occasionally before but particularly after that
resolution. As with the issue of separatism, on which the Soviets also
may have felt vulnerable, so too with the issue of international terrorism,
the Soviet public position was clear—and negative—whatever the actual
clandestine policy.

Public statements against any kind of terrorism, more clearly of a
propagandistic nature, poured forth in a torrent in 1981, in response to
American accusations of Soviet support (and control) of international
terrorism. There were innumerable direct assertions of Soviet opposition
to terrorism, in principle and universally, by Soviet commentators and

official sources including an official TASS statement, and even leaders such as Ustinov, who declared:

> terrorism is an instrument of extremism and neo-fascism, one of the most terrible manifestations of the moral and political crises of capitalist society...Terrorism is absolutely alien to socialism's very nature...the USSR has always been and remains an opponent in principle to the theory and practice of terrorism, including terrorism in international relations.[222]

Aside from direct denials of this type, Soviet responses fell into two categories, neither of which defended the use of terror itself by anybody. (This despite the fact that, in reporting specific terroristic acts of a national liberation movement in the past, they had occasionally expressed "understanding" for the use of such methods.[223]) The responses in 1981 were either a defense of the national liberation movements' legitimate use of armed struggle, distinguishing between this and terrorism, or they were counter-accusations, not entirely new, that it was the imperialist states that were actually engaged in terrorism against innocent people.

Colonel Dolgopolov had argued, in response to earlier American accusations, that national liberation movements rejected terrorism in favor of mass action for the simple reason that only the latter was effective against a colonial war machine.[224] However unfactual this argument was, it was a rare attempt of the Soviets to provide what appeared to them to be a logical reason for disproving the Western accusations—a reason that reflected their own objection to the use of terror. It may have been Soviet sensitivity to the fact that some movements did employ terror that prevented Soviet responses from following the Dolgopolov example or taking the trouble to explain the different forms of armed struggle, and on that basis to claim that national liberation movements did not use that particular form. Instead, most Soviet responses simply claimed that Western accusations, which identified the national liberation struggle with the use of terrorism—and international terrorism, at that—were merely designed to discredit the national liberation struggle and, indirectly, Soviet support of this struggle.[225]

It was in this torrent of protestations of innocence that one could find Soviet condemnations of terrorism of the most general kind. These became somewhat more specific, with the horrors and dangers of terrorism being mentioned, when the second type of defense was used: that is, going on the offensive: this was the argument, that it was in fact the imperialists that used "state terrorism...as part and parcel of [their] strategy of enslaving and subjecting the developing nations," including acts of terrorism against leaders of the national liberation movements.[226] This line was not fully expressed at the highest levels, but

Andrei Gromyko did employ it indirectly when, at the United Nations, he countered the American charges of terrorism with accusations of American support for "aggressor" policies and interference in the affairs of other peoples.[227] Brezhnev, speaking to the twenty-sixth CPSU Congress, did not choose this response, but rather the one that accused the West of maligning the national liberation movements, although this accusation was tucked into his comments on the aggressive and interfering nature of American policies.[228] Similarly, Brezhnev's message to the 1981 Council of the Afro-Asian Solidarity Organization meeting in Aden combined both, a bit more explicitly. The message said: "Widely using terror and violence against the fighting peoples, the imperialists slander the national liberation movement by putting on it the label of 'international terrorism.'"[229]

In all of these charges, one thing was clear: the Soviet Union did not want to be accused of supporting terrorism or to admit that terrorism was employed by groups that they were clearly and openly supporting. Whatever their attitude toward armed struggle, the Soviets clearly perceived that terrorism, particularly international terrorism, had nothing but negative connotations in the minds of people in the world. Presumably for this reason Gorbachev included a paragraph in his twenty-seventh CPSU Congress speech on the struggle against international terrorism. It was probably this perception, rather than the military or ideological arguments invoked by some, which led to the apparently generally held view that the use of terrorism by national liberation movements was on the whole counter-productive.

Conclusions

A general preference for political means or the avoidance of armed struggle was perceivable in the works of civilian theoreticians. Employing Leninist admonitions against "putchism" or adventurism, there were many voices against the precipitous, if any, use of force. The requisites of a revolutionary situation and a mass-based movement both channeled the means to be used in the direction of political–organizational and ideological work, that is, peaceful means. There were those who saw a complementary auxiliary role for armed actions; indeed, few actually rejected the use of force out of hand, preferring rather to subordinate it even to the point of almost discounting its efficacy and certainly its essentiality. They were particularly concerned with the challenge offered by violence-centred views popular among national liberation movements, such as the ideas of Franz Fanon and the Chinese. Such views challenged the Soviet view of Marxist–Leninist revolutionary doctrine and also introduced such non-Soviet features as spontaneity and priority for the countryside. Much of this opposition, however, was influenced also by the more pragmatic interest in détente and/or the prevention of conflicts, including concern over escalation of local wars. Thus, the condemnation of the use of armed struggle, even in the criticism of Chinese doctrine, was often couched in détente-related terms. Similarly, détente itself was invoked by these opponents of force, as a factor that reduced if not eliminated the need for armed struggle.

At the other end of the spectrum, there were a number of theoreticians who explicitly supported the idea of armed struggle. For most it was simply a matter of defending the right to use this form of struggle, but for some, armed struggle was seen as inevitable, an integral or even essential part of a movement's struggle. For those accepting, possibly even advocating, the use of force, the divisibility of détente was espoused, disclaiming any limitation détente might place on the struggle of national liberation (or revolutionary) movements—and ignoring any damage this might cause to détente (possibly out of opposition to détente itself). The military provided some fuel for this position, either categorizing wars of national liberation under the rubric of just wars rather than local wars (by definition subject to escalation), or by eliminating the concept of inevitable escalation with regard to local wars. The military was by no means uniform, however, in its appraisal of local wars and the possibility of escalation, leading to some differences of view regarding the inevitability as well as desirability of armed struggle among military commentators themselves. It would appear that, as a more sophisticated approach to local wars was developed, wars of national liberation became more problematic for these theorists, but as the views regarding escalation became more varied such wars could be more easily accommodated. The military leadership appeared to tend toward the older concern regarding escalation, possibly preferring stability to the risks involved in armed conflicts, but their views were not unequivocal.

The same may actually be said with regard to the civilian leadership of the Soviet Union. Avoiding, on the whole, any explicit expression of preferences regarding means, some leaders such as Andropov and Kosygin did speak of people's rights to fight for their independence. Brezhnev, Andrei Gromyko, and the ideological watchdog Suslov divided détente to accommodate this struggle, and Ponomarev appeared actually to favor the recourse to arms. Yet Andropov qualified his position by frequent warnings regarding the risks of escalation and instability, while Brezhnev refrained from clear support even at the 1976 CPSU Congress, retreating from what had possibly been a positive position. Podgornyi expressed Soviet preferences for political over armed means in his 1977 African trip, which position was upheld by Gorbachev at the 1986 CPSU Congress.

While a slight chronological tendency may have been discernible with regard to the leadership (the mid-1970s a high point, declining in the early 1980s), no such time factor was evident with regard either to the military or the civilian theoreticians, the differing views within each group spanning the 1970s and early 1980s. Nor does there appear to have been any institutional factor. As in the issues already seen in the preceding chapter, so too on the issue of armed struggle, the Central Committee's leading International Department experts were not entirely in agreement. Brutents and only slightly less Ul'ianovskii took the anti-armed struggle view; Zagladin took a more middle position—though not the extreme advocacy of armed struggle position. Surprisingly, the Ideology Department's Marxist–Leninist Institute specialist Sobolev was at the peaceful means end of the spectrum, while not unexpectedly the *World Marxist Review* editor, the conservative Zarodov, was at the other end. Similarly, Agaev, of the Workers' Movement Institute, supported armed struggle, as did Starushenko (and Tarabrin) of the Africa Institute, who had expressed conservative attitudes on other issues as well. Starushenko's director, Anatolii Gromyko was not, however, as interested in armed conflict, and his former director, Solodovnikov, was even less so. Simoniia and his director Primakov appeared to be at even greater odds over the issue. As might have been expected, however, the U.S.A.– Canada Institute analysts adopted a position consistent with détente, the Far Eastern specialists a position consistent with an anti-Maoist view, and at least some Latin Americanists a view influenced by the failure of the peaceful path in Chile and the successful armed path in Nicaragua.

With regard to types of armed struggle to be employed, there appears to have been far fewer divergencies of views. Guerrilla warfare, associated with the priority of the countryside (and the Chinese), was condemned by many, particularly among the military. On the whole, such warfare was acceptable only as a prelude to the clearly preferred form of struggle, conventional warfare by regular forces. This preference suited—and presumably was dictated by—the Marxist propensity for the city, the seat of the proletariat and, in terms of the Third World, of the colonial power. A reappraisal may have been suggested by some commentators following the successful guerrilla struggle in Nicaragua, but there were no signs of this as an overall preference.

If guerrilla warfare was questionable, the use of terror was even less desirable. Though acknowledged by some as a possible auxiliary means, if under proper control, terror was generally repugnant for both ideological and pragmatic reasons. At the ideological level, this type of indiscriminate action against civilians resembled anarchism, unrelated to, even defying, the steady rules of historical development. At the pragmatic level, it was deemed counter-productive, repelling rather than attracting people to the cause. For both these reasons sabotage was preferred over terror. Indeed, most commentators, particularly among the military, rejected anything but mass action, by definition conducted by a regular army, possibly with guerrilla assistance.

These views may or may not have guided the leadership level. Leadership pronouncements were unequivocal in their condemnation of terrorism, indicating at the very least an objection to being publicly associated with this type of action even when employed by groups favorably regarded by Moscow. To some degree this opposition was also conveyed privately to the movements, suggesting that the leadership did share some of the theoreticians' general preferences and priorities: sabotage over terror, guerrilla over sabotage, regular (conventional) warfare over guerrilla, political means over armed struggle.

Notes

1 Y. Zhukov, L. Delyusin, A. Iskenderov, and L. Stepanov, *The Third World*, Progress, Moscow, 1970, p. 23.
2 Ibid.
3 Ibid.
4 Ibid., pp. 22–4.
5 E.M. Primakov, *Vostok posle krakha kolonial'noi sistemy*, Nauka, Moscow, 1982, pp. 109–10.
6 Editorial, "Lenin and the National Liberation Movement", *Asia and Africa Today*, no. 2 (1982): 5.
7 Ibid.
8 Vl. Fedorov, "'Levyi ekstremizm v politicheskoi zhizni stran Vostoka," *Aziia i Afrika segodnia*, no. 5 (1983): 13–16.
9 Ibid., pp. 13–14 (emphasis mine).
10 K. N. Brutents, *Sovremennye natsional'no-osvoboditel'nye revoliutsii*, Politizdat, Moscow, 1974 (citations from K. N. Brutents, *National Liberation Revolutions Today*, Progress, Moscow, 1977), vol. I. p. 67.
11 Ibid., p. 65,
12 Ibid., pp. 159–60.
13 Ibid., pp. 65, 159, 292; and K. N. Brutents, *Osvobodivshiesia strany v 70-e gody*, Politizdat, Moscow, 1979, p. 8.
14 Karen Brutents, *The Newly Free Countries in the Seventies*, Progress, Moscow, 1983, p. 136. This whole chapter was added in the English version, so this sentence was not to be found in the Russian edition. Neither edition discussed the issue of means to anywhere near the same extent as the earlier study.
15 R. A. Ul'ianovskii, *Funktsii gosudarstva v nezavisimykh stranakh Afriki*, Nauka, Moscow, 1972, p. 283.
16 R. A. Ul'ianovskii, *Ocherki natsional'no-osvoboditel'noi bor'by: voprosy teorii i praktiki*, Nauka, Moscow, 1976 (citations from the English translation: Rostislav Ulyanovsky, *National Liberation: Essays on Theory and Practice*, Progress, Moscow, 1978), p. 236.
17 Ibid., pp. 70, 197.
18 Ibid., p. 70.
19 Ibid., p. 71.
20 Ibid., p. 197.
21 Ibid., pp. 196, 199.
22 Ibid., pp. 195, 201.

23   Ibid., p. 72.
24   Rostislav Ulyanovsky, *Present-day Problems in Asia and Africa*, Progress, Moscow, 1980, pp. 171–2. This section was not in the Russian edition at all (R. A. Ul'ianovskii, *Sovremennye problemy Azii i Afriki*, Nauka, Moscow, 1978).
25   R. Ul'ianovskii, "Nauchnyi sotsializm i Frants Fanon," *Aziia i Afrika segodnia*, no. 5 (1978): 21. See also Ulyanovsky, *Present-day Problems*, pp. 234–5.
26   Ul'ianovskii, "Nauchnyi sotsializm," pp. 20–2.
27   R. A. Ul'ianovskii, "Nauchnyi sotsializm i Amilkar Kabral," *Aziia i Afrika segodnia*, no. 12 (1978): 31; Ulyanovsky, *Present-day Problems*, p. 229. This same point was made by V. Solodovnikov and O. Martyshin, "Nasledie Amilkara Kabrala," *Aziia i Afrika segodnia*, no. 7 (1983): 42–5.
28   A. V. Gordon, *Problemy natsional'no–osvoboditel'noi bor'by v tvorchestve Frantsa Fanona*, Nauka, Moscow, 1977, pp. 77–80, 88–91; Ul'ianovskii, "Fanon," pp. 21–2.
29   Gordon, *Problemy*, p. 105, 126.
30   Ibid., p. 106.
31   See chapter 3.
32   O. Yuriev, "Sources and Substance of Non-Marxist Socialism," *New Times*, no. 32 (1973): 18.
33   Ibid.
34   Ibid.
35   Ibid.
36   Zhukov et al., *Third World*, p. 23.
37   Evgeny Tarabrin, "Peking's Manoeuvres in Africa," *New Times*, no. 6 (1972): 19.
38   *Sovetskaia Rossiia*, 31 October 1974 (Mikhailov); *Izvestiia*, 20 April 1974 (Mitin); Dmitry Volsky, "Dangerous Fancy: The Twisted Maoist Picture of the Modern World," *New Times*, no. 35 (1974): 14–16; Vikenty Matveyev, "Détente and Conflicts," *New Times*, no. 46 (1974): 4–5; Zinovy Mirsky, "Maoist Ideology: Behind the Facade," *New Times*, no. 7 (1975): 20–1; I. Belyaev, "Peking's African Policy," *Far Eastern Affairs*, no. 3 (1975): 58–71; V. Krivtsov, "The Maoists Foreign Policy Strategy," *Far Eastern Affairs*, no. 3 (1978): 48–60; V. Krivtsov, "China's Anti-Socialist Policy vis-à-vis Developing States," *Far Eastern Affairs*, no. 2 (1980): 89–101.
39   V. G. Solodovnikov and V. V. Bogoslovsky, *Non-Capitalist Development: An Historical Outline*, Progress, Moscow, 1975, p. 18.
40   Ibid., p. 228.
41   Ibid., pp. 162, 228.
42   A. Kiva, "Imperializm i strany sotsialisticheskoi orientatsii. Stat'ia pervaia naudrug," *Aziia i Afrika segodnia*, no. 8 (1980): 8–9. See also E. Tarabrin, "Neokolonializm na sovremennom etape," *Aziia i Afrika segodnia*, no. 1 (1978): 13–14.
43   *Izvestiia*, 8 September 1978.
44   A. Krasilnikov, "Peking's Treacherous Course and the Liberation Struggle in Southern Africa," *Far Eastern Affairs*, no. 2 (1981): 64–73.
45   A. I. Sobolev, "Leninskaia kontseptsiia mnogoobraziia putei sotsial'nogo razvitiia," *Voprosy istorii KPSS*, no. 4 (1980): 41–52.
46   Ibid., p. 49 (emphasis mine).
47   Ibid., pp. 49–50.
48   Ibid., p. 50.
49   Ibid., p. 51.
50   Ibid., pp. 51–2.
51   See Daniel Papp, "National Liberation during Détente: The Soviet Outlook," *International Journal* 32 (1976–77): 82–99.
52   E. Zhukov, "The Impact of the Changes in International Relations on the National Liberation Struggle," *International Affairs*, no. 12 (1973): 27–28.
53   Georgii Kim, *The Socialist World and the National Liberation Movement*, Novosti, Moscow, 1978, pp. 65, 77.
54   Zhukov, "Impact," p. 28.
55   G. Kim, "National Liberation Movement: Topical Problems," *International Affairs*, no. 9 (1984): 51–2; G. Kim, "Razriadka i sotsial'nyi progress v stranakh Azii i

Afriki," *Aziia i Afrika segodnia*, no. 11 (1978): 6 (though Kim also spoke of détente as restraining the West); An. Gromyko, "Sovetskaia politika mira," *Aziia i Afrika segodnia*, no. 1 (1981): 3; I. Ivanov, "Osvobodivshiesia strany: razriadka i razvitie," *Aziia i Afrika segodnia*, no. 8 (1980): 4.

56 Ivanov, "Osvobodivshiesia strany," p. 5.
57 *Izvestiia*, 25 May 1975.
58 N. Inozemtsev, "O novom etape v razvitii mezhdunarodnykh otnoshenii," *Kommunist*, no. 15 (1973): 97.
59 V. Zhurkin, "Détente and International Conflicts," *International Affairs*, no. 7 (1974): 90; or V. V. Zhurkin and E. M. Primakov, *Mezhdunarodnye konflikty*, mezhdunarodnye otnosheniia, Moscow, 1972, p. 19.
60 V. V. Zhurkin, "Razriadka i politika SShA v mezhdunarodnykh konfliktakh," *SShA: ekonomika, politika i ideologiia*, no. 2 (1977): 12–13.
61 V. Kremeniuk and Vl. Lukin, "Imperializm i razvivaiu shchiesia strany: evoliutsiia vzaimootnoshenii," *Aziia i Afrika segodnia*, no. 12 (1983): 4–7; V. Kremeniuk, "Sistema vzaimodeistviia mezhdunarodnykh konfliktov sovremennosti," in V. I. Gantman, *Mezhdunarodnye konflikty sovremennosti*, Nauka, Moscow, 1983, pp. 236–92.
62 A. Kiva, "The Changing Africa," *New Times*, no. 7 (1976): 18; D. Volsky, "Peaceful Coexistence and the Third World," *New Times*, no. 33 (1972): 4–5.
63 Volsky, "Coexistence," pp. 4–5.
64 D. Volsky, "Taking Up A Point," *New Times*, no. 22 (1978): 30 and "Behind the Conflict in Angola," *New Times*, no. 38 (1975): 8.
65 Vl. Shelepin, "European Détente and the Third World," *New Times*, no. 38 (1975): 4.
66 K. Brutents, "A Great Force of Modern Times," *International Affairs*, no. 3 (1981): 77; see also chapter 5 below.
67 Ibid., pp. 83–4, 77.
68 Ulyanovsky, *National Liberation*, pp. 199–201.
69 Zhurkin and Primakov, *Mezhdunarodnye konflikty*, p. 24; Gantman, *Mezhdunarodnye konflikty sovremennosti*, pp. 40–2.
70 Zhurkin and Primakov, *Mezhdunarodnye konflikty*, p. 20.
71 Ibid., pp. 20–1; Gantman, *Mezhdunarodnye konflikty sovremennosti*, pp. 4–5, 63.
72 Gantman, *Mezhdunarodnye konflikty sovremennosti*, pp. 79, 257–92; *Pravda*, 22 July 1973 (Arbatov) and Soviet television, December 1980.
73 Soviet television, 24 November 1980.
74 *Literaturnaia gazeta*, 1 January 1981, pp. 14–15; A. Bovin, "Neprekhodiashchee znachenie Leninskikh idei," *Kommunist*, no. 10 (1980): 75.
75 Kim, *Socialist World*, p. 77; *Pravda*, 20 June 1981.
76 S. Madzoevskii, "Iuzhnoafrikanskii uzel mirovoi politiki," *Mirovaia ekonomika i mezhdunarodnye otnosheniia*, no. 7 (1977): 21 (emphasis mine).
77 V. Zagladin, "XXVI s'ezd KPSS i mirovoi revoliutsionnyi protsess," *Mirovaia ekonomika i mezhdunarodnye otnosheniia*, no. 4 (1981): 12; P. I. Manchkha, *Aktual'nye problemy sovremennoi Afriki*, Politizdat, Moscow, 1979, p. 201.
78 See below.
79 See Joan Barth Urban, "Contemporary Soviet Perspectives on Revolution in the West," *Orbis* 14, no. 4 (1976): 1361–5, 1371; Jerry Hough, "The Evolving Soviet Debate on Latin America," *Latin American Research Review* 16, no. 1 (1981): 131–2; Pedro Ramet and Fernando Lopez-Alvez, "Moscow and the Revolutionary Left in Latin America," *Orbis* 28, no. 2 (1984): 348–51.
80 Urban, "Contemporary Soviet Perspectives," 1361–5, 1371; Edme Dominguez Reyes, "Soviet Academic Views on the Caribbean and Central America," Conference paper, Washington, 1985, pp. 5–6.
81 S. L. Agaev, "Levyi radikalizm, revoliutsionnyi demokratizm i nauchnyi sotsializm v stranakh Vostoka," *Rabochii klass i sovremennyi mir*, no. 3 (1984): 134–5. See also Reyes, "Soviet Academic Views," pp. 22–3.
82 G. B. Starushenko, "XXV s''ezd KPSS o progressivnykh izmeneniiakh v osvobodivshikhsia stranakh i povyshenii ikh roli v mirovom razvitii, " *Voprosy istorii KPSS*, no. 7 (1976): 49.
83 Gleb Starushenko, "Chosen Path," *New Times*, no. 40 (1980): 18.

84   G. Starushenko, "International Law and National Liberation," *International Affairs*, no. 2 (1983): 80–1, 83.
85   A. A. Gromyko and G. B. Starushenko, "Sotsial'nye i natsional'nye faktory razvitiia osvobodivshikhsia stran," *Sotsiologicheskie issledovaniia*, no. 1 (1983): 3–9.
86   An. A. Gromyko, "XXVI s'ezd KPSS i zadachi sovetskoi afrikanistiki," *Narody Azii i Afriki*, no. 4 (1981): 6.
87   Anatoly Gromyko, *Africa: Progress, Problems, Prospects*, Progress, Moscow, 1981, p. 141.
88   E. A. Tarabrin, *USSR and Countries of Africa*, Progress, Moscow, 1980 (Russian edition 1977), p. 14; E. A. Tarabrin, "Afrika na novom vitke osvoboditel'noi bor'by," *Mirovaia ekonomika i mezhdunarodnye otnosheniia*, no. 2 (1979): 45–7.
89   N. Simoniya, "The October Revolution and National Liberation Movements," ₅*International Affairs*, no. 12 (1979): p. 61 (emphasis in original).
90   R. G. Landa, "A. V. Gordon. Problemy natsional'no–osvoboditel'noi bor'by v tvorchestve Frantsa Fanona," *Narody Azii i Afriki*, no. 6 (1977): 215.
91   Vl. Maksimenko, "Ob ideinom nasledii Fanona," *Aziia i Afrika segodnia*, no. 10 (1977): 63.
92   P. Shastitko, "Revoliutsiia dolzhna umet' zashchishchat'sia," *Aziia i Afrika segodnia*, no. 1 (1982): 2.
93   A. A. Ivanov, "Avangard revoliutsionnogo dvizheniia v Afrike," *Nauchnyi kommunizm*, no. 4 (1976): 89.
94   Interview with Stanley Mabizela, "Southern Africa: Backstage of the Racists" Manoeuvres," *World Marxist Review* 27, no. 7 (1984): 130. See also Vusizwe Seme, "On the Various Forms of Revolutionary Struggle." *African Communist*, no. 71 (1977): 31. Syrian Communist party leader Khaled Bagdesh also supported armed struggle, criticizing the Social Democrats for "putting 'democracy' above everything and therefore refusing to support the armed struggle in Africa": Khaled Bagdesh, "Social Reformism and the National Liberation Movement," *World Marxist Review* 22, no. 8 (1979): 8.
95   *Pravda*, 26 August 1977; cited in Judson Mitchell, "The Restructuring of International Relations," paper delivered to the International Association for Soviet and East European Studies, Washington, 1985, p. 13.
96   D. Baratashvili, "Lenin's Doctrine of the Self-determination of Nations and the National Liberation Struggle," *International Affairs*, no. 12 (1970): 12.
97   V. Sidenko, "The Truth versus Lies," *New Times*, no. 19 (1977): 18–21.
98   E. Tarabrin, "Neo-colonialism—A new System of Dependence and Enslavement," *International Affairs*, no. 11 (1978): 61; Starushenko, "XXV s'ezd KPSS," p. 49; N. Simoniya, "Mighty Tide of National Liberation," *New Times*, no. 50 (1980): 22–3.
99   *New Times*, no. 9 (1978): 1.
100 See also TASS, 21 November 1978; *Izvestiia*, 17 January 1978; *Sovetskaia Rossiia*, 14 February 1978.
101 *Izvestiia*, 24 August 1978.
102 See, for example, K. I. Zarodov, "O nekotorykh perspektivakh razvitiia mirovogo revoliutsionnogo protsessa v svete idei XXVI s'ezda KPSS," *Voprosy istorii KPSS*, no. 9 (1981): 33–4.
103 Mark Katz, *The Third World in Soviet Military Thought*, Johns Hopkins University Press, Baltimore, 1982. For earlier authoritative works on this subject, see Raymond Garthoff, *Soviet Military Policy: A Historical Approach*, Praeger, New York, 1966, and Thomas Wolfe, *Soviet Strategy at the Crossroads*, Harvard University Press, Cambridge, Mass., 1964.
104 Katz, *Third World*, pp. 21–6.
105 Ibid., p. 24 (Col.-Gen. Lomov).
106 Gen. I. Shavrov, "Lokal'nye voiny i ikh mesto v global'noi strategii imperializma": Part I, *Voenno-istoricheskii zhurnal*, no. 3 (1975): 57–66; Part II, *Voenno-istoricheskii zhurnal*, no. 4 (1975): 90–7; Gen. Shavrov (ed.), *Lokal'nye voiny: istoriia i sovremennost'*, Voenizdat, Moscow, 1981.
107 Shavrov, "Lokal'nye voiny," from Katz, *Third World*, p. 75.

108 Col. G. Malinovskii, "Lokal'nye voiny v zone natsional'no–osvoboditel'nogo dvizh-eniia," *Voenno-istoricheskii zhurnal*, no. 5 (1974): 73–6.
109 Ibid., p. 70. See Col. E. Rybkin, "Voiny sovremennoi epokhi i ikh vliianie na sotsial'nye protsessy," *Kommunist Vooruzhennykh Sil*, no. 11 (1970): 9–16; Col. E. Rybkin, "Leninskie printsipy sotsiologicheskogo analiza voin i sovremennost'," in Maj.-Gen. A. S. Milovidov and Col. V. G. Kozlov (eds.), *Filosofskoe nasledie V. I. Lenina i problemy sovremennoi voiny*, Voenizdat, Moscow, 1972, pp. 31–52; Col. E. Rybkin, "XXV s'ezd KPSS i osvoboditel'nye voiny sovremennoi epokhi," *Voenno-istoricheskii zhurnal*, no. 11 (1978): 10–17.
110 Katz, *Third World*, p. 70.
111 Malinovskii, "Lokal'nye voiny," p. 92. (He said that these inner-state differences would not become wars and could be solved peacefully, if the imperialists did not intervene and exploit the situation.) In 1983 Malinovskii offered a new classification based on "neo-colonialist wars," i.e., wars of imperialists against dependent states and peoples, and imperialists against newly independent states. The examples were El Salvador, Zaire, Cambodia, Laos, and South Vietnam: Col. G. Malinovskii, "Neo-kolonial'nye voiny imperializma," *Voenno-istoricheskii zhurnal*, no. 5 (1983): 60.
112 Shavrov, "Lokal'nye voiny," pt. I, p. 63.
113 V. L. Tiagunenko et al., *Vooruzhennaia bor'ba narodov Afriki za svobodu i nezavisimost'*, Ministerstvo Oborony–SSSR, Nauka, Moscow, 1974, p. 51.
114 Rybkin, "XXV s'ezd," p. 14.
115 Tiagunenko et al., *Vooruzhennaia bor'ba*, pp. 329–30.
116 Col. E. Dolgopolov, "Razoblachenie burzhuaznykh i maoistskikh fal'sifikatorov istorii lokal'nykh voin," *Voenno-istoricheskii zhurnal*, no. 6 (1980): 58.
117 Maj.-Gen. D. Volkogonov, "Klassovaia bor'ba i sovremennost'," *Kommunist Vooru-zhennykh Sil*, no. 4 (1979): 12.
118 Tiagunenko et al., *Vooruzhennaia bor'ba*, p. 53. It was also to be found in innumerable articles in *Krasnaia zvezda*, e.g. 20 December 1973 (after the Central Committee plenum, following the Yom Kippur war); 20 December 1974; 1 May 1979.
119 We shall examine the escalation issue below.
120 Malinovskii, "Lokal'nye voiny v zone," p. 92.
121 Rybkin, "XXV s'ezd," p. 14.
122 Tiagunenko et al., *Vooruzhennaia bor'ba*, pp. 53, 72–5, 328.
123 Dolgopolov, "Razoblachenie burzhuaznykh," p. 61.
124 Ibid., pp. 61–2.
125 Col. G. Kirilenko, "Blizhnii Vostok: opasnye manevry imperializma i sionizma," *Kommunist Vooruzhennykh Sil*, no. 10 (1983): 87.
126 For example, Belyi in Col. Tushkevich et al., *Marksizm–Leninizm o voine i armii*, Voenizdat, Moscow, 1968, p. 72; Marshal Sokolovskii, *Voennaia strategiia*, Voenizdat, Moscow, 1965, 1968; or V. Perfilov, "Limited Warfare in US Foreign Policy," *Voennaia mysl*, no. 4 (1971): 107; cited in Rajan Menon, *Soviet Power and the Third World: Aspects of Theory and Practice*, Yale University Press, New Haven, Conn., 1986. For a discussion covering the 1960s, see Christofer Jones, "Just Wars and Limited Wars: Restraints on the Use of the Soviet Armed Forces," *World Politics* 28, no. 1 (1975): 44–67; and Katz, *Third World*, pp. 38–9.
127 Col. N. Nikitin, "Nekotorye operativno–takticheskie uroki lokal'nykh voin imper-ializma," *Voenno-istoricheskii zhurnal*, no. 12 (1978): 66 (emphasis mine).
128 Dolgopolov, "Razoblachenie burzhuaznykh," pp. 62–3. For a later apparent reversal, at least regarding Soviet aid, see chapter 5.
129 *Krasnaia zvezda*, 11 June 1978 (in response to the Shaba crisis).
130 Col. A. Levchenkov, "War and Politics," *Soviet Military Review*, no. 12 (1983): 21.
131 *Sovetskaia voennaia entsiklopediia*, vol. 7, Voenizdat, Moscow, pp. 564–5; translated by Harriet Fast Scott and William Scott, *The Soviet Art of War*, Westview, Boulder, Colo., 1982, p. 247 (emphasis mine).
132 Milovidov and Kozlov, *Filosofskoe nasledie*, pp. 48, 16–14. See Menon, *Soviet Power*.
133 Shavrov, "Lokal'nye voiny," pt. II, p. 94. See also Menon, *Soviet Power*.
134 Shavrov, "Lokal'nye voiny," pt. II, p. 97.
135 Katz, *Third World*, pp. 73–6, 142; Shavrov, "Lokal'nye voiny," pt. I, p. 61.

136 Shavrov, "Lokal'nye voiny," pt. I, p. 61.
137 V. M. Kulish (ed.), *Voennaia sila i mezhdunarodnye otnosheniia*, Mezhdunarodnye otnosheniia, Moscow, 1972, p. 47; see Katz, *Third World*, p. 90 (n. 2) and Menon, *Soviet Power*, for comments on Kulish.
138 Malinovskii, "Lokal'nye voiny v zone," p. 97.
139 In Katz, *Third World*, p. 97.
140 Maj.-Gen. Volkogonov et al., *Voina i armiia*, Voenizdat, Moscow, 1977, pp. 249–50.
141 Lt.-Gen. D. Volkogonov, "The Logic of Retaliatory Measures," *Soviet Military Review*, no. 6 (1984): 55; D. Volkogonov, "The Soviet Army: A Factor in Peace and Security," *Soviet Military Review*, no. 2 (1984): 3.
142 Maj.-Gen. V. Matsulenko, "Some Lessons of Imperialist Local Wars," *Soviet Military Review*, no. 10(1984): 45.
143 *Pravda*, 12 July 1982; 25 July 1981; 7 November 1981.
144 Private Interviews with and lectures by Soviet scholars.
145 Menon, *Soviet Power*, pp. 72–4; Michael McGwire, *Soviet Military Objectives*, Third Draft, Brookings, February 1985, p. 23.
146 Moscow radio, 4 April 1971; 22 December 1971 (Andropov).
147 *Pravda*, 4 July 1972.
148 TASS, 12 January 1978.
149 E.g. M. Suslov, "Kommunisticheskoe dvizhenie v avangarde bor'by za mir, sotsial'noe i natsional'noe," *Kommunist*, no. 11 (1975): 7.
150 Boris Ponomarev, "The World Situation and the Revolutionary Process," *World Marxist Review* 19, no. 6 (1974): 10–11.
151 See below, 1980 article by Ponomarev in *Kommunist*.
152 A. A. Gromyko, "Programma mira v deistvii...," *Kommunist*, no. 14 (1975): 9.
153 *Pravda*, 25 February 1976.
154 *Pravda*, 23 April 1976; *Leninskoe znamia*, 23 February 1979 (FBIS, III, 5 April 1979, R-8).
155 *Pravda*, 23 April 1976.
156 TASS, 29 March 1977.
157 TASS, 29 March 1977; *Pravda*, 31 March 1977.
158 TASS, 31 March 1977. Podgornyi was relieved of his duties as president of the Supreme Soviet shortly after his return from Africa, a move that must have miffed his African hosts but was most likely unconnected with the trip.
159 *Pravda*, 23 June 1978.
160 TASS, 28 June 1978.
161 *Pravda*, 3 November 1977.
162 B. Ponomarev, "Neodolimost' osvoboditel'nogo dvi zehnnia," *Kommunist*, no. 1 (1980): 2–27.
163 *Pravda*, 23 February 1981.
164 *Pravda*, 28 April 1981; TASS, September 1982; TASS, 27 October 1982. See chapter 5.
165 *Pravda*, 22 December 1982.
166 Ibid.; *Pravda*, 23 November 1982; 16 June 1983.
167 *Pravda*, 7 January 1983.
168 *Izvestiia*, 29 October 1983 (Aliev); *Pravda*, 30 July 1983 (Zimianin).
169 *Pravda*, 26 October 1985.
170 Tiagunenko et al., *Vooruzhennaia bor'ba*.
171 Ibid., pp. 54, 332.
172 Ibid., pp. 43–4.
173 Ibid., p. 46.
174 Ibid., p. 55, quoting Giapp.
175 Ibid., p. 55.
176 Ibid., p. 56.
177 Ibid., p. 364.
178 Ibid., p. 350.
179 Ibid., p. 354.
180 Ibid., p. 337.

181 Ibid., p. 338.
182 Ibid., p. 356.
183 Outside assistance was also a factor, as we shall see below.
184 Ibid., pp. 55, 369–70.
185 Ibid., p. 371 (see chapter 5 below).
186 Sergio Vieira, "Stage of Fundamental Change," *World Marxist Review*, no. 1 (1981): 21–2.
187 See Ulyanovsky, *Present-day Problems*, pp. 223–4 (not in Russian edition).
188 E.g., A. Kudriavtsev, op. cit., p. 89; Solodovnikov and Bogoslovsky, *Non-capitalist Development*, p. 228; Dolgopolov, "Razoblachenie burzhuaznykh," p. 62; Krivtsov, "Maoists' Foreign Policy," p. 53; Krivtsov, "China's Anti-socialist Policy," p. 35.
189 G. Mos'ko, "K voprosu o maoistskoi teorii 'narodnoi voiny'," *Voenno-istoricheskii zhurnal*, no. 3 (1979): 59.
190 Ibid.
191 Ibid., pp. 60–1.
192 Ibid., p. 63.
193 Malinovskii, "Lokal'nye voiny," p. 94.
194 N. Mel'nik, "V bor'be za nezavisimost'," *Voenno–istoricheskii zhurnal*, no. 11 (1984): 58.
195 Tarabrin, "Afrika na novom vitke," p. 45.
196 G. Kim, "Osnovopolozhniki marksizma i osvobozhdenie Vostoka," *Aziia i Afrika segodnia*, no. 3 (1971): 4.
197 Sobolev, "Leninskaia kontseptsiia," p. 50.
198 Ibid. Also criticized were the various concepts of urban guerrilla, attributed to Latin Americans.
199 Fedorov, "Levyi ekstremizm," p. 13.
200 Ul'ianovskii, "Frants Fanon," p. 21.
201 Ibid., p. 22. See also Ulyanovsky, *Present-day Problems*, p. 235.
202 Col. V. Andrianov, "Partizanskaia voina i voennaia strategiia," *Voenno-istoricheskii zhurnal*, no. 7 (1975): 29–31. Katz, *Third World*, p. 82, pointed to the same article's praise for the flexibility of guerrilla warfare.
203 T. E. Vorozheikina, "Revoliutsionnye organizatsii Sal'vadora i narodnoe dvizhenie," *Latinskaia Amerika*, no. 7 (1982): 23–6; S. A. Mikoian, "Ob osobennostiakh revoliutsii v Nikaragua i ee urokakh s tochki zreniia teorii i praktiki osvoboditel'nogo dvizheniia," *Latinskaia Amerika*, no. 3 (1980): 34–44. See above, n. 85 and 86, and Mark Katz, "The Soviet–Cuban Connection," *International Security* 8, no. 1 (1983): 89–93.
204 See Hough, "Evolving Soviet Debate." One interviewee has claimed that the staff of Latinskaia Amerika were more "radical" than its parent organization, the Latin American Institute. See Reyes, "Soviet Academic Views," p. 6.
205 Tiagunenko et al., *Vooruzhennaia bor'ba*, pp. 44–5.
206 Ibid., p. 301.
207 Ibid., p. 302.
208 Ibid., p. 361.
209 See William Pomeroy (ed.), *Guerrilla Warfare and Marxism*, Lawrence and Wishart, London, 1969, pp. 75–121; Feliks Gross, *Violence in Politics*, Mouton, The Hague, 1972, p. 32; Nathan Leites, *A Study of Bolshevism*, Free Press, Glencoe, Ill., 1953, p. 341; Stefan Possony, *A Century of Conflict*, Regenoy, Chicago, 1953, pp. 224–5; Ze'ev Avyensky, *Personal Terror (Hateror Haishi)*, Kibbutz HaMeuchad, Tel Aviv, 1977; Yonah Alexander (ed.), *International Terrorism: National, Regional, and Global Perspectives*, Praeger, New York, 1976, pp. 115–116.
210 Dolgopolov, "Razoblachenie burzhuaznykh," pp. 61–2.
211 Ibid.
212 Sobolev, "Leninskaia kontseptsiia," pp. 49–50.
213 "Revolution and Democracy: International Science Conference," *World Marxist Review* 22, no. 10 (1979): 38 (Antonio Jannazzo).
214 Ibid., p. 39 (Tommy O'Flaherty).
215 Fedorov, "Levyi ekstremizm," pp. 13–16.

216　E.g., *Pravda*, 7 January 1973; *Pravda*, 19 December 1973; TASS, 27 November 1972; TASS, 20 May 1974.
217　E.g., Vladimir Terekhov, "International Terrorism and the Fight Against It," *New Times*, no. 11 (1974): 20–1.
218　*New York Times*, 27 September 1972.
219　*Izvestiia*, 30 July 1974.
220　See Galia Golan, *The Soviet Union and the Palestine Liberation Organization*, Praeger, New York, 1980, pp. 219–27, for Soviet responses to specific acts of terror.
221　Robert Freedman, "Soviet Policy Towards International Terrorism," in Alexander, *International Terrorism*, pp. 115–47.
222　*Pravda*, 21 February 1981.
223　E.g., *Pravda*, 4 March 1973.
224　Dolgopolov, "Razoblachenie burzhuaznykh," pp. 61–2.
225　E.g., Malinovskii, "Neokolonial'nye voiny," p. 62; An. Gromyko, "XXVI s'ezd," p. 10; Gromyko and Starushenko, "Faktory razvitiia," p. 6; A. Iskenderov, "Developing Countries: Improving the World Climate," *International Affairs*, no. 10 (1981): p. 42; G. Kim, "The National Liberation Movement Today," *International Affairs*, no. 4 (1981): 36; G. Kim, "Sovetskii Soiuz i natsional'no–osvoboditel'noe dvizhenie," *Mirovaia ekonomika i mezhdu narodnye otnosheniia*, no. 9 (1982): 31; *Pravda*, 1 February 1981; *Izvestiia*, 15 October 1981.
226　V. Iordansky, "The Policy of Neo-colonialism in Action". *International Affairs*, no. 6 (1981): 84. See also V. Efremov, "Mezhdunarodnyi terrorizm–orudie imperializma i reaktsii," *Aziia i Afrika segodnia*, no. 7 (1981): 24–6; *Izvestiia*, 15 October 1981 (An. Gromyko); *Izvestiia*, 8 February 1981; *Izvestiia*, 17 June 1981; *Pravda*, 1 February 1981; *Pravda*, 19 October 1981.
227　TASS, 22 September 1981.
228　*Pravda*, 23 February 1981.
229　TASS, 20 March 1981.

5

Relations with the Soviet Union and the Socialist World

Introduction

Soviet theoretical works and discussions could not be expected to be particularly explicit or revealing concerning the actual role the Soviet Union played or should play with regard to the national liberation movements. Nevertheless, views expressed on particular issues might well serve as indicators of preferred policies or attitudes. The relative importance or place of the national liberation movements in the overall world revolutionary process was probably one such indicator, those according them a more significant place presumably being among the more willing to provide Soviet assistance or advocating Soviet involvement. Traditionally, at least, that has been the case since the early Comintern debates on the subject. Related to this was the issue of not only what, if anything, the national liberation movement contributed, but also what potential it had for actually becoming part and parcel of the revolution, that is, for becoming a socialist revolution. Conversely, the importance of the Soviet Union to the national liberation struggle, that is, the dichotomy between those who saw Soviet input as crucial and those who emphasized the irrevocable historical and/or internal processes at play, may have been an indicator of policy preferences. A third possible indicator was the characterization of Western policy regarding the national liberation movement, a higher hostility interpretation of Western behaviour indicating, perhaps, advocacy of greater Soviet involvement, or the necessity for Soviet involvement, although it might equally be argued that those who depicted an aggressive, intervening West may have been signalling that Soviet intervention or involvement would be too risky.

While this discussion was connected with the subject of the conditions in which national liberation movements were born (see chapter 1), it had relevance for the subject of Soviet involvement as well. More to the point was the matter of just what form this Soviet input was to take or what type of Soviet input was required as distinct from indigenous forces. The issue was clouded somewhat by the Soviets' perceived need to respond to Third World and possibly domestic opponents of détente, to the Chinese challenge, and to American accusations of Soviet involvement. Finally, the attitude toward local conflicts and force projection, some of which was seen in the previous chapter, was ultimately connected with positions regarding the role to be played, the appraisal of the possibility of escalation being an indicator of willingness or lack of willingness to have Soviet involvement.

The Place of National Liberation Movements in the World Revolutionary Process

The formula generally accepted placed the national liberation movements among the main revolutionary forces of the world revolutionary process in the present era, along with the socialist world and the international working class. There were, however, varied opinions as to just how important and in what way the national liberation movements contributed to this process. Judging from the criticism expressed by party theoreticians such as Ul'ianovskii and Brutents, or the institutes' commentators such as Simoniia and Solodovnikov, there were two extreme positions: that which overestimated the role of the national liberation movements, viewing them as the central element in the revolutionary process and as vehicles for socialist transformation; and, at the other end of the spectrum, the position that belittled their role altogether, emphasizing the contradictory, non-socialist, potential of the movements.[1] Often the criticism of the first position was phrased as attacks on the Chinese attitude, but Ul'ianovskii and Solodovnikov, for example, made no mention of the Chinese in referring to those who overestimated the socialist nature of the national liberation movement in their conclusions that some of these movements had actually, already, created socialist states.[2] Such criticism was a clear indication that this view was indeed held by some other than the Chinese, but it is more likely that the spectrum ended with persons who advocated greater attention to the national liberation movements rather than those who adopted the Roy–Chinese position of the absolute centrality of these movements.

At least the generally expressed opinions tended to reflect such a view. These included such characterizations of the national liberation movements as "reserves of world socialism," and an "inseparable," "organically linked" part of the world revolutionary process, which had "merged with" or formed with the other components "one revolutionary current" or "one revolutionary tide." These optimistic characterizations were occasionally fortified with examples of Third World states which had become socialist or with general enthusiasm about the inevitable eventual socialist result.

Some of this enthusiasm was expressed in references to the new phenomena of people's democracies in the Third World,[3] but mainly it appeared to be connected with more general propagandistic–exhortative statements rather than with the more academic analyses. Examples of this could be found in a 1978 *Izvestiia* article on the appearance of a book of Brezhnev speeches, a Zagladin article in *Kommunist* (1972), a Ponomarev speech cited by Entin in 1978, a *Pravda* editorial in 1979, a Lenin anniversary editorial in *Asia and Africa Today* (English version only) in 1982, and a *New Times* article in 1980.[4]

Even these more enthusiastic appraisals had caveats, in some cases. The *Izvestiia* commentary, for example, spoke of "one revolutionary current" dependent upon the degree to which the national liberation movements became socialist. The same caveat had been added by Zagladin himself, who in 1981 was much less optimistic when he wrote that the Third World was still far from real socialism.[5] Given Zagladin's negative (to the point of dogmatic) appraisal of nationalism, which we have already seen in his 1973 book, this later position was probably a more accurate reflection of his attitude. Primakov, writing in *Pravda* in 1982, used the term "organically linked," but he too saw this as a function of the increasing identification with socialism.[6] Kortunov and Kim both spoke of the national liberation movements as "accelerating" the world revolutionary process, and Kim appeared to become increasingly optimistic over the years.[7] Thus, in 1976 Kim was still emphasizing the movements' need for the Soviet Union, but by 1978 he wrote of a mutual need whereby the socialist world could not be secure without the national liberation revolution.[8] He spoke in 1981 of the national liberation movements as an "inalienable part" of, and in 1984 as "indissolubly linked" to, the world revolutionary process,[9] arguing that there was an objective and a subjective union of the revolutionary forces, despite what he alluded to as "reversals" cited by critics.[10] Kim quoted Lenin to the effect that the "socialist revolution will not be *solely, or chiefly*, a struggle of the revolutionary proletariat in each country against their bourgeoisie—no, it will be a struggle of all the imperialist-oppressed colonies and countries, of all dependent countries, against international imperialism."[11]

As distinct from an almost unidentifiable extreme position more alluded to than specified, and the above apparently enthusiastic positions which on occasion went so far as to ascribe to the national liberation movements a certain centrality in a "unified" revolutionary stream, a somewhat more middle, pragmatic position was quite prevalent. This was the position advocated previously by the Central Committee's experts Ul'ianovskii, Brutents, and to a slightly lesser degree Manchkha. Brutents and Ul'ianovskii took upon themselves explicitly to argue against both extremes—both analysts argued that the national liberation movements were often overrated ("by leftist opportunists") and were not truly socialist; both pointed out that, although they were "needed," or "paved the way," they could not be seen as "reserves" for the world revolutionary movement.[12] Brutents, for example, warned that: "One should bear in mind that in purpose, motive forces, social make-up and ideology the national liberation movement has a different character, as compared with the working-class movement for socialism."[13] And Ul'ianovskii cited Lenin's rebuff to Roy that the latter "was going too far when he claimed that the main role in the world revolutionary process had now passed over to the East." Indeed, Ul'ianovskii claimed, Lenin believed national liberation could come for the peoples of the East only through alliance with the world proletariat.

The overall thrust of their arguments, however, was clearly in defense of the national liberation movements, urging measured optimism regarding their eventual outcome but clearly according them an important, perhaps even essential, role in the world revolutionary process. Brutents employed the same Lenin quote as Kim on the relative importance of the national liberation movements vis-à-vis the revolutionary proletariat (which would not be the *chief* revolutionary vehicle). Implying that it was their sheer numbers that made the peoples of the Third World so important, Brutents explained that the national liberation movements were "the main channel through which the bulk of mankind—hundreds of millions of men and women in Asia, Africa, and substantially Latin America as well—are involved in the worldwide revolutionary process."[14] This alone would make the national liberation movement the "chief" revolutionary movement, but it also contributed to world revolution; first, by helping prove that the revolutionary process was indeed worldwide, and that capitalism/imperialism was in a state of crisis; and second, by hampering the action of the imperialists, diverting their energies away from their conflict with the proletariat in Europe—a defensive role which in time grew into an offensive one against imperialism as such.[15] "'The very success of the revolutionary struggle on a world scale,'" Brutents quoted Lenin, "'now depended upon...joint action'" as the Third World became, according to Brutents, "one of the most important front lines" in the social–ideological struggle of our times; the national liberation struggle constituted "the field of confrontation" of the two world systems.[16] In this sense, he maintained that even the growth of the socialist system "has not reduced the importance of its alliance with the forces of national liberation."[17] Allowing for the fact that not all national liberation movements would actually arrive at socialism, Brutents nonetheless meticulously demonstrated the "specific form" of revolution which accounted for the difference between a classical bourgeois revolution and that of the national liberation movements, leading the latter to assume an inherently progressive social potential which would go over to socialism."[18]

A later article by Brutents, and his 1979 book, were somewhat less sanguine about the unity of revolutionary forces after independence, implying less optimism about the ultimate outcome of the national liberation movement.[19] The 1979 book was far less explicit or effusive about the positive role played by the national liberation movements, pointing to negative developments—and speaking of a new phase in the relationship—once these movements came to power. Yet there does not appear to have been a total retreat on his part from what was in any case a cautious but basically positive concept of the importance of the movements. Indeed, in pointing to the negative phenomena after independence, Brutents added: "This does not mean that the progressive potential...is no longer there."[20]

Ul'ianovskii too employed the quote from Lenin on the national liberation movements' assumption of the "chief role" in the revolutionary process, claiming that Lenin was "categorical" in his belief that the socialist revolution could not be limited to the proletarian revolution in each country.[21] In two articles separated by ten years, Ul'ianovskii presented virtually the same characterization of the national liberation movements as a "key component" of the world revolutionary process, which was historically necessary for the security of the European revolution. They would lead to the collapse of colonialism, "drastically weakening" world capitalism, and would eventually "grow over" into socialism.[22]

As we have seen, in his 1976 and 1978 books and his arguments with Simoniia, Ul'ianovskii expressed his faith in the socialist potential inherent in national liberation movements, as well as his conviction that the national liberation movements "have become one of the cardinal areas of the world-wide confrontation between the forces of socialism and the forces of imperialism."[23] Thus, his position was a relatively consistent one, even with his occasional, realistic, warnings not to idealize or overrate these movements and the absolute inevitability of their all becoming socialist.[24] Indeed, like Brutents, he became somewhat more measured in his optimism regarding this last; in his 1978 book his criticism was mainly for those who overrated the potential. Characteristic, on the whole, of Ul'ianovskii and Brutents, as well as of Kim's attitude, was the use of statements by Lenin on the revolutionary struggle as a "combined" one which necessitated the joining of the proletarian revolution in capitalist countries with that of the national liberation movements, and that this linkage was clearly *in the interests* of the socialist world.[25] In the case of both Ul'ianovskii and Brutents, however, the cautionary statements, and warnings not to mistakenly identify the movements with real socialism, became more frequent (at least in their books of the late 1970s), while Kim became more optimistic.

The leading Africanists, Manchkha, Solodovnikov, and Anatolii Gromyko—representing the party as well as the Africa Institute—appeared to be somewhat less forthcoming on the spectrum of positions regarding the place of national liberation movements in the world revolutionary process. None denied them a role certainly; indeed, Manchkha saw them as an "inseparable part," and Solodovnikov said their victories were welcomed as victories for Marxism–Leninism, "for progress over reaction."[26] Solodovnikov spoke of the mutual interests of the three currents, of a "political union" against imperialism, in which each could tie up the imperialists' energies, relieving the pressures on the other fronts. Thus, on occasion the national liberation movements could and did help the socialist states and created more favorable conditions for the proletarian struggle in the capitalist world.[27] Similarly, Gromyko spoke of the "objective" alliance and mutual assistance of all three because of their common enemy.[28]

The Africanists also all spoke of the tendency of these revolutions to grow into socialist revolutions. Yet all three exhibited somewhat less confidence about the ultimate outcome, emphasizing more the complexities of their progress and the differences between them, on the one hand, and socialist revolution, on the other. Solodovnikov was slightly more optimistic in his 1975 book with Bogoslovskii than in his earlier works, but even here, in the context of criticism of the Chinese, he argued that, although the socialist revolution needed national liberation revolutions as well as revolutions in the capitalist countries, it would be incorrect to see the former as the main struggle of our day.[29]

Just below these leading Africanists in this scale of interest in the movements, one might place a cluster of commentators, with varied professional affiliations, who saw the national liberation movements not so much as having merged with or as being inseparably linked with the other revolutionary forces, but rather as their allies. This characterization seemd to accord the movements a more subordinate, less certain, place in the revolutionary process. It was a view that regarded them as important, as Starushenko (for example) pointed out, insofar as their future direction might tip the scales in the East–West struggle, but the overall thrust was in the direction of the movements' need for and dependence upon the other components of the revolutionary process, rather than on their contribution to this process.[30] Kiva and Gavrilov were probably in this category, for although Gavrilov, for example, cited Lenin's reference to the national liberation movements' role in eclipsing the proletariat revolution in the capitalist countries as the "sole," even "chief," revolutionary struggle, his inordinate emphasis on the difficulties Lenin faced in imposing this position on the communist movement and the problematics of the view suggested a hint of criticism or at least restrained enthusiasm on Gavrilov's part.[31] The placement of Kiva and Gavrilov in the more skeptical school of thought may be substantiated by the fact that both were to side, on the whole, with Simoniia's critical position in debates in 1976 and 1978.[32] This restraint was somewhat clearer in Kortunov, despite his comment that the national liberation movements accelerated the world revolutionary process; and it was still clearer in articles by Krasin, particularly one in *Rabochii klass i sovremennyi mir* in January 1977.[33]

With some exceptions, all of the preceding represented gradations rather than opposing views within the overall position favoring an interest in the national liberation movements. The other end of the spectrum included decidedly negative views which appeared to be arguing against even the more realistic or pragmatic supporters of the movements, though not necessarily for a *total* lack of involvement. None, for example, openly espoused the extreme view, attacked by Brutents, Ul'ianovskii, Solodovnikov, and others, denying any revolutionary or positive role to the national liberation movements. Their counter-accusations, however, suggested more than slight reservations regarding what they may have viewed as excessive interest in these movements. Mirskii, who sided openly with Simoniia in the controversy over the latter's book, appeared to share Simoniia's pessimism over the nature and, therefore, overall direction of the national liberation movements.[34] While both (but Mirskii more than Simoniia) were a bit more positive in the late 1970s with regard to regimes that appeared to be approaching people's democracies,[35] they nonetheless emphasized the primarily bourgeois–democratic nature of the national liberation revolutions and (according to Simoniia) their similarity to past bourgeois revolutions.[36] Such characterization would hardly rate them comparable status with the socialist states and the international proletariat in the world revolutionary process. Indeed, as we have already seen, Simoniia saw most of them going in the opposite (capitalist) direction, which certainly would not render the national liberation movements essential, even positive, to the revolutionary process.

As we have seen, Zagladin too was pessimistic about the direction taken by the national liberation movements, viewing them as no different from classical bourgeois nationalism, willing to give them credit only when and so far as they actually became socialist.[37] Others, such as the Zhukov et al. study of 1970, more directly attacked a view which accorded too great an importance to the national liberation movements, arguing that the "focus" of world revolution was the socialist countries, and that the chief struggle in the world, as pointed out by Lenin, was between imperialism and Soviet Russia.[38] Vladimir Li appeared to share the same sentiments when he said that the national liberation movements, were in the vanguard of the world revolutionary process and could aggravate the crisis of imperialist countries, but:

> [they] cannot play a decisive role in the world struggle against imperialism or determine the historical future of world socialism, that is, they cannot exert a decisive influence on the resolution of the principal contradiction of the present epoch, the transition from capitalism to socialism...the present-day national liberation movement is one of the main (but in no sense the decisive or leading) currents in the world revolutionary process...[39]

Iskenderov, in a similar context, asserted that the socialist world system was "the decisive force" against imperialism.[40] The generally conservative Fedoseev study went even farther when it stated:

> The idea that the national liberation movement plays a special role is contrary to Marxism–Leninism. Its exponents are unaware of the international situation serving as the setting of the anti-imperialist struggle and slip into nationalistic influences...To trace the weakening of imperialism exclusively to the national liberation struggle, and to proclaim it the main and decisive revolutionary factor, is to forget that the incontestable victories of that struggle are confined to at least socially and economically developed regions where the objective conditions for socialism, especially an industrial basis, are practically non-existent. [But] the Leninist doctrine of socialist revolution postulates as prerequisites of success in a socialist overturn a combination of subjective and objective conditions, the existence of revolutionary forces and of essential material production resources...The successes of the national liberation struggle of the predominantly peasant countries of the East would have been unthinkable without the revolutionary struggle of the world proletariat and its chief gain—the world socialist system.[41]

Fedoseev's last point—the centrality of the socialist world for the success of the national liberation movements—was directed here, and by others, against too high an estimation of the movements and, by extrapolation, against too much involvement with them (as well, undoubtedly, as a reminder to the Third World that it needed the Soviet Union and not vice versa). It was also the case, however, that those who alloted the movements a more significant, even essential, role also evoked the centrality of the Soviet position—or at least the importance of the socialist world for the success of the national liberation movements—apparently in justification of a greater Soviet role. To say, therefore, that the national liberation movements needed the socialist world, or that Soviet input was crucial to the success of these movements, did not necessarily mean that the Soviet Union *should*—or, conversely, should *not*—become involved. Nor did this necessarily indicate what type of involvement was called for, although the reasons provided by way of explanation usually indicated just what type of role was envisaged for the Soviet Union. These difficulties of analysis notwithstanding, there were (albeit often only nuanced) discernible differences on this issue as well.

Soviet Assistance

INTERVENTION

As might have been expected, Ul'ianovskii and Kim, but also, with some reservations, the slightly less enthusiastic Solodovnikov, and Manchkha, all spoke of the "obligation" or duty of the socialist world to help the national liberation movements. (Kim spoke of this as a "basic law".[42]) And Starushenko provided the "legal" justification for the "right" of the socialist states to render assistance.[43] They all argued that, by helping these movements, the socialist world would be better able to influence their future socio-political orientation. Indeed, this was the main reason given by Brutents and later by Ul'ianovskii;[44] but there were also more pessimistic analysts, such as, apparently, Gavrilov, who explicitly advocated Soviet assistance as the only factor that could sway these movements from a bourgeois to a socialist path.[45] Yet it was probably more typical for those critical of the potential of the national liberation movements simply to refrain from advocating assistance, as we shall see below.

The views regarding and defining Soviet assistance fell along a spectrum not necessarily identical to the spectrum of views on the importance of the movements. At one end one might place the advocates of a maximalist—possibly even (military) interventionist—position. There were few clear-cut examples of this position, although Starushenko, in providing the legal justification for outside support, appeared to be advocating even military intervention. Thus, he spoke of Soviet assistance of all kinds against the (imperialist) export of counter-revolution.[46]

In a sense, this was the most forthcoming Soviet attitude: that which advocated all types of Soviet aid, including military assistance, in conjunction with the effort against the export of counter-revolution. The references to the export of counter–revolution were numerous, and were not confined to any one period prior to Brezhnev's death. Vladimir Li, for example, employed it in 1971, Starushenko, as we have seen, in 1976, Manchkha in his 1979 book, Zarodov in 1981, Gromyko on one occasion in 1981, Primakov in a 1982 *Pravda* article.[47] The same point was made in a *Narody Azii i Afriki* editorial on the 1981 twenty-sixth CPSU Congress, as well as in a 1981 *New Times* rebuttal to Italian Communists' criticism.[48] Shastitko, while not speaking of counter-revolution, actually employed the example of the Red Army's role in Mongolia in a 1980 article, making the point of the Soviet Union's duty to help national liberation movements.[49] Anatolii Gromyko also left out any reference to fighting counter-revolution on most occasions, but he was most explicit in a 1978 article in which he spoke of Soviet aid to "repulse aggression" while helping to build up the defense capabilities of new states.[50] Tarabrin had already made the same point in a 1977 book (for which Gromyko had written the introduction), in which he quoted Brezhnev (from 1967) regarding a "militant union with peoples which still have to carry on an armed struggle against the colonialists."[51]

In trying to determine if the above commentators were actually advocating direct involvement by the Soviet Union, or even by other socialist states such as Cuba, certain difficulties arise. Shastitko and Tarabrin, for example, would appear to have been most forthcoming. Yet in the case of Shastitko, the reference to the Mongolian–Red Army example was followed by an article he wrote two years later entitled "The Revolution Must Defend Itself." The title at least indicated a more reserved attitude, although the text of the article could well have been construed in either direction in its references to the need of the new states for socialist assistance.[52] Tarabrin, who appeared to be strongly in favor of a maximum commitment in his 1977 book, tempered this somewhat in a 1980 *MEMO* article in which he seemed to play down Soviet assistance, insisting, for example, that the Cuban brigade had been sent to Angola without any prior consultation with Moscow and then only *after* an independent government had been established.[53] A 1978 article had upheld the right to "outside support to help against aggression," but only in reference to states (while national liberation movements were to have the right to use "any means" at their disposal).[54] Soviet sensitivity on this point was evidenced by an *Izvestiia* article in 1978, which explained that socialist military assistance of this type was sent only on request of "lawful governments," a clarification that ruled out intervention on behalf of movements not yet in power.[55]

While Starushenko and the earlier Tarabrin and Shastitko items seemed to condone direct intervention even for movements, most Soviet statements favoring some type of intervention were at best vague when it came to the distinction between aid to governments and to national liberation movements. A 1977 *Novoe vremia* article, which spoke favorably of Soviet military assistance specifically to such movements, elucidated that what was meant was the supply of weapons, ammunition, and military equipment and the training of soldiers and officers of the liberation movements' military branches.[56]

This was a rare comment in its explicitness, as was a *Narody Azii i Afriki* article by V. Katsman in 1980, which mentioned training camps (as well as party and press centers) provided by the socialist countries for national movements on the territory of the front-line states in Africa.[57]

The problem with analyzing what has been mentioned above in the context of intervention is not just that, on the whole, such references applied only to states, but also that many of these calls for "active counter-action" (Manchkha) and the struggle against the export of counter-revolution were followed by caveats which raised some doubt as to the extent of commitment actually intended by the author. Manchkha, for example, in what appeared to be a fulsome call for Soviet assistance against the export of counter-revolution, citing the assistance given Mongolia and the central Asian republics by Soviet defensive power, then added: "As is known, the Soviet Union renders the African countries considerable assistance. But one must take into account the circumstances whereby, in contrast to the Soviet republics and Mongolia, the African countries of socialist orientation are situated thousands of kilometers from the Soviet Union..." in addition to "other differences."[58] His conclusion appeared to be that indigenous processes and forces were to be the key. The references of Primakov, Li, Solodovnikov, and even (though much less so) Starushenko to Moscow's role in combating the export of counter-revolution may also have been intended as less than Soviet or socialist bloc intervention, for they all spoke in terms of the Soviet Union as a deterrent force, to prevent the West from acting.[59] Similarly, Anatolii Gromyko's position also saw the Soviet role as one of deterrent, on the one hand putting a "Soviet Union first" argument, and on the other, referring to the role of indigenous and contiguous forces.[60] Indeed, in an article on the tasks of Soviet African studies after the twenty-sixth CPSU Congress, Gromyko listed the types of assistance the Soviet Union should render the national liberation movements (and Third World states), omitting any reference to the military sphere altogether: he discussed only the political–diplomatic, economic, and ideological spheres.[61]

NON-INTERVENTION

The preceding qualifiers were indicative of three varied, though often overlapping or simultaneously expressed, views of a non-interventionist Soviet role which roughly emphasized the indigenous forces, or the Soviet Union as a deterrent holding off the West at the global level, or, simply, the need to take care of the Soviet Union first. The indigenous forces argument was usually employed in Soviet references to the undesirability or lack of feasibility of trying to export revolution. This, in turn, was employed to counter outside accusations of Soviet expansionism, but it may well have been intended domestically to hold interventionist-leaning persons in check. Inasmuch as the analysts who employed the argument were usually also those who urged all-round, even military, assistance to the national liberation movements, it may be that this view was in part defensive—an explanation, so to speak, as to just how far they thought this outside help should go, without, however, fighting the battle for the movements. This was clearly the thrust of Kim's position and, most often, that of Solodovnikov when they spoke, repeatedly, of economic and political, and only occasionally of military, assistance, in combination with indigenous social and economic forces rather than the export of revolution.[62]

Iskenderov spoke of Soviet aid to accelerate the national liberation process, but he too made a clear point against the export of revolution; like the International Department's Midtsev, he emphasized indigenous forces engaged in natural, inevitable processes.[63] Anatolii Gromyko, arguing against the export of revolution, on at least one occasion specified the Soviets' task as one of holding off the West on the international scene.[64] He even claimed that, in so doing, the Soviet Union bore the brunt of the struggle, but, as he explained in another article the same year, the local battle was the responsibility of the indigenous forces, the front-line states, the Organization of African Unity, and the United Nations.[65]

If all of the above analysts spoke of multi-faceted Soviet aid even as they emphasized indigenous forces and/or the primary Soviet role as one of deterrence at the superpower level, there was a more minimalist position which spoke only of the deterrence role. Advocates of this position included Kremeniuk, Entin, a *Kommunist* article by Skorov in 1974, and the hard-line study edited by Fedoseev which defined Soviet help only as "weakening" imperialism.[66] Kremeniuk, Entin, and the 1970 Zhukov study all spoke of the altered balance of forces in the world as a factor aiding national liberation movements; but this was evoked in the more passive context of the weakening of imperialism, which created the possibility for the movements to act more quickly, implicitly or explicitly, because the existence of the socialist world restrained or held imperialism in check.[67]

Zagladin, too, took the position that "every revolutionary force and every national (or regional) detachment of revolutionaries itself defines and solves the problems facing its country (region). No one solves the problem for them."[68] He saw the role of the Soviet Union in the realm of "the state of affairs in the world as a whole, the correlation of forces between socialism and imperialism, the forces of liberation and the forces enslaving the peoples, the forces of peace and war," which all greatly influenced the course and results of the struggle.[69] Beyond that, Zagladin saw the Soviets' role only in what he called "international, moral backing" for the movements.

Krasin, one of the more pessimistic of the party analysts regarding the national liberation movements, spoke in terms of each component of the world revolutionary process having its own task. The task of the Soviet Union was in the East–West struggle at the superpower level, or, as Krasin put it on another occasion, to prevent world holocaust and maintain peace.[70] This view defined national liberation as a global or international issue, not in the sense of demanding a Soviet role locally or regionally, but rather in the sense that a strong Soviet Union was necessary for the local movement to succeed.[71] Only a strong Soviet bloc could deter the West or preserve the peace necessary for progress at the local level. As Krasin put it, Soviet concern for its "state interests, of the interests of a nation building a new society, does not run counter to proletarian internationalism; on the contrary, as history shows, it is a factor making for a change in the world balance that accords with the interests of all progressives."[72]

This, then, was the "Soviet Union first" attitude. It was enunciated by some, such as Anatolii Gromyko, Kim, and Brutents, in addition to or as a condition for other Soviet aid; it was advocated by others, such as Krasin and, earlier, the Zhukov study, as almost the only type of Soviet role.[73] It is difficult to determine if the assertion of this basically highly restrained attitude toward the national liberation movements was a function of time rather than differing viewpoints. The appearance of this attitude in the late 1960s–early 1970s, even as official policy, has already been noted and documented in Western literature.[74] The Zhukov study, or a *Pravda* commentary after the December 1973 Central Committee plenum by V. Petrov, may serve as examples of the early 1970s call for a reappraisal of the "real requirements" of the national liberation movements, and their placement in a lower category, with the "urgent tasks of the world socialist system" assuming first, specified, priority.[75]

Even later, as the Soviet Union was pursuing what could be called an interventionist policy in the Third World, the "Soviet Union first" attitude could still be found, for example in a commentary for the October celebrations in 1977, which said: "By insuring the favorable conditions for building Communism in our country and the defense of the USSR's state interests, this policy also contributes to strengthening the position of world socialism, to the people's struggle for national liberation and social progress, to preventing aggressive wars and to achieving general and complete disarmament."[76] And, as we have already seen, the less anti-interventionist but nonetheless restrained attitude regarding the Soviets' role (e.g., those who saw the Soviet role only as a deterrent at the global level) appeared at various times throughout the 1970s.

Yet the sudden appearance, beginning in 1981, of a spate of articles evoking the "Soviet Union first" attitude, even from Kim (in 1982) as well as Brutents and Gromyko, the last in three different journals in 1981, would suggest some particular trigger or policy decision.[77] Economic motivation was suggested by the appearance of two articles by economists of the Institute for the Economy of the Socialist States in 1982. One of these, by Yurii Novopashin in *Voprosy filosofii*, argued that domestic economic problems of the Soviet Union and the socialist bloc (which hurt the Soviets' ability to serve as an example) might necessitate a rethinking of aid to the Third World. Taking a "Soviet Union first" attitude, this article argued that "socialism influences the revolutionary process by its very existence and development."[78] Similarly, two articles appeared in *Mezhdunarodnaia zhizn'* in the first half of 1984 quoting Lenin to the effect that "the socialist countries would mainly influence the world revolutionary process through their economic successes."[79] This was a view implied, perhaps more expectedly, by Mirskii (in conjunction with Latin Americanist Maidanik) in 1981 as well.[80]

Before turning to hypotheses as to just what precipitated this line, still one more attitude should be noted at what may have been the furthest end of the Soviet commitment spectrum. This was the almost totally passive role advocated, at least on occasion, by Simoniia or the Zhukov study, defining the Soviets' main influence as one of serving as an example, although both would allow the additional role as a force weakening imperialism.[81] Simoniia, in one of his more optimistic articles, spoke of the new socialistically minded countries' dependence upon Soviet economic and, in some cases, military assistance (defined only as "strengthening the defense potential").[82] Gromyko too, in his 1981 book, made the statement that the "Soviet state exerts [the influence of a socialist revolution on backward countries and peoples] primarily through the strength of socialism's example and through its revolutionary experience." Gromyko did go on to speak of lending "effective support" to the national liberation movements, even to the point of placing "all its might at the disposal of peace and progress," as in the cases of Vietnam, Angola, Ethiopia, and Afghanistan. And he even mentioned "support" for states of socialist orientation struggling against imperialist export of counter-revolution. Yet the general tenor of the book suggested that Gromyko was, perhaps, trying to juggle his old view with a newer line—which he himself may have been responsible for introducing.[83]

The views of Ul'ianovskii and Brutents incorporated many of the above positions, but, given their importance in the Soviet party hierarchy on this subject, their positions warrant particular attention.[84] Ul'ianovskii, with no discernible changes over time, accepted the deterrent role of the Soviet bloc as a check on imperialism because of the altered balance of forces in the world. He even spoke of deflecting the imperialists' energies to the socialist world, freeing the national liberation movements to operate without interference.[85] He was willing to go further, advocating economic, political, and, when necessary, military aid; but he explained the last (on one occasion at least) only as the supply of weapons.[86] He stopped short of anything more involved, explicitly ruling out the "export of revolution," invoking the responsibility of indigenous forces.[87]

In his 1976 book, Ul'ianovskii spoke of the "people" themselves as the "decisive" factor in the national liberation struggle, even if they were in need of Soviet assistance.[88] By 1978, he was willing to point with pride to Soviet "direct help" to the liberation movements against the Portuguese, specifically the case of Angola; but aside from "all-round aid," he emphasized the Soviet Union's contribution by "its very existence, and the extension of its political influence."[89] Although he included military assistance in this "all-round aid," he explained in the earlier book, citing Lenin, that military aid was to be considered only "if it actually was a question of the already formed internal conditions essential for the victory of the developing revolution and upholding its gains." The thrust of his argument was that such conditions were far from existing in the Third World yet, and that intervention from outside to accelerate or impose such conditions was beyond the tasks of the socialist world—the main task of which was to deter the West and, possibly, to provide arms.[90]

Brutents employed a more complex approach to say virtually the same things as Ul'ianovskii. He divided the Soviet role into an "objective" and a "subjective" one—which might also translate into a passive versus an active one—although he stopped short of an interventionist position. Explaining the "objective" role, Brutents said that "the very existence of the USSR is in many ways the material, moral–political, and frequently ideological...mainstay for the struggle of the national liberation forces (even when their socio-political makeup and anti-Communist prejudices may prevent the Soviet Union from giving them direct support)."[91] This objective role consisted primarily of the weakening of imperialism and the deterrence factor inherent in the new balance of forces.[92] The subjective role was also essential, however; for, according to Brutents, "The Soviet Union...exerts a much more substantial influence when its objective role can be backed up by alliance and interaction with the forces of national liberation, active and direct assistance and concerted action," defined as "Soviet support on the state to state level, through political parties and mass bodies, etc."[93] If, however, the national liberation forces could not be seen as a "reserve" of the world revolution, so too the leading force of the world revolution could not substitute for indigenous national liberation forces in the latter's struggle.[94]

Echoing earlier comments by Ul'ianovskii, Brutents said that "the fact that the international working class has the vanguard role to play in the anti-imperialist struggle, that the socialist system is the leading force of the world revolutionary process, and that they exert an important political and ideological influence on the national liberation movement does not yet mean that they provide that movement with leadership or guidance, not in world-historical but in concrete political terms."[95] Brutents acknowledged the importance of international conditions and factors, but, like Ul'ianovskii, concluded that in the final analysis "the decisive role" belonged to conditions within the local countries and the national liberation forces themselves.[96]

It is difficult to know if it was intended as a hint or not, similar to Manchkha's comment on the differences between the Mongolian–central Asian revolutions and those of Africa, but Brutents twice within a few pages of his 1974 book referred to the geographic proximity of the early national liberation revolutions helped by the Soviet Union.[97] Whether or not this was intended to draw a distinction—and a reservation—regarding the possibility of Soviet intervention today, a later article by Brutents, noting the importance of both the deterrent factor and direct Soviet assistance, ended on the "Soviet Union first" theme: "The more the state of détente and peace is established in the world, and the more the positions of world socialism and its main force, the Soviet Union, are consolidated, the more favorable become the conditions for successful struggle for national liberation and social emancipation and against imperialism."[98] Indeed, in his 1979 book he singled out the Soviets' "authority and weight in the international arena" as the vehicle for Soviet solidarity, although he referred to the assistance granted *states*, such as Angola and Ethiopia, in protecting their independence (in the case of Angola, once it was won).[99]

DÉTENTE AND SOVIET ASSISTANCE

The above comments by Brutents on détente and the conditions favorable to the national liberation struggle could also be interpreted as another, related, set of indicators regarding the Soviet role. The favorable conditions for the national liberation struggle created by détente *could* be interpreted to mean a peaceful situation in which the Soviet bloc might dare, with little risk, to intervene on behalf of the movements. Conversely, it could be argued, a cold war situation—one in which the West was perceived as aggressive, intervening, and violent—would not be conducive to any Soviet action of this type, at least not if risks were to be kept at a minimum. Yet, as we have seen in the discussion of means, the détente argument was actually used—and explained—as the policy that might preclude any need for Soviet intervention, with the peaceful atmosphere, the superpower relationship, and disarmament all creating a low-risk situation for the movements themselves. This view, by implication, might see an aggressive, interfering West as a condition that would necessitate outside assistance to the liberation struggle.

The key to these varied positions would appear to have been the explanations employed to defend détente, and Western behaviour. For example, when Tarabrin defended détente he made it quite clear, as we have seen, that détente did not mean either a ban on the use of all possible means by the movements, or the use, by states, of "outside support to repel aggression."[100] His defense of détente pointed to the achievements of the national liberation movements—including the examples of Angola, Ethiopia, Guinea-Bissau, Mozambique, and others— in the era of détente, owing in part to the restraining influence of détente on neo-colonialism.[101] The same position was taken by Zarodov, who, employing dialectics, tried to answer several critics at one time. Basically, he argued that détente did not apply to the national liberation struggle or "active Soviet support" of this struggle. Nor did it mean that the imperialists were so willing to have peace that they had lost all aggressiveness, to the point that the national liberation movements could get along without their alliance with Moscow.[102] All this even though détente, world peace, and the absence of cold war were all obviously deemed positive.

The inapplicability of détente to the national liberation struggle was singled out by Starushenko, who explicitly said that détente excluded war but not national liberation struggles, since "laws of revolutionary progress could not be prohibited."[103] This was echoed in a *Novoe vremia* editorial in February 1978, as well as in an *Izvestiia* article in August 1978 (which nonetheless spoke of crisis management and peaceful solution of conflicts, presumably insofar as they were not connected with the national liberation movements).[104] Kiva spoke in 1976 of the advances made by the movements in recent years as a result of Soviet deterrence and détente (which tied the hands of the imperialists). In that article it was not clear if he meant that there was therefore no need for Soviet intervention or that such assistance could be given without great risk.[105] A later, 1984, article by Kiva was somewhat clearer; it strongly defended the Soviets' right to support national liberation movements in their struggle against a more aggressive West.[106] He argued against "indifference" and for "internationalism," making the point that socialist assistance had foiled the attempt of the West, in the past, to employ détente as a means of freezing the national liberation process or, after détente, to separate the movements from their socialist allies so as to weaken and defeat them.

Ul'ianovskii, who as we have already seen was relatively though not fully reserved on the involvement spectrum, expressed what may have been contradictory positions. In his 1978 book and in a *New Times* article in 1977, he defended the détente policy with the assertion that this policy did not mean accepting imperialism: "On the contrary, it creates conditions for the activation of the people's fight for political, social, and economic self-determination...The struggle by the CPSU for détente presupposes unflagging performance by the Soviet Union and the entire socialist community of their internationalist duty to render political, economic, and military support to the revolutionary movements."[107] Yet in his volume on national liberation, written a year earlier and issued in English in 1978, Ul'ianovskii devoted an entire chapter to détente, the thrust of which was that détente restrained the West, with the result that:

> Under the conditions of universal peace and security of the peoples not a single nation or state will be the loser... *Today socialism's positions are so powerful that imperialism cannot expect to attain its aims by unleashing an armed conflict. Realizing this, the more foresighted capitalist politicians are compelled to accept the alternative of peaceful coexistence.*[108]

The comments of Anatolii Gromyko were somewhat ambiguous on the issue of détente and intervention. Like Tarabrin and Kiva, he cited Angolan, Ethiopian, and other examples of Soviet assistance, listing the many successes of national liberation movements in the era of détente, even *thanks to* détente. Linking this with the Soviet deterrent role which tied the hands of the imperialists (détente "made it a good deal more difficult for imperialism to interfere, particularly by military force"), the argument was much the same, but Gromyko on the whole emphasized, repeatedly, the benefits the national liberation movements could derive, for their own growth and development, from the peaceful, less tense, safer atmosphere of détente.[109] This was the position more generally expounded, explaining the value of detente for the movements on the grounds, implicitly, that détente obviated the need for Soviet bloc intervention. There may have been some internal contradictions or purposeful obfuscation in the use of the many national liberation victories, including Angola, to prove this point; but the line clearly taken by many was *not* the divisibility of détente but rather the harmful effects that cold war, international tension, and the absence of détente would have on the liberation struggle.

Novoe vremia commentator Dmitrii Vol'skii had explained in 1972 that the cold war spawned local "hot wars' on the former colonial periphery," while cold war hindered development, so that détente was not only beneficial but vital to the Third World, to prevent the danger of war.[110] He reiterated this line, even while supporting Soviet aid to national liberation movements, arguing that "coercion and force of arms"—the opposite of détente—was what helped the racists in South Africa, for example, to stay in power. Détente, disarmament, and so forth would create the conditions wherein the struggling people could not be "victims of violence."[111] Referring to the "Soviet Union first" Zhukov explained that cold war increased imperialist determination to stamp out the national liberation movements and served to inculcate particular stubbornness against them, while détente would have the opposite effect.[112] This was the position taken in a *Kommunist* article in 1974, which criticized many in the Third World who did not appreciate that détente, particularly the arms limitations, was creating an international climate which would exclude the possibility for imperialism to achieve its efforts by violent means.[113]

In a similar vein, Iskenderov called for military détente as part of a "healthier international climate which, in turn, would benefit peaceful development in the Third World."[114] Zhurkin, as we have seen, explained the benefits of détente in this manner, arguing that the *opponents* of détente encouraged the exacerbation of conflicts (the context was Western "anti-détentists," but given his views, his target may be presumed to have been more universal), and that on the whole détente exerted a restraining influence on the Americans' use of force.[115] Primakov, as we have seen, appeared to share Zhurkin's views, emphasizing the collaborative side of détente for preventing or containing conflicts.[116]

Kim produced a different argument, which was apparently directed against those within the Soviet Union who opposed détente on the grounds that it prevented full Soviet assistance to the Third World. Albeit speaking of states, he argued that détente made it easier for new states to withdraw from international blocs (read "Western"), and to rid themselves of foreign bases, alliances, and commitments imposed on them by the imperialists. This in turn permitted a reduction in the phenomenon of anti-Sovietism or anti–communism ("the more odious forms of ideological enmity"). The result was contacts which would have been "unthinkable during the cold war."[117] In addition, Kim made the more standard argument that, far from handicapping revolutionary development, a relaxed, cooperative international atmosphere facilitated such change by limiting the imperialists and reducing the pressures and burdens on the local revolutionaries.[118]

Brutents remained consistent in his defense of détente not as a policy facilitating intervention but rather as one obviating the need for it. In a *Pravda* article, answering the accusation that détente was "at the expense" of the Third World, Brutents said:

> The cold war and its very atmosphere are a breeding ground for the intensification of anti-democratic trends in international relations and the violation of the rights of the developing states...It was precisely in this period that imperialism often made use of the military cudgel against the peoples who were striving for liberation from colonial

and semi-colonial dependencies...Relaxation of tension is considerably
changing the situation in this respect, too.[119]

Exactly the same position was included in Brutents's book of 1979,
with the conclusion that détente seemed to restrain the imperialists.[120]
He elaborated on this more extensively in a 1981 article, in which he said
that the Third World was only just beginning to understand and take
an interest in détente.[121] Rather than counter their skepticism with the
division of détente argument, he emphasized the beneficial consequences
of a relaxed international climate and disarmament for the Third World
forces.[122] Coupled with his comments on the national liberation forces
themselves constituting the decisive factor for their own struggle, this
position would appear to be, like Ul'ianovskii's, one of restraint with
regard to risk-taking even in the era of détente.

Image of the West

If arguments defending détente with regard to the national liberation
movements could be interpreted in two entirely different ways, this was
no less the case with regard to the estimates of imperialist aggressiveness
and its consequences for the national liberation struggle. There does
not appear to be any correlation between relatively pro-interventionist
(or high commitment) attitudes and the increasingly aggressive picture
of the West presented in the 1980s—those who had been high on the
interventionist scale, such as Tarabrin or Starushenko, remained so.
There does, however, appear to have been some connection between
the increasingly pessimistic view of the West (which began roughly with
the aftermath of the invasion of Afghanistan, mushrooming in the first
year of the Reagan administration), and a turn toward greater restraint
and "Soviet Union first" attitudes on the part of observers who had
been characterized by more or less restrained attitudes to begin with.
This was also the period of serious economic deterioration for the
Soviet Union, which may have played a role in these attitudes. Indeed,
these were basically the same people who had defended détente on the
grounds that it minimized the need for or risk of outside intervention.

   Arbatov, who as head of the USA and Canada Institute was also a
chief defender of détente, saw the rise in international tension and the end
of détente as a factor that clearly increased the risk inherent in escalation
to superpower confrontation in the case of Third World conflicts.[123]
This was also the position taken by Kremeniuk and Burlatskii and, as
we have seen, by Primakov.[124] Kremeniuk, however, displayed some
ambivalence when he argued that escalation was inevitable only for those
conflicts in which the United States had a commitment; where there was

no such commitment, the rendering of Soviet assistance did not appear to risk escalation.[125]

Participating in the same discussion with Arbatov, Zagladin emphasized the domestic processes position, arguing that in a situation of tension these inevitable processes *"threatened the world* with extraordinary conflicts."[126] Unlike Arbatov and Kremeniuk, however, who tended to seek cooperation with the United States for crisis control, Zagladin's conclusions were not entirely clear. By confining his arguments to the issue of poverty and development, he did appear to be limiting the Soviet role to the economic sphere. In any case, neither he nor Arbatov so much as mentioned Soviet aid or support, while emphasizing the globally dangerous potential of the Third World in the era of increased tensions. Zagladin displayed a similar ambiguity in a 1984 article in which he appeared to take the more interventionist line by referring to American attempts to export counter-revolution. Yet he made no mention of the Soviet need to combat this; nor, for that matter, did he mention any Soviet role. Rather, he took an almost "Soviet Union first" attitude in speaking of Soviet strength to protect its own gains.[127]

The influential journalist Aleksandr Bovin, then a member of the party's Auditing Commission, who expressed pragmatic but sometimes varying views of the national liberation movements, concluded from what he saw as the Americans' greater degree of aggressiveness that "the complexity of the situation and the presence of opposing aspirations make the need to refrain from sudden movements and to preserve reason a particularly pressing one.[128] On the other hand, Bovin himself, a few months later, in a vein similar to a number of other commentaries responding to American accusations of Soviet encouragement of terrorism, declared continued Soviet assistance to national liberation movements even as the United States was stepping up its own "interventionist activities" against them.[129] Indeed, it was in response to the American accusations that the idea of opposing the export of counter-revolution was repeated, though as already noted there were those who limited their response to these charges to the argument that the Soviets did not export revolution and to an emphasis on local processes and forces. A number of the commentaries focusing on increased Western aggressiveness were, in fact, responses (or, rather, counter–charges) to the American terrorism charges, and as such they were *not* typified by a call for or declarations of high Soviet commitment.[130] Three years later Bovin was joining observers like Brutents, who argued that reduced tensions and stability would be beneficial for the Third World, and that confrontational situations would only prevent "economic decolonialization."[131]

On the whole, the greater aggressiveness argument implied higher risk and coincided with an increasing trend in the literature of the 1980s toward a more minimalist or restrained Soviet role. This did not mean that the converse had been true, in other words, that those who had perceived the West at less aggressive in the area of détente had taken a more interventionist position. As we have seen, the higher estimate of aggressiveness—which resulted not from a theoretical or ideological shift, but from the factual end of détente and the advent of higher international tensions—was employed to justify the same restrained position that the defense of détente argument had been used to justify previously. Or, at most, the changed appraisal of the West moved the protagonist somewhat further along the spectrum in the direction of greater restraint. The other, interventionist, end of the spectrum, however, does not appear to have been particularly affected by the higher risk situation or estimate.

The View of the Military

The view of the military regarding the Soviet commitment to national liberation movements may be more easily determined through another set of indicators; it too was not one monolithic set of judgments. As we have seen, Soviet military commentators periodically divided wars into complex and varying typologies, according to which, it might be argued, only one category unequivocally warranted direct Soviet involvement: wars in defense of the socialist system or wars between the two world systems, socialism and capitalism. National liberation wars, as we have seen, were traditionally viewed as just wars and therefore, presumably, were also deserving of Soviet support or involvement. With the varying typologies, some of which placed national liberation wars in the general, non-ideological, category of local wars, there arose questions as to the danger of escalation and, therefore, the risk involved in the granting of Soviet aid. The parameters by which one might judge the attitudes of Soviet military thinkers on the issues of Soviet involvement with wars of national liberation might therefore include the possibility of escalation (which we have examined in the previous chapter) and the role of the Soviet armed forces, as well as the question of détente.

Extrapolating from the possibility of escalation, which we have already considered, it is possible to say that the military commentators who supported the idea of local wars in the belief that escalation need not inexorably occur may have been advocating Soviet involvement. Indeed, in some cases the low-risk argument implicit in the avoidance-of-escalation claim was explicitly linked to a Soviet role. Colonel Malinovskii went so far as to speak of "communist" assistance for national liberation wars, the Soviet element actually providing a deterrent to imperialist intervention (and, therefore, to escalation), while tipping the scales in favor of the national liberation movements.[132] Malinovskii spoke of support "in every possible way" and of "efforts of the socialist states," but he failed to specify anything but public pressures with regard to what type of involvement he envisaged for the Soviet bloc. The thrust of his 1974 and 1978 articles was in the direction of actual Soviet intervention, but in a 1983 article Malinovskii elaborated on a theme, hinted at in 1974, which seemed to favor other than military action by the socialist states. Without changing his position, examined above, on the possibility of avoiding escalation, Malinovskii said that, beyond the material and technical aid, political and diplomatic support were of such importance that the "militarily–technologically stronger" party might not win.[133] The latter referred to the imperialists, but it is possible that some other party was also meant. Whether this was a hint at a milder, more restrained, line or not, the same 1983 article praised the "decisive merit" of Soviet and socialist states' assistance in the defense of Angola, Ethiopia, and Afghanistan in presenting a joint "rebuff" to imperialist forces. These examples clearly indicated support for relatively direct military aid.

A less explicit article by Major-General V. Matsulenko in 1984 expressed much the same line regarding the Soviet ability to deter an American use of nuclear arms (with the example of Vietnam), implying at least a low-risk situation for the implementation of what he called the "duty" to support the struggle of the national liberation movement.[134] The Volkogonov study, in its references to the idea that the socialist deterrent might prevent escalation, also spoke of a Soviet "all-round support and aid" in what appeared to be advocacy of Soviet role in local wars.[135] Indeed, Volkogonov has been cited by a Western source as one of several proponents of the projection of Soviet power overseas.[136] In particular, the volume he edited in 1977, with its extensive treatment of local wars and the "external functions" of the Soviet army, though not explicitly defining the latter as intervention in national liberation wars, did make a connection between the two. The external function of the Soviet army was still described as defense of the socialist fatherland and the socialist system, but the discussions of the importance of the study of local wars for the Soviet army and the use of local wars by the imperialists to impede the progress of socialism suggested a link which, given the possibility of avoiding escalation, broadened the Soviet army's external function.[137] A later article by Volkogonov, in 1984, defined the external role of the Soviet armed forces in the same way, speaking of the

> multifarious assistance to the national liberation movements...[which] manifests itself in holding in check, through political means, imperialists' aggressive intentions against developing countries, in supplying

their armies, in some cases, with the requisite equipment, training their military personnel, etc. All this testifies to the fact that the armed forces of the socialist community direct their efforts to halt the export of the imperialist counter-revolution and also reveals the truly internationalist nature of the Soviet Armed Forces.

Linking this to the escalation issue, he added that each time the West had launched a local war it had been forced to retreat because of "the strength and resolve of the socialist system"—the explanation a few months later being that the West was not willing to use nuclear weapons because of the Soviet nuclear capability and the knowledge that the West could not win a nuclear war. [138]

The work generally cited[139] as having signalled the breakthrough of this kind of thinking, the 1972 study edited by retired Colonel V. Kulish, also linked the avoidability of escalation with an expanded external function of the Soviet army.[140] On this point, it was argued that

greater importance is being attached to the Soviet Union's military presence in various regions throughout the world, reinforced by an adequate level of strategic mobility for its armed forces [necessary in] connection with the task of preventing local wars and also in those cases in which military support must be furnished to those nations fighting for their freedom and independence against the forces of international reaction and imperialistic interventions.[141]

More significant, in view of its author, was a volume by the head of the Main Political Administration of the Soviet armed forces, General A. A. Epishev. Writing in 1973, Epishev defined the "external function" of the Soviet armed forces as fighting the export of counter-revolution, and he made an explicit link with the national liberation struggle when he said:

Today the defense of the socialist fatherland is closely tied to giving comprehensive assistance to national liberation movements, progressive regimes, and new states who are fighting imperialist domination. Thus, the function of each socialist army to defend its own fatherland and to defend the socialist community as a whole objectively merges with the liberation struggle of the international working class, the national liberation movement of all progressive humanity.[142]

This position was echoed in 1980 in a study by Colonel K. Vorob'ev, who said, "The activity of the socialist armies, primarily of our Armed Forces, in present-day circumstances with full justification might be

classified as one of the most important sides of their external function, directed at the suppression of the export of imperialist counter-
revolution."[143]

In explaining the implementation of this function, however, neither Epishev nor Vorob'ev was particularly forthcoming. Vorob'ev
specified only assistance in building up the new states' national armies,
"giving them experience in building up the military and so forth," and
Epishev spoke only generally of "military assistance."[144] Moreover, in
listing the tasks of the external function, Vorob'ev, at least, spoke first of
defense of the socialist fatherland, second, of the defense of the socialist
states, and third, of the above aid to "people of countries liberated from
imperialist dependence." That is, the external function did *not* seem to
include either direct involvement or even, specifically, aid to national
liberation movements. This view would correspond more closely to the
less restrained civilian views, such as those of Tarabrin, which carefully
noted Soviet military intervention at the invitation of legitimate ruling
governments. Later Vorob'ev did speak of peoples engaged in the
national liberation struggle, but he mentioned this only at the end of an
article which concentrated on the main role of the Soviet armed forces
as protecting the socialist system.[145] Epishev too seemed to focus on
post-independence assistance in his definition of the "external function,"
and he almost never referred even to this function in his later speeches
and writings.[146]

Colonel Rybkin was much clearer in his categorization of war and
the defense of wars of national liberation. He not only spoke positively of
military assistance "from the countries of socialism" to "oppressed and
dependent nations waging wars," but he also argued that the victory
or defeat of a nation waging such a war could change the international
balance of forces—a fact that made them of more than local significance,
presumably warranting a Soviet role.[147] Another at least partially military volume went further and, like Starushenko, justified the rights of
national liberation movements to outside assistance, elaborating on just
what type of assistance this meant.[148] This was contained in the 1974
work produced by the Defense Ministry Historical Institute in conjunction
with the Africa Institute. This volume, citing examples of socialist
assistance in the struggle against the export of counter-revolution,
referred to the dispatch of weapons, military equipment, advisers,
and instructors to China and Spain in the 1930s, including "also the
participation of Soviet volunteer soldiers in the armed struggle."[149] It
was not clear if this example was intended for today, however, for
the study went on to say that the post-World War II change in the
international correlation of forces made it possible for the Soviet Union
to halt imperialist action by the mere *threat* of intervention.[150] Taking
credit for an improved international climate within which to operate,

thanks mainly to its own deterrent value and political activities, the Soviet Union was nonetheless said to continue to render "constant military and economic assistance and political support" to the national liberation struggle. Here the examples given focused on arms supplies and military training provided to the Algerians; but aside from the role of the Soviet armed forces as "a source of military experience" for the new states, no further use of Soviet military involvement was mentioned.[151]

Soviet training was advocated, in time, by many Soviet military commentators, as was even the use of Soviet advisers, although there was no mention of Soviet advisers actually with the national liberation forces themselves.[152] The dispatch of socialist though not necessarily Soviet forces was apparently advocated by various observers who praised the Cuban role in Angola,[153] and the use of even Soviet forces was implied in Malinovskii's inclusion of Afghanistan along with Ethiopia and Angola in a list of examples of positive aid.[154] These examples need not apply directly to national liberation movements as distinct from Third World states, but an article by Captain 1st Rank Iu. Osipov in 1978 and one by Colonel A. Leont'ev in 1979 referred to the Mongolian cases (Osipov) as well as the Chinese and Spanish civil war examples, in which, as Leont'ev put it, "Loyal to internationalism, the Soviet people fought for freedom."[155]

Soviet military attitudes favoring interventionism or at least the minimum of restraint may have been implied in positions regarding détente, as was the case to some degree among the civilian commentators. Mark Katz has argued that Soviet military thinkers began to support détente when, with the change of thinking regarding escalation, they perceived détente not as an obstacle to military activity abroad, but actually as an atmosphere conducive to this pursuit.[156] While it is difficult to find evidence specifically of this view,[157] as with the civilian commentators, one can find a division of the concept of détente which provided room for Soviet action on behalf of national liberation movements, beyond or despite the confines of détente. An early example of this view, provided by Katz, was an article by Colonel N. Vetrov in 1971.[158] Volkogonov also divided détente, as we have seen in the previous chapter, when he asserted that "the Soviet Union's decisive support for socialist Vietnam, revolutionary Ethiopia, people's democratic Yemen, new Angola, and the progressive forces of Kampuchea in no way contradicts our adherence to a policy of peaceful coexistence..."[159] This distinction was made by the otherwise relatively restrained Defense Ministry–Academy study as well, arguing that "There can be no peaceful coexistence when the issue is one of internal processes of class and national-liberation struggle in capitalist countries or in colonies. The principle of peaceful coexistence is not applicable to relations between the oppressors and oppressed, between the colonizers and the victims of the colonial yoke."[160]

Katz has claimed that the Soviet military was uniform and consistent in its opposition to détente, eagerly grasping at the divisibility of détente argument in order to eliminate the constraints on military activity abroad.[161] Indeed, one would be hard put to find among the military commentators the opposite view of détente presented by many civilians, namely, that détente eliminated the need for outside intervention on behalf of the national liberation movements. Nonetheless, as we have seen, there does not appear to have been total unanimity among these military commentators regarding such issues as escalation, nor apparently on the issue of Soviet power projection. This would suggest that at least some military thinkers did not enthusiastically support the idea of Soviet military intervention on behalf of the national liberation movements (or in Third World conflicts in general). The warnings regarding the risks of escalation expressed, for example, by Milovidov, Belyi, Nikitin, Dolgopolov, and to some degree Shavrov, may have been indicative of opposition to Soviet involvement in what they saw as high-risk situations.[162] One of these, Colonel Dolgopolov, specifically warned of the possibility of direct Soviet–American confrontation.[163] Inasmuch as he had also expressed positive evaluations of the military in the Third World, one wonders if he was not making a case for relying on indigenous forces to handle things themselves.[164] Indeed, he did make the argument against the export of revolution as distinct from (and in favor of) reliance upon indigenous forces.[165] In so doing it was notable that, although he used the divisibility of détente argument, he did so not in justification of the Soviets' right to help national liberation movements despite superpower détente, but, rather, of the rights of the national liberation movements themselves to fight:

> As to the principle of peaceful coexistence, it embraces *only the sphere of interstate relations* and does not abolish and cannot abolish the class struggle. In the course of this *every people* has a right to respond to aggressive imperialist policy by all means available to it, *including to defend their interests by beginning national liberation war*, with arms in hands.[166]

By implication, at least, this would appear to contradict the power projection advocated above (although a later article by Dolgopolov expressed a decidedly more interventionist position).[167] Even the earlier generally interventionist volume edited by Kulish contained what may have been some reservations about too active a Soviet role. At least in one place it stated that, unlike the Americans, the USSR "has its own historical, economic, and geographic peculiarities which will not allow it or require it to maintain a military presence in remote regions of the world." Moreover, in another place it was argued that the Americans were creating trouble in remote areas so as to "force the socialist countries to further distribute their forces among many centers of resistance and thereby weaken their direct resistance to the USA."[168] While somewhat contradictorily, in another place such a presence was advocated, but more for deterrent purposes (preventing escalation) than for purpose of intervention:

> the knowledge itself of the Soviet military presence in a given area in which a conflict may be developing can serve to restrain the imperialists [and] prevent them from causing violence against the local population and eliminate the threat to overall peace and international security. It is precisely this type of role that is played by the ships of the Soviet navy in the Mediterranean Sea.[169]

Much more recently, at a time (in 1984) when Dolgopolov appeared to be taking a more activist line along with what appeared to be the usual power projection position of Volkogonov and others, Major-General A. Skryl'nik published an article in the *Soviet Military Review* which described the role of the Soviet armed forces entirely and exclusively in terms of defense of the socialist system, with no mention of any external function beyond the socialist system of states.[170] Even though he did mention that imperialism sought to suppress "the people's movement for national and social emancipation," he drew no other conclusion than that the Soviet armed forces had "historical responsibility for the fate of the Soviet state and socialist community," and that they were created for the purpose of "defending the revolutionary gains and the creative labor of the builders of the new society."[171] The tasks of the Soviet armed forces, therefore, was to "safeguard the USSR's security in peacetime, and to help avert another world war, thereby making a sizeable contribution to protecting world peace."[172] A similarly minimalistic, though less explicit, position was reflected in an article by Colonel-General G. Sredin in the same issue. Entitled "Real Socialism and the Leninist Peace Policy," this article discussed in detail the benefits of the détente of the 1970s, and the shift to aggressiveness on the part of the United States in the 1980s—without, however, so much as a mention of the Third World or national liberation movements.[173]

According to one Western observer, the minimalist position, at least with regard to Africa, was advocated by some in the military on the grounds that Soviet intervention diverted needed resources and capabilities from the more essential border with the Chinese.[174] This view, purportedly to be found among those responsible for Soviet conventional forces (or more generally responsible for the security of the Sino-Soviet border, such as General V. I. Petrov), advocated a limitation on Soviet Third World involvement.[175] The same Western analyst, however, has pointed out that Petrov was associated with the more activist position, interested in local wars and believing in the avoidability of escalation; and indeed, he was the commander of Soviet forces aiding Ethiopia against Somalia and reportedly favored the Soviet decision to invade Afghanistan.[176]

The lack of unanimity, or perhaps the existence of a debate on this issue, was reflected somewhat in the public positions of the Soviet military leadership as well. The then defense minister Grechko advocated a role for the Soviet military abroad in a 1974 *Voprosy istorii KPSS* article, which said that the role of the Soviet forces was "not limited to their task of defending our Motherland and the other socialist countries";[177] he added the task of opposing Western attempts at "counter-revolution...in whatever distant region of our planet [they] may appear." While not specifying just what form this opposition to counter-revolution was to take or, more importantly, if this also applied to military intervention on behalf of national liberation movements, the article's overall thrust did appear to be in the direction of an interventionist role for the Soviet army. It has been claimed, however, that Grechko, in argument with Admiral Gorshkov, was in fact much more restrained regarding such a role than was the commander of the Soviet navy.[178] Gorshkov, in his 1978 book, clearly indicated a role for the Soviet navy overseas, in peacetime as well as wartime, in relation to local as well as world war, with interventionist rather than solely deterrent implications.[179]

On the other hand, a warning against local wars, presumably even wars of national liberation, because of the possibility of escalation, was contained in an article by the then chief of the general staff, Marshal Ogarkov, in the *Sovetskaia voennaia entsiklopediia* of 1979.[180] Minister of Defense Ustinov (following Grechko's death in 1976) was also more restrained in speaking of a Soviet military presence all over the globe, but his implied threats that the United States would suffer if it continued its policy of local conflicts, and that Soviet power might be brought to bear, suggested a possibly activist interventionist policy.[181] A clue, perhaps pointing nonetheless to a more restrained policy preference, may be found in Ustinov's declarations to the effect that Soviet military doctrine was designed to protect the Soviet Union. He spelled this out to the Vietnamese in 1982 when he said that the Soviet Constitution saw defense of the socialist homeland as the primary task of the state and people, according the Soviet armed forces the task of defending "the accomplishments of socialism, the peaceful labor of the Soviet people, and the sovereignty and territorial integrity of the Soviet Union."[182] On another occasion he added the "security of our friends and allies," but he followed this with the comment that the Soviet Union would use all its might "if need be...to protect the peaceful labor of the Soviet people and the peoples of the fraternal socialist states."[183] One might interpret this to mean willingness to use nuclear power only in the latter case but a willingness, nonetheless, to use lesser force for "friends and allies"—whoever they may be. Yet the aggressive picture painted of American military involvement all over the globe, described as "nothing but political adventurism," suggested an atmosphere, at least, that was not conducive to similar Soviet adventurism.

Involved here, however, was a debate over more basic issues—world stability versus revolutionary activity, and theater warfare versus nuclear war. The latter issue, at least in the 1980s, did not concern itself directly with the Third World or power projection except perhaps in terms of reducing the Soviet military role to one of only protecting the continental USSR and socialist bloc (including perhaps a peripheral power projection role for the navy) for the purposes of theater warfare in Europe instead of a more distant power projection to the Third World. In this context, it is possible that the discussion of local wars and escalation was connected not with the issue of Third World intervention but analogously with the issue of theater warfare and the possibility of escalation (or possibly lack of escalation) in Europe.[184]

Leadership Views

It was, of course, the political leadership which ultimately determined the Soviet policy position regarding the role of the Soviet Union in national liberation conflicts, although the leadership pronouncements were understandably lacking in the nuanced analyses and explanations of at least the civilian commentators. Changes in the Soviet policy line were clearly apparent in the leadership's pronouncements throughout the 1970s and early 1980s. The 1971 twenty-fourth CPSU Congress, while quite positive on the Third World, was only partially forthcoming regarding the Soviet role. Brezhnev, in his speech to the Congress, did adopt the optimistic view which saw the national liberation movement progressing inexorably toward socialism, praising in detail the states of socialist orientation which had grown out of the national liberation struggle. This optimism notwithstanding, Brezhnev saw the national liberation movement as an ally of the world revolutionary process, clearly subordinate to the vanguard of that process: the world communist movement. He was less explicit than he had been at the previous (1966) CPSU Congress regarding the divisibility of détente, though he said that, together with pursuing peace, "the Soviet Union will continue to wage a resolute struggle against imperialism...we shall, as in the past, give undeviating support to the peoples struggling for democracy, national liberation and socialism." This came as a declaratory statement at the close of the speech, with neither amplification, introduction, nor explanation. No mention was made of aid to the movements as such, although Brezhnev spoke of aid (political, economic and the training of cadres) to the new states.

On the other hand, Brezhnev also struck another note. In addition to the efforts to ensure peaceful conditions for the construction of communism in the USSR, he mentioned the Soviets' efforts to "unmask and frustrate the actions of the aggressive imperialist forces and to defend socialism, the freedom of peoples, and peace." Yet he appeared to sum up the Soviet role, in this context, by declaring that the Soviet Union had "everything necessary—an honest policy of peace, military might, the solidarity of the Soviet people—*to ensure the inviolability of our borders against any encroachments and to defend the goals of socialism.*"[185]

Ponomarev, writing on the Congress, picked up the "Soviet Union first" theme, quoting Lenin to the effect that Soviet Russia's main channel of influence would be economic, and that, therefore, augmented Soviet economic might was of primary importance, in that it guaranteed greater Soviet leverage in the world and "strengthening of the base" of the fight against imperialism.[186] In his speech to the Congress, Gromyko too spoke of ensuring favorable conditions for the building of communism, as well as averting world war, as the main tasks of Soviet foreign policy. He did speak of the Soviets' role in defending Third World countries against aggression and of "internationalism" as part of Soviet policy, but he also warned against "ultra-revolutionary verbiage" and "ostentatious, theatrical ultra-radicalism."[187] He also failed to mention the national liberation movements as such.

In speeches on the occasion of a Fidel Castro visit in 1972, there were more forthcoming statements, as was to be expected, in defense of the unfolding détente opposed by Castro. It was directly in response to Castro's (and the Chinese) challenge on the issue of revolution in the Third World that Brezhnev spoke of the divisibility of détente at least in the ideological sphere.[188] On the same occasion, Kosygin went further, when, defending peaceful coexistence, he said: "But this in no way signifies a denial of the right of the peoples, arms in hands, to oppose aggression or to strive for liberation from foreign oppression. This is a sacred and inalienable right, and the Soviet Union invariably helps peoples that have risen in struggle against colonialism..."[189] Undoubtedly prompted by Castro's complaints, this more militant line was not representative of either Kosygin or most other official pronouncements at the time, although the divisibility of détente was already standard for Suslov. In his role as ideological watchdog, Suslov was always to qualify détente regarding ideological competition. While this usually meant division of détente regarding Soviet support of (proletarian) revolutionary action around the world, in a July 1975 *Kommunist* article Suslov defined détente in Brezhnev's terms of 1966 as excluding "class peace between...the colonialists and the victims of colonial oppression, or between the oppressors and the oppressed."[190]

The emergence of this more interventionist line as officially declared policy was signalled by Andrei Gromyko in a *Kommunist* article two months later, not too long before the twenty-fifth CPSU Congress.[191] Gromyko took the line, to be repeated at the Congress, that détente opened new opportunities for cooperation with new states. While this was not specifically the divisibility of détente argument, it was sufficiently vague as to be interpreted in this, as well as the opposite, way. That he did *not* intend the more moderate view (that détente eliminated the necessity for Soviet intervention) was strongly suggested by his mention not only of the USSR's "internationalist duty" on the side of "fighters for independence and progress," but also of the "substantial role...played by our moral and material support" for the peoples of Bangladesh, Guinea-Bissau, South Vietnam, Cambodia, Laos, Mozambique, and others.

This indeed was exactly the line taken by Brezhnev in his report to the twenty-fifth Congress.[192] There, he argued at some length that détente and revolution were not contradictory, although this was clearly asserted defensively. Paraphrased, he said: to those who say that détente helps the capitalists and freezes the revolution, we say that détente helps *our* development, and revolution cannot be frozen because it is the result of intrinsic processes, and, anyway, we can see that détente clearly has *not* prevented revolution. Nonetheless, Brezhnev did preface these remarks with the comment that "it could not be clearer that détente and peaceful coexistence refer to relations between states." Like the Gromyko article, Brezhnev was effusive in his praise of the role played by the Soviet Union in the victories of Guinea-Bissau–Cape Verde, Mozambique, and Angola (in the case of the last, claiming that help from "progressives" had been given to the new *state*), speaking of "every kind of support" and declaring that "Our party supports and will continue to support peoples who are fighting for their freedom."

Andropov echoed some of this Brezhnev line, at least in a warning to the West not to expect the Soviet Union "to renounce its solidarity with those who are waging a struggle against exploitation and colonial oppression" even in the era of détente.[193] Yet certain other remarks in this same speech suggested that he might not have been particularly enthusiastic about Soviet intervention. In addition to slogans regarding the undesirability of exporting revolution and implying that indigenous forces were the bearers of revolution, he offered only "our sympathies" to peoples fighting "foreign interventionists." Clarifying this somewhat, he argued that there was "no sane alternative to détente" in the era of nuclear weapons and that, therefore, the ideological struggle should not be at the cost of peace. In this context, he criticized the Chinese for stirring up conflicts.

Basically, however, the tone set by Brezhnev at the Congress was that followed in speeches by Soviet leaders and official pronouncements; the obligation to the national liberation movements was enshrined in the Soviet Constitution of 1977 and, again, was spelled out in the Soviet Government Statement on Africa, issued in June 1978.[194] Suslov maintained his less explicit but overall advocacy of "unswerving" Soviet support for the national liberation struggle.[195] And, as might have been expected, Ponomarev went even further, citing the case of China in the 1930s and 1940s as an example of Soviet activity on behalf of national liberation movements, praising the later role in Africa as well.[196] Also expectedly, Podgornyi, on his 1977 trip to Africa, was relatively fulsome in his declarations of Soviet support, although in his speech in Mozambique, where he was particularly forthcoming, he added the caveat (regarding economic aid) that "we do not have extensive means."[197] This would suggest that he at least was concerned about the economic burden at a time of general economic strain at home.

Speaking at an election meeting in 1979, Brezhnev maintained the more interventionist line, explaining that "support for the struggle of the peoples for national liberation and social progress is a principle of our foreign policy recorded in the Constitution of the USSR...We are proud of the unselfish aid which the Soviet Union and other countries of the socialist community have given, for instance, to the peoples of Angola and Ethiopia...[198]

In the same round of election speeches, Andropov again struck a slightly different note. He set out as Moscow's primary attribute in international affairs its deterrent quality because of its military might, and he saw this military strength as the Soviets' main responsibility or role.[199] Coupling this with détente, in defense against Western accusations of Soviet meddling, he emphasized the intrinsic processes argument, stating that it would be "extremely unreasonable and dangerous to jeopardize détente" each time these inevitable processes took place. Although directed to the West, the absence of the divisibility of détente line and the apparently "Soviet Union first" deterrent limited role position suggested that the above comment may have had a domestic target as well. Slightly earlier, he had defended détente with the argument that it hurt capitalist society and the West by preventing them from employing tactics of diktat and pressure; that is, the argument that détente limited the West, by implication, preventing any need for Soviet intervention.[200] Moreover, Andropov's overall conclusion for Soviet foreign policy was the need for restraint and détente, making no mention of a role in the Third World or regarding national liberation movements.

In 1980 Ponomarev published an article in *Kommunist* which seemed to have everything in it, from the more interventionist line of the 1976 Congress (and the future 1981 Congress) to the apparently more restrained line of Andropov.[201] On the one hand, Ponomarev spoke at length of the power of indigenous trends and the impossibility of exporting revolution, citing Lenin against "leftist" adventurists. Yet he went on to declare the battle against the export of counter-revolution, and characterized the national liberation movements as an "inseparable element" in the world revolutionary process. He attacked the concept that revolution depended upon a conflict situation, arguing that détente and revolution could go together and that détente provided the possibility for the Third World to develop peacefully. Moreover, he implied the Soviet deterrent role idea but he also added that the Soviet Union provided "sympathies," "solidarity, and support" for the movements despite détente. He offered no concrete examples, however, but this may have been because he was also answering Western accusations of Soviet meddling.

If Ponomarev's policy statement was ambiguous, Brezhnev's speech to the twenty-sixth CPSU Congress was less so. Although Brezhnev devoted less attention to the Third World and particularly to national liberation movements than in his 1976 speech, and waxed somewhat less enthusiastic, he not only reaffirmed the commitment made in the earlier Congress but added the apparently stronger reference against the export of counter-revolution.[202] Thus, at the very same time that at least some of the presumably more influential theoreticians such as Brutents and Anatolii Gromyko were raising the "Soviet Union first" argument, the party leadership appeared still to be at the stage of a more activist orientation, if perhaps less enthusiastically optimistic. Brezhnev's rules of conduct proposal later in 1981 may have been a sign of greater willingness to restrain the Soviet role in the Third World, although it referred primarily to states and, insofar as it was relevant to movements, called for peoples' rights basically to self-determination. Another sign that Brezhnev himself might have been retreating from the interventionist position, however, was his September 1982 speech, calling on both East and West to refrain from activity in the Third World.[203] This was followed by his October talk with Soviet military leaders, in which he stressed Soviet economic problems, the implication being the need for a more restrained policy.[204]

Following Brezhnev's death, the changes apparent earlier in the theoreticians' works began to emerge in leadership pronouncements. In his speeches to the Central Committee plena in November 1982 and even more so in June 1983, Andropov struck a much more hesitant note, casting some doubt on the inevitability of socialism as the end product of the national liberation movements, opposing the export of revolution without any mention of counter-revolution, and repeating his earlier line against "a contest of ideas" turning into military confrontation.[205] Gone were the glowing references to past Soviet support; the only example for relations with the Third World was that of India—not a national liberation movement, not even a "socialist-oriented" state. Instead, there was the quote from Lenin that "the main influence on the world revolutionary process is exerted by our economic policy."[206] Indeed, in the June speech Andropov called for a revision of the party's foreign policy program.[207] Speaking of the complexities of the Third World states, he asserted that: "It is one thing to proclaim socialism as a goal and another thing to build it." He even added that Soviet help would be "to the extent of our possibilities," and that ultimately these states had to rely on themselves primarily. He had nothing to say of national liberation movements as such.

None of this was particularly new for Andropov, nor was it very different from many of the views already expressed by even party theoreticians. It was new, however, for the leadership level, as evidenced by Gromyko's speech to the June 1983 plenum, which bore more resemblance to past pronouncements than to Andropov's line.[208] By the fall of 1983, Gromyko had come around, at least insofar as his October speech to the UN was an indication.[209] Others, such as party secretary Zimyanin and Andropov-promoted Politburo member Aliev, reflected the more minimalistic positions of the Soviet Union's task as protecting the gains of socialism and the Soviet state, echoing Andropov's comments that no problem needed a military solution and that ideological battle should not be permitted to escalate to military conflict.[210] This having been said by Gromyko, for example, Soviet support for peoples fighting for freedom and independence was asserted. But, unlike his comments of earlier years, Gromyko did *not* list this as one of the tasks of Soviet foreign policy, in addition to those of preserving peace, pursuing détente, curbing the arms race, and promoting cooperation.[211] Party secretary Kapitonov, who had earlier spoken simply of Soviet support for national liberation movements, now added the phrase of Lenin that the Soviet Union could exert its main influence on the revolutionary process through its economic policy, the strengthening of the Soviet Union serving the interests of all.[212] Aliev, too, suggested that the new Soviet reticence was connected with economic problems when he said in Hanoi that, in helping the Vietnamese economy, the "Soviet people have to share with you even things they also need."[213] The brief Chernenko period did witness some return in Soviet leadership pronouncements to the national liberation movements and the need to assist them. This did not, however, include any return to the fight against counter-revolution argument or the more fulsome commitments of the twenty-fifth CPSU Congress type, or even of the 1981 Congress type.

With Gorbachev there appears to have been a return to Andropov's positions, including almost total absence of references to the national liberation movements. In an early speech, in March 1985, the most Gorbachev had to offer them was "sympathies"; he did not even offer that in his mammoth speech to the twenty-seventh CPSU Congress in February 1986.[214] The Congress resolutions remedied at least this omission by reaffirming the CPSU's "immutable solidarity with the forces of national liberation and social emancipation."[215] Nothing more was said, however, of a Soviet role.

Moreover, the only reference to the problem of the export of counter-revolution came in a strange context, in Gorbachev's speech, as one in a list of negative phenomena (including political assassinations and hijackings) defined as "international terrorism." On this point, and a few others, the party's program was somewhat different. It spoke not only of "profound sympathy" and "solidarity" but also of "support [for] the struggle of peoples who are still under the yoke of racism" and apartheid; it also spoke against the "export of counter-revolution" and proclaimed that "the Soviet Union resolutely opposes attempts to halt and reverse the course of history by force."[216] Yet limits appeared to be set on just what this opposition, or the support for the movements, would take. The program declared, as had Andropov earlier, that people in the developing countries would progress "mainly through their own efforts" with Soviet assistance only "to the extent of its capabilities." Moreover, the program reiterated a "Soviet Union first" position not only in its list of foreign policy priorities (which had solidarity with national liberation struggles at the very end of the list), but also in its declaration that socialism proved its advantages "by the force of its example in all areas of social life—by the dynamic development of the economy, science and culture, by the enhancement of the living standard of the working people, and by the deepening of socialist democracy."[217]

The post-Brezhnev period generally saw a drawing together of the leadership positions and those of most of the theoreticians (with the exception mainly of military commentators), away from the advocacy of too great a commitment or involvement on behalf of the national liberation movements, toward a more "Soviet Union first" orientation. The reasons for this were not explicitly indicated by the published works of either leadership or theoreticians; references to the West's increased aggressiveness, or to the complexities, that is, the difficulties, of the Third World situation, were not necessarily the explanations proffered for the more cautious policy. They may, nonetheless, have referred to factors which did influence the change, that is, to the higher risk situation in the post-détente, Reagan administration atmosphere; the lack of return or difficulties encountered even in the Third World countries in which the Soviets had invested heavily, such as Angola and Mozambique and even Ethiopia; the tenacity and cost (not necessarily economic) of the Afghan problem.

At the same time, these were years of serious domestic economic difficulties which presumably dictated cutbacks or at least some restraints in foreign expenditure. These difficulties may have prompted renewed interest in détente and a concomitant concern (or understanding) that a less restrained policy would hurt the chances of East–West accord. Nor can the succession issue, with its changing power relations within the Kremlin, be ruled out as a contributing factor to the emergence of different views which ultimately resulted in what appears to have been a change in the official line.

Notes

1   Rostislav Ul'ianovskii, *Ocherki natsional'no-osvoboditel'noi bor'by: voprosy teorii i praktiki*, Nauka, Moscow, 1976 (citations from the English translation; Rostislav Ulyanovsky, *National Liberation: Essays on Theory and Practice*, Progress, Moscow, 1978), p. 383; K. N. Brutents, *Sovremennye natsional'no-osvoboditel'nye revoliutsii*, Politizdat, Moscow, 1974 (citations from K. N. Brutents, *National Liberation Revolutions Today*, Progress, Moscow, 1977), vol. I, pp. 48–9, 68; V. G. Solodovnikov, *Afrika vybiraet put'*, Nauka, Moscow, 1970, p. 135; N. A. Simoniia, *Strany Vostoka: puti razvitiia*, Nauka, Moscow, 1975, *passim.*
2   Ulyanovsky, *National Liberation*, p. 383; Solodovnikov, *Afrika*, p. 135.
3   See chapter 4.
4   *Izvestiia*, 24 August 1978; V. V. Zagladin, "Revoliutsionnyi protsess i mezhdunarodnaia politika KPSS," *Kommunist*, no. 13 (1972): 14–26; V. V. Zagladin, "XXVI s"ezd KPSS i mirovoi revoliutsionnyi protsess," *Mirovaia ekonomika i mezhdunarodnye otnosheniia*, no. 4 (1981): 3–19; L. M. Entin, *Politicheskie sistemy razvivaiushchikhsia stran*, Mezhdunarodnye otnosheniia, Moscow, 1978, p. 109; *Pravda*, 23 November 1974; V. Shelepin, "The Socialist World and the Developing Countries," *New Times*, no. 9 (1980): 20–3; "Lenin and the National Liberation Movement," *Asia and Africa Today*, no. 2 (1982): 2–5.
5   Zagladin, "Revoliutsionnyi protsess," p. 18; Zagladin, "XXVI s"ezd," p. 7.
6   *Pravda*, 11 August 1982.
7   Vadim Kortunov, "The Working Class...The Leading Revolutionary Force of Our Time," *New Times*, no. 11 (1972): 19; G. Kim, "Razriadka i sotsial'nyi progress v stranakh Azii i Afriki," *Aziia i Afrika segodnia*, no. 11 (1979): 2.
8   G. Kim, "World Socialism and the National Liberation Movement," *Far Eastern Affairs*, no. 2 (1976): 47–50; G. Kim, *The Socialist World and the National Liberation Movement*, Novosti, Moscow, 1978, pp. 6–8.
9   G. Kim, "The National Liberation Movement Today," *International Affairs*, no. 4 (1981): 27; G. Kim, "National Liberation Movement: Topical Problems," *International Affairs*, no. 9 (1984): 43.
10 Kim, "National Liberation Movement Today," p. 30.
11 Kim, "Topical Problems," p. 43.
12 Brutents, *Revolutions*, vol. I, pp. 15, 68; Ulyanovksy, *National Liberation*, pp. 383–4; his introduction to I. L. Andreev, *Nekapitalisticheskoe razvitie*, Politizdat, Moscow, 1974, p. 21; R. A. Ul'ianovskii, *Sovremennye problemy Azii i Afriki*, Nauka, Moscow, 1978, p. 87.
13 Brutents, *Revolutions*, vol. I, p. 306.
14 Ibid., p. 7.
15 Ibid., pp. 13, 16.

244   *A Soviet Theory of National Liberation*

16 Ibid., pp. 14–15, 51.
17 Ibid., p. 15.
18 Ibid., pp. 24, 35, 48–9, 68.
19 K. N. Brutents, "A Great Force of Modern Times," *International Affairs*, no. 3 (1981): 81.
20 K. N. Brutents, *Osvobodivshiesia strany v 70-e gody*, Politizdat, Moscow, 1979, pp. 65, 77, 149–50.
21 R. A. Ulyanovsky, "Leninism, Soviet Experience and the Newly Free Countries," *New Times*, no. 1 (1971): 18.
22 Ibid., pp. 19–20; R. Ul'ianovskii, "O natsional'nom osvobozhdenii i natsionalizme," *Aziia i Afrika segodnia*, no. 10 (1980): 2.
23 Ulyanovsky, *National Liberation*, p. 383; R. A. Ul'ianovskii, "O nekotorykh voprosakh marksistsko–leninskoi teorii revoliutsionnogo protsessa," *Novaia i noveishaia istoriia*, no. 4 (1976): 72–83; R. Ulyanovsky, "An Epochal Prediction That Has Come True," *New Times*, no. 22 (1977): 18. Ul'ianovskii, *Sovremennye problemy* pp. 38, 40.
24 Ibid., p. 87.
25 Brutents, *Revolutions*, vol. I, p. 14; Ulyanovsky, "Leninism," p. 18; R. Ulyanovsky, "Lenin and the National Liberation Movement," *New Times*, no. 16 (1970): 8; Ul'ianovskii, "O natsional'nom osvobozhdenii," p. 2; Kim, *Socialist World*, pp. 6, 8, 56.
26 Solodovnikov, *Afrika*, p. 169; P. I. Manchkha, *Aktual'nye problemy sovremennoi Afriki*, Politizdat, Moscow, 1979, p. 305.
27 Solodovnikov, *Afrika*, p. 169.
28 An. Gromyko, "Lenin i Afrika," *Aziia i Afrika segodnia*, no. 5 (1980): 2–4; An. Gromyko, "Sovetskaia politika mira i Afrika," *Aziia i Afrika Segodnia*, no. 1 (1981): 2–5; An. Gromyko, "Za mir i svobodu narodov," *Aziia i Afrika segodnia*, no. 8 (1981): 52; An. Gromyko, *Africa: Progress, Problems, Prospects*, Progress, Moscow, 1981, pp. 35, 75–6, 79, 81.
29 V. G. Solodovnikov and V. V. Bogoslovsky, *Non-capitalist Development: An Historical Outline*, Progress, Moscow, 1975, p. 166. The authors distinguished between two extremes and said that before the October Revolution the national liberation movements had led to bourgeois revolutions only, but in the era of world transformation to socialism "all the objective possibilities" existed for the growing over into a socialist revolution (p. 89).
30 G. B. Starushenko, "XXV s''ezd KPSS o progressivnykh izmeneniiakh v osvobodivshikhsia stranakh i povyshenii ikh roli v mirovom razvitii," *Voprosy istorii KPSS*, no. 7 (1976): 49.
31 Iu. Gavrilov, "V. I. Lenin i istoricheskie sud'by antikolonial'noi bor'by," *Aziia i Afrika segodnia*, no. 3 (1980): 2–5.
32 A. I. Borisov and N. B. Aleksandrov, "Obsuzhdenie knigi N. A. Simoniia 'Strany Vostoka: puti razvitiia'", *Narody Azii i Afriki*, no. 3 (1977): 59 (Gavrilov); unsigned, "Natsional'no-osvoboditel'noe dvizhenie: nekotorye voprosy differentsiatsii," *Aziia i Afrika segodnia*, no. 6 (1978): 29 (Kiva).
33 Kortunov, "The Working Class," p. 19; Yuri Krasin, "The International and the National in the Revolutionary Process," *New Times*, no. 7 (1981): 18–19; Iu. A. Krasin, "Uzlovaia problema strategii kommunistov," *Rabochii klass i sovremmennyi mir*, no. 1 (1977): 35–49.
34 Borisov and Aleksandrov, "Obsuzhdenie knigi," 57–8; K. Maidanik and G. Mirskii, "Natsional'no-osvoboditel'naia bor'ba: sovremennyi etap," *Mirovaia ekonomika i mezhdunarodnye otnosheniia*, no. 6 (1981): 17–31.
35 See chapter 4.
36 Maidanik and Mirskii, "Natsional'no-osvoboditel'naia bor'ba," pp. 57–8. N. Simoniya, "The October Revolution and National Liberation Movements," *International Affairs*, no. 12 (1979): 64–5.
37 Zagladin, "XXVI s''ezd," p. 7; V. V. Zagladin and F. D. Ryzhenko, *Sovremennoe revoliutsionnoe dvizhenie i natsionalizm*, Politizdat, Moscow, 1973, p. 89.
38 Y. Zhukov, L. Delyusin, A. Iskenderov, and L. Stepanov, *The Third World*, Progress, Moscow, 1970, pp. 29–30. Krasin, and to a lesser degree Kortunov, made

similar points, which might place them in this category, though they were on the whole less negative.

39 Vl. Li, "The Role of the National Liberation Movement in the Anti-Imperialist Struggle," *International Affairs*, no. 12 (1971): 72.

40 A. Iskenderov, "World Socialism and the National Liberation Movement," *New Times*, no. 25 (1972): 23.

41 P. N. Fedoseev, *Leninizm i natsional'nyi vopros v sovremennykh usloviiakh*, Politizdat, Moscow, 1974 (citations from the English translation, Institute of Marxism–Leninism, CC, CPSU: P. N. Fedoseyev, *Leninism and the National Question*, Progress, Moscow, 1977), pp. 471–2.

42 Ulyanovsky, "Leninism, Soviet Experience," p. 18; Kim, *Socialist World*, pp. 18–19; Kim, "Razriadka i sotsial'nyi progress," p. 2; Kim, "World Socialism," p. 51; G. Kim, "Sovetskii Soiuz i natsional'no-osvoboditel'noe dvizhenie," *Mirovaia ekonomika i mezhdunarodnye otnosheniia*, no. 9 (1982): 30; Solodovnikov, *Afrika*, p. 168.

43 Starushenko, "XXV s"ezd," p. 49; Gleb Starushenko, "Chosen Path," *New Times*, no. 40 (1980): 18; G. Starushenko, "International Law and National Liberation," *International Affairs*, no. 2 (1983): 83.

44 Brutents, *Revolutions*, vol. I, pp. 59, 124; vol. II, p. 183. See also R. Ulyanovsky, "Paths and Prospects of National Democracy," *New Times*, no. 14 (1978): 20; Ul'ianovskii, *Sovremennye problemy*, 62; Manchkha, *Aktual'nye problemy*, p. 30; Solodovnikov and Bogoslovksy, *Non-capitalist Development*, p. 89, and Kim, "Razriadka i sotsial'nyi progress," p. 2.

45 Gavrilov, "V. I. Lenin," pp. 2–5.

46 Starushenko, "XXV s"ezd," p. 48. However, in a later article, with Gromyko, Starushenko was no longer so forthcoming, even adding a caveat that the movements should be loyal to the interests of the whole world revolutionary current if they wanted assistance: A. A. Gromyko and G. B. Starushenko, "Sotsial'nye i natsional'nye faktory razvitiia osvobodivshikhsia stran," *Sotsiologicheskie issledovaniia*, no. 1 (1983): 3–4. Given Starushenko's position even in 1983 (see *International Affairs*, no. 2 (1983): p. 83), the moderation must have been the contribution of his co-author, the more important Anatolii Gromyko.

47 Li, "Role of the National Liberation Movement," p. 71; Solodovnikov and Bogoslovsky, *Non-capitalist Development*, p. 184; Starushenko, "XXV s"ezd," p. 48; Manchkha, *Aktual'nye problemy*, p. 33; K. I. Zarodov, "O nekotorykh perspektivakh razvitiia mirovogo revoliutsionnogo protsessa v svete idei XXVI s"ezda KPSS," *Voprosy istorii KPSS*, no. 9 (1981): 33; An. A. Gromyko, "XXVI s"ezd KPSS i zadachi sovetskoi afrikanistiki," *Narody Azii i Afriki*, no. 4 (1981): 10; *Pravda*, 11 August 1982; Gromyko, *Africa: Progress*, p. 104.

48 Editorial, "XXVI s"ezd KPSS i problemy natsional'no-osvoboditel'nogo dvizheniia," *Narody Azii i Afriki*, no. 3 (1981): 5; E. Fryazin, "The Communists and the Fight for Peace," *New Times*. no. 47 (1981): 15.

49 P. Shastitko, "Vstrecha s Leninym," *Aziia i Afrika segodnia*, no. 4 (1980): 6.

50 Anatoly Gromyko, "African Realities and the 'Conflict of Strategy' Myth," *New Times*, no. 51 (1978): 4.

51 E. A. Tarabrin (ed.), *USSR and Countries of Africa*, Progress, Moscow, 1980 (Russian edition 1977), pp. 12, 129.

52 P. Shastitko, "Revoliutsiia dolzhna umet' zashchishchat'sia," *Aziia i Afrika segodnia*, no. 1 (1982): 2–5. He said that the "alliance with the socialist community gives even a small, militarily, and economically weak state the possibility of retaining its sovereignty and upholding its revolutionary gains irrespective of its geographic location." One may also contrast the deputy chairman of the Soviet Afro-Asian Solidarity Committee, A. Dzasokhov's, 1971 comments on the Soviet Union as the "shield" of the national liberation movements "of the emerging states," with his later (1984) emphasis on the need for peace and the Soviets' role in obtaining peace and arms limitation in the interests of the national liberation movements: "Developing Countries: A New Stage in the Struggle for Peace and Social Progress," *International Affairs*, no. 1 (1984): 36; "Africa: The Basic Trend," *New Times*, no. 21 (1971): 29.

53   E. Tarabrin, "Afrika: osvoboditel'naia bor'ba i proiski imperializma," *Mirovaia ekonomika i mezhdunarodnye otnosheniia*, no. 6 (1980): 72–4.

54   Y. Tarabrin, "The National Liberation Movement: Problems and Prospects," *International Affairs*, no. 2 (1978): 61. See also E. Tarabrin, "Afrika na novom vitke osvobodi tel'noi bor'by," *Mirovaia ekonomika i mezhdunarodnye otnosheniia*, no. 2 (1979): 41–7.

55   A. Voronov, *Izvestiia*, 10 October 1978. See also F. Voloshin in *Sel'skaia zhizn'*, 28 November 1979 (FBIS, III, 30 November 1979, J-1), who added that there was "not a single Soviet soldier in Africa."

56   V. Sidenko, "SSSR–Afrika: real'nosti protiv lzhi," *Novoe vremia*, no. 19 (1977): 19–20. Manchkha also mentioned training in the Soviet Union: *Aktual'nye problemy*, p. 309.

57   V. Ia. Katsman, "Osnovnye cherty vneshnei politiki afrikanskikh gosudarstv sotsialisticheskoi orientatsii," *Narody Azii i Afriki*, no. 3 (1980): 28.

58   Manchkha, *Aktual'nye problemy*, p. 35.

59   Primakov, *Pravda* 11 August 1982; (see also E. Primakov, "Osvo bodivshiesia strany v mezhdunarodnykh otnosheniiakh," *Mirovaia ekonomika i mezhdunarodnye otnosheniia*, no. 5 (1982): 22–)6; Li, "Role of the National Liberation Movement," p. 71; Solodovnikov and Bogoslovsky, *Non-capitalist Development*, p. 217; Solodovnikov, *Afrika*, p. 169; Starushenko, "XXV s"ezd," p. 48.

60   An. Gromyko, "The Imperialist Threat to Africa," *International Affairs*, no. 7 (1981): 47–53; An. A. Gromyko, "XXV s"ezd," pp. 9–10; Gromyko, "Sovetskaia politika," p. 2.

61   Gromyko, "XXVI s"ezd," p. 11.

62   Kim, *Socialist World*, p. 72; G. Kim, "Sovetskii Soiuz i natsional'no-osvoboditel'noe dvizhenie," *Mirovaia ekonomika i mezhdunarodnye otnosheniia*, no. 9 (1982): 29–30; Kim, "National Liberation Movement," p. 43; *Pravda*, 20 June 1981; V. G. Solodovnikov, *Problemy sovremennoi Afriki*, Nauka, Moscow, 1973, pp. 279–81.

63   Iskenderov, "World Socialism," p. 24; Midtsev, *Izvestiia*, 7 August 1979.

64   Gromyko, "Sovetskaia politika," p. 2.

65   Ibid., p. 2; Gromyko, "XXVI s"ezd," pp. 6–7.

66   V. Kremeniuk and V. Lukin, "Imperializm i razvivaiushchiesia strany: evoliutsiia vzaimootnoshenii," *Aziia i Afrika segodnia*, no. 12 (1983): 4–7; Entin, *Politicheskie sistemy*, p. 30; Fedoseyev, *Leninism*, pp. 470–1; G. Skorov, "Imperializm i razvivaiushchiesia strany: antagonizm uglubliaetsia," *Kommunist*, no. 18 (1974): 99.

67   Kremeniuk and Lukin, "Imperializm," pp. 3–4; Entin, *Politicheskie sistemy*, p. 30; Zhukov et al., *Third World*, p. 31. See also *Izvestiia* editorial, 28 September 1975.

68   V. Zagladin, "XXVI s"ezd," p. 16.

69   Ibid. He had expressed this same line, speaking of intrinsic processes rather than the export of revolution, in an interview to *Der Stern*, 31 January 1980.

70   Yuri Krasin, "The International and the National in the Revolutionary Process," *New Times*, no. 7 (1981): 19.

71   Ibid.

72   Ibid.

73   Gromyko, "Imperialist Threat," pp. 47–53; Gromyko, "XXVI s"ezd," pp. 9–10; Gromyko, "Sovetskaia politika," p. 2; Kim, "Sovetskii Soiuz," pp. 29–30; Brutents, "A Great Force," pp. 83–4; Krasin, "International and National," p. 19; Zhukov et al., *Third World*, p. 31.

74   See Elizabeth Kridl Valkenier, "Soviet Economic Relations with the Third World," in Roger Kanet (ed.), *The Soviet Union and The Developing Nations*, Johns Hopkins University Press, Baltimore, 1974, pp. 215–36; or Oye Ogunbadejo, "Soviet Policies in Africa," *African Affairs* 79, no. 316 (1980): 301–2.

75   Zhukov et al., *Third World*, pp. 33–4; *Pravda*, 21 December 1973.

76   *Pravda*, 1 November 1977.

77   Gromyko, "XXVI s"ezd," pp. 3–13 (which nonetheless has the "counter-revolution" formula); Gromyko, "Imperialist Threat," pp. 47–53; Gromyko, "Sovetskaia politika," p. 2; Kim, "Sovetskii Soivz," pp. 29–30; Brutents, "A Great Force,"

pp. 83–4. See also Krasin, who apparently always held this view: "Uzlovaia problema," pp. 35–50; Krasin, "International and National," p. 19.

78 Iu. Novopashin, "Vozdeistvie real'nogo sotsializma na mirovoi revoliutsionnyi protsess metodologicheskie aspekty," *Voprosy filosofii*, no. 8 (1982): 6; cited in Thomas Zamostny, "Moscow and the Third World: Recent Trends in Soviet Thinking," *Soviet Studies* 36, no. 2 (1984): 231–2. The second article was by P. Ia. Korbelev, who, like Novopashin, also worked at the Institute for Economics of the World Socialist System; but he published his article in *Narody Azii i Afriki*, no. 2 (1982): "Ekonomicheskoe sotrudnichestvo SSSR afrikanskimi gosudarstvami", pp. 8–9.

79 A. Kodachenko, "Strategiia nezavisimogo razvitiia osvobodivshikhsia stran," *Mezhdunarodnaia zhizn'*, no. 1 (1984): 54; Sh. Sanakoiev, "The Great Transforming Force in World Relations," *International Affairs*, no. 8 (1984): 11.

80 Maidaneik and Mirskii, "Natsional'no-osvoboditel'naia bor'ba," p. 3.

81 N. Simoniya, "The October Revolution and the National Liberation Movements," *International Affairs*, no. 12 (1979): 60–7; N. Simoniya, "Mighty Tide of National Liberation," *New Times*, no. 50 (1980): 21–3.

82 N. Simoniia, "Sovremennyi etap osvoboditel'noi bor'by," *Aziia i Afrika segodnia*, no. 5 (1981): 16.

83 Gromyko, *Africa: Progress*, pp. 99–102.

84 This is not to say that Zagladin or Primakov were necessarily less important, but Brutents and Ul'ianovskii addressed this issue more directly and thoroughly than did Zagladin and even Primakov, whose views have been noted in the preceding pages.

85 Ul'ianovskii, *Sovremennye problemy*, p. 33; Ulyanovsky, "Epochal Prediction," p. 18. See also Ulyanovsky, *National Liberation*, p. 235; Ulyanovsky, "Leninism," p. 18; R. Ulyanovsky, "Lenin and the National Liberation Movement," *New Times*, no. 16 (1970): 8.

86 Ulyanovsky, *National Liberation*, pp. 235, 350; Ulyanovsky, "Epochal Prediction," p. 18; Ulyanovsky, "Paths and Prospects," p. 19.

87 Ulyanovsky, *National Liberation*, p. 215.

88 Ibid., p. 349. See also Ulyanovsky, "Epochal Prediction," p. 20.

89 Ul'ianovskii, *Sovremennye problemy*, pp. 34–5, 64.

90 Ulyanovsky, *National Liberation*, pp. 196, 349. In his 1972 book Ul'ianovskii had said, "In reality, on the international level the working class of the socialist countries emerges as a vanguard force, rendering a growing influence on the development of states of socialist orientation. However, it does not and cannot exercise direct state leadership over this development. This can be done only by the national working class in the very states of socialist orientation..." (R. A. Ul'ianovskii, *Funktsii gosudarstva v nezavisimykh stranakh Afriki*, Nauka, Moscow, 1972, p. 23).

91 Brutents, *Revolutions*, vol. I. p. 59.

92 Ibid., pp. 57–63.

93 Ibid., pp. 58–9.

94 Ibid., p. 306.

95 Ibid., p. 68 (emphasis mine).

96 Ibid., vol. II, p. 2332.

97 Ibid., vol. I, pp. 61, 64.

98 Brutents, "A Great Force," p. 84.

99 Brutents, *Osvobodivshiesia strany*, pp. 131–2, 151–2.

100 Tarabrin, "National Liberation Movement," p. 61.

101 E. Tarabrin, "Neokolonializm na sovremennom etape," *Aziia i Afrika segodnia*, no. 1 (1978): 12.

102 Zarodov, "O nekotorykh perspektivakh," p. 33.

103 Starushenko, "XXV s"ezd," p. 49.

104 Unsigned, "Who is Impeding Detente?" *New Times*, no. 9 (1978): 1. See also *Novoe vremia*, no. 27 (1978): 39; *Izvestiia*, 24 August 1978.

105 Alexi Kiva, "The Changing Africa," *New Times*, no. 7 (1976): 18.

106 A. Kiva, "Natsional'no-osvoboditel'noe dvizhenie: nekotorye osobennosti sovremennogo etapa razvitiia," *Aziia i Afrika segodnia*, no. 11 (1983): 3.

107   Ulyanovsky, "Epochal Prediction," p. 20; Ul'ianovskii, *Sovremennye problemy*, p. 63.

108   Ulyanovsky, *National Liberation*, pp. 196–201.

109   Gromyko, "Sovetskaia politika," p. 3; Gromyko, "Za mir," p. 52; Gromyko, *Africa: Progress*, p. 40. For the benefit of states, Gromyko (as well as others) also argued that détente would positively affect the Soviets' economic assistance, because it would reduce the need for high Soviet military expenditures (*Africa: Progress*, pp. 158–9).

110   D. Volsky, "Peaceful Co-existence and the Third World," *New Times*, no. 33 (1972): 4. He espoused the "Soviet Union first"–deterrent ideas: "The strengthening of the position of the socialist community improves the international position of the developing countries too" (p. 5).

111   D. Volsky, "Taking Up A Point," *New Times*, no. 22 (1978): 30.

112   E. Zhukov, "The Importance of the Changes in International Relations on the National Liberation Struggle," *International Affairs*, no. 12 (1973): 27–8.

113   Skorov, "Imperializm," p. 108.

114   A. Iskenderov, "Developing Countries: Improving the World Climate," *International Affairs*, no. 10 (1981): 44. The détente-for-development line was expounded at length by IMEMO deputy director Ivan Ivanov in "Osvobodivshiesia strany: razriadka i razvitie," *Aziia i Afrika segodnia*, no. 8 (1980): 3.

115   V. V. Zhurkin, "Razriadka i politika SShA v mezhdunarodnykh konfliktakh," *SShA: ekonomika, politika i ideologiia*, no. 2 (1977): 4–13.

116   Primakov, "Osvobodivshiesia strany," p. 20.

117   Kim, "Socialist World," p. 75.

118   Ibid., pp. 75–8.

119   *Pravda*, 30 August 1973.

120   Brutents, *Osvobodivshiesia strany*, p. 128.

121   Brutents, *Revolutions*, vol. I, pp. 17–18; Brutents, "A Great Force," pp. 77. 83.

122   Brutents, "A Great Force," pp. 77, 83.

123   Moscow television, 24 November 1980.

124   V. A. Kremeniuk, "Sovetsko–amerikanskie otnosheniia i nekotorye problemy osvobodivshikhsia gosudarstv," *SShA: ekonomika, politika i ideologiia*, no. 6 (1982): 17; Fedor Burlatskii, *Literaturnaia gazeta*, 28 January 1981.

125   V. A. Kremeniuk, *SShA: Bor'ba protiv natsional'no-osvoboditel'nogo dvizheniia*, Mysl', Moscow, 1983, p. 289.

126   Moscow domestic television, 24 November 1980.

127   V. Zagladin, "Sixty-seven Steps Along the Road to Lasting Peace," *New Times*, no. 45 (1984): 6–7.

128   *Literaturnaia gazeta*, 1 January 1981, pp. 4–15. Here Bovin was pessimistic, even cynical, about the potential of the national liberation movements. See also his July 1980 article in *Kommunist*, in which he spoke of the need for "caution, circumspection, and self-control": A. Bovin, "Neprekhodiashchee znachenie Leninskikh idei," *Kommunist*, no. 10 (1980): 75.

129   Moscow domestic radio, 3 May 1981; B. Orekov, *Pravda*, 13 February 1981; S. Kondrashov, Moscow radio in English to North America, 14 February 1981; V. Zorin, Moscow radio in English to North America, 22 February 1981. See also E. S. Troitskii, "Kritika neokolonialistskikh fal'sifikatsii idei V. I. Lenina po problemam natsional'no-osvoboditel'nogo dvizheniia," *Voprosy istorii KPSS*, no. 7 (1980): 79–80, after the invasion of Afghanistan; and A. Sovetov, "1980 In Retrospect," *International Affairs*, 1 (1981): 8. There had been a spate of similar articles in 1978 responding to the Zaire (Shaba) crisis and to comments by President Carter regarding the Soviet Union as a threat to détente (Iu. Zhukov, *Pravda*, 24 March 1978; A. Maslennikov, *Pravda*, 15 July 1978; A. Voronov, *Izvestiia*, 10 October 1978; interview with Anat. Gromyko, "Imperialism Against Africa," *New Times*, no. 28 (1978): 18–20.)

130   E.g., V. Iordansky, "The Policy of Neo-colonialism in Action," *International Affairs*, no. 6 (1981): 85–90; Moscow domestic radio with journalists Strelnikov and Gerasimov, 20 February 1981; Iu. Zhukov, *Pravda*, 22 November 1981; Iu. Rudnev, *Sovetskaia Rossiia*, 5 February 1981; *Izvestiia*, 17 January 1981. For the opposite view, i.e., a reference to counter-revolution, see V. Nekrasov, *Pravda*, 19 October 1981.

131 *Izvestiia*, 12 November 1984.
132 Lt.-Col. G. Malinovskii, "Lokal'nye voiny v zone natsional'no-osvoboditel'nogo dvizheniia," *Voenno-istoricheskii zhurnal*, no. 5 (1974): 97–8; Col. G. Malinovskii, "Lokal'naia voina," in *Sovetskaia voennaia entsiklopediia*, vol. 5, Voenizdat, Moscow, 1978, p. 22.
133 Col. G. Malinovskii, "Neokolonial'nye voiny imperializma," *Voenno-istoricheskii zhurnal*, no. 5 (1983): 64.
134 Maj.-Gen. V. Matsulenko, "Some Lessons of Imperialist Local Wars," *Soviet Military Review*, no. 10 (1984): 45.
135 Maj.-Gen. D. Volkogonov et al., *Voina i armiia: filosofskosotsiologicheskii ocherk*, Voenizdat, Moscow, 1977, pp. 248–9.
136 Harriet Fast Scott and William F. Scott, *The Soviet Art of War*, Westview, Boulder, Colo., 1982, p. 251.
137 Volkogonov et al., *Voina i armiia*, pp. 248–9, 353–4. See Scott and Scott, *Soviet Art of War*, pp. 250–2. Carl Jacobsen quotes V. Ustimenko: "Especially now echoes the Leninist definition according to which to be an internationalist signifies to do 'the maximum in one country for the development, support of and victory of the revolution in all countries'...this may be expressed in a moral–political and in a material way, and in necessary cases also in military support for the toilers who are battling with imperialist aggression": V. Ustimenko, *Vestnik protivovozdushnoi oborony*, no. 1 (1975): 12–13; cited in C. G. Jacobsen, *Soviet Strategic Initiatives*, Praeger, New York, 1979, p. 29.
138 Lt.-Gen. D. Volkogonov, "The Soviet Army: A Factor in Peace and Security," *Soviet Military Review*, no. 2 (1984): 3; "The Logic of Retaliatory Measures," *Soviet Military Review*, no. 6 (1984): 56.
139 Jacobsen, *Soviet Strategic Initiatives*, pp. 15–18; Scott and Scott, *Soviet Art of War*, p. 242; Mark Katz, *The Third World in Soviet Military Thought*, Johns Hopkins University, Baltimore, 1982, p. 67.
140 V. M. Kulish (ed.), *Voennaia sila i mezhdunarodnye otnosheniia*, Mezhdunarodnye otnosheniia, Moscow, 1972, pp. 136–9. For a critique of the Western interpretations of the external function of the Soviet armed forces, see Rajan Menon, *Soviet Power and the Third World*, Yale University Press, New Haven, Conn., 1986, pp. 19–86.
141 Menon, *Soviet Power*, pp. 19–86; cited in Scott and Scott, *Soviet Art of War*, p. 242.
142 A. A. Yepishev, *Mighty Weapon of the Party*, Voenizdat, Moscow, 1973; cited in Frank Fukuyama, "Civil–Military Relations," Rand Report, Santa Monica, Calif., 1986, p. 19.
143 K. A. Vorob'ev, *Vooruzhennye sily razvitogo sotsialisticheskogo obshchestva*, Voenizdat, Moscow, 1980; in Scott and Scott, *Soviet Art of War*, p. 255. Somewhat less strong, but envisaging a similar role for the Soviet navy, was Col.-Gen. S. A. Tushkevich, *Sovetskie Vooruzhennie Sily*, Voenizdat, Moscow, 1978, p. 470.
144 Scott and Scott, *Soviet Art of War*, p. 256; and Fukuyama, "Civil–Military Relations", p. 19.
145 Col. K. Vorobyov, "Socialist Army: Essence and Purpose," *Soviet Military Review*, no. 7 (1984): 5–8.
146 Fukuyama, "Civil–Military Relations," p. 40.
147 Col. E. Rybkin, "XXV s"ezd KPSS: osvoboditel'nye voiny sovremennoi epokhi," *Voenno-istoricheskii zhurnal*, no. 11 (1978): 13–15.
148 V. L. Tiagunenko et al., *Vooruzhennaia bor'ba narodov Afriki za svobodu i nezaviimost*, Ministerstvo oborony SSSR, Nauka, Moscow, 1974, p. 409.
149 Ibid., p. 407.
150 Ibid., p. 408.
151 Ibid., p. 410.
152 Lt.-Col. N. Khmara, "Nekotorye osobennosti grazhdanskikh voin v sovremennuiu epokhu," *Kommunist Vooruzhennykh Sil*, no. 16 (1971): 23; Col. Iu. Dolgopolov, "Razvivaiushchiesia strany Azii, Afriki i Latinskoi Ameriki," *Kommunist Vooruzhennykh Sil*, no. 16 (1975): 79.

153 Dolgopolov, "Razvivaiushchiesia strany," p. 74; Col. G. Malinovskii, "Natsional'no-osvoboditel'noe dvizhenie na sovremennom etape," *Kommunist Vooruzhennykh Sil*, no. 24 (1979): 33; Lt.-Col. N. Khibrikov, "Krushenie kolonial'noi sistemy imperializma: osvobodivshiesia strany Azii, Afriki i Latinskoi Ameriki," *Kommunist Vooruzhennykh Sil*, no. 6 (1978): p. 74. See Katz, *The Third World*, p. 139.

154 Malinovskii, "Natsional'no-osvoboditel'noe," p. 33; Capt. 1st rank, Iu. Osipov, "V. I. Lenin, KPSS ob internatsional'nom kharaktere zashchity zavoevanii sotsializma," *Kommunist Vooruzhennykh Sil*, no. 13 (1978) 76; Col. V. Solovyov, "Army of Internationalists,: *Soviet Military Review*, no. 4 (1980): 4. See Katz, *The Third World*, p. 139.

155 Osipov, "V. I. Lenin," p. 76; Col. A. Leont'ev, *Krasnaia zvezda*, 1 May 1979.

156 Katz, *The Third World*, p. 79. He actually dates it to the 1971 CPSU Congress, when Brezhnev made a statement on aid to national liberation movements (see below).

157 Katz, *The Third World*, p. 103, cites the example of B. Vesnin, "Boevoi avangard bor'by za mir, protiv agressivnoi politiki imperializma," *Kommunist Vooruzhennykh Sil*, no. 11 (1978): 25, on gains made during détente.

158 Col. N. Vetrov, "Problems of War and Peace and the World Revolutionary Process," *Voennaia mysl'*, no. 8 (1971): 18; in Katz, *The Third World*, p. 80.

159 Maj.-Gen. D. Volkogonov, "Klassovaia bor'ba i sovremennost'," *Kommunist Vooruzhennykh Sil*, no. 4 (1979): 12.

160 Tiagunenko et al., *Vooruzhennaia bor'ba*, p. 53.

161 Katz, *The Third World*, pp. 51–2, 79. See Galia Golan, "Internal Factors in Soviet Foreign Policy," unpublished paper, Hebrew University of Jerusalem, 1975, for similar conclusions.

162 See chapter 4. Even Volkogonov worried about escalation, but he did come down on the side of the "external function," as we have seen.

163 Col. E. Dolgopolov, "Razoblachenie burzhuaznykh i maoistskikh fal'sifikatorov istorii lokal'nykh voin," *Voenno-istoricheskii zhurnal*, no. 6 (1980): 62.

164 See chapter 2.

165 Dolgopolov, "Fal'sifikatorov," p. 58.

166 Ibid., p. 58.

167 Maj.-Gen. Ye. Dolgopolov, "On Principle of Equality," *Soviet Military Review*, no. 1 (1984): 49. Though he refrained from any reference to fighting "counter-revolution" and ignored the divisibility of détente argument (despite the fact that he mentioned accusations of violations to détente and did emphasize government invitations), he heartily supported aid to national liberation movements with copious examples from China to El Salvador (pp. 49–50).

168 Kulish, *Voennaia sila*, pp. 99, 102.

169 Ibid., p. 103.

170 Maj.-Gen. A. Skrylnik, "Under Lenin's Banner," *Soviet Military Review*, no. 4 (1984): 5–7.

171 Ibid., pp. 6–7.

172 Ibid., p. 7.

173 Col.-Gen. G. Sredin, "Real Socialism and the Leninist Peace Policy," *Soviet Military Review*, no. 4 (1984): 3–4.

174 Peter Vanneman and W. Martin James, "The Role of Opinion Groups in the Soviet African Policy Process," *Journal of Contemporary African Studies* 2, no. 2 (1983): 225–6.

175 Ibid., p. 226.

176 Ibid., p. 233.

177 A. Grechko, "Rukovodiashchaia rol' KPSS v stroitel'stve armii razvitogo sotsialisticheskogo obshchestva," *Voprosy istorii KPSS*, no. 5 (1974): 24.

178 MccGwire, *Soviet Military Objectives*, Third Draft, Brookings Institution, Washington D.C., February 1985, p. 23; Michael MccGwire and John McDonnell, *Soviet Naval Influence*, Praeger, New York, 1977, p. 34.

179 Admiral S. G. Gorshkov, *Sea Power and the State*, Pergamon, Oxford, 1979, pp. 217–21, 234–53. On Grechko and Gorshkov, see Menon, *Soviet Power*.

180 Marshal Ogarkov, "Voennaia strategiia," *Sovetskaia voennaia entsiklopediia*, vol. 7, Voenizdat, Moscow, 1979, p. 565.
181 *Pravda*, 25 July 1981; 7 November 1981; 20 August 1982.
182 *Tapchi quan doi nhan dan* (Hanoi); cited in Fukuyama, *Civil–Military Relations*, p. 36.
183 *Pravda*, 7 November 1981.
184 See Coit Blacker, in Robert Byrnes, *After Brezhnev*, Indiana University Press, Bloomington, 1983, pp. 159–60, or MccGwire, *Military Objectives*; Nofra Trulock, "Weapons of Mass Destruction in Soviet Military Strategy," unpublished paper, no date.
185 *Pravda*, 31 March 1971 (emphasis mine). In 1966 he had said: "Naturally there can be no peaceful coexistence when it comes to internal processes of the class and national liberation struggle in the capitalist countries or the colonies. The principle of peaceful coexistence is not applicable to the relations between the oppressors and the oppressed, between the colonialists and the victims of colonial oppression."
186 Boris Ponomarev, "Under the Banner of Marxism–Leninism and Proletarian Internationalism," *World Marxist Review* 14, no. 6 (1971): 1.
187 *Pravda*, 4 April 1971.
188 *Pravda*, 28 June 1972.
189 *Pravda*, 4 July 1972.
190 M. Suslov, "Kommunisticheskoe dvizhenie v avangarde bor'by za mir, sotsial'noe i natsional'noe osvobozhdenie," *Kommunist*, no. 11 (1975): 7.
191 A. Gromyko, "Programma mira v deistvii," *Kommunist*, no. 14 (1975): 3–20.
192 *Pravda*, 25 February 1976.
193 *Pravda*, 23 April 1976.
194 *Pravda*, 23 June 1978.
195 Moscow domestic radio, 1 September 1978 (to the opening of the Central Committee's Institute of Social Sciences).
196 *Pravda*, 13 December 1978 (speech to *World Marxist Review* conference in Sofia).
197 TASS, 31 March 1977.
198 *Pravda*, 2 March 1979.
199 *Pravda*, 23 February 1979.
200 TASS, 5 August 1978.
201 B. Ponomarev, "Neodolimost' osvoboditel'nogo dvizheniia," *Kommunist*, no. 1 (1980): 11–27.
202 *Pravda*, 24 February 1981.
203 TASS, 20 September 1982.
204 TASS, 27 October 1982.
205 *Pravda*, 23 November 1982; *Pravda*, 16 June 1983.
206 *Pravda*, 23 November 1982. He appeared to take the line of his earlier speeches, such as the one of April 1982, when he asserted Soviet responsibility for its own defense and that of the socialist states plus solidarity with foreign communists (*Pravda*, 23 April 1982).
207 *Pravda*, 16 June 1983.
208 *Pravda*, 17 June 1983.
209 TASS, 5 October 1983 (Gromyko).
210 *Pravda*, 30 July 1983 (Zimianin); *Izvestiia*, 29 October 1983 (Aliev). Stephen Sestanovich was the first to point out these changes: *Washington Post*, 20 May 1984.
211 TASS, 5 October 1983. Gromyko's earlier pronouncements had generally listed the national liberation movements after the Soviet Union and socialist community among Soviet foreign policy commitments (e.g. A. Gromyko, "Leninskaia vneshniaia politika v sovremennom mire," *Kommunist*, no. 1 (1981): 18; "Leninskaia strategiia mira: edinstvo teorii i praktiki," *Kommunist*, no. 4 (1976): 17).
212 Ivan Kapitonov, "A Working Class Party: The Whole People's Party," *World Marxist Review* 26, no. 7 (1983): 8–9. For earlier comments see Moscow domestic radio, 20 April 1979.
213 *Izvestiia*, 29 October 1983.
214 *Pravda*, 12 March 1985, 26 February 1986.

215 *Political Report of the CPSU Central Committee to the 27th Party Congress*, Novosti, Moscow, 1986, pp. 151–2.
216 *Pravda*, 26 February 1986.
217 Zagladin, commenting on the new program, again quoted Lenin that "socialism influences world development particularly through its economic policy," referring also to the period of "economic difficulties" of the Soviet Union in the mid-1970s, which, he claimed, led to US aggressiveness to exploit Soviet weakness (Prague radio, 7 February 1986).

Conclusions

It is not possible to deduce one consistent Soviet theory of national liberation movements from the foregoing positions on conditions, composition, means, and so forth. Rather, it is possible to discern one relatively consistent theory of an orthodox, or conservative, nature, and several other fragmented theories of a more sophisticated and realistic nature.

The conservative approach viewed the class, not the nation or ethnic group, as the central feature even of a national liberation movement, with socioeconomic factors as the major determinants of the emergence of such a movement rather than more subjective factors or even external factors. With these priorities, the proletariat was seen as the only group capable of genuine understanding of, and even loyalty to, the national cause—which was basically a social cause. Therefore, despite its small size, often artificially bloated by the inclusion of working groups of a non-proletarian nature, the proletariat was considered the most important group within a movement and the group that should dominate. Every other class, or even strata, was by nature bourgeois or petty bourgeois and not to be trusted. While one might enter into alliances with the petty bourgeoisie and the peasants, leadership was to remain in the hands of the urban proletariat. Such an alliance might dictate a mass organizational structure and united front tactics, but the role of a communist party would be central, or else the creation of a vanguard Marxist–Leninist party based on scientific socialism was viewed as a necessity. The ideology of nationalism was totally unacceptable in any of its forms (including religious ideologies or pan-Africanism, etc.), inasmuch as nationalism by definition was a class philosophy serving the bourgeoisie (or the petty bourgeoisie) and producing particularism and exclusiveness, even racism. The only basic conceptual framework acceptable was that of Marxism–Leninism, with aspirations for a society based on scientific socialism which would include, as a primary component, a vanguard Marxist–Leninist party.

Given the conservatives' view of the national liberation struggle as one no less dictated by class (socioeconomic) interests than other social struggles, the national revolution would be no different from past (European) bourgeois revolutions *unless* led by the proletariat—in which case it was to be inspired by the model of the October revolution. In this sense, the conservative view overestimated rather than underestimated the socialist potential of these movements, provided they were guided by a Marxist–Leninist world view, party, and aspirations. This approach thus led to precipitous expectations and demands for Marxist–Leninist scientific socialist features, with the accompanying tendency toward total rejection of the movement in the absence of such features. In either case, as strict Marxist–Leninists (or at least Marxists), the conservatives did not view the national liberation movements as a central element of the world revolutionary movement, adhering to the primacy of the socialist camp and the subordination of the movements. This view itself, however, dictated two attitudes toward the role of the Soviet Union: one that precluded maximum Soviet involvement because of the lack of importance (or truly socialist nature) of the national liberation struggle; and one that envisaged maximum Soviet assistance in the overall interests of world revolution. In the latter, the revolutionary process and ideological struggle were not to be subordinated to or restrained by détente or fear of local wars and their escalation. In keeping with the latter view, armed struggle was deemed legitimate, possibly even necessary, though it was to be combined with political–organizational work conducted in and focused upon the city.

Challenging this orthodox school were a number of theories which tended in another general, more realistic, direction. Without extolling the primacy of nations or ethnic groups and categories in Third World society, these observers acknowledged the nonetheless central role played by these concepts as the subject of national liberation. Thus, national (including spiritual), cultural, and psychological oppression played a dominant role in the awakening of a people and the formation of a movement. If socioeconomic (class) factors played a less dominant role, then, according to most of these analysts, the class character of the movement and even of its leadership was of less significance.

This was an analysis that recognized the barely class-differentiated nature of Third World societies—and with this the virtual absence of a proletariat—and the dominance of the petty bourgeoisie and even national bourgeoisie, particularly in the leadership. Eschewing peasant leadership (despite their great numbers), its advocates appeared to maintain the orthodox priority of the town over the countryside. But within the town the petty bourgeoisie, particularly the intellectuals, and even the national bourgeoisie, were regarded as more positive than negative for the national liberation struggle. The dual nature of all the non-proletarian groups was recognized (i.e., the potential for reactionary as well as progressive tendencies); but, unlike the conservative school, most of these analysts advocated encouragement of the positive elements rather than rejection of the whole. Given this approach, a genuine united front alliance with a mass party was the only acceptable, or practical, organizational option. The absence of a proletariat precluded, therefore, not only proletariat leadership but also an organizational structure patterned on a Marxist–Leninist vanguard party.

The ideologies of the movements received the same realistic appraisal from these theorists. A basic world view devolved from the nation as the central analytic tool was acknowledged and even credited with certain positive features. Moreover, even nationalism, the ideology born of such an approach, was positively appraised, reservations about its value at future stages of development notwithstanding. Indeed, some analysts were even this generous with regard to various offshoots of nationalism such as populism, Fanon-type "social nationalism," religious nationalism, pan-Africanism, and the like. Their negative features were pointed out, particularly their potential for petty bourgeois, anti-proletariat or even racist features, but their expediency was recognized and to some degree even praised.

Searching for a way to accept what they realistically viewed as the major ideological trends of the national liberation movements, these analysts offered a differentiated approach. That is, by defining and refining the concept of nationalism (for example) they could find at least one type that could be regarded positively, thereby preventing rejection of the ideology as a whole. The same technique was applied to the future society aspired to or posited by the basic conceptualization implicit in these ideologies. Arguing that it was unrealistic to apply a strict yardstick of scientific socialism, these theoreticians posited the idea of revolutionary democracy, with varying attributes. And when even this proved disappointing, they spoke of left–wing revolutionary democracy, some even redefining the whole concept of revolutionary democracy in hope of finding some basis for a potential for the eventual emergence of scientific socialism. In this regard they accepted, in theory, the necessity of a vanguard Marxist–Leninist party, but saw this as a long-term requirement, wholly premature at the present stage of development. Basically, these analysts appeared to be arguing that, while ideologically national liberation movements had a potential for scientific socialism, this was not an ideology suitable for the present stage and, therefore, should not be demanded or expected of them. Indeed, a degree of capitalism must be expected to persist, a realistic view neither rejecting them because of this nor trying to impose ideological aspirations inappropriate or unacceptable to them at this stage—for such "voluntarism" simply would not work.

Thus, it was out of a sense of realism, and the belief that these movements, for the sheer numbers they represented if for no other reason, constituted an important part of today's revolutionary struggle, that these analysts explained that they were *not* in fact genuinely Marxist–Leninist or scientific–socialist. Moreover, this high estimation of the importance of the national liberation movements did not lead to advocacy of maximum Soviet assistance, namely, intervention. Indeed, while various types of assistance were supported, most of the realists advocated relatively minimalist-type aid, viewing the Soviets' role as a purely deterrent one vis-à-vis the West or even merely serving as an example, with development of the "Soviet Union first" heralded as the best type of "aid" the Soviets could offer. Even those realists who appeared to advocate somewhat more, such as military assistance, added sufficient caveats as to make this a relatively minimalist position. The reason for this hesitancy would appear to have been possibly their belief that movements had to go their own way, according to their own inner tendencies, but, perhaps more importantly, an interest in the preservation of détente (concern over local wars and escalation). The latter dictated a general opposition to the use of armed struggle, although the occasional realist recognized the tendency of the movements to use these means (just as some conservatives eschewed armed struggle in favor of political–ideological work).

Points on which less controversy appears to have existed were the general undesirability of separatism, the opposition to terrorism, the priority of the town over the countryside, and the acceptance of a mass party form of organization for at least the early stage of a national liberation struggle. There were some nuances even on these issues, but general agreement was more the norm. Agreement or disagreement on any issue does not appear, however, to have been a function of bureaucratic or institutional allegiances among Soviet theoreticians. Certain analysts themselves were consistent in their approach to the various issues and over a period of time, but colleagues in the same organization (party or research institute, possibly the Foreign Ministry) did not necessarily share the same views.

Differing positions within the same institute were of possibly less significance than differences that were apparent within the Central Committee apparat. While the Ideological Department was, as might be expected, consistently associated with the orthodox approach, the International Department spoke with several voices. First deputy chief of the Department, Zagladin, was a major exponent of the orthodox view, in one case choosing as his vehicle a symposium conducted not by his own department but by the apparently more congenial (for his ideas) Ideological Department. Yet the men next in line to him in the International Department, Brutents and (only slightly less) Ul'ianovskii, were major exponents of the realistic tendencies. These more innovative Third World specialists found a common language with the American- ists, at least from the USA–Canada Institute, presumably because of the latter's support for détente, and also with most Africanists. Yet one of the staunchest exponents of the orthodox school was deputy head of the Africa Institute Starushenko, joined often in his views by other analysts from his Institute, even as the directors of this Institute were much closer to the realistic end of the spectrum. Analysts from the military establishment exhibited much the same inconsistency, taking opposing sides on issues such as the risks of local war and the role of the Soviet Union. They were relatively consistent, however, in their defence of the role of the local military in national liberation movements and the importance of conventional over guerrilla or other methods.

This picture of varied views, controversy, and institutional inconsistency strongly suggests an ongoing debate not only sanctioned by the Communist party but actually conducted within as well as outside the party. How much this debate affected or was affected by the Soviet leadership itself remains enigmatic. In at least one case, that of the role to be played by the Soviet Union, the theoreticians, both inside and outside the party apparat, appear to have preceded the leadership, either influencing or at least paving the way for a position taken subsequently by the leadership. It was on this issue, too, that a time factor was apparently operative, a more "Soviet Union first" position gaining strength over time. In this regard it may be that objective circumstances (economic problems, end of détente, failures in the Third World) induced the leadership to accept the more realistic views appearing among the theoreticians. This may also have been the case with regard to the idea of a vanguard Marxist–Leninist party. Reservations among even Central Committee theorists regarding this idea may well have penetrated leadership echelons, eventually precipitating a change in the latter's positions.

Thus, the picture that emerges is by no means entirely the monolithic image of leadership positions merely elaborated upon, explained, justified, and propagated by teams of loyal theorists, each perhaps appealing to his or her own selected audiences. While there were undoubtedly those who did fit that pattern of regime spokesperson, the movement of ideas appears to have been at least in two directions, if not actually from the theorists to the policy-makers. Moreover, the absence of one clear line even among the theorists attests to the fluidity of the whole process.

Nor was there total consistency among the leadership itself, variations among individuals receding as a certain evolution of views and changing objective circumstances emerged. The most striking divergence was that of Andropov, whose declared positions strongly resembled those of the realists. Once Andropov took over the party leadership, his became the dominant view, expressed even by the leadership and continued subsequently by Gorbachev. Brezhnev himself, however, exhibited an increasingly realistic position, foreshadowing the change that was to appear after his death. Similarly, the leadership of the military, perhaps no less involved in the ongoing debate, had exponents of realism, at various times in the form of Ustinov, as well as Ogarkov. Of significance in the military as well as political realm, however, was the fact that a position taken by a leadership figure such as Ustinov, or Suslov (considered the ultimate authority for the International Department as well as the Ideological Department), or Ponomarev, who was directly responsible for the International Department, did not prevent dissent and public discussion among subordinates.

Even without one clear line of an exclusive, fully consistent theory regarding national liberation movements, policy did have to be made. To what degree actual policy decisions were affected by the above debates, ambiguities, and changes may emerge from an investigation of Soviet behavior itself. At the very least, such an investigation will provide indicators as to which position or tendency did receive official legitimation in policy. For each tendency carried with it policy conclusions and options, determining the approach to the objective set of circumstances and the concrete factors at play at any given time.

PART II

Soviet Policy Toward National Liberation Movements

6
Patterns of Soviet Behavior

The preceding discussion of Soviet theoretical positions with regard to national liberation movements revealed a perhaps startling variety of views, even conflicting ones, among those responsible for explaining (and possibly shaping) Soviet policies in this realm. To some extent this diversity reached even into the Soviet leadership, although to just what degree leadership pronouncements reflected rather than generated or dictated the still broader range of views at lower party and at academic levels remains unclear. An examination of actual Soviet behavior may shed some light on the connection between policy and theory; it may well answer the question as to which of the theoretical positions was actually the dominant or "victorious" one. At the very least, it may be said that it was against this backdrop of diversity and debate that Soviet policy toward each movement was determined and pursued.

Soviet Support for the Movements

Actual Soviet behavior with regard to the various national liberation movements has been multi-faceted, in some cases apparently inconsistent, and to some degree selective. Before examining just how and why the Soviets have behaved in a particular way toward a particular movement, a primary distinction must be made between those movements supported and those not supported by Moscow. This distinction alone is more complex than might be presumed, particularly when dealing with a relatively long time-span, but a preliminary categorization may be made excluding the finer points of the nature of such support or the instruments of this support. Table 6.1, then, refers to the basic Soviet position in the post-Khrushchev period. The relative vagueness of these categories ("Virtually never," "At times," "Most of the time") is due, in part, to the fact that the Soviets were late in supporting some movements, for example the PLO or the Tamils, only sporadic in supporting other movements, such as the Eritreans or the Kurds.[1] In fact, in some cases, such as that of the FROLINAT or the Congo NLF, the existence of Soviet support at anytime is not clear.

Leaving aside for the time being the distinctions between rival organizations within one nation or national movement, certain categories

Table 6.1 Degree of Soviet Support

Country	Movement	SOVIET SUPPORT		
		Virtually never	At times	Most of the time
Afghanistan	Baluchi		x	
Angola	MPLA			x
	FNLA	x		
	UNITA	x		
Burma	Deren, Shan,	x		
	Kachin, Kayah, Mon			
Chad	FROLINAT		x	
Ethiopia				
Eritrea	ELF		x	
	EPLF		x	
	ELF–PLF		x	
Tigre	TPLF	x		
Guinea-Bissau/Cape				
Verde	PAIGC			x
India	Sikh	x		
Iran	Kurd		x	
	Baluchi		x	
	Khuzistan-Arabistan	x?		
	Liberation Front			
Iraq	Kurd KDP		x	
Israel				
Palestine	PLO — Fatah			x
	PFLP			
	DFLP			
Mozambique	FRELIMO			x
	COREMO	x		
Morocco			x	
Western Sahara	Polisaro		x	
Namibia	SWAPO			x
	SWANU	x		
Nigeria	Biafra — Ibo	x		
Oman	Dhofar — PFLOAG		x	
Pakistan	Baluchis		x	
	Pathans		x	
	Bengali			x
Philippines	Moro	x	(x)	
Rhodesia/Zimbabwe	ZAPU			x
	ZANU	x		
South Africa	ANC			x
	PAC	x		
Sri Lanka	Tamil		x	
Sudan				
Southern Sudan	Anyanya	x		
	SPLM		x	
Turkey	Kurd – KPP		x	
Vietnam	Vietcong – NLF			x
Zaire	Congo National			
Katanga	Liberation Front		x	

Table 6.2 Degree of Support by Type of Movement

Support (most of the time)	
FRELIMO	
MPLA	
PAIGC	
SWAPO	Anti-colonials
NLF	
ZAPU	
*ANC	Anti-colonial (?)
*PLO	
Bengalis	Separatist
Sporadic support	
Baluchis (Iran)	
Baluchis (Pakistan)	
Dhofaris	
Eritreans	
FROLINAT	Separatists
Katangans (Congo NLF)	
Kurds (Iran, Iraq, Turkey)	
Pathans	
Tamils	
*Polisario	Separatist (?)
Virtually no support	
Anyanya, SPLM	
Burmese minorities	
Baluchis–Afghanistan	
Ibos	
Khuzistanis (ALF)	Separatists
Moros	
Sikhs	
Tigrean	

* "internal" or unclassifiables

are easily discernible even within this broad—and vague—distinction regarding support (see table 6.2). At least one of each of the classical anti-colonial movements (MPLA, PAIGC, FRELIMO, ZAPU, SWAPO, NLF) may be found in the "Most of the time" support category, and these movements constitute two-thirds of this category (six out of nine). Of the remaining three movements in this category, the PLO and ANC are considered anti-colonial even though they might objectively be considered part of a separate grouping of "internal" movements, which, along with the Polisario, defy classification.

Looked at somewhat differently, the striking feature of this table is that, with only one exception, all of the movements *not* supported by the Soviets, or only sporadically supported by them, are separatist

Table 6.3 Nature and Instruments of Soviet Behavior

	Military involvement against	Political opposition	No role	Propaganda support	Political diplomatic support	Humanitarian and financial aid	Indirect arms	Direct arms	Training in bloc or third country	Military advisers on the spot	Proxy military advisers on the spot	Naval activity	Proxy military intervention	Direct military intervention
Anti-colonial														
FRELIMO				x	x	x		x	x					
MPLA				x	x	x		x	x		x		x	
PAIGC				x	x	x		x	x		x	x		
SWAPO				x	x	x		x	x					
NLF				x	x	?	x	?	x					
ZAPU				x	x	x		x	x					
Separatist														
Anyanya	x	x												
Baluchis (Afghn.)	?					?	?	?	?					
Baluchis (Iran)				0	0	0	0		0?					
Baluchis (Pak.)				x	x	0	0		0?					
Bengalis						x?	x?		?					
Burmese minorities		x										x		
Dhofaris				x	x	x	x	?	x		0			
Eritreans	x	x		0		0	0	?	0			x		
FROLINAT		x	0	0	0		0?							
Ibos	x	x												

Table 6.3 Nature and Instruments of Soviet Behavior (cont.)

	Military involvement against	Political opposition	No role	Propaganda support	Political diplomatic support	Humanitarian and financial aid	Indirect arms	Direct arms	Training in bloc or third country	Military advisers on the spot	Proxy military advisers on the spot	Naval activity	Proxy military intervention	Direct military intervention
Separatist (cont.)														
Katangans			0	0	0	0	0?		?					
Kurds (Iran)	x	x		0	0	0	0	?	?					
Kurds (Iraq)				0	0	0	0	0	0					
Kurds (Turkey)				0	0	0	0	?	?					
Khuzistan			x?	0*										
Moros		0	0	0	0	0	0	?	?					
Pathans		x												
Sikhs		x	0	0			0							
SPLM								0?						
Tamils	x?	x	0	0										
Tigreans														
"Internal"														
ANC				x	x	x	x	x	x					
PLO				x	x	x	x	x	x	**	***	x		
Polisario				0	0	?		?	?					

0 = sporadically   x = most of the time   * = very briefly   ** = Soviet team there briefly   *** = Cubans reportedly there at one time.

Table 6.4 Indication of Political Support (prior to statehood)

	May Day slogans																CPSU Congresses			50th anniversary celebrations '72	60th anniversary celebrations '82	Funerals			Diplomatic status for Moscow office
	'70	'71	'72	'73	'74	'75	'76	'77	'78	'79	'80	'81	'82	'83	'84	'85	'71	'76	'81			Brezhnev '82	Andropov '84	Chernenko '85	
Anti-colonial																									
FRELIMO		nr	nr	nr	nr	nr	nr	nr	nr	nr	nr	nr	nr	nr	nr	nr	a★	nr	nr	a	nr	nr	nr	nr	
MPLA		nr	nr	nr	nr	nr	nr	nr	nr	nr	nr	nr	nr	nr	nr	nr	a★	nr	nr	a	nr	nr	nr	nr	
PAIGC	nr	nr	nr	nr	nr	nr	nr	nr	nr	nr	nr	nr					sp	sp	nr	sp	nr	nr	nr	nr	
SWAPO							x	x	x						x	x	a★	a★		a	sp	a	a	a	
NLF	x	x	x	(x)	(x)	nr	nr	nr	nr	nr	nr	nr	nr	nr	nr	nr	sp	nr	nr	a	nr	nr	nr	nr	
ZAPU							x	x	x	nr	nr	nr	nr	nr	nr	nr	a★	nr		a	nr	nr	nr	nr	x
Separatist																									
Anyanya/SPLM																									
Baluchis (Afgh.)																									
Baluchis (Iran)																									
Baluchis (Pak.)																									
Bengalis																									
Burmese minorities																									
Dhofaris																									
Eritreans																									
FROLINAT																									
Ibos																									
Katangans																									

Table 6.4 Indication of Political Support (prior to statehood) (cont.)

	May Day Slogans																CPSU Congresses			50th anniversary celebrations '72	60th anniversary celebrations '82	Funerals			Diplomatic status for Moscow office
	'70	'71	'72	'73	'74	'75	'76	'77	'78	'79	'80	'81	'82	'83	'84	'85	'71	'76	'81			Brezhnev '82	Andropov '84	Chernenko '85	
Separatists (cont.)																									
Kurds (Iran)																									
Kurds (Iraq)																	a★			a					
Kurds (Turkey)																									
Khuzistan																									
Moros																									
Pathans																									
Sikhs																									
Tamils																									
Tigreans																									
"Internal"																									
ANC														x	x	x		a★	a★	a		a	a	a	?
PLO														x	x	x		a★	a	sp	sp	a	a	a	x
Polisaro																									

x = mentioned   a = attended   a★ = spoke to party organization   sp = spoke   (x) = changed from "People fighting" to people who achieved victory   nr = not relevant (after independence) movements; there are no anti-colonial movements in these categories, and there is only one separatist movement (possibly two with the Dhofar case) in the "Most of the time" support category. At first glance, then, the Soviet claim to support anti-colonialism as part of its revolutionary mission to overthrow capitalism in its imperialist stage would appear to be confirmed in practice, while its theoretical opposition to separatism would appear to be confirmed by the more reserved, that is, sporadic, support or downright negative behavior toward secessionist movements. A look at the nature and instruments of Soviet support or lack of support provides greater detail and gradations regarding Soviet behavior but does not significantly change this picture (see tables 6.3 and 6.4).

Means and Types of Soviet Support: The Anti-colonials

On the whole, Soviet treatment of anti-colonial movements *prior to independence* has been relatively uniform. It has been composed of propaganda and political–diplomatic, humanitarian, and financial support, coupled with direct arms supplies and training (in the Soviet bloc or a third country). These have generally been overtly and directly accorded, although some aid has gone through the OAU–Liberation Committee, and in the case of Vietnam almost all went through North Vietnam. Soviet support has not included advisers on the spot or military intervention, only rarely the use of proxies, and on only one occasion naval activity. This last was in fact an unusual occurrence, probably the result of Soviet naval assistance to a neighboring state (Guinea) which hosted the national liberation movement (PAIGC). In this instance, Soviet naval units patrolling the coast of Guinea in 1973 (because of past Portuguese attacks on Guinea) intervened on behalf of PAIGC when they intercepted the fleeing assassins of PAIGC leader Amilcar Cabral.[2] This was, however, the only, and a totally isolated, case of known Soviet naval involvement on behalf of an anti-colonial liberation movement. PAIGC was relatively unusual also in that it had what might be called proxy military advisers on the spot, namely Cubans.

While the Cubans are stated here as proxies or surrogates for the Soviet Union, such a characterization is far from certain.[3] The Cubans, from the early 1960s, had their own revolutionary ambitions for the Third World, which, from the mid-1960s, extended well beyond Latin America (and by the 1970s replaced Latin America) as a target area. Moreover, in the 1960s, though not the 1970s, such revolutionary ambitions were not always condoned (and were sometimes opposed) by the Soviet Union. Thus, when the Cubans first made contact with PAIGC, during a 1964–65 trip to Africa by Che Guevara, it was probably a totally independent act.[4] The Soviets, who had some contact in the early 1960s, followed these Cuban contacts with arms and training in the Soviet Union and Czechoslovakia (in addition to training provided in Algeria, Cuba, North Vietnam, and China) in the 1960s, as well as propaganda and political–diplomatic support by the end of the 1960s.[5] In 1970 this aid was expanded significantly (after the Portuguese raids on Conakry which included attacks on PAIGC facilities[6]), but the Soviets reportedly refused to have its advisers on the spot.[7] Cubans, however, are said to have fought on the spot with PAIGC as early as the late 1960s, though they may have simply entered in with PAIGC units from Guinea rather than being stationed inside Guinea-Bissau.[8] The Soviets did send medical teams to work with PAIGC in the areas held by the movement as well as Soviet journalists and delegations, all apparently beginning in 1970.[9] Visits to Moscow by PAIGC officials, including Amilcar Cabral, were a fairly regular occurrence. In October 1973, the Soviets recognized the independent state declared by PAIGC in the liberated areas and sent an ambassador the following spring.[10] This move was accompanied by the dispatch of more sophisticated weapons including SA-7s,[11] but Moscow did not alter its refusal to have Soviet military advisers on the spot—even in liberated "independent" areas of Guinea–Bissau.

Soviet support of some type for the MPLA apparently started with the beginning of the armed struggle in the early 1960s but was relatively limited and sporadic.[12] While this included propaganda and possibly some arms and/or financing, significant aid apparently resulted primarily from the Neto visit to Moscow in 1964 (a trip reportedly arranged by the Portuguese Communist party).[13] This aid included arms and training in the Soviet Union as of 1965, in time in Czechoslovakia, Bulgaria and East Germany.[14] Soviet advisers may have been involved in MPLA training in Algeria, Congo-Brazzaville and Egypt; North Koreans were also involved in training MPLA.[15] Political ties developed rapidly after 1964, if not earlier, and Neto visits to the Soviet Union, including participation in Soviet events (party congresses, etc.), became a standard (usually yearly) affair.[16] The Cubans, too, trained the MPLA in Congo-Brazzaville following Neto's meeting with Che Guevara there in 1965.[17] This visit also resulted in the training of MPLA people in Cuba as of 1966.[18] According to some Western sources, the MPLA, like PAIGC, actually had Cuban advisers on the spot in the late 1960s.[19] While there may have been very small numbers of Cuban advisers actually in Angola, they reportedly entered only sporadically with MPLA forces from the Congo. Actual stationing of Cuban advisers inside Angola reportedly occurred only in the late spring of 1975, during the civil war, when 230 Cubans arrived.[20] The Cuban presence became an actual interventionary combat force in late October and early November 1975.[21]

The Soviets, however, apparently had a very much less satisfactory relationship with Neto than did the Cubans. In 1972–73 Moscow reduced (possibly even halted) its material support, and again, just one month before the Portuguese coup in April 1974, it suspended arms deliveries, resuming them only six months after the coup, in the Fall of 1974.[22] Total Soviet military aid from the 1960s up to March 1975 was said to have been $54 million, a figure much smaller than aid given by non-Soviet bloc sources to other movements in Angola. In the spring of 1975 Soviet military aid was significantly increased, reaching $30 million between March and July 1975 alone and $80 million in August–November 1975.[23] Soviet equipment was airlifted in for the intervening Cubans in October 1975, just prior to Angolan independence (and after the South African and Zaire interventions).[24] The Soviets did not, however, send advisers prior to independence, reportedly refusing an MPLA request in August 1975.[25] Cuban involvement with the MPLA was quantitatively and qualitatively quite different from that with PAIGC, small numbers of advisers in combat being different from a several–thousand-strong expeditionary force. Moreover, Soviet logistic assistance indicated Soviet–Cuban cooperation bordering on a proxy relationship insofar as Moscow actively supported Cuban actions perceived as serving Soviet interests. However, Soviet transportation of Cuban troops, Soviet naval activity, and the dispatch of Soviet personnel all occurred only after Angolan independence on 11 November 1975.[26]

As in the cases of PAIGC and the MPLA, FRELIMO, the liberation movement of the third Portuguese colony, Mozambique, also received Soviet propaganda support and some arms from its creation in 1962, and possibly training for personnel sent to Algeria and Egypt later in the 1960s.[27] In the 1970s the Soviets reportedly gave FRELIMO sophisticated weapons such as rocket launchers and SA-7 missiles;[28] the East Germans and Czechs reportedly provided arms and equipment, the Bulgarians, medical assistance.[29] Che Guevara's 1964–65 trip also resulted in Cuban training for FRELIMO, in Cuba and, according to some sources, in Mozambique itself, although there are no reports of a combat role as in Guinea–Bissau or Angola.[30] FRELIMO had more aid and direct support from the Chinese (as we shall see below), but the Soviets consistently provided aid, arms, and training as well as propaganda and political support, particularly after 1970. The last was expressed equally among FRELIMO, PAIGC, and MPLA at the Soviet-sponsored (World Peace Council) conference in Rome in 1970 for solidarity with the struggle in the Portuguese colonies. Following this conference, a FRELIMO delegation traveled to Moscow, and aid was apparently stepped up.[31] Such trips became fairly regular, with Mozambique leader Samora Machel leading a delegation (received by Ponomarev) in June 1973.[32]

Unlike the cases of Guinea-Bissau and Angola, the Soviets do not appear to have sent medical teams or delegations (with the exception of journalists) to liberated areas of Mozambique until after the 1974 coup in Portugal.[33] In all three cases, the Soviets were quite open, even boastful, about their aid to the anti-Portuguese liberation struggle. They publicized—at the time—their own and the movements' acknowledgments even of Soviet training and arms supplies.[34] The only case of defensiveness about such aid could be discerned during the Angolan civil war of 1974–75. Soviet aid to the MPLA at this time was equally open, but was explained or justified as being in response to "the request not only of the movements themselves but of the OAU, which is not in a position to offer them extensive help and has, both in its documents and through special missions, repeatedly addressed such a request to all countries of the world."[35] On the whole, the Soviets did not in fact send much of their aid to the Portuguese movements through the OAU–Liberation Committee, preferring to maintain direct contact.[36]

Aside from the presence of Cuban advisers (and the one exceptional incident of Soviet naval activity), the pattern set with regard to the anti-Portuguese movements was the same regarding the other anti-colonial movements. Quantitatively, however, the anti-Portuguese movements received less than the later aid to the other African anti-colonials (ZAPU and SWAPO).[37]

The Zimbabwean movement, ZAPU, founded in 1961, reportedly made its first contacts with the Soviet Union and Eastern Europe in the early 1960s through the South African ANC.[38] Indeed, it was with the ANC that ZAPU carried out its first major guerrilla operation in 1967, but that cooperation was not repeated in future actions.[39] The Soviets have dated their support to ZAPU (and the Zimbabwean cause) to 1965, at which time Moscow reportedly provided ZAPU financing, political and propaganda support, arms and training in the Soviet Union.[40] ZAPU also trained in North Korea and, in time, in Algeria and Egypt, possibly with Soviet instructors at least in the last two.[41] Later still (in the mid-1970s), Bulgaria also hosted trainees,[42] and the Soviets along with Cubans may have trained ZAPU people in Zambia; after Angolan independence, Soviet and Cuban instructors trained ZAPU people there.[43] Still later, at the end of the 1970s, East Germans were also helping ZAPU, apparently in Angola.[44]

Despite many rumors to the contrary, born of the Angolan experience, no Soviet or Cuban advisers were ever reported inside Zimbabwe. The Cubans did however train ZAPU's rival, ZANU, in Mozambique (and Ethiopia) in the late 1970s, as well as in Cuba from the mid-1960s.[45] The Soviets also provided ZAPU rocket launchers including SA-7s in the second half of the 1970s.[46] Unlike the anti-Portuguese cases, however, Soviet publicity for its material aid to ZAPU only very rarely specified military aid of any kind until after Zimbabwean independence.[47] Training of ZAPU people in the Soviet Union was acknowledged, but no mention was made of such training overseas.[48] Political support, however, was open and active. ZAPU leader Nkomo and lesser delegations visited the Soviet Union (and Eastern Europe) regularly and participated in the various Soviet party congresses, holidays, and international events.[49] A publicized meeting between Nkomo and Podgornyi also occurred during the latter's 1977 African trip while ongoing contacts were apparently supervised by Soviet Africanist, ambassador to Zambia, Solodovnikov.[50] Moreover, the Soviets championed the Zimbabwean cause in their own international pronouncements, particularly in the second half of the 1970s. Nonetheless, the Zimbabwean cause, like that of the other southern African movements, did not always appear in central Soviet foreign policy pronouncements, even in this period; for example, various regions and causes were mentioned in Brezhnev's important Tula speech of January 1977, but Africa was excluded altogether.[51]

Some support for SWAPO was rendered in the early 1960s along with Soviet contacts with the other African anti-colonial movements. This support, including some arms and money, began apparently in 1962, four years after the founding of SWAPO in 1958.[52] Propaganda and political support differed little from the other anti-colonial movements. SWAPO participated with all the others in the various meetings organized by the Soviets, and SWAPO leaders regularly visited the Soviet Union. Military assistance, however, in the form of arms and equipment would appear to have been smaller than that accorded the other movements, prior to the Angolan war.[53] Reports of increases after this time, coupled with estimates that Soviet aid had not previously been great, indicate a somewhat more restrained relationship until the second half of the 1970s.[54] After 1975, however, the Soviets not only greatly increased (qualitatively as well as quantitatively) their military aid to SWAPO, but they also began training SWAPO people in Angola.[55] A 1976 turn to Cuba, with a meeting with Castro in Africa in 1977, followed by two trips to Cuba that year by SWAPO leader Sam Nujoma, led to the opening of a SWAPO office in Havanna and training by Cubans in Angola as well as in Cuba.[56] A 1979 African trip by East German Defense Minister Hoffman occasioned effusive promises of military aid, although GDR aid had been reported in 1977 and in 1978, SWAPO opened an office in East Berlin. East Germans at some time began training SWAPO in Angola.[57]

As in the case of ZAPU, this assistance has almost never been acknowledged beyond general statements of, at most, "all-round" or material support.[58] Only in an article by Nujoma in *World Marxist Review* did the Soviets indirectly permit a more explicit reference to the military nature of their assistance (the same time as a similar reference to

ZAPU).[59] Soviet sources have acknowledged the presence in the Soviet Union of SWAPO "activist" students and the granting of medical aid, equipment, and vehicles as well as financial assistance, though nothing has been admitted about training SWAPO in Africa.[60] Indeed, when two Soviet advisers were killed, with SWAPO fighters in Angola, by South African troops, the Soviets claimed they had been serving with the Angolan army (and that their wives were killed along with them).[61] Open political support became increasingly vociferous in the late 1970s and early 1980s; Nujoma made as many as three trips to Moscow in 1976 and, like Nkomo, met with Podgornyi during the latter's 1977 African trip. He made only two trips from 1978 to 1981, including attendance at the 1981 CPSU Congress.[62] In 1987 SWAPO (followed shortly but the ANC) became the first African movement to open a permanent office in Moscow, "accredited," according to the Soviets, to the Soviet Afro-Asian Peoples Solidarity Committee.

All of the African anti-colonial movements maintained regular exchanges with the Soviets, their leaders or high-level officials visiting the Soviet Union once, often twice, a year, although with the exception of the new SWAPO office, none apparently has had an office in Moscow. The visiting delegations were usually the guests of the Afro-Asian Peoples Solidarity Committee, meeting with Central Committee International Department chief Boris Ponomarev and, usually, his deputy Ul'ianovskii. The only exception to this was a PAIGC meeting with President Podgornyi, but this occurred in November 1973, after Soviet recognition of the Guinea-Bissau republic declared a month earlier.[63] All, except SWAPO and ZAPU, attended the CPSU congresses in 1971, 1976, and 1981; SWAPO and ZAPU after 1971. Only PAIGC addressed a Congress, in 1971. The others addressed party organizations. All attended the decennial celebrations of 1972 and 1982, PAIGC again speaking at the first, SWAPO at the second. No African liberation struggle was specified in the May Day slogans until 1977, when Zimbabwe and Namibia were singled out (along with South Africa). This occurred from 1977 to 1979, disappeared from 1980 to 1982 and returned, with specific mention of Namibia (and South Africa and the Palestinians) from 1983 to 1985.

Military relations were similar, even to the types of weapons supplied (T-34 and T-54 tanks, 122 millimetre rocket launchers, light arms, armoured personnel carriers, and in most cases SA-7 rockets). The only exception in the military area was the Cuban involvement with PAIGC and MPLA on the spot, particularly the combat role in Angola, and the one incident of Soviet naval activity which occurred with PAIGC. Naval activity of any type was notably absent from all but this one case, including Angola (until after independence). As noted, Soviet military aid was apparently more extensive in the last half of the 1970s, that is, after the anti-Portuguese movements had achieved independence, but acknowledgment of this aid was much less direct or open than in the earlier (anti-Portuguese) cases. Indeed, not only was the cautiousness about committing Soviet personnel on the spot or direct Soviet intervention maintained in the latter period, but the use of proxies for such activity was totally absent in the non-anti-Portuguese movements, at all times.

The one anti-colonial movement that does not fit into these general patterns of Soviet behavior is the South Vietnamese NLF (Vietcong). Propaganda and political support were accorded throughout the movement's existence. Inasmuch as the Vietcong was a movement created, staffed, and apparently run by North Vietnam, a direct Soviet relationship is difficult to trace. With the exception of medical supplies, Soviet aid, including arms, would appear to have been channeled exclusively through North Vietnam. For example, in 1972 the NLF received Sagger anti-tank weapons and SA-7s, but these appeared at the same time in the North and may have been distributed to the Vietcong from there.[64] Soviet naval activity in the South was altogether limited, and on the one occasion when it did occur it had nothing to do with the Vietcong. (In the Spring of 1972, Soviet ships appeared for a few days in the South China Sea some 500 nautical miles from the US Fleet in the Gulf of Tonkin, following a US hit on a Soviet merchant ship in Haiphong.[65]) There were no Soviet advisers in the South (indeed, there were no Soviet advisers outside of Hanoi for the most part), and it is not even clear if Vietcong trained in the Soviet Union except as participants in groups sent by North Vietnam.[66]

On the other hand, political contacts were quite open and fulsome. The NLF had offices in the Soviet Union, Cuba, and some East European countries.[67] In Moscow this office was accorded diplomatic status, with an NLF "ambassador" presenting his credentials to the Afro-Asian Peoples Solidarity Committee or, by 1973, to the Supreme Soviet.[68] From the creation of the Provisional Revolutionary Government of South Vietnam in 1969, the NLF representation was said to be ambassador of this entity, but NLF delegations were often still invited only by the Afro-Asian Peoples Solidarity Committee (AAPSCO). They were occasionally received, however, not only by Ponomarev but also by other CPSU secretaries and/or Politburo members such as Shelepin, Grishin, Demichev, and Solomenstev.[69] From its creation in 1960, the NLF sent regular delegations to Moscow; however, Soviet delegations (youth, etc.) visited southern liberated areas only after 1974. Included in the former were NLF delegations to the CPSU Congress of 1971—with a talk by the NLF—and fiftieth anniversary celebrations. Similarly, the Soviet May Day slogans consistently specified the cause of the

Vietnamese people, even when no other national liberation struggle was so mentioned.

The Secessionists

While there is not exactly an abundance of information on Soviet relations even with the anti-colonial national liberation movements, there is extraordinarily little with regard to the secessionist movements. Moreover, Soviet behavior with these movements has been much more varied, inconsistent, and contradictory.

The most striking feature of Soviet behavior in this category is direct Soviet military involvement, albeit on a limited scale, against four, possibly five, movements: the Anyanya (South Sudan), the Eritreans (Ethiopia), the Ibos (Biafra), the Kurds (Iraq), and, the Tigreans (Ethiopia) possibly. In all of these cases, the Soviets provided arms to the central governments seeking to put down the rebellion and provided advisers, in some cases in combat positions. For example, Soviet pilots reportedly flew combat missions against the Anyanya and Iraqi Kurds in 1969–71 and 1974–75, respectively;[70] after 1977 Soviet advisers reportedly served in command positions against the Eritreans, and the Soviet navy shelled Eritrean positions from offshore.[71] In the 1967–70 Nigerian war the Soviet navy made two visits to Nigerian ports, probably more as a show of political rather than military support, but Moscow also provided the central government with significant weapons in both type and quantity.[72] Czechoslovakia, Algeria, and possibly Poland also supplied arms.[73]

Proxies may have been employed against Biafra, inasmuch as Egyptian and, reportedly, East German pilots flew combat missions.[74] In Eritrea, however, the Cubans apparently refused to play any military role, at least not directly. South Yemen also, reportedly, refused to join the Soviets against Eritrea, pulling out the 1,000 troops they had had fighting in the Ogaden.[75] East Germans were reported fighting in Eritrea, however, in 1979.[76] In the cases of the Ibos and Anyanya, Soviet military involvement (against the movement) was consistent; in the Eritrean and Kurdish cases, it was sporadic; that is; it followed a period of support for the movement. The same distinction applied to public acknowledgement of the Soviet role: in the two cases in which the negative Soviet role was consistent, the Soviets have been willing to acknowledge a role, although such acknowledgment came after the rebellions were defeated, and even then without specifics as to just how much and in what way they had been involved militarily.[77] In the two cases in which the involvement alternated with periods of support, the negative Soviet role has not been publicized.[78]

Political (including propaganda) opposition accompanied the above cases of military opposition, with the Kurds and Eritreans portrayed as right-wing nationalists and separatists, supported by outside reactionaries or imperialists. In the case of Eritrea, these were said to be "certain Arab states" seeking to create an "Arab lake" of the Red Sea, just as the West was accused of stirring up the Ibos for the mineral wealth of Biafra.[79] Nonetheless, the Ibos, Eritreans, and particularly the Kurds were presented with some sympathy as peoples with almost legitimate claims merely dominated by reactionary–extremists or manipulated by outside forces, or both.

In a later period, the early 1980s, the south Sudanese were also acknowledged (in at least two brief references) as having legitimate claims which were being violated. By this time, however, it was no longer the Anyanya but the Sudanese Peoples Liberation Movement that was said to be seeking more than local demands. Nonetheless, there have been no other signs of a change to actual support for them prior to the overthrow of Numeri in 1985.[80] The movement itself said in late 1985 that it had no contact with the Soviet Union.[81]

In three other cases—the Sikhs, the Moros, and the Burmese minorities—Soviet opposition has been limited to the political/propaganda sphere, with no military involvement, direct or by proxy. Little has been said by the Soviets of the Burmese minorities, but they are occasionally referred to, negatively, as separatists, incited by imperialist forces from outside.[82] The Sikhs too are condemned in this way, said specifically to be incited by Pakistan and the United States so as to dismember India.[83]

The Moros, mentioned only slightly more frequently than the Burmese minorities, have generally been condemned as separatists with occasional reference to Chinese influences.[84] However, an interesting lapse in this occurred at one point. One day before the agreement was reached between the Moros and Manila via the Islamic Conference (and especially Libya) on 24 December 1976, *Pravda* was referring derogatorily to the "so-called Moro National Liberation Front," a line consistent with previous pronouncements; a few days after the accord, *Pravda* justified the Moros' cause, explicitly, as socioeconomic–political rather than ethnic or religious.[85] A second positive account appeared in early 1977, calling on the government to meet Moro demands. By the Fall, however, as the cease-fire completely disintegrated, reporting became noncommittal, reverting, in October, to the former epitaph of "secessionist," with the explanation that "facts" had recently come to light demonstrating Chinese influence with the Moslems' People's Liberation Army.[86] Subsequently, the Moros were once again referred to only as Moslem separatists, if at all, and the Soviets denied any connection with them.[87] The brief reversal in reporting was most likely connected with Libya's involvement with the Moros, although Libyan (and PLO) support, arms supplies, and apparently training preceded and succeeded the short-lived Soviet political/propaganda support.[88] There is no evidence that Libya and the PLO acted in any way as proxies of Moscow with regard to the Moros, although the arms provided were probably of Soviet manufacture. A second reversal in the Soviet position including possibly even arms supplies from Eastern Europe has been rumored in 1987. This would coincide with a deterioration in Soviet relations with the Aquino government in Manila.

There are four movements with which the Soviets would appear to have had no direct contact or played any (at least overt) role, positively or negatively. The sparsity of comment on them (in one case none at all) may not mean total Soviet indifference, however. In three of the four cases, Soviet comments have even been positive, though actual involvement remains unknown, even doubtful. Thus, the Arabistan Liberation Movement (ALF) of Khuzistan in Iran has virtually never been mentioned by the Soviet Union, despite the fact that Iraq (at least in the 1960s and 1970s) and Libya are said to support it.[89] There is no reason to assume that their support bears anything of a surrogate character, although Soviet arms may have found their way to the ALF through these channels. At least, the Khomeni regime has accused the Soviets of inciting the Arab separatists, but it is not clear that there was in fact any significant connection between the ALF and the communists active in that part of Iran in 1979.[90]

The case of the Tamils, at first similar to those of the Sikhs or the Moros insofar as the Soviets took a negative position, has undergone some evolution. As in the case of the Sikhs, the Tamils were originally condemned as "chauvinists," provoked by outside elements seeking to harm India.[91] Yet this position was gradually modified to one acknowledging Tamil interests, and then to one championing their "just grievances" and "national rights."[92] Moreover, although Western elements were still charged with provoking trouble, the Sri Lankan government was also held accountable.[93] Whether this gradual, and limited, shift to public support has been accompanied by assistance of any kind is difficult to determine. None has been rumored, despite India's and the PLO's involvement with the movement.[94] A reversal occurred in 1987, however, when the Soviets resumed criticism of the Tamils condemning some elements as extremists. This reversal coincided with the dispatch of the Indian peace-keeping force to Sri Lanka and its clashes with the Tamils, in other words, a change in the position of Moscow's ally, India.

There is even more ambiguity over the Soviet role with regard to the FROLINAT in Chad and the Katangans inside and outside the Shaba area in Zaire. Direct Soviet references to each conflict portray them not as nationalist conflicts but rather as socioeconomic–political struggles of a revolutionary nature against a reactionary government and imperialist intervention. In this context, the Soviets have occasionally supported FROLINAT's political claims to power.[95] It is possible, though disputed, that Soviet aid, at least in the form of arms, may be going to FROLINAT through Libya, whose intervention in Chad also received Soviet political support.[96] Libya's involvement with FROLINAT (as well as with the Moros and Khuzistan) is most likely totally independent of the Soviet Union, given the nature of the Soviet–Libyan relationship.[97] In the Katangan–Shaba case, however, the Cubans have apparently been involved, at any rate in training (in Angola) and equipping the Congolese National Liberation Front (with Soviet arms), suggesting at least Soviet approval.[98] Indeed, one report claimed that East Germans were training this movement, and United States intelligence sources reported "direct Soviet involvement" in Cuban training and arming of the Katangans.[99] Yet no evidence has been found to corroborate either a Soviet or an East German role.[100] And the Cubans claim to have disarmed the Katangans after Shaba II (1978).[101] Moscow did give political support to the upheavals in Shaba, describing them as popular "anti-government" uprisings because of economic and political discontent, rather than as ethnic or national claims.[102] Denying any involvement of the Soviet Union or Cuba, Soviet reporting sought to disassociate itself by citing "foreign press reports" of the role of the Congolese National Liberation Front, although it did admit the participation of Katangan exiles in the uprising.[103]

The FROLINAT and Katangans are perhaps borderline cases, which bring us to the much larger category of secessionist movements sporadically supported by the Soviets. Here the most striking examples are two movements that the Soviets supported and then actively participated in suppressing: the Kurds (of Iraq) and the Eritreans.

Soviet support for the Eritreans was covert, and genuine evidence of it is extremely difficult to uncover. There were reports as early as 1965 of Soviet arms shipments to the Eritreans, and in 1967 the Bulgarians were said to be sending arms as well.[104] There were subsequent reports of Czechoslovak and Hungarian arms supplies.[105] One of these reports claimed that the Soviets (and Chinese) had agreed to train the Eritreans as well.[106] Just where the Soviets trained them is not clear (possibly in Algeria or other Arab countries), for there were no Soviet advisers in Eritrea and reportedly no Eritreans were sent to the Soviet Union.[107] They were, however, sent to Cuba as of the late 1960s (as well as China), and some Cuban advisers apparently served with the Eritreans in the late 1960s.[108] In addition, the main source of Eritrean support came from the Arabs, including Egypt, Iraq, Syria, the PDRY, Libya, and Fatah.[109] Thus Soviet weapons undoubtedly reached the Eritreans through these channels; indeed, some sources, including an Eritrean leader, claim that all Soviet arms were supplied indirectly, through the Syrians.[110] Some of this may have been with Soviet cooperation, but the Arabs' (possibly even the Cubans') contacts with the Eritreans were most likely independent rather than proxy actions (as evidenced by later friction when the Soviets abandoned their support for the Eritreans).[111]

In the early 1970s, however, what little direct Soviet assistance existed reportedly declined significantly, drawing to a total halt after the 1974 Ethiopian revolution.[112] Political support was equally covert, despite the original pro-Eritrean position of the Soviet Union in the 1949–50 UN discussions of the issue. The number of times Soviet publications even mentioned Eritrea up to 1974 can perhaps be counted on no more than one hand.[113] Even these very rare references were generally neutral or only mildly supportive of the Eritrean cause, usually (but not always) implying that the problem had been solved by the federal arrangement worked out with the Ethiopian government.[114] A striking exception to this was an isolated Radio Moscow broadcast in 1971, which referred to the "ultra-nationalist liberation front operating for several years in the Eritrean Province."[115] The more typical Soviet silence on the issue was broken only at the end of 1974. Two months after the Ethiopian revolution, a background article guardedly sympathetic to the Eritreans appeared in *New Times*. Allowing, virtually for the first time, that such an Eritrean problem existed, this article claimed that it would now be justly solved by the new government.[116] After that, Soviet opposition gradually became apparent, as we have seen.[117]

Despite the actual Soviet assistance to the suppression of the Eritrean rebellion after 1977, there were reports of continued Soviet contacts (reportedly through the Italian Communist party and the Cubans) with the Eritrean groups (both the ELF and EPLF at various times), including trips to Moscow by ELF leader Ahmad Nasir in 1978 and 1980.[118] These were apparently efforts to mediate a solution, but they suggested that once again Moscow was willing to maintain a covert relationship with the Eritreans. Indeed, according to one report, the Soviets refused an Ethiopian request for further aid in putting down the rebellion. In his 1980 speech honoring Mengistu, Brezhnev made a pointed reference to the Soviet's own needs; and a comment on Moscow Radio by the influential Aleksandr Bovin in 1984 spoke of Ethiopia's need to solve its own problems.[119] If any Soviet relationship has been maintained with the Eritreans, there is no indication that it is characterized in any way by actual support. Indeed, public Soviet references in the late 1970s and early 1980s (including Bovin's above comments) have remained consistently negative toward the Eritrean movements.[120] Moscow has condemned them as separatists, isolated from their own people and manipulated by outside forces; some accounts even deny the Eritreans' existence as a nation.[121]

The Kurdish case has been different in that Soviet support for the Iraqi Kurds, when it occurred, was much more open and extensive. From 1946 until 1958, exiled Kurdish leaders found refuge in the Soviet Union, and Kurdish fighters trained in the Soviet Union as well as in Eastern Europe.[122] Though not publicized, arms supplies were apparently directly allocated to the Kurds. And political support was open, active and accompanied by propaganda.[123] Following the return of the Kurdish leaders to Iraq in 1958, the Soviet–Kurdish relationship underwent many vacillations, depending upon the Soviet–Iraqi relationship at any given time. It is not at all clear just when the Soviets suspended arms supplies and training: political propaganda vacillated between full support for the Kurdish cause to accusations that outside provocateurs and "extremist elements" on both sides were stirring up strife between the Kurds and the Iraqi government.[124] Actual, if not propaganda, support would appear to have tapered off in the late 1960s, probably coming to a halt after the Kurd–Iraqi government agreement of 1970. The United States (together with Iran and later Israel) took up the Iraqi Kurds in the summer of 1972, according to one report planting Soviet weapons with the rebels so as to implicate Moscow and sour Iraqi–Soviet relations.[125] Yet a Kurdish delegation participated in the December 1972 fiftieth anniversary celebrations of the Soviet Union in Moscow, and as late as 1973 the Soviets were still openly meeting with Kurdish leaders (Suslov received a delegation in August 1972 in Moscow, Ponomarev met with a delegation in Baghdad in November 1973) as efforts to inlcude the Kurds in the new Iraqi National Front were still underway in Baghdad.[126] Only in the beginning of 1974 did the Soviet press speak of communist–Kurdish clashes, and then begin condemnation of right-wing Kurdish elements for continuing the struggle.[127]

One similarity to the Eritrean case was that, even as the Soviets were assisting militarily in the Kurds' suppression, they were indirectly justifying this by claiming that the central government was willing to accord the minority its rights.[128] The end of the rebellion in 1975 saw no significant change or shift back to overt Soviet support for the Kurds, either in propaganda or in political statements. References to the Kurds, although positive about their rights, remained relatively rare.[129] This was the case to some degree even after the 1978 deterioration in Soviet–Iraqi relations, but there have been some reports of Soviet contacts with Kurds in 1979–80 and of Iraqi Communist party cooperation with them since 1980.[130] There is no evidence, however, of Soviet arming and/or training.

Soviet relations with the Kurds of Iran and of Turkey, like those with the Baluchis and Pathans, rarely, if ever, achieved the public expression—and never the military involvement (against)—characteristic of the relationship with the Iraqi Kurds. In all four of these cases, Soviet assistance has been covert and, therefore, very difficult to determine, with only rare if any propaganda–political support. In the pre-Khomeni period, the Soviets were more involved with the Kurds of Iraq than with those of Iran or Turkey. While the Soviets were actively engaged against the Iraqi Kurds in the early and mid-1970s, they could hardly be expected to encourage the Kurds just across the borders. There have been reports over the years of Soviet and/or local communist contacts with the Kurds in both Iran and Turkey, but one can only assume that there was also Soviet training and arms supplies of some kind, probably indirect.[131] According to one report, the Turkish Kurds may have received some Soviet support through the Palestinians, though the same report notes Soviet and Turkish communist reticence regarding the generally radical Kurdish organizations, at least in the 1970s.[132] This was said to have changed once these groups, particularly the Kurdish Workers Party (KPP), were mainly in exile.[133] Indeed, there were Turkish Communist party declarations of support for the Kurdish issue in the early 1980s (as there had been in the early 1970s),[134] and there was a 1983 *Pravda* comment condemning the trial of members of the KPP in Turkey.[135] Other comments critical of Turkish treatment of the Kurds could be found in Soviet journals in the early 1980s and in the *World Marxist Review* in 1985.[136] On the whole, Soviet propaganda support has been limited to either indirect reporting or publications not intended for foreign consumption.[137]

After the Iranian revolution, there were rumors, as well as Iranian accusations, of Soviet aid (including arms) to the Kurds in Iran. The Soviets vehemently denied these accusations, attributing the Kurdish disturbances in northern Iran to the work of reactionary and imperialist provocateurs.[138] At the same time, they reported Iranian condemnation of "separatism."[139] Nonetheless, Soviet reporting generally portrayed the Iranian Kurds positively, even urging the central government not to "ignore" the Kurds' "just" demands. Implicitly, sometimes even explicitly Khomeni's use of force against the Kurds was condemned.[140] Such reporting, most frequent during the 1979 fighting, continued into the 1980s, even prior to, as well as after, the deterioration of Soviet–Iranian relations in 1982. The Soviets denied the charges of separatism against the Kurds and, increasingly, condemned the central government.[141] Yet for all the propaganda support, Western observers believe that the Soviets have not provided the Iranian Kurds with arms or other material assistance in their struggle against Khomeni.[142] According to the Kurds, in 1980 their request to Moscow for arms, particularly SA-7s, was turned down.[143]

Soviet support for the Pathans and Baluchis in Pakistan and the Baluchis of Iran resembles that of the Kurds in Iran and Turkey in its clandestine nature, only rarely expressed in propaganda. The Soviets may have armed the Pakistani Baluchis in their 1973–77 uprising (and possibly the Pathans) through the Iraqis. In 1973, at least, Soviet arms were found in the Iraqi Embassy in Islamabad, and were claimed by the Pakistanis to be intended for the Baluchis and Pathans.[144] This channel reportedly was closed when the Iraq–Iran accord was signed in 1975. It is not clear if it was reopened after renewed deterioration in Iraq–Iran relations. Nor is it entirely certain that Iraq operated on behalf of Moscow rather than independently. Indeed, one report claims that the Soviets did *not* provide any kind of support to the Baluchi insurgents, and even sought to restrain Afghan aid to the Pathans in that period.[145] Soviet statements on the issue had wavered in the 1960s and early 1970s, according to one interpretation becoming decreasingly supportive in 1973, when there was even a warning against "bourgeois nationalism."[146] On the other hand, another source claims that during Bhutto's 1972 trip to Moscow the Pakistani leader was told that, should the situation warrant, Moscow would support the "national liberation movements" in Pakistan in the future just as it had supported the Bengalis the previous year.[147] During Daoud's 1974 trip to Moscow, however, the Soviets offered only the mildest of sympathy for the Afghan leader's demands regarding Paktoonistan. On that occasion Podgornyi spoke only of the "legitimate rights of peoples in Asia."[148]

With the improvement of Afghan–Pakistani relations in 1976, the Soviets refrained from any public position on the Baluchis and Pathans, although it is not known if they actually ceased material assistance and any training they may have been providing (presumably in the Soviet Union).[149] Pakistan claimed that the Soviets and East Europeans were sending arms to the Baluchis through Afghanistan at least prior to 1976.[150] It has been suggested, however, that Daoud's willingness to reduce (or end) his support for the Baluchis and Pathans in Pakistan and to improve relations with Pakistan may even have been at Soviet instigation.[151]

The Soviet invasion of Afghanistan led to a spate of reports on Soviet assistance to the Baluchis and Pathans in Pakistan. According to a number of sources, the Soviets have been arming and, together with the Cubans, training Baluchis and Pathans, both in Afghanistan and in the Soviet Union, for guerrilla warfare inside Pakistan.[152] Others have claimed, however, that, despite the opportunity and perhaps the logical interest in doing so, the Soviets have not in fact been arming or training these groups.[153] Nonetheless, in late 1985 and early 1986, the Soviets began publicly supporting the armed clashes between Pathans and Pakistani forces in the Kyber Pass. Moscow ascribed these skirmishes not to nationalist Pathan aspirations, however, but to Pathan opposition to the presence of Afghan rebel troops in their area and its use by Pakistan to transmit aid to the rebels in Afghanistan.[154]

There is even less evidence of any Soviet support for the Baluchis in Iran. Iraqi arming of this group from 1973 to 1975 was not apparently Soviet-manipulated support.[155] In the Khomeni period, there have been accusations of Soviet arming of the Iranian Baluchis.[156] Yet the Soviet media (and the Tudeh) have not been particularly supportive in the few references they have made to the Baluchis. Indeed, in 1981 both the Soviets and the Tudeh spoke critically of "reactionary gangs" among the Baluchis. They warned against outside plots to foment counter-revolution (in part traceable to the refugees from Afghanistan).[157] However, at least one Soviet-sponsored broadcast (of the National Voice of Iran) did urge the government to improve the situation so as to prevent exploitation of the poor conditions for the purposes of counter-revolution.[158]

The pattern of Soviet relations with the Baluchis of Afghanistan is confused and contradictory, probably because of the far from clear tribal and clan nature of the rebellion in Afghanistan. Generally supporting the Pathan majority in Afghanistan over the years, the Soviets' only sign of support for the Baluchis came in the changes after the 1978 coup. A Soviet-type federal system with unusual (for their size) rights for the Baluchis was introduced, suggesting some political support by the Soviets for their cause.[159] According to some reports—not particularly friendly to the Soviet Union—the Baluchis accepted the pro-Soviet regime in Afghanistan, receiving in return not only national rights but also training (reportedly from Cubans as well as Soviet advisers in Afghanistan and the Soviet Union) for guerrilla warfare in Pakistan and Iran as well as for combating the rebels in Afghanistan.[160] According to other reports, however, the early (1978) Baluchi support for the Marxist regime in Afghanistan disintegrated, with ninety per cent of the Baluchis fleeing to neighboring Iran, from whence they have been seeking to assist the remaining Baluchis in Afghanistan *against* Soviet forces there.[161] These Baluchis do not apparently have any ties to the Afghan Islamic rebels but, like many other tribal groups, are nonetheless said to be fighting the Soviets. If this is the case, as it appears to be, it is not at all clear just how, or even if, the Soviets have been willing or able to assist the Baluchis elsewhere, namely, in Pakistan and Iran.

The two cases of relatively consistent, open, and fulsome Soviet support for a secessionist movement are those of the Bengalis of East Pakistan and the Dhofaris of Oman, though the latter do not, strictly speaking, compose a secessionist movement. In the case of Bangladesh, the Soviets reportedly "expressed sympathy" for the Bengali cause "for years" before the Bengalis declared independence in 1971 and the Indo-Pakistani war broke out.[162] Yet there is no evidence of this sympathy or of actual support before 1969; nor is there any sign of Soviet recognition of the East Bengalis as a "people" prior to the war. A *New Times* article in early 1970 was critical of the treatment of East Pakistan, referring positively to "Bengalese national bourgeoisie, intellectuals and democratic middle strata" claims; but, unlike Indian references, Soviet media did *not* use the term "Bangladesh" instead of East Pakistan.[163] The Soviets went so far as to offer a different version of a joint communiqué with India in September 1971, replacing the words "East Bengal" in every instance with "East Pakistan."[164] Even during the fighting, there was only an exceptional Soviet reference to the "Bengali people,"[165] and it was only at the end of the war that the Soviets spoke of the "national movement of East Bengal," although *Pravda*, a few days earlier, spoke of the "people's liberation war" in East Pakistan.[166] Nonetheless, Moscow accorded increasing political and propaganda support from early 1970 until the outbreak of hostilities in December 1971, championing the "legitimate and inalienable rights" of the population of East Pakistan.[167]

While not going as far as the Indian government in this period, the Soviets did generally assist the East Pakistani cause at the UN prior to the war, and they played an active role in pressing the Pakistani government to accede to at least some of the demands of the Awami League.[168] Though not officially recognizing the Awami League-created government-in-exile (recognition came only after independence, 4 January 1972), the Soviets did apparently have some cooperative relationship with it.[169] At the least, they demanded that the Awami League be included in any negotiations.[170] The communists also participated in the five-party consultative committee set up to advise the government-in-exile.[171] On the other hand, despite communist participation, there have been no reports of Soviet aid to the guerrilla army organized in India (with Indian aid) and infiltrated into East Pakistan. Nonetheless, during the war the Soviets vetoed early efforts at the UN to obtain a cease-fire on the grounds that the fate of the refugees and of the "civilian population of East Pakistan" remained unresolved.[172] And they airlifted arms and equipment to India for the struggle. There was no sign, however, of arms or any other non-political Soviet assistance to the Bengalis themselves.

The Soviets did send ships of their Pacific Fleet to the Bay of Bengal, according to one account in order to prevent American intervention in East Pakistan.[173] Such use of the Soviet navy was an unprecedented act on behalf of a secessionist movement; indeed, it was virtually unprecedented, as we have seen, regarding any kind of a national liberation movement. It came, however, not only after the United States had sent its own fleet to the Bay of Bengal.[174] Soviet support for the East Pakistanis, later East Bengalis and, after independence, Bangladeshis, was openly acknowledged both during and after the war, although nothing but political support has ever been mentioned.[175] Indeed, it remains unclear if there *was* anything but political support, aside from the use of the Soviet navy—which itself was probably connected more with India than with Bangladesh, as we shall see below.

The Dhofar rebellion began in 1965 under the Dhofar Liberation Front (founded in 1962) as a secessionist movement. In 1968 the secessionist elements were replaced by a revolutionary leadership pursuing revolution throughout Oman and the Persian Gulf.[176] Thus the movement's name was eventually changed to the People's Front for the Liberation of Oman and the Arab Gulf (PFLOAG). Given this transformation, the PFLOAG, like the Liberation Front of Bahrain and various revolutionary movements in Latin America, does not belong in the category of secessionist movements, or even in the general category of national liberation movements as defined in this study. This was at first implicitly recognized by the Soviets themselves, for they depicted the rebellion as a national liberation struggle of Omanis (fighting in the Dhofar province) against the British colonialist ruler served by the Sultan and his local mercenaries.[177] Never abandoning the idea of British and later other "imperialist" involvement (likening it to South Vietnam[178]), Soviet propaganda in time referred to the rebellion as a struggle against the Sultan of Oman, and occasionally, but not always, for revolutionary change in the entire Gulf.[179]

Soviet political and propaganda support for the movement was open and relatively consistent, tapering off only as the rebellion diminished in the late 1970s and early 1980s.[180] There were even publicly acknowledged visits by PFLOAG delegations to Moscow, on a yearly basis beginning in 1969, and by Soviet journalists to Dhofar.[181] Soviet aid to the rebellion was openly acknowledged, but this was always in very general terms, with no mention of military or even material support of any kind.[182] Just what type of material support the Soviets actually gave the Dhofar rebellion is unclear. Some accounts claim that the Soviets never accorded direct assistance but rather aided South Yemen in *its* assistance to the Dhofaris.[183] This indirect aid reportedly took the form of arms deliveries through the Peoples Democratic Republic of Yemen (PDRY), training by the Cubans in the PDRY,[184] and, in 1973, Soviet naval transport of PDRY troops and equipment to the Oman border.[185] Libya and Iraq also provided aid, including, presumably, Soviet arms, but these were probably independent acts. Others claim that Soviet support began, on a small scale and reluctantly, in 1970, increasing in 1972.[186] This included not only arms deliveries but also training in the Soviet Union, following the trip by a PFLOAG delegation to Moscow in 1971. Whether direct or indirect, a decline in Soviet aid by the mid-1970s was said to have contributed to the Dhofaris' losses of 1976, arousing consternation in Aden.[187] As late as 1984, however (a year before the opening of Soviet–Omani diplomatic relations), the Omani government claimed that the Soviets were still sending aid.[188]

The relatively uniform picture of Soviet relations with anti-colonial movements is clearly not repeated with regard to the secessionists. The general range of behavior is varied and erratic, from involvement in suppression at one end of the scale, to arming, training, and political support, *sporadically*, at the other end. The only cases of consistent support, which in fact are the only two cases of naval activity, may have been exceptions in themselves: support for Bangladesh, which could be regarded as part of a Soviet effort on behalf of a state ally (India), and the Dhofar case (perhaps similar in the sense that it was aid to the PDRY), which is not, strictly speaking, a case of a national liberation movement. With these two exceptions, then, the Soviets do not appear to have rendered consistent or full assistance to this type of movement, and in most cases seem to have been reluctant even to acknowledge a Soviet connection. Thus, no separatist movement has ever been mentioned in the May Day slogans, and, with the exception of the Kurds of Iraq in 1971, no secessionist has ever been listed as participating in a CPSU congress. Similarly, no secessionists, with the exception again of the Kurds (in 1972 but not 1982), have been mentioned as attending the USSR decennials. The Kurds and the Dhofaris were the only secessionists whose visits to the Soviet Union were noted publicly, the Kurds only in the early 1970s, the Dhofaris throughout the 1970s. No secessionist was mentioned as being present at the Brezhnev, Andropov, or Chernenko funerals in the 1980s.

Very little is known about Soviet military relationships with secessionist movements. It is even unclear as to whether any secessionist, with the exception of the Kurds (on occasion), has received direct arms supplies. While there is much uncertainty regarding training and even indirect arms supplies, these do appear to have been relatively common types of aid when Moscow *was* supporting a movement. As in the case of the anti-colonials, the Soviets have never sent advisers on the spot, and there is only one case of a possible proxy involvement in support of a movement—the case of Cubans in Eritrea prior to 1974, though there is no evidence that this was not an independent Cuban matter. Similarly there has been no case of proxy or direct Soviet military intervention and only two cases of any Soviet naval involvement, both of which constituted assistance to *states* (the PDRY and India) neighboring on and battling the country in which the movement was operating (Oman and Pakistan).

The "Internal" Movements

Soviet behavior toward the ANC has been identical to the pattern regarding the anti-colonial movements, though Soviet aid to the ANC may predate that to the other African movements (of which the ANC was and is by far the oldest, formed in 1912). Inasmuch as it was the South African Communists who virtually established the ANC military wing in 1961, one may safely assume that Soviet training and arming dates back at least to this year and probably earlier. Contacts are said to have been made by the ANC, through the South African Communist party, for arms and training when the ANC was banned and forced into exile in 1960.[189] Until 1975, this training was probably provided in the Soviet bloc, possibly Egypt and Algeria; after 1976, Soviet advisers began training ANC people in Angola and possibly Mozambique.[190] The Mozambique connection, to the degree that it existed, was virtually terminated after the Mozambique–South African agreement of 1984. Although the Soviets have a large diplomatic staff in Botswana and use that as a contact point with the ANC, they apparently are not training ANC people there.[191] Cubans too are involved in ANC training in Angola, apparently as a result of ANC leader Tambo's meeting with Castro in 1977 and his subsequent trip to Cuba the same year.[192] ANC training in Cuba may also have resulted from those contacts. East Germans are also training ANC people in Angola, and the GDR provides functional assistance such as the publication of ANC materials (including editing its journal *Secheba*), cadre training, and information assistance.[193] For many years, the ANC has had an office in East Germany; it opened one in Moscow in 1987, attached to the AAPSCO. There has been no sign of Soviet or Soviet bloc or Cuban personnel with ANC units operating in South Africa itself, nor of any direct Soviet military involvement.

As in the case of the other African anti-colonial movements, the ANC began to receive more and better arms in the late 1970s, after the independence of the Portuguese colonies, some of which could now be used not only as training sites but also as conduits for direct arms supplies to the ANC (and SWAPO).[194] These arms reportedly include tanks, long-range artillery, SA-7s, and rocket launchers.[195] While the Soviets have openly acknowledged non-military aid, such as books and supplies for ANC schools in Zambia and Tanzania, and have published innumerable expressions of solidarity and of ANC gratitude for Soviet support and assistance, they have not publicly acknowledged the military side of this assistance. The most they have intimated publicly has been "all-round help" or "material" as well as moral support, but even these expressions are rarely employed.[196] *International Affairs* published an interview with ANC general secretary Alfred Nzo who noted diplomatic, moral, and material support, under the last referring only to information and communications.[197]

On the other hand, the South African Communist party journal *African Communist* has been quite open about Soviet military as well as other aid to African liberation movements, including the ANC.[198]

Political support, however, has been widely publicized and propaganda coverage quite fulsome. ANC leaders have been frequently visiting the Soviet Union since the 1960s, usually once or twice a year, and they have participated fully in important Soviet occasions. Thus, ANC leaders attended the CPSU congresses (speaking to party organizations), attended the decennial celebrations (addressing those of 1982), and attended all the Soviet leadership funerals in the 1980s. They have usually been received by Ponomarev and Ul'ianovskii or Brutents, and one occasion (1971) by party secretary Katushev. Participating in the various conferences and events organized by the Soviet Union for anti-colonial movements (such as the 1969 Khartoum meeting), ANC leaders also met with Podgornyi during his 1977 African trip (at which time Tambo said that the Soviets were always willing to increase their military assistance when asked—a comment not reported in the Soviet media).[199] On the whole, the ANC has been accorded the same treatment (though over a longer period) as ZAPU and SWAPO, including references in May Day slogans, and with a slightly higher status in terms of visits to the Soviet Union and media attention.

The PLO too has been treated by the Soviet Union according to the pattern set for anti-colonial movements, although the Palestinian cause has achieved a more central position in Soviet political pronouncements, and more propaganda attention, than any other movement with the exception of the Vietnamese. After an initial period of coolness, the Soviets agreed to contacts with the PLO in 1968, four years after its creation.[200] This was the result of a trip to Moscow by Arafat as a member of an Egyptian delegation. An independent trip by an Arafat delegation in 1970 was followed by indirect Soviet arms deliveries to the movement, which became direct deliveries in 1972.[201] In time, these arms deliveries included the same types of weapons sent to the anti-colonial movements, that is, tanks, rocket launchers, light weapons, and SA-7s, although apparently they were not everything the PLO requested.[202] Even prior to 1968, there were Palestinian students studying in the Soviet Union; but after Arafat's visit Palestinians began training in the Soviet Union, Eastern Europe, North Korea, and, in time, Cuba as well as the PDRY and possibly other Arab countries, with Soviet and possibly Cuban advisers.[203] The PLO itself became a conduit for training and arms for other movements, such as the Eritreans, but it is not certain that this activity has been at the behest of the Soviet Union (particularly since various PLO factions often help movements not supported by Moscow).

While Soviet advisers train the PLO in third countries, there do not appear to have been Soviet advisers with Palestinian forces in Lebanon. At most, one team or more visited PLO units there prior to the 1982 war. There were reports of Cubans and Libyans training PLO forces in Lebanon, but the proxy nature of this presence is by no means certain, particularly with regard to the Libyans and perhaps even the Cubans.[204] Following the 1982 war and the PLO split, Soviet material aid and training for Arafat's Fatah forces fell to nearly zero, although the East Germans apparently continued training. Soviet aid was resumed in 1987. Assistance to the other organizations has continued and even been augmented with regard to the PFLP and DFLP of Habash and Hawatmeh, respectively. As with the ANC and other anti-colonials (aside from the anti-Portuguese movements), Soviet military aid, when given, has been publicized by Moscow in only a general fashion, for example, by references to assistance in "deeds" not just words or "material" aid, with only rare mention specifically of military aid.[205]

As to actual assistance in the field, neither the Soviets nor their possible proxies have ever intervened militarily on behalf of the PLO, even on the occasions when the organization was under severe attack and in danger of liquidation, as in the 1970 civil war in Jordan, the 1976 civil war in Lebanon, the 1982 Israeli war in Lebanon, and the siege of Arafat at Tripoli in 1983. During the 1970, 1976 and 1982 wars, Soviet naval activity in the form of the augmentation of their Mediterranean squadron was undertaken, but in all three cases this was in response to American naval activity: in 1970, an American threat to intervene against *Syria*; in 1976, the evacuation of US personnel from Lebanon; in 1982, after the movement of the US fleet in the early days of the war.[206] The 1982 case of naval activity, coming as it did only during the period of risk of an all-out Israeli–Syrian war, resembled the 1970 warning, primarily to the United States in connection with Syria. Nonetheless, insofar as it provided even political backing for the fighting Palestinians as well, it may be construed as a type of assistance very rarely accorded a national liberation movement, although it fell far short of the type of military aid requested or needed by the PLO.[207]

Open political and propaganda support for the Palestinians built up gradually from the late 1960s, from isolated acknowledgment of the Palestinians as a people in 1968 and of the PLO as a national liberation movement in 1969 to fully fledged, open, and even high-level championing of the cause in more than the local or regional context in the 1970s and 1980s.[208] Since 1970, PLO delegations have regularly visited the Soviet Union (some trips being postponed or cancelled when certain disputes have clouded the relationship), and high-level Soviet visitors to the area—including Politburo members—have often met with PLO delegations in countries such as Syria. The PLO was authorized to open an office in Moscow (and one in East Berlin) in 1974; it actually did this in 1975 and received diplomatic status as an embassy in 1981—status granted no other liberation movement with the exception of the Vietnamese. Similarly, Arafat, usually received by Ponomarev, was also occasionally received by Foreign Minister Gromyko and even Brezhnev in Moscow.

The PLO, like the anti-colonial movements, has participated since 1971 in all the functions and anniversaries of the Soviet Union, including the CPSU congresses (from 1976 onwards) and the funerals in the 1980s. Unlike the NLF and PAIGC, however, it has never been invited to speak at the congresses (though in 1976 and at the 1982 decennial celebrations it did address party or military organizations). In the reporting of Brezhnev's funeral (but not the others), the PLO delegation was listed last of the national liberation movements, non-ruling parties, and anyone else reported by name (although, unlike the secessionists, the PLO was at least reported). When the anti-colonial movements and the ANC were mentioned in the 1977–79 May Day slogans, the PLO was omitted, but it was mentioned with them when the slogans again referred to all of these movements from 1983 to 1985.

If the ANC and, to a slightly lesser degree, the PLO have been treated the same way as anti-colonials, the Polisario bears greater resemblance to the secessionists in Soviet behavior (and possibly in fact, though not in Soviet propaganda). The ambiguity so characteristic of Soviet involvement with secessionists is noticeable in the case of the Polisario as well, and reports of actual aid are conflicting and difficult to document. While the Polisario clearly has Soviet arms, including T-54 tanks, and, reportedly, SA-7 missiles, these have been supplied from Algeria and, until 1983, Libya.[209] Whether this has been done at Soviet behest is difficult to ascertain. Arms shipments to Angola in January 1976 transiting Algeria were said to have contained arms for the Polisario as well, or at least were in part diverted by the Algerians to the Polisario.[210] One account claims this to have been Soviet-directed aid, abandoned in the late 1970s.[211] There have been no reports, however, of training, nor of any Soviet acknowledgment of concrete assistance to the movement. But in response to accusations of such aid, the Soviets have, at least on a few occasions, denied giving any assistance, either directly or through Algeria and Libya.[212]

Nonetheless, Moscow has increasingly expressed its political support for the Polisario. Historically, despite the fact that Soviet retrospective accounts recount the launching of the Polisario in 1973 (and the beginning of the "national liberation struggle" in 1958), there was no mention of the issue or the movement before the 1975 conflict with Spain, at which time the struggle was presented as a legitimate one against Spanish imperialism. Once the battle became one against Morocco (and for a while Mauritania), Moscow adopted an almost neutral public position, only gradually in 1976, and more strongly from 1977, expressing support for the Polisario.[213] Criticism of Morocco remained relatively restrained, on some occasions absent altogether (from reporting on Morocco or

North Africa),[214] although on the whole Soviet presentations of the problem have championed the Polisario's demands and the rights of the people of the Western Sahara.[215]

However, despite reporting the 1976 creation of the Saharan Arab Democratic Republic (SADR), and the recognition of the state by as many as fifty states and various organizations, the Soviet Union itself has not yet recognized the republic.[216] Indeed, no Warsaw Pact state has done so, although the Cubans (and the Yugoslavs) have.[217] Nor has Moscow ever acknowledged any Soviet contacts of any kind with SADR or the Polisario movement. In answer to a direct question regarding aid from "progressive forces," asked by a Soviet reporter in Algiers, a Polisario leader was quoted in *Novoe vremia* as naming only Algerian aid.[218] No Polisario delegation has been listed at any Soviet function since the movement's creation, be it CPSU congresses, USSR anniversaries, or leaders' funerals, with the one exception of participation in an East Berlin conference in 1980 sponsored by the *World Marxist Review*.[219] And, as has been the case with the secessionists, no mention has been made of the Western Sahara in May Day slogans.

Internal Factors Influencing Soviet Support

IDEOLOGY

A major question, not easily answered, is to what degree a movement's basic principles and/or objectives have operated as factors regarding Soviet behavior. The first difficulty arising is trying clearly to label the basic ideological orientation of a given movement, inasmuch as many movements have used Marxist phraseology, and may even have been staffed by many Marxists, without being what the Soviets would call a Marxist–Leninist movement.

Soviet designations themselves are problematic and, in fact, quite often inconsistent. This inconsistency not only has been a function of time and support, but is apparent even within the same time-frame in relation to one and the same movement. Even the NLF, which is probably the only movement that Moscow has clearly categorized as Marxist–Leninist, was not generally described as such until retrospective accounts. While it was engaged in its struggle, the NLF was referred to as a "patriotic," sometimes "progressive patriotic," movement.[220]

It is conceivable that the Soviets had tactical reasons for ignoring, even refuting, any claims that national liberation movements were Marxist, preferring the united front approach for mass appeal (and to counter accusations of involvement). Yet even without using the term "Marxist–Leninist," much inconsistency has been evident in Soviet characterization of the movements. The MPLA, for example, was described in 1961 as having grown out of Marxist circles; in 1971 it was said to have a democratic nature with socialist leanings.[221] Yet a 1963 discussion said nothing of this, and an article the same year spoke of it only as a united front of "all patriotic forces."[222] Retrospective accounts have been only somewhat more consistent. Ul'ianovskii, for example, claimed in 1982 that Neto had formed "truly Marxist views" by 1974; but the same article in a book a year later omitted this sentence, stating rather that Neto and the other MPLA leaders did not use the term "socialism," concentrating on the national stage of their movements.[223] Only after independence, at its 1976 plenum, did the MPLA, according to Ul'ianovskii, embark on a "revolutionary democratic" course in the direction of socialism. Another retrospective account also labeled the MPLA's struggle as "national democratic."[224] The other two anti-Portuguese movements were given even less attention in the sphere of ideology. FRELIMO was portrayed as an anti-colonial movement, and PAIGC, if characterized at all, was described by one account as at least led by a Marxist (in an article disagreeing with accounts that Cabral had been merely a nationalist or even an adherent of the idea of Negritude).[225] Ul'ianovskii said that Cabral, without using the term "socialist," did believe in the transformation of the national liberation movement into a "social revolution" and acknowledged that his views were "akin to those of socialist revolution."[226]

The International Department's Africanist Manchkha referred in 1975 to ZAPU, SWAPO, and the ANC as revolutionary democratic parties, and *Izvestiia* spoke of them as movements struggling for national *and social* liberation.[227] Yet not all accounts portrayed them this way, if they referred to ideological aspects at all. Discussions of ZAPU, for example, almost always spoke only of the national aspect of the struggle, with one account explaining that even workers had first to think of national liberation from colonial powers, while another characterized ZAPU (and the ZAPU–ZANU Patriotic Front) as patriotic national forces.[228] There was even a suggestion of Soviet dissatisfaction over the less than revolutionary nature of ZAPU's ideology when *African Communist* criticized the Zimbabwe movement for its "non-class" ideology and its nationalist views which ill equipped it for class struggle.[229] SWAPO's ideology was also described in conflicting ways. Some accounts in the first half of the 1970s referred to its revolutionary democratic nature but most portrayed it only as a national movement.[230] Somewhat more attention was devoted to its ideology after a new SWAPO program was adopted in 1976. Since this time, SWAPO could, and has been said to, have a social as well as a national side, with an orientation toward scientific socialism.[231] Two commentators even claimed that SWAPO sought to build a people's democracy.[232] On the other hand, one account allowed for such an orientation but argued that this was not

Marxist–Leninist.[233] And many other accounts ignore these aspirations, continuing to note only the more general national demands. Often the more radical, ideologically directed, statements are in fact comments by SWAPO leaders in the Soviet media rather than characterizations by the Soviets themselves.[234]

Similar inconsistencies have been apparent with regard to the ANC. Despite the above mentioned characterization by Manchkha as a revolutionary democratic movement, the ANC has much more frequently been referred to as a national democratic movement, albeit one seeking social as well as national changes.[235] Thus, *Pravda* has used both the terms "democratic front" and "national patriotic front."[236] Careful to explain that this nationalism does not mean racism or black chauvinism, the Soviets have said that even the communists in South Africa are struggling for a "national democratic revolution."[237] Thus while the three movements, ZAPU, SWAPO, and the ANC, are often lumped together under the revolutionary democratic rubric, there has been much greater variety in the descriptions of their ideologies, with ZAPU and the ANC appearing more often as national democratic and SWAPO often as espousing scientific socialism.

The PLO, like ZAPU, though more so, has actually been criticized for its exclusively nationalist ideology. Soviet historical accounts speak of the early years of the PLO, particularly Fatah, as strongly influenced by "bourgeois reaction," and they have actually criticized the movement for failure to introduce any ideological or Marxist content.[238] Some accounts claim that this situation improved in the early to mid-1970s when progressive forces began to dominate, adding social to national demands and leading "if not to Marxist–Leninist then at least to revolutionary democracy."[239] Yet even as this was said, there were critical comments as to the lack of an ideological substance or social program in the PLO because of bourgeois influences,[240] and in 1977 the deputy head of the Foreign Ministry's Middle East section published a generally critical article.[241] Acknowledging the PLO as a basically revolutionary and progressive movement, the author nonetheless condemned the lack of a sufficiently elaborated program for social transformation (because of the bourgeois–nationalist nature of the leadership), concluding that it was "premature to speak of the victory of a national democratic direction" in the Palestinian movement.[242] The PLO was said, therefore, to be insufficiently revolutionary or progressive. While most of this criticism has been implicitly or explicitly directed against the dominant Fatah, the actually Marxist organizations, the PFLP and the DFLP, have not been accorded much better treatment. Though acknowledged to be Marxist "to some extent" and leftist–revolutionary, they have occasionally been characterized (not by name) as "leftist–extremists" typical of petty bourgeois influence.[243]

Such attention to the ideological basis of a movement was unusual particularly for the three "internal" movements. The Polisario, for example, has received virtually no attention in terms of ideology. It has been described as a national liberation movement with national aspirations only. The only exception to this appears to have been a *Voprosy istorii* account which spoke of the Polisario favoring a "national democratic" state introducing "radical social transformations."[244] This sparsity of any ideological references is more typical of Soviet treatment of the secessionists.

Although the Sikhs, for example, have been clearly labeled reactionary and the Burmese minorities "feudal,"[245] the more usual approach to these secessionist movements opposed by the Soviets has been simply to label them "separatist," as if that term said it all. This was the case with Anyanya, the Tigreans, and the Moros, though the last was said to be motivated by legitimate social and economic grievances during the very brief period of Soviet political support.[246] A sign of change in the Soviet attitude toward the south Sudanese was the characterization of the Sudanese People's Liberation Movement as "democratic," in a 1985 *World Marxist* review article.[247] This new movement of the south Sudanese would appear to be ideologically more acceptable than the anti-communist Anyanya, although the change in Soviet attitude was relatively late in coming, suggesting other than ideological considerations.[248]

There has been a bit more subtlety with regard to those movements originally supported and then abandoned. To a slight degree, the Ibos might be included in this group. There were some references to the "progressive" nature of this people prior to Moscow's support for the central government.[249] Even after the shift, when the Soviets characterized the government as "progressive," the Ibos were called "separatist," but the term "reactionary" was not used. The Kurds, much more clearly and frequently, have been termed "progressive" and "democratic" in the Iraqi, Iranian, and Turkish cases. During the periods of Soviet opposition, in the Iraqi case, reactionary elements were said to have taken over, and in the Turkish case it has been acknowledged that there were reactionary as well as democratic elements in the movement, with different objectives, as we shall see below.[250] The Eritreans (and Tigreans) have been regarded similarly: during the period of clandestine support nothing was said of their ideology, but after the Soviet reversal the explanation was that the movement had been progressive so long as it was aimed against the reactionary monarchy, but *became* reactionary when it continued its struggle against the progressive revolutionary regime of Mengistu.[251]

These shifts would certainly suggest adherence to the often cited theoretical argument in Soviet literature that it is not the actual ideology of a

nationalist movement that makes it progressive (or not), but the nature
of the object against which it is struggling, that is, the overall political
situation.[252] Nonetheless, in the case of Bangladesh the reactionary
nature of the Pakistani government was not sufficient to elicit ideological
agreement with the major Bengali movement, the Awami League. In
1970 the Soviets spoke of the National Awami Party as the focus of
progressive forces, and on at least one occasion they indirectly labelled
the League "bourgeois chauvinists."[253] Only in October 1971 was the
incarcerated Awami League leader Rahman termed "a progressive" along
with the rest of the leadership of that party, marking a change in the overall characterization of the League.[254] The other secessionist movements,
including the Baluchis, the Pathans, and the Tamils, have usually been
referred to in national terms with no indication of their ideological bent.
When the Tamils were criticized in 1987 they were accused of "juggling
with Marxist phraseology" without in fact having any genuine ideology
or platform.[255] Only exceptionally have the Iranian Baluchis been termed
"reactionary" (in the period of their assistance to the rebels in Afghanistan). Similarly, the FROLINAT in Chad and the Katangans have
been described with little ideological amplification, although both have
been described as revolutionary groups with legitimate socioeconomic
and political grievances against reactionary regimes.[256] The PFLOAG
has been described similarly, with "people's democratic" objectives, as
we shall see below, but Soviet characterizations have not gone beyond
the terms "patriotic" or "national" or "anti-feudalist" in describing the
nature of their movement.[257]

The Soviet characterization of a movement (reactionary, progressive, national democratic, revolutionary democratic, socialist oriented,
Marxist–Leninist) in itself has been inconsistent, suggesting that support
dictated the ideology characterization rather than the opposite. If one
considers the actual ideological basis of each movement, it becomes
even more difficult to ascertain any correlation between basic ideological
orientation and Soviet support, or the lack of it. Non-Soviet analyses,
and often the movements themselves, present, roughly, the following
characterizations, albeit with their own definitions of Marxism.

The NFL were basically Marxist–Leninist, despite the effort to operate
as a broader nationalist front. Relatively close to genuine Marxist would
be FRELIMO and the PAIGC. Further along the scale, toward the center,
is the ANC, in which the Marxist trend is strong but not the sole
determining one, and SWAPO, with ZAPU clearly in the center if not
to the right of center of the spectrum and the PLO to the right of that.
(Although inside the PLO there are two Marxist factions, the PFLP and
DFLP, besides the dominant non-Marxist Fatah.) Of the separatists there
are two—possibly three—movements that could be termed Marxist:
the EPLF of the Eritreans, the PFLOAG (Dhofaris), and, possibly, the

Baluchis of Pakistan. The Polisario, the Moros, the Katangans, and some others may be said to have left-wing tendencies of varying degrees and at various times, but they are not generally considered Marxist or even somewhat Marxist movements. The Kurds of Turkey are divided, with some Marxist, even radical groups among them, though this is not generally the case with the Kurds of Iraq or Iran.

There is certainly no way to prove that the relative Marxist orientation of the three anti-Portuguese movements was *not* a factor in the higher degree of open support the Soviets accorded them. It was in connection with these movements that the two highest instances of support occurred: naval assistance to PAIGC (albeit the least Marxist of the three) and the Cuban military intervention (with Soviet assistance) for the MPLA, which was the highest type of support ever given a movement. Similarly, the second highest type of support was given another relatively Marxist movement, the Dhofaris, for whom support was relatively open and included indirect naval assistance. There were, however, two non-Marxist movements which received this higher degree of Soviet support, particularly unusual for a secessionist: the Benghalis and the PLO. Moreover, neither the Marxist NLF nor the relatively Marxist FRELIMO received this kind of assistance.

Short of these higher degrees of support, there were or have been apparently no distinctions made between more and less Marxist movements among the anti-colonials (aside from May Day slogans on the NLF in the early 1970s) and among the secessionists. Thus, ZAPU, SWAPO, and the ANC were treated more or less equally, SWAPO gaining significant Soviet military aid somewhat later than the even less Marxist ZAPU. And indeed, ZAPU itself was favored over its Marxist rival ZANU. On the other hand, the EPLF, despite its Marxist orientation, was actually actively suppressed with Soviet assistance during one period. Indeed, even in the later period of renewed Eritrean contact with the Soviet Union, the contacts were not with the Marxist EPLF but with the right-of-center ELF. And in the earlier period of support, what support was given the EPLF was both limited and covert, although the Cubans were involved.

Similarly, even if the Pakistani Baluchis are Marxist, what Soviet support has existed has not been overt or of the highest categories. Yet the Iraqi Kurds, before the period of Soviet-assisted suppression, were quite openly assisted by Moscow despite their non-Marxist orientation. Indeed, the movements that occasionally or even usually received the most commonly accorded Soviet assistance (propaganda, political, training, and arms, even indirect) have comprised Marxists, less Marxists, and non-Marxists alike, with support for the anti-colonials and support or lack of support for the secessionists generally eluding ideological lines.[258] While information is lacking, there are at least two or three movements with which the Soviets were uncomfortable about their non-Marxist orientation))the PLO, ZAPU, and SWAPO—but this discomfort did not, as far as can be determined, affect Soviet support, though as we shall see below it may have affected some Soviet maneuvering regarding factions.

Ideological dissonance has been discernible with regard to objectives as well, the large degree of inconsistency, particularly with regard to the secessionists, making it difficult to classify objectives as a factor for Soviet support. The Soviets have clearly *not* wanted to appear to be supporting separatism, and for this reason they generally publicly espouse only the objective of autonomy, claiming to reject those movements demanding secession, that is, independence. Thus, in connection with the movements they have actually (and actively) opposed (the Ibos, Anyanya, the Tigreans, and at certain times the Eritreans and the Iraqi Kurds), they have claimed that there is actually regional autonomy and, therefore, no justification for waging a struggle. The implication here is that the Soviets would have supported, or even did support, them when their demands were limited to autonomy. In this way they explain their cessation of support for the Kurds and Eritreans, claiming that the central governments had become willing to grant this autonomy.[259] Yet there was never support for Anyanya or the Tigreans, or, probably, the Ibos, no matter what their demands, while there was support for the Eritreans and Kurds at times, despite their demands for independence.

It is true that in all of these cases public Soviet positions favored autonomy, and no more (although there were some rare Soviet references to their 1949–50 support in the UN for Eritrean independence).[260] According to some Soviet claims, the Sudanese Communist party even had a resolution calling for autonomy of the southern Sudan,[261] and there were some comments on the Ibos' right to autonomy. Yet what changed was not the movements' delineation of their objectives, but rather the Soviets' definition of these objectives in accord with the Soviet decision to support a movement or not, and *this* decision was determined by other factors. In the cases of the Sikhs, the Moros, the Burmese minorities, the Tigreans, and occasionally the Eritreans, however, the Soviets have gone so far as to imply if not state that their lack of support for these movements is based on the illegitimacy even of the objective of autonomy, on the grounds that none of them actually constitutes a nation.[262] Yet the instances of support for the Eritreans and, briefly, even the Moros belies this "explanation," while support for ethnic groups elsewhere (for example, the Katangans, the Tamils, the Dhofaris) raises further doubts. Nor could the absence of any Soviet position regarding the Arabs of Khuzistan be accounted for if the determining factors were the movement's objectives.

If lack of support was justified ostensibly by the criterion of the legitimacy of a movement's objectives—specifically, autonomy—the granting of support was also presented as a function of the movement's ostensible goals. Thus, when supported, the Kurds were claimed to be seeking only regional autonomy, not independence.[263] In regard to the Tamils, the Kurds of Turkey, and Iran, or even the Iraqi Kurds and Eritreans, the Soviets condemned "extremists" within each group who sought independence and defended those who sought regional autonomy.[264] Indeed, Moscow did support only autonomy for these movements, though it is by no means certain that this was the ultimate objective of the movements themselves, which, in fact, generally sought full independence. The same dissonance has probably existed between Soviet definitions of objectives and those of the Baluchis and the Pathans. In the case of the Dhofaris, it is not certain that there was actually Soviet support in the pre-1968 separatist stage, while in the post-1968 stage the movement was no longer a national liberation but rather a revolutionary movement for all of Oman. (Moscow called for a genuinely independent, democratic, and sovereign Oman, including Dhofar.)[265] This was the way the Soviets depicted the objectives of the FROLINAT and the Katangans (and briefly the Moros) as well, ignoring or denying any ethnic goals. (Yet the same demands for improved socioeconomic conditions for the Katangans, for example, were not supported for the Sikhs—for whom neither the socioeconomic nor ethnic claims were acknowledged by Moscow.[266]

Even in the case of Bangladesh, the Soviets rejected the Bengalis" demand for independence for some time. According to some reports, Moscow pressed India to abandon its support for the idea, calling rather for autonomy.[267] As late as the fall of 1971, a Soviet communiqué with Algeria spoke of respect for the "national unity and territorial integrity" of Pakistan (and India), while the Awami League complained—in what was seen as a reference to the Soviet Union—of the narrow self-interest and world strategy "which was holding outside powers back on the issue of independence."[268] However, despite a long period of hesitation, the Soviets did eventually change their position, and from mid-October 1971 on they supported India's efforts on behalf of Bangladesh independence (though they did not *explicitly* or publicly espouse this objective until after the war). Indeed, they only rarely referred to the Awami League's demand even for autonomy.[269] Support for Bengali independence was explained on one occasion on the grounds that the movement had sought only autonomy, had been refused, and therefore had been forced to seek independence.[270] This explanation was more accurate regarding Soviet positions than those of the Bengalis, but in any case it was never sufficiently convincing for the Soviets to apply it to movements whose independence the Soviets indeed opposed (no matter how similar were the movements' grievances).

A second case of support even for independence may be that of the Polisario. Such support is at least implied in Soviet references to the existence of SADR and of its recognition by so many countries. Similarly, the Soviets support OAU and UN resolutions for "self-determination and independence" for the Western Sahara. Nevertheless, the Soviets themselves have not recognized the state, explaining that they have refrained from doing so out of "discretion as befits a great power."[271] Indeed, even as they acknowledge Soviet support for the OAU and UN position, their assertion of their own position omits the word "independence," speaking only of self-determination. Thus, while leaving little doubt as to their support for this objective, they are careful to maintain a fine distinction regarding their own commitment.[272]

In all of the above cases, however, no matter how much support the Soviets actually have given, or how the Soviets struggle to define or redefine the goals, the objective of independence has been problematic for Moscow. Even in the case of the Palestinians, the Soviets explicitly opposed the idea of an independent Palestinian state until 1974 (they even refrained from adding the word "national" to the formula for the "legitimate" rights of the Palestinians until November 1973), and disagreement has persisted over the location of such a state, that is, between the PLO objective of a democratic, secular state in all of Palestine and a mini-state in the West Bank and Gaza Strip only.[273]

The Soviets have argued that it is simply unrealistic to think that Israel could be supplanted by a Palestinian state. Neither Soviet support for the PLO itself, beginning in 1968, nor the various increments in this support (1972, direct arms; 1975, opening of a Moscow office; 1981, diplomatic status) appear to have been dependent upon the PLO's own position regarding this objective. Similarly, the Soviet advocacy of Security Council resolution 242, despite the continued PLO rejection, does not appear to have affected Soviet support for the organization, though this as well as the statehood issue have been serious sources of discord between the two at various times. At one point these issues were even part of a rift and open polemics between Moscow and the small Marxist PFLP organization within the PLO.[274] Later, positions appeared to be reversed when the Soviets accused Arafat of abandoning the idea of an independent state in favor of a Jordanian–Palestinian confederation. This disagreement had less to do with the confederation idea (which did not necessarily rule out an independent state, according to Arafat) than with its tactical implications, as we shall see below.[275]

The third "internal" movement, the ANC, was treated by Moscow similarly to the more standard anti-colonial movements in the sense that full independence was an objective unreservedly espoused by both Moscow and the movement. In this case, independence meant fully free elections with equal suffrage for all races, thereby transferring the power to the black majority.[276] In 1928 Stalin proposed to the Comintern, with South African Communist opposition, the idea of a black republic as a solution, but this objective has not been heard in the post-World War II period, and certainly it preceded, and differed significantly from, Pretoria's idea of "homelands."[277]

With regard to the anti-colonial movements proper, the matter of objectives has been less problematic for the Soviet Union. Rather than a deterrence to Soviet support, the goal of independent statehood may well have been an incentive favoring support. The only possible exception to this might be the brief difference of opinion between SWAPO and the Soviet Union over interim goals, specifically Security Council resolution 435. While SWAPO accepted this resolution outlining a settlement of the Namibian issue, Moscow abstained in the UN vote. It did not actually veto it, however, because of SWAPO and African support, but it objected to the idea of UN-supervised elections without prior withdrawal of South African forces from Namibia.[278] Though this did indicate dissonance with regard to immediate objectives, it did not entail disagreement in principle over the broader objectives of the movement. More important, it did not in any way affect Soviet support for SWAPO. And in time, the Soviets did accept the resolution, joining the movement in demanding its implementation.[279]

In summary, it cannot be said that ideological considerations, both basic conceptualization and objectives, were totally absent from Soviet calculations. There are cases of high support coinciding with ideological agreement, particularly the one case of highest Soviet support. Yet the more numerous cases of support for non-ideologically compatible, or at least less congenial, movements, plus the cases of outright opposition even to ideologically acceptable movements, as well as the cases of dissonance in objectives, all suggest that ideological factors have played only a very limited role, if any, in the determination of Soviet support. Karen Brutents's assertion that support for national liberation movements should not rest on ideological agreement would appear to be the dictum guiding actual policy, despite the variety of views expressed within the Soviet Union.[280] Moreover, the ideological factor as a consideration does not appear to have varied within the time-period studied here, with increasing support after 1975 going to non-Marxist and closer-to-Marxist movements alike.

COMPOSITION, LEADERSHIP, AND ORGANIZATION

From the point of view of the social composition of the leadership and the movement at large, it might be said that the cases of absence of Soviet support (and actual opposition) have all been cases of non-proletariat movements. But the same may also be said of virtually every movement supported, for only one movement has been acknowledged by the Soviets as having a proletarian leadership—that of the NLF—and only one as having "proletariat or semi-proletarian" cadres—the ANC.[281] Nor does there appear to have been any distinction in Soviet support regarding the class that did have predominance, be it petty bourgeoisie, bourgeoisie, or peasantry, particularly inasmuch as the vast majority of movements have been peasant movements with petty bourgeois leadership. Indeed, even the NLF, as well as the ANC, was said to have been mainly a peasant movement.[282] SWAPO, though unacknowledged by the Soviets, has something of a proletarian base, but in neither this case nor those of the NLF and ANC has any proletarian coloring earned a movement significantly different behavior from Moscow (with the exception of mention of the Vietcong in May Day slogans in the early 1970s, an honor accorded all the anti-colonials, briefly, only in the late 1970s, and in the 1980s to SWAPO, ANC, and the PLO, plus the NLF and PAIGC speech to the 1971 CPSU Congress).

On the other hand, the bourgeois nature of the PLO has been criticized by the Soviets, but there has been no apparent reduction of support (just as ideological criticism has not affected support).[283] Another albeit brief instance of Soviet criticism of the composition of a movement occurred in 1970 with regard to the Awami League, but that was in fact before the Soviets expanded their support beyond the National Awami party.[284] On the whole, there have been few Soviet references to the social composition of the movements supported.

It is very difficult to determine to what degree the leader of a movement has himself affected Soviet behavior. Indeed, Soviet discussion (interviews, biographies, etc.) of the leaders have been limited almost entirely to the anti-colonials and the two "internals" which are treated like anti-colonials (ANC, PLO). The only exceptions appear to be the leaders of the PFLOAG and, sporadically, the Iraqi KDP, whose trips to Moscow have at least been reported. The lack of coverage for secessionist leaders may have more to do with general public Soviet reticence regarding these movements than with actual approval or disapproval of a particular leader. With regard to the others, the general Soviet approach appears to have been to accept the leadership it has found in the movements, glossing over differences and urging unity where rivalries have existed. Thus, the dominant group accepting the continued leadership of Nujoma in SWAPO was supported when a group of more militant black nationalists broke off in rebellion against Nujoma's methods in the mid-1970s. The Soviets did not even report the problem directly, referring only to American efforts to split the liberation forces, and they did not alter their aid because of the conflict.[285] Similarly, there was no alteration of Soviet relations with the ANC leadership when it faced similar problems with a break-away group in 1975. Nevertheless, despite the public Soviet enthusiasm for Cabral (PAIGC), Machel (and before him Mondlane—FRELIMO), Neto (MPLA), Nujoma (SWAPO), Nkomo (ZAPU), Tambo (ANC), and Arafat (PLO), there have apparently been problems between Moscow on the one hand, and, at least, Neto, Nkomo, and Arafat on the other.

In the case of Neto, this may even have affected Soviet support for the MPLA. While Soviet opposition to Neto did not lead to a shift of support to a rival movement (UNITA or FNLA), it did result in a brief period of reported support for a rival faction (led by Daniel Chipenda) within the MPLA. This was preceded and then accompanied by a reduction and even suspension of arms supplies pending the settlement of the internal strife.[286] Once Neto was victorious in this internal struggle, however, the Soviets resumed arms supplies, and even increased their support despite their disdain for him.[287] This disdain apparently had less to do with ideology (Neto was a Soviet-oriented Marxist) or policy issues than simply with personality problems; it continued even into the post-independence period, as evidenced by the reported Soviet role in the 1977 coup attempt against Neto.[288]

Independently of their dissatisfaction with Neto, which only temporarily affected actual Soviet support for the MPLA, the Soviets did urge cooperation and unity between the Angolan movements. Aside from a possible very early, very limited, connection with FNLA, the Soviets consistently opposed and directly criticized the rival movements. Nonetheless, presumably in keeping with their united front approach, and in time to prevent civil war,[289] the Soviets tended to overestimate the chances for unity and recommended cooperation right up to the time of Cuban intervention and, according to an Angolan source, even up to a few days prior to independence.[290] Moscow apparently did, however, bring pressure upon the OAU, and its president at the time, Idi Amin, to limit its recognition to the MPLA alone.[291]

The previously mentioned possibility of Soviet dissatisfaction with the ideological bent of ZAPU was part of speculation over a change in Soviet attitude toward Joshua Nkomo in the late 1970s.[292] There is in fact little evidence that the Soviets were planning to abandon Nkomo, despite the fact that there were Soviet contacts with his rival Robert Mugabe of ZANU. The 1976 alliance of ZAPU and ZANU, creating the Patriotic Front (PF), did lead to open and positive Soviet references to Mugabe and ZANU, and there was reportedly even a Mugabe trip to the Soviet Union in 1978.[293] Mugabe also met with Castro, in Angola in 1977 and again in Ethiopia in 1978; the latter was followed by a trip to Cuba.[294] One result of these encounters was Cuban and Ethiopian training of ZANU people in Ethiopia and Cuban training in Mozambique.[295]

Theoretically, this was training of PF forces, but the forces in Mozambique were virtually all ZANU people, and Nkomo reportedly opposed joint training anywhere else (refusing to have his own people train in Ethiopia or ZANU people to train with ZAPU in Zambia).[296]

All of these developments led to rumors that Moscow was considering a shift to the Marxist Mugabe, and Mugabe made it clear that he was willing (even seeking) Soviet assistance.[297] There apparently was a conflict within ZANU over this matter, some activists preferring alliance with the Soviets so as to gain more and better arms.[298] Yet ZANU accounts and Mugabe's treatment of the Soviets after independence indicate that Moscow in fact gave very little if any assistance to ZANU.[299] While there may have been a brief flirtation with Mugabe, the Soviets remained loyal to Nkomo, Cuban and Ethiopian aid notwithstanding.[300] As in the case of Angola—indeed, more openly and consistently—the Soviets, throughout the Zimbabwean struggle, favored unification of the national liberation movements, often claiming that such unification existed even when it did not. Thus they publicly minimized the differences between the movements, encouraging cooperation, regardless of their exclusive support for one of them. Soviet praise for unification efforts even of the military wings suggested that Soviet interest in amalgamation into one movement or front was genuine, in keeping with the united front idea.[301]

As in the case of ZAPU, the Soviets have generally preferred the non-Marxist leader and organization over the Marxist ones within the PLO. At one point the Soviets were at odds with one of the Marxist groups, George Habash's PFLP, and engaged in open polemics with the group. Basically, this group, which had some early Chinese connections, was too radical for Moscow in both its objectives and methods. The other Marxist group, Nayif Hawatmeh's DFLP, has been closer to Moscow, but, like the PFLP, it has been too small to offer an alternative to Fatah.[302]

Unlike any other case, the Soviets have openly criticized "bourgeois" and "non-ideological" elements in the PLO, referring indirectly to Arafat and his Fatah organization. They have also long criticized the lack of unity within the PLO altogether. Until the post-1982 crisis in the PLO, however, the Soviets clearly acknowledged (by their support of all kinds) the political and military dominance of Fatah over the other organizations within the movement. Their criticism in no way affected their aid to the movement; nor was it translated into activity to replace Fatah or Arafat with one of the Marxist groups. There were numerous signs of discord between Arafat and Moscow over the years, with Arafat cancelling trips to Moscow in 1976 and again in 1981 apparently because of dissatisfaction with Soviet aid to the PLO in Lebanon. After the 1982 Lebanese war there were open signs of Soviet dissatisfaction, resulting in the gradual but almost total reduction of Soviet training and arming of Fatah, a refusal to invite Arafat to the Soviet Union, and actual Soviet criticism of Arafat, both publicly and privately, in connection with his political moves with King Hussein.[303] There may even have been an attempt to curry favor with high officials of Fatah (and close associates of Arafat's) when they expressed reservations about these policies, though it is difficult to know if the Soviets actually believed that Arafat might be replaced by one of them.[304] Regarding those Fatah and non-Fatah forces that actually did seek to unseat Arafat, the Soviets actually maintained a neutral position. Even while criticizing Arafat, mildly and usually indirectly, Moscow neither assisted nor supported the rebels in any way. It did strengthen its ties with the Marxist organizations, but even in dealing with them the Soviets strongly opposed a formal split in the PLO and the creation of a rival organization.[305] Thus they urged all concerned (including the Syrians) to find a compromise solution in hopes of achieving unity and even mediated an internal PLO settlement in 1986–87.

Despite their disagreement with Arafat's post-1982 tactics, the Soviets have not assisted in overthrowing him, although they have probably tried to use the split to restrain some of his policy preferences even in a reunited PLO. The reasons for this reluctance fully to break with Arafat may be found not only in the limited size, power, and prestige of the alternative groups or leaders, but also in the affinity of Moscow and Arafat's *basic* positions regarding a Middle East settlement, as distinct from the "rejectionist" alternatives within the PLO. The disagreement was over Arafat's new American-oriented tactics. While the Soviets' dissatisfaction with the leadership led them temporarily to reduce material aid to Arafat's own forces, they were been careful not to permit this to affect support, political and material, for the PLO as a whole.

One phenomenon which occurred with the PLO, and which raises questions about Soviet policies regarding the organization of other movements, was the creation of a Palestinian Communist party in late 1981. This had been preceded by two earlier attempts to create a communist Palestinian liberation movement (1970, al-Ansar; 1973, the Palestine National Front) as a member organization in the broader PLO framework. Presumably an effort to achieve a degree of influence over the roof-organization, none of these was, however, necessarily envisaged as an alternative or rival to the PLO itself. Indeed, in the case of the PNF and the PCP, the new organs provided a vehicle for legal or semi-legal activity in the occupied territories (in which the PLO itself was banned). Yet they also strove to expand their presence within the PLO and especially in its highest organs. Al-Ansar and the PNF generally failed (and disappeared); the later PCP achieved somewhat greater success. The creation of the PCP, however, was most likely connected with growing Soviet support for the idea of an independent Palestinian state which demanded a clearer Soviet delineation between Jordan and

Palestinian territories envisaged for the future state. This was reflected first by the creation of a Palestinian Communist organization (out of the West Bank branch of the Jordanian Communist party) in 1974, and then a full-fledged communist party in late 1981, officially 1982.[306]

There were two precedents of the same general period for the creation of a communist party alongside an existing national liberation movement: the People's Revolutionary party of South Vietnam (1982) and the Communist party of East Pakistan (1969?). The three cases together might suggest that the Soviets authorized or sought the creation of a communist party when they became committed to independence or foresaw it as inevitable, regardless of the nature of the movement (anti-colonial, separatist, "internal"). Yet there are caveats which may render these cases exceptions rather than the rule.

Aside from the fact that it is not at all certain that the Soviets agreed with the idea of Bangladesh independence prior to the war, the party itself was *not* the Communist party of Bangladesh until December 1971. It was, in fact, the Eastern branch of the clandestine Pakistan Communist party, the Eastern and Western branches of which had little contact with each other. This Eastern branch was not only by far the larger branch (an estimated 2,500 members as distinct from 500 in West Pakistan), but it also had an historical continuity as part of the Bengali branch of the Indian Communist Party prior to the creation of Pakistan (and the split of Bengal).[307] It emerged publicly in 1969 as the Communist party of East Pakistan when it sent a delegation to the 1969 Moscow Conference of Communist and Workers' Parties.[308] Yet a relatively detailed 1970 Soviet account of the political forces and organizations in East and West Pakistan failed to mention anything but the banned Pakistan Communist party.[309] Nonetheless, the "Central Committee of the Communist Party of East Pakistan" was noted as sending greetings to the CPSU Congress of March 1971.[310]

At the least, there is some uncertainty that this party actually achieved independent status prior to Moscow's recognition of Bangladesh statehood, although it did have something of an independent historical and organizational base, from the time of the creation of East (and West) Pakistan in 1949. Its preferred ally (and target for penetration) was the National Awami party, described by Moscow as the leader of the progressive forces of East Pakistan; but when the communists sought membership in the Bangladesh government-in-exile in India, they cooperated with the Awami League insofar as that party permitted.[311] The South Vietnamese PRP was even more doubtful, in that it was little more than the southern branch of the Vietnamese Communist party based in Hanoi.[312] It was purposely *not* given the status of a communist party (for reasons of southern politics), while its independence of Hanoi was highly questionable. It must also be noted that the creation of the

PRP did not necessitate Soviet approval inasmuch as the Vietnamese Communist party was generally independent of the Soviets at the time. One explanation of Hanoi's decision to create the PRP was the desire to have a local instrument for control of the NLF; indeed, PRP people permeated the movement, particularly the control organs.[313]

While the creation of the above three parties did provide, in each case, a nascent organizational structure appropriate to an anticipated independent state, such a step did not in fact constitute the norm. Indeed, in one case just the opposite process was true; that is, a local communist party was actually dissolved to create a national liberation movement. This occurred in 1956, when the Angolan Communist party was amalgamated with other groups, just one year after its own creation, to form the MPLA.[314] These origins probably account for the close relationship that the MPLA maintained with the Portuguese Communist party. Such a relationship was *not* evident on the part of the other two anti-Portuguese movements, PAIGC and FRELIMO. Nor was there any attempt to create a communist party in Guinea-Bissau or Mozambique, or in the other two African countries containing anti-colonial movements: Zimbabwe and Namibia. Thus, aside from the somewhat ambiguous case of South Vietnam, there was no Soviet attempt to create or maintain a communist party alongside an anti-colonial movement, even when independence was clearly supported and even imminent.

The same could be said for virtually all the other movements as well. With the possible exception of East Pakistan, no communist party has been created for a secessionist nation or alongside a secessionist movement even when supported by the Soviets. Similarly, unlike the Palestinians, the other "internal" case—that of the Polisario—saw no creation of a communist party. What did occur for the "internals," and the secessionists supported by Moscow, was Soviet encouragement of cooperation between the movement and the existing central communist party of the country, when such a party existed. Such cooperation was successfully achieved between the ANC and the South African Communist party, Africa's oldest communist party, founded in 1921, ten years after the ANC. Whatever the historical reasons for its creation, this party has provided cadres and leadership, particularly for the military wing of the ANC, as well as other types of assistance. Communists have played a large role inside the ANC itself, although they achieved membership in its highest body only in June 1985. This cooperation has been the subject of some dispute within the ANC—not, apparently, so much because of opposition to Moscow, but because of racial preferences for black nationalism on the part of some (and just plain nationalism as distinct from Marxism for others). Nonetheless, ANC–South African Communist party cooperation is almost exceptional, not only in its closeness and openness, but also by virtue of the fact that the ANC has maintained its independence.[315]

Cooperation has been sought and often achieved between the communist parties of Turkey, Iraq, and Iran and the local Kurds, between that of Sri Lanka and the Tamils (to a lesser degree), and between that of Pakistan and the Baluchis and Pathans; cooperation between the Tudeh and the Arabs of Khuzistan was rumored but was never in any way acknowledged by communist or Soviet sources. In the case of the Polisario, there has been political support by the Moroccan Communist party, but the major cooperative relationship has been with the Algerian Communist party rather than the party in Rabat (presumably because of Soviet–Moroccan relations, as we shall see below). In the absence of a "central" party, cooperation has been sought in some cases with an outside communist party—for example, the Eritreans' cooperation with the Italian Communist party, although this, like the Algerian–Polisario case, may not have been at Soviet instigation, as demonstrated by continued Italian communist support of the Eritreans even after the change in the Soviet position regarding Eritrea.

Other instances of cooperation may also have been at least partially independent of Moscow. Many Iraqi communists, for example, were themselves Kurds, and some even split off to fight in Kurdistan when Moscow withdrew its support of the Kurds. There was a similar case of a split in the Syrian Communist party in the early 1970s, in part over Soviet reticence at the time fully to endorse the Palestinians. With the case of the Turkish Kurds, cooperation of the communist party was apparently encouraged, but, according to one report, Kurdish communists in Turkey were ordered by the Communist party to leave the various Kurdish organizations and limit their organizational ties to the Communist party alone.[316] In the case of the PFLOAG, FROLINAT, and the Katangans, there were no local or even neighboring communist parties with which to encourage cooperation, but in the Katangan case there was cooperation with the MPLA and Cubans in Angola, and in the case of Dhofar, with the ruling Marxists of South Yemen.

It is difficult to determine if cooperation with an existing communist party—locally or beyond the border—has been a condition for Soviet support to a secessionist movement; it clearly has not been with regard to anti-colonials. The fact that the Soviets have not sought to create communist parties for the separatist areas (Kurdistan, Baluchistan, etc.) would suggest the limits of Soviet commitment, and, specifically, their lack of interest in independence as distinct from autonomy, and/or the belief that success is not inevitable. In this sense, Bangladesh could be the exception that proves the rule: creation of a party when independence is supported and deemed likely. Presumably the same could be said for non-secessionists as well as in the case of the South Vietnamese and Palestinians. Yet, given the caveats noted above regarding at least the Vietnamese and Pakistani cases, plus the fact that the Soviets did not create parties for the anti-colonials such as Zimbabwe, Namibia, Angola, Guinea-Bissau, and Mozambique, no general conclusion is readily apparent.

Even if one were to conclude that the creation of a communist party was an indication of Soviet commitment and interest in independent statehood, the opposite need not be true. Failure to create a party is not necessarily an indication of the absence of such a commitment or interest, at least not in the anti-colonial situation. Indeed, in the purely anti-colonial struggle, the Soviets may actually prefer the broadly based movement, as the sole vehicle for national struggle, to a communist party, as is suggested by the dissolution of the Angolan Communist party. Alternatively, the decision to create a communist party where none existed may not be a matter of preferences for one organizational framework or another but, rather, a function of local, possibly regional, circumstances which might mitigate for or against such a party.

Soviet preferences for as broadly based unity as possible, at least for the anti-colonial movements, have been apparent in the admonitions not only for unification within the movements, but also for unity or at least cooperation between movements within one country. One Soviet account claims that such unity was actually achieved among the Angolan movements, and that the rival UNITA and FNLA rebelled only after independence; other accounts portray UNITA and sometimes FNLA as splinter groups with no basis in the country.[317] Nonetheless, cooperation with one or both of them was continuously advocated by the Soviets, who did not accord the MPLA official status as the sole legitimate representative of the Angolan people prior to independence. This did not, however, affect Soviet assistance or political support. Nor, as we have seen, did it prevent the Soviets from pressing for exclusive recognition for the MPLA from the OAU. The long sought unity was achieved among the Zimbabweans, although this apparently had little to do with any activity on the part of the Soviets. It did however permit Moscow to refer to the resultant Patriotic Front as the sole legitimate representative of the Zimbabwean people and—at least theoretically—to distribute its aid in a less discriminatory fashion.[318] Yet, in fact, Soviet practice and policy changed little, suggesting that factors other than the organizational framework dictated Soviet support.

Unity has been recommended for the organizations of Namibia, but support has always gone exclusively to SWAPO, acknowledged by Moscow as the sole legitimate representative of the Namibian people (albeit some years after the UN accorded SWAPO that status in 1973).[319] The rival SWANU, if referred to, has been depicted as a particularistic ethnic-based group (of the Hereros).[320] The NFL of South Vietnam was also accorded that status, to distinguish it not from rival liberation organizations but from the colonial regime and its organizations. PAIGC had no rival liberation group with which to contend, possibly accounting for the fact that it was not referred to by Moscow as the sole legitimate representative. Yet FRELIMO, which did have a small rival liberation group (said to have no roots in the country),[321] was similarly treated; that is, like the other anti-Portuguese movements, it was not designated the sole legitimate representative, suggesting that such a characterization has less to do with organizational questions than with other problems such as inclusion in negotiations—of which there were none for the Portuguese colonies. This might account for the fact that, alone among the "internals," the PLO has been accorded such status. Official Soviet acknowledgment of the PLO as the sole legitimate representative of the Palestinians occurred quite late (1978), at a time of no significant organizational development but, as we shall see below, at a time of quite significant development in the realm of negotiations.[322]

With regard to the other two "internals" (Polisario and ANC), Soviet treatment is somewhat less clear. While there is no rival liberation organization to the Polisario, Moscow has only sporadically referred to it as the sole legitimate representative,[323] on some occasions speaking of it only as "the most influential political and military force in the western Sahara national liberation movement," the "most influential organ," or "the spokesman" of the people.[324] Nonetheless, the frequent positive references to the recognition of SADR, under the leadership of the Polisario, suggests that it is not an organizational problem dictating this apparently different approach.

In the case of the ANC, this movement, so fully supported by the Soviets, has also only very rarely been referred to as the sole legitimate representative. If any characterization is employed at all, it is usually "the true [or genuine] representative of the African people in South Africa."[325] In May 1985, one Soviet source called it "*an* organization at the forefront of the fight against the racist regime."[326] The Soviets have advocated the idea of unity within a broadly based mass front, sometimes defining the ANC as that mass organization. This hesitancy to demand (or accord) total exclusivity for the ANC may be a reflection of ANC policies, at least insofar as that organization has advocated the creation of a single (legal) front for all the liberation forces. In this connection, the Soviet Union has supported the UDF, created in 1983, calling it a "roof organization" operating under the same principles as the ANC.[327] Inasmuch as the illegal ANC fully endorses (and is often identified with) the UDF, there is no problem here of rivalry. Rather, the UDF clearly suits Moscow's preference for mass-based united fronts, without impeding in any way support for the ANC. The Soviet position may also reflect the situation in South Africa, which includes a very large number of anti-regime organizations involved one way or another in the liberation struggle. The Soviets, therefore, leave the way open for contact and possibly cooperation with others, such as the Black Consciousness groups, and support a broad front.[328] This does not prevent them from concentrating their support on the ANC and the South African Communist party. Nor does it prevent them from condemning actual rivals to the ANC such as PAC[329] or, possibly, Gatsha Buthelezi's Inkatha, although a Soviet representative met with Buthelezi in Washington in 1982.[330]

If organizational criteria are at all in effect, there is even less evidence of it with regard to the secessionist movements. Organizationally, there would appear to be little difference between those supported by the Soviets and those opposed. One source has claimed that the Soviets have refrained from helping the Baluchis of Pakistan because of the disarray within the movement.[331] Similar reservations may exist over the Kurds in Turkey, as there have been signs of Soviet concern over the lack of unity among them.[332] And Moscow has implied such a criterion in its discussion, for example, of the disarray within the Eritrean movement and the existence of three rival movements.[333] Generally, however, the *opposed* movements have not been dealt with in such detail. Indeed, even the movements supported have been presented more or less monolithically, and also with little detail.

Even when the secessionist movements have been referred to as representing or leading their people's struggle (as in the case of the Congolese National Liberation Front, the FROLINAT, the PFLOAG, or the Kurdish Democratic Party), exclusivity has been neither claimed nor denied. The PFLOAG, for example, has been called the "largest, most active detachment" of the revolutionary liberation forces, seeking to unite "all patriotic, national forces."[334] In the case of Bangladesh, the National Awami Party was favored by the Soviets until the Awami League's overwhelming victory in the December 1970 elections—after which only the League was mentioned in Soviet media. Insofar as the East Pakistani Communists sought broadly based representation in the government-in-exile and participated in the five-party consultative committee, they appeared to be seeking a broad front.[335] None of this found its way into any Soviet statements (or even later histories), however. Nor does it appear to have been a factor in Soviet support, although it is probably safe to assume that Moscow did urge broad fronts for the secessionist movements in most instances.

Soviet interest in unity may have expressed itself upon occasion in another form, that is, in efforts to create links between the countries. This has been accomplished in the form of regional meetings of movements, such as the 1969 Khartoum conference of pro-Soviet movements or the 1970 Rome meeting of anti-Portuguese movements.[336] The former was in fact perceived as an effort to bypass the OAU–Liberation Committee, inasmuch as aid through this channel often assisted training actually given by the Chinese in Tanzania, for example.[337] The Soviets encouraged—and possibly instigated—the joint actions of ZAPU and the ANC against the Rhodesian government in 1967 and claimed that there was much more cooperation than actually existed.[338] In 1970 an *Izvestiia* article called upon SWAPO to cooperate with the other movements in southern Africa, citing positively the case of ANC–ZAPU cooperation, and in 1973 the *World Marxist Review* extolled what it presented as SWAPO–MPLA, SWAPO–ANC, ANC–ZAPU, and ZAPU–FRELIMO cooperation (although actually FRELIMO was working with ZANU).[339]

While apparently encouraged and considered desirable, such cooperation was by no means a condition or a determinant of Soviet support. Nor does it appear to have been sought outside of Africa. Such cooperation has existed between the PLO and other liberation movements, notably the Eritreans, the Kurds of Turkey, and possibly the Moros. Yet there is no evidence that this cooperation was instigated or even condoned by Moscow; in the case of the Eritreans, it became a source of discord. An exception to this may have been cooperation between the different contingents of the Kurds, the Baluchis, and the Pathans across the state lines dividing each of these peoples. As is generally the case with the secessionists, however, there is very little evidence to go on and, no Soviet mention of the possibility, with the exception of occasional general references to the problems of each of these peoples as a whole.[340] Rather, on many occasions Soviet support for one segment of the people (the Turkish or Iranian Kurds) has not coincided with the support for another segment (the Iraqi Kurds) or vice versa. Conversely, Soviet opposition to one segment (Baluchis in Afghanistan) may generate opposition to another segment's (Baluchis of Iran) helping them. In this last case, cooperation may operate as a deterrent to Soviet support and thus be a factor, but it is both too complex and too specific an example to warrant a generalization.

MEANS

The issue of armed struggle versus political means and/or negotiations, as well as the type of armed struggle, has been the source of some disagreement between Moscow and many movements. It is by no means certain that the Soviets have viewed agreement on this matter as a criterion for support, or if the means chosen have precipitated Soviet opposition to a movement. With regard to the movements more or less consistently opposed (the Ibos, the Anyanya, the Tigreans, the Sikhs, the Moros, and the Burmese minorities), the Soviets have argued that the central government offers a peaceful solution and, therefore, that the movement has been responsible for the introduction of force. Inasmuch as Moscow has denied the justice of these movements demands altogether (with the brief exception of the Moros and possibly, also briefly, the Ibos), the issue of *means* does not appear to have been the determining factor. Indeed, the means chosen by these movements have differed little from those employed by movements that have been supported by Moscow. Nor has this factor been singled out by Moscow as even the ostensible reason for Soviet opposition. Moreover, there is no indication that the Soviets did or would have supported these movements in the absence of armed struggle.

With regard to the movements sporadically supported, the means employed have been the same in the periods of support as in the periods of opposition. What has differed has been the Soviet attitude regarding the legitimacy of the struggle altogether, that is, opposition to the Eritreans' or to the Kurds' persistence in their demands, despite what Moscow claimed as the central governments' willingness to accord autonomy. It is conceivable that the Soviets would have continued to champion the Iraqi Kurds' and the Eritreans' causes had they refrained from the use of armed struggle after Moscow's attitude toward the central government changed to one of close friendship. Indeed, Moscow has urged the government to choose a political situation over civil war in the case of Eritrea, for example.[341] The fact remains, however, that it was the change in attitude toward the central government, not the movements' choice of methods (which remained consistent), that occasioned the reversal of Soviet support for the movement. Armed struggle in the new circumstances simply made the conflict too acute to permit either continued support or even neutrality. Still later, after further changes regarding the central government—in Iraq, for example—the Soviets may have returned to support for armed struggle, for in 1980 the Iraqi Communist party spoke of the fact that the Kurds were compelled to use force because of Bagdad's intransigence.[342] The brief period of support for the Moros included, by implication, support for their use of force. The Soviets' call then for the government to make concessions was explicitly linked to the cease-fire—and was not repeated when the cease-fire was acknowledged to have broken down.[343] While the early Soviet support for the Eritreans was so clandestine that no public evidence is available upon which to judge the Soviet attitude, retrospective accounts as early as 1974 have been critical of the Eritreans' use of force.[344] Retrospective accounts of the Kurds' struggle, however, have been favorable to the use of armed struggle by the Kurds in the period prior to the 1970 agreement.[345]

As in the case of the Eritreans, so too with most of the secessionists with regard to availability of information on just what means the Soviets have recommended. Public expression of support either for armed struggle or political means need not reflect what means the Soviets have actually advocated—or opposed, although where public pronouncements are available the relative weights may suggest something of Soviet preferences. In most cases of the secessionists supported by Moscow, only a political solution or political means (if any) have been mentioned publicly. In the case of the Tamils, the Soviets apparently did urge, or have urged, political means exclusively. When the central Tamil group, the Tigers, fought the India peace-keeping force, the Soviets not only condemned its rejection of political means but also condemned it as "terrorist."[346] Such a characterization, and indeed any condemnation, had been totally absent when the same types of armed struggle were employed, by the same group, during the period of Soviet support. With regard to the Bengalis it was only in retrospect that they have justified the Bengalis' resort to violence, and then only implicitly. Indeed, one of the grievances of the various breakaway communist groups in Pakistan in the late 1960s early 1970s was the Soviet rejection of guerrilla warfare and preference for a political solution.[347] The evidence generally indicates that Moscow persisted in this attitude in 1971 as well, seeking to restrain both the Bengalis and India up to approximately six weeks before the war—at which time, according to one account, the Soviet position changed in response to Pakistani refusal to compromise.[348] In the case of the Tamils, Soviet support was quite limited, while aid to the Bengalis was quite fulsome, though directed apparently through India. In neither case does Soviet opposition to their use of armed struggle appear to have been the decisive factor; political support, at the least, was offered in both cases even as armed struggle was opposed.

In the case of the Baluchis and Pathans of Pakistan, and the Baluchis of Iran, most observers believe that the Soviets have not favored armed struggle, even during the Baluchi uprising of 1973–77.[349] It is possible though that, at least in the case of the Pathans, the Soviets have supported the armed actions of 1985.[350] Altogether, Soviet support of the Baluchis (of Iran as well) and Pathans has vacillated a great deal over the years, while the use of armed struggle by the movements themselves has remained relatively consistent. Thus, as in the case of the Iraqi Kurds and the Eritreans, Soviet preferences regarding means in the Baluchi and Pathan cases would appear to be a function of the overall position and goals at the time. Armed struggle would be considered more or less harmful to Soviet interests; at some times it might even prevent or discourage Soviet support, while at other times it would be considered less harmful and, therefore, tolerable if not actually encouraged. Just what the determining factor has been we shall see below, but the Soviet attitude to the means used would be only an outgrowth of this other factor or factors.

In the case of the Iranian Kurds, at least in the period of some Soviet support for the movement in the early Khomeni period, armed struggle was publicly defended (it was said that the government left no alternative), but both sides were repeatedly urged to seek a political solution, and the weight of Soviet opinion was heavy in the direction of political rather than armed struggle.[351] The same defense of the resort to arms was evident with regard to the FROLINAT and Katangan cases, but in the latter (and possibly the former) the Soviets may have preferred abstention from the use of force.[352] The Cubans, at any rate, claimed to the United States that they had opposed the Katangans' incursion into Shaba, and this may have been the Soviets' position as well.[353] The Dhofar case, similar to the Chad and Zaire situations of what the Soviets have portrayed as internal revolutionary insurrections, has varied from the general Soviet preference for political means. Rather than encourage a political solution, with the occasional justification of armed struggle, in the Dhofar case the Soviets apparently supported the use of force even to the point of trying to convert the guerrilla forces into a more acceptable (to the Soviets) "military army."[354] (The military forces of the rest of the secessionists, if described *at all*, have usually been characterized as "guerrillas"—or, in the case of movements opposed by Moscow, as "insurgents" or "rebels.")

Soviet preferences regarding the anti-colonials have been only somewhat clearer than those regarding the secessionists, but if the latter *tended* to elicit greater Soviet support for political rather than armed means, the anti-colonials have received less hesitant support for their armed struggle. At the very least, the Soviets have been much more open and even enthusiastic about reporting the use of armed struggle, though even in their moments of greatest enthusiasm they have not neglected to encourage political means as well. Moreover, there have also been instances of opposition and efforts at restraint with regard to armed struggle. Yet in only one *possible* case has there been even a hint that the choice of means might have influenced Soviet backing, as we shall see below.

There were a number of instances in the course of the Vietnam war in which Moscow appeared to advocate political means, specifically negotiations, over continuation or augmentation of the military struggle.[355] Most of these instances were reflected in controversies between Moscow and Hanoi, but there were also times, apparently, when the NLF too was involved. For example, pro-Soviet elements are said to have been purged from the NLF in 1968 (after the Tet offensive) because they favored greater emphasis on political rather than military means.[356] The military means, if any, to be used were apparently in keeping with Soviet preferences for regular rather than guerrilla forces (while the Chinese urged only guerrilla action in the South).[357] After the Paris agreement, in 1973 and possibly 1974, the Soviets reportedly were "fainthearted" about a return to armed struggle to topple Thieu.[358] Inasmuch as Soviet aid to North Vietnam is said to have been quite limited in this period, there may be reason to believe that Moscow's support was indeed affected by Hanoi's choice of military means. Moscow's political support for the Vietnamese, however, was not, as far as can be determined, ever reduced because of this, though it is entirely possible that the Soviets also urged more flexible Vietnamese positions in the negotiations, even while supporting the more inflexible public demands of both the NLF and Hanoi.[359]

In Africa at roughly the same time, the Soviets fully supported the armed struggle of the anti-Portuguese movements (aside from the brief suspension of aid to the MPLA apparently connected with organizational and personnel issues). Yet they appeared to prefer political methods as an important part of, if not the only, means to be used. The Portuguese government was said to be unlikely to agree to any acceptable conditions for negotiations, leaving the movements no choice but to abandon peaceful means and opt for prolonged armed struggle.[360] At the same time, it was emphasized that these movements were willing to negotiate, and that they considered political means no less important than armed struggle.[361] In one article, FRELIMOs armed struggle was even said to be part of the political battle, while PAIGC's struggle was described as *primarily* political.[362]

In keeping with this, the internal organizational and social activities of these movements in the areas they had liberated was given coverage by the Soviets, and retrospective accounts have emphasized the movements' (particularly PAIGC's) appreciation of the value of political work without glorification of armed struggle.[363] Whether a sign of Soviet commitment or simply approval, PAIGC's military effort was singled out as one of a "regular people's army," combined with guerrilla forces.[364] Indeed the Soviets urged PAIGC to convert its forces into a regular army, although this was not done. MPLA and FRELIMO were described by one 1974 study as being at the earlier or lesser stage of "guerrilla" warfare, but in retrospect the MPLA's battle has been variously termed guerrilla, guerrilla/conventional, and, in another 1974 study, a guerrilla war which developed into a conventional war.[365] The MPLA's rejection of terrorism has been commended, but nowhere has actual approval or disapproval for any of the methods used been expressed.[366] In fact, there does not appear to have been Soviet disapproval even of FRELIMO's use of Chinese training and tactics.

The only sign of active Soviet pursuit of political over armed struggle in connection with the anti-Portuguese movements would appear to have been limited to efforts to achieve a peaceful resolution of the problems between the different Angolan movements, though it was in this struggle that the Soviets offered their greatest support. Most of their more direct support was rendered the MPLA after formal independence, but even that which arrived earlier (particularly large arms supplies) was accompanied by efforts to forestall military conflict.[367] There is some controversy over the sincerity of these efforts, but it appears that the Soviets advised some sort of coalition not only in connection with the 1974 Alvor Agreement but in the months prior to independence as well, even as they assisted the MPLA in its military struggle.[368]

The position with regard to ZAPU was much more complicated. One of the persistent complaints against ZAPU over the years, and one of the (many) factors behind the split and creation of ZANU in 1963, was the movement's preference for political over military means.[369] ZAPU was much better armed than ZANU but generally was reluctant to engage in battle.[370] There is no indication, however, that this was necessarily the result of Soviet influence or preferences. ZAPU was the first major movement in Zimbabwe to approach the Soviet Union, before the ZANU break-off, and there appeared to be agreement on the issue of political versus military means rather than one side pressing the other or choosing the other for this reason. In an article criticizing ZANU, the Soviets accused the Chinese of inciting the Africans to armed struggle, and Moscow commended ZAPU's appreciation of the value of political means.[371] The armed actions undertaken by ZAPU together with the ANC in 1967 were in fact uncharacteristic, both for ZAPU (and the ANC) and for the Soviet Union, particularly because they preceded rather than followed intensive political work. One observer has explained this anomaly by citing the dominant influence at the time of Cuban concepts of struggle.[372] In any case, the Soviets appeared to support, possibly even encourage, Nkomo's talks with Smith in 1974 and the negotiating efforts of 1974–75.[373]

On the other hand, in 1977 the Soviets appeared to be trying to convert the ZAPU military arm (ZIPRA) into a conventional force. This would be in keeping with Soviet preferences for regular over guerrilla forces, and need not indicate an actual intention to commit such forces in all-out war. Indeed, as early as the 1967 joint ZAPU–ANC action, praised if not actually encouraged by Moscow, conventional rather than guerrilla techniques were used.[374] However, there were also reports in 1977 that the Soviets were not only preparing for but actually were encouraging such an offensive.[375] It was at this time that Moscow clearly opposed the various negotiating efforts, and there were the rumors of a possible switch to Mugabe, who *was* willing to fight. *Pravda* even quoted Mugabe on the futility of political means (strikes, passive resistance) and the efficacy *only* of armed struggle.[376]

While there is little evidence that the Soviets actually contemplated a shift to Mugabe there were reportedly some (possibly the Soviet military mission sent to Zambia to reorganize ZAPU's army in 1978)[377] who recommended such a move, while others (apparently the Soviet ambassador to Zambia, Africanist Solodovnikov) preferred the political path. In any case, Soviet propaganda from 1977 on spoke of the intensified armed struggle and generally condemned the various attempts at negotiations, although continuing to emphasize the desirability of a dual approach—military and political means.[378] In fact, the Soviets appeared to favor negotiations, but not in the framework of those actually taking place (under Western auspices).[379] Similar ambivalence characterized their response to the Lancaster House talks in 1979, Soviet media praising the PF's flexibility while condemning the forum.[380] Moreover, there was not in fact a deployment of ZAPU forces in 1977 or after, and there were even subsequent reports of ZAPU dissatisfaction over Soviet arms deliveries. It is by no means certain, however, that the inadequacy of Soviet aid, if it in fact existed, was a form of Soviet pressure or an expression of Soviet hesitancy regarding armed struggle. Nkomo himself was apparently still opposed to a large military move.[381] The Soviet media, in any case, never expressed any dissatisfaction with ZAPU's methods, referring to terrorist actions only generally, if at all, as acts of sabotage.[382]

A somewhat similar picture of ambivalence emerges over the Soviet attitude to SWAPO's armed struggle. As in the case of the other African movements, here too armed struggle has not been openly condemned, particularly after Soviet involvement with SWAPO increased in the second half of the 1970s. In 1970, for example, a Soviet journal published SWAPO claims that non-violence was not effective and, therefore, had given way to armed struggle; but it also claimed that strikes, civil disobedience, demonstrations, and meetings continued to be used together with armed struggle.[383] A footnote in a *World Marxist Review* article in 1973 "defined" SWAPO's meaning of the term "armed struggle" by referring the reader to an article on strikes in Namibia as an example of "struggle."[384] By the mid-1970s, however, the public Soviet position supported armed struggle, even quoting SWAPO leaders to the effect that this was the "only" effective means.[385] Some of these accounts were derogatory about negotiations, warning against political maneuvres, even as they asserted that SWAPO was ready for talks at any time.[386] In the 1980s, support for armed action has become still more enthusiastic. Not only has guerrilla warfare against "industrial–military targets" been praised,[387] but SWAPO has been said to have grown over the years from small detachments of guerrillas to a "people's liberation army" conducting a "real peoples war."[388] Nonetheless, most of these accounts have spoken of simultaneous political work, even negotiations, though not negotiations of the type initiated by the West.[389] Indeed, there were even reports, at least in the 1978–79 period, that Moscow was restraining SWAPO (ostensibly because of ideological disagreement, or in order to await the termination of the struggle in Zimbabwe).[390] This would roughly correspond to the time of the 1978–79 problems within SWAPO over the issue of negotiations or intensified armed struggle (which was complicated by opposition to Nujoma's leadership, as we have seen).[391] If the Soviets were indeed restraining SWAPO in this period, they would have sided with the majority position favoring negotiations. Yet Soviet rejection of resolution 435 at that time suggests the opposite position, as do contemporary Soviet media. And other Western observers claim that the Soviets were not in fact restraining SWAPO,[392] although Moscow did come around to accepting resolution 435.

In summary, the armed struggle waged by the anti-colonials evoked some ambivalence on the part of the Soviets. In all cases, both political and armed means have been encouraged, with occasional preference for one over the other—to some degree depending upon the framework of the proposed negotiations. Soviet hesitation over guerrilla warfare has been apparent in the effort to convert, or at the very least to portray, these struggles as conventional or mixed guerrilla–conventional ones. Such portrayal has generally implied support. With the possible but unlikely exception of a rumored shift to Mugabe in the late 1970s, there is no evidence that the Soviet attitude to the means employed has actually influenced Soviet support one way of another. Restraint may have been attempted (in the NLF, ZAPU, SWAPO, and possibly even MPLA cases), but if so this did not actually affect relations.

The ANC would appear to fall within this same pattern of ambivalence, with the Soviets at least occasionally emphasizing if not pressing for political over armed means. The fact that the South African Communists were those who set up (in 1961) and still run the military wing of the ANC (Umkonto we Sizwe) is certainly evidence of Soviet support for the use of armed struggle.[393] There is also praise of armed struggle, including relatively detailed accounts of what are called guerrilla or sabotage actions, said to be directed against military–industrial targets (though traitors have also been mentioned as targets).[394] ANC (and South African Communists) have been frequently quoted on the need for intensification of the armed struggle or, at the least, the legitimacy of all means including armed struggle.[395] Yet the ANC more than any other movement has developed an instrumental theory of armed struggle by which military or para-military action is seen not as a means to win independence (majority rule), but as "a catalyst" for "inspiring the masses" and forging a "mass political movement" in order to achieve political goals.[396] Thus, as the Soviets have explained, the ANC has rejected terrorism so as not to alienate the whites with whom they might one day cooperate.[397] They formed a para-military arm for guerrilla actions against military and industrial targets, but they have not been said to have either a guerrilla or regular army.[398] They have also been cited as opposing the absolutization of the use of armed struggle.[399] Political work, the Soviets have maintained, has been an equal part of the ANC's tasks, including not only organization and propaganda but also political means of struggle (e.g., strikes, political agitation, student protests).[400]

It is not entirely clear just where the Soviets stood during the internal ANC debates of 1975–78 and 1984–85 over the relative weight of armed versus political methods, but on at least one occasion they were accused of trying to direct the ANC toward "diplomacy" rather than armed struggle.[401] It may have been in the context of these debates that Soviet publications spoke of the priority of political work, or at least put strong emphasis on political work and the specific rejection of terrorism.[402] One authoritative account even spoke of the need for protracted political preparations before armed struggle could take any serious form.[403] Yet in the 1970s, at least, there was no lack of references to the desirability of armed struggle combined with political work. In the pre-1985 Congress debates Soviet preferences appear to have been clearer, with reported efforts to restrain the ANC. The *World Marxist Review* (after a South African government call for the ANC to abandon violence) did publish one ANC view on armed struggle as the main means of action, with arguments as to why it should be stepped up.[404] Yet articles in March and April 1985 in *Mezhdunarodnaia zhizn'* spoke of both military and political means with political and organizational work and mass political action as the "most important" tasks, higher in priority than armed struggle.[405] Reporting on the Congress itself, the Soviets referred indirectly to the debate, claiming that unity was preserved on the basis of decisions "to step up the struggle," including the "broadening of the political and military offensive." Ignoring Western reports of the victory of those who had sought stepped-up violence, now even to include "soft targets" (i.e. terrorism), the Soviets blithely placed "armed actions against apartheid" *last* in the list of actions (strikes, protest demonstrations) praised at the Congress for inspiring the masses.[406] This account did mention, however, the ANC's rejection of negotiations "under present conditions."

According to a Western source, the Ccmmunist commander of the military wing, Joe Slovo (the first white elected to the ANC executive board, which occurred at this Congress), opposed the idea of terrorism, that is, actions against civilians, and spoke of concentrating even more on political organizing (even as he spoke of extending the range of military actions) and exploiting the "combat potential for political motion."[407] Yet in an interview with a non-Soviet magazine a year later, Slovo spoke of the essential role played by "revolutionary violence," and of the possibility of hitting civilians (who were in the vicinity of military targets or were defined as military personnel by virtue of belonging to the "white farmer class"). [408] Thus Slovo himself expressed contradictory views, for even as he praised such actions, he reiterated the need for a combination of political and armed means. Armed struggle for him was "inspirational," for emboldening the masses, but it was not the means by which to achieve victory.

After the 1985 Congress, the Soviet media appeared to fall in line with the Congress's more hard-line decisions when they reported an ANC executive member, on stages of "national uprising," quoted as saying: "a people's war is not merely possible, it is now inevitable." [409] This was quite new language for the Soviet media in the context of South Africa, but a few months later the same journal took a contradictory position when it claimed that an increasing number of whites favored negotiations with the ANC, and that the South African government would not be able to resist pressures for a peaceful solution. [410] Moreover, an interview with Joe Slovo failed to mention armed struggle at all, devoting much attention to strike activities and legal actions, implying that the violence (which was not, however, condemned) was the spontaneous work of young people acting on their own initiative. [411] Similar omissions were apparent in Soviet articles late in 1985, although the existence of a "revolutionary situation" was noted. [412] Whether this represents continued disagreement or not, there has been no sign of any alteration in the Soviets' fulsome support for the ANC before or after the Congress.

While the Soviet attitude toward the means used by the ANC resembles that regarding the anti-colonial movements, the attitude toward the PLO has been significantly less ambivalent. Both before and after the beginning of Moscow's involvement with the movement, Soviet officials and even the media expressed opposition to the use of armed struggle by the Palestinians. While generally referring to the use of terror, this opposition was explicitly applied to the idea of guerrilla warfare as well. [413] Indeed, this difference of opinion over means was the source of some conflict between Moscow and various elements within the PLO over the years, particularly with George Habash's PFLP.

Early criticism of the idea of guerrilla warfare for the PLO was expressed directly, in comments to the effect that suitable conditions did not exist or were not effective in the case of the Palestinians, as well as in criticism of the Chinese for encouraging adventurist ideas among the Palestinians of a "people's war." [414] An early commentary clearly stated that guerrilla war could not regain the lost territories, and the idea of armed struggle was condemned as "extremist" or adventuristic. [415]

This blanket condemnation of armed struggle of any kind, including guerrilla warfare, was apparently altered in the early 1970s, a distinction finally being made between terror and other types of armed action. Thus, in 1970 the Soviets reportedly urged Arafat to restrict such actions to sabotage only, and this within the occupied territories.[416] That this was preferred over terrorism as such (international or within the territories and Israel) was demonstrated by both the public, often vociferous, Soviet criticism of Palestinian terrorism and by the attempts (a) to dissociate the PLO publicly from such actions (by claiming them to be the work of splinter groups or even of Israeli intelligence); (b) to portray them as sabotage or guerrilla acts against military installations or personnel; and/or (c) to ignore them altogether.[417] This public stance was accompanied by repeated comments in the Soviet press and to Arafat himself, on the occasion of PLO visits to the Soviet Union, for example, in 1973 and 1974.[418] *Pravda* said in 1972 that "adventuristic" attacks on non-military targets were bad for the Palestinian image, and *Izvestiia* in 1974 expressed disapproval of the PLO's methods.[419] The 1974 Soviet break with Habash and both the private and public polemics between the two focused on this issue as well as others. There was some talk of a change in the Soviet position when it patched up its rift with Habash, whose people began to train first in Cuba and then in the Soviet Union after 1978; but according to some sources, the Soviets still sought to restrain Habash on this issue.[420]

Many Soviet condemnations of terrorism did express approval of sabotage and operations against military targets, that is, guerrilla warfare. Some retrospective Soviet accounts have even explained that it was the PLO's failure to organize guerrilla warfare that had led to the use of terror, though most accounts have claimed that terror was part of the "extremist" errors of the PLO in its early stages (and leadership), rejected by the mature PLO.[421] The idea of non-terroristic armed struggle was apparently condoned, for the occupied territories, with the creation of the PNF in 1973. This group was said to have been formed in part to organize armed resistance in the territories. Yet in 1974 a journalist who accompanied Arafat to Moscow said that the Soviets still opposed armed struggle, preferring political solutions (even in these crisis situations).[422] Indeed, the PNF did concentrate on political activity, and the idea of armed struggle rarely appeared in Soviet comments on the PLO or the Palestinian question.

Not only was armed struggle generally opposed for the PLO, but the idea of a political solution was emphasized and proposed in a number of ways by the Soviets. Almost all of the comments critical of terror or even guerrilla warfare urged an understanding of the importance of political and diplomatic struggle. Certain radical states (Algeria, Iraq, and the PDRY) were even criticized for "practically ignoring the non-military methods of resolving the Palestinian problem, clearly underestimating political means of struggle."[423] For many years the Soviets sought PLO acceptance of Security Council resolution 242 so that they could participate in negotiations at an international conference. This involved Moscow in a double problem with the PLO; for this position entailed not only the idea of a negotiated solution, but also acceptance of Israel—both of which were not entirely amenable to the PLO. These pressures dissipated when it appeared that the PLO might opt for exclusively American mediation on the basis of resolution 242, but the Soviets have neither abandoned their advocacy of political means nor supported the idea of armed struggle as a result. Rather, they have continued to press even the Palestinians to opt *only* for an international conference to negotiate a settlement (with Soviet participation and guarantees).[424]

As in other cases (of states as well as national liberation movements[425]), Soviet support and even arms deliveries and training have not been affected by the basic preference for political means over military ones. There have been serious complaints by Arafat over the years (even to the point of postponing visits to the Soviet Union) about Moscow's refusal to supply the quantity and types of weapons requested. It is difficult to determine, however, if this has been an attempt to use arms supplies as a lever of control intended to limit the armed struggle. Typical of their preference for regular over guerrilla forces, the Soviets did begin to convert PLO forces in Lebanon into a conventional army in the early 1980s or possibly slightly earlier.[426] Arafat reportedly was interested in such a transformation, even though it would render the PLO much less suited to the type of struggle it waged best, with no hope of becoming a match for the Israeli army in conventional warfare. It also rendered the PLO vulnerable during the long conversion process.[427] Just what the conversion was intended for is not clear, but, as in the case of ZAPU, it did not necessarily indicate a readiness to have the movement go into battle. Rather, it illustrated Soviet preferences for the type of warfare Moscow understood, despite the handicaps or delays it created for the movement.

Thus, with regard to the PLO as with anti-colonial movements, Soviet opposition to the means of struggle chosen has not been, apparently, strong enough or significant enough to affect actual support for the movement. Soviet willingness, despite the continued expression of such opposition, to assist in training and arming (possibly with some limitations and different priorities) clearly suggests that the means chosen by a movement is not a primary factor—if a factor at all—in Soviet calculations. It is almost ironic that Soviet aid began to fall off (for Fatah) when Arafat was attacked internally for preferring political over military means. Yet, the dispute within the PLO was not only over this issue. More important, Soviet opposition to Arafat was over the vehicle being considered by Arafat for a political settlement—the Americans—not the choice itself.[428]

The last case, that of the Polisario, may be somewhat different, placing it closer to the secessionists in the area of the Soviets' position on means. Although *occasionally* Soviet media have referred to the Polisario's use of armed struggle in the form of guerrilla warfare,[429] the vast majority of pronouncements speak only of, and advocate, a political solution. Without in any way criticizing the Polisario's use of force—the implication is generally that Morocco has rejected peaceful means—the Soviets have claimed that "progressives want a political not military solution."[430] In keeping with this, the Soviets have espoused—and encouraged—the UN and OAU idea of a referendum in the western Sahara, as well as direct negotiations.[431] According to Moscow, Morocco accepted the former, but rejected the latter.[432] There are no reports of conflict between the Soviets' clearly stated preference for political means and the Polisario's use of armed struggle (with Algerian help), but if such disagreement does exist, there is no sign that it has affected what support the Soviets have been willing to render. As in the case of many separatist movements, it is difficult to know if the Soviets would be willing to become more directly involved if there were no actual fighting, but it may be said that this has not interfered with Moscow's political support for the movement.

External Factors

THE CHINESE

Given the Soviet tendency to criticize the Chinese (and vice versa) in every possible context, it is not surprising to find Soviet rhetoric against the Chinese with regard to national liberation movements. This is particularly the case in view of the centrality of such movements, and the Third World in general, in Chinese theory. Moreover, the Sino-Soviet dispute resulted in actual competition for the loyalty not only of communist parties and states, but also—sometimes even primarily—of the national liberation movements. What is difficult to determine, however, is when the competition was merely rhetoric and when it actually determines Soviet behavior.

In the case of the NLF, there would appear to be little doubt that Chinese interest in the movement and in the conflict in Vietnam was of great concern to Moscow, prompting increased Soviets involvement in the mid-1960s.[433] It may be argued that the Soviets wanted an end to the conflict so as to limit whatever gains the Chinese might elicit from the ongoing war. There were, for example, differences between the Soviets and the Chinese over the desirability of increased fighting in the South (the Chinese favoring, Soviets opposing).[434] Yet, to slacken support in any way because of this would only have served to strengthen the Chinese position with the Vietnamese. As it was, the Soviets strove to prove their interest—and to discredit the Chinese—in what was actually competition with Beijing from Moscow's point of view.

While the Soviets sought Vietnamese loyalty in the Sino-Soviet conflict, they did not actually demand exclusivity in their aid. Indeed, they proposed a joint assistance plan (refused by the Chinese), in part to embarrass the Chinese, in part because Chinese cooperation was needed to transport Soviet aid. Nonetheless, from the Soviet point of view, this was a zero-sum competition insofar as Soviet default promised to redound to the Chinese and future Chinese influence. The details of the Sino-Soviet competition in Vietnam and the ways in which it moulded Soviet behavior on specific issues are quite complex.[435] But this competition clearly played a role in Soviet calculations and behavior, for simple geo-political as well as ideological reasons. This is not to say that the Soviets would *not* have supported the communist-led national liberation struggle if there had been no Chinese factor; but the degree and type of Soviet involvement may well have been different.

A similarly central function of the Chinese factor was probably to be found in the case of Bangladesh, regardless of the separatist nature of this movement. In this case, it was not a question of competing with Chinese support for the movement (and the state behind the movement), but actually the opposite: supporting the movement because of the relationship with China of the state (Pakistan) opposing the movement—and an interest in maintaining an anti–Chinese position of the state (India) that supported the movement.

The role of Soviet–Pakistani and Soviet–Indian relations in Moscow's position vis-à-vis the East Bengalis will be discussed below. The Chinese factor enters, however, insofar as Pakistan's increasingly positive relationship with Beijing impelled the Soviets to abandon efforts to improve their own relations with Islamabad and actually oppose it, from early 1970 apparently, and therefore to support the East Pakistanis. According to one account, Soviet fear of improving Chinese–Indian relations also spurred Moscow to take a decisively pro-Indian (and, therefore, pro-Bengali) position in India's dispute with Pakistan.[436] However, the Soviet–Indian Friendship Treaty of August 1971 and the subsequent support for the Bengalis was also said to have been the result, at least in part, of Soviet concern over the revelation of a Chinese–American rapprochement.[437] At the very least, it may be said that Moscow became involved, even to the point of naval activity, in order to counter what it perceived as Chinese gains or threats. Other calculations played a perhaps equally central role, but the Chinese factor was a most significant one, particularly in the initial formulation of the Soviet position. Soviet propaganda itself gave some attention to this factor, exploiting the situation not only to discredit the Chinese for "selling out" a national liberation movement so as to pursue their own interests, but also to explain Moscow's position against what it called Chinese–American collusion to back the Pakistani government against the Bengalis in order to combat India as the leader of the Third World.[438]

The significance of the Chinese factor in the Bangladesh case is substantiated to some degree by the different behavior of the Soviets toward the Baluchis and Pathans of Pakistan. As we shall see below, Soviet support for these peoples varied in accord with a number of local and regional factors; and in an earlier period—the 1960s—Soviet efforts to compete with China for Pakistani favor were said to have caused Moscow to abandon its support for the Pathans and Baluchis.[439] Pakistan's refusal to cooperate with the Soviets against the Chinese has been said to have prompted whatever support the Soviets gave the Baluchis and Pathans after Bhutto's visit to Moscow in 1972 (similar to the Bengali case).[440] Yet, Chinese–Pakistani relations do not appear to have been a cause for Soviet concern later in the 1970s, which may be the reason for a different (less favorable) Soviet attitude toward the dismemberment of Pakistan and, therefore, much less commitment to these movements than to the Bengalis. While the absence of the Indian factor, as well, contributed to the different Soviet behavior, it is reasonable to assume that, had there been a significant Chinese–Pakistani relationship, particularly during the 1973–77 Baluchi uprising, the Soviets may well have been more forthcoming on behalf of the Baluchis.

The only other movement in Asia in which the Chinese factor has played a role and/or is cited in Soviet propaganda is the case of the Moros.[441] The brief Soviet support for this movement from the cease-fire and peace talks of December 1976 to the fall of 1977 probably had little to do with the Chinese. The cessation of this support, however, was directly explained by the fact that the Moslem People's liberation Army (New People's Army), with which the Moros were cooperating, was under the influence of the Chinese (a link Moscow claimed to have only recently discovered).[442] There may be some truth to this claim, inasmuch as the Moros reportedly rejected the NPA's offers of cooperation until roughly the fall of 1977.[443] Yet, if the Chinese factor was indeed the central one, it is not clear why the Soviets opposed the Moros in the earlier period, calling them the "so-called Moro National Liberation Front" and condemning them as separatists, for a number of years prior to the 24 December 1976 cease-fire.[444] It would appear that in this case the Chinese factor was there, to be exploited in propaganda, but that Chinese support for the movement was not necessarily the cause or central factor in the varying Soviet positions against and for and again against the Moros or, conversely, the Philippine government.

It is possible, though, that Soviet opposition to the Moros was influenced by a desire to offset or compete with an improvement in Chinese–Philippine relations. Marcos opened relations with the Chinese before the Soviets and sent his daughter to visit China in June 1977, some months before the Soviet ambassador presented his credentials in Manila.[445] This connection is further suggested by the fact that, at least in 1979, the Soviets sought to discredit the Chinese by comments that Peking was supporting the "separatists" even as it was improving relations with Manila.[446] It may also have been operative in 1975 when first China, then the Soviet Union, achieved diplomatic relations with the Philippines. At this time, the Soviets opposed the Moros and the Chinese supported them.[447]

If competition with the Chinese was the decisive factor, this factor had the opposite effect with regard to the Philippines and the Moros than it had with apparently the more hopeless (for the Soviets) case of Pakistan and the Bengalis. In the Philippine case, the threat of improved state relations with China may ultimately have prompted Soviet opposition to the movement so as to compete with the Chinese in currying favor with the government, rather than with the movement.

A similar effect *may* be discernible with regard to the Eritreans *prior* to the 1974 Ethiopian revolution. Both the Soviets and the Chinese supported the Eritreans in the 1960s. In 1971, China and Ethiopia opened diplomatic relations, leading to a cessation of Chinese support for the movement.[448] The Ethiopian–Chinese rapprochement did not, however, result in greater Soviet support to the Eritreans. Actually, somewhat less Soviet support may have been the result, in an effort to compete with the Chinese for relations with Haile Selassie. This hypothesis is supported by—and would explain—a surprising propaganda comment by Moscow in 1971 which referred to the "ultra nationalist liberation front operating for several years in the Eritrea province."[449] Inasmuch as Soviet media virtually never mentioned Eritrea in those years, such a negative comment was particularly outstanding. This apparent deviation, with its Chinese connection, notwithstanding, the real Soviet reversal regarding the Eritreans came only later and independently of any Chinese factor. Then, after 1974, the Soviets sought to discredit the Chinese in the eyes of the new Ethiopian regime by claiming that Peking was aiding the "separatists" in Eritrea, along with the CIA.[450] Competition with the Chinese has not, however, been a significant feature of Soviet–Ethiopian relations since 1974, or of the Soviet position on the Eritrean question.

While the above are the only cases of Chinese–state relations affecting Soviet behavior toward a movement, the Soviet explanation in the case of the Moros raises the question as to whether Chinese involvement with a movement in any way affected Soviet behavior toward that movement. It has been argued, at least with regard to the African movements, that Moscow has supported only those movements exclusively loyal to it in the Sino-Soviet context.[451] In defence of this thesis, one may point to the 1969 Soviet convening of the movements it supported (PAIGC, FRELIMO, MPLA, ZAPU, SWAPO, and the ANC), which was condemned by the Chinese with anti-Soviet statements by movements aligned with Peking (COREMO, PAC, UNITA, and ZANU).[452] In turn, the Soviets have condemned the Chinese for "splittist" actions in Guinea-Bissau, Angola, Mozambique, Zimbabwe, Namibia, and South Africa, illustrating these accusations by examples of Chinese contacts with (or encouragement of extremists in) the MPLA, SWAPO, SWANU (Namibia), PAC, and the ANC in the early 1970s.[453]

It has been said that the reason the Soviets did not shift to ZANU in the late 1970s, and did not on the whole respond to Mugabe's requests for aid, was Mugabe's refusal to break with China or take a position in the Sino–Soviet dispute.[454] This was despite the fact that Chinese aid had apparently slackened after Mao's death, prompting Mugabe to turn to Moscow.[455] The same problem reportedly drew SWAPO to request significant increases in Soviet aid, which request was also said to have met with a Soviet demand for SWAPO to abandon the Chinese.[456] The Soviets reportedly voiced opposition to SWAPO's refusal to take sides (with Moscow) in the Sino-Soviet conflict.[457] A break-away group from the ANC in 1975 also claimed that the Soviets, through the communists in the ANC, were dragging the movement into the Sino-Soviet conflict (apparently by demands for anti-Chinese statements, which were indeed issued).[458] It has also been claimed that the Soviets' involvement with the MPLA was generated by Chinese support for the MPLA's rivals, the FNLA and then UNITA.[459] On the other hand, it has been argued that Chinese support for a movement, the PLO, actually generated the Soviet decision to take up the PLO's cause after initial hesitations (from 1964 to 1968).[460] The opposite might be argued in the Biafra case, where the Chinese supported the Biafrans and the Soviets the Nigerian government.

In all of the above, anti-colonialist, secessionist, and internal movements alike, Soviet support for some movements and opposition to others has been said to have been dependent upon the Chinese attitude toward the movement—eliciting either support or opposition as a Soviet response or as Soviet demands for exclusive loyalty. Without rejecting the importance of the Chinese factor in some instances, it may be argued, first, that Soviet opposition to the Biafrans, for example, predated any Chinese position,[461] while support for movements such as ZAPU and the ANC predated the creation of their rival groups (ZANU and PAC), which probably turned to China at least in part because the Soviets were already involved with—and remained loyal to—the older organization.

Second, although the Soviets may well have sought ZANU condemnation of the Chinese, as they did with the ANC and SWAPO, connections with the Chinese do not seem to have disqualified all, if any, movements for Soviet support. SWAPO, for example, did not terminate its (albeit already reduced) Chinese aid, and yet it did receive increased Soviet assistance. Nujoma continued to visit China even as he visited the Soviet Union and drew closer to Moscow. More significantly, perhaps, the Soviets were willing to aid FRELIMO despite that movement's quite close and dominant relationship with China. Other instances of simultaneous Soviet and Chinese support have included the cases of the Eritreans in the 1960s, the Dhofaris and PAIGC briefly in the 1960s, the PLO, the NLF, and even the FNLA at various times. Even the MPLA and the ANC have been recipients of Chinese aid and/or training.[462] When armed conflict actually came between the rival Angolan movements, Chinese support particularly for UNITA may, nonetheless, have been at least one of the factors in the Soviets' decision to assist the MPLA so heavily, although, as we have seen, Moscow did not rule out a coalition and, more importantly, Chinese aid itself had been greatly reduced by this time.[463] Nor does it seem to be the case, with regard to the PLO, that four years of exclusive Chinese aid suddenly triggered Soviet interest in 1968. The Chinese connection may have been a contributing factor in Soviet calculations, but it probably was not the central one. And as in other cases, a severing of PLO relations with China was not apparently a condition for Soviet support; for, although those relations were reduced, they were not totally eliminated. (PLO, even Fatah, officials visited China from time to time on a fairly regular basis.)

LOCAL, REGIONAL AND GLOBAL FACTORS

The secessionist movements appear to have been the ones most affected by local and to some degree regional considerations. The key to support or opposition or fluctuations in Soviet behavior almost always has been connected with local considerations, that is, the Soviet relationship with the government involved, and in some cases regional considerations, such as Soviet relations with neighboring states; on one or two occasions, global considerations have played a part. (It may be argued that ultimately all Soviet regional and local interests are posited on a global interest in gaining positions—strategic, political, etc.—vis-à-vis the West, but our interest here is in factors more directly motivating Soviet behavior.)

In the case of the Anyanya, for example, whatever Soviet interests were in the region as a whole and in Sudan as an ally of Egypt, the factor that most determined Soviet behavior on the southern Sudanese question was Moscow's relationship with the Sudanese government itself; the desire to maintain a close relationship with Numeri dictated Soviet willingness to assist this government in putting down the rebellion. The Sudan's close relationship with Moscow's chief Middle East ally at the time, Egypt, may well have influenced the Soviet's decision, just as the absence of any global risks may have contributed to the calculations. One can only theorize as to the role of other factors. For example, would Soviet behavior have been different had this been an ideologically closer movement, or if the means chosen had been non-violent or the objectives different? As we have already seen, Marxist ideology and even non-violence and/or limited objectives have not always been a guarantee of Soviet support (nor has Chinese involvement). On the other hand, signs of a reversal of the Soviet position in favor of the rebels, now in a different organizational framework, in southern Sudan in the 1980s would probably be the result of shifting Soviet–Sudanese relations, particularly in the context of the Soviet–Ethiopian alliance (Ethiopia became the principal supplier of the southern Sudanese) rather than any factor emanating from the new movement itself.[464]

Soviet opposition to the Sikhs may be seen in a similar way, that is, Moscow's alliance with India being the overriding factor determining behavior toward the movement, with regional factors such as Pakistani support for the Sikhs compounding Soviet opposition. While this opposition has not taken the form of active assistance in the repression of the Sikhs, as it did in the Anyanya case, this may be because the Indians have not requested such assistance, rather than a sign of Soviet reservations. Similarly, opposition to the various movements in Burma is most likely a function of Soviet friendship with Burma, the lack of more direct Soviet involvement probably being a function of Burma's efforts to maintain a semblance of neutrality.

It is in the cases of fluctuating support and opposition that one can most readily perceive the role of local factors. In the Eritrean case the Soviet relationship with the central government dictated Soviet behavior toward the movement. A general opposition to Haile Selassie's government, coupled with a desire to maintain relations with it, prompted assistance to the Eritreans but of a clandestine and limited nature. As we have seen, competition with the Chinese, at one point, for positive relations with the Ethiopian government may have affected this, but the real switch in Soviet behavior, namely, opposition to the Eritreans, came when the central government changed. Similarly, in the case of the Tigreans, who may never have been supported by Moscow, active Soviet opposition came in response to the request of what was now a friendly government in Addis Ababa.

With regard to the Kurds of Iraq, one can virtually trace Soviet support or lack of support for the movement along the lines of Soviet–Iraqi relations. When these were good, the Kurds were neglected, even actively opposed; when they were bad, the Kurds were helped. This connection worked both ways, for Baghdad was probably more interested in good relations with Moscow when it was having trouble with the Kurds, and less dependent upon and interested in the Soviets when this internal problem was more or less settled.[465] It might be argued that Moscow supported the movement even in periods of good relations with the government so as to create such a dependence by perpetuating a crisis situation. But in fact, as far as can be determined, the Soviets were not willing to help the movement when this threatened to jeopardize relations with Baghdad.

Other factors may also enter the picture: a desire to prevent further deterioration in relations with a less than friendly government may prompt a cautious attitude on the part of the Soviets with regard to the movement, rather than a fully supportive one. Yet in the two cases of an active Soviet turnabout (the Eritreans and the Iraqi Kurds), the only independent variable has been the Soviet relationship with the central government.

In the case of the Moros, an only-correct relationship with the central government was not sufficient to induce even limited Soviet support for the movement inasmuch as the Soviets were seeking to improve their relationship with the government. The fleeting support for the Moros occurred only when the central government appeared to be finding an accommodation with them, ending when this government was again involved in hostilities against the movement. It is possible, however, that the Soviets did support the Moros, however briefly, because of dissatisfaction over the pace of Soviet–Philippino relations, abandoning the Moros when Marcos finally accepted a Soviet candidate for ambassador to Manila in late 1977.[466] An extraneous factor may also have influenced the brief Soviet digression, that is, Qadaffi and the Islamic Conference's role in bringing about the cease-fire. This factor was not sufficient, however, to sustain a permanent Soviet change in the face of renewed Manila–Moro hostilities. The rumored renewed support for the Moros in 1987 could be more directly tied to growing Soviet criticism of the Aquino government. The Soviet attitude toward the movement would in this case clearly be a consequence of the changing Soviet relationship with the local government.

Support for the Kurds of Turkey or Iran may follow a similar pattern, though regional factors may also enter the picture. For example, in both cases, as in the case of the Philippines and pre-1974 Ethiopia, the Soviets have striven to maintain correct relations with the central government and, therefore, have limited whatever support, if any, was given the movement. Moreover, while actively engaged in suppressing the Kurds of Iraq, the Soviets could not have been expected to lend much support to those in Turkey and Iran, thus introducing, possibly, a regional factor. In the case of Turkey, negative fluctuations with the government in Ankara have generated somewhat greater support for the Kurds at various times, while also, improved government relations in the 1970s may have limited this support—which has rarely been very open at any time.

In the case of Iran, however, the picture is less clear with regard to all the movements there. It may not have been the relationship with the central government that regulated Soviet support for the Kurds or Baluchis or the Arabs of Khuzistan. A desire to maintain correct relations with the Shah may have limited Soviet support in the 1970s, but it is difficult to explain the increase in support of the Kurds, and (according to some claims), briefly, the Baluchis and even the Arabs of Khuzistan, *prior* to the deterioration in Soviet relations with Khomeini's Iran. It is conceivable that this Soviet support was merely exploitation of the chaotic situation in Iran (which was being exploited by the Kurds themselves), designed to maintain maximum options pending stabilization of the central regime. This was at best, however, quite limited support and may not even have existed in the case of the Baluchis and Khuzistan. In the case of the Kurds, the Soviet propaganda support persisted, more predictably, after the deterioration in Soviet–Khomeini relations, though this deterioration has not generated any increase of Soviet support as far as can be determined. With regard to the Baluchis, the regional factor of Iranian Baluchi assistance to Baluchi rebels in Afghanistan probably accounts for Soviet reluctance to offer them any support, whatever Moscow's relations with Khomeini. It may be that the situation has returned to that of the period of the Shah, that is, to one of only limited clandestine support, if any, to the movements in Iran while the Soviets seek to prevent a deterioration in state-to-state relations.

Regional combined with local factors are most likely responsible for Soviet behavior regarding the Baluchis and Pathans of the Pakistan–Afghanistan area. Moscow's pursuit of improved relations with Pakistan after the 1971 war apparently accounts for the lack of serious support to either the Baluchis or Pathans in the 1970s. There are reports that the rise of the initially pro-Soviet Daoud regime in Afghanistan prompted Soviet support for Afghanistan's demands regarding Paktoonistan, but Pakistani–Afghan rapprochement (possibly encouraged by Moscow) put an end to this.[467] With the 1978 coup, or later with the Soviet invasion of Afghanistan, Moscow reportedly began to support both minorities more actively, guiding the Pathans (and possibly the Baluchis) in the direction of their brethren in Pakistan, against the Pakistani government.[468] The decisive factors here are not only the relationship of the Pakistani government to Moscow but the rebellion in Afghanistan as well. The only surprising fact is that, despite the "logic" of Soviet support to the anti-Pakistani movements, from Afghanistan as well as inside Pakistan, this support appeared only quite late. It may be that other factors, such as the Chinese or global (American) factors, account for this restraint, for the Soviets may have been concerned that threatening Pakistan in such a way might lead to greater American and Chinese involvement with Pakistan. The change that appeared to have occurred, at least with regard to the Pathans in 1985, was presumably been connected with the degree of Pakistani assistance to the Afghan rebels that the Soviets were willing to tolerate. It was not clear however, just how much assistance the Soviets actually accorded the Pathans. The issue of the Baluchis appears to be a bit more complex because of the ambiguous role of the Baluchis in the Afghan rebellion.

Both regional and local factors probably account for Soviet involvement with the Dhofaris. It is difficult to know if one preceded the other, or if one would have been sufficient cause without the other. The Soviets opposed the regime of Oman, and it is possible that a global factor—British assistance to the Sultan–played a large role in this. The regional factor was quite important, however, primarily because the PDRY was involved and sought Soviet assistance. It was also a factor once Iran became involved and a power struggle for the Gulf evolved, with its global implications not only in connection with Britain but also with U.S. military plans, as perceived by Moscow. One could argue that these three factors (global, regional, and local) also determined the cessation of Soviet support for the Dhofaris, when the PDRY and Oman came to agreement in 1982, opening the way for Soviet–Omani diplomatic relations in 1985. The Dhofari rebellion was more or less extinguished by the time of the 1982 agreement, however, and one can only speculate as to whether the Soviets would have continued to support it without the South Yemenis. Moscow did not try to revive it in that period, despite at least an additional year of anti-Omani propaganda in other (global) contexts prior to the opening of Soviet–Omani relations. This would suggest that the regional factor was the dominant one with regard to the PFLOAG itself.

The case of the Tamils is more clearly one of dominant regional factors. Local factors might well dictate no Soviet support or any position regarding the movement, given Soviet interests in maintaining at least correct relations with the Sri Lanka government (port facilities being a part of this interest).[469] Indeed, this factor may account for initial silence on the part of the Soviets, and the restrained nature of their support for the Tamils. It may well be that the only reason for the limited support the Soviets did eventually express is the fact that India was assisting the Tamils, providing them refuge and probably more direct aid. This explanation appears all the more likely in view of the reversal in the Soviet position and condemnation of the Tamils when they came into conflict with Indian peace-keeping forces—and Indian abandonment of the Tamils' armed struggle in 1987.

Regional as well as local considerations may have guided Soviet behavior regarding the FROLINAT and the Katangans, given the Libyan interest in one and the Angolan interest in the other. The global factor may also have entered (it was certainly proclaimed as the main reason by Soviet propaganda) with the involvement of West European powers. Ultimately, it may well be the global factor that renders these cases of interest to Moscow, but, by the same token, it may be just this factor that prompts Moscow to limit its involvement and its support.

The global factor may have played an important role, along with the local factor, with regard to the Ibos. According to some accounts, there was Soviet sympathy for the Ibos during a period of poor Sovi-et–Nigerian relations prior to the coup of 1966, although there was no actual Soviet support for them against the central government.[470] After the coup of 1966, and particularly after the rise of General Gowon, the potential for improved Soviet–Nigerian relations apparently prompted a Soviet position more favorable to the central government. But the factor that may have tipped the scales in the direction of significant Soviet assistance against the Ibos was a global one: the refusal of Britain and the united States to provide the type of assistance requested by Gowon. Gowon apparently did not turn to the Soviets until the United States and Britain had refused to meet his requests.[471] Nor did Soviet propaganda fully turn against the Ibos until this time.[472] The motivating factor for the Soviets, then, would have been the local one—to improve relations with the government—complemented by the direct global competition with the West, even though few Western states were actually siding with the Ibos. Regional factors were also at play, for the OAU opposed changes of boundaries generally and the secession of Biafra specifically. Just how great a role this regional factor played is difficult to determine, but, combined with the local and even global considerations, it must have eased the decision.

Local, regional, and global factors, as well as the Chinese factor, were at play in the case of Bangladesh. Soviet efforts to improve relations with Pakistan (including Moscow's bid for an Asian Security Pact) were increasingly thwarted by 1969, leading to a more favorable Soviet posi-tion regarding East Pakistan in early 1970. Pessimism over relations with Pakistan, which was drawing increasingly close to China, provided the local incentive for Soviet support, but the regional factor—the role of India—was significant. The fact that Moscow did not go as far as India, and, until relatively late, sought to change India's position and policies, suggests, however, that the local consideration—the wish to avoid total alienation of Pakistan—was of equal significance. Only when it was clear that no compromise was possible with Islamabad did the Soviets opt for the Indian—and East Pakistani—position. The Chinese and global factors were also of importance here, however; for by this time the Pakistanis had mediated an American–Chinese rapprochement, placing the local East–West Pakistan and regional Pakistan–India conflicts on a global scale. With the Soviet decision to support the East Bengalis, the regional and global considerations became dominant, with Soviet military behavior directed at assisting India and deterring American interference for the sake of Soviet regional interests. Thus, it was not East Pakistan or the Bengalis that were of interest to Moscow, but India and the influence of China and the United States in the region.

With regard to the anti-colonial movements, there was almost no local factor as such, for the local regime was, by definition, representative of other regional or more usually global powers. Local circumstances, including the relative strength of an anti-colonial movement, may have played a role regarding the degree or type of Soviet support, but the dilemma of choosing between the regime and a national liberation movement was not present in the anti-colonial cases.

Only in the case of the NLF did the local factor play more than the obvious role (of prompting support for the movement against the regime), if one defines North Vietnam as a local rather than regional actor vis-à-vis the conflict in South Vietnam. In this case the local consideration of maintaining good relations with North Vietnam was of central importance and greatly influenced Soviet behavior toward the movement. What greatly complicated Soviet calculations, and ultimately guided them, however, were the regional and global factors, that is, the competition with China (as we have seen) and the American involvement against the movement (and North Vietnam). In this sense Moscow had to measure its moves not only against the criterion of Chinese benefit or loss but also from the point of view of the global and regional setting, be it damage to the U.S.–Soviet relationship, the risk of U.S.–Soviet confrontation, expansion of the conflict in the region, or the global and regional implications regarding the prestige and credibility of both superpowers. Soviet preference for genuine negotiations was probably motivated by such concerns as the expansion of American intervention elsewhere in the region and damage to the emerging Soviet–U.S. détente, but also by the fear of the American–Chinese rapprochement, as well as the situation on the ground. Yet these concerns had to be weighed against possible damage to Soviet–North Vietnamese relations, which might in turn accrue to the Chinese benefit, and against the political propaganda benefits being derived by Moscow from America's unpopular involvement in the protracted war and the benefits accruing to the Soviets from their active "anti-imperialist" stand.

Thus, even the global and regional factors were multi-faceted and difficult to isolate. On the whole, however, it was Moscow's global–regional (including China) interests that dictated Soviet positions. An example of this may have been Moscow's willingness for a compromise solution in the South, against the will of Hanoi, on the issue of Thieu's continued participation in the government. With their major interest (U.S. withdrawal) to be achieved, the Soviets were probably confident that their local allies (the NLF and Hanoi) would have little difficulty gaining victory, albeit without Soviet involvement.[473]

In the African context, the global factors may have been less acute but they have been no less operative. If in the Vietnamese case the overriding Soviet objective was expulsion of the Western powers, so too in Africa the primary consideration has been the weakening of the Western presence or influence, be it the NATO state of Portugal in Guinea-Bissau–Cape Verde, Mozambique, and Angola or the British via the Rhodesians in Zimbabwe. With the revolution in Portugal it became more a matter of combating other external influences, specifically the United States in Angola. In the Zimbabwean case, after the Angolan war, American involvement together with the British largely dictated Soviet behavior, particularly on the issue of negotiations, which were under U.S.–British auspices. It may have been this American involvement in the second half of the 1970s that prompted the increase in Soviet aid and support to the remaining African liberation movements (ZAPU, SWAPO, ANC) in the same period. Regional factors, however, also played a large role in this increase. The victories of the anti-Portugese movements cleared the way for increased Soviet aid, for they provided new training sites and supply routes via the new states. These facilities not only made intensification of the struggles in southern Africa possible, but they also provided a direct channel for Soviet assistance formerly dependent to some degree on the OAU—through which assistance was channelled for the movements' training by Chinese, for example, in Tanzania. The OAU, as a regional factor, has been involved in other ways in Soviet calculations.

With regard to the anti-Portugese movements, Moscow generally acted in accord with OAU decisions, though in the Angolan inter-movement struggle the Soviets moved in opposition to the OAU and the initial positions of some states in the region, including Zambia and Mozambique. Both states eventually came round, as did the OAU, but the Soviets' willingness to defy them (though it did actively try to change their minds) demonstrated the priority of global over regional considerations.[474] Another regional factor that entered was South Africa, whose threatening position toward and actual moves into Angola in June and especially October 1975 may have been the decisive factor in the Soviet (and Cuban) decision to expand their involvement.[475] Certainly,

South African cooperation with UNITA and FNLA, and the incursion in the north by American-backed Zaire, brought regional factors into the forefront. (It was also these factors that brought the OAU to reverse its position.)

Similarly, the danger of South African interference may have prompted greater Soviet aid to the Zimbabweans, although one observer has claimed that the fears of South African involvement made Moscow cautious, particularly with regard to committing advisers on the spot.[476] As we have seen, however, the Soviets have never committed advisers on the spot to a movement prior to independence. Cautiousness, and a willingness to negotiate, was characteristic of the front-line states, a regional factor that may have caused the Soviets to respond relatively positively to negotiations for Zimbabwe in the mid-1970s. By the later period, however, the American factor was probably overriding. The fact that the negotiations were now directly sponsored by the United States and Britain may account for Moscow's divergence from the front-line states' (and its own) position. Nonetheless, the PF's (ZAPU and ZANU) decision to pursue these talks did not evoke any kind of reduction in Soviet support.

A very similar pattern appears with regard to Namibia, where the Soviets view the local–regional conflict in global terms, that is, in terms of a struggle against Western-oriented South Africa. The involvement and support of the front-line states is a regional factor operating in favor of Soviet aid. Yet, as in the Zimbabwean case, the front-line states' cautiousness and preference for negotiations has created problems for the Soviets, given the Western domination of these negotiations (Soviet reservations over resolution 435, for example). By the same token, it is possible that, as in the case of Zimbabwe, Moscow's greater assistance in the second half of the 1970s was at least in part prompted by increased American involvement. If the name of the game is competition with the West, then Moscow's solution, when opposing the movement over Western settlement plans, has been not to pressure the movement through reduced assistance, but rather to offer generous support for the movement in hopes of demonstrating the value and reliability of the Soviet link.

The ANC, for the most part, follows the pattern of the anti-colonial movements, whereby the local actor, the state, is perceived more or less as a constant—a constant of a hostile "Western" imperialist nature. Regional and global factors strengthen both this perception and the support of the movement. African concensus for the ANC and against the South African regime fortifies if not actually causes Soviet interest, while Western, particularly American, support for the regime adds a global element to Soviet involvement. There is some irony in this, for although Soviet support for the ANC is at least in part the result of the pursuit of good relations in the region as a whole, the states of the region themselves do not always follow this policy. Fear of South African retaliation often limits the degree of assistance the neighboring states are willing to provide; Botswana, Zimbabwe, and especially Mozambique are prime examples of such ambivalency. In the case of Mozambique, an actual agreement was reached with Pretoria (the Nkomati Accord of 1984) leading to the exit or curtailment of whatever ANC personnel were operating from there. In this respect, the fears of the states in the region may influence Soviet calculations as to the advisability of armed actions by the ANC. And the Soviets themselves may also prefer to avoid provocation of South African incursions. (The Soviets have sought, for example, to limit the level of combat between South Africa and Angola).

Soviet cautiousness, so far as it exists, may be connected not only with the fears of the front-line states but also with concern over the global nature of any conflict in southern Africa. Particularly since the Angolan war, and with continued American backing of UNITA, a threat to a front-line state could occasion American involvement or gains. Nkomati might in fact be proof of this, demonstrating the precariousness of the Soviet position in competition with the West in Africa.

In the case of the PLO it is difficult to distinguish between local and regional actors, but for the purposes of analysis the local element may be seen as Israel, the regional actors as the surrounding states. Within this framework, the local factor operates almost as a given, as it did in the anti-colonial cases: the local state is viewed by the Soviets as a "Western" imperialist, with little to no variation in Soviet behavior on the bilateral level. Regional and global factors, however, have played a very large, even determining, role.

Regional factors prompted Soviet support for the PLO finally in the late 1960s, particularly when Egypt began to accord the Palestinian issue a certain centrality. The Soviet falling-out with Egypt led to a strengthening of Soviet ties with alternative clients in the region, including the PLO, resulting in direct arms supplies to the movement. Regional factors were also behind Soviet support for the PLO in the Lebanese civil war of 1976 when Moscow opposed the Syrian move into Lebanon. Indeed, it has largely been regional factors, that is, the political importance rendered the Palestinian cause by the Arab states, that has sustained Soviet involvement (and financed it). Regional factors have even influenced, in part, the Soviet response to the internal problems of the PLO in the mid-1980s, with the Soviet alliance with Syria balanced by a Soviet effort to improve relations with less radical Arab states such as Jordan (but also Egypt), prompting relative Soviet neutrality in the PLO dispute. In this dispute, however, one can also see the importance of the global factor—the major problem from the Soviet point of view

having been Arafat's flirtation with the idea of an American-mediated
solution. Moscow's interests in Jordan led to a certain restraint in Soviet
criticism of Arafat's dealings with Jordan, despite Syria's opposition.
Considerations regarding the Syrians themselves also led to Soviet
reluctance to assist in a Syrian takeover of the PLO. Yet the danger of a
PLO move to the Americans prompted what no other disagreement
between Moscow and the PLO had in the past: a reduction, possibly even
suspension, of military aid to Fatah. This did not, however, resulted in
any change in military aid to the other PLO organizations or in overall
political support. Indeed, as in the anti-colonial cases, competition with
the United States has engendered still greater political support so as
to demonstrate the value of alliance with Moscow over whatever the
Americans might offer.

The global factor has acted as a stimulus to greater Soviet support
at various times in the past, as well as, for example, the official
recognition of the PLO as the sole legitimate representative almost
days after the Camp David agreement in 1978. The patching up of
Moscow's rift with Habash, and agreement to train his forces, may also
have been the result of the Camp David accords. The Soviet agreement
to the idea of a Palestinian state began to take form apparently with the
American involvement in the Middle East peace efforts in 1973, and
it came out openly when Kissinger was progressing toward a separate
Israeli–Jordanian partial settlement in the summer of 1974, just prior to
the Rabat conference's decision to propose such a state (which operated
as a regional factor).

The global, and to some degree regional, factors have also operated,
on occasion, as limiting factors on Soviet behavior toward the PLO.
Concern over the threatened Israeli–US intervention in the Jordanian
civil war in 1970 prompted the Soviets to restrain the Syrian intervention
on the side of the PLO. Soviet concern over escalation of hostilities
with Israel over Lebanon prompted the Soviets both to seek an end
to the 1976 Lebanese civil war and to limit the aid they gave the PLO
during and after the conflict. Similarly, the lack of Soviet involvement
on behalf of the PLO against the 1982 Israeli invasion of Lebanon was
most likely dictated by a desire to avoid escalation into regional and
possibly even global conflict. (Although, as we have seen, the Soviets
have never intervened on behalf of a national liberation movement.)
Moreover, Soviet interests in preventing an exclusively American settlement probably prompted the Soviets to agree in 1977 to a compromise
formula for the convening of an international conference which would
include the Soviet Union, partially at the expense of PLO participation.
In sum, the more salient global nature of the Palestinian issue, as distinct
from that of many other movements, may be responsible for the higher
degree of Soviet involvement with the movement—and this despite

numerous disagreements with the movement. It may also, however, account for a certain amount of Soviet cautiousness, particularly with regard to the means employed by the movement and, most recently, for the ambivalence apparent in Soviet behavior toward the movement.

Finally, the case of the Polisario is also problematic in terms of distinguishing between local and regional factors. As already noted, the Soviets prefer to cast this conflict in anti-colonial terms, but their behavior runs closer to the secessionist pattern. The vicissitudes, particularly the limited nature, of Soviet support would appear to be related to what could be called local interests, that is, Soviet–Moroccan relations. At the early stages, at least, Moscow's desire to maintain good (commercial) relations with Morocco appear to have held Moscow back. The fact that, even as support has been rendered, it has been done so indirectly, through other states in the area and even through communist parties other than the Moroccan one, further supports the importance of the local factor. Soviet commentators themselves acclaim the positive aspects of Soviet–Moroccan relations, including Soviet assistance to Morrocco, despite what on one occasion was refered to as "differing views on the Western Sahara."[477] Regional factors have not been ignored, however. Indeed, the degree of Soviet support actually accorded may well be the result of the deep involvement of Algeria and the backing given the Polisario by the OAU.[478] The juggling of these local versus regional interests is typified by the Soviets' reluctance to recognize SADR (Morocco broke relations with Cuba when Havana did so), even as they cite, positively, the decisions of other states to do so. Even if the Soviets were to run the political risk of recognizing SADR, it appears that more direct and fulsome Soviet aid to the Polisario will continue to be limited by the desire to maintain a relatively good relationship with Rabat.

Other Variables

A number of other factors may contribute to Soviet decision-making in connection with the degree and type of support, if any, to be rendered a movement. A movement's chance for success, the degree of risk involved for the Soviets, and the importance of the area from Moscow's point of view may all play a role. The time factor, such as different behavior corresponding to different periods, possibly in connection with the Soviet succession issue, cannot be ruled out.

The evidence of these factors, however, is extremely contradictory. One might argue, for example, that the movements operating on or near Soviet borders (Iran, Turkey, Afghanistan) are of much greater importance to Moscow than those further away, such as in southern Africa. Yet no such consistency appears in Soviet behavior. The economic or strategic importance of an area might be of significance. Moroccan phosphates would appear to be a decisive factor regarding the Polisario. Yet economic and even strategic assets (ports, airfields, etc.) could probably be found for virtually any area without necessarily explaining why the Soviets chose to support (and how much) a government rather than a movement or vice versa. Arguments of this type have been almost overwhelming with regards to the Baluchis and Pathans, possibly even the Kurds and the Arabs of Khuzistan, yet they do not account for the lack of Soviet support at various times, if at all. The degree of risk actually involved, or, in other worlds, the danger of regional conflagration and/or global confrontation, should evoke a more limited Soviet involvement with a movement. Indeed, it does appear to play such a role, as we have seen in the previous sections, in Soviet considerations regarding armed struggle and negotiations. In the cases of the MPLA and the PLO, this may even have taken the form of Soviet restraint.

Yet the volatility of an area and the potential risk for the Soviets do not necessarily limit Soviet involvement or determine its positions. In the same MPLA and PLO cases the higher risk, for both regional and global reasons, has not deterred a high degree of Soviet involvement. In fact, as we have seen, the global and regional elements, despite their higher risk potential, may actually have contributed to greater Soviet involvement. The same might be said for the case of the NLF, or the Bengalis. It is in fact in the "riskier" cases that the Soviets have been willing to take even higher risk positions, be it with regard to the means employed, the objectives, or even the types of involvement. Conversely, the lower-risk conflicts, generally the secessionist ones, in which local factors are central, have not seen greater risk-taking behavior on the part of the Soviets. Even willingness to support armed struggle, possibly only on a limited basis, is more apparent in various higher-risk situations connected with the anti-colonials than in many lower-risk situations of many secessionists. This is not to say that the risk involved does not enter into Soviet calculations: it would not make sense for Moscow *not* to weigh the likelihood of risk. But the perception of risk, and the willingness to accept varying degrees of risk, do not fall into any clear pattern with regard to national liberation movements, short of the fact that the Soviets are not willing to intervene militarily on behalf of any movement or send on-the-spot advisers prior to independence.

No greater consistency can be found with regard to chances for success. One might argue that the Soviets are more consistent in their support for the anti-colonials because of the belief in the inevitability of their victory. This may well explain the clear difference between Soviet behavior toward anti-colonials, on one hand, and the lack of consistency toward the secessionists, on the other. The somewhat greater willingness to support armed struggle for the anti-colonials and the ANC than for the secessionists and the PLO may be connected with this factor inasmuch as compromise, specifically, a limitation of objectives, is more possible with the secessionists than in the all-or-nothing situation of the anti-colonials. Whether the chance of success is a criterion within the secessionist category, or the internals, is not clear, however. It may well have been a factor in the decision regarding the Bengalis, or conversely, the Ibos, but it does not appear clearly applicable or decisive regarding the Tamils or the Kurds, or the Katangans or even the PLO.

The time factor *may* be relevant, following periodization suggested in part by the Soviet theoretical discussions: the early 1970s, a period of restraint; the mid- to late 1970s, a period of greater involvement; the 1980s, a return to restraint. In Africa there would appear to be some logic to this, with 1975–76 marking the beginning of quite extensive Soviet involvement, so that the movements supported in the late 1970s received more than those whose struggle had ended in 1974–75. Yet alternative explanations might be that the Portuguese revolution—and the inter-movement conflict in Angola—created a specific situation which had not existed previously. Following the end of this struggle and of the Portuguese Empire, resources and efforts could be concentrated on the remaining movements, the fighting in Angola having provided a more tolerant regional response to Soviet involvement. Within the movements themselves, such a sequential explanation has been given: with the end of the anti–Portuguese struggle came the turn of southern Africa; with the independence of Zimbabwe came the turn of SWAPO and the ANC.

Another feature of the same periodization, however, is the appearance of the Americans, at least in the form of diplomacy designed to resolve the conflicts with American assistance. Whatever the explanation, the periodization itself is not entirely valid. Not only has there been no significant change in the 1980s, but the changes within the 1970s were not entirely consistent. While it is true that the quantity of Soviet aid has been far greater since 1975, actual Soviet (and Cuban) involvement has never reached the same proportions or form since the Angolan war. Even as the Soviets appeared to be more supportive of armed struggle in the late 1970s, they did not make as direct a contribution (or encourage the Cubans to do so) as previously. Moreover, no similar periodization emerges with respect to the non-African movements. This may be explained by the fact that, with the exception of the NLF and PLO, the non-African movements were all secessionist, in which instances local (and other) factors were the highly individual and fluctuating variables. Whatever the explanation, no consistent periodization is observable outside Africa or between Africa and other areas, and not entirely within Africa.

The absence of clear periodization raises doubts about a role for the succession struggle within the Soviet leadership. If the contention is that

Brezhnev's advanced age and poor health paralyzed Soviet policy during his last years, there is no evidence that this was the case with regard to the national liberation movements. No significant changes appeared at the end of the 1970s or the beginning of the 1980s except those directly related to local and/or regional factors: the PDRY–Oman agreement of 1982 ended whatever was left of Yemeni— and Soviet—aid to the Dhofaris; the post-Lebanese war split in the PLO led to a reduction of aid to Fatah, but not to the PLO as a whole; the victory in Zimbabwe may have led to the opposite of retreat, that is, a step-up in aid to SWAPO. There was the lack of Soviet assistance to the PLO in the time of critical danger during the Lebanese war, but this Soviet reticence was *not* a change; rather, it was entirely characteristic of Soviet behavior toward the PLO and national liberation movements in general. In the post-Brezhnev period, one might point to the Soviets' restraining position regarding the ANC, at least prior to the latter's 1985 congress, but there does not appear to have been any correponding policy regarding SWAPO. While it is not known (to this author) just what the Soviets have been advising such movements as the Kurds, for example, in the wake of the Soviet–Iraqi rapprochement, the Pathans were encouraged to act against Pakistan.

It would appear, therefore, that the same internal and particularly the external factors discussed above are at play, rather than some overall policy shifts determined by the changes in the Soviet leadership. The priority accorded Soviet domestic reform and economic interests by Gorbachev may lead to limitations on Soviet support for national liberation movements. Indeed, the first year of Gorbachev's rule, including the twenty-seventh Congress, revealed signs of a "Soviet Union first" policy dictated by economic limitations. Gorbachev's theory of global interdependence and his aspirations for regional stability may dictate a still more cautious policy of involvement. The strikingly miniscule, virtually non-existent, attention accorded these movements by Gorbachev in his mammoth speech to the twenty-seventh CPSU Congress certainly suggested such a direction. Yet neither the theoretical discussions nor the official rhetoric, including that of the Soviet leadership, nor actual Soviet behavior indicates withdrawal or drastic reduction of Soviet involvement (of various types) with these movements. Rather, where the theory, the rhetoric, and the behavior coincide, beginning in the early 1980s, if not earlier, is their generally pragmatic, relatively cautious tactical approach to the national liberation movements.

Notes

1   In 1968 the Dhofari liberation movement was converted into a revolutionary movement for all of Oman and even the Gulf; therefore its inclusion here is purely tentative. Similarly, the FROLINAT is more a political movement for rule in Chad than a strictly national liberation movement.

2   Bradford Dismukes and James McConnell, *Soviet Naval Diplomacy*, Pergamon Press, New York, 1979, p. 131; Stephen S. Kaplan, *Diplomacy of Power*, Brookings Institution, Washington, D.C., 1981, p. 564. Soviet involvement was not acknowledged by Soviet reporting on the capture of the assassins: *Pravda*, 22 and 24 January 1973, 6 March 1973; and *Izvestiia*, 24 January 1973 referred only to the Guinean navy.

3   See Mark Katz, "The Soviet-Cuban Connection," *International Security* 8, no. 1 (1983): 88-112; Zdenek Cervenka and Colin Legum, "Cuba: The New Communist Power in Africa," *African Contemporary Record* (1977-78): A103-16; (1979-80): A162-72; Abraham Lowenthal, "Cuba's African Adventure," *International Security* 2, no. 1 (1977): 3-10.

4   William LeoGrande, "Cuban-Soviet Relations and Cuban Policy in Africa," *Cuban Studies* 10, no. 1 (1980): 5; Cervenka and Legum, "Cuba" (1977-78): A102-3.

5   Kaplan, *Diplomacy of Power*, p. 547; Thomas Henriksen, "People's War in Angola, Mozambique and Guinea-Bissau," *Journal of Modern African Studies* 14, no. 3 (1976): 390; Donald Alberts, "Armed Struggle in Angola," in Bard O'Neill et al., *Insurgency in the Modern World*, Westview, Boulder, Colo., 1980, p. 265n.

6   Stephen Hosmer and Thomas Wolfe, *Soviet Policy and Practice Toward Third World Countries*, Lexington Books, Lexington, Mass., 1982, p. 49; Kaplan, *Diplomacy of Power*, p. 548.

7   Ibid., p. 548.

8   Seth Singleton, "Soviet Policy and Socialist Expansion in Asia and Africa," *Armed Forces and Society* 6, no. 3 (1980): 353; Arthur Jay Klinghoffer, *The Angolan War*, Westview, Boulder, Colo., 1980, pp. 110-111. Cabral denied the presence of any Cubans except medical personnel in testimony before the U.S. Congress *(Report on Portuguese Guinea and the Liberation Movement*, Subcommittee on Africa, Committee on Foreign Affairs, House of Representatives, U.S. Government Printing Office, 1970, p. 12).

9   *Pravda*, 14 November 1973; Moscow radio, 27 November 1972; Radio Peace and Progress, 24 January 1972; Moscow radio, 26 February 1972.

10   TASS, 1 October 1973, urged all countries to recognize the new state, though actual independence with UN acceptance came only in November 1974. Luis Cabral led an official delegation which was received by Podgornyi (TASS, 24 November 1973), though the Soviet ambassador went only in May 1974 (Radio Moscow radio, 13 May 1974).

11   Alberts, "Armed Struggle," p. 265n.; *Africa Confidential* 15, no. 8 (1974): 5; Anthony Wilkinson, "Insurgency in Rhodesia 1956-1973," *Adelphi Paper*, no. 100 (1973): 26.

12   John Marcum, *The Angolan Revolution*, vol. 1, MIT University Press, Cambridge, Mass., 1969, pp. 28, 250, 253; vol. II, 1978, pp. 14-15, 171; Jiri Valenta, "The Soviet-Cuban Intervention in Angola," *Studies in Comparative Communism* 11, nos. 1 and 2 (1978): 6-7; unsigned, "The National Liberation Movement in Angola," *International Affairs, no. 8 (1961): 106*.

13   Unsigned, "Angola after Independence," *Conflict Studies*, no. 64 (1975): 5; Klinghoffer, *Angolan War*, p. 17; Jiri Valenta, "Soviet Decision-making on the Intervention in Angola," in David Albright, *Communism in Africa*, Indiana University Press, Bloomington, 1980, p. 95.

14   Unsigned, "Angola after Independence", p. 5; Klinghoffer, *Angolan War*, p. 17. Marcum, *The Angolan Revolution*, vol. II, p. 172.

15   Alberts, "Armed Struggle," p. 249; interview with Gerald Bender.

16   Klinghoffer, *Angolan War*, p. 17.

17   LeoGrande, "Cuban-Soviet Relations," pp. 488-9; Arthur Jay Klinghoffer, "The Soviet Union and Angola," in Robert Donaldson (ed.), *The Soviet Union in*

    the Third World: Successes and Failures, Westview, Boulder, Colo., 1981, p. 110, Cervenka and Legum, "Cuba," p. 103, say that Cuban contacts predated the Soviet ones and that there are reports of Cubans training Angolans in Algeria as early as 1963: Ian Greig, *The Communist Challenge to Africa*, Foreign Affairs Publishing Co., Richmond, Surrey, 1977, p. 94.

18　Marcum, *The Angolan Revolution*, vol. II, p. 225; David Ottaway and Marina Ottaway, *Afrocommunism*, Africana Publishing Co., New York, 1980, p. 7.

19　Ottaway and Ottaway, *Afrocommunism*, p. 33; Singleton, "Soviet Policy," p. 353.

20　Marcum, *The Angolan Revolution*, vol. II, p. 273; Klinghoffer, "Soviet Union and Angola," p. 111; Kaplan, *Diplomacy of Power*, p. 194; Valenta, "Decision-making," pp. 99-112.

21　Marcum, *The Angolan Revolution*, vol. II, p. 273; Klinghoffer, "Soviet Union and Angola," p. 111; Gerald Bender, "Angola, the Cubans, and American Anxieties," *Foreign Policy*, no. 31 (1978): 12.

22　Marcum, *The Angolan Revolution*, vol. II, p. 201; *African Contemporary Record* (1975-76): A-5; Colin Legum and Tony Hodges, *After Angola: The War over Southern Africa*, African Publishing Company, New York, 1978, p. 22; Ottaway and Ottaway, p. 7; Bender "Angola, the Cubans," p. 23; John Marcum, "Lessons of Angola," *Foreign Affairs* 54, no. 3 (1976): 413.

23　Klinghoffer, *Angolan War*, pp. 27-8; Valenta, "Decision-making," p. 100; Marcum, "Lessons of Angola," p. 413.

24　Dismukes and McConnell, *Soviet Naval Diplomacy, p. 144;* Kaplan, *Diplomacy of Power*, p. 194; Bender, "Angola," p. 12; Marcum, *The Angolan Revolution*, vol. II, pp. 263-75; Klinghoffer, *Angolan War*, p. 111.

25　Merritt Robins, "The Soviet-Cuban Relationship," in Roger Kanet (ed.), *Soviet Foreign Policy in the 1980s*, Praeger, New York, 1985, p. 158; John Stockwell, *In Search of Enemies*, W.W. Norton, New York, 1978, p. 194; Klinghoffer, *Angolan War*, p. 19 (with the exception of one GRU officer).

26　Robins, "Soviet-Cuban Relationship", p. 158; Stockwell, *Enemies*, p. 194; Klinghoffer, *Angolan War*, p. 19;

27　Richard Bissell, "Southern Africa: Testing Détente," in Grayson Kirk and Nils Wessell, *The Soviet Threat: Myths and Realities*, Academy of Political Science, New York, 1978, p. 90; Allen Isaacman and Barbara Isaacman, *Mozambique: From Colonialism to Revolution 1900-1982*, Westview, Boulder, Colo., 1983, p. 105; Greig, *Communist Challenge*, p. 94, said Cubans trained them in Algeria from approximately 1963. By 1970 Cubans were also training them in Tanzania: Wilkinson, "Insurgency," p. 47.

28　Wilkinson, "Insurgency," p. 26; Witney Schneidman, "The Process of Liberation," *Africa Today* 22, no. 3 (1977): 58.

29　*Christian Science Monitor*, 26 June 1978, said the GDR offered comprehensive aid in 1969; George Glass, "East Germany in Black Africa," *The World Today*, (August 1980): 305, said this aid began in 1973; Schneidman, "Process of Liberation," p. 58.

30　LeoGrande, "Cuban-Soviet Relations," p. 5; Valenta, "Decision-making," p. 110; P. M. Whitaker, "The Revolution of Portuguese Africa," *Journal of Modern African Studies* 8, no. 6 (1970): 15-35, said that Cubans were with all the anti-Portuguese movements after Che's trip.

31　*Africa Contemporary Record* (1970-71): A-55; TASS, 25 February 1971, reported trip.

32　Moscow radio, 14, 15 June 1973.

33　A women's delegation went in June 1974 (TASS, 13, 15 June 1974). Journalists visited Angola, but *New Times*, no. 46 (1974): 14, made a point of mentioning that almost no Soviets ever went there and that there was "no Soviet citizen" there at the time.

34　E.g., Moscow radio, 26 February 1972, 9 September 1972, 11 April 1973, 24 April 1973; Radio Peace and Progress in Portuguese, 24 January 1972; TASS, 13 April 1972 (Cabral thanks); Samora Machel, "The Fight of Mozambique," *New Times*, no. 28 (1973): 22; V. Molchanov, "The People's War in Mozambique," *New Times*, no. 26 (1972): 11; Vasily Solodovnikov, *African Fights for Independence*, Novosti, Moscow, 1970, p. 65.

35　*Izvestiia*, 26 December 1975.

36 In 1974 the Soviets announced that they gave the OAU Liberation Committee £4 million sterling in medical equipment and food (Moscow radio, 5 August 1974). It is difficult to know if this was a typical sum, but in May 1973 the Soviets announced with some pride and fanfare that they had just donated $29,000 to the OAU Liberation Committee (TASS, 16 May 1973).

37 Ottaway and Ottaway, *Afrocommunism*, p. 33; *Africa Contemporary Record* (1978-79): A-19.

38 Richard Gibson, *African Liberation Movements*, Oxford University Press, 1972, p. 164; Henry Slater, "The Politics of Frustration: The ZAPU-ZANU Split in Historical Perspective," *Kenya Historical Review* 3, no. 2 (1975): 272, said 1962.

39 Wilkinson, "Insurgency," pp. 24-5.

40 Moscow radio, 13 March 1976; but there was pro-ZAPU propaganda as early as 1962 (e.g., L. Demkina, "Anti-enslavement Grows." *International Affairs*, no. 11 (1962), and 1961 (unsigned, "Leaders of the National Liberation Movement of the Federation of Rhodesia and Nyasaland," *International Affairs*, no. 11 (1961): 86-7).

41 Wilkinson, "Insurgency," p. 26.

42 Richard Bissell, "Southern Africa: Testing Détente," in Kirk and Wessell, *Soviet Threat*, p. 95; David Martin and Phyllis Johnson, *The Struggle for Zimbabwe*, Faber and Faber, London, 1981, p. 87; Grayson Kirk, "Politics and Violence in Rhodesia," *African Affairs* 74, no. 294 (1975): 9-10.

43 Cervenka and Legum, "Cuba," p. A-113; Daniel Papp, "The Soviet Union and Southern Africa," in Donaldson, *Soviet Union in the Third World*, p. 79; Oye Oguhbadejo, "Soviet Policies in Africa," *African Affairs* 79, no. 316 (1980): 310-11; Colin Legum, "The Soviet Union, China and the West in South Africa," *Foreign Affairs* 54, no. 4 (1976): 755; George Shepherd, "Socialist State Strategy and Arms in Southern Africa," *Issue*, 9, nos. 1-2 (1979): 49; Kaplan, *Diplomacy of Power*, p. 601. Cubans also trained ZAPU in Tanzania in the early 1970s: Wilkinson, "Insurgency," p. 47.

44 *Africa Research Bulletin* (April 1979): 5243.

45 Ibid. (May 1979): 5282; *Africa Contemporary Record*, (1975-76): B-643; (1979-80): A-167. *Africa Contemporary Record* (1977-78) said that Zambia would not permit Soviets or Cubans to train ZAPU there, although Cubans were known at least to accompany ZAPU people en route to and from their bases in Zambia. A ZAPU statement on this appeared in the *Daily Gleaner* (Kingston), 31 May 1978.

46 Wilkinson, "Insurgency," p. 26.

47 For example, E. A. Tarabrin (ed.), *SSSR i strany Afriki, Mysl'*, Moscow, 1977 (English version: *USSR and Countries of Africa*, Progress, Moscow, 1980, pp. 129-35) has much on Soviet military aid to the anti-Portuguese movements, but it speaks only of "all-round aid" in reference to the southern African movements. Ul'ianovskii spoke of all types of aid, including military, to "contingents of the national liberation movement," implying southern Africa as well, but he did not specify it; he did specify military aid to the anti-Portuguese movements. R. A. Ul'ianovskii, *Ocherki natsional'no-osvoboditel'noi bor'by*, Nauka, Moscow, 1976 (English version: R. A. Ulyanovsky, *National Liberation*, Progress, Moscow, 1978, p. 350). Nkomo mentioned military aid publicly (e.g., BBC-TV, 9 May 1977 interview), but such references were usually not reported by Soviet media. An exception was an article by Nkomo in *World Marxist Review*, February 1978 ("Zimbabwe: A Turning Point"), in which he spoke of arms supplies (p. 95). Another exception was Moscow radio, 9 September 1972.

48 M. Ibragimov, "Reshitel'naia podderzhka," *Azilia i Afrika segodnia*, no. 2 (1979): 12-13.

49 The first CPSU Congress attended was only in 1976, but ZAPU did participate in the 50th anniversary celebrations of 1972 and other events throughout the 1970s.

50 *Pravda*, 5 March 1977.

51 TASS, 8 January 1977. (Brezhnev spoke of the United States, Western Europe, and the Middle East, including Lebanon.)

52 William Griffith, "Soviet Power and Policies in the Third World: The Case of Africa," in *Prospects for Soviet Power in the 1980's*, Adelphi Paper, no. 152 (1979): 43; K. W. Grundy, *Guerrilla Struggle in Africa*, Grossman Publishers, New York, 1981,

p. 110. A SWAPO source dates the contacts with Moscow, at the latter's initiative, from 1963: Andreas Shipanga, *The Role of the Soviet Union*, vol. 1, 1982, p. 692; cited in Franz Ansprenger, *Die SWAPO*, Kaiser Verlag, Munich, 1984, p. 83.

53 Papp, "The Soviet Union," p. 79.

54 Legum, "Soviet Union, China and the West," p. 758; *Africa Contemporary Record* (1976-77): A-27, A-55; (1982-83): A33.

55 Kaplan, *Diplomacy of Power*, p. 601. There was one report that this increase preceded the Angolan war, after two trips to Moscow by Nujoma in 1973: *Africa Contemporary Record* (1973-74): A-79.

56 Cervenka and Legum, "Cuba," pp. A-113-14; *Africa Research Bulletin* (April 1977): 4407; *Facts and Reports* 6, no. 5 (10 March 1976), although a SWAPO interviewee suggested that the Cubans had trained them previously.

57 *Facts and Reports* 8, no. 22 (10 November 1978); *Africa Contemporary Record* (1982-83): A-38; Ottaway and Ottaway, *Afrocommunism* p. 33; *Africa Research Bulletin* (May 1979): 5282. Glass, "East Germany," pp. 306-11, said that GDR aid began earlier.

58 E.g., "Iug Afriki: revoliutsionnyi protsess neobratim," *Aziia i Afrika segodnia*, no. 9 (1979): 25; S. Nuioma, "My uvereny v svoei pobede," *Kommunist*, no. 17 (1980): 104.

59 Sam Nujoma, "Namibia at the Threshold of Independence," *World Marxist Review*, no. 2 (1978): 94, repeated in a quote in Iu. Gorbunov, "Namibiia: militarizatsiia obrechennogo rezhima," *Aziia i Afrika segodnia*, no. 8 (1982): 29.

60 Ibragimov, "Reshitel'naia podderzhka," pp. 12-13; M. Ibragimov, "Golos sovetskoi obshchestvennosti - golos solidarnosti," *Aziia i Afrika segondnia*, no. 7 (1978): 4-5.

61 *Pravda*, 20 September 1981.

62 This was after Zimbabwe's independence: *Africa Contemporary Record* (1981-82): A-170. He addressed an accompanying party organization meeting, as was the case in 1976, rather than the Congress itself.

63 TASS, 24 November 1973.

64 Kaplan, *Power of Diplomacy*, pp. 342, 349; Bruce Porter, *The USSR in Third World Conflicts*, Cambridge University Press, Cambridge, 1984, pp. 22-3.

65 Kaplan, *Power of Diplomacy*, p. 100.

66 Ibid.

67 Opened first in Cuba 1963, East Germany and Czechoslovakia, 1964, the USSR 1965: Donald Zagoria, *The Vietnam Triangle*, Pegasus, New York, 1967, p. 49.

68 *Pravda*, 31 August 1973. See Douglas Pike, *Viet-Cong: The Organization and Techniques of the NLF of South Vietnam*, MIT University Press, Cambridge, Mass., 1966, pp. 342-3.

69 *Pravda*, 17 March 1971, 3 June 1971, 2 June 1974.

70 Paul Henze, "Arming the Horn 1960-1980," The Wilson Center, Working Paper no. 43 (July 1982): 32; Kaplan, *Power of Diplomacy*, pp. 170, 488-9, 504; Ogunbadejo, "Soviet Policies," p. 310. Hosmer and Wolfe, *Soviet Policy and Practice*, p. 130, say no hard evidence but persistent rumors of Soviet pilots.

71 Hosmer and Wolfe, *Soviet Policy and Practice*, p. 93; *Le Monde*, 15 September 1978; *The Guardian*, 2 February 1978; Peter Vanneman and Martin James, "Soviet Intervention in the Horn of Africa," *Policy Review*, no. 5 (1978): 26; *Hoover Yearbook 1984*, Palo Alto, 1984, pp. 23-4.

72 Porter, *The USSR*, pp. 96, 105; David Morrison, "Tropical Africa: The New Soviet Look," *Mizan* (August 1971): 52; John Stremlau, *The International Politics of the Nigerian Civil War*, Princeton University Press, Princeton, N. J. 1977, p. 79; Ogunbadejo, "Soviet Policies," pp. 308-9.

73 Porter, *The USSR*, p. 103.

74 Ibid, p. 106; Hosmer and Wolfe, *Soviet Policy and Practice*, p. 31; John Mauer and Richard Porth (eds.) *Military Intervention in the Third World*, Praeger, New York, 1984, pp. 54-5.

75 The Eritreans claimed that the Cubans were involved: *Africa Research Bulletin* (December 1978): 4914-15; see also *Hoover Yearbook 1984*, pp. 23-4; Hosmer and Wolfe, *Soviet Policy and Practice*, p. 149; Bruce Porter, "Moscow and Mengistu," Radio Liberty, 401/80, 27 October 1980; Ottaway and Ottaway, *Afrocommunism*,

p. 184; Jorge Dominguez, "Political and Military Limitations and Consequences of Cuban Policies in Africa," *Cuban Studies* 10, no. 2 (1980): 2-35; Harry Brind, "Soviet Policy in the Horn of Africa," *International Affairs* (London) 60, no. 1 (1981): 78; Gordon Adams, "Cuba and Africa: The International Politics of the Liberation Struggle," *Latin American Perspectives* 8, no. 1 (1981): 108-25. On the South Yemenis, see *International Herald Tribune*, 23 June 1978, although *Africa Contemporary Record* (1977-78): A-415, said Yemini pilots were there in early 1978. See also Bereket Habte Selassie, *Conflict and Intervention in the Horn of Africa*, Monthly Review Press, London, 1980, pp. 143-6.

76 DPA, 23 November 1979.

77 *Pravda*, 29 May 1974; Rostislav Ulyanovsky, "Leninism: The Soviet Experience and Newly-free Countries," *New Times*, no. 2 (1971): p. 23; Ulyanovsky, *National Liberation*, p. 141.

78 Although during the oppression of the Iraqi Communist party in 1978 the Soviets did recall the fact that Iraqi Communists had fought with the ruling Ba'ath against the Kurds (TASS, 17 June 1978).

79 *Pravda*, 2, 24 February 1975, 15 March 1978; *Izvestiia*, 9 February 1975 (Eritrea); P. N. Fedoseev et al., *Leninizm i natsional'nyi vopros v sovremennykh usloviiakh*, Politizdat, Moscow, 1974 (English version: P. N. Fedoseyev (ed.), *Leninism and the National Question*, Progress, Moscow, 1977) p. 483; *Pravda*, 21 October 1966; *Izvestiia*, 21 March 1967, 24 November 1968; Radio Peace and Progress in English, 26 February 1969 (Ibos).

80 A. A. Gromyko and G. B. Starushenko, "Sotsial'nye i natsional'nye faktory razvitiia osvobodivshikhsia stran," *Sotsiologicheskie issledovaniia*, no. 1 (1983): 8-9; D. M. Eremeev, "Anatomiia etnicheskikh konfliktov," *Aziia i Afrika segodnia*, no. 6 (1981): 15; Muhammed Ibrahim Nugug, "At the Beginning of a Difficult State," *World Marxist Review*, no. 9 (1985): 89.

81 Al-Sharq al-Awsat (Saudi Arabia), 6 December 1985 (interview with J. Garang).

82 Ulyanovsky, "Leninism," p. 23; A Malov, "Milestone for Burma," *New Times*, no. 30 (1971): 23; A. Malov, "Burma's Progress," *New Times*, no. 1 (1974): 14; K. Pavlov, "Peking's Chauvinists' Duplicity," *New Times*, no. 4 (1974): 12.

83 E.g., L. Yelin, "Write These Things or Else," *New Times*, no. 19 (1984): 17; L. Zhegalov, "Divide and Destabilize," *New Times*, no. 14 (1984): 12-13; L. Zhegalov, "The Nation is Continuing Along the Road," *New Times*, no. 48 (1985): 24-5.

84 *Izvestiia*, 18 February 1979; TASS, 29 October 1977, 29 November 1977, 13 April 1979; *Za rubezhom*, 19 July 1979; Radio Peace and Progress in Mandarin to Southeast Asia, 15 October 1977, 23 November 1977, 5 February 1978, 11 March 1978, 5 August 1978, 14 July 1979.

85 *Pravda*, 29 December 1976.

86 *Pravda*, 6 February 1977, 24, 30 September 1977, 15 October 1977. The condemnations began again after the 10 October killing by the Moros of a leading Philippino general and several other high-ranking officers: *Far Eastern Economic Review* (4 November 1977): 29.

87 An academically objective account in 1981 referred sympathetically to the Moros' lack of rights but then spoke of Chinese support for "separatists" including the Moros: Eremeev, "Anatomiia," p. 15.

88 *Far Eastern Economic Review* (14 January 1977): 18-19, claims that Gadaffi had supported the Moros since the late 1960s, arming the MNLF when it emerged in 1972.

89 *Hoover Yearbook 1982*, pp. 24-5.

90 *New York Times*, 13 June 1979; Alvin Rubinstein, *Soviet Policy Towards Turkey, Iran and Afghanistan*, Praeger, New York, 1982, p. 103.

91 *Pravda*, 8 August 1983.

92 Moscow radio, 9 September 1983; K. P. Silva, "Championing Independence, Democracy and Progress," *World Marxist Review*, no. 8 (1984): 34; Pieter Keuneman, "The Background of the Conflict," *World Marxist Review*, no. 2 (1984): 65; A. Mikhailov, "Trudnye vremena," *Aziia i Afrika segodnia*, no. 3 (1985): 32-5.

93   Mikhailov, "Trudnye Vremena," pp. 32-5; A. Ulansky, "Mossad Steps In?" *New Times*, no. 27 (1984): 17.
94   The London *Observer* (9 December 1984) cited a Tamil source on training by Habash's PFLP in Syria.
95   Soviet television, 4 September 193 (Bovin); *Pravda*, 20 May 1983, 30 June 1983.
96   Ibid. for political support. For contradictory views on Soviet involvement see *Africa Contemporary Record* (1981-82): 174; David Smock and Norman Miller, "Soviet Designs in Africa," *American University Field Staff Reports*, no. 17 (1980): 3; Hosmer and Wolfe, *Soviet Policy and Practice*, p. 41; S. N. MacFarlane, "Intervention and Security in Africa," *International Affairs* (U.S.) 60, no. 1 (1984): 59; Robert Legvold, "The Super Rivals: Conflict in the Third World," *Foreign Affairs* 57, no. 4 (1979): 768.
97   William Gutteridge, "Libya: Still a Threat to Western Interests?" *Conflict Studies*, no. 160 (1984): 13-14. Although relations have improved significantly from the open hostility of the early 1970s up the reported *drafting* of a Friendship Treaty in 1983, the fact is that no such treaty has been signed and many differences exist between the two states. See Lisa Anderson, "Qadhafi and the Kremlin," *Problems of Communism* 34, no. 5 (1985): 29-44.
98   Peter Mangold, "Shaba I and Shaba II," *Survival* 21, (1979): 108-9; Bender, "Angola, the Cubans," p. 15; Hosmer and Wolfe, *Soviet Policy and Practice*, p. 86.
99   Colin Legum, "It's Germans Not Cubans," *New Republic* (24 June 1978); Hosmer and Wolfe, *Soviet Policy and Practice*, p. 87.
100   Raymond Garthoff, *Détente and Confrontation*, Brookings Institution, Washington, D.C., 1985, pp. 624-6.
101   Robins, "Soviet-Cuban Relationship," p. 159.
102   A. A. Gromyko, "Imperialism Against Africa," *New Times*, no. 78 (1978): 18; Vladimir Kirsanov, "The Shaba Uprising and NATO Interferences," *New Times*, no. 22 (1978): 13.
103   Ibid.
104   *Christian Science Monitor*, 17 March 1967; *New York Times*, 3 March 1967; Kaplan, *Power of Diplomacy*, p. 610; Philippe Leymarie, "Le Conflit d'Erythrée: Trois fronts, une guerre de liberation nationale," *Revue Française d'études politiques Africaines* 13, no. 148 (1978): 63; Don Connell, "The Unknown War in Eritrea," *The Nation*, 3 March 1979: 238-9; Jack Kramer, "Ethiopia's Unknown War," *The Nation* 11 August 1979: 104.
105   Richard Lobban, "Eritrea Liberation Front: A Close-up View," *Munger Africana Library Notes*, no. 13 (September 1972): 13, said that 18 tons of Czech arms intended for the Eritreans were seized in Khartoum in June 1965. Henze, "Arming the Horn"; Paul Henze, "Communism and Ethiopia," *Problems of Communism* 30, no. 3 (1981): 61.
106   *New York Times*, 3 March 1967.
107   Henze, "Communism and Ethiopia," p. 61; Paul Henze, *Russians and the Horn*, European American Institute for Security Research, Paper no. 5, 1983, p. 17; Don Connell, "The Birth of the Eritrean Nation," *Horn of Africa* 3, no. 1 (1980): 23; Taye Geremaw, "Rebellion in Eritrea," *Survival* 13, no. 8 (1971): 277.
108   Connell, "Birth," p. 23; Hoover Institute Archives, Jack Kramer Collection, unidentified report: "Today, deep in the barren mountains of a vast black African territory, there are Cubans seeking a revolution," p. 1.
109   Henze, "Communism and Ethiopia," p. 61; Connell, "Birth," p. 23; Lobban, "Eritrea Liberation Front," p. 13; Geremaw, "Rebellion," p. 277.
110   LeoGrande, "Cuban-Soviet Relations," p. 28; Zdenek Cervenka, "Eritrea: Struggle for Self-determination," *Afrika Spektrum* (Hamburg) 12, no. 1 (1977): 42; Connell, "Birth," p. 23; John Campbell, "Points of Conflict," *Survival* 13, no. 8 (1971): 270.
111   See, e.g., dispute with the Iraqis over Eritrea: Frank Fukuyama, "The Soviet Union and Iraq since 1968," Rand Corporation, July 1980, p. 59.
112   Interviews with U.S. officials; Pierre Rondot, "La guerre d'Erythrée," *Revue Française d'études politiques Africaines*, no. 73 (1972): 27-8; unsigned, "The Eritrean Conflict," *Africa Currents*, no. 7 (1976-77): 19.
113   G. B. Aleksandrenko, *Burzhuaznyi federalizm*, Izdatel'stvo Akademii Nauk Ukrainskoi SSR, Kiev, 1962, pp. 202-4; M. I. Ivanitskii, *Put' k nezavisimosti. Iz istorii*

resheniia voprosa o sud'be byvshikh ital'ianskikh kolonii 1945-1950, Izdatel'stvo Akademii Nauk Ukrainskoi, SSR, Kiev, (1962)pp 3-5, 6-7, 18-40, 104-29; A. N. Stepunin, *Efiopiia*, Mysl', Moscow, 1965, pp. 20, 70, 78-80; D. R. Voblikov, *Gosudarstvennyi stroi Efiopii*, Gosudarstvennoe izdatel'stvo iuridicheskoi literatury, Moscow, 1957, pp. 3, 13-40; G. V. Fokeev, *Vneshniaia politika stran Afriki*, Mezhdunarodnye otnosheniia, Moscow, 1968, pp. 119-21; I. Etinger, *Mezhgosudarstvennye otnosheniia v Afrike: politicheskie problemy, evoliutsiia, organizatsionnye formy*, Nauka, Moscow, 1972.

114 Aleksandrenko, *Federalizm*, was an exception to this; he was critical of the federal arrangement and its provisions for Eritrea.

115 Moscow radio, 3 January 1971.

116 B. Gorbachov, "The Situation in Eritrea," *New Times*, no. 46 (1974): 20.

117 *Pravda*, 2, 11, 15, and 24 February 1975, 5 March 1975; *Izvestiia*, 9 February 1975 (though still not oppositional); D. Borisov, "The Developments in Ethiopia," *New Times*, no. 8 (1975): pp. 10-11. The Cubans and the Italian Communist party did not change their positions; see, for example, interviews with Eritrean leaders in *l'Unita*, 7 November 1977, 18 April 1978; ANSA, 1 April 1978, and even criticism of the Soviet Union in *L'Unita*, 22 September 1977.

118 *Africa Confidential* 19, no. 14 (1978): 3; 21, no. 8 (1980): 3; 21, no. 2 (1980): 3; 21, no. 16 (1980): 2; *Africa Research Bulletin* (August 1978): 4926; Andrew Lycett, "States within States," *The Middle East*, no. 75 (1981): 28; *Africa*, no. 34 (1978): 35. The Soviet yearbook refers to negotiations mediated by the PDRY, Cuba, and GDR in 1978 which failed because of "separatist" EPLF pre-conditions and objectives: *Mezhdunarodnyi ezhegodnik, politika i ekonomika 1979*, Politizdat, Moscow, 1979, p. 281.

119 *Pravda*, 28 October 1980; Moscow radio, 1 April 1984.

120 E.g., Soviet television, 1 April 1984, 6 May 1984; *Krasnaia zvezda*, 11 September 1982; V. Sharayev, "Milestone in Ethiopian History," *International Affairs*, no. 10 (1984): 36; I. Ivanov, "Osvobodivshiesia strany: razriadka i razvitie," *Aziia i Afrika segodnia*, no. 8 (1980): 2-3; G. Gal'perin, "Etiopiia: nekotorye aspekty natsional'nogo voprosa," *Aziia i Afrika segodnia*, no. 8 (1979): 24-5; Gennady Gabrielyan, "In Step With the Whole Country," *New Times*, no. 30 (1984): 26.

121 E.g., *Pravda*, 15 March 1978; *Izvestiia*, 4, 6 May 1977, 16 June 1977, 2 August 1977; Moscow radio, 28 April 1977. Gennady Gabrielyan, "In the Liberated Areas of Eritrea,: *New Times*, no. 16 (1979): 30, said there was no such thing as an Eritrean nation. P. I. Manchkha virtually said the same in his 1979 book, *Aktual'nye problemy sovremennoi Afriki*, Politizdat, Moscow, 1979, p. 132, as did G. Gal'perin, "Eritreiskaia problema," *Novoe vremia*, no. 5 (1979): 26-7; An. A. Gromyko, "Opyt resheniia natsional'nogo voprosa v SSSR i afro-aziatskii mir," *Narody Azii i Afriki*, no. 6 (1982): 24; G. Tanov, "At Odds with Logic," *New Times*, no. 14 (1979): 14.

122 Paul Viotti, "Iraq: The Kurdish Rebellion," in O'Neill et al., *Insurgency in the Modern World*, pp. 194, 201-2; Ya'acov Ro'i, *From Encroachment to Involvement: A Documentary Study of Soviet Policy in the Middle East, 1945-1973*, John Wiley, New York, 1974, p. 315.

123 See, for example, acknowledgment of past aid (TASS 23 June 1971), although during the fighting in 1974, *Pravda* (19 May 1974) referred to the 1961-70 civil war negatively, with no mention of Soviet aid.

124 Ro'i, *From Encroachment*, p. 509; *Pravda*, 11 March 1971; Aryeh Yodfat, *Arab Politics in the Soviet Mirror*, Israel Universities Press, Jerusalem, 1973, pp. 181-91; John Campbell, "The Soviet Union and the Middle East," in Roger Kanet (ed.), *The Soviet Union and the Developing Nations*, Johns Hopkins University Press, Baltimore, 1974, p. 165.

125 *The Village Voice*, 16 February 1976 (Pike Report).

126 *Pravda*, 19 December 1972; Moscow radio, 30 August 1972, 2 December 1973; TASS, 15 November 1973, 1 December 1973.

127 Moscow radio in Arabic, 11 January 1974; *Pravda*, 25 July 1974.

128 TASS, 11 March 1974; *Pravda*, 26 April 1974; Moscow radio, 25 June 1974; Moscow radio in Arabic, 8 March 1974.

129   E.g., Radio Peace and Progress in Arabic, 3 April 1980, 31 March 1984 (on the occasion of the Iraqi Communist party's anniversary).
130   Edgar O'Ballance, "The Kurdish Factor in the Gulf War," *Military Review* (June 1981): 14-16; Rubinstein, *Soviet Policy*, p. 116; *Hoover Yearbook 1981*, p. 7; *1983*, p. 22; *1984*, p. 28; Chris Kutschera, "Inside Kurdistan," *The Middle East* (September 1985): 10-12; Kadhim Habib and Ali Ileri, "What Lies Behind an Anti-people Conspiracy?" *World Marxist Review*, no. 4 (1985): 125-6 (very favorable to the Kurds).
131   O'Ballance, "The Kurdish Factor"; Martin van Bruinessen, "The Kurds," *Merip Reports (February 1984): 6-12.*
132   Van Bruinessen, "The Kurds." There was a report in 1983 of Iraqi Communist party claims to have helped Kurdish groups fight off Turkish army units in the border area, but the incident is not clear: *MEED* 22 (1983): 69.
133   *MEED* 22 (1983): 69.
134   *Hoover Yearbook 1971*, pp. 268-9; *1972*, p. 238; *1980*, pp. 217, 452; *1981*, p. 453; *1985*, p. 534.
135   *Pravda*, 5 June 1983.
136   Eremeev, "Anatomiia," pp. 15-16; M. Lazarev, "Sovremennyi etap natsional'nogo razvitiia stran zarubezhnogo Vostoka," *Aziia i Afrika segodnia*, no. 12 (1979): 49-51; Habib and Ileri, "What Lies Behind," pp. 125-6.
137   E.g., a Soviet broadcast in Turkish (11 March 1979) praising the Kurdish autonomy in Iraq: G. Chipashvili and K. Angosi, "The Struggle Continues: Concerning Events in Iranian Kurdistan," *Tibilisi Kommunisti* (October 1979) in Georgian in FBIS/Soviet Union, 28 December 1979, M4-6; Soviet television, 18 November 1979 (Bonn).
138   *Pravda*, 24 March 1979; Moscow radio in Persian, 3 August 1979; TASS, 14 April 1979; TASS statement, 4 September 1979; TASS, 2 October 1979, said Israel was supplying the arms.
139   TASS, 4 April 1979.
140   *Pravda*, 25 and 31 August 1979, 4 September 1979 (with Tudeh letter favorable to the Kurds); Moscow radio, 4 and 7, September 1979, 20 November 1979 (Bovin); Moscow radio in Persian, 3 September 1979. *Pravda*, 20 September 1979, spoke of conflicting views within the Iranian leadership on how to handle the Kurds, and Moscow radio, 5 September 1980 condemned Khomeini's response to the "legitimate" Kurdish demands.
141   *Pravda*, 15 June 1982; TASS, 27 April 1982; National Voice of Iran (in Persian from the Soviet Union), 28 June 1983- although in 1981 at least the Tudeh was critical of the Kurds (*Hoover Yearbook 1982*, p. 21, referring to a June 1981 Tudeh letter).
142   Rubinstein, *Soviet Policy*, pp. 115-16 (says may be clandestine arms deliveries); Wayne Limberg, "The USSR and the Persian Gulf: Continuity vs. Change," paper delivered to the III World Congress of Soviet and East European Studies, Washington, D.C., 1985; *Hoover Yearbook 1980*, 1981.
143   Dr. Abder-Rahman Ghassemlou (head of the KPD), interviewed in *The Middle East* (July 1980): 19.
144   Shirin Tahir-Keli, "External Dimensions of 'Regionalism' in Pakistan," *Contemporary Asia Review 1*, no. 1 (1977): 89; *Hoover Yearbook 1974*, p. 519. Iraq reportedly was encouraging the idea of "greater Baluchistan" as an anti-Iranian move because of Iranian support for the Kurdish rebellion against Baghdad.
145   Selig Harrison, "Nightmare in Baluchistan," *Foreign Policy*, no. 32 (1978): 159.
146   Ibid., pp. 158-9; Rubinstein, *Soviet Policy*, p. 139.
147   Tahir-Keli, "External Dimensions," p. 89; Bhabani Sen Gupta, *Soviet Asian Relations in the 1970s and Beyond*, Praeger, New York, 1976, p. 90.
148   *Pravda*, 6 June 1974, carries the speeches and communiqué; in the former, Daoud spoke of the fate of the "Pushtan and Baluchi brethren," and Rubinstein, *Soviet Policy*, p. 141, claims TASS omitted this line. TASS in *Pravda*, 6 June 1974, does, however, include it. According to Olaf Caroe, *The Pathans*, Oxford University Press, 1978, p. 529, the Soviets offered Daoud only mild support on the Paktoonistan issue at this time.
149   Tahir-Kheli, "External Dimensions," p. 90.
150   *Hoover Yearbook 1976*, p. 357.

151 *Hoover Yearbook 1975*, p. 398; Rubinstein, *Soviet Policy*, pp. 140-1. However, it may have been due to improved Afghan-Iranian relations: Tahir-Khell, "External Dimensions," p. 89.

152 *Business Week*, 21 January 1980, p. 51; *Hoover Yearbook 1983*, p. 207; *Sunday Times* (London), 7 March 1982; R. G. Wirsing, *The Baluchis and the Pathans*, Minority Rights Group Report, London, post-1980, p. 15.

153 Legvold, "Super Rivals," p. 771; William Griffith, "The USSR and Pakistan," *Problems of Communism* 31 (1982)," 412-13; Selig Harrison, "A Breakthrough in Afghanistan," *Foreign Policy*, no. 51 (1983): 21; Dev Murarka, "Growing Fears in Moscow," *Middle East International*, 7 January 1983, p. 8; Jamal Rasheed, "All Eyes on Baluchistan," *Middle East International*, 15 January 1982.

154 *Pravda*, 6, 12, 15, and 28 December 1985; *Izvestiia*, 30 December 1985 (accused the Pakistanis of genocide); *Krasnaia zvezda*, 8 December 1985.

155 Harrison, "Nightmare," pp. 151, 155.

156 E.g., Tehran radio (in Arabic), 20 March 1980.

157 National Voice of Iran, 3 April 1981; Moscow radio in Persian, 15 February 1981; TASS, 26 May 1981.

158 National Voice of Iran, 3 April 1981.

159 Wirsing, *Baluchis and Pathans*, pp. 13-14; R. Wirsing, "South Asia: The Baluch Frontier Tribes of Pakistan," in R. Wirsing, *Protection of Ethnic Minorities Comparative Perspectives*, Pergamon Press, New York, 1981, p. 301.

160 *Business Week*, 21 January 1980, p. 51 (said trained by Cubans as well as Soviets in Afghanistan with 8,000 in the Soviet Union); *Hoover Yearbook 1983*, p. 207; Radio Tehran, 20 March 1980. Drew Middleton of the *New York Times* spoke of 300 Soviet experts helping the Baluchis (Wirsing, *Baluchis and Pathans*, p. 15).

161 A Dastarac and M. Levant, "What Went Wrong in Afghanistan?" *Merip Reports* (July–August 1980): 10. AFP, 5 February 1980, spoke of Baluchi resistance fighters taking refuge from Afghanistan in Iran. This was one of many reports of Iranian denials that Tehran was helping these rebels, who were assisted by local Iranian Baluchis.

162 Bhabani Sen Gupta, "Moscow and Bangladesh," *Problems of Communism* 24 (1975): 59.

163 V. Sosnovsky, "Election Campaign in Pakistan," *New Times*, no. 10 (1970): 11. William Barnds, "Moscow and South Asia," *Problems of Communism* 21 (1972): 25, said the Indians were concerned over this Soviet ambiguity. India recognized Bangladesh 7 December 1971, according to Barnds, having waited this long because of Soviet pressure.

164 Sen Gupta, *Soviet-Asian Relations*, p. 157; *Pravda*, 30 September 1971 (although the TASS version in English left the term "East Bengal"); see also Robert Jackson, *South Asian Crisis*, Praeger, New York, 1975, pp. 83, 194.

165 *Izvestiia*, 12 December 1971 (Kudriavtsev). One TASS release a month earlier (15 November 1971) in English spoke of the "peaceful Bengali people."

166 Moscow radio in Arabic, 20 December 1971; *Pravda*, 16 December 1971. The term "Bangladesh" was finally used in TASS 31 December 1971 quoting Indira Gandhi, and in *Pravda*, 16 January 1972, which spoke of the post-liberation struggle of the people of Bangladesh.

167 Communiqué with Indira Gandhi, *Pravda*, 30 September 1971.

168 Jackson, *South Asian Crisis*, pp. 103-5.

169 Ibid. Jackson claims that the Soviet press published condolences on the death of Soviet cosmonauts in July 1971 from the "acting President of the Democratic Republic of Bangladesh," but I have not been able to find any such reference in the Soviet press.

170 Ibid., p. 90.

171 Ibid., p. 78.

172 *Soviet News*, no. 5617, 7 December 1971.

173 Hosmer and Wolfe, *Soviet Policy and Practice*, p. 150, citing Soviet Ambassador to India.

174 Kaplan, *Power of Diplomacy*, p. 104; Garthoff, *Détente and Confrontation*, p. 273.

175 E.g., *Pravda*, 27 December 1971.

176   Fred Halliday, *Arabia without the Sultans*, Vintage, New York, 1974, p. 327.
177   See, for example, A. Vasilyev, "Rebels Against Slavery," *New Times*, no. 38 (1971): 27-30; *Pravda*, 3 August 1971; Moscow radio in Arabic, 8 July 1972.
178   Moscow radio in Persian, 7 February 1975, 27 October 1975.
179   E.g., TASS, 9 January 1973; Moscow radio in Arabic, 24 March 1973; *Krasnaia zvezda*, 13 January 1974; *Pravda*, 11 June 1975. Usually the idea of Gulf liberation was ignored, even when the full name of the movement was given, and references tended to be to the PFLO (e.g. *Pravda*, 26 April 1973; *Sovetskaia Rossiia*, 11 June 1975; Radio Peace and Progress in Arabic, 13 and 21 January 1975).
180   In 1982 a PDRY-Omani agreement brought an end to PDRY support for the already dwindling rebellion *(Hoover Yearbook 1984*, p. 72). The Soviet Union and Oman opened diplomatic relations in the Fall of 1985.
181   E.g., Moscow radio, 21 September 1971; Moscow radio in Arabic, 12 February 1974, 6 May 1979; TASS, 20 February 1975.
182   E.g., Moscow radio, 19 September 1973; Radio Peace and Progress in Arabic, 10 June 1975; in English, 13 May 1974; Radio Moscow in Arabic, 17 January 1974, 12 February 1974; *Krasnaia zvezda*, 10 April 1975; *Sovetskaia Rossiia*, 11 June 1975. An exception to this was an enthusiastic interview with a delegation leader in 1971 (Moscow radio, 21 September 1971) who spoke of "all possible help."
183   Garthoff, *Détente and Confrontation*, p. 669; Valerie Yorke, "The Sultan Keeps His Eye on Dhofar," *Middle East International*, 12 March 1982, p. 12; Paul Viotti, "Politics in the Yemens and the Horn of Africa: Constraints on a Superpower," in Mark Kauppi and Craig Nation, *The Soviet Union and the Middle East in the 1980's*, Lexington Books, Lexington, Mass., 1983, p. 217.
184   *Middle East International*, 12 March 1982, p. 11-12.
185   Dismukes and McConnell, *Soviet Naval Diplomacy*, p. 137.
186   Halliday, *Arabia without the Sultans*, pp. 390, 401; Hosmer and Wolfe, *Soviet Policy and Practice* p. 49. Dismukes and McConnell, *Soviet Naval Diplomacy*, p. 137, said that there was a complaint in 1970 of the "tokenism" of Soviet aid.
187   Viotti, "Iraq: The Kurdish Rebellion", p. 217.
188   *Al-Majales* (Kuwait), 21 April 1984 (interview with Omani official).
189   Gibson, *African Liberation Movements*, p. 65.
190   *Africa Contemporary Record* (1981-82): B-695; (1982-83): A-38; Kaplan, *Power of Diplomacy*, p. 601; *Africa Confidential* 19, no. 24 (1978): 1; Daniel Papp, "The Soviet Union and Southern Africa," in Donaldson, *Soviet Union*, pp. 79-82.
191   Papp, "Soviet Union and Southern Africa," p. 81.
192   Cervenka and Legum, "Cuba," p. A-113; *Africa Contemporary Record* (1981-82): B-695; (1982-83): A-38. Cubans were training ANC people in Algeria from approximately 1963: Greig, *Communist Challenge*, p. 94.
193   Greig, *Communist Challenge*, p. 94; Glass, "East Germany," pp. 309-11; interview with Colin Legum.
194   Papp, "Soviet Union and Southern Africa"; *Africa Contemporary Record* (1978-79): A19.
195   Papp, "Soviet Union and Southern Africa", p. 79; *Africa*, no. 57 (1976): 23.
196   TASS, 6 December 1972 (on the occasion of the ANC's fiftieth anniversary); TASS, 7 January 1979 (citing ANC officials).
197   Alfred Nzo, "South Africa: The Struggle Continues," *International Affairs*, no. 5 (1983): 109.
198   E.g., Vusizwe Seme, "On the Various Forms of Revolutionary Struggle," *African Communist*, no. 71 (1977): 34.
199   *Africa Research Bulletin* 14, no. 3 (1977): 4376.
200   Galia Golan, *The Soviet Union and the Palestine Liberation Organization*, Praeger, New York, 1980, pp. 5-14.
201   Bard O'Neill, *Armed Struggle in Palestine: A Political-Military Analysis*, Westview, Boulder, Colo., 1978, p. 195; Lester Sobel (ed.), *Palestinian Impasse: Arab Guerrillas and International Terror*, Facts on File, New York, 1977, p. 117; Robert Freedman, "The Soviet Policy Towards International Terrorism," in Yonah Alexander (ed.), *International Terrorism: National, Regional and Global Perspectives*, Praeger, New York,

1976, p. 125; *New York Times*, 17 September 1972; *l'Orient le Jour* (Lebanon), 27 September 1972.

202 Golan, *Soviet Union and the PLO*, pp. 207-8.

203 Ibid., P. 213; Leonard Shapiro, "The Soviet Union and the PLO," *Survey*, no. 23 (1977-78): 206; Ran Merom, "The Soviet Concept of Guerrilla Warfare and Retaliation," *International Problems* (Israel) 16, nos. 3-4 (1977): 78-91.

204 *Al-Nahar* (Lebanon), 24 July 1978 (Soviet denial of this *Pravda*, 7 May 1978).

205 E.g., *Pravda*, 16 September 1977 (quoting Kaddumi during a trip to Moscow).

206 Dismukes and McConnell, *Soviet Naval Diplomacy*, p. 171; Kaplan, *Power of Diplomacy*, p. 194; Galia Golan, "The Soviet Union and the Israeli Action in Lebanon," *International Affairs* (Britain) 59, no. 1 (1982-83): 8.

207 Golan, "Soviet Union and Israeli Action," p. 12; Galia Golan, "The Soviet Union and the PLO since Lebanon," *Middle East Journal* 40, no. 2 (1986): 288-9.

208 Golan, *Soviet Union and the PLO*, pp. 5-14.

209 *Africa Contemporary Record* (1981-82): A67; Garthoff, *Détente and Confrontation*, p. 669; Smock and Miller, "Soviet Designs in Africa," p. 3; *New York Times*, 17 February 1980; George Henderson, "Libya and Morocco – Marriage of Necessity," *Middle East International*, no. 260 (11 October 1985): 18; John Damis, "The Western Sahara Conflict: Myths and Realities," *Middle East Journal* 37, no. 2 (1983): p. 173; Tony Hodges, "The Endless War," *Africa Report* 27, no. 4 (1982): 10-11.

210 Kaplan, *Power of Diplomacy*, p. 199; Hosmer and Wolfe, *Soviet Policy and Practice*, pp. 71-2.

211 David Albright, "The Middle East and Africa in Recent Soviet Policy", Kanet, *Soviet Foreign Policy*.

212 Moscow radio in Arabic, 14 August 1979; 20 October 1979.

213 E.g., TASS, 29 February 1976; 6 March 1976; K. Andreev, "Zapadnaia Sakhara," *Novoe Vremia*, no. 24 (1977): 24-5.

214 Critical or mildly critical on Moscow radio in Arabic, 20 October 1977; TASS, 8 November 1977; *Izvestiia*, 17 July 1983; L. P. Andreev and N. P. Podgornova, "Zapadnaia Sakhara: poiski uregulirovaniia," *Narody Azii i Afriki*, no. 4 (1984): 99-102; D. B. Malisheva, "Zapadnaia Sakhara," *Voprosy istorii*, no. 8 (1983): 95; Andreev, "Zapadnaia Sakhara," p. 25. Criticism was absent from A. Shvedov and A. Podtserob, "The Soviet Union and North African Countries," *International Affairs*, no. 6 (1983): 54-62, usual in Moscow radio in French to North Africa as well.

215 E.g., *Pravda*, 2 February 1978; 8 October 1983.

216 On Algerian recognition and Moroccan break in relations, TASS, 29 February 1976; 6 and 7 August 1976. On other states' recognition, Moscow radio, 14 September 1979; Malisheva, "Zapadnaia Sakhara," p. 97; K. Andreev, "Referendum ili eskalatsiia?," *Novoe vremia*, no. 50 (1981): 12.

217 Ignacio Klick, "Success for Polisario," *Middle East International*, 11 January 1985, p. 11; George Jaffe, "The Issue is Sovereignty," *Middle East International*, 8 March 1985, p. 12.

218 M. Sadek, "My stremimsia k nezavisimosti, k miru," *Novoe vremia*, no. 40 (1979): 14-15.

219 Unsigned, "Against Imperialism, For Social Progress" (International Scientific Conference in Berlin), *World Marxist Review*, no. 4 (1981): 72.

220 E.g., introduction to interview, "Nguyen Huu Tho," *New Times*, no. 52 (1973): 6; E. Vasilkov, "Leading Political Force of South Vietnam," *New Times*, no. 23 (1973): 6; I. Ivkov, "Preserve and Consolidate Peace in South Vietnam," *New Times*, no. 33 (1974): 4. For retrospective categorization see K. N. Brutents, *Sovremennge natsional'no-osvoboditel'nye revoliutsii*, Politizdat, Moscow, 1974 (English version: K. N. Brutents, *National Liberation Movements Today*, Progress, Moscow, 1977, vol. I, p. 86).

221 L. Nekrasova, "Partiia narodnogo dvizheniia za osvobozhdenie Angoly," *Mirovaia ekonomika i mezhdunarodnye otnosheniia*, no. 9 (1961): 138; unsigned, "The Ways of the Anti-imperialist Struggle in Tropical Africa," *World Marxist Review*, no. 8 (1971): 34.

222 Iu. Borisoglebskii, "Agostin'o Neto," *Mirovaia ekonomika i mezhdunarodnye otnosheniia*, no. 10 (1963): 139; unsigned, "Angola's National Forces," *International Affairs*, no. 3 (1963): 117.

223 R. Ul'ianovskii, "Agostin'o Neto," *Aziia i Afrika segodnia*, no. 2 (1982); 26; R. A. Ulyanovsky et al., *Fighters for National Liberation*, Progress, Moscow, 1984, pp. 114-15 (R. Ul'ianovskii, *Bortsy za natsional'nuiu svobodu*, Politizdat, Moscow, 1983).

224 I. Strekalova, "SVAPO: 20 let upornoi bor'by," *Aziia i Afrika segodnia*, no. 4 91980): 25.

225 V. Solodovnikov and O. Martyshin, "Nasledie Amilkara Kabrala," *Aziia i Afrika segondnia*, no. 7 (1983): 42; Alexander Ignatov, "Secret War Against Africa," *New Times*, no. 25 (1973): 29; unsigned, "Southern Africa: Armed Struggle against Imperialism," *World Marxist Review*, no. 5 (1973): 30-1.

226 Rostislav Ulyanovsky, "Scientific Socialism and Amilcar Cabral," *Asia and Africa Today*, no. 2 (1979): p. 47; Ulyanovsky et al., *Fighters*, p. 164.

227 P. I. Manchkha, "Kommunisty, revoluitsionnye demokraty i nekapitalisticheskii put' razvitiia v stranakh Afriki," *Morovaia ekonomika i mezhdunarodnye otnosheniia*, no. 10 (1975): 58; *Izvestiia*, 8 July 1977.

228 M. Braginskii et al., "Rabochii klass Afriki," *Aziia i Afrika segodnia*, no. 8 (1979): 51; Z. A. Samoilov, "Bor'ba patriotov Zimbabve," *Narody Azii i Afriki*, no. 2 (1978): 31.

229 John Ngara, "The Internal Settlement and the Zimbabwean Revolution," *African Communist*, no. 75 (1978): 81.

230 E.g., P. I. Manchkha, "Narodnaia Organizatsiia Iugo-Zapadnoi Artki," in *Bol'shaia Sovetskaia Entsiklopediia*, vol. 17, Izdatel'stvo "Sovetskaia entsiklopediia," Moscow, p. 256.

231 E.g., Iu. Gorbunov, "SVAPO: chetvert' veka bor'by," *Aziia i Afrika segodnia*, no. 4 (1985): 32; Iu. Gorbunov, "Obychai narodnosti ovambo," *Aziia i Afrika Segodnia*, no. 7 (1978): 61; I. Strekalova, *Aziia i Afrika Segodnia*, no. 6 (1977): 18-19; K. Borishpolets and A. Kovalenko, "Namibiiskaia stavka imperializma," *Aziia i Afrika segodnia*, no. 1 (1984): 35.

232 V. Shubin, "Manevry rasistov obrecheny na proval," *Aziia i Afrika Segodnia*, no. 6 (1977) pp. 18-19; I. Ul'ianovskaia, "Bantustany Namibii: bitaia stavka rasistov," *Aziia i Afrika segodnia*, no. 5 (1978): p. 11.

233 N. Kosukhin, "Kharakternye cherty avangardnykh partii trudiashchikhsia," *Asiia i Afrika segodnia*, no. 2 (1983): 2.

234 E.g., Moscow radio, 12 May 1976; Dzhon Ia Otto, "Novyi etap bor'by naroda Namibii," *Aziia i Afrika segodnia*, no. 1 (1978): 18; Sam Nujoma, "Namibia at the Threshold of Independence," *World Marxist Review*, no. 2 (1978): 93; unsigned, "Against Imperialism" p. 71.

235 E.g., I. Iastrebova, "Khartiia Svobody – programma deistvii patriotov," *Aziia i Afrika segodnia*, no. 6 (1980): 14-15.

236 *Pravda*, 7 October 1978 (democratic); 15 May 1982 (national).

237 Iastrebova, "Khartiia Svobody," p. 14; Iu. Bochkarev, "Bankrotstvo rasistskogo rezhima," *Novoe vremia*, no. 33 (1985): 19.

238 E. Dmitriev, *Palestinskii uzel*, Mezhdunarodnye otnosheniia, Moscow, 1978, p. 65; R. Landa, "Iz istorii Palestinskogo dvizheniia soprotivleniia (1967-1971 g.g.)," *Narody Azii i Afriki*, no. 4 (1976): 29; E. D. Pyrlin, "Palestinskoe natsional'no-osvoboditel'noe dvizhenie i blizhnevostochnoe uregulirovanie," *Sovetskoe gosudarstvo i pravo*, no. 10 (1977): 96-8; E. Dmitriev, *Put' k miru na Blizhnem Vostoke*, Mezhunarodnye otnosheniia, Moscow, 1974, p. 64.

239 *Izvestiia*, 30 July 1974 (comment by editor Tolkunov); E. Dmitriev, "Blizhnii Vostok: vazhnyi faktor uregulirovaniia," *Kommunist*, no. 2 (1976): 101. Some accounts dated the change as early as the 1967 replacement of Shukeiry: Dmitriev, *Palestinskii Uzel*, p. 68.

240 E.g., *Izvestiia*, 30 July 1974 (on the eve of an Arafat visit).

241 Pyrlin, "Palestinskoe...dvizhenie."

242 Ibid., pp. 97-8.

243 Ibidl.; Landa, "Iz istorii Palestinskogo dvizheniia," pp. 20-7; R. Landa, "Sovremennyi etap bor'by Palestinskogo dvizheniia soprotivleniia" (1971-76), *Narody Azii i Afriki*, no. 5 (1976): 17.

244 Malisheva, "Zapadnaia Sakhara," p. 96.
245 L. Yelin, "Write the Right Things or Else," *New Times*, no. 19 (1984): 17; L. Zhegalov, "The Nation is Continuing Along Its Road," *New Times*, no. 48 (1985): 24; Ulyanovsky, "Leninism," p. 23.
246 *Pravda*, 29 December 1976.
247 Nugud, "At the Beginning," p. 89.
248 Anyanya was described as anti-Communist in Grundy, *Guerrilla Struggle*, p. 124.
249 Unsigned, "Soviet View on Nigeria," *Mizan* 9, no. 2 (1967): 70-2; Arthur Jay Klinghoffer, "The USSR and Nigeria: The Secession Question," *Mizan*, 10, 2: 64; Morrison, "Tropical Africa," p. 52; *Pravda*, 8 March 1967; Moscow radio in English to Africa, 11 August 1978, explained that the question of support was not dependent upon whether or not the movement was progressive (implying that it was) but on whether its cause, the separation of Biafra, served the progressive interests of Nigeria and Africa.
250 *Hoover Yearbook 1981*, p. 453 (Turkish Communist party statement).
251 Gal'perin, "Efiopiia," pp. 24-5; Gabrielyan, "In Step," p. 28; Moscow radio in English to Africa, 11 August 1978.
252 This was stated in Moscow radio in English to Africa, 11 August 1978, citing *African Communist* and mentioning the cases of Eritrea and Biafra.
253 Sosnovsky, "Election Campaign," p. 11; unidentified General Secretary of the Communist party of East Pakistan, "Leninism is Our Guide," *World Marxist Review*, no. 5 (1970): 35-6.
254 TASS (in English), 7 October 1971; Moscow radio in English to South Asia, 23 November 1971.
255 TASS, 26 May 1981.
256 E.g., Vladimir Kirsanov, "The Shaba Uprising and NATO Interference," *New Times*, no. 22 (1978): 12-13; Victor Sidenko, "The Lessons of Shaba," *New Times*, no. 23 (1978): 8-9; Soviet television, 4 September 1983; *Pravda*, 30 June 1983.
257 Radio Peace and Progress in English, 11 February 1974; Moscow radio in Arabic, 12 February 1974; *Krasnaia zvezda*, 10 April 1973.
258 For similar findings for an earlier period see Stephen Gibert, "Wars of Liberation and Soviet Military Aid Policy," *Orbis* 10, no. 3 (1966): 839-58.
259 Ulyanovsky, *National Liberation*, pp. 138-40; Fedoseyev, *Leninism*, p. 478 (Kurds); Gal'perin, "Eritreiskaia problema," p. 25; G. Gal'perin, "Natsional'no-demokrat-icheskie preobrazovaniia v Efiopii," *Aziia i Afrika segodnia*, no. 8 (1976): 11; Sharayev, "Milestone," p. 36; Borisov, "Development in Ethiopia," p. 10.
260 Aleksandrenko, *Burzhuaznyi federalizm*, p. 202; Ivanitzkii, *Put'*, pp. 3-5; Voblikov, *Efiopiia*, p. 13.
261 Gromyko and Starushenko, "Faktory razvitiia," p. 8; I. R. Grigulevich and S. Iu. Kozlov, *Rasy i narody: sovremennye etnisheskie i rasovye problemy*, Nauka, Moscow, 1974 (R. N. Ismagilova chapter in English version, *The Ethnic Factor in Modern Africa*, Progress, Moscow, 1977, p. 202).
262 V. Cherepakhin, "Where Tracks Lead," *New Times*, no. 25 (1985): 9; *Pravda*, 9 January 1973, 23 December 1976; Ulyanovsky, "Leninism," p. 23; Moscow radio in English to Africa, 11 August 1978; Manchkha, *Aktual'nye problemy*, p. 132 (by implication). Gal'perin, "Eritreiskaia problema," pp. 26-7; Tanov, "At Odds with Logic," p. 14; Gavrielyan, "Liberated Areas," p. 30.
263 E.g., G. S. Akopian, "O dvukh tendentsiiakh natsionalizma ugnetennykh i razviv-aiushchikhsia natsii (K postanovke voprosa)," *Narody Azii i Afriki*, no. 5 (1970): 9; *Pravda*, 11 March 1971.
264 E.g., *Hoover Yearbook 1981*, p. 453, citing speech by Turkish Communist official; TASS 11 April 1979; Moscow radio in Persian, 27 November 1979; Moscow radio, 5 September 1980; *Pravda*, 11 March 1971, 14 May 1974, 4 August 1983; *Izvestiia*, 13 September 1977; Pieter Keuneman, "The Background of the Conflict," *World Marxist Review*, no. 2 (1984): 66. Although there have been at least two cases of implied support for an independent Kurdistan: Chipash-vili and Angosi, "The Struggle Continues,"; Moscow radio, 20 November 1979 (Bovin).

265 TASS, 9 August 1974.
266 Once (1942), the pro-Soviet Indian Communist party had listed the Sikhs among the "natives" deserving autonomy (Marcus Franda, "Communism and Regional Politics in East Pakistan," *Asian Survey* 7 (1970): 593). In the Sikh uprising of the 1980s, however, Soviet statements rejected anything but the full integration of the Sikhs, denying, as we have seen, any separate national identity for them (V. Krasilnikov, "Central Government and States in India," *International Affairs*, no. 11 (1985): 125-6; Zhegalov, "The Nation," pp. 24-5; Alexander Ter-Grigoryan, "Overcoming Divisions," *New Times* no. 23 (1984): 24-5; L. Zhegalov, "Behind the Terrorists," *New Times*, no. 36 (1985): 7-8; I. Yeling, "Lal Singh and Others," *New Times*, no. 38 (1985): 16-17; L. Zhegalov, "Imperialist Plottings Against India's Unity," no. 42 (1985): 12-13; Cherepakhin, "Where Tracks Lead," p. 9).
267 Barnds, "Moscow and South Asia," p. 25; Jackson, *South Asian Crisis*, p. 83; General Secretary, Communist party of East Pakistan, "Leninism," pp. 35-6.
268 Moscow radio, 8 October 1971 (Soviet–Algerian communiqué). Jackson, *South Asian Crisis*, pp. 86n, 89, citing *New Statesman*, 9 October 1971, on Soviet pressures on India against independence.
269 *Pravda*, 23 November 1971, 16 December 1971. Usually references were only to refugees and the legitimate interests of the people of East Pakistan (e.g., TASS, 7, 15, and 16 October 1971, 9 November 1971).
270 *Pravda*, 16 December 1971.
271 Konstantin Andreyev, "Western Sahara Tangle," *New Times*, no. 15 (1987), p. 27. See also Andreev and Podgornova, "Zapadnaia Sakhara," pp. 102-3; Andreev, "Zapadnaia Sakhara," pp. 12-13; Malisheva, "Zapadnaia Sakhara," p. 96.
272 Ibid. (all); Moscow radio in Arabic, 2 March 1981; *Pravda*, 28 March 1981; 8 October 1983.
273 See Golan, *Soviet Union and the PLO*, pp. 50-112.
274 Ibid., pp. 87-8.
275 Golan, "Soviet Union and the PLO Since Lebanon," pp. 293-4.
276 See, e.g., Iastrebova, "Khartiia Svobody," p. 15.
277 A breakaway group of black nationalists who were expelled from the ANC in 1975 actually criticized the SACP for rejecting this idea, which ran counter to the Communists' and the ANC's belief in multi-racial cooperation (T. Bonga et al., "Statement on the Expulsion from the ANC (SA)," London, 27 December 1975 (Hoover Archives), p. 12).
278 *Pravda*, 1 October 1978, 26 February 1979; Veniamin Midtsev, "Manoeuvres of the Racists and their Friends," *New Times*, no. 29 (1980): 10; Veniamin Midtsev, "Abetting the Racists," *New Times*, no. 45 (1979): 13; Iu. Borisoglebskii, "Likvidatsiia ochagov kolonializma i rasizma – velenie vremeni," *Mezhdunarodnaia zhizn'*, no. 7 (1979): 27n.
279 E.g., Midtsev, "Manoeuvres," p. 10; Strekalova, "SVAPO," p. 27.
280 Brutents, *National Liberation Movements*, vol. II, p. 207.
281 Ibid., vol. I, p. 86; Ulyanovsky, *National Liberation*, p. 344. South African Communist leader Joe Slovo told the *World Marxist Review* that the working class had a special role to play with the national liberation alliance (led by the ANC) so as to prevent "a repetition of what has happened in other parts of Africa, where the fruits of sacrifice and victory of the indigenous people were undermined by new exploiters with black faces": Joe Slovo, "When the Situation is Red Hot," *World Marxist Review*, no. 10 (1985): 57.
282 Brutents, *National Liberation Movements* vol. I, pp. 91-2.
283 *Izvestiia*, 30 July 1974 (Tolkunov).
284 Sosnovsky, "Election Campaign," p. 10; General Secretary, Communist Party of East Pakistan, "Leninism," p. 35.
285 N. D. Turkatenko, "Raschety i proschety Vashingtona v Iuzhoi Afrike," *SShA: ekonomika, politika, ideologiia*, no. 2 (1977): 33.
286 Bender, "Angola," p. 22; Marcum, "Lessons," p. 413; Marcum, *Angolan Revolution*, p. 383; Klinghoffer, *Angolan War*, p. 18; Legum, "Soviet Union, China," p. 749.
287 Ibid. (all).

288 Bender, "Angola, the Cubans," p. 23; Thomas Henrikson, "Angola, Mozambique, The Soviet Union: Liberation and the Quest for Influence," in W. Weinstein and T. Henrikson (eds.), *Soviet and Chinese Aid to African Nations*, Praeger, New York, 1980, p. 66.
289 See below.
290 In 1973, for example, they made much ado over the MPLA-FNLA agreements (unsigned, "Angola's Fight for Freedom," *New Times*, no. 5 (1973) p. 16). See Gerald Bender (interview); Valenta, "Soviet-Cuban Intervention," pp. 10, 13.
291 *African Development* (January 1976): 18; Klinghoffer, *Angolan War*, pp. 61-71.
292 *Africa Confidential* 19, no. 18 (1978): 2; Samoilov, "Bor'ba," pp. 32-3; John Ngara, "The Internal Settlement and the Zimbabwean Revolution," *African Communist*, no. 75 (1978): 80-1.
293 Ngara, "The 'Internal Settlement,'" p. 136; *The Guardian*, 28 March 1976. Soviet coverage of Mugabe: TASS, 20 and 22 October 1978; *Pravda*, 23 May 1977.
294 *The Punch* (Ikeja), 22 August 1978; William Griffith, "Soviet Policy in Southern Africa," MIT paper, 1979, p. 9.
295 Ottaway and Ottaway, *Afrocommunism*, p. 99; *The Guardian*, 28 April 1977; *Africa Confidential* 20, no. 9 (1979): 2; *Africa Contemporary Record (1975-76): B-643*.
296 *New African* (May 1979): 35 (Mugabe interview); *Africa Contemporary Record* (1979-80): A-167.
297 *Le Monde*, 4 May 1979 (Mugabe interview); *The Guardian*, 16 May 1979.
298 Martin and Johnson, *Struggle for Zimbabwe*, p. 164; Martin Meredith, *The Past is Another Country*, Pan Books, London, 1979, p. 160; *Africa Confidential* 19, no. 7 (1978): 1.
299 *Jeune Afrique*, 19 March 1980, p. 33 (Mugabe press conference); Papp, "Soviet Union and Southern Africa," p. 82 (citing *Newsweek* interview, 2 October 1978); Meredith, *The past*, p. 351; Martin and Johnson, *Struggle for Zimbabwe*, p. 304; *African Index* 2 no. 13 (1979): 47. According to *The Observer*, 2 July 1979, a ZANU official said that after being refused Soviet arms three times ZANU would not ask again because "we are not willing to be humiliated."
300 There was a report *(Sunday Times, 17 October 1979)* that the Soviets conditioned further aid to ZAPU on its gaining control over ZANU; but there is no evidence that such an ultimatum, if delivered, was ever carried out by the Soviets.
301 E.g., TASS, 20 March 1973, 4 April 1977; Moscow radio in English to southern Africa, 23 January 1978; Samoilov, "Bor'ba," pp. 49-50; unsigned, "Iug Afriki: revoliutsionnyi protsess neobratim," *Aziia i Afrika segodnia*, no. 9 (1979): 23; Veniamin Midtsev, "Relapse of Colonialism," *New Times*, no. 7 (1980): 18; A. Runov, "Death Throes of Racist Regime," *International Affairs*, no. 1 (1977): 69-73.
302 See Golan, *Soviet Union and Palestine*, pp. 143-79; Galia Golan, "The Soviet Union and the PLO in Kauppi and Nation, *Soviet Union and the Middle East*, pp. 192-3. See below for other disagreements.
303 Golan, "Since Lebanon," *passim*.
304 Ibid., p. 302. The Soviets reportedly invited Salah Khalaf and Faruk Kaddumi to Moscow after these two expressed dissatisfaction with the Arafat-Hussein February 1985 accord, but the Chernenko funeral intervened.
305 Golan, "Since Lebanon," p. 303.
306 "Palestine Communists" were said to have sent greetings to the 1971 CPSU Congress, but there does not appear to have been a separate organizational framework for them at that time: *XXIV S"ezd Kommunisticheskoi Partii Sovetskogo Soiuza*, vol II, Politizdat, Moscow, 1971, p. 584.
307 Franda, "Communism and Regional Politics," p. 600; Robert Scalapino, "Communism in Asia: Towards a Comparative Analysis," in Robert Scalapino (ed.), *Communism and Revolution in Asia: Tactics, Goals and Achievements*, Prentice-Hall, Englewood Cliffs, N.J., 1965, p. 32; *Hoover Yearbook 1971*, pp. 654-5; *1972*, p. 565; *1973*, p. 532.
308 Head of Delegation, Communist Party of East Pakistan, *World Marxist Review*, no. 9 (1969): 11.
309 Sosnovsky, "Election Campaign."
310 *XXIV S"ezd*, vol. II, p. 584.

311 Franda, "Communism and Regional Politics," p. 600; Jackson, *South Asian Crisis*, p. 78; Sosnovsky, "Election Campaign," p. 11; unidentified General Secretary of the Communist party in East Pakistan, "Leninism," *World Marxist Review*, no. 5 (1970): 35-6.

312 Pike, *Viet-Cong*, p. 217.

313 Zagoria, *Vietnam Triangle*, p. 116.

314 Ottaway and Ottaway, *Afrocommunism*, p. 100.

315 *Africa Confidential* 19, no. 1 (1978): 3; *Africa Contemporary Record* (1977-78): A-28; Colin Legum, "The USSR and Africa: The African Environment," *Problems of Communism* 27 (1978): 15.

316 Martin van Bruinessen, "The Kurds in Turkey," *Merip Reports* (February 1984): 8.

317 A. M. Khazanov, "Angola: bor'ba za nezavisimost'," *Voprosy istorii*, no. 8 (1978): 118-19; unsigned, "Southern Africa: Armed Struggle Against Imperialism," *World Marxist Review*, no. 5 (1973): 29; Alexander Ignatov, "Secret War Against Africa," *New Times*, no. 25 (1970): 29; unsigned, "Angola's National Forces," *International Affairs*, no. 3 (1963): 117.

318 Samoilov, "Bor'ba," p. 34; *Izvestiia*, 15 October 1977; E. Tarabrin, "Afrika na novom vitke osvoboditel'noi bor'by," *Mirovaia ekonomika i mezhdunarodnye otnosheniia*, no. 2 (1979): 45; Manchkha, *Aktual'nye problemy*, p. 284.

319 Idid.; *Pravda*, 27 March 1977.

320 V. Shubin, "SWAPO: At the Forefront of the Struggle," *International Affairs* no. 6 (1985): 101.

321 Unsigned, "Southern Africa: Armed Struggle," p. 30.

322 The Soviet press but not official speeches, communiqués, etc., had been referring to the PLO as the sole legitimate representative since 1975.

323 TASS, 29 February 1976, 6 March 1976; Andreev, "Zapadnaia Sakhara," p. 24.

324 Andreev, "Zapadnaia Sakhara," p. 24; Andreev, "Referendum," p. 12; K. Andreev, "Zapadnaia Sakhara. Trudnye poiski uregulirovaniia," *Novoe vremia*, no. 34 (1979): 14.

325 *Pravda*, 8 January 1982; Leonid Skuratov, "Ever-mounting Tide," *New Times*, no. 2 (1982): 21.

326 Unsigned, "South Africa: The Struggle Continues," *International Affairs*, no. 5 (1985): 105.

327 *Pravda*, 7 October 1978 (on uniting into a single democratic front); 15 May 1982 (on UDF); unsigned, "Southern Africa: Backstage of the Racists' Manoeuvres," *World Marxist Review*, no. 7 (1984): 128; Iu. Bochkarev, "Bankrotstvo rasistskogo rezhima," *Novoe vremia*, no. 33 (1985): 19; A. Urnov, "Iuzhnoafrikanskii uzel," *Mirovaia ekonomika i mezhdur narodnye otnosh niia*, no. 5 (1984): 118-21.

328 Winrich Kuhne, "Der Befreiungskampf in Sudafrika: von 'Black Consciousness' zu 'Black Power,'" *Stiftung Wissenschaft und Politik*, 1981, English summary. Visiting American Africanists were told in Moscow that the Soviet Union was willing to have contacts with groups other than the ANC, specifically the UDF: Peter Clement, "Moscow and Southern Africa," *Problems of Communism* 24 (1985): 46.

329 E.g., *Pravda*, 12 April 1979; A. Krasilnikov, "Peking's Treacherous Course and the Liberation Struggle in Southern Africa," *Far Eastern Affairs*, no. 2 (1981): 65-6; A. Krasil'nikov, "Politika Pekina protiv osvoboditel'noi bor'by v Afrike," *Aziia i Afrika segodnia*, no. 5 (1973): 25.

330 *Africa Contemporary Record* (1982-83): A-160; David Albright, "New Trends in Soviet Policy Toward Africa," *Africa Notes* (515), no. 27 (1984): 7-8. The ANC reportedly held some meetings with him as well, in 1982 or 1983 and in 1979: Tom Lodge, "The African National Congress in South Africa, 1967-1983: Guerrilla War and Armed Propaganda," *Journal of Contemporary African Studies* 3, no. 1/2 (1983-84): 173.

331 James Rasheed, "All Eyes on Baluchistan," *Middle East International*, 15 January 1982, pp. 10-11.

332 van Bruinessen, "The Kurds," pp. 10-11; *Hoover Yearbook 1980*, p. 217.

333 Manchkha, *Aktual'nye problemy*, pp. 133-4.

334 *Krasnaia zvezda*, 10 April 1975. See also *Pravda*, 11 June 1975.

335 Jackson, *South Asian Crisis*, pp. 78-9.

336 On anti-Portuguese cooperation see editorial, "Solidarnost' kontinentov: novaia vekha," *Aziia i Afrika segodnia*, no. 12 (1975): 7-9.

337 See, for example, Gibson, *African Liberation Movements*, p. 9.

338 Ibid., pp. 164-6; Martin and Johnson, *Struggle for Zimbabwe*, p. 10; unsigned, "Southern Africa," pp. 28-9; V. L. Tiagunenko et al., *Vooruzhennaia bor'ba narodov Afriki za svobodu i nezavisimost'*, Ministerstvo-oborny SSSR Nauka, Moscow, 1974, p. 305.

339 *Izvestiia*, 1 February 1970; unsigned, "Southern Africa," p. 31.

340 For example, Lazarev, "Sovremennyi etap," pp. 22-5; Eremeev, "Anatomiia," pp. 12-16.

341 Ulyanovsky, *National Liberation*, p. 353; *Pravda*, 11 February 1975; 13 March 1978.

342 *Hoover Yearbook 1981*, p. 7.

343 *Pravda*, 6 February 1977, 2 June 1977, 24 September 1977.

344 Gorbachov, "The Situation in Eritrea," p. 20; *Pravda*, 9 February 1975.

345 Ulyanovsky, *National Liberation*, pp. 138-40; Fedoseyev, *Leninism*, p. 478.

346 Silva, "Championing Independence," p. 34; Keunemen, "Background of Conflict," pp. 65-7; Volkov, "Extremes," p. 21.

347 Franda, "Communism and Regional Politics," pp. 597, 601-3. See also, Ulyanovsky, *National Liberation*, p. 142 on being forced to seek separation. *Pravda*, 22 December 1971, however, accused the Chinese of inciting the people of East Pakistan to take up arms.

348 Jackson, *South Asian Crisis*, p. 88. See also Barnds, "Moscow and South Asia," p. 25.

349 See, for example, Harrison, "Nightmare," p. 159; Dev Murarka, "Growing Fears in Moscow," *Middle East International*, 7 January 1983; p. 8; Griffith, "USSR and Pakistan," p. 38; Legvold, "Super Rivals," p. 771.

350 *Pravda*, 24, 28 December 1985; *Izvestiia*, 24 and 30 December 1985.

351 Moscow radio, 7 September 1979, 20 November 1979 (Bovin), 5 September 1980; TASS, 3, 4 September 1979; 11 and 25 October 1979; *Pravda*, 20 September 1979.

352 Bender, "Angola, The Cubans," p. 15.

353 Robins, "Soviet-Cuban Relationship," p. 159, citing *New York Times*, 26 May 1978.

354 *Pravda*, 3 August 1971.

355 Zagoria, *Vietnam Triangle*, pp. 46, 105; Chester Bain, *Vietnam: The Roots of Conflict*, Prentice-Hall Inc., Englewood Cliffs, N.J., 1967, p. 162.

356 William Duiker, *The Communist Road to Power*, Westview Press, Boulder, Co., 1981, p. 277.

357 Ibid., pp. 245-56.

358 Ibid., p. 304.

359 Ibid., Charles McLane, "The Russians and Vietnam," *International Journal*, no. 24 (1968-69): 56-9.

360 Khazanov, "Angola," p. 117; unsigned, "The Way of the Anti-imperialist Struggle in Tropical Africa," *World Marxist Review*, no. 8 (1971): 31.

361 Ibid.; Moscow radio, 12 February 1972; Ul'ianovskii, "Neto," p. 25; Ul'ianovskii, "Kabral," pp. 31-2.

362 Unsigned, "Anti-imperialist Struggle," p. 31; unsigned, "Southern Africa," p. 21.

363 Unsigned, "Southern Africa," p. 21;

364 Tiagunenko et al., *Vooruzhen-naia bor'ba*, pp. 277, 330.

365 Ibid., p. 330; A. I. Sobolev, "Leninskaia kontseptsiia mnogoobraziia putei sotsial'nogo razvitiia," *Voprosy istorii KPSS*, no. 4 (1980): 49; G. Malinovskii, "Lokal'nye voiny v zone natsionali'no-osvobodite'nogo dvizheniia," *Voenno-istoricheskii zhurnal*, no. 5 (1974): 94; Khazanov, "Angola," p. 120.

366 Tiagunenko et al., *Vooruzhennaia bor'ba*, p. 361.

367 Klinghoffer, *Angolan War*, p. 18; Bender, "Angola, the Cubans," p. 21 and interview; Legvold, "Super Rivals," p. 772.

368 See discussion above on organization and different groups in Angola.

369   Martin and Johnson, *Struggle for Zimbabwe*, p. 146; *Le Monde Diplomatique* (May 1970): 11; John Day, "The Insignificance of Tribe in the African Politics of Zimbabwe-Rhodesia,"*Journal of Commonwealth and Comparative Politics* 18, no. 1 (1980): 89-93; Th. Gerald-Scheepers, "African Resistance in Rhodesia," *African Perspectives*, no. 1 (1976): 125-6; Slater, *"Politics of Frustration,"* pp. 263-6.

370   *New African* (November 1978): 81; (May 1979): 34; *Africa*, no. 75 (1977): 25.

371   Evgeny Tarabrin, "Peking's Manoeuvres in Africa," *New Times*, no. (1972): 19; Tiagunenko et al., *Vooruzhennaia bar'ba*, p. 73.

372   Lodge, "African National Congress," p. 160.

373   Moscow radio in English to Africa, 14 January 1975; Moscow radio, 13 August 1975; Radio Peace and Progress in English, 18 and 31 December 1974, 30 December 1975; *Africa Contemporary Record* (1975-76): A-105.

374   Martin and Johnson, *Struggle for Zimbabwe*, p. 10.

375   *To the Point* 7, no. 31 (1978): p. 13; Christopher Coker, "Decolonization in the Seventies: Rhodesia and the Dialectic of National Liberation," *Round Table*, no. 274 (1979): 122-36; *Africa Confidential* 19, no. 21 (1978): 1.

376   *Pravda*, 23 May 1977.

377   *Daily Telegraph*, 28 May 1979.

378   E.g., Anatoly Gromyko, "Neo-colonialism's Manoeuvres in Southern Africa," *International Affairs*, no. 12 (1977): 98-9; Samoilov, "Bor'ba", p. 33.

379   E.g., *Izvestiia*, 26 January 1978 (on the desirability of negotiations but not these negotiations); *Pravda*, 28 March 1978.

380   See *Pravda*, 23 September 1979, or Moscow radio in English, 15 and 21 May 1979, 6 December 1979, although *Izvestiia*, 16 August 1979, called them "a force,"

381   *Africa Research Bulletin*, 1-28 February 1978 (*Financial Times*, 4 February 1978); *Africa Confidential* 20, no. 9 (1979): 2.

382   Tiagunenko et al., *Vooruzhennaia bor'ba*, p. 300; unsigned, "Southern Africa," p. 29.

383   Alexander Ignatov, "Battle for Freedom," *New Times*, no. 20 (1970): 16.

384   Unsigned, "Southern Africa," p. 29.

385   *Pravda*, 24 October 1976; *Krasnaia zvezda*, 25 May 1977; TASS, 11 December 1976, 2 July 1977; Radio Peace and Progress, 18 August 1975; Otto, "Novyi etap bor'by," p. 18. Manchkha, *Aktual'nye problemy*, p. 264, said that SWAPO reached the "natural conclusion" that peaceful means would not do.

386   TASS, 11 August 1976; Turkatenko, "Raschety," p. 33; Otto, "Novyi etap bor'by," p. 18; unsigned, "Iug Afriki," pp. 23-4; *Krasnaia zvezda*, 25 May 1977.

387   *Pravda*, 10 October 1983; Andrei Urnov, "The Windhoek Farce," *New Times*, no. 29 (1985): 22; V. Shubin, "Fictions and Realities," *New Times*, no. 50 (1985): 13; A. Kiva, "The Struggle against the Remnants of Colonialism and Neo-colonialism," *International Affairs*, no. 3 (1981): 51-2.

388   Moscow radio, 26 August 1983; Iu. Gorbunov, "Militarizatsiia obrechennogo rezhima," *Aziia i Afrika segodnia*, no. 8 (1982): 29.

389   *Pravda*, 31 July 1984; TASS, 11 August 1976; Otto, "Novyi etap bor'by," p. 18; K. Vitaliev, "Imperialist Policy and the Conflict in South Africa," *International Affairs*, no. 11 (1982): 46.

390   *Africa Contemporary Record* (1978-79): A-19-20.

391   *Africa Confidential* 19, no. 13 (1970): 1; 20 no. 8 (1979): 1.

392   Griffith, "Southern Africa," p. 11; Katz, "Soviet-Cuban Connection," p. 97. (Both of these authors claimed that the Soviets urged armed struggle because they did *not* want Namibian victory for fear the new state would be too independent, or, put differently, because the longer the conflict, the more dependent SWAPO would become upon the Soviet Union.)

393   Umkonto we Siswe was actually set up by joint decision of the ANC and the SACP to undertake sabotage, preceding (if necessary) guerrilla war: Lodge, "African National Congress," p. 159.

394   *Pravda*, 26 April 1978; Moscow radio in English, 5 August 1981; V. Shubin, "ANK: gody podpol'ia i vooruzhennoi bor'by," *Aziia i Afrika segodnia*, no. 1 (1982): 35-6; Leonid Skuratov, "Ever-mounting Tide," *New Times*, no. 2 (1982): 22.

395 *Pravda*, 8 January 1982, 22 May 1983; Vusizwe Seme, "On the Various Forms of Revolutionary Struggle," *African Communist*, no. 17 (1977): 31; Sergei Petukhov, "Oliver Tambo: We Are Committed Internationalists," *New Times*, no. 2 (1980): 22-3.
396 "South Africa" (interview with Alfred Nzo), *International Affairs*, no. 5, (1983): 108.
397 Tiagunenko et al., *Vooruzhennaia bor'ba*, pp. 301, 361; A. A. Ivanov, "Avangard revoliutsionnogo dvizheniia v Afrike," *Nauchnyi kommunizm*, no. 4 (1976): 89.
398 Iastrebova, "Khartiia Svobody," pp. 14-15. Indeed, Shubin ("ANK," p. 35) even said that the ANC was unable to set up a guerrilla movement for massive resistance, and therefore employed strikes and other means, although guerrilla ranks swelled after Soweto. The Defence Ministry study (Tiagunenko et al., *Vooruzhennaia bor'ba*, pp. 310, 316) referred to sabotage acts perpetrated by "guerrillas."
399 Francis Meli at Berlin Conference, "Against Imperialism, for Social Progress," *World Marxist Review*, no. 3 (1981): 78.
400 Ibid.; Shubin, "ANK," p. 36; Petukhov, "Oliver Tambo," pp. 22-3.
401 *Economic and Political Weekly* (Bombay) 11, no. 4 (1976): 112-13.
402 Ivanov, "Avangard revoliutsionnogo," p. 89; Skuratov, "Ever-mounting Tide," pp. 22-3; "Against Imperialism for Social Progress, International Scientific Conference in Berlin," *World Marxist Review*, no. 4 (1981): 71-2.
403 Brutents, *National Liberation Revolutions*, vol. I, p. 136, said this did not mean rejection of armed actions but rather that it took time to prepare for war.
404 "Southern Africa: Backstage of the Racists' manoeuvres," *World Marxist Review*, no. 7 (1984): 130.
405 "Dvizhenie soprotivleniia rasistam usilivaetsia," *Mezhdunarodnaia zhizn'*, no. 4 (1985): 131 (Nzo interview); V. Shubin, "Mezhdu nakoval'nei i molotom," *Mezhdunarodnaia zhizn'*, no. 3, (1985): 36-7.
406 V. Shubin, "What the Camera is Not Focussed On," *New Times*, no. 31 (1985): 10-11.
407 *The Guardian*, 11 August 1985.
408 *AfricAsia*, no. 33 (1986): 15-16. Slovo called for "mass political struggle coupled with an intensification of revolutionary violence" in *The Guardian*, 17 August 1986.
409 Oliver Tambo, "Rumbling Volcano," *New Times*, no. 38 (1985): p. 26 (quoting Johny Makatini). See also Temba Hlanganani, "The Greatest Moment of My Life," *African Communist*, no. 103 (1985): 22-9.
410 M. Zaripov, "Designs on the Zambezi," *New Times*, no. 45 (1985): 25.
411 Slovo, "Situation is Red Hot," pp. 56-7.
412 V. Rasnitzyn, "The Apartheid Regime under Seige," *International Affairs*, no. 10 (1985): 118-20; B. Asoyan, "The Apartheid System is Doomed," *International Affairs*, no. 11 (1985): pp. 53-9.
413 See Golan, *Soviet Union and Palestine*, pp. 210-27.
414 Fahmi Salfiti, "The Situation in Jordan and Communist Tactics," *World Marxist Review*, no. 11 (1968): 46; *Za rubezhom*, 6-12 June 1969; John Cooley, *Green March, Black September*, Frank Cass, London, 1973, p. 166 (Shelepin); *At'talia* (Cairo) (June 1970): 59-67; cited in Ro'i *From Encroachment*, p. 527 (Ul'ianovskii).
415 George Mirsky, "Israel: Illusions and Miscalculations," *New Times*, no. 39 (1968): 7; "Special Document," *Journal of Palestine Studies* 2, no. 1 (1972): 96.
416 Aryeh Yodfat, "The USSR and the Palestinians," *New Outlook*, no. 19 (1976): 31.
417 See Golan, *Soviet Union and Palestine*, pp. 210-27. for examples.
418 Yodfat, "USSR and Palestinians," p. 32; *al-Nahar*, 7 December 1974.
419 *Pravda*, 29 August 1972; *Izvestiia*, 30 July 1974.
420 *Al-Manar*, 29 April 1978.
421 Golan, *Soviet Union and Palestine*, p. 216.
422 *Al-Nahar*, 7 December 1974.
423 Pyrlin, "Palestinskoe...dvizhenie," p. 101.
424 See Golan, *Soviet Union and Palestine*, pp. 113-42, and Golan, "Soviet Union and the PLO since Lebanon," p. 304.
425 E.g., Egypt prior to the 1973 war, Syria after the 1982 Lebanon war.
426 Raphael Israeli, *The PLO in Lebanon: Selected Documents*, Weidenfeld and Nicolson, London, 1983, pp. 74-139.

427 Helena Cobban, *The Palestinian Liberation Organization*, Cambridge University Press, 1984, p. 254.
428 See Golan, "Soviet Union and the PLO since Lebanon."
429 Moscow radio, 14 September 1979; Andreev, "Zapadnaia Sakhara," p. 25; Andreev, "Zapadnaia Sakhara. Trudnye poiski uregulirovaniia," p. 14.
430 Moscow radio, 17 August 1979; Moscow radio in Arabic, 19 February 1976, 14 August 1979, 2 March 1981; Andreev and Podgornova, "Zapadnaia Sakhara," pp. 98–103.
431 Malisheva, "Zapadnaia Sakhara," pp. 96–7; *Izvestiia*, 18 December 1981.
432 *Izvestiia*, 17 July 1983, 28 July 1984.
433 See Zagoria, *Vietnam Triangle, passim*, and especially p. 52.
434 Ibid., p. 105.
435 Ibid., *passim*.
436 Barnds, "Moscow and South Asia," pp. 22–3.
437 Jackson, *South Asian Crisis*, p. 72; G. W. Choudhury, "Dismemberment of Pakistan, 1971: Its International Implications," *Orbis* 18, no. 2 (1974): 181–2; Bhabani Sen Gupta, "Moscow and Bangladesh," *Problems of Communism* 24, no. 2 (1975): 59.
438 *Izvestiia*, 12 December 1971; *Pravda*, 22 December 1971.
439 Tahir-Keli, "External Dimensions," pp. 88–9.
440 Ibid.
441 The insurgents in Burma were said to have had some Chinese aid, at least as of the early 1970s, but the involvement of pro-Chinese Communists and Kuomintang Chinese defies any clear connection or conclusion. See Justus M. van der Kroef, "The Soviet Union in Southeast Asia," in Roger Kanet, *The Soviet Union and Developing Nations*, Johns Hopkins University Press, Baltimore, 1975, p. 115; *Asia 1979 Yearbook*, p. 156.
442 Radio Peace and Progress, 15 October 1977.
443 *Far Eastern Economic Review*, 1 April 1977, p. 13; 25 November 1977, pp. 28–9.
444 *Pravda*, 23 December 1976, 9 January 1973.
445 *Asia 1978 Yearbook*, p. 293.
446 TASS, 13 April 1979; Radio Peace and Progress in Mandarin, 14 July 1979. See also *Asia 1979 Yearbook*, p. 283.
447 Sen Gupta, *Soviet-Asian Relations*, p. 237.
448 Henze, "Arming the Horn," p. 32.
449 Moscow radio, 3 January 1971.
450 *Pravda*, 13 September 1978.
451 E.g., Legum, "Soviet Union, China," *passim*; Colin Legum, "National Liberation in Southern Africa," *Problems of Communism* 24 (1975): 7; Legum, "African Environment,: p. 15.
452 Gibson, *Africa Liberation Movements*, p. 9; W. A. C. Adie, "The Communist Powers in Africa," *Conflict Studies*, no. 10 (1970–71): 3; *Africa Confidential*, no. 3 (1969): 8; no. 17 (1972): 4.
453 E.g., Krasilnikov, "Politika Pekina," p. 25; A. Krasilnikov, "Peking's Policy and the Revolutionary-Democratic Forces in Portugal," *Far Eastern Affairs*, no. 3 (1976): 139–43; Krasil'nikov, "Peking's Treacherous Course," 65–6; Tarabrin, "Peking's Manoeuvres," p. 19; V. Sofinsky and A. Khazanov, "PRC Policy in Tropical Africa," *Far Eastern Affairs*, no. 3 (1978): 77–8; Pyotr Manchkha, "Maoist Subversion in Africa," *New Times*, no. 5 (1976): 25–7; *Izvestiia*, 11 January 1979; V. Solodovnikov and V. Bogoslovsky, *Non-capitalist Development*, Progress, Moscow, 1975, pp. 228–9.
454 Legum, "Africa Environment," p. 15. The East Germans reportedly tried to persuade Mugabe to condemn the Chinese (*Africa Contemporary Record* (1978–79): 17–19).
455 *Africa Confidential* 19, no. 7 (1978): 1; Ottaway and Ottaway, *Afrocommunism*, p. 34.
456 Legum, "Soviet Union, China and the West," p. 758.
457 Shipanga, in Ansprenger, *Die SWAPO*, pp. 85–6.
458 Bonga, et al., "Expulsion from the ANC," p. 18.
459 Kaplan, *Diplomacy of Power*, p. 195; George Yu, "China's Impact," *Problems of Communism*, no. 1 (1978): 47–9; Colin Legum, "International Rivalries in the Southern Africa Conflict," in Gwendolen Carter and Patrick O'Meara, *Southern Africa: The*

Continuing Crisis, Indiana University Press, Bloomington, 1979, p. 12; Colin Legum and Tony Hodges, *After Angola: The War Over Southern Africa*, Africana Publishing House, New York, 1978, p. 5; Jiri Valenta, "The Soviet-Cuban Intervention in Angola," *Studies in Comparative Communism* 11, nos. 1 and 2 (1978): 7; *Sunday Times*, 17 October 1976; William Griffith, "Soviet Policy in Southern Africa," MIT, January 1979, pp. 3-5.

460 Oded Eran, "The Soviet Union and the Palestine Guerrilla Organization," Tel Aviv University, 1971, p. 5.

461 Porter, *USSR in Third World Conflicts*, pp. 109-11.

462 Marcum, *Angolan Revolution*, vol. II p. 230; Klinghoffer, *Angolan War*, p. 104; *Sunday Times*, 3 February 1975. Tambo travelled to China in 1983: Pan-African News Agency, 29 July 1983, in *Facts and Reports* 13 (1983): p. 3.

463 Marcum, *Angolan Revolution*, p. 265; Klinghoffer, *Angolan War*, pp. 104-6.

464 John Murray Brown, "Sadiq Out Front," *Middle East International* (7 February 1986): 11.

465 See Fukuyama, "Soviet Union and Iraq," p. 39.

466 *Asia 1978 Yearbook*, p. 243, said the Philippines turned down at least one name because the proposed ambassador had KGB links.

467 Olaf Carol, *The Pathans*, Oxford University Press, 1975, p. 529; Tahir-Kheli, "External Dimensions," pp. 89-90. For opposite view on Daoud period, see A. G. Noorani, "Soviet Ambitions in South Asia," *International Security* 4, no. 3 (1979-80): 43.

468 Wirsing, *Baluchis and Pathans*, pp. 13-16; Dastarac and Levant, "What Went Wrong," pp. 9-10; *Business Week*, 21 January 1980, p. 51.

469 Richard Remnek, "Soviet Policy in the Horn of Africa: The Decision to Intervene," in Donaldson, *Soviet Union in the Third World*, p. 130.

470 E.g., Porter, *USSR in Third World Conflicts*, p. 96.

471 Ibid. p. 98; Stemlau, *International Politics*, pp. 26-30.

472 Klinghoffer, "USSR and Nigeria," pp. 64-5; unsigned, "Soviet Views on Nigeria," pp. 71-3; "Soviet Thoughts on Nigeria Crisis," *Mizan*, 9, no. 4 (1967): 174.

473 Duiker, *Communist Road*, pp. 295-9.

474 Porter, *USSR in Third World Conflicts*, pp. 154-5; Klinghoffer, *Angolan War*, pp. 62-71; Marcum, *Angolan Revolution*, vol. II, pp. 262-3; Papp, "Soviet Union and Southern Africa," p. 80.

475 Klinghoffer, *Angolan War*, pp. 62-71; Marcum, *Angolan Revolution*, pp. 266-75.

476 Seth Singleton, "Soviet Policy and Socialist Expansion in Asia and Africa," *Armed Forces and Society* 6, no. 3 (1980): 361.

477 Moscow radio in French to North Africa, 2 March 1980. See also, TASS, 2 March 1976; Moscow radio in Arabic, 2 March 1982; *Pravda*, 21 May 1982 (Brutents in Morocco).

478 One account claims that the Algerians conditioned transit of Soviet aid to the MPLA on assistance to the Polisario. Moscow then halted such assistance when it no longer needed the Algerians for Angola and was therefore able to return to its interest in maintaining good relations with Morocco (David Albright, "The Middle East and Africa in Recent Soviet Policy," in Kanet, *Soviet Foreign Policy*, p. 293). No such reduction in at least Soviet political (and possibly material) support was in fact noticeable.

Index

Academy of Sciences
  Ministry of Defense joint study on
    armed struggle 173–4, 184
  non-party research institutes 5
Afghanistan 34, 107, 181, 229, 232
  as base for guerrilla warfare inside
    Pakistan 282
  national liberation movements 8
  rebellion, as factor in Soviet-Pakistan
    relations 331–2
  see also Baluchi
Africa
  African socialism 111, 112
  cooperation between liberation groups
    311
  national liberation struggles 79, 180
  Podgorny tour 180
  Soviet assistance 217, 234, 335
  vanguard revolutionary democratic
    parties 132, 134
  see also individual states
African Nationalist Council (ANC) 3, 9,
    262
  cooperation with South African
    Communist Party 306–7, 318
  cooperation with ZAPU 271
  ideology 295
  leaders' visits to Soviet Union 288
  Soviet support 286–8, 296, 309, 336–7
  Soviet views of means of struggle
    318–20
  Soviet views of ideology 293, 299–300
  see also Tambo
Afro-Asian Peoples Solidarity Committee
    (of Soviet Union) 273, 274
Agaev, S. schema for revolutionary
    democracy 125–8, 166–7
aid and assistance
  from socialist world 215
  against counter-revolutions 215–16, 217,
    231
  in relation to détente 222–6
  in relation to estimates of Western
    aggressiveness 226–8
  in relation to "Soviet Union first"
    attitude 219–20, 226, 240 242, 256,
    342
  types of 217, 218, 221–2
  views of the military 228–36
  see also support

Algeria 173, 179
  Communist Party cooperation with
    Polisario 307
  liberation movement organization 79,
    189
  military training 232
  objectives of armed struggle 186
Andreev, on social class and national
    liberation struggles 54, 56, 61, 64–5,
    67, 69
Andropov, Y. 257
  on armed struggle 180, 182–3, 238
  on role of Soviet Union 239, 240–1
  on socialism and party creation 136
  on the rise of national liberation
    movements 38, 40
Angola 129, 168, 173, 223
  Communist Party and origins of MPLA
    306
  Cuban advisers 269
  Cuban brigade assistance 216, 232
  national liberation movements 8, 308
  Soviet assistance 221, 222, 229, 232, 242,
    335
  see also FNLA; MPLA; UNITA
anti-colonial movements 3, 8
  degree of Soviet support 263, 268, 300,
    334
  means and type of Soviet support 264,
    266, 268–75, 308
  Soviet view of means of struggle 314–18
Anyanya 9, 262, 275, 328
Arabs of Khuzistan 9
Arafat, Y. 288, 289–90, 302, 338
  relations with Soviet Union 303–4,
    322–3
Arbatov, G. 5
  on détente 226
armed struggle 3, 155–6
  and détente 162–6, 169–70, 179–80, 197
  Chinese support for 160–1
  factors influencing strategy 186–7
  Soviet criticisms of 156–9, 161, 174, 175,
    183, 196–7
  Soviet tolerance of 166–70, 174, 180–1, '
    197, 315, 318
  spontaneity versus organization 187–8
  typology of 184, 187
  typology of conflicts 173–4
  weapons and training 188